Frommer's
South Florida 2002

POSTCARDS FROM

D0205866

Biscayne National Park and the Florida Keys offer some of the best snorkeling and scuba diving in South Florida. See chapters 10 and 11. © Stephen Frink / Waterhouse Stock Photography.

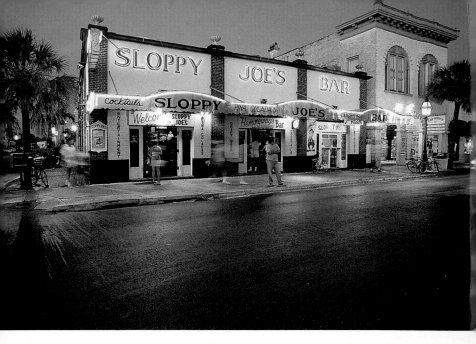

Stop in at Sloppy Joe's, the quintessential Key West watering hole. See chapter 11 for more on Key West's nightlife. © *Darrell Ray Jones / The Stock Market.*

Every winter, millions of sunbathers head for the warm, pristine beaches of South Florida. See chapter 1 for a list of the best beaches in the region. © *Trevor Wood / Tony Stone Worldwide.*

See the house where "Papa" Hemingway wrote some of his most famous works and check out other Hemingway haunts while in Key West. See chapter 11. © Michael Ventura Photography.

Built alongside the ruins of oil magnate Henry Flagler's incredible Overseas Railroad, the Seven-mile Bridge is an excellent vantage point from which to view the stunning waters of the Keys. See chapter 11.
© Michael Ventura Photography.

Take a boat tour through the wilds of Everglades National Park—you're almost guaranteed to glimpse a gator. See chapter 10. © D.E. Cox/Tony Stone Images.

It's hard to walk anywhere in Miami's South Beach without encountering magnificent examples of Art Deco architecture. See chapter 7. © Stuart Westmorland/Tony Stone Images.

Sip cocktails at a hotel bar, see a show, or dance the night away at a South Beach club; when the sun goes down, Miami just begins to heat up. See chapter 9 for more on Miami's nightlife.
© Catherine Karnow Photography.

Miami Beach—home to a multitude of hotels, clubs, and crowded beaches—offers a great nightlife, but if you're looking for peace and quiet, look elsewhere. See chapter 5 for information on accommodations in Miami.
© Alan Schein/The Stock Market.

The oldest hotel in Coral Gables, the stately Biltmore is a National Historic Landmark—one of only two operating hotels in Florida so designated. See chapter 5. © *Darrell Jones Photography.*

South Florida has the largest concentration of Art Deco architecture in the United States. See chapter 7 for information on walking tours of South Beach's Art Deco District.
© *Gail Mooney/Kelly/Mooney Photography.*

Every year, eager baseball fans from across the country flock to Florida for spring training. See chapter 13.
© M. Timothy O'Keefe Photography.

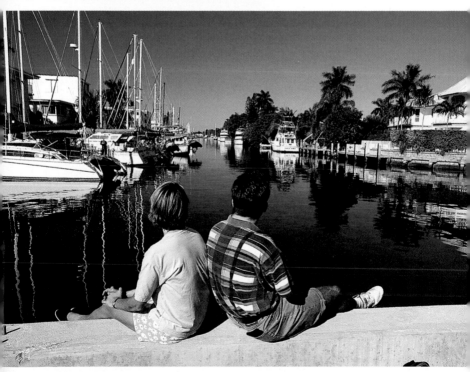

You'll have no trouble renting a boat or hopping on a water taxi when you visit Fort Lauderdale's Isle of Venice, the "yachting capital of the world." See chapter 12.
© Jeff Greenberg / Silver Images.

Known as the "Taj Mahal of North America," The Flagler Museum features a 55-room Edwardian-style mansion and stunning grounds. See chapter 12. © M. Timothy O'Keefe Photography.

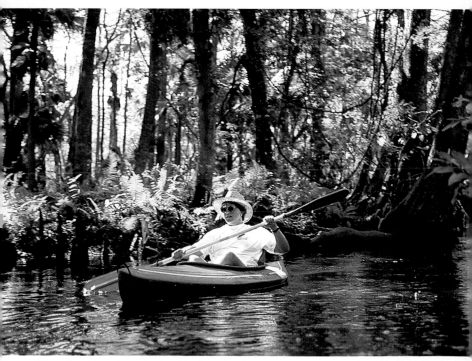

Taking a kayak trip down the Loxahatchee River is a great way to see the abundance of plant and animal life found on South Florida's Treasure Coast. See chapter 13. © Murry H. Sill/Silver Images.

When should I travel to get the best airfare?
Where do I go for answers to my travel questions?
What's the best and easiest way to plan and book my trip?

frommers.travelocity.com

Frommer's, the travel guide leader, has teamed up with **Travelocity.com**, the leader in online travel, to bring you an in-depth, easy-to-use resource designed to help you plan and book your trip online.

At **frommers.travelocity.com**, you'll find free online updates about your destination from the experts at Frommer's plus the outstanding travel planning and purchasing features of Travelocity.com. Travelocity.com provides reservations capabilities for 95 percent of all airline seats sold, more than 47,000 hotels, and over 50 car rental companies. In addition, Travelocity.com offers more than 2,000 exciting vacation and cruise packages. Travelocity.com puts you in complete control of your travel planning with these and other great features:

> **Expert travel guidance from Frommer's** - over 150 writers reporting from around the world!

> **Best Fare Finder** - an interactive calendar tells you when to travel to get the best airfare

> **Fare Watcher** - we'll track airfare changes to your favorite destinations

> **Dream Maps** - a mapping feature that suggests travel opportunities based on your budget

> **Shop Safe Guarantee** - 24 hours a day / 7 days a week live customer service, and more!

Whether traveling on a tight budget, looking for a quick weekend getaway, or planning the trip of a lifetime, Frommer's guides and Travelocity.com will make your travel dreams a reality. You've bought the book, now book the trip!

A New Star-Rating System & Other Exciting News from Frommer's!

In our continuing effort to publish the savviest, most up-to-date, and most appealing travel guides available, we've added some great new features.

Frommer's guides now include a new **star-rating system.** Every hotel, restaurant, and attraction is rated from 0 to 3 stars to help you set priorities and organize your time.

We've also added **seven brand-new features** that point you to the great deals, in-the-know advice, and unique experiences that separate travelers from tourists. Throughout the guide look for:

Finds	Special finds—those places only insiders know about
Fun Fact	Fun facts—details that make travelers more informed and their trips more fun
Kids	Best bets for kids—advice for the whole family
Moments	Special moments—those experiences that memories are made of
Overrated	Places or experiences not worth your time or money
Tips	Insider tips—some great ways to save time and money
Value	Great values—where to get the best deals

We've also added a **"What's New"** section in every guide—a timely crash course in what's hot and what's not in every destination we cover.

Other Great Guides for Your Trip:

Frommer's Florida

Florida from $70 a Day

Frommer's Portable Miami

Frommer's Caribbean Cruises & Ports of Call

Frommer's®

South Florida
including Miami & the Keys

2002

by Lesley Abravanel

Here's what the critics say about Frommer's:

"Amazingly easy to use. Very portable, very complete."

—Booklist

"The only mainstream guide to list specific prices. The Walter Cronkite of guidebooks—with all that implies."

—Travel & Leisure

"Complete, concise, and filled with useful information."

—New York Daily News

"Hotel information is close to encyclopedic."

—Des Moines Sunday Register

Hungry Minds™

Best-Selling Books • Digital Downloads • e-Books • Answer Networks •
e-Newsletters • Branded Web Sites • e-Learning
New York, NY • Cleveland, OH • Indianapolis, IN

About the Author

Lesley Abravanel is a freelance journalist and a graduate of the University of Miami School of Communication. When she isn't combing South Florida for the latest hotels, restaurants, and attractions, she is on the lookout for vacationing celebrities, about whom she writes in her weekly columns, "Nocturnal Admissions," for miami.citysearch.com and "Velvet Underground," for the *Miami Herald*'s weekly entertainment newspaper, *The Street*. She is also the Miami correspondent for *Black Book Magazine*.

Published by:

Hungry Minds, Inc.

909 Third Ave.
New York, NY 10022

ISBN 0-7645-6458-7
ISSN 1530-8758

Editor: Lorraine Festa
Production Editor: M. Faunette Johnston
Cartographer: Elizabeth Puhl
Photo Editor: Richard Fox
Production by Hungry Minds Indianapolis Production Services

Special Sales

For general information on Hungry Minds' products and services, please contact our Customer Care department; within the U.S. at 800-762-2974, outside the U.S. at 317-572-3993 or fax 317-572-4002. For sales inquiries and reseller information, including discounts, bulk sales, customized editions, and premium sales, please contact our Customer Care department at 800-434-3422.

Manufactured in the United States of America

5 4 3 2 1

Contents

7 What to See & Do in Miami · 156

8 Miami Shopping · 188

9 Miami After Dark · 202

10 South Florida Side Trips: The Everglades & Biscayne National Park · 219

11 The Keys · 236

12 The Gold Coast: Hallandale to the Palm Beaches   290

13 The Treasure Coast: Stuart to Sebastian   352

Index   376

List of Maps

Acknowledgments

To my mother and father, without whose influence, encouragement, and support, I would never have ended up in Miami doing what I'm doing. To Michael Sasser and Phil LaPadula, whose assistance I'd have been lost without. To Matt Hannafin and Heidi Sarna for cruising with me and steering me here. To my friends—you know who you are—who applauded my jumping ship to embark on this interesting journey. And finally, to "Aunt" Trish—the Thelma to my Louise—who emerged from the girl at the valet as my sister in schlepping, whining, dining, and enlightening, and, last but not least, Mrs. Ritchie, for inspiring me to express myself and aspire to greatness.

—Lesley Abravanel

An Invitation to the Reader

In researching this book, we discovered many wonderful places—hotels, restaurants, shops, and more. We're sure you'll find others. Please tell us about them, so we can share the information with your fellow travelers in upcoming editions. If you were disappointed with a recommendation, we'd love to know that, too. Please write to:

Frommer's South Florida including Miami & the Keys 2002
Hungry Minds, Inc. • 909 Third Avenue • New York, NY 10022

An Additional Note

Please be advised that travel information is subject to change at any time—and this is especially true of prices. We therefore suggest that you write or call ahead for confirmation when making your travel plans. The authors, editors, and publisher cannot be held responsible for the experiences of readers while traveling. Your safety is important to us, however, so we encourage you to stay alert and be aware of your surroundings. Keep a close eye on cameras, purses, and wallets, all favorite targets of thieves and pickpockets.

New! Frommer's Star Ratings & Icons

Every hotel, restaurant, and attraction listing in this guide has been ranked for quality, value, service, amenities, and special features using a star-rating scale. In country, state, and regional guides, we also rate towns and regions to help you narrow down your choices and budget your time accordingly. Hotels and restaurants in the Very Expensive and Expensive categories are rated on a scale of one (highly recommended) to three stars (exceptional). Those in the Moderate and Inexpensive categories rate from zero (recommended) to two stars (very highly recommended). Attractions, towns, and regions are rated according to the following scale: zero stars (recommended), one star (highly recommended), two stars (very highly recommended), and three stars (must-see).

In addition to the rating system, we also use seven icons to highlight insider information, useful tips, special bargains, hidden gems, memorable experiences, kid-friendly venues, places to avoid, and other useful information:

Finds	Fun Fact	Kids	Moments	Overrated	Tips	Value

The following abbreviations are used for credit cards:

AE American Express	DC Diners Club	V Visa
DISC Discover	MC MasterCard	

FROMMERS.COM

Now that you have the guidebook to a great trip, visit our website at **www.frommers.com** for travel information on nearly 2,000 destinations. With features updated regularly, we give you instant access to the most current trip-planning information available. At Frommers.com, you'll also find the best prices on air fares, accommodations, and car rentals—and you can even book travel online through our travel booking partners. At Frommers.com, you'll also find the following:

- Daily Newsletter highlighting the best travel deals
- Hot Spot of the Month/Vacation Sweepstakes & Travel Photo Contest
- More than 200 Travel Message Boards
- Outspoken Newsletters and Feature Articles on travel bargains, vacation ideas, tips & resources, and more!

What's New in South Florida

At last, South Florida has broken free from its tired stereotypes. No longer equated with sleepy retirement communities and rowdy spring-break beaches, South Florida's varied regions, from the Palm Beaches down to the Key, offer something for everyone. Here's a rundown of what's new.

MIAMI A cash crop of luxury hotels, restaurants, and nightclubs has sprouted throughout Miami. But hold on to your wallets—there are still plenty of deals to be found. And though Miami is a seasonal destination, what used to be a completely somber summer in the city has been resurrected as a lively, cheaper, albeit much hotter, time to visit. For complete information on Miami, see chapters 4 through 9.

Accommodations Two **Ritz-Carlton** hotels (✆ **800/241-3333**) have opened—on South Beach (1 Lincoln Rd.) and Key Biscayne (415 Grand Bay Drive). A third location, in Coconut Grove (2700 Tigertail Ave.), is scheduled to open October 2001. To compete with the hauter-than-thou Delano Hotel on South Beach, the **Shore Club**, 1901 Collins Ave. (✆ **305/695-3100**), was scheduled to open at press time, practically next door. To fill the void of a luxury hotel near downtown Miami, the **Mandarin Oriental** (✆ **305/913-8288**) has opened on at 500 Brickell Key Drive. For the shabby chic set, the **Townhouse**, 150 20th St. (✆ **877/534-3800**), has opened on South Beach, and is making a splash with

rooftop waterbeds and hallway exercise equipment. Also scheduled for 2001 opening, is Casa Tua, an outrageous, and outrageously priced, boutique property at 1700 James Ave. (✆ **305/673-1010**). The Ritz Plaza, taken over by W Hotels, has been resuscitated from its decrepit state into a revitalized stylish boutique hotel. We await the opening of **W Miami** (✆ **877-W-HOTELS**) and its wing of oceanfront rooms in the fall of 2002.

Dining Soon, Miami will have three new sushi options. **Nobu,** a hot New York sushi import, will be opening in 2001, at Shore Club (1901 Collins Ave., South Beach; ✆ **305/695-3100**), as will **Sushi Samba** (at the corner of Pennsylvania Avenue and Lincoln Road; no phone at press time); **Bond St. Lounge,** located at Townhouse Hotel, 150 20th St., South Beach (✆ **305/534-3800**) opened in December 2000. **Azul** (✆ **305/913-8258**), at the new Mandarin Oriental, 500 Brickell Key Drive, is a superb Global Fusion restaurant that's worth busting the bank account for.

Sightseeing Work continues on the **Miami Beach Cultural Park** in South Beach, which includes the new Arquitectonica-design home of the **Miami City Ballet,** the Miami Beach Regional Library, which broke ground in January 2001, the **Bass Museum of Art,** and a sculpture garden. The Bass (✆ **305/673-7530**) has expanded and received a dramatically new look by world-renowned Japanese architect

Arata Isozaki. Additions include triple the amount of exhibition space, an outdoor sculpture terrace, and a museum cafe.

Shopping Merrick Park, an upscale shopping center, has opened in Coral Gables and features the city's first Dean & DeLuca gourmet grocery, in addition to Armani, Yves St. Laurent, and a host of other pricey stores. In South Beach, the area between Fifth and Eighth streets on Collins Avenue features a slew of high-end stores; new additions include Intermix and Club Monaco. Lincoln Road continues to become an outdoor mall, recently adding Bebe to the mix with Victoria's Secret on the horizon.

After Dark   At press time, the hottest nightspots are located on the still sizzling South Beach. However, over the causeway, a burgeoning nocturnal buzz is emanating from the once desolate area of **downtown Miami,** off of Biscayne Boulevard and into the newly hip **Design District** (NE 36th Street to 41st Street and NE Second Avenue to N Miami Avenue), in which after-hours clubs and a few funky nightspots have cropped up. South Beach's **Rumi,** 330 Lincoln Rd. (✆ 305/672-4353), scheduled to open summer 2001, will be a high-style, high-concept supper club featuring haute, Floribbean cuisine.

THE GOLD COAST   For complete information on this region, see chapter 12.

Accommodations   The $600 million **Diplomat Resort Country Club and Spa,** 3555 South Ocean Drive (✆ 800/327-1212), has been thoroughly revamped to a 1,060-room full- service beach resort and convention center with a 155-acre golf course. The **Marriott Harbor Beach Resort,** 3030 Holiday Drive, (✆800/222-6543) has undergone over $20 million in renovations, adding a 24,000-square-foot European spa. Las Olas Boulevard's quaint **Riverside Hotel,** 620 E. Las Olas Blvd. (✆ 800/325-3280), intends to expand its capacity to 221 rooms by February 2002. Palm Beach's stately **Breakers Hotel,** 1 S. County Rd. (✆ 800/833-3141), received a $100 million renovation, which added the Oceanfront Spa and Beach Club and expanded the Breakers Ocean Course to a 6,200-yard, par-70 championship golf course.

Dining   The Boca Raton Resort and Club, 501 E. Camino Real (✆ 800/327-0101), has added two new restaurants: **Lucca,** a Tuscan-style waterfront restaurant designed by David Rockwell and run by Drew Nieporent's Myriad Restaurant Group, and **27 Ocean Blue,** an eclectic restaurant fusing Pacific Rim, Caribbean, Southern, Hawaiian, and New World cuisines.

Shopping   West Palm Beach's **City Place**, 222 Lakeview Ave. (✆ 561/835-0862), is not unlike Coconut Grove's CocoWalk or Fort Lauderdale's Beach Place shopping, dining, and entertainment complexes. The $550 million outdoor Mediterranean-style complex features 78 stores, including Macy's and FAO Schwarz, a multiplex movie theater, and several restaurants such as Legal Seafoods and the Cheesecake Factory.

The Best of South Florida

There's much more to South Florida than the neon-hued nostalgia of *Miami Vice* and pink flamingos. In fact, what used to be a relatively sleepy, beach vacation destination has awoken from its humid slumber, upped its tempo, and finally earned its place in the Palm Pilots of cutting-edge jet-setters worldwide. But don't be fooled by the hipper-than-thou celebrity-drenched playground commonly known as South Beach. While the chic elite do, indeed, flock to Miami's coolest enclave, it is surprisingly accessible to the average Joe, Jane, or José. For every Phillippe Starck–designed, bank-account-busting boutique hotel on South Beach, there's a kitschy, candy-coated Art Deco–rated one that's much less taxing on the pockets. For each Pan-MediterAsian haute cuisinerie, there's always the down-home, no-nonsense Cuban bodega offering hearty food at ridiculously cheap prices.

Beyond the whole "scene," Miami has an endless number of sporting, cultural, and recreational activities to keep you entertained. Did I mention our sparkling beaches that are beyond compare? Crystal-clear waters span a turquoise horizon and sandy beaches are filled with palm fronds and seashells. Plus there's excellent shopping and other nightlife activities that include ballet, theater, and opera.

Cross over the bridge onto the mainland, be it the Keys, the Gold Coast, or the Treasure Coast, and you've just exposed yourself not only to more UV rays, but to a world of cultural, historical, and sybaritic surprises. In these spots you can take in a spring baseball game, walk in the footsteps of Papa Hemingway, get up close and personal with the area's sea life, or just soak up the serenity of unspoiled landscapes.

Forget what you've heard about South Florida being Heaven's Waiting Room. That slogan is as passé as the concept of Early Bird dinners (which you can still get—they just no longer define the region). In fact, according to some people, South Florida *is* heaven. So what are you waiting for?

1 Frommer's Favorite South Florida Experiences

- **Driving along A1A:** The oceanfront route that runs north up Miami Beach, through Sunny Isles and Hollywood into Fort Lauderdale, embodies the essence that is South Florida. From time-warped hotels steeped in Art Deco kitsch to multi-million-dollar modern high-rises, A1A is one of the most scenic, albeit heavily trafficked, roads in all of Florida. See chapter 7.

- **Sunset in Key West:** You haven't seen the sun set properly until you've seen it in all its fiery glory at the southernmost point in the United States, at Mallory Square, in Key West. Brace yourself for a stellar solar performance in which this leading actress in the sky is

Florida

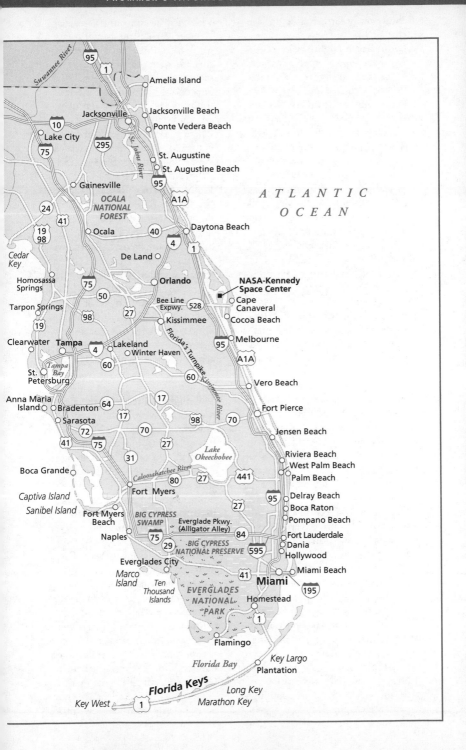

always ready for her close-up. See chapter 11.

- **South Beach Nightlife:** Leonardo DiCaprio spent a recent New Year's Eve at Tantra, a grass-floored restaurant/lounge in which Marrakesh meets Miami Beach. Madonna and Gwyneth spent theirs at 320 Lincoln Rd., where Studio 54 is resurrected in its full, glitzy glory. Best of all, these were *not* private parties. Where else can us ordinary folk brush elbows with—or spill Cosmopolitans on—Hollywood starlets, entertainment moguls, and living legends, but in one of South Beach's hot clubs, bars, and restaurants, many of which don't get going until the crack of dawn? See chapter 9.

- **Airboat Ride through the Outskirts of the Everglades:** Unfettered by jet skis, cruise ships, and neon bikinis, the Everglades are Florida's outback, resplendent in its swampy nature, which is best explored via an airboat that can navigate its way through the most stubborn of sawgrass, providing you with an up-close and personal view of the land's inhabitants, from alligators and manatees to raccoon and Florida panther. See chapter 10.

- **Dining at Big Fish Restaurant on the Miami River:** Some consider dining on the Miami River to be industrial chic; others consider it seedy in a *Miami Vice* sort of way. However you choose to look at it, by all means *do* look at it, as the sleepy Miami River is nestled below the sweeping downtown Miami skyline, reminding you that even though you're in a major metropolis, things in this often frenetic city are capable of slowing down to a more soothing pace. See chapter 6.

- **Vizcaya Museum and Gardens:** Built in 1916 as the winter home of industrialist James Deering, this Italian Renaissance–style manse on the water is the San Simeon, the Xanadu of Miami, featuring 34 rooms of antiques, art, and tapestries, 10 acres of Italian gardens, statues, and fountains, and a picture-perfect view of the skyline and Key Biscayne. See chapter 7.

- **Wolfie Cohen's Rascal House:** You *will* wait on line at South Florida's landmark diner, but it's never dull as the cacophony of mostly northeastern U.S. accents will keep you entertained until you are seated in what seems to be an ancient vinyl booth, at which an octogenarian waitress will serve you corned beef sandwiches, brisket, or potato pancakes, and, if you're lucky, she may tell you about the time Sinatra and his Rat Pack came in way back when. See chapter 6.

- **Moonlight Concerts at the Barnacle State Historic Site:** Once a month, on or near the full moon (except during July and August), the Barnacle State Historic Site hosts a concert in the backyard of their charming 1908 bungalow built on 5 acres of waterfront property. Listeners are welcome to picnic and bask in this sublime setting for a mere $5. See chapter 7.

- **Midnight Snacking at Versailles:** This iconoclastic, gaudy Cuban diner in the heart of Little Havana is humming with the buzz of old-timers reminiscing about Pre-Castro Cuba, local politicos trying to appease them, and a slew of detached people only there for the fantastically cheap, authentic Cuban fare. Much like its French namesake in whose image it's been literally mirrored, Miami's

Versailles provides a palatial view of Miami's ever changing Cuban landscape. See chapter 6.

- **Watching the Cruise Ships Set Sail from South Pointe Park:** Unless you're already on a boat, you can't get a better view of the monstrous cruise ships leaving the Port of Miami than from South Pointe Park, located at the southern tip of South Beach. If you stare long enough, you *will* feel like you're moving, which is almost as much fun as being on board. See chapter 7.

- **Lunch at News Café on Ocean Drive:** The quintessential South Beach experience, lunching at News Café is more of a spectator sport than a dining experience. What the Big Mac is to McDonald's, people watching is to News Café, whose Ocean Drive location is one of the best sidewalk spots from which to observe the wacky, colorful mix of pedestrians on parade. See chapter 6.

- **Relishing the View from Bill Baggs Cape Florida State Recreation Area:** You haven't truly seen South Florida until you've checked out the view from the southern point of Key Biscayne. Whether it's the turquoise water or the sight of Stiltsville—seven still-inhabited aquatic cabins dating back to the 1930s, perched smack in the middle of the Biscayne Channel—it may take a little coercing to get you to leave. See chapter 7.

- **Scuba Diving Off Jupiter Beach:** In 1988, Jupiter lifeguard Peter Leo spotted an anchor and a cannon while on his routine morning swim. Turns out, they belonged to what is believed to be the shipwreck of a Spanish galleon dating back to the 16th or 17th century. Giving literal meaning to South Florida's Treasure and Gold coasts,

this wreck is worth holding your breath for. See chapter 12.

- **Happy Hour at Mai Kai:** Where Polynesia meets Fort Lauderdale, Mai Kai is the trippiest tiki hut this side of Tahiti, with its sarong-clad bartenders, a fiery hula show, and an exhaustive menu of frozen concoctions. See chapter 12.

- **Discovering your Inner Flipper at the Dolphin Research Center:** Learn to communicate with and touch the mammals at the non-profit Dolphin Research Center in Marathon Key, home to a school of approximately 15 dolphins. See chapter 11.

- **Eyeing the Estates on Palm Beach:** The winter playground for the *Lifestyles of the Rich and Famous* set, Palm Beach is lined with jaw-dropping palatial estates. While many of them are hidden behind towering shrubbery, head south on South County Road, where you will see some of the most opulent homes ever built. Make sure someone holds the steering wheel if you're driving, because you *will* do a double-take. See chapter 12.

- **Lounging Poolside at the Delano:** In addition to tanning, the scene here is about striking a pose and pretending not to notice the others doing so. If you're staying at the Delano, and if you're savvy enough to score one of the luxe lounges, prepare to overhear some interesting conversations between the movers and shakers who bake here. See chapter 5.

- **Boating through the Intracoastal Waterway:** The waterway that connects the natural bays, lagoons, and rivers along Florida's East Coast snakes around all the way from the Florida–Georgia Border to the port of Miami. A ride through the Fort Lauderdale Intracoastal provides a sublime view of million-dollar waterfront houses. See chapter 12.

- **Having a Postbeach Beer at Jimbo's on Key Biscayne:** Who knew that a dive housed in a wooden shack in the mangroves of Virginia Key, serving beer from a cooler, would become one of Miami's best-kept local secrets? That is, until now. See chapter 6.

- **Visiting a Salsa Club:** If the only salsa you're familiar with is the kind you put on your tacos, go to La Covacha (West Miami) or Bongo's Cuban Cafe (downtown Miami), and watch some of the city's best dancers show off their fancy, sassy footwork. See chapter 9.

2 The Best Beaches

- **For Tranquility:** Matheson Hammock Park Beach (© 305/ 665-5475) in South Miami features an enclosed man-made lagoon that is flushed naturally by the tidal action of the adjacent Biscayne Bay. The serene beach is surrounded by the bay's warm, calm waters and a backdrop of tropical hardwood forest. See chapter 7.

  The beach at **Bahia Honda State Park** (© 305/872-2353), in Bahia Honda Key, is one of the nicest and most peaceful in Florida, located amidst 635 acres of nature trails and even a portion of Henry Flagler's railroad. See chapter 11.

- **For Water Sports: Hobie Beach,** located on the south side of Key Biscayne's Rickenbacker Causeway, is one of the most popular beaches for water-sport enthusiasts, featuring jet-ski, sailboat, windsurfing, and sailboard rentals, shade, if necessary, from the Australian pine, and a sublime view of the picturesque downtown Miami skyline. See chapter 7.

- **For People Watching: Lummus Park Beach** is world renowned, not necessarily for its pristine

sands, but for its more common name of **South Beach,** on which seeing, being seen, and, at times, the obscene, go hand in hand with the sunscreen and beach towels. See chapter 7.

Not nearly as scenic, but still heavily populated, is **Fort Lauderdale Beach,** the site of many a bacchanalian spring break, Frankie and Annette, and, now, an eclectic—albeit calmer—mix of young, buff beach bums. See chapter 12.

- **For Nature Lovers: MacArthur Beach** in West Palm Beach is considered by many nature enthusiasts to be the most beautiful nature park in South Florida, with a nice stretch of beach set against a lush and diverse background of foliage, plus a state-of-the-art nature center and renowned sea turtle awareness program. See chapter 12.

- **For Nude Sunbathing:** For that all-over tan, the place to be is **Haulover Beach** (© 305/944-3040), nestled between the Intracoastal Waterway and the ocean, on the north end. A gay, nude beach is also there, as is an area for

Impressions

What could be better than to sit on the beach playing cards in my shirt-sleeves in January?

—Anonymous Miami Beach Resident

nude volleyball. Sunscreen on this beach is a commodity. See chapter 7.

- **For Seclusion:** The producers of *Survivor* could feasibly shoot their show on the ultra-secluded, picturesque, and deserted **Virginia Key,** on Key Biscayne, where people go purposely not to be found. See chapter 7.
- **John U. Lloyd State Park** (© 954/923-6711) in Dania Beach is unfettered by high-rise condos, T-shirt shops, and hotels, and remains intact with an untouched shoreline surrounded by a canopy of Australian pine to ensure that your seclusion is, indeed, highly guarded. See chapter 12.
- **For Gay Beach-goers:** South Beach's **12th Street Beach** is the

beach of choice for gay residents and travelers who come to show off just how much time they've spent in the gym, and, of course, catch up on the latest gossip and upcoming must-attend parties and events. Oftentimes, this beach is the venue for some of the liveliest parties South Beach has ever seen. See chapter 7.

- **For Kids:** Miami's **Crandon Beach** (© 305/361-5421) is extremely popular for families with kids because of the shallow water created by a neighboring sandbar. Convenient parking, picnic areas, a winding boardwalk, and a multiethnic mix of families grilling, dancing, and relaxing are the benchmarks of this beach. See chapter 7.

3 Best Hotel Bets

- **Best Historic Hotel:** With a guest registry that reads like a who's who of history crossed with an engrossing whodunit, the monumental, Mediterranean-revivalist–style **Biltmore Hotel** (© 800/727-1926 or 305/445-1926) opened its doors in 1926. Guests ranging from Al Capone to the duke and duchess of Windsor loved the stately hotel so much that they never left, so say those who claim the hotel is haunted. Ghosts aside, this national landmark boasts the largest hotel pool in the continental United States and a 300-foot bell tower modeled after the Cathedral of Seville. See chapter 5.
- **Best Cheap-Chic Hotel:** South Beach's **Townhouse** (© 877/534-3800 or 305/534-3800) is a funky six-story 1930s building featuring exercise equipment in the hallways, laundry machines in the lobby, and a roof deck with waterbeds surrounding a glow-in-the-dark water tower. Rooms start at just $99. See chapter 5.

- **Best Celebrity-Saturated Hotel:** The **Delano** (© 800/555-5001 or 305/672-2000) is a celebrity magnet, attracting stars and starlets who you'd only find at the most A-list Hollywood parties. The hotel's star power makes up for its sterile rooms. See chapter 5.
- **Best Role-Playing Hotel:** With rooms such as "Me Tarzan, You Vain," or "Best Whorehouse," South Beach's **Pelican Hotel** (© 800/7-PELICAN or 305/673-3373) takes the concept of escapism to an entirely new level. See chapter 5.
- **Best Out-of-Place Bed-and-Breakfast:** Located on the outskirts of gritty, bustling downtown Miami is the historic **Miami River Inn** (© 800/468-3589 or 305/325-0045), housed in five restored clapboard buildings dating back to 1906. By the looks of this place, you could swear you were somewhere in New England until you stepped out for a breath of the balmy air. See chapter 5.

- **Best Hotel in a League of Its Own: Jules' Undersea Lodge** (② 305/451-2353) in Key Largo really gives you the low-down on the full Keys experience by requiring all guests to scuba 30 feet underwater to get to their rooms, which are literally located under the sea, in the mangrove habitat of Emerald Lagoon. See chapter 11.
- **Best Art Deco Hotel:** The **Raleigh Hotel** (② 800/848-1775 or 305/534-6300) in Miami is the reigning diva of Deco, dating back to 1940, featuring one of the most photographed palm-lined swimming pools reminiscent of the days of Esther Williams. See chapter 5.
- **Best Gatsby-esque Hotel:** As you drive up to the **Breakers** (② 800/833-3141) in posh Palm Beach, you can't help but feel the spirit of Jay Gatsby beckoning you into this mammoth Italian Renaissance–style hotel. See chapter 12.
- **Best Beach Hotel:** The **Beach House Bal Harbour** (② 877/782-3557 or 305/865-3551) was inspired by the great beach homes of the Hamptons, Nantucket, and Coastal Maine, and when you stay here, you will feel like someone's houseguest rather than an anonymous hotel guest. See chapter 5.
- **Best Inexpensive Hotel:** It's hard to find a hotel on South Beach with both good value and excellent service, but the **Crest Hotel Suites** (② 800/531-3880 or 305/531-0321) delivers and peaks as one of Miami's best bargains and coolest hotels. See chapter 5.

  In Key West, the **Grand** (② 888/947-2630), despite its name, will not leave you with a huge tab at the end of your stay. The rooms in this hotel are bright and airy and the proprietor works hard to keep you happy. See chapter 11.

The **Blue Seas Courtyard** (② 877/225-8373) in Lauderdale-by-the-Sea is a terrific deal that's just 1 block from the beach and features rooms drenched in Haitian and Peruvian art, as well as a garden pool. See chapter 12.
- **Best for Families:** In Miami, the **Sonesta Beach Resort Key Biscayne** (② 800/SONESTA or 305/361-2021) is known for its complimentary children's programs led by trained counselors who supervise kids, grouped by age, in pool and beach activities and on field trips including dinner and a movie and museum excursions. Fees apply for meals/certain excursions. See chapter 5.

  In Fort Lauderdale, **Marriott's Harbor Beach** (② 800/222-6543) has the Beachside Buddies program for children ages 5 to 12, offering half-day and all-day children's activities that range from seashell collecting to hula hoop contests. The 8,000-square-foot, free-form swimming pool, expansive sand beach, and instant access to water toys keep kids entertained. See chapter 12.

  The **Boca Raton Resort & Club** (② 800/327-0101) has three activity programs designed for distinct age groups: Boca Tots (ages 3 to 5), Boca Bunch (ages 6 to 11) and Boca Sport (ages 12 to 17). Upon registering children in the program, each parent is given a beeper with a 60-mile radius so that they may be contacted at any time. See chapter 12.
- **Best for Romance:** In Miami, the **Hotel Place St. Michel** (② 800/848-HOTEL or 305/444-1666) is a cozy European-style hotel whose wood-floored dark-paneled rooms are adorned in antiques, transporting you from sunny Florida to gay Paris. See chapter 5.

Imagine an intimate haven on your own private island and you've got **Little Palm Island** (℡ 800/343-8567), located just 3 miles offshore in the Florida Keys, accessible only by boat or seaplane, and quite possibly the closest thing to paradise, with only one telephone on the entire island. See chapter 11.

In Palm Beach, modeled after a quaint English inn, the **Chesterfield Hotel** (℡ 800/243-7871) is absolutely seductive, thanks in part to its sexy, sultry Leopard Lounge, its cozy fireside library, and Churchill's Cigar Room. See chapter 12.

- **Best Guesthouses/B&Bs:** The **Villa Paradiso Guest House** (℡ 305/532-0616) may be smack in the heart of frenetic South Beach, but once you're inside you're worlds away, with rooms facing a sun-drenched courtyard and a host who is genuinely glad to see you, unlike some of the more attitudinal staff found in other nearby hotels. See chapter 5.

In Fort Lauderdale, **La Casa Del Mar** (℡ 954/467-2037) is located right on the beach and offers cozily appointed rooms with names such as Stolen Kiss. Owners Larry and Lee bend over backward to make sure your stay is a fantastic one. See chapter 12.

4 Best Dining Bets

- **Best for Celebrating a Big Deal:** The **Forge Restaurant,** 432 Arthur Godfrey Rd. (at 41st Street), Miami Beach (℡ 305/538-8533), is a multichambered, ornately decorated (and priced) monument known for its decadent wines, steak, and fish. See chapter 6.

- **Best Romantic Restaurant: La Vieille Maison,** 770 East Palmetto Park Rd., Boca Raton (℡ 561/391-6701), is housed in a 1920s-era structure, with a stunning courtyard, superlative haute French cuisine, and intimate, private dining rooms. See chapter 12.

- **Best Waterfront Dining:** Ensconced in a tiki hut on Key Biscayne's Virginia Key, the **Bayside Seafood Restaurant,** 3501 Rickenbacker Causeway, Virginia Key (℡ 305/361-0808), is surrounded by a mangrove-studded lagoon and offers a simple menu with a simply unbelievable view of the downtown skyline. See chapter 6. **Louie's Backyard,** 700 Waddell Ave., Key West (℡ 305/294-1061), offers Caribbean cuisine and one of the best views of the gulf you'll ever have. See chapter 11.

- **Best Restaurant Worth the Wait for a Table:** The legendary South Florida institution known as **Joe's Stone Crab Restaurant,** 11 Washington Ave., Miami Beach (℡ 305/673-0365), refuses to take reservations, but that doesn't stop people from clawing their way into the restaurant for a table despite a wait that's often in excess of 3 hours. See chapter 6.

- **Best Cuban Restaurant:** There's always a debate on who has the best, most authentic Cuban cuisine, but for those of you who

Impressions

I come to Miami to relax, so I've never had a power lunch or dinner there.

—Madonna

have never been to Havana, **Versailles,** 3555 SW 8th St. (at SW 36th Ave.), Little Havana (© 305/444-0240), is *the* quintessential Cuban diner, featuring enormous portions at paltry prices. See chapter 6.

• **Best Steak House: New York Prime,** 2350 NW Executive Center Dr., Boca Raton (© 561/998-3881), may be part of a South Carolina–based chain, but its steaks are a cut above the rest. The only problem may be scoring a reservation. See chapter 12.

In addition to the **Forge Restaurant** (see above), **Christy's,** 3101 Ponce de León Blvd., Coral Gables (© 305/446-1400), is the Miami carnivore's choice, with superb steaks and famous Caesar salad. See chapter 6.

• **Best New World Cuisine:** It's a toss-up between the restaurants of the original founders of this palate-pleasing fusion of Florida and Caribbean (Floribbean) ingredients: **Norman's,** 21 Almeria Ave., Coral Gables (© 305/446-6767, owned by James Beard chef Norman van Aken; and **Chef Allen's,** 19088 NE 29th Ave., Aventura (© 305/935-2900), owned by chef Allen Susser. Whichever chef's cuisine you choose, they both do wonders with mangoes. See chapter 6.

• **Sexiest Restaurant: Tantra,** 1445 Pennsylvania Ave., Miami Beach (© 305/672-4765), was founded on an ancient Middle Eastern philosophy of sensuality and brings a bit of exotic Marrakesh to South Beach with an aphrodisiac-inspired menu, grass-lined floors, and an equally sultry crowd that isn't afraid of getting in touch with their sensual side. See chapter 6.

• **Best Scene: China Grill,** 404 Washington Ave., Miami Beach (© 305/534-2211), is a cavernous,

cacophonous Pan-Asian eatery whose portions are large enough to feed an entire continent and whose clientele is as stellar as its food. **Joia,** 140 Ocean Dr., Miami Beach (© 305/674-8855), exemplifies South Beach's spin on *La Dolce Vita* with its fine Italian cuisine, celebrity clientele, and requisite paparazzi hiding nearby in the bushes. See chapter 6.

• **Best Sunday Brunch: Nemo,** 100 Collins Ave., Miami Beach (© 305/532-4550), turns its open kitchen into your kitchen for a help-yourself-to-anything, calorie-busting Sunday brunch of gourmet fare and insanely good desserts. See chapter 6. **Mark's at the Park,** 344 Plaza Real (Mizner Park), Boca Raton (© 561/395-0770), features a gourmet all-you-can-eat $19 brunch—an unheard-of value in swanky Mizner Park. See chapter 12.

• **Best View: Big Fish,** 55 S. Miami Rd., Miami (© 305/373-1770), is all about gritty-chic, located on the Miami River, where tugboats and cargo ships slink by as you indulge in fresh fish and sip good Italian wine under the glow of the brilliant downtown skyline hovering above. The **Poet's Café at Power Studios,** 3701 NE 2nd Ave., Miami (© 305/576-1336), offers a diverse, reasonably priced menu and is housed in the SoHo-esque Design District's multimedia nocturnal fun house known as Power Studios. The ambient rooftop dining area provides an excellent overview of the burgeoning Design District, as well as featured classic films every evening, projected onto a big screen and the walls of the neighboring buildings. See chapter 6.

• **Best Haute Cuisine: Mark's Las Olas,** 1032 E. Las Olas Blvd., Ft. Lauderdale (© 954/463-1000), and **Mark's South Beach,** Hotel Nash, 1120 Collins Ave., Miami Beach (© 305/604-9050), are both owned by celebrity chef Mark Militello, whose New American cuisine restores the faith of gourmands whose palates once belonged to the Pan-Asian Fusion movement. See chapters 12 and 6.

- **Best People Watching: News Café,** 800 Ocean Dr., Miami Beach (© 305/538-6397), and 2901 Florida Ave., Coconut Grove (© 305/774-6397), practically invented the sport of people watching, encouraging its customers to sit at an outdoor table all day, if they want, lingering over the passing parades of people while sipping a cappuccino. The Delano Hotel's pricey **Blue Door** restaurant, 1685 Collins Ave., Miami Beach (© 305/674/6400), provides a front-row seat to the hordes of hipsters who flock there. See chapter 6.

- **Best Comfort Food: Big Pink,** 157 Collins Ave., Miami Beach (© 305/532-4700), serves kitsch in large doses, featuring TV dinners served in trays. Fun, funky, and the food's pretty good, too. See chapter 6.

- **Best Italian Food: Café Prima Pasta,** 414 71st St., Miami Beach (© 305/867-0106), can scare any vampire away with its garlic-infused Italian fare that lures a casual-chic crowd which spills out onto the street on a nightly basis. See chapter 6. **Tuscan Today Trattoria,** 1161 N. Federal Hwy, Ft. Lauderdale (© 954/566-1716), churns out primo Tuscan fare in its imported-from-Italy wood-burning brick oven. See chapter 12.

- **Best Kids' Restaurant: Game-Works,** 5701 Sunset Dr. in the Shops at Sunset Place, South Miami (© 305/667-4263) is the brainchild of co-owner Steven Spielberg, whose virtual reality and video games contribute to the actual reality of kids cleaning their plates so that they can play. See chapter 7.

- **Best Mexican:** The fresh, authentic Mexican fare at **El Rancho Grande,** 1626 Pennsylvania Ave., Miami Beach (© 305/673-0480), will have you swearing off Taco Bell forever. See chapter 6. **Carlos and Pepe,** 1302 SE 17th St., Ft. Lauderdale (© 954/467-7192), wouldn't dare serve bagged tortilla chips with its addictive spicy salsa and homemade Mexican cuisine. See chapter 12.

- **Best Star-Studded Sushi Restaurant: Bambu,** 1661 Meridian Ave., Miami Beach (© 305/531-4800), was created when it-girl Cameron Diaz decided there wasn't a fabulous sushi joint in the city she comes to often. Known more as "the Cameron Diaz restaurant" than anything else. See chapter 6.

- **Best Seafood: Grillfish,** 1445 Collins Ave., Miami Beach (© 305/538-9908), and 2325 Galliano St., Coral Gables (© 305/445-6411), is simple, unpretentious, and serves the freshest fish in town any which way you desire. See chapter 6.

- **Best Late-Night Dining:** In addition to the 24-hour **News Café** (see above and chapter 6) and the **Big Pink** (see above and chapter 6), **Lester's Diner,** 250 State Rd. 84, Ft. Lauderdale (© 954/525-5641), is a 24-hour institution, serving classic greasy-spoon fare at ridiculously cheap prices. The **Floridian,** 1410 E. Las Olas Blvd., Ft. Lauderdale (© 954/463-4041), serves everything from eggs to steaks, 24 hours a day. See chapter 12 for Lester's and the Floridian.

- **Kitschiest Dining: Wolfie Cohen's Rascal House,** 17190 Collins Ave., North Miami Beach (© 305/947-4581), is a must for those looking for a retro-fabulous South Florida experience, with a wait staff as old as the vinyl booths and the best corned beef on rye this side of the Lower East Side.

See chapter 6. **Green Turtle Inn,** Mile Marker 81.5, Islamorada (© 305/664-9031), is an old-fashioned Florida Keys institution since 1947 featuring moderately priced steaks, stone crabs, and, yes, turtle, to the tune of campy pianist Tina Martin. See chapter 11.

Planning a Trip to South Florida

As diverse as South Florida is, it's also a very seasonal destination. Peak season in South Florida runs from October to March. And while peak season is the most popular time to visit, pre- and postseason offer you a less congested, less expensive travel experience. It all depends on how much heat you can take. Regardless of when you choose to travel, a little advanced planning will make the most of your trip.

1 Visitor Information

Note: For more detailed information on the Keys, Fort Lauderdale, Boca Raton, and other cities on Florida's Gold and Treasure coasts, see chapters 11 to 13. Visitors from outside the United States should also see chapter 3 for entry requirements and other pertinent information.

The **Greater Miami Convention and Visitor's Bureau,** 701 Brickell Ave., Miami, FL 33131 (© **800/283-2707;** www.tropicoolmiami.com), is the best source for specialized information about the city and its beaches. Even if you don't have a specific question, you should request a free copy of *Tropicool,* the bureau's greater Miami and the beaches vacation planner. And remember that just because information on a particular establishment you're inquiring about is not available doesn't mean the place no longer exists. The GMCVB only endorses member businesses.

The **Greater Miami and Beaches Hotel Association,** 407 Lincoln Rd., Miami Beach, FL 33139 (© **800/531-3553**), provides information on accommodations and tours.

Because Miami is such a vast city, some of the more popular neighborhoods have their own chambers of commerce that will provide you with specific information on events, accommodations, and attractions in their areas. The following are some of them:

- **Miami Beach Chamber of Commerce,** 420 Lincoln Rd., Miami Beach, FL 33139 (© 305/672-1270).
- **Coral Gables Chamber of Commerce,** 50 Aragon Ave., Coral Gables, FL 33134 (© 305/446-1657).
- **Coconut Grove Chamber of Commerce,** 2820 McFarlane Rd., Coconut Grove, FL 33133 (© 305/444-7270).
- **Florida Gold Coast Chamber of Commerce** (representing Bal Harbour, Sunny Isles, and Surfside), 1100 Kane Concourse, Bay Harbor Islands, FL 33154 (© 561/866-6020).

For information on visiting the Fort Lauderdale area, the **Greater Fort Lauderdale Convention & Visitor's Bureau,** 1850 Eller Dr., Suite 303, Ft. Lauderdale, FL 33316 (© **954/765-4466**; www.sunny.org), offers a 71-page vacation planner as well as maps and other helpful information on the area and its beaches.

The **Palm Beach County Convention and Visitors Bureau,** 1555 Palm Beach Lakes Blvd., Suite 204, West Palm Beach, FL 33401 (© **561/471-3995**; www.palmbeachfl.com), offers maps, brochures, and, if you request it, a coupon book of over $500 in savings in the Palm Beach area. Ask for it!

Because there are so many islands in the Florida Keys, the best place for information is at www.florida-keys. fl.us/chamber.htm, where you can send e-mail requests to each individual Florida Keys chamber of commerce. To call, contact the chambers of commerce at the following numbers: Key Largo © **305/451-4726**; Islamorada © **800/FAB-KEYS** or 305/664-4503; Marathon © **800/262-7284** or 305/743-5417; Lower Keys © **800/872-3722**; Key West © **305/294-2587**.

For the Everglades, the **Tropical Everglades Visitor's Center,** 160 U.S. Hwy. 1, Florida City, FL 33034 (© **305/245-9180**), will provide you with information on tours, sites, and parks in the area.

For information on traveling throughout Florida, including a calendar of events, a guide to accommodations, and a list of useful websites, contact **Visit Florida,** P.O. Box 1100, 66 E. Jefferson St., Tallahassee FL 32302 (© **888-7-FLA-USA**; www. flausa.com). Visit Florida also has an office in London, Roebuck House, Palace Street, London SW1 E 5BA (© 071/630-6602).

2 Money

For as many palm trees as there are in South Florida, there are just as many, if not more, ATM machines linked to a major national network that will likely include your bank at home. Using common sense at ATM machines is first and foremost. Avoid withdrawing money at those machines located on sparsely populated streets; machines are available in many hotels, at most major tourist attractions, shopping malls, and even restaurants and nightclubs.

ATMS

Cirrus (© 800/424-7787; www. mastercard.com/atm/) and **Plus** (© 800/843-7587; www.visa.com/ atms) are the two most popular networks. **Bank of America** (© 800/932-2265) ATMs (automated teller machines) are among the most prevalent throughout South Florida; check the back of your ATM card to see which network your bank belongs to. Use the toll-free numbers to locate ATMs in your destination. Be sure to check the daily withdrawal limit before you depart.

TRAVELER'S CHECKS

Traveler's checks are something of an anachronism from the days before the ATM made cash accessible at any time. The only sound alternative to traveling with dangerously large amounts of cash, traveler's checks were as reliable as currency, unlike personal checks, but could be replaced if lost or stolen, unlike cash.

These days, traveler's checks seem less necessary because most cities have 24-hour ATMs that allow travelers to withdraw small amounts of cash as needed—and thus avoid the risk of carrying a fortune around an unfamiliar environment. Many banks, however, impose a fee every time a card is used at an ATM in a different city or bank. If you're withdrawing money every day, you might be better off with traveler's checks—provided that you don't mind showing identification every time you want to cash a check.

You can get traveler's checks at almost any bank. **American Express** offers denominations of $10, $20, $50, $100, $500, and $1,000. You'll pay a service charge ranging from 1% to 4%.

You can also get American Express traveler's checks over the phone by calling ℂ 800/221-7282; by using this number, Amex gold and platinum cardholders are exempt from the 1% fee. AAA (Automobile Association of America) members can obtain checks without a fee at most AAA offices.

Visa offers traveler's checks at Citibank locations nationwide, as well as at several other banks. The service charge ranges between 1.5% and 2%; checks come in denominations of $20, $50, $100, $500, and $1,000. **MasterCard** also offers traveler's checks. Call ℂ 800/223-9920 for a location near you.

CREDIT CARDS

Credit cards are invaluable when traveling. They are a safe way to carry money and provide a convenient record of all your expenses. You can also withdraw cash advances from your credit cards at any bank (though you'll start paying hefty interest on the advance the moment you receive the cash, and you won't receive frequent-flyer miles on an airline credit card). At most banks, you don't even need to go to a teller; you can get a cash advance at the ATM if you know your PIN (personal identification number). If you've forgotten your PIN or didn't even know you had one, call the phone number on the back of your credit card and ask the bank to send it to you. It usually takes 5 to 7 business days, though some banks will provide the number over the phone if you tell them your mother's maiden name or pass some other security clearance.

What Things Cost in Miami	U.S. $	UK £
Taxi from the airport to the city center	$22.30	13.51
Taxi from Miami International Airport to Miami Beach	$24	16.80
Local telephone call	.35	.24
Double room at the Delano (peak season)	$375	262.50
Double room at the Biscayne Bay Marriott (peak)	$194	135.80
Double room at the Hampton Inn, Coconut Grove (peak)	$134	93.80
Lunch for one at News Café	$12	8.40
Lunch for one at Front Porch Café	$8	5.60
Dinner for one at The Forge (without wine)	$ 50	35
Dinner for one at Van Dyke Café (without wine)	$16	11.20
Dinner for one at Versailles (without wine)	$8	5.60
Beer	$3.50	2.80
Martini	$9	6.30
Coca-Cola in restaurant	$2	1.40
Cup of coffee	$1.25	.88
Cup of Cuban coffee	$1	.70
Movie ticket	$7.75	5.43
Cover charge to a nightclub on South Beach	$15	10.5

At this writing the price conversion above was computed at the rate of $1 equals 70p.

THEFT Almost every credit-card company has an emergency toll-free number that you can call if your wallet or purse is stolen. They may be able to wire you a cash advance off your credit card immediately, and in many places, they can deliver an emergency credit card in a day or two. The issuing bank's toll-free number is usually on the back of the credit card—though of course that doesn't help you much if the card was stolen. The toll-free information directory will provide the number if you dial ℂ 800/555-1212. Citicorp Visa's U.S. emergency number is ℂ 800/336-8472. American Express cardholders and traveler's check holders should call ℂ 800/221-7282 for all money emergencies. MasterCard holders should call ℂ 800/307-7309.

If you opt to carry traveler's checks, be sure to keep a record of their serial numbers separately from the checks so that you're ensured a refund in just such an emergency.

Odds are that if your wallet is gone, the police won't be able to recover it for you. However, after you realize that it's gone and you cancel your credit cards, it is still worth informing them. Your credit-card company or insurer may require a police report number.

3 When to Go

Contrary to popular belief, the notion of sunny Florida isn't always 100% correct. While the term is hardly an oxymoron, when it comes to weather, sunny Florida undergoes major mood swings. While it may be pouring on the ocean side of Miami Beach, on the bay side the only thing pouring down are UV rays.

Rain showers aside, the most pressing concern for every South Florida visitor is the dreaded "H" word—the unpredictable, unstoppable hurricane. Official hurricane season is from August to November, and while the hurricane's actual pattern is unpredictable, for the most part, the meteorologists at the National Hurricane Center in Coral Gables are able to give fair enough warning so that people can take proper precautions. One of the safest places during a hurricane happens to be in a hotel, because most hotels are sturdy enough to withstand high winds and they have generators in case of power failures. Hurricanes rarely last more than 48 hours, and once the storm has passed, the weather is unbelievably beautiful.

For many people, the worst time to come to South Florida is during the summer, when temperatures are usually scorching, humidity is oppressive, and rain at 4pm is a daily occurrence. Europeans love South Florida summers and are undeterred by the heat. Others, however, prefer to come during the peak season of October to April. Wintertime in South Florida is spectacular—not too hot, not too cool. Temperatures can, however, dip down into the low 50s during a cold front, and it's most amusing to see the Northeast transplants whipping out their leather and fur coats.

Weather aside, peak season in South Florida means more tourists, snowbirds, and models. You always know the season has begun when you notice the lithe, beautiful people carrying big black portfolios and rushing off to "go-sees" and photo shoots. Another season marker is the influx of celebrities, who also call South Florida their winter home away from home.

In the summer, South Florida practically comes to a standstill as far as special events, cultural activities, and overall pace is concerned. Locals love it; it is their time to reclaim their cities. Tourists may want to take advantage of the summers down here as long as they can stand the heat. If you can brave the temperature, you will not have to face the long lines in restaurants and at attractions that you will encounter during peak season.

For some people, however, the lines and the waiting is all part of the allure of South Florida, as they provide an opportunity to see and be seen.

Miami's Average Monthly High/Low Temperatures & Rainfall

	Jan	Feb	Mar	Apr	May	June	July	Aug	Sept	Oct	Nov	Dec
Avg. High (°F)	76	77	80	83	86	88	89	90	88	85	80	77
Avg. Low (°F)	60	61	64	68	72	75	76	76	76	72	66	61
Avg. High (°C)	24.4	25	26.7	28.3	30	31.1	31.7	32.2	31.1	29.4	26.7	25
Avg. Low (°C)	15.6	16.1	17.8	20	22.2	23.9	24.4	24.4	24.4	22.2	18.9	16.1
Avg. Rain (in.)	2.0	2.1	2.4	3.0	5.9	8.8	6.0	7.8	8.5	7.0	3.1	1.8

SOUTH FLORIDA CALENDAR OF EVENTS

January

FedEx Orange Bowl Classic, Miami. Football fanatics flock down to the big Orange Bowl game (oddly taking place not at the Orange Bowl in seedy downtown, but at the much more savory Pro Player Stadium) on New Year's Day, featuring two of the year's best college football teams. Tickets are available from March 1 of the previous year through the Orange Bowl Committee (© **305/371-4600**), but call early as they sell out quickly.

Polo Season, Palm Beach. Join the crisp and clean Ralph Lauren–clad polo fanatics including actor Tommy Lee Jones and socialite Ivana Trump at the Palm Beach Polo and Country Club for polo season. Call © **561/793-1440** for details. Begins in early January.

Three Kings Parade, Miami. Miami's Cuban community makes up for the fact that Castro banned this religious celebration over 25 years ago by throwing a no-holds-barred parade throughout the streets of Little Havana's Calle Ocho neighborhood, usually the first Sunday of January. Call (© **305/447-1140.**

Art Deco Weekend, South Beach. Gain a newfound appreciation for the Necco-wafered Art Deco buildings, deco furniture, history, and fashion at this weekend-long festival of street fairs, films, lectures, and other events (© **305/672-2014**). Mid- to late January.

Martin Luther King Jr. Day Parade, Miami. The culmination of the week's celebration of Dr. King's birthday, this parade occurs in the troubled neighborhood of Liberty City, along NW 54th Street, between NW 12th and 32nd avenues. For information, call © **305/636-1924.** Mid-January.

Taste of the Grove Food and Music Festival, Coconut Grove. Brave massive crowds of hungry folk at this fund-raising festival featuring booths from various neighborhood eateries hawking their goods for the price of a few prepurchased tickets. Call © **305/444-7270.** Usually third weekend in January.

Royal Caribbean Golf Classic, Key Biscayne. Watch as pro golfers such as Lee Trevino tee off for over $1 million at this tournament played on the scenic Crandon Park Golf Course. Call © **305/374-6180.** Late January.

Palm Beach International Art and Antiques Fair, West Palm Beach. With antiques and art older than some of Palm Beach's very own residents, this fair has become a premier stomping ground for domestic artifacts. Call ℂ **561/220-2690.** Late January or early February.

Key West Literary Seminar, Key West. Literary types get a good reason to put down the books and head to Key West. This annual 3-day event features a different theme every year, such as "The Memoir" and "Science Fiction," and a roster of incredible authors, writers, and other literary types such as Joyce Carol Oates, Barbara Ehrenreich, and Jamaica Kincaid. The event is so popular it sells out well in advance, so call early for tickets (available for individual lectures or events, or the entire 3-day conference). For information call ℂ **888/293-9291** or visit www. keywestliteraryseminar.org.

February

Miami Film Festival. Not exactly Cannes, the Miami Film Festival sponsored by the Film Society of America is an impressive 10-day celluloid celebration, featuring world premiers of Latin American, domestic, and other foreign and independent films. Actors, producers, and directors show up to plug their films and participate in Q & A sessions with the audiences. Call ℂ **305/377-FILM.** Early to mid-February.

Everglades Seafood Festival, Florida City. What seems like schools of fish-loving people flock down to Florida City for a 2-day feeding frenzy, in which Florida delicacies from stone crab to gator tails are served from shacks and booths on the outskirts of this quaint old Florida town. Free admission (ℂ **941/695-4100**). First full weekend in February.

Homestead Rodeo. Say hee-haw to one of South Florida's only rodeo shows featuring clowns, competitions, and bucking broncos. (ℂ **305/247-3515**). Early February.

Coconut Grove Arts Festival, Coconut Grove. Florida's largest art festival features over 300 artists who are selected from thousands of entries. Possibly one of the most crowded street fairs in South Florida, the festival attracts art lovers, artists, and lots of college students who seem to think this event is the Mardi Gras of art fairs. Call ℂ **305/447-0401** for information. Presidents' Day Weekend.

Miami International Boat Show, Miami Beach. Agoraphobes beware, as this show draws a quarter of a million boat enthusiasts to the Miami Beach Convention Center. Some of the world's priciest megayachts, speedboats, sailboats, and schooners are displayed for purchase or for gawking. Call ℂ **305/531-8410.** Mid-February.

Winter Equestrian Festival, West Palm Beach. With over 1,000 horses and three grand-prix equestrian events, the Palm Beach Polo Club's winter festival is an equestrian's dream (ℂ **561/798-7000**). Late February.

Doral Ryder Golf Open, West Miami. Another prestigious annual golf tournament swings into Miami at the legendary courses at the Doral Resort and Club. Call ℂ **305/477-GOLF.** Late February.

Hatsume Fair, Delray Beach. A 2-day fair celebrating the first buds of spring in a state that barely has seasons may seem like an odd notion, but the Hatsume Fair takes place at the Morikami Japanese Museum and Gardens—a place where visitors can appreciate truly exotic flora and fauna. Call ℂ **561/495-0233.** Last weekend in February.

March

Winter Party, Miami Beach. Gays and lesbians from around the world book trips to Miami as far as a year in advance to attend this weekend-long series of parties and events benefiting the Dade Human Rights Foundation. Travel arrangements can be made through Different Roads Travel, the event's official travel company, by calling ✆ **888/ROADS-55,** ext. 510. For information on the specific events and prices, call ✆ **305/538-5908** or visit www.winterparty.com. Early March.

Italian Renaissance Festival, Miami. Villa Vizcaya gets in touch with its Renaissance roots at this festival, which features strolling musicians, stage plays, and a cast of period-costumed characters who do their best to convince you that you're in a time warp. Call ✆ **305/250-9133.** Mid-March.

Miami Gay & Lesbian Film Festival, Miami Beach. This 10-day event is the Sundance of festivals for gay and lesbian films and filmmakers. It features an impressive roster of independent and commercial films, plus appearances by some of the films' directors, actors, and writers. Call ✆ **305/532-7256.** Mid-March.

Calle Ocho Festival, Little Havana. What Carnivale is to Rio, the Calle Ocho Festival is to Miami. This 10-day extravaganza, also called Carnival Miami, features a lengthy block party spanning 23 blocks, live salsa music, parades, and, of course, tons of savory Cuban delicacies. Those afraid of mob scenes should avoid this party at all costs (✆ **305/644-8888**). Mid-March.

Grand Prix of Miami, Homestead. A little bit of Daytona in Miami, the Grand Prix is a premier racing event, attracting celebrities, Indy car drivers, and curious spectators who get a buzz off the smell of gasoline. Get tickets early, as this event sells out quickly. Call ✆ **305/250-5200.** Late March.

Ericsson Open, Key Biscayne. Sampras, Agassi, Kournikova, and the Williams sisters are only a few of the grand slammers who appear at this, one of the world's foremost tennis tournaments. Tickets for the semifinals and finals are hard to come by, so order early. Call ✆ **305/446-2200.**

April

World Cup Polo Tournament, Palm Beach. The last tournament of the polo season, this event draws the diamond-studded mallet set who gather one more time in the name of scene and sport. Call ✆ **561/793-1440.** Mid-April.

PGA Seniors Golf Championship, Palm Beach Gardens. This is the oldest and most prestigious of the senior golf tournaments in which aging swingers prove they've still got spunk in their swing (✆ **561/624-8400**). Mid-April.

Little Acorns International Kite Festival, South Beach. A great event for the kids and kids at heart, this kite festival is a true spectacular in the sky, attracting thousands of expert flyers and their flying works of art from 5th to 15th streets. Kids can build their own kites and scrounge for candy, which is dropped piñata-style along the beach. Sandy candy—and kids—aside, the event's free, which makes it even more popular with parents looking for ways to entertain without having to pay a Disneyesque price tag. Call ✆ **888/298-9815.** Third weekend in April.

Sunfest, West Palm Beach. Sleepy downtown West Palm comes alive at the end of April for this street fair and concert, featuring big-name entertainment, food stands, a youth fair, and hordes of people. Admission charges are reasonable, but, unless there's someone performing who you must see, not always worth the price. Stick to the free nontented area on Clematis Street for excellent people watching (© 561/659-5992). Late April.

Texaco Key West Classic, Key West. This catch-and-release fishing competition offers $50,000 in prizes to be divided between the top anglers in three divisions: sailfish, marlin, and light tackle. You won't believe the size of some of these catches. Call © 305/294-4042. Late April.

Conch Republic Celebration, Key West. Residents of Key West fancy themselves to be members of an independent Conch Republic. This local pride is demonstrated in this soiree honoring the founding fathers of this small island "nation." Call © 305/296-0123. Late April.

May

Shell Air & Sea Show, Fort Lauderdale. It's a tough call as far as what's more crowded—the air, the sea, or the ground, which attracts over 2 million onlookers craning their necks for a view of big-name airwolves such as the Blue Angels and the Thunderbirds. Remember: It's an *air* and *sea* show, not a car show, so consider leaving yours at the hotel. Call © 954/467-3555. Early May.

Cajun Zydeco Crawfish Festival, Fort Lauderdale. A little bit of Nawlins in South Florida. Enjoy the crawfish delicacies at this 3-day festival paying homage to all things hot, spicy, and, er, crunchy. Call © 954/761-5934. Early May.

Arabian Nights Festival, Opa-Locka. A colorful celebration of Opa-Locka's Moorish architecture, this festival features a mix of entertainment, food, and fantasy inspired by Arabian culture (© 305/758-4166). Mid-May.

June

Coconut Grove Goombay Festival, Coconut Grove. They may say it's better in the Bahamas, but that's questionable after you've attended Miami's own Bahamian bash, featuring lots of dancing in the streets, marching bands, scorching Caribbean temperatures, and the ever buzz-worthy and refreshing Goombay punch (© 305/372-9966). Early June.

July

Independence Day, Miami. Watch as one of the nation's most spectacular skylines is further illuminated with the masterful display of professional fireworks throughout the entire city. Best views are from Key Biscayne and Bayfront Park. For specific information on July 4 events, contact the local newspapers.

Lower Keys Underwater Music Fest, Looe Key. When you hear the phrase "the music and the madness," you may want to think of this amusing aural aquatic event in which boaters head out to the underwater reef at the Looe Key Marine Sanctuary, drop speakers into the water, and pipe in all sorts of music, creating a disco-diving spectacular. Considering the heat at this time of year, underwater is probably the coolest place for a concert. Call © 800/872-3722. Early July.

Miccosukee Everglades Festival, Miami. South Florida's Native American community celebrates their own unique heritage with music, food, and fanfare including shriek-inducing alligator wrestling. Call © 305/223-8380 for prices and information. Early and late July.

Hemingway Days Festival, Key West. The legendary author is alive and well—many times over—at this celebration of the literary world's most famous papa, to which eerily accurate Hemingway clones flock in the hopes of winning the big look-alike contest. Call ℂ **305/ 294-4440.** Mid- to late July.

Wine and All That Jazz, Boca Raton. Though the experts may recommend water as the ideal summer thirst quencher, the organizers of this event prefer the fruits of the vine. Sip over 100 vintages to the tune of jazz at this swank wine-tasting party at the end of July. Call ℂ **561/278-0424.**

Beethoven by the Beach, Fort Lauderdale. The Florida Philharmonic takes Beethoven to the beach with its summer music festival, featuring symphonies, chamber pieces, and piano concertos. Call ℂ **954/ 561-2997.**

August

This month is possibly the most scorching, which is why event planners try to avoid it altogether. Your best bet? The beach, the pool, or anywhere with air-conditioning.

September

Festival Miami, Miami. The University of Miami School of Music presents a 4-week program of performing arts, classical, jazz, and world music. For a schedule of performances, call ℂ **305/284-4940.** Mid-September.

October

Caribbean Carnival, Miami. If you've never been to the Caribbean, then this is your introduction to the colorful, multicultural island nations of Trinidad, Jamaica, Haiti, St. Vincent, Barbados, and St. Croix, as natives from the islands participate in a masquerade parade in their traditional costumes. Call ℂ **305/653-1877.** Early October.

Columbus Day Regatta, Miami. On the day that Columbus discovered America, the party-hearty discover their fellow Americans' birthday suits, as this bacchanalia in the middle of Biscayne Bay encourages participants in this so-called regatta (there is a boat race at some point during the day, but most people are too preoccupied to notice) to strip down to their bare necessities and party at the sandbar in the middle of the bay. You may not need a bathing suit, but you will need a boat to get out to where all the action is. Consider renting one on Key Biscayne, which is the closest to the sandbar.

Fort Lauderdale International Boat Show, Ft. Lauderdale. The world's largest boat show, this one's got boats of every size, shape, and status symbol displayed at the scenic Bahia Mar marina and four other locations in the area. Traffic-phobes beware. Call ℂ **954/764-7642.** Mid-October.

Fantasy Fest, Key West. Mardi Gras takes a Floridian holiday as the streets of Key West are overtaken by wildly costumed revelers who have no shame and no parental guidance. This week-long, hedonistic, X-rated Halloween party is not for children under 18. Make reservations in Key West early, as hotels tend to book up quickly during this event. Call ℂ **305/296-1817.** Last week of October.

November

Blues Festival at Riverwalk, Fort Lauderdale. The scenic landscape of downtown Fort Lauderdale's Riverwalk will make your own personal blues go away, but you'll want to immerse yourself in the music of big-name performers who sing and play the blues at various venues. Call ℂ **954/761-5934.** Early November.

South Florida International Auto Show, Miami Beach. Cars are everywhere—literally—at this massive auto show, displaying the latest and most futuristic modes of transportation on the market. Try to take public transportation or call a cab to get to this gridlocked event. Call ✆ **305/947-5950.** Early November.

Jiffy Lube Miami 300 Weekend of NASCAR, Homestead. World-class racing takes place on Miami's world-class 344-acre motor sports complex. Rev your engines early for tickets to this event (✆ **305/230-5200**). Mid-November.

Miami Bookfair International, downtown Miami. Bibliophiles, literati, and some of the world's most prestigious and prolific authors descend upon downtown Miami for a week-long homage to the written word, which also happens to be the largest book fair in the United States. The weekend street fair is the most well attended of the entire event, in which regular folk mix with wordsmiths such as Tom Wolfe and Jane Smiley while indulging in snacks, antiquarian books, and literary gossip. All lectures are free, but they fill up quickly, so get there early. Call ✆ **305/237-3258** for lecture schedules. Mid-November.

White Party Week, Miami and Fort Lauderdale. This week-long series of parties to benefit AIDS research is built around the main event, the White Party, which takes place at Villa Vizcaya and sells out as early as a year in advance. Philanthropists and celebrities such as Calvin Klein and David Geffen join thousands of white-clad mostly gay men (and some women) in what has become one of the world's hottest and hardest-to-score party tickets. Call ✆ **305/667-9296** or visit www.whitepartyweek.com for a schedule of parties and events. Thanksgiving week.

Santa's Enchanted Forest, Miami. Billing itself as the world's largest Christmas theme park, Santa's Enchanted Forest is an assault on the eyes, with thousands of lights lining Tropical Park plus rides, games, and lots of food. A great place to bring younger kids. Call ✆ **305/893-0090.** Early November to mid-January.

December

Winterfest Boat Parade, Fort Lauderdale. People who complain that the holiday season just isn't as festive in South Florida as it is in colder parts of the world haven't been to this spectacular boat parade along the Intracoastal Waterways. Forget decking the halls. At this parade, the decks are decked out in magnificent holiday regalia as they gracefully—and boastfully—glide up and down the water as if it were a sheet of ice. If you're not on a boat, the best views are from waterfront restaurants or anywhere you can squeeze in along the water. Call ✆ **954/767-0686.** Mid-December.

King Mango Strut, Coconut Grove. This parody of the by-the-book Orange Bowl parade is a hilarious march featuring people in crazy costumes and on outrageous floats making a mockery of recent scandals and controversies having to do mostly with Miami politics. Call ✆ **305/444-7270.** December 30.

King Orange Jamboree Parade, Miami. Consider this festive, nocturnal New Year's Eve parade to be the beginning of the many tailgate parties preceding the next day's Orange Bowl football game. Call ✆ **305/539-3000.**

4 Health & Insurance

STAYING HEALTHY

Tantamount to staying well in South Florida (and maintaining a sunny disposition) is sunscreen. Even on the cloudiest of days, you *will* feel the effects of the powerful UV rays, so it's best to take precautions at all times. Limit your exposure to the sun, especially during the first few days of your trip and thereafter from 11am to 2pm. Use a sunscreen with a high sun protection factor (SPF) and apply it liberally. Remember that children need more protection than adults do.

Should you be in South Florida during a tropical storm or hurricane, it is essential to drink bottled water, as the public water supply can become contaminated. Another concern of late are mosquitoes and the viruses they carry. Mosquito repellent, especially if you travel to the Everglades and other swampy areas and parks, is a good idea.

WHAT TO DO IF YOU GET SICK AWAY FROM HOME

It can be hard to find a doctor you can trust when you're in an unfamiliar place. Try to take proper precautions the week before you depart, to avoid falling ill while you're away from home. Amid the last-minute frenzy that often precedes a vacation break, make an extra effort to eat and sleep well—especially if you feel an illness coming on.

If you worry about getting sick away from home, you may want to consider **medical travel insurance** (see the section on travel insurance below). In most cases, however, your existing health plan will provide all the coverage you need. Be sure to carry your identification card in your wallet.

If you suffer from a chronic illness, consult your doctor before your departure. For conditions like epilepsy, diabetes, or heart problems, wear a **Medic Alert Identification Tag** ((C) **800/825-3785;** www.medicalert.org), which will immediately alert doctors to your condition and give them access to your records through Medic Alert's 24-hour hotline. Membership is $35, plus a $15 annual fee. If you have dental problems, a nationwide referral service known as **1-800-DENTIST** ((C) **800/336-8478**) will provide the name of a nearby dentist or clinic.

Pack prescription medications in your carry-on luggage. Carry written prescriptions in generic, not brand-name form, and dispense all prescription medications from their original labeled vials. Also bring along copies of your prescriptions in case you lose your medicine or run out.

If you wear contact lenses, pack an extra pair in case you lose one.

If you do get sick, you may want to ask the concierge at your hotel to recommend a local doctor—even his or her own. This will probably yield a better recommendation than any toll-free number would. If you can't find a doctor who can help you right away, try the emergency room at the local hospital. Many emergency rooms have walk-in clinics for emergency cases that are not life-threatening. You may not get immediate attention, but you won't pay the high price of an emergency room visit (usually a minimum of $300 just for signing your name, on top of whatever treatment you receive).

INSURANCE

There are three kinds of travel insurance: trip cancellation, medical, and lost luggage coverage. **Trip cancellation insurance** is a good idea if you have paid a large portion of your vacation expenses up front. The other two types of insurance, however, don't make sense for most travelers. Rule number one: Check your existing policies before you buy any additional coverage.

Your existing health insurance should cover you if you get sick while on vacation (though if you belong to an HMO, you should check to see whether you are fully covered when away from home). For independent travel health insurance providers, see the information later in this chapter. Your homeowner's insurance should cover stolen luggage. The airlines are responsible for $1,250 on domestic flights if they lose your luggage; if you plan to carry anything more valuable than that, keep it in your carry-on bag.

Some credit- and charge-card companies may insure you against travel accidents if you buy plane, train, or bus tickets with their cards. Before purchasing additional insurance, read your policies and agreements over carefully. Call your insurers or credit/charge-card companies if you have any questions.

Some credit cards (American Express and certain gold and platinum Visa and MasterCards, for example) offer automatic flight insurance against death or dismemberment in case of an airplane crash.

If you require additional insurance, try one of the companies listed below. But don't pay for more than you need. For example, if you need only trip cancellation insurance, don't purchase coverage for lost or stolen property. Trip cancellation insurance costs approximately 6% to 8% of the total value of your vacation.

Among the reputable issuers of travel insurance are: **Access America,** 6600 W. Broad St., Richmond, VA 23230 (© 800/284-8300); **Travel Guard International,** 1145 Clark St., Stevens Point, WI 54481 (© 800/ 826-1300); **Travel Insured International, Inc.,** P.O. Box 280568, East Hartford, CT 06128 (© 800/243-3174); **Travelex Insurance Services,** P.O. Box 9408, Garden City, NY 11530-9408 (© 800/228-9792).

Drivers Alert Network (DAN) specializes in accident and medical care and insures scuba divers (© 800/ 446-2671 or 919/684-2948).

5 Tips for Travelers with Special Needs

FOR TRAVELERS WITH DISABILITIES A disability shouldn't stop anyone from traveling. There are more resources available than ever before. *A World of Options,* a 658-page book of resources for disabled travelers, covers everything from biking trips to scuba outfitters. It costs $35 ($30 for members) and is available from **Mobility International USA,** P.O. Box 10767, Eugene, OR, 97440 (© **541/343-1284,** voice and TDD; www.miusa.org). Annual membership for Mobility International is $35, which includes their quarterly newsletter, *Over the Rainbow.* In addition, Twin Peaks Press, P.O. Box 129, Vancouver, WA 98666 (© **360/694-2462),** publishes travel-related books for people with disabilities.

Moss Rehab Hospital (© **215/ 456-9600)** has been providing friendly and helpful phone advice and referrals to disabled travelers for years through its **Travel Information Service** (© **215/456-9603;** www. mossresourcenet.org).

You can join the **Society for the Advancement of Travel for the Handicapped (SATH),** 347 Fifth Ave., Suite 610, New York, NY 10016 (© **212/447-7284;** fax 212/725-8253; www.sath.org) for $45 annually, $30 for seniors and students, to gain access to their vast network of connections in the travel industry. They provide information sheets on travel destinations and referrals to tour operators that specialize in traveling with disabilities. Their quarterly magazine,

Open World for Disability and Mature Travel, is full of good information and resources. A year's subscription is $13 ($21 outside the U.S.).

Car Rentals   Many of the major car-rental companies now offer hand-controlled cars for disabled drivers. **Avis** can provide such a vehicle at any of its locations in the U.S. with 48-hour advance notice; **Hertz** requires between 24 and 72 hours of advance reservation at most of its locations. **Wheelchair Getaways** (© 800/ 873-4973; www.blvd.com/wg.htm) rents specialized vans with wheelchair lifts and other features for the disabled in more than 100 cities across the U.S.

Travelers with disabilities may also want to consider joining a tour that caters specifically to them. One of the best operators is **Flying Wheels Travel,** 143 West Bridge (P.O. Box 382), Owatonna, MN 55060 (© 800/535-6790). They offer various escorted tours and cruises, with an emphasis on sports, as well as private tours in minivans with lifts. Other reputable specialized tour operators include **Access Adventures** (© 716/ 889-9096), which offers sports-related vacations; **Accessible Journeys** (© 800/TINGLES or 610/521-0339), for slow walkers and wheelchair travelers; Guided Tour, Inc. (© 215/782-1370); **Wilderness Inquiry** (© 800/728-0719 or 612/ 379-3858); and **Directions Unlimited** (© 800/533-5343).

You can obtain a copy of *Air Transportation of Handicapped Persons* by writing to Free Advisory Circular No. AC12032, Distribution Unit, U.S. Department of Transportation, Publications Division, M-4332, Washington, DC 20590.

In addition, both **Amtrak** (© 800/ USA-RAIL; www.amtrak.com) and **Greyhound** (© 800/752-4841; www. greyhound.com) offer special fares and services for the disabled. Call at least a week in advance of your trip for details.

The **National Park Service** issues free "Golden Access Passports" that entitle disabled people and a guest of their choice to free admission into national parks, forests, and wildlife refuges. Get them at park entrances.

Vision-impaired travelers should contact the **American Foundation for the Blind,** 11 Penn Plaza, Suite 300, New York, NY 10001 (© 800/ 232-5463), for information on traveling with seeing eye dogs.

FOR GAY & LESBIAN TRAVELERS   South Florida, particularly Key West, South Beach, and Fort Lauderdale, has a thriving gay community, supported by a wide range of services and establishments. There are several local gay-oriented publications full of information on gay and gay-friendly events, businesses, and services. *TWN, Wire, Hot Spots,* and *Miamigo* are among the free publications available for free in boxes on street corners, in stores, and on newsstands.

For a map and directory of gay businesses or a copy or the gay and lesbian community calendar sponsored by the **Dade Human Rights Foundation,** call © 305/572-1841. For a copy of the calendar and other information, you can also visit www.dhrf. com. Two organizations that are extremely helpful for gay and lesbian travelers are the **Miami Dade and South Beach Business Guild** (better known as the Gay Chamber of Commerce; © 305/751-8855), and the **Gay and Lesbian Community Center of Fort Lauderdale** (© 954/ 563-9500).

The **International Gay & Lesbian Travel Association (IGLTA)** (© 800/ 448-8550 or 954/776-2626; fax 954/ 776-3303; www.iglta.org) links travelers with the appropriate gay-friendly service organization or tour specialist. With around 1,200 members, it offers quarterly newsletters, marketing mailings, and a membership directory that's updated quarterly. Membership often includes gay or lesbian businesses but is open to individuals for $150 yearly, plus a $100 administration fee for new members. Members are kept informed of gay and gay-friendly hoteliers, tour operators, and airline and cruise-line representatives. Contact the IGLTA for a list of its member agencies that are tied into IGLTA's information resources.

General gay and lesbian travel agencies include **Family Abroad** (© 800/999-5500 or 212/459-1800; gay and lesbian); **Above and Beyond Tours** (© 800/397-2681; mainly gay men); and **Yellowbrick Road** (© 800/642-2488; gay and lesbian).

There are also two good biannual English-language gay guidebooks, both focused on gay men but including information for lesbians as well. You can get the *Spartacus International Gay Guide* or *Odysseus* from most gay and lesbian bookstores, or order them from Giovanni's Room (© 215/923-2960), or A Different Light Bookstore (© 415/431-0891; www.adlbooks.com). Both lesbians and gays might want to pick up a copy of *Gay Travel A to Z*. The **Ferrari Guides** (www.q-net.com) is yet another very good series of gay and lesbian guidebooks.

Out and About, 8 W. 19th St., #401, New York, NY 10011 (© 800/929-2268 or 212/645-6922), offers guidebooks and a monthly newsletter packed with good information on the global gay and lesbian scene. A year's subscription to the newsletter costs $49. *Our World,* 1104 N. Nova Rd., Suite 251, Daytona Beach, FL 32117 (© 904/441-5367), is a slicker monthly magazine promoting and highlighting travel bargains and opportunities. Annual subscription rates are $35 in the U.S., $45 outside the U.S.

FOR SENIORS Don't be shy about asking for discounts, but always carry some kind of identification, such as a driver's license, that shows your date of birth. Also, mention the fact that you're a senior citizen when you first make your travel reservations. For example, both Amtrak (© 800/USA-RAIL; www.amtrak.com) and Greyhound (© 800/752-4841; www.greyhound.com) offer discounts to persons over 62. And many hotels offer seniors discounts; Choice Hotels (Clarion Hotels, Quality Inns, Comfort Inns, Sleep Inns, Econo Lodges, Friendship Inns, and Rodeway Inns) give 30% off their published rates to anyone over 50, provided you book your room through their nationwide toll-free reservations numbers (that is, not directly with the hotels or through a travel agent). In most cities, people over the age of 60 qualify for reduced admission to theaters, museums, and other attractions, and discounted fares on public transportation.

Members of the **American Association of Retired Persons (AARP),** 601 E St. NW, Washington, DC 20049 (© **800/424-3410** or 202/434-2277), get discounts not only on hotels but on airfares and car rentals, too. AARP offers members a wide range of special benefits, including *Modern Maturity* magazine and a monthly newsletter.

The **National Council of Senior Citizens,** 8403 Colesville Rd., Suite 1200, Silver Spring, MD 20910 (© **301/578-8800**), a nonprofit organization, offers a newsletter six times a year (partly devoted to travel tips) and discounts on hotel and auto rentals; annual dues are $13 per person or couple.

Mature Outlook, P.O. Box 9390, Des Moines, IA 50306 (© **800/336-6330**), began as a travel organization for people over 50, though it now caters to people of all ages. Members receive discounts on hotels and receive a bimonthly magazine. Annual membership is $19.95, which entitles members to discounts, and, often, free coupons for discounted merchandise from Sears.

Golden Companions, P.O. Box 5249, Reno, NV 89513 (© 702/324-2227), helps travelers 45-plus find compatible companions through a personal voice-mail service. Contact them for more information.

The *Mature Traveler,* a monthly 12-page newsletter on senior citizen travel, is a valuable resource. It is available by subscription ($30 a year) from GEM Publishing Group, Box 50400, Reno, NV 89513-0400. GEM also publishes *The Book of Deals,* a collection of more than 1,000 senior discounts on airlines, lodging, tours, and attractions around the country; it's available for $9.95 by calling © 800/460-6676. Another helpful publication is *101 Tips for the Mature Traveler,* available from Grand Circle Travel, 347 Congress St., Suite 3A, Boston, MA 02210 (© 800/221-2610 or 617/350-7500).

Grand Circle Travel is also one of the hundreds of travel agencies specializing in vacations for seniors (see above). Many of these packages, however, are of the tour-bus variety, with free trips thrown in for those who organize groups of 10 or more. Seniors seeking more independent travel should probably consult a regular travel agent. **SAGA International Holidays,** 222 Berkeley St., Boston, MA 02116 (© 800/343-0273), offers inclusive tours and cruises for those 50 and older. SAGA also sponsors the more substantial "Road Scholar Tours" (© 800/621-2151), which are fun-loving but with an educational bent.

If you want something more than the average vacation or guided tour, try **Elderhostel** (© 877/426-8056; www.elderhostel.org) or the University of New Hampshire's **Interhostel** (© 800/733-9753), both variations on the same theme: educational travel for senior citizens. On these escorted tours, the days are packed with seminars, lectures, field trips, and sightseeing, all led by academic experts. **Elderhostel,** 75 Federal St., Boston, MA 02110-1941 (© 877/426-8056; www.elderhostel.org), arranges study programs for those age 55 and over (and a spouse or companion of any age) in the U.S. and in 77 countries around the world. Most courses last about 3 weeks and many include airfare, accommodations in student dormitories or modest inns, meals, and tuition. Write or call for a free catalog, which lists upcoming courses and destinations. **Interhostel** takes travelers 50 and over (with companions over 40), and offers 2- and 3-week trips, mostly international. The courses in both these programs are ungraded, involve no homework, and often focus on the liberal arts. They're not luxury vacations, but they're fun and fulfilling.

Although all the **specialty books** on the market are U.S.-focused, three do provide good general advice and contacts for the savvy senior traveler. Thumb through *The 50+ Traveler's Guidebook* (St. Martin's Press), *The Seasoned Traveler* (Country Roads Press), or *Unbelievably Good Deals and Great Adventures That You Absolutely Can't Get Unless You're Over 50* (Contemporary Books). Also check out your newsstand for the quarterly magazine *Travel 50 & Beyond.*

FOR FAMILIES Several books on the market offer tips to help you travel with kids. Most concentrate on the U.S., but two, *Family Travel* (Lanier Publishing International) and *How to Take Great Trips with Your Kids* (The Harvard Common Press), are full of good general advice that can apply to travel anywhere. Another reliable tome, with a worldwide focus, is *Adventuring with Children* (Foghorn Press).

Family Travel Times is published six times a year by TWYCH (Travel with Your Children; ☎ 888-822-4388 or 212/477-5524), and includes a weekly call-in service for subscribers. Subscriptions are $40 a year for quarterly editions. A free publication list and a sample issue are available by calling or sending a request to the above address.

Families Welcome!, 92 N. Main St., Ashland, OR 97520 (☎ 800/326-0724 or 541/482-6121), is a travel company specializing in worry-free vacations for families.

FOR STUDENTS The best resource for students is the Council on International Educational Exchange, or CIEE (www.ciee.org). They can set you up with an ID card (see below), and their travel branch, Council Travel Service (☎ 800/226-8624; www.counciltravel.com), is the biggest student travel agency operation in the world. It can get you discounts on plane tickets, rail passes, and the like. Ask them for a list of CTS offices in major cities so that you can keep the discounts flowing (and aid lines open) as you travel.

From CIEE you can obtain the student traveler's best friend, the $18 **International Student Identity Card (ISIC).** It's the only officially acceptable form of student identification, good for cut rates on rail passes, plane tickets, and other discounts. It also provides you with basic health and life insurance and a 24-hour help line. If you're no longer a student but are still under 26, you can get a **GO 25 card** from the same people, which will get you the insurance and some of the discounts (but not student admission prices in museums).

In Canada, **Travel CUTS,** 200 Ronson St., Ste. 320, Toronto, ONT M9W 5Z9 (☎ 800/667-2887 or 416/614-2887; www.travelcuts.com), offers similar services. **Campus Travel,** 52 Grosvenor Gardens, London SW1W 0AG (☎ 020/7730-3402; www.campustravel.co.uk), opposite Victoria Station, is Britain's leading specialist in student and youth travel.

FOR WOMEN Several websites offer women advice on how to travel safely and happily. The **Executive Woman's Travel Network** (www.delta.com/womenexecs/) is the official women's travel site of Delta airlines; it offers women tips on staying fit while traveling, eating well, finding special airfares, and dealing with many other gender-based travel issues. **WomanTraveler** (www.womantraveler.com) is an excellent guide that suggests places where women can stay and eat in various destinations. The site is authored by women and includes listings of women-owned businesses such as hotels, hostels, etc.

Several books on the market cater to the concerns of the female traveler. Look into the Virago *Women's Travel Guides.* The series is excellent but new, and covers only three cities to date: London, San Francisco, and Amsterdam. *Safety and Security for Women Who Travel,* by Sheila Swan Laufer and Peter Laufer, is well worth buying, and *Adventures in Good Company: The Complete Guide to Women's Tours and Outdoor Trips* is a very good resource.

FOR SINGLE TRAVELERS Many people prefer traveling alone—save for the relatively steep cost of booking a single room, which usually costs well over half the price of a double. **Travel Companion** (☎ 516/454-0880) is one of the nation's oldest roommate finders for single travelers. Register with them and find a trustworthy travel mate who will split the cost of the room with you and be around as little, or as often, as you like during the day.

Several tour organizers cater to solo travelers as well. **Experience Plus** (☎ 800/685-4565) offers an interesting selection of single-only trips.

Travel Buddies (℃ 800/998-9099 or 604/533-2483) runs single-friendly tours with no singles supplement. The **Single Gourmet Club,** 133 E. 58th St., New York, NY 10022 (℃ 212/980-8788; fax 212/980-3138), is an international social, dining, and travel club for singles, with offices in 21 cities in the U.S. and Canada, and one in London.

You may also want to research the *Outdoor Singles Network,* P.O. Box 781, Haines, AK 99827. An established quarterly newsletter since 1989 for outdoor-loving singles, ages 19 to 90, the network will help you find a travel companion, pen-pal, or soulmate within its pages. A 1-year subscription costs $45, and your own personal ad is printed free in the next issue. Current issues are $15. Write for free information or check out the group's website at www.kcd.com/bearstar/osn.html.

6 Getting There

BY PLANE

Miami is one of American Airlines' (℃ 800/433-7300; www.aa.com) biggest hubs, and most major domestic airlines fly to and from many Florida cities, including Continental (℃ 800/525-0280; www.continental.com), Delta (℃ 800/221-1212; www.delta.com), Northwest/KLM (℃ 800/241-6522; www.nwa.com), TWA (℃ 800/221-2000; www.twa.com), United (℃ 800/241-6522; www.united.com), and US Airways (℃ 800/428-4322; www.usairways.com).

Several budget airlines also fly to South Florida, including **Southwest Airlines** (℃ 800/435-9792; www.southwest.com), **Air Tran** (℃ 800/AIR-TRAN; www.airtran.com), **Spirit** (℃ 800/772-7117; www.spiritair.com), and **Jet Blue** (℃ 800/538-2583; www.jetblue.com).

If you're planning to visit Florida from another country, see chapter 3 for information on which international carriers serve the Miami area.

Passengers within the same airplane cabin are rarely paying the same fare for their seats. Business travelers who need to purchase tickets at the last minute, change their itinerary at a moment's notice, or get home before the weekend pay the premium rate, known as the full fare. Passengers who can book their ticket long in advance, who don't mind staying over Saturday night, or who are willing to travel on a Tuesday, Wednesday, or Thursday after 7pm, will pay a fraction of the full fare. On most flights—even the shortest hops—the full fare is close to $1,000 or more, but a 7-day or 14-day advance purchase ticket is closer to $200 to $300. Here are a few other easy ways to save:

1. Periodically airlines lower prices on their most popular routes. Check your newspaper for advertised discounts or call the airlines directly and ask if any **promotional rates** or special fares are available. You'll almost never see a sale during the peak travel months or during the Thanksgiving or Christmas seasons, but in periods of low-volume travel, you should pay no more than $400 for a cross-country flight. If your schedule is flexible, ask if you can secure a cheaper fare by staying an

---

Tips **Flying in Comfort**

You'll find the most legroom in a bulkhead seat, in the front row of each airplane cabin, or in an emergency exit row.

Tips   Fly for Less

When booking airfare to Miami, consider flying into the Fort Lauderdale/ Hollywood International Airport for considerably cheaper fares. The airport is only a half hour from downtown Miami.

extra day or by flying midweek. (Many airlines won't volunteer this information.) If you already hold a ticket when a sale breaks, it may even pay to exchange your ticket, which usually incurs a $50 to $75 charge.

Note, however, that the lowest-priced fares are often nonrefundable, require advance purchase of 1 to 3 weeks and a certain length of stay, and carry penalties for changing dates of travel.

2. **Consolidators,** also known as bucket shops, are a good place to find low fares. Consolidators buy seats in bulk from the airlines and then sell them back to the public at prices below even the airlines' discounted rates. Their small-boxed ads usually run in the Sunday travel section at the bottom of the page. Before you pay, however, ask for a confirmation number from the consolidator and then call the airline itself to confirm your seat. Be prepared to book your ticket with a different consolidator—there are many to choose from—if the airline can't confirm your reservation. Also be aware that bucket shop tickets are usually nonrefundable or rigged with stiff cancellation penalties, often as high as 50% to 75% of the ticket price. **Council Travel** (© 800/226-8624; www.counciltravel.com) and **STA Travel** (© 800/781-4040; www.sta.travel.com) cater especially to young travelers, but their bargain-basement prices are available to people of all ages.

Travel Bargains (© 800/AIR-FARE; www.1800airfare.com) was formerly owned by TWA but now offers the deepest discounts on many other airlines, with a 4-day advance purchase. Other reliable consolidators include **1-800-FLY-CHEAP** (www.1800 flycheap.com); **TFI Tours International** (© 800/745-8000 or 212/736-1140), which serves as a clearinghouse for unused seats; or "rebators" such as **Travel Avenue** (© 800/333-3335 or 312/876-1116) and the **Smart Traveller** (© 800/448-3338 in the U.S. or 305/448-3338), which rebate part of their commissions to you.

3. Book a seat on a **charter flight.** Discounted fares have pared the number available, but they can still be found. Most charter operators advertise and sell their seats through travel agents, thus making these local professionals your best source of information for available flights. Before deciding to take a charter flight, however, check the restrictions on the ticket: You may be asked to purchase a tour package, to pay in advance, to be amenable if the day of departure is changed, to pay a service charge, to fly on an airline you're not familiar with (this usually is not the case), and to pay harsh penalties if you cancel—but be understanding if the charter doesn't fill up and is canceled up to 10 days before departure. Summer charters fill up more quickly than others and are almost sure to

fly, but if you decide on a charter flight, seriously consider cancellation and baggage insurance.

4. Join a travel club such as **Moment's Notice** (© 718/234-6295) or **Sears Discount Travel Club** (© 800/433-9383, or 800/255-1487 to join), which supply unsold tickets at discounted prices. You pay an annual membership fee to get the club's hotline number. Of course, you're limited to what's available, so you have to be flexible.

BY CAR

Although four major roads run to and through Miami—I-95, S.R. 826, S.R. 836, and U.S.1—chances are you'll reach Miami and the rest of South Florida by way of I-95. This north–south interstate is South Florida's lifeline and an integral part of the region. The highway connects all of Miami's different neighborhoods, the airport, the beaches, and all of South Florida to the rest of the country. Miami's road signs are notoriously confusing and notably absent when you most need them. Do not exit from the highway if you aren't sure where you're going. Some exits are not impervious to unsavory neighborhoods. Study the map of I-95 so that you are familiar with its placement on the map and how it pertains to the rest of South Florida.

Other highways that will get you to Florida include I-10, which originates in Los Angeles and terminates at the tip of Florida in Jacksonville, and I-75, which begins in North Michigan and runs through the center of the state to Florida's west coast.

If you plan to be in your car quite a bit during your visit, you may want to join the **American Automobile Association (AAA)** (© 800/596-2227; www.aaa.com), which has hundreds of offices nationwide. Members receive excellent maps, emergency road service, and, upon request, planned, detailed itineraries.

For information on car-rental companies with offices in South Florida, see "Getting Around," in chapter 4.

Saving Money on a Rental Car Car-rental rates vary even more than airline fares. The price you pay will depend on the size of the car, where and when you pick it up and drop it off, the length of the rental period, where and how far you drive it, whether you purchase insurance, and a host of other factors. A few key questions could save you hundreds of dollars:

- Are weekend rates lower than weekday rates? Ask if the rate is the same for pickup Friday morning, for instance, as it is for Thursday night.
- Is a weekly rate cheaper than the daily rate? Even if you only need the car for 4 days, it may be cheaper to keep it for 5.
- Does the agency assess a drop-off charge if you don't return the car to the same location where you picked it up? Is it cheaper to pick up the car at the airport compared to a downtown location?
- Are special promotional rates available? If you see an advertised price in your local newspaper, be sure to ask for that specific rate; otherwise you may be charged the standard cost. Terms change constantly.
- Are discounts available for members of AARP, AAA, frequent-flier programs, or trade unions? If you belong to any of these organizations, you may be entitled to discounts of up to 30%.
- How much tax will be added to the rental bill? Local tax? State tax?
- What is the cost of adding an additional driver's name to the contract?
- How many free miles are included in the price? Free mileage is often

Cyber Deals for Net Surfers

It's possible to get some great deals on airfare, hotels, and car rentals via the Internet. Grab your mouse and surf before you take off—you could save a bundle on your trip. The websites highlighted below are worth checking out, especially since all services are free. Always check the lowest published fare, however, before you shop for flights online.

Arthur Frommer's Budget Travel (www.frommers.com) Home of the Encyclopedia of Travel and *Arthur Frommer's Budget Travel* magazine and daily newsletter, this site offers detailed information on 200 cities and islands around the world, and up-to-the-minute ways to save dramatically on flights, hotels, car reservations, and cruises.

Microsoft Expedia (www.expedia.com) The best part of this multipurpose travel site is the "Fare Tracker." You fill out a form on the screen indicating that you're interested in cheap flights from your hometown, and, once a week, they'll e-mail you the best airfare deals on up to three destinations. The site's "Travel Agent" will steer you to bargains on hotels and car rentals, and with the help of hotel and airline seat pinpointers, you can book everything right on line. This site is even useful once you're booked. Before you depart, log on to Expedia for maps and up-to-date travel information, including weather reports and foreign exchange rates.

Travelocity (www.travelocity.com) This is one of the best travel sites out there, especially for finding cheap airfare. In addition to its "Personal Fare Watcher," which notifies you via e-mail of the lowest airfares for up to five different destinations, Travelocity will track the three lowest fares for any routes on any dates in minutes. You can book a flight right then and there, and if you need a rental car or hotel, Travelocity will find you the best deal via the SABRE computer reservations system (another huge travel agent database). Click on "Last Minute Deals" for the latest travel bargains, including a link to "H.O.T. Coupons" (www.hotcoupons.com), where you can print out electronic coupons for travel in the U.S. and Canada.

The Trip (www.thetrip.com) This site is really geared toward the business traveler, but vacationers-to-be can also use The Trip's exceptionally powerful fare-finding engine, which will e-mail you every week with

negotiable, depending on the length of your rental.

• How much does the rental company charge to refill your gas tank if you return with the tank less than full? Though most rental companies claim these prices are "competitive," fuel is almost always cheaper in town. Try to allow enough time to refuel the car yourself before returning it. Some companies offer "refueling packages," in which you pay for an entire tank of gas up front. The price is usually fairly competitive with local gas prices, but you don't get credit for any gas remaining in the tank. If a stop at a gas station on the way to the airport will make you miss your plane, then the best city-to-city airfare deals for as many as 10 routes. The Trip uses the Internet Travel Network, another reputable travel agent database, to book hotels and restaurants.

E-Savers Programs Several major airlines offer a free e-mail service known as E-Savers, via which they'll send you their best bargain airfares on a regular basis. Here's how it works: Once a week (usually Wednesday), or whenever a sale fare comes up, subscribers receive a list of discounted flights to and from various destinations, both international and domestic. Here's the catch: These fares are usually only available if you leave the very next Saturday (or sometimes Friday night) and return on the following Monday or Tuesday. It's really a service for the spontaneously inclined and travelers looking for a quick getaway. But the fares are cheap, so it's worth taking a look. If you have a preference for certain airlines (in other words, the ones you fly most frequently), sign up with them first.

Here's a partial list of airlines and their websites, where you cannot only get on the e-mailing lists, but also book flights directly:

- **American Airlines:** www.aa.com
- **British Airways:** www.british-airways.com
- **Canadian Airlines International:** www.cdnair.ca
- **Continental Airlines:** www. continental.com
- **Northwest Airlines:** www.nwa.com
- **TWA:** www.twa.com
- **US Airways:** www.usairways.com
- **United Airlines:** www.united.com
- **Virgin Airways:** www.virgin.com

One caveat: You'll get frequent-flier miles if you purchase one of these fares, but you can't use miles to buy the ticket.

Smarter Living (www.smarterliving.com) If the thought of all that surfing and comparison shopping gives you a headache, then head right for Smarter Living. Sign up for their newsletter service, and every week you'll get a customized e-mail summarizing the discount fares available from your departure city. Smarter Living tracks more than 15 different airlines, so it's a worthwhile time-saver.

by all means take advantage of the fuel purchase option. Otherwise, skip it.

Demystifying Renter's Insurance
Before you drive off in a rental car, be sure you're insured. Hasty assumptions about your personal auto insurance or a rental agency's additional coverage could end up costing you

tens of thousands of dollars—even if you are involved in an accident that was clearly the fault of another driver.

If you already hold a **private auto insurance** policy, you are most likely covered in the United States for loss of or damage to a rental car, and liability in case of injury to any other party involved in an accident. Be sure to find out whether you are covered in the area you are visiting, whether your policy extends to all persons who will be driving the rental car, how much liability is covered in case an outside party is injured in an accident, and whether the type of vehicle you are renting is included under your contract. (Rental trucks, sports utility vehicles, and luxury vehicles such as the Jaguar may not be covered.)

Most **major credit cards** provide some degree of coverage as well—provided they were used to pay for the rental. Terms vary widely, however, so be sure to call your credit-card company directly before you rent.

If you are **uninsured,** your credit card provides primary coverage as long as you decline the rental agency's insurance. This means that the credit card will cover damage or theft of a rental car for the full cost of the vehicle. (In a few states, however, theft is not covered; ask specifically about state law where you will be renting and driving.) If you already have insurance, your credit card will provide secondary coverage—which basically covers your deductible.

Credit cards **will not cover liability,** or the cost of injury to an outside party and/or damage to an outside party's vehicle. If you do not hold an insurance policy, you may seriously want to consider purchasing additional liability insurance from your rental company. Be sure to check the terms, however: Some rental agencies only cover liability if the renter is not at fault; even then, the rental company's obligation varies from state to state.

Bear in mind that each credit-card company has its own peculiarities. Most American Express Optima cards, for instance, do not provide any insurance. American Express does not cover vehicles valued at over $50,000 when new, luxury vehicles such as the Porsche, or vehicles built on a truck chassis. MasterCard does not provide

coverage for loss, theft, or fire damage, and only covers collision if the rental period does not exceed 15 days. Call your own credit-card company for details.

The basic insurance coverage offered by most car-rental companies, known as the **Loss/Damage Waiver (LDW)** or **Collision Damage Waiver (CDW),** can cost as much as $20 per day. It usually covers the full value of the vehicle with no deductible if an outside party causes an accident or other damage to the rental car. In all states but California, you will probably be covered in case of theft as well. Liability coverage varies according to the company policy and state law, but the minimum is usually at least $15,000. If you are at fault in an accident, however, you will be covered for the full replacement value of the car but not for liability. Some states allow you to buy additional liability coverage for such cases. Most rental companies will require a police report in order to process any claims you file, but your private insurer will not be notified of the accident.

Package Deals   Many packages are available that include airfare, accommodations, and a rental car with unlimited mileage. Compare these prices with the cost of booking airline tickets and renting a car separately to see if these offers are good deals.

Arranging Car Rentals on the Web Internet resources can make comparison shopping easier. **Microsoft Expedia** (www.expedia.com) and **Travelocity** (www.travelocity.com) help you compare prices and locate car-rental bargains from various companies nationwide. They will even make your reservation for you once you've found the best deal.

BY TRAIN
Amtrak (© 800/USA-RAIL; www. amtrak.com) isn't the best option, but

it's the only option if you don't want to fly or drive down to South Florida. Two trains leave daily from New York—the Silver Meteor at 7:50pm and the Silver Star at 11:50am. They both take from 26½ to 29 hours to complete the entire journey to Miami. At press time, the lowest-priced round-trip ticket from New York to Miami cost $169 for a coach seat, climbing to $426 for a sleeper.

Miami's Amtrak terminal is located at 8303 NW 37th Ave. Unfortunately, no major car-rental companies are located at the train station, so you will have to go 5 miles to the airport to rent a car. Taxis meet each Amtrak arrival, and the fare to downtown Miami will cost about $24.

If you want to travel to South Florida with your car, you can avoid most of I-95 by taking the Amtrak East Coast Auto Train. The 16½-hour ride, connecting Lorton, Virginia (outside of Washington, D.C.), with Sanford, Florida (outside of Orlando), has a glass-domed viewing car and includes breakfast and dinner in the ticket price. Round-trip fares are approximately $170 one-way for adults, $85 for children under 12, and $300 for your car.

MONEY-SAVING PACKAGE DEALS

Before you start your search for the lowest airfare, you may want to consider booking your flight as part of a travel package.

Package tours are not the same as escorted tours. They are simply a way to buy airfare and accommodations (and sometimes rental cars) at the same time. For Miami and many other destinations in South Florida, a package can be a smart way to go. In many cases, one that includes airfare, hotel, and car rental will cost you less than the hotel alone would have had you booked it yourself. That's because packages are sold in bulk to tour operators, who resell them to the public at a cost that drastically undercuts standard rates.

Packages, however, vary widely. Some offer a better class of hotels than others. Some offer the same hotels for lower prices. With some packagers, your choice of accommodations and travel days may be limited. Which package is right for you depends entirely on what you want.

Here are a few tips to help you tell one from the other and figure out which one is right for you:

- **Read this guide.** Do a little homework; read up on the region. Compare the rack rates that we've published to the discounted rates being offered by the packagers to see what kinds of deals they're offering—if you're actually being offered a substantial savings, or if they've just gussied up the rack rates to make their offer *sound* like a deal. If you're being offered a stay in a hotel I haven't recommended, do more research to learn about it, especially if it isn't a reliable brand name like Holiday Inn or Hyatt. It's not a deal if you end up at a dump.

- **Read the fine print.** Make sure you know *exactly* what's included in the price you're being quoted, and what's not. Are hotel taxes and airport transfers included, or will you have to pay extra? Before you commit to a package, make sure you know how much flexibility you have, say, if your kid gets sick or your boss suddenly asks you to adjust your vacation schedule. Some packagers require iron-clad commitments, while others will go with the flow, charging minimal fees for changes or cancellations.

- **Use your best judgment.** Stay away from fly-by-nights and shady packagers. If a deal appears to be too good to be true, it probably is. Go with a reputable firm with a proven track record. This is where your travel agent can come in handy; he or she should be knowledgeable about different packagers, the deals they offer, and the general rate of satisfaction among their customers.

So how do you find a package deal? The best place to start your search is the travel section of your local Sunday newspaper. Also check the ads in the back of national travel magazines like *Travel & Leisure, National Geographic Traveler,* and *Condé Nast Traveller.* **Liberty Travel** (℃ **888/271-1584** to be connected with the agent closest to you; www.libertytravel.com), one of the biggest packagers in the Northeast, often runs a full-page ad in the Sunday papers. You won't get much in the way of service, but you will get a good deal. **American Express Vacations** (℃ **800/241-1700;** www.leisureweb. com) is another option. Check out its **Last Minute Travel Bargains** site, offered in conjunction with **Continental Airlines** (www6.americanexpress. com/travel/lastminutetravel/default. asp), with deeply discounted vacation packages and reduced airline fares that differ from the E-saver bargains that Continental e-mails weekly to subscribers. **Northwest Airlines** offers a similar service. Posted on Northwest's website every Wednesday, its **Cyber Saver Bargain Alerts** offer special hotel rates, package deals, and discounted airline fares.

Another good resource is the airlines themselves, which often package their flights together with accommodations. Fly-by-night packagers are uncommon, but they do exist; when you buy your package through the airline, however, you can be pretty sure that the company will still be in business when your departure date arrives. Among the airline packagers, your options include **American Airlines FlyAway Vacations** (℃ 800/ 321-2121), **Delta Dream Vacations** (℃ 800/872-7786), and **US Airways Vacations** (℃ 800/455-0123). Pick the airline that services your hometown most often.

The biggest hotel chains, casinos, and resorts also offer package deals. If you already know where you want to stay, call the resort itself and ask if they can offer land/air packages.

For information on package tours to South Florida, consult the following companies: **CWS Tours & Transportation** (℃ 407/448-3969; www. cwstours.com/sfltour.htm), **Eyre Tour and Travel** (℃ 800/321-EYRE; www. eyre.com), **Miami City Web** (℃ 888/ MIAMI-MALL or 305/715-9080; www.miamicity.net).

7 The Top Websites for Miami & South Florida

GENERAL SOUTH FLORIDA SITES

Digital City South Florida on AOL
Keyword: South Florida

Click here for entertainment, dining, sports, and festival information produced in cooperation with the *Sun-Sentinel.* This site includes a lively forum, where you can read comments from others or post a question of your own. Digital City is also available on the Web at southflorida.digitalcity.com.

FLA USA
www.flausa.com

A product of Florida's official tourism bureau, this extensive website includes information on attractions, beaches, golfing, and water sports, as well as airport information, weather, and maps. The beach guide is nicely organized by region, and there's advice on Florida's natural attractions in the "Activities" section.

Florida Association of Convention and Visitors Bureaus
www.facvb.org

Links to more than a dozen bureaus throughout the state, including several in South Florida. Most of the sites include information on attractions, dining, lodging, and shopping.

Florida State Parks
www8.myflorida.com/communities/learn/
  stateparks

Though the home page is awkwardly designed (this is a government site, after all), you can find parks by clicking on "Park Maps" or "Park Index." From there, you can learn about camping at each park, including information on fees, nearby attractions, and facilities.

Just Go: South Florida
www.justgo.com/southflorida

Dining, music, theater, and movies are listed and reviewed on this site. Just Go does a nice job of spotlighting upcoming concerts and makes it easy to find restaurants by cuisine and neighborhood.

See Florida
www.see-florida.com

A nicely organized guide to theme parks, marine attractions, museums, boating, fishing, and much more. See Florida includes guides to many of South Florida cities and has advice for first-time visitors to the Sunshine State.

SoFla.com
www.sofla.com

A comprehensive site covering all aspects of South Florida, including shopping, sports, recreation, movies, events and relocation information.

CITY GUIDES & ENTERTAINMENT SITES

City guides are a good way to get acquainted with what's going on in Miami. While some are geared toward residents, they are still excellent resources for travelers who want to get the local scoop on nightlife, restaurants, and places to shop.

About.com: Miami for Visitors
gomiami.about.com

Primarily a collection of websites for travelers to Miami, you'll find sections on culture, fishing, and shopping, among many others. While you won't find in-depth stories here, the site does include some short features on Miami, such as one on what to do if it's too cold for the beach. All these features are rich with links to other relevant websites.

CitySearch: Miami
miami.citysearch.com

This site offers listings and reviews for Miami arts and entertainment events, restaurants, shopping, and attractions. CitySearch is part of a national network of city guides, and has editorial reviews as well as Web pages paid for by restaurants and other businesses. CitySearch clearly labels its pages as either "editorial profile" or advertiser's "website." Click on the calendar link for events recommended by the editors. The extensive shopping listings range from clothing to specialty stores and include updates on sales. Along with Sidewalk, CitySearch is a leading directory for arts and dining in Miami.

Discover: Key West
key-west.com

A well-rounded guide to Key West, including an events calendar and extensive listings for attractions, sightseeing and ecotours, theater, and art galleries. You'll also find a dining guide, lodging options, and sections on dining, fishing, and shopping.

Gay Key West Travel Guide
www.gaykeywestfl.com

A guide to gay-friendly lodgings, restaurants, and clubs.

Miami.com

www.miami.com

Featuring local news and information from the *Miami Herald,* Miami.com features up-to-date information on events and entertainment options in Miami-Dade and Broward counties. It also features links to many attractions and Florida travel sites.

Time Out: Miami

www.timeout.com/miami

This site offers reviews and listings for attractions, entertainment, restaurants, hotels, and shopping, and includes categories for kids and gays and lesbians. Time Out is a lively guide with a youthful approach, but has features for everyone, including festival previews. Unlike some other city guides, Time Out: Miami makes a concerted effort to cater to tourists as well as locals. The listings appear uninfluenced by ads, because there are no ads visible here. Plus, the site's clean design makes it a pleasure to navigate.

Tropicool Miami (Miami Convention & Visitors Bureau)

www.miamiandbeaches.com

This nice site will provide you with a good overview of Miami and its beckoning beaches. Sure, the content is a bit sales-heavy, but it's still informative. You won't find detailed listings for restaurants and hotels, but there is general information about Miami's dining and arts scene, as well as advice about shopping and lodging in various districts. If you want more, you can order the print guide through the website or by calling a toll-free number.

NEWSPAPERS & MAGAZINES

One of the best ways to take a city's pulse is to browse through the virtual pages of its newspapers and magazines. Now, you no longer have to go to a newsstand to browse through Miami's news sources, which also contain entertainment information.

Miami Herald

www.herald.com

Miami's leading news source can give you a sense of what's going on in the city, but don't expect extensive entertainment listings.

Miami New Times

www.miaminewtimes.com

Miami's leading alternative weekly includes features and listings for music, theater, film, and more. Click on "Music" and then "Concerts This Week" to see listings ranging from the Florida Philharmonic to the Blues Festival.

Sun-Sentinel: Showtime

www.sun-sentinel.com/showtime

Here's a nice roundup of music, theater, sports, and dining choices in South Florida, with coverage of local festivals and events. For hard news and weather, see www.sun-sentinel.com.

DINING GUIDES

Get a taste of Miami's restaurants with online reviews. You can also find extensive restaurant listings at Sidewalk, CitySearch, and some other city guides (see above).

CuisineNet

www.cuisinenet.com

Listings and reviews for Miami and 15 other U.S. cities. Each restaurant has a capsule review compiled by CuisineNet and ratings based on surveys received from site users. For many restaurants, only two or three people have bothered to submit ratings, so they may not be statistically significant. However, comments can be instructive, as CuisineNet's readers discuss service, parking, free birthday desserts, and a host of other insightful topics.

Zagat Restaurant Survey

www.zagat.com

Reviews of top restaurants for Miami and many other U.S. cities. Zagat has made a name for itself as the people's choice, as its listings are based on extensive surveys.

TICKETS

If you want to purchase concert, theater, or sporting event tickets, try the following online services:

TicketMaster

www.ticketmaster.com

A national outlet, TicketMaster sells tickets for sports, theater, and concerts—and tacks on a hefty service charge. You can also buy tickets through Culturefinder.com and reach TicketMaster through CitySearch.

TicketWeb

www.ticketweb.com

TicketWeb sells theater and concert tickets, usually for a much lower service charge than TicketMaster. Ticket-Web is best for events at smaller venues—many of the larger arenas and halls are locked into exclusive deals with large ticket sellers and do not sell through other outlets.

GETTING AROUND

Get acquainted with the airport, check options for getting from the airport to your hotel, and learn how the locals get around at a fraction of the cost of a cab.

Miami-Dade Transit

www.co.miami-dade.fl.us/mdta/

Though this is a terribly slow-loading site, it does have basic information on bus and rail lines in and around Miami.

Miami International Airport

www.miami-airport.com

This site features a terminal map, airline counter locations, car-rental information, taxi and van advice, and other services to help you get around this labyrinthine airport.

Supershuttle: Miami

www.supershuttle.com/mia.htm

For single travelers this shuttle can be considerably cheaper than taking a cab. The site includes sample fares and toll-free reservation lines.

3

For Foreign Visitors

The pervasiveness of American culture around the world may make you feel that you know the U.S. pretty well, but leaving your own country still requires an additional degree of planning. This chapter will help prepare you for the more common problems that visitors may encounter.

1 Preparing for Your Trip

ENTRY REQUIREMENTS

Immigration laws are a hot political issue in the United States these days, and the following requirements may have changed somewhat by the time you plan your trip. Check at any U.S. embassy or consulate for current information and requirements. You can also plug into the **U.S. State Department's** Internet site at **http://state.gov**.

VISAS The U.S. State Department has a **Visa Waiver Pilot Program** allowing citizens of certain countries to enter the United States without a visa for stays of up to 90 days. At press time these included Andorra, Argentina, Australia, Austria, Belgium, Brunei, Denmark, Finland, France, Germany, Iceland, Ireland, Italy, Japan, Liechtenstein, Luxembourg, Monaco, the Netherlands, New Zealand, Norway, San Marino, Slovenia, Spain, Sweden, Switzerland, and the United Kingdom. Citizens of these countries need only a valid passport and a round-trip air or cruise ticket in their possession upon arrival. If they first enter the United States, they may also visit Mexico, Canada, Bermuda, and/or the Caribbean islands and return to the United States without a visa. Further information is available from any U.S. embassy or consulate. Canadian citizens may enter the United States without visas; they need only proof of residence.

Citizens of all other countries must have (1) a valid passport that expires at least 6 months later than the scheduled end of their visit to the United States, and (2) a tourist visa, which may be obtained without charge from any U.S. consulate.

OBTAINING A VISA To obtain a visa, the traveler must submit a completed application form (either in person or by mail) with a 1½-inch square photo, and must demonstrate binding ties to a residence abroad. Usually you can obtain a visa at once or within 24 hours, but it may take longer during the summer rush from June through August. If you cannot go in person, contact the nearest U.S. embassy or consulate for directions on applying by mail. Your travel agent or airline office may also be able to provide you with visa applications and instructions. The U.S. consulate or embassy that issues your visa will determine whether you will be issued a multiple- or single-entry visa and any restrictions regarding the length of your stay.

British subjects can obtain up-to-date passport and visa information by calling the **U.S. Embassy Visa Information Line** (© 0891/200-290) or the **London Passport Office** (© 0990/ 210-410 for recorded information).

IMMIGRATION QUESTIONS

Telephone operators will answer your inquiries regarding U.S. immigration policies or laws at the **Immigration and Naturalization Service's Customer Information Center** (�C 800/375-5283). Representatives are available Monday through Friday from 9am to 3pm. The INS also runs a 24-hour automated information service for commonly asked questions at ℂ **800/755-0777.**

MEDICAL REQUIREMENTS

Unless you're arriving from an area known to be suffering from an epidemic (particularly cholera or yellow fever), inoculations or vaccinations are not required for entry into the United States. If you have a disease that requires treatment with narcotics or syringe-administered medications, carry a valid signed prescription from your physician to allay any suspicions that you may be smuggling narcotics (a serious offense that carries severe penalties in the U.S.).

For HIV-positive visitors, requirements for entering the United States are somewhat vague and change frequently. According to the latest publication of *HIV and Immigrants: A Manual for AIDS Service Providers,* although INS doesn't require a medical exam for everyone trying to come into the United States, INS officials may keep out people who they suspect are HIV positive. INS may stop people because they look sick or because they are carrying AIDS/HIV medicine.

If an HIV-positive noncitizen applying for a nonimmigrant visa knows that HIV is a communicable disease of public health significance but checks "no" on the question about communicable diseases, INS may deny the visa because it thinks the applicant committed fraud. If a nonimmigrant visa applicant checks "yes," or if INS suspects the person is HIV positive, it will deny the visa unless the applicant asks for a special waiver for visitors. This waiver is for people visiting the United States for a short time, to attend a conference, for instance, to visit close relatives, or to receive medical treatment. It can be a confusing situation, so for up-to-the-minute information concerning HIV-positive travelers, contact the Centers for Disease Control's **National Center for HIV** (ℂ **404/332-4559;** www.hivatis.org) or the **Gay Men's Health Crisis** (ℂ **212/367-1000;** www.gmhc.org).

DRIVER'S LICENSES Foreign driver's licenses are mostly recognized in the U.S., although you may want to get an international driver's license if your home license is not written in English.

CUSTOMS Every visitor over 21 years of age may bring in, free of duty, the following: (1) 1 liter of wine or hard liquor; (2) 200 cigarettes, 100 cigars (but not from Cuba), or 3 pounds of smoking tobacco; and (3) $100 worth of gifts. These exemptions are offered to travelers who spend at least 72 hours in the United States and who have not claimed them within the preceding 6 months. It is altogether forbidden to bring into the country foodstuffs (particularly fruit, cooked meats, and canned goods) and plants (vegetables, seeds, tropical plants, and the like). Foreign tourists may bring in or take out up to $10,000 in U.S. or foreign currency with no formalities; larger sums must be declared to U.S. Customs on entering or leaving, which includes filing form CM 4790. For more specific information regarding U.S. Customs, call your nearest U.S. embassy or consulate, or the U.S. Customs office at ℂ **202/927-1770** or www.customs.ustreas.gov.

INSURANCE

Although it's not required of travelers, health insurance is highly recommended. Unlike many European countries, the United States does not usually offer free or low-cost medical

Impressions

The waves come rolling as the bright moon shines up above.
Old folks stroll along the beach with boys and girls in love.
Aaah, this is Miami Beach, where the moonlit waters flow.
And folks from 'round the world come here to avoid the winter snow.

—Anonymous

care to its citizens or visitors. Doctors and hospitals are expensive, and in most cases will require advance payment or proof of coverage before they render their services. Policies can cover everything from the loss or theft of your baggage and trip cancellation to the guarantee of bail in case you're arrested. Good policies will also cover the costs of an accident, repatriation, or death. For more information see "Health & Insurance," in chapter 2. Packages such as **Europ Assistance** in Europe are sold by automobile clubs and travel agencies at attractive rates. **Worldwide Assistance Services, Inc.** (© **800/821-2828**) is the agent for Europ Assistance in the United States.

Though lack of health insurance may prevent you from being admitted to a hospital in nonemergencies, don't worry about being left on a street corner to die: The American way is to fix you now and bill the living daylights out of you later.

INSURANCE FOR BRITISH TRAVELERS Most big travel agents offer their own insurance and will probably try to sell you their package when you book a holiday. Think before you sign. **Britain's Consumers' Association** recommends that you insist on seeing the policy and reading the fine print before buying travel insurance. The **Association of British Insurers** (© **020/7600-3333**) gives advice by phone and publishes the free *Holiday Insurance,* a guide to policy provisions and prices. You might also shop around for better deals: Try **Columbus Travel Insurance Ltd.** (© 020/7375-0011), or, for students, **Campus Travel** (© 020/7730-2101).

INSURANCE FOR CANADIAN TRAVELERS Canadians should check with their provincial health plan offices or call **HealthCanada** (© 613/957-2991) to find out the extent of their coverage and what documentation and receipts they must take home in case they are treated in the United States.

COMPREHENSIVE INSURANCE PLANS The best insurance for all travelers, however, is a comprehensive policy that includes coverage for, among other things, trip cancellation, delay, and medical expenses. Without insurance, you will lose most, if not all, of your money. Default insurance comes in handy if your tour company, cruise line, or airline goes out of business. Trip delay covers those expenses that arise because of bad weather—something that is not uncommon in South Florida, especially during hurricane season. **Access America** (© 800/284-8300) and **Travel Guard International** (© 800/826-1300) offer comprehensive insurance within the U.S. Residents of the United Kingdom and Australia should contact the **Association of British Insurers** (© 020/7600-3333) and the **Insurance Council of Australia** (© 03/9614-7924), respectively.

MONEY

CURRENCY The U.S. monetary system is painfully simple: The most common bills (all ugly, all green) are the $1 (colloquially, a "buck"), $5, $10, and $20 denominations. There are also $2 bills (seldom encountered), $50 bills, and $100 bills (the last two are usually not welcome as payment for small purchases). Note that a newly redesigned $100 and $50 bill were introduced in 1996, a redesigned $20 bill in 1998, and new $10 and $5 notes were introduced in 2000. Despite rumors to the contrary, the old-style bills are still legal tender.

There are six denominations of coins: 1¢ (1 cent, or a penny); 5¢ (5 cents, or a nickel); 10¢ (10 cents, or a dime); 25¢ (25 cents, or a quarter); 50¢ (50 cents, or a half dollar); and, prized by collectors, the rare $1 piece (the older, large silver dollar and the newer, small Susan B. Anthony coin). A new gold $1 piece was introduced in 2000.

Note: The foreign exchange bureaus so common in Europe are rare even at airports in the United States, and nonexistent outside major cities. It's best not to change foreign money (or traveler's checks denominated in a currency other than U.S. dollars) at a small-town bank, or even a branch in a big city; in fact, leave any currency other than U.S. dollars at home—it may prove a greater nuisance to you than it's worth.

TRAVELER'S CHECKS Though traveler's checks are widely accepted, make sure that they're denominated in U.S. dollars, as foreign currency checks are often difficult to exchange. The three traveler's checks that are most widely recognized—and least likely to be denied—are **Visa, American Express,** and **Thomas Cook.** Be sure to record the numbers of the checks, and keep that information separately in case they get lost or stolen. Most businesses are pretty good about taking traveler's checks, but you're better off cashing them in at a bank (in small amounts, of course) and paying in cash. Remember: You'll need identification, such as a driver's license or passport, to change a traveler's check.

CREDIT CARDS & ATMS Credit cards are the most widely used form of payment in the United States: Visa (BarclayCard in Britain), **MasterCard** (EuroCard in Europe, Access in Britain, Chargex in Canada), **American Express, Diners Club, Discover,** and **Carte Blanche.** You must have a credit or charge card to rent a car. There are, however, a handful of stores and restaurants that do not take credit cards, so be sure to ask in advance. Most businesses display a sticker near their entrance to let you know which cards they accept. (*Note:* Often businesses require a minimum purchase price, usually around $10, to use a credit card.)

It is strongly recommended that you bring at least one major credit card. Hotels, car-rental companies, and airlines usually require a credit-card imprint as a deposit against expenses, and in an emergency a credit card can be priceless.

You'll find automated teller machines (ATMs) on just about every block—at least in almost every town—across the country. Some ATMs will allow you to draw U.S. currency against your bank and credit cards. Check with your bank before leaving home, and remember that you will need your personal identification number (PIN) to do so. Most accept Visa, MasterCard, and American Express, as well as ATM cards from other U.S. banks. Expect to be charged up to $3 per transaction, however, if you're not using your own bank's ATM.

One way around these fees is to ask for cash back at grocery stores that accept ATM cards and don't charge usage fees. You'll have to purchase something first, however, and often the amount of additional cash you can get back is modest.

SAFETY
GENERAL SAFETY SUGGESTIONS While tourist areas are generally safe, U.S. urban areas tend to be less safe than those in Europe or

Travel Tip

Be sure to keep a copy of all your travel papers separate from your wallet or purse, and leave a copy with someone at home should you need it faxed in an emergency.

Japan. You should always stay alert. This is particularly true of large U.S. cities. It is wise to ask your hotel front desk staff or the city's or area's tourist office if you're in doubt about which neighborhoods are safe.

Avoid deserted areas, especially at night, and don't go into public parks at night unless there's a concert or similar occasion that will attract a crowd.

Avoid carrying valuables with you on the street, and don't display expensive cameras or electronic equipment. If you are using a map, consult it inconspicuously—or better yet, try to study it before you leave your room. Hold onto your pocketbook, and place your billfold in an inside pocket. In theaters, restaurants, and other public places, keep your possessions in sight.

Remember also that hotels are open to the public, and in a large hotel, security may not be able to screen everyone entering. Always lock your room door—don't assume that once inside your hotel you are automatically safe and no longer need to be aware of your surroundings.

DRIVING SAFETY Driving safety is important too, especially given the highly publicized carjackings of foreign tourists in Florida. Question your rental agency about personal safety and ask for a traveler safety brochure

when you pick up your car. Obtain written directions—or a map with the route clearly marked—from the agency showing how to get to your destination. (Many agencies now offer the option of renting a cellular phone for the duration of your car rental; check with the rental agent when you pick up the car.) If possible, arrive and depart during daylight hours.

Recently, more and more crime has involved cars and drivers. If you drive off a highway into a doubtful neighborhood, leave the area as quickly as possible. If you have an accident, even on the highway, stay in your car with the doors locked until you assess the situation or until the police arrive. If you're bumped from behind on the street or are involved in a minor accident with no injuries and the situation appears to be suspicious, motion to the other driver to follow you. Never get out of your car in such situations. Go directly to the nearest police precinct, well-lit service station, or 24-hour store.

Always try to park in well-lit and well-traveled areas if possible. Never leave any packages or valuables in sight. If someone attempts to rob you or steal your car, don't try to resist the thief/carjacker—report the incident to the police department immediately by calling ☎ **911.**

2 Getting to the United States

British Airways (☎ 081/897-4000 from within the UK) offers direct flights from London to Miami (and Orlando), as does **Virgin Atlantic** (☎ 012/937-47747 from within the

UK). Canadian readers might book flights with **Air Canada** (☎ 800/776-3000), which offers service from Toronto and Montreal to Miami and Tampa.

Miami International Airport is a hub for flights to and from Latin America. Carriers include **Aerolinas Argentinas** (© 800/333-0276), **Aeromexico** (© 800/245-8585), **American Airlines** (© 800/433-7300), **Avianca** (© 800/284-2622), **Lan Chile Airlines** (© 800/735-5526), and **Varig Brazilian Airlines** (© 800/468-2744).

AIRLINE DISCOUNTS The idea of traveling abroad on a budget is something of an oxymoron, but travelers can reduce the price of a plane ticket by several hundred dollars if they take the time to shop around. For example, overseas visitors can take advantage of the APEX (Advance Purchase Excursion) reductions offered by all major U.S. and European carriers. For more money-saving airline advice, see "Getting There," in chapter 2. For the best rates, compare fares and be flexible with the dates and times of travel.

IMMIGRATION AND CUSTOMS CLEARANCE Visitors arriving by air, no matter what the port of entry, should cultivate patience and resignation before setting foot on U.S. soil. Getting through immigration control may take as long as 2 hours on some days, especially on summer weekends, so be sure to have this guidebook or something else to read. Add the time it takes to clear Customs, and you'll see that you should make a 2- to 3-hour allowance for delays when you plan your connections between international and domestic flights.

In contrast, for the traveler arriving by car or rail from Canada, the border-crossing formalities have been streamlined to the vanishing point. People traveling by air from Canada, Bermuda, and some places in the Caribbean can sometimes clear Customs and Immigration at the point of departure, which is much quicker.

3 Getting Around the United States

BY PLANE Some large airlines (for example, Northwest and Delta) offer travelers on their transatlantic or transpacific flights special discount tickets under the name **Visit USA,** allowing mostly one-way travel from one U.S. destination to another at very low prices. These discount tickets are not on sale in the United States and must be purchased abroad in conjunction with your international ticket. This system is the best, easiest, and fastest way to see the United States at low cost. You should obtain information well in advance from your travel agent or the office of the airline concerned, since the conditions attached to these discount tickets can be changed without advance notice.

BY TRAIN International visitors can also buy a **USA Rail Pass,** good for 15 or 30 days of unlimited travel on Amtrak (© **800/USA-RAIL;** www.amtrak.com). There are six regional options to choose from: National, East Coast, West Coast, Eastern U.S., Western U.S., and Far Western U.S. The pass is available through many foreign travel agents. Prices in 2001 for a 15-day pass (not available for all regions) are $210 to $295 off-peak, $260 to $440 peak; a 30-day pass costs $265 to $385 off-peak, $320 to $550 peak. (With a foreign passport, you can also buy passes at some Amtrak offices in the United States, including locations in San Francisco, Los Angeles, Chicago, New York, Miami, Boston, and Washington, D.C.) Reservations are generally required and should be made for each part of your trip as early as possible.

BY BUS Although bus travel is often the most economical form of public transit for short hops between U.S. cities, it can also be slow and uncomfortable—certainly not an option for everyone (particularly when Amtrak, which is far more luxurious, offers similar rates). **Greyhound/Trailways** (℃ **800/231-2222**), the sole nationwide bus line, offers a **Domestic Ameripass,** which must be purchased before coming to the United States, or at the Greyhound International Office at the Port Authority Bus Terminal in New York City. The pass can be obtained from foreign travel agents and costs less than the domestic version. In 2001, passes were priced as follows: 7 days ($185), 10 days ($235), 15 days ($285), 21 days ($335), 30 days ($385), 45 days ($419), or 60 days ($509). Regional passes, for varying trip lengths, are also available. Foreign travelers can get more info on the pass at **www.greyhound.com**, or by calling ℃ 212/971-0492 (14:00–21:00 GMT or 2–9pm EST) or 402/330-8552 (all other times). In addition, special rates are available for senior citizens and students.

BY CAR The most cost-effective, convenient, and comfortable way to travel around the United States is by car. The interstate highway system connects cities and towns all over the country; in addition to these high-speed, limited-access roadways, there's an extensive network of federal, state, and local highways and roads.

In South Florida, you *will* need a car, as public transportation is somewhat of an oxymoron in this region.

There is no subway system and the bus system is excruciatingly slow.

Some of the national car-rental companies include **Alamo** (℃ 800/327-9633), **Avis** (℃ 800/331-1212), **Budget** (℃ 800/527-0700), **Dollar** (℃ 800/800-4000), **Hertz** (℃ 800/654-3131), **National** (℃ 800/227-7368), and **Thrifty** (℃ 800/367-2277).

Local car-rental companies that either deliver and pick up your rental car at your hotel or pick you up and take you to their office include **Marlin's International Auto Rental** (℃ 305/636-4107), **Al's Rent-A-Car** (℃ 305/887-4226), and **Inter American Car Rental** (℃ 305/534-1100).

If you plan on renting a car in the United States, you probably won't need the services of an additional automobile organization. If you're planning to buy or borrow a car, automobile association membership is recommended. **AAA,** the **American Automobile Association** (℃ **800/222-4357;** www.aaa.com) is the country's largest auto club and supplies its members with maps, insurance, and, most important, emergency road service. The cost of joining runs from $63 for singles to $87 for two members, but if you're a member of a foreign auto club with reciprocal arrangements, you can enjoy free AAA service in America. See "Getting There," in chapter 2 for more information.

 FAST FACTS: For the Foreign Traveler

Automobile Organizations Auto clubs will supply maps, suggested routes, guidebooks, accident and bail-bond insurance, and emergency road service. The **American Automobile Association (AAA)** is the major auto club in the United States. If you belong to an auto club in your home country, inquire about AAA reciprocity before you leave. You may be able to join AAA even if you're not a member of a reciprocal club; to inquire, call ℃ 800/222-4357 (www.aaa.com). AAA is actually an organization of regional auto clubs, so look under "AAA Automobile Club" in the White Pages of the telephone directory. AAA has a nationwide emergency road service telephone number (℃ 800/AAA-HELP).

Business Hours Offices are usually open weekdays from 9am to 5pm. Banks are open weekdays from 9am to 3pm or later and sometimes Saturday mornings. Stores, especially those in shopping complexes on South Beach, in Coconut Grove, and in Key West, tend to stay open late: until about 9pm on weekdays and as late as 11 pm on weekends.

Currency See "Entry Requirements," and "Money," under "Preparing for Your Trip," above.

Currency Exchange Foreign exchange bureaus in South Florida are, unfortunately, foreign to the area. There are currency exchanges at the Miami International Airport, such as **Miami Currency Exchanges** (© 305/ 876-0040). **Abbot Foreign Exchange,** 230 NE 1st St. (© 305/374-2336), is located in downtown Miami and is open on weekdays from 8am to 5pm and on Saturday from 8am to 2pm.

Drinking Laws The legal age for purchase and consumption of alcoholic beverages is 21; proof of age is required and often requested at bars, nightclubs, and restaurants, so it's always a good idea to bring ID when you go out. On South Beach, in particular, the clubs and bars have become stricter since they raised the minimum age of entry from 18 to 21. Beer and wine can often be purchased in supermarkets, but liquor laws vary throughout the state.

Do not carry open containers of alcohol in your car or any public area that isn't zoned for alcohol consumption. The police can, and probably will, fine you on the spot. And nothing will ruin your trip faster than getting a citation for DUI ("driving under the influence"), so don't even think about driving while intoxicated.

Electricity Like Canada, the United States uses 110 to 120 volts AC (60 cycles), compared to 220 to 240 volts AC (50 cycles) in most of Europe, Australia, and New Zealand. If your small appliances use 220 to 240 volts, you'll need a 110-volt transformer and a plug adapter with two flat parallel pins to operate them here. Downward converters that change 220–240 volts to 110–120 volts are difficult to find in the United States, so bring one with you.

Embassies & Consulates All embassies are located in the nation's capital, Washington, D.C. Some consulates are located in Miami and are listed below. Travelers from other countries can get telephone numbers for their embassies and consulates by calling directory information in Washington, D.C. (© **202/555-1212**).

In South Florida, the **Canadian Consulate** is located at 200 S. Bayshore Dr., Miami, FL 33131 (© 305/579-1600). The **British Consulate** is located at the Brickell Bay Tower, Suite 2110, 1001 S. Bayshore Dr., Coconut Grove, FL 33131 (© 305/374-1522). **Brazil's Consulate General** is located at 2601 S. Bayshore Dr., Suite 800, Coconut Grove, FL 33133 (© 305/285-6200).

Emergencies Call © **911** to report a fire, call the police, or get an ambulance anywhere in the United States. This is a toll-free call (no coins are required at public telephones).

If you encounter traveler's problems, check the local telephone directory to find an office of the **Traveler's Aid Society,** a nationwide, nonprofit, social service organization geared to helping travelers in difficult straits. Their services might include reuniting families separated while traveling, providing food and/or shelter to people stranded without cash, or even emotional counseling. If you're in trouble, seek them out.

Gasoline (Petrol) Petrol is known as gasoline (or simply "gas") in the United States, and petrol stations are known as both gas stations and service stations. Gasoline costs about half as much here as it does in Europe (about $1.70 per gallon at press time), and taxes are already included in the printed price. One U.S. gallon equals 3.8 liters or 0.85 Imperial gallons.

Holidays Banks, government offices, post offices, and many stores, restaurants, and museums are closed on the following legal national holidays: January 1 (New Year's Day), the third Monday in January (Martin Luther King Jr. Day), the third Monday in February (Presidents' Day, Washington's Birthday), the last Monday in May (Memorial Day), July 4 (Independence Day), the first Monday in September (Labor Day), the second Monday in October (Columbus Day), November 11 (Veterans' Day/Armistice Day), the fourth Thursday in November (Thanksgiving Day), and December 25 (Christmas). Also, the Tuesday following the first Monday in November is Election Day and is a federal government holiday in presidential election years (held every 4 years, and next in 2004).

Legal Aid The foreign tourist will probably never become involved with the American legal system. If you are "pulled over" for a minor infraction (for example, of the highway code, such as speeding), never attempt to pay the fine directly to a police officer; this could be construed as attempted bribery, a much more serious crime. Pay fines by mail, or directly into the hands of the clerk of the court. If accused of a more serious offense, say and do nothing before consulting a lawyer. Here, the burden is on the state to prove a person's guilt beyond a reasonable doubt, and everyone has the right to remain silent, whether he or she is suspected of a crime or actually arrested. Once arrested, a person can make one telephone call to a party of his or her choice. Call your embassy or consulate.

Mail If you aren't sure what your address will be in the United States, mail can be sent to you, in your name, c/o General Delivery at **Miami's Main Post Office,** 2200 Milam Dairy Rd., Miami, FL 33152 (© 305/639-4280); in **Broward County,** 1801 Polk St., Hollywood, FL 33020 (© 954/923-0201); and in **Palm Beach County,** 14280 Military Trail, Delray Beach, FL 33484 (© 561/498-8504). The addressee must pick mail up in person and must produce proof of identity (driver's license, passport, etc.). Most post offices will hold your mail for up to 1 month and are open Monday to Friday from 8am to 6pm, and Saturday from 9am to 3pm.

Generally found at intersections, mailboxes are blue with a red-and-white stripe and carry the inscription U.S. MAIL. If your mail is addressed to a U.S. destination, don't forget to add the five-digit postal code (or ZIP code) after the two-letter abbreviation of the state to which the mail is addressed.

At press time, domestic postage rates were 20¢ for a postcard and 34¢ for a letter. For international mail, a first-class letter of up to one-half ounce costs 80¢ (60¢ to Canada and Mexico); a first-class postcard costs 70¢ (50¢ to Canada and Mexico); and a preprinted postal aerogramme costs 70¢.

Newspapers The *Miami Herald* is the premier daily newspaper in South Florida, particularly in Miami–Dade County. The *Ft. Lauderdale Sun Sentinel* is Broward County's daily newspaper and the *Palm Beach Post* and *Key West Citizen* cover local and national news. The *Miami New Times* and *Broward/Palm Beach New Times* are free weekly alternative newspapers with comprehensive calendars and event listings as well as local items of interest.

Taxes In the United States there is no value-added tax (VAT) or other indirect tax at the national level. Every state, county, and city has the right to levy its own local tax on all purchases, including hotel and restaurant checks, airline tickets, and so on. A 6% state sales tax (plus 0.5% local tax, for a total of 6.5% in Miami) is added on at the register for all goods and services purchased in Florida. In addition, most municipalities levy special taxes on restaurants and hotels. In Surfside, hotel taxes total 10.5%; in Bal Harbour, 9.5%; in Miami Beach (including South Beach), 11.5%; and in the rest of Dade County, a whopping 12.5%. In Miami Beach, Surfside, and Bal Harbour, the resort (hotel) tax also applies to hotel restaurants and restaurants with liquor licenses.

Telephone, Telegraph, Telex & Fax The telephone system in the United States is run by private corporations, so rates, especially for long-distance service and operator-assisted calls, can vary widely. Generally, hotel surcharges on long-distance and local calls are astronomical, so you're usually better off using a **public pay telephone,** which you'll find clearly marked in most public buildings and private establishments as well as on the street. Convenience grocery stores and gas stations always have them. Many convenience groceries and packaging services sell **prepaid calling cards** in denominations up to $50; these can be the least expensive way to call home. Many public phones at airports now accept American Express, MasterCard, and Visa credit cards. **Local calls** made from public pay phones in most locales cost either 25¢ or 35¢. Pay phones do not accept pennies, and few will take anything larger than a quarter.

Most long-distance and international calls can be dialed directly from any phone. **For calls within the United States and to Canada,** dial 1 followed by the area code and the seven-digit number. **For other international calls,** dial 011 followed by the country code, city code, and telephone number of the person you are calling.

Calls to area codes **800, 888,** and **877** are toll-free. However, calls to numbers in area codes **700** and **900** (chat lines, bulletin boards, "dating" services, and so on) can be very expensive—usually a charge of 95¢ to $3 or more per minute, and they sometimes have minimum charges that can run as high as $15 or more.

For **reversed-charge or collect calls** and for person-to-person calls, dial 0 (zero, not the letter O) followed by the area code and number you want; an operator will then come on the line, and you should specify that you are calling collect, or person-to-person, or both. If your operator-assisted call is international, ask for the overseas operator.

For **local directory assistance** ("information"), dial 411; for long-distance information, dial 1, then the appropriate area code and 555-1212.

Telegraph and telex services are provided primarily by Western Union. You can bring your telegram into the nearest Western Union office (there are hundreds across the country) or dictate it over the phone (© 800/ 325-6000). You can also telegraph money or have it telegraphed to you very quickly over the Western Union system, but this service can cost as much as 15% to 20% of the amount sent.

Most hotels have **fax machines** available for guest use (be sure to ask about the charge to use it), and many hotel rooms are even wired for guests' fax machines. A less expensive way to send and receive faxes may be at stores such as Mail Boxes Etc., a national chain of packing service shops (look in the Yellow Pages directory under "Packing Services").

There are two kinds of telephone directories in the United States. The so-called **White Pages** list private households and business subscribers in alphabetical order. The inside front cover lists emergency numbers for police, fire, ambulance, the Coast Guard, poison-control center, crime victims hotline, and so on. The first few pages will tell you how to make long-distance and international calls, complete with country codes and area codes. Government numbers are usually printed on blue paper within the White Pages. Printed on yellow paper, the so-called **Yellow Pages** list all local services, businesses, industries, and houses of worship according to activity with an index at the front or back. (Drugstores/ pharmacies and restaurants are also listed by geographic location.) The Yellow Pages also include city plans or detailed area maps, postal ZIP codes, and public transportation routes.

Time The continental United States is divided into **four time zones:** eastern standard time (EST), central standard time (CST), mountain standard time (MST), and Pacific standard time (PST). Alaska and Hawaii have their own zones. For example, noon in Miami (EST) is 11am in Chicago (CST), 10am in Denver (MST), 9am in Los Angeles (PST), 8am in Anchorage (AST), and 7am in Honolulu (HST).

Daylight saving time is in effect from 1am on the first Sunday in April through 1am on the last Sunday in October, except in Arizona, Hawaii, part of Indiana, and Puerto Rico. Daylight saving time moves the clock 1 hour ahead of standard time.

Tipping Tipping is so ingrained in the American way of life that the annual income tax of tip-earning service personnel is based on how much they should have received in light of their employers' gross revenues. Accordingly, they may have to pay tax on a tip you didn't actually give them.

Here are some rules of thumb:

In hotels, tip **bellhops** at least $1 per bag ($2 to $3 if you have a lot of luggage) and tip the **chamber staff** $1 to $2 per day (more if you've left a disaster area for him or her to clean up, or if you're traveling with kids and/or pets). Tip the **doorman** or **concierge** only if he or she has provided you with some specific service (for example, calling a cab for you or obtaining difficult-to-get theater tickets). Tip the **valet parking attendant** $1 every time you get your car.

In restaurants, bars, and nightclubs, tip **service staff** 15% to 20% of the check, tip **bartenders** 10% to 15%, and tip **valet parking attendants** $1 per vehicle. Tip the **doorman** only if he has provided you with some specific service (such as calling a cab for you). Tipping is not expected in cafeterias and fast-food restaurants. Many restaurants on South Beach include a 15% tip in the check due to the enormous influx of European tourists who are not accustomed to tipping. Keep in mind that this amount is the *suggested* amount and can be adjusted, either higher or lower, depending on your assessment of the service provided. Because of this tipping-included policy, South Beach wait staff are best known for their lax or inattentive service. Make sure to always read the bottom of your check to see if tipping is included. People tend to get ripped off because they assume the tip is not included.

Tip **cab drivers** 15% of the fare.

As for other service personnel, tip **skycaps** at airports at least $1 per bag ($2 to $3 if you have a lot of luggage) and tip **hairdressers** and **barbers** 15% to 20%.

Tipping ushers at movies and theaters and tipping gas station attendants is not expected.

Toilets You won't find public toilets or "restrooms" on the streets in most U.S. cities, but they can be found in hotel lobbies, bars, restaurants, museums, libraries, department stores, railway and bus stations, or service stations. Note, however, that restaurants and bars in resorts or heavily visited areas may reserve their restrooms for the use of their patrons. Some establishments display a notice that toilets are for the use of patrons only. You can ignore this sign, or, better yet, avoid arguments by paying for a cup of coffee or a soft drink, which will qualify you as a patron. Large hotels and fast-food restaurants are probably the best bet for good, clean facilities. If possible, avoid the toilets at parks and beaches, which tend to be dirty.

4

Getting to Know Miami

It's really not that difficult to learn the lay of the land in the magic city. Miami is a little less than 2,000 square miles and it comprises unique and densely populated neighborhoods.

1 Orientation

ARRIVING

Originally carved out of scrubland in 1928 by Pan American Airlines, **Miami International Airport (MIA)** has become 2nd in the United States for international passenger traffic and 10th in the world for total passengers. Despite the heavy traffic, the airport is quite user-friendly and not as much of a hassle as you'd think. And, unlike most airports, you'll even find signs printed in both Spanish and English. You can change money or use your Honor or Plus System ATM card at Nation's Bank of South Florida, located near the exit. Visitor information is available 24 hours a day at the **Miami International Airport Main Visitor Counter,** Concourse E, 2nd level (✆ **305/876-7000**). Information is also available at **www.miami-airport.com**. Because MIA is the busiest airport in South Florida, travelers may want to consider flying into the less crowded **Fort Lauderdale–Hollywood International Airport (FLL)** (✆ **954/359-1200**), which is closer to north Miami than MIA, or the **Palm Beach International Airport (PBI)** (✆ **561/471-7420**), about 90 minutes away.

GETTING INTO TOWN

The airport is located about 6 miles west of downtown and about 10 miles from the beaches, so it's likely you can get from the plane to your hotel room in less than half an hour. Of course, if you're arriving from an international destination, it will take more time to go through Customs and Immigration.

BY CAR   All the major car-rental firms operate off-site branches reached via shuttle from the terminals. See "Getting Around," later in this chapter, for a list of major rental companies. Signs at the airport's exit clearly point the way to various parts of the city. If you're arriving late at night, you might want to take a taxi to your hotel and have the car-rental firm deliver a car to your hotel the next day.

BY TAXI   Taxis line up in front of a dispatcher's desk outside the airport's arrivals terminals. Most cabs are metered, though some have flat rates to popular destinations. The fare should be about $20 to Coral Gables, $18 to downtown, and $24 to South Beach, plus tip, which should be at least 10% and more for each bag the driver handles. Depending on traffic, the ride to Coral Gables or downtown takes about 15 to 20 minutes, and to South Beach, 20 to 25 minutes. One of the more reliable companies in the city is **Yellow Cab** (✆ **305/444-4444**).

BY LIMO OR VAN Group limousines (multipassenger vans) circle the arrivals area looking for fares. Destinations are posted on the front of each van, and a flat rate is charged for door-to-door service to the area marked.

SuperShuttle (*☎* **305/871-2000;** www.supershuttle.com/mia.htm) is one of the largest airport operators, charging between $10 and $20 per person for a ride within the county. Its vans operate 24 hours a day and accept American Express, MasterCard, and Visa. This is a cheaper alternative to a cab, but be prepared to be in the van for quite a while, as you may have to make several stops to drop all passengers off before you reach your own destination.

Private limousine arrangements can be made in advance through your local travel agent. A one-way meet-and-greet service should cost about $50.

BY PUBLIC TRANSPORTATION Public transportation in South Florida is a major hassle bordering on a nightmare. Painfully slow and unreliable, buses heading downtown leave the airport only once per hour (from the arrivals level), and connections are spotty at best. It could take about an hour and a half to get to South Beach. Journeys to downtown and Coral Gables are more direct. The fare is $1.25, plus an additional 25¢ for a transfer.

VISITOR INFORMATION

The best up-to-date information is provided by the **Greater Miami Convention and Visitor's Bureau,** 701 Brickell Ave., Suite 700, Miami, FL 33131 (© 800/ 933-8448 or 305/539-3000; fax 305/530-3113; www.tropicoolmiami.com). Several chambers of commerce in Greater Miami will send out information on their particular neighborhoods; for addresses and numbers, please see "Visitor Information," and "Money," in chapter 2.

When you arrive at the Miami International Airport, you can pick up visitor information at the airport's main visitor counter on the second floor of Concourse E. It's open 24 hours a day.

Always check local newspapers for special things to do during your visit. The city's only daily, the *Miami Herald,* is a good source for current events listings, particularly the "Weekend" section in Friday's edition and the paper's entertainment weekly offshoot, *The Street,* available free every Friday in freestanding boxes anchored to city streets. Even better is the free weekly alternative paper, the *Miami New Times,* found in bright red boxes throughout the city.

Information on everything from dining to entertainment in Miami is available on the Internet at **www.miami.citysearch.com**.

CITY LAYOUT

Miami may seem confusing at first, but it quickly becomes easy to negotiate. The small cluster of buildings that make up the downtown area is at the geographical heart of the city. In relation to downtown, the airport is northwest, the beaches are east, Coconut Grove is south, Coral Gables is west, and the rest of the city is north.

FINDING AN ADDRESS Miami is divided into dozens of areas with official and unofficial boundaries. Street numbering in the city of Miami is fairly straightforward, but you must first be familiar with the numbering system. The mainland is divided into four sections—NE, NW, SE, and SW—by the intersection of Flagler Street and Miami Avenue. Flagler divides Miami from north to south and Miami Avenue divides the city from east to west. Street numbers (1st Street, 2nd Street, and so forth) start from here and increase as you go further out from this intersection, as do numbers of avenues, places, courts, terraces, and lanes. Streets in Hialeah are the exceptions to this pattern; they are listed separately in map indexes.

Numerical addresses are descriptive, with the first digits giving the cross streets. For example, 12301 Biscayne Blvd. is located at 123rd Street and 501 Ocean Dr. is at 5th Street. It's also helpful to remember that avenues generally run north–south, while streets go east–west.

Getting around the barrier islands that make up Miami Beach is somewhat easier than moving around the mainland. Street numbering starts with 1st Street, near Miami Beach's southern tip, and increases to 192nd Street, in the northern part of Sunny Isles. Collins Avenue makes the entire journey from head to toe. As in the city of Miami, some streets in Miami Beach have numbers as well as names. When they are part of listings in this book, both names and numbers are given.

You should know that the numbered streets in Miami Beach are not the geographical equivalents of those on the mainland, but they are close. For example, the 79th Street Causeway runs into 71st Street on Miami Beach.

STREET MAPS   It's easy to get lost in sprawling Miami, so a reliable map is essential. The Trakker Map of Miami is a four-color accordion map that encompasses all of Dade County. The map is available at newsstands and shops throughout South Florida or online at www.trakkermaps.com.

Some maps of Miami list streets according to area, so you'll have to know which part of the city you are looking for before the street can be found. All the listings in this book include area information for just this reason.

THE NEIGHBORHOODS IN BRIEF

South Beach—The Art Deco District   Though there are many monikers used to describe Miami's publicity darling—Glitter Beach, SoBe, America's Riviera, Hollywood South, Manhattan South—South Beach is a uniquely surreal, Dalí-esque cocktail of cosmopolitan influences with a splash of saltwater thrown in to remind you that you're not in a concrete jungle anymore. South Beach's 15 blocks and 10 miles of beach are alive with a frenetic, circus-like atmosphere and are center stage for a motley crew of characters, from eccentric locals, senior citizens, snowbirds, and college students to gender benders, celebrities, club kids, and curiosity-seekers. Individuality is as widely accepted on South Beach as Visa or MasterCard. Bolstered by a Caribbean-chic cafe society and a sexually charged, tragically hip nightlife, people watching on South Beach is almost as good as a front row seat at a Milan fashion show. Sure, the beautiful people do flock here, but the models aren't the only sights worth drooling over. The thriving Art Deco District within South Beach contains the largest concentration of Art Deco architecture in the world. In 1979, much of South Beach was listed in the National Register of Historic Places. The pastel-hued structures are supermodels in their own right—only these models improve with age.

Miami Beach   Before South Beach's late '80s renaissance, during the fabulous '50s, Miami Beach was America's true Riviera. The stomping ground of choice for the Rat Pack and notorious mobsters such as Al Capone, its huge self-contained resort hotels were vacations unto themselves, providing a full day's worth of meals, activities, and entertainment. Then, in the 1960s and 1970s, people who fell in love with Miami began to buy apartments rather than rent hotel rooms. Tourism declined, the Rat Pack fled to Vegas, Capone disappeared, and many area hotels fell into disrepair.

However, since the late 1980s, Miami Beach has experienced a tide of revitalization. Huge beach hotels are finding their niche with new international tourist markets and are attracting large convention crowds. The **Miami Beach Convention Center,** 1901 Convention Center Dr., Miami Beach, FL 33139 (© **305/673-7311**), has more than 1 million square feet of exhibition space. New generations of Americans have discovered the qualities that originally made Miami Beach so popular, and they are finding out that the sand and surf now come with a thriving international city.

Surfside, Bal Harbour, and **Sunny Isles** make up the north part of the beach. Hotels, motels, restaurants, and beaches line Collins Avenue. For visitors, it seems that, with some outstanding exceptions, the farther north one goes, the cheaper lodging becomes. All told, excellent prices, location, and facilities make Surfside and Sunny Isles attractive places to stay, although a little rough around the edges. A South Beach–like revitalization is in the works, and, while it's highly unlikely these areas will ever become as chic as South Beach, there is potential, especially as South Beach falls prey to the inevitable spoiler known as commercialism. Keep in mind that beachfront properties are at a premium, so many of the area's moderately priced hotels have been converted to condominiums, leaving fewer and fewer affordable places to stay.

In exclusive Bal Harbour, where well-paid police officers are instructed to ticket drivers who go above the 30 mph speed limit, the Rodeo Drive of Miami known as the Bal Harbour Shops attracts shoppers who don't flinch at four-, five-, and six-figure price tags. Few hotels remain amid the many beachfront condominium towers. Fancy homes, tucked away on the bay, hide behind gated communities.

Note that **North Miami Beach,** a residential area near the Dade–Broward County line, is a misnomer. It is actually northwest of Miami Beach on the mainland and has no beaches. North Miami Beach is part of North Dade County and has some of Miami's better restaurants and shops. Located within North Miami Beach is the posh residential community of **Aventura,** best known for its high-priced condos, Turnberry Isle Resort, and the Aventura Mall. Also, South Beach, the historic Art Deco District, is treated as a separate neighborhood.

Key Biscayne   Miami's forested and secluded Key Biscayne is technically one of the first islands in the Florida Keys. However, this island is nothing like its southern neighbors. Located south of Miami Beach, off the shores of Coconut Grove, Key Biscayne is protected from the troubles of the mainland by the long Rickenbacker Causeway and a $1 toll. Key Biscayne is largely an exclusive residential community, with million-dollar homes and sweeping water views, although it also offers visitors great public beaches, some top resort hotels, and several good restaurants. Hobie Beach, adjacent to the causeway, is the city's premier spot for sailboarding and jet-skiing (see "Watersports," in chapter 7). On the island's southern tip, Bill Baggs State Park has great beaches, bike paths, and dense forests for picnicking and partying.

Downtown   Miami's downtown boasts one of the world's most beautiful cityscapes. Unfortunately, that's about all it offers. During the day, a vibrant community of students, businesspeople, and merchants make their way through the bustling streets. Vendors sell fresh-cut pineapples and mangos while young Latin American consumers on shopping sprees lug bags and boxes. At night, downtown is desolate and not a place in which you'd want to get lost. The downtown area does have a mall (Bayside Marketplace, where many cruise passengers come to browse), some culture (Metro-Dade Cultural Center), and a few decent restaurants (see chapter 6), as well as the new American Airlines Arena. A downtown revitalization project is in the works, in which a cultural arts center, among other things, is expected to bring downtown back to life.

Design District   With restaurants springing up between galleries and furniture stores galore, the Design District is, as locals say, the new South Beach, adding a touch of New York's SoHo to an area formerly known as downtown Miami's "Don't Go." The district, which is a hotbed for furniture import companies, interior designers, architects, and more, has also become a player in Miami's ever-changing nightlife, with a cavernous nightclub–restaurant–production/recording studio–live music venue that has become hipster central for South Beach expatriates and artsy bohemian types. In anticipation of its growing popularity, the district has also banded together to create an up-to-date website, **www.designdistrict.com**, which includes a calendar of events and is chock-full of information. The district is loosely defined as the area bounded by NE 2nd Avenue, NE 5th Avenue East and West, and NW 36th Street to the South.

Biscayne Corridor   From downtown near Bayside to the 70s, where trendy curio shops and upscale restaurants are slowly opening, Biscayne Boulevard is aspiring to reclaim itself as a safe thoroughfare where tourists can wine, dine, and shop. Previously known for sketchy, dilapidated 1950s- and '60s-era hotels that had fallen on hard times, residents fleeing the high prices of the beaches in search of affordable housing are renovating Biscayne block by block, making this once again famous boulevard worthy of a Sunday drive. With the trendy Design District immediately west of 36th and Biscayne by 2 blocks, there is hope for the area.

Little Haiti   During a brief period in the late 1970s and early '80s, almost 35,000 Haitians arrived in Miami. Most of the new refugees settled in a 200-square-block area north of downtown. Extending from 41st to 83rd streets and bordered by I-95 and Biscayne Boulevard, Little Haiti is a neighborhood with at least 60,000 residents, more than half of whom were born in Haiti. Tourists are not recommended to venture into this neighborhood.

Little Havana   If you've never been to Cuba, just visit this small section of Miami and you'll come pretty close. The sounds, tastes, and rhythms all remind you of Cuba's capital city. Some even jokingly say you don't have to speak a word of English to live an independent life here. Street signs are in Spanish and English. Cuban coffee shops, tailor and furniture stores, and inexpensive restaurants line "Calle Ocho" (pronounced *Ka*-yey *O*-choh), SW 8th Street, the region's main thoroughfare. Salsa and merengue beats ring loudly from old record stores while old men in *guayaberas* smoke cigars over their daily game of dominoes. Although the spotlight was focused on the area during the Elian Gonzalez situation in 2000, the area was previously noted for the groups of artists and nocturnal types who have moved their galleries and performance spaces here, sparking a culturally charged neo-bohemian nightlife.

Coral Gables   "The City Beautiful," created by George Merrick in the early 1920s, is one of Miami's first planned developments. But this is not Levittown. The houses here were built in a Mediterranean style along lush tree-lined streets that open onto beautifully carved plazas, many with centerpiece fountains. The best architectural examples of the era have Spanish-style tiled roofs and are built from Miami oolite, native limestone commonly called "coral rock." The Gables's European-flared shopping and commerce center is home to many thriving corporations. Some of the city's best restaurants, headed by world-renowned chefs, are located here. You'll also find landmark hotels, great golfing, and upscale shopping.

Coconut Grove   There was a time when Coconut Grove was inhabited by artists, intellectuals, hippies, and radicals, but times have changed. Gentrification has pushed most

---

Fun Fact **The Mistress of Miami**

From 10,000 B.C. to about 1875, much of Miami was a swamp until an unsuspecting woman named Julia Tuttle arrived to collect her inheritance—a large swath of swamp in the Miami area. Over the next 20 years, Tuttle acquired much more property throughout the Miami area and prepared it for the major development that exists today. Following Tuttle, Henry Morrison Flagler arrived in Miami circa 1895. A developer and Standard Oil cohort of J. D. Rockefeller, Flagler had no intention of traveling down to Miami's swampland and instead focused on building a railroad that began at the northern tip of Florida and ended in Palm Beach. A hopeful Tuttle contacted Flagler with a proposal asking him to extend his railroad down to Miami in exchange for half of her property. Flagler declined the offer until a cold front froze out most of northern Florida, and, ultimately, all the tourists. It was then that Flagler decided to see Miami for himself. What he found was a warm tropical paradise, and, ultimately, a partner in Tuttle. Train service to Miami began in April 1896 and the swampy city has never been the same.

---

alternative types out, leaving in their place a multitude of commercialized cafes, boutiques, and nightspots. The intersection of Grand Avenue, Main Highway, and McFarlane Road pierces the area's heart. Right in the center of it all is CocoWalk and the Shops at Mayfair, filled with lovely boutiques, eateries, and bars. Sidewalks here are often crowded, especially at night, when University of Miami students who frequent this adopted college town come out to play.

Coconut Grove's link to the Bahamas dates from before the turn of the 20th century, when islanders came to the area to work in a newly opened hotel called the Peacock Inn. Bahamian-style wooden homes built by these early settlers still stand on Charles Street. Goombay, the lively annual Bahamian festival, celebrates the Grove's Caribbean link and has become one of the largest black

heritage street festivals in America (see "South Florida Calendar of Events," in chapter 2).

Southern Miami–Dade County   To locals, South Miami is both a specific area, southwest of Coral Gables, and a general region that encompasses all of southern Dade County and includes Kendall, Perrine, Cutler Ridge, and Homestead. For the purposes of clarity, this book has grouped all these southern suburbs under the rubric "Southern Miami–Dade County." Similar attributes unite the communities: They are heavily residential, and all are packed with shopping malls amidst a few remaining plots of farmland. Tourists don't usually stay in these parts, unless they are on their way to the Everglades or the Keys. However, Southern Miami–Dade County contains many of the city's top attractions (see chapter 7), making it likely you'll spend some time here.

---

2 Getting Around

Officially, Dade County has opted for a "unified, multimodal transportation network," which basically means you can get around the city by train, bus, and taxi. However, in practice, the network doesn't work too well. Things may improve when the city completes its transportation center in 2005, but until then, unless you are going from downtown Miami to a not-too-distant spot, you are better off in a rented car or a taxi.

With the exception of downtown Coconut Grove and South Beach, Miami is not a walker's city. Because it is so spread out, most attractions are too far apart to make walking between them feasible. In fact, most Miamians are so used to driving that they do so even when going just a few blocks.

BY PUBLIC TRANSPORTATION

BY RAIL   Two rail lines, operated by the **Metro-Dade Transit Agency** (© **305/770-3131**; www.co.miami-dade.fl.us/mdta/), run in concert with each other.

Metrorail, the city's modern high-speed commuter train, is a 21-mile elevated line that travels north–south, between downtown Miami and the southern suburbs. Locals like to refer to this semi-useless rail system as Metro*fail*. If you are staying in Coral Gables or Coconut Grove, you can park your car at a nearby station and ride the rails downtown. However, that's about it. Unfortunately for visitors, the line's usefulness is limited. The first addition to the system, scheduled for completion in mid-2001, will only extend the rail from the Okeechobee station to just west of the Palmetto Expressway. There are plans to extend the system to service Miami International Airport, but until those tracks are built, these trains don't go most places tourists go, with the exception of Vizcaya in Coconut Grove. Metrorail operates daily from about 6am to midnight. The fare is $1.25.

Metromover, a 4.4-mile elevated line, connects with Metrorail at the Government Center stop and circles downtown. This is a good way to get to Bayside if you don't have a car. Riding on rubber tires, the single-car train winds past many of the area's most important attractions and shopping

> ### Joy Ride
> Metromover offers a fun, futuristic ride that you might want to take to complement your downtown tour.

and business districts. You may not go very far, but you will get a beautiful perspective from the towering height of the suspended rails. System hours are daily from about 6am to midnight. The fare is 25¢.

BY BUS   Miami's suburban layout is not conducive to getting around by bus. Lines operate and maps are available, but instead of getting to know the city, you'll find that relying on bus transportation will acquaint you only with how it feels to wait at bus stops. In short, a bus ride in Miami is grueling. You can get a bus map by mail, either from the Greater Miami Convention and Visitor's Bureau (see "Visitor Information," in chapter 2) or by writing the Metro-Dade Transit System, 3300 NW 32nd Ave., Miami, FL 33142. In Miami, call © **305/770-3131** for public-transit information. The fare is $1.25.

BY CAR

Tales circulate about vacationers who have visited Miami without a car, but they are very few indeed. If you are counting on exploring the city, even to a modest degree, a car is essential. Miami's restaurants, attractions, and sights are far from one another, so any other form of transportation is impractical. You won't need a car, however, if you are spending your entire vacation at a resort, are traveling directly to the Port of Miami for a cruise, or are here for a short stay centered in one area of the city, such as South Beach, where everything is within walking distance and parking is a costly nightmare.

When driving across a causeway or through downtown, allow extra time to reach your destination because of frequent drawbridge openings. Some bridges open about every half hour for large sailing vessels to make their way through the wide bays and canals that crisscross the city, stalling traffic for several minutes.

RENTALS   It seems as though every car-rental company, big and small, has at least one office in Miami. Consequently, the city is one of the cheapest places in the world to rent a car. Many firms regularly advertise prices in the neighborhood of $140 per week for their economy car. You should also check first with the airline you have chosen. There are often special discounts when you book a flight and reserve your rental car simultaneously. A minimum age, generally 25, is usually required of renters. Some rental agencies have also set maximum ages. A national car-rental broker, **A Car Rental Referral Service** (© 800/ 404-4482), can often find companies willing to rent to drivers over the age of 21 and can also get discounts from major companies as well as some regional ones.

National car-rental companies with toll-free numbers include **Alamo** (© 800/327-9633), **Avis** (© 800/331-1212), **Budget** (© 800/527-0700), **Dollar** (© 800/800-4000 or 800/327-7607), **Hertz** (© 800/654-3131), **National** (© 800/328-4567), and **Thrifty** (© 800/367-2277). One excellent company that has offices in every conceivable part of town and offers extremely competitive rates is **Enterprise** (© 800/325-8007). Call around and comparison shop—car-rental prices can fluctuate more than airfares. For information on car-rental insurance, see "Getting There," in chapter 2.

Many companies offer cellular phones or electronic map rental. It might be wise to opt for these additional safety features, although the cost can be exorbitant; the phone especially can come in handy if you get lost.

Finally, think about splurging on a convertible. Not only is it one of the best ways to see the beautiful surroundings, but it's an ideal way to perfect a tan! At most companies, the price for convertibles is approximately 20% more.

PARKING   Always keep plenty of quarters on hand to feed hungry meters. Or, on Miami Beach, stop by the chamber of commerce at 1920 Meridian Ave. or any Publix grocery store to buy a magnetic **parking card** in denominations of $10, $20, or $25. Parking is usually plentiful (except on South Beach and Coconut Grove), but when it's not, be careful: Fines for illegal parking can be stiff.

In addition to parking garages, valet services are commonplace and often used. Expect to pay from $5 to $15 for parking in Coconut Grove and on South Beach's busy weekend nights.

LOCAL DRIVING RULES   Florida law allows drivers to make a right turn on a red light after a complete stop, unless otherwise indicated. In addition, all passengers are required to wear seat belts, and children under 3 must be securely fastened in government-approved car seats.

BY TAXI

If you're not planning on traveling much within the city, an occasional taxi is a good alternative to renting a car. If you plan on spending your vacation within the confines of South Beach's Art Deco District, you might also want to avoid

the parking hassles that come with renting your own car. Taxi meters start at
$1.50 for the first quarter-mile and 25¢ for each one-eighth mile. There are
standard flat-rate charges for frequently traveled routes—for example, Miami
Beach's Convention Center to Coconut Grove would cost about $16.

Major cab companies include **Metro** (© **305/888-8888**), **Yellow** (© **305/
444-4444**), and, on Miami Beach, **Central** (© **305/532-5555**).

BY BIKE

Miami is a biker's paradise, with several scenic places in which to spin your
wheels, including most of Miami Beach, where the hard-packed sand and board-
walks make it an easy and scenic route. However, unless you are a former New
York City bike messenger, you won't want to use a bicycle as your main means
of transportation.

For more information on bicycles, including where to rent the best ones, see
chapter 7, "What to See & Do in Miami."

FAST FACTS: Miami

Airport See "Orientation," earlier in this chapter.

American Express You'll find American Express offices in downtown
Miami at 330 Biscayne Blvd. (© **305/358-7350**); 9700 Collins Ave., Bal
Harbour (© **305/865-5959**); and 32 Miracle Mile, Coral Gables
(© **305/446-3381**). Offices are open weekdays from 9am to 5pm and
Saturday from 10am to 4pm. The Bal Harbour office is also open on
Sunday from noon to 6pm. To report lost or stolen traveler's checks,
call © **800/221-7282**.

Area Code The original area code for Miami and all of Dade County
was 305. That is still the code for older phone numbers, but all phone
numbers assigned since July 1998 have the area code 786 (SUN). For all
local calls, even if you're calling across the street, you must dial the
area code (305) or (786) first. Even though the Keys still share the Dade
County area code of 305, calls to there from Miami are considered long
distance and must be preceded by 1-305. (Within the Keys, simply dial
the seven-digit number.) The area code for Fort Lauderdale is 954; for
Palm Beach, Boca Raton, Vero Beach, and Port St. Lucie, it's 561.

Business Hours Banking hours vary, but most banks are open weekdays from 9am to 3pm. Several stay open until 5pm or so at least 1 day
during the week, and many banks feature automated teller machines
(ATMs) for 24-hour banking. Most stores are open daily from 10am to
6pm; however, there are many exceptions. Shops in the Bayside Marketplace are usually open until 9 or 10pm, as are the boutiques in
Coconut Grove. Stores in Bal Harbour and other malls are usually open
an extra hour one night during the week (usually Thursday). As far as
business offices are concerned, Miami is generally a 9-to-5 town.

Car Rentals See "Getting Around," earlier in this chapter.

Climate See "When to Go," in chapter 2.

Curfew Although not strictly enforced, there is an alleged curfew
in effect for minors after 11pm on weeknights and midnight on

weekends in all of Miami–Dade County. After those hours, children under 17 cannot be out on the streets or driving unless accompanied by a parent or on their way to work. Somehow, however, they still manage to sneak out and congregate in popular areas such as Coconut Grove and South Beach.

Dentists **A&E Dental,** 11400 N. Kendall Dr., Mega Bank Building (② 305/ 271-7777), offers round-the-clock care and accepts MasterCard and Visa.

Doctors In an emergency, call an ambulance by dialing ② **911** from any phone. The Dade County Medical Association sponsors a **Physician Referral Service** (② **305/324-8717**) weekdays from 9am to 5pm. **Health South Doctors' Hospital,** 5000 University Dr., Coral Gables (② **305/666-2111**), is a 285-bed acute-care hospital with a 24-hour physician-staffed emergency department.

Driving Rules See "Getting Around," earlier in this chapter.

Drugstores See "Pharmacies," later in this section.

Embassies/Consulates See chapter 3.

Emergencies To reach the police, ambulance, or fire department, dial ② **911** from any phone. No coins are needed. Emergency hotlines include **Crisis Intervention** (② **305/358-HELP** or 305/358-4357) and the **Poison Information Center** (② 800/282-3171).

Eyeglasses **Pearle Vision Center,** 7901 Biscayne Blvd. (② **305/754-5144**), in Miami, can usually fill prescriptions in about an hour.

Hospitals See "Doctors," earlier in this section.

Information See "Visitor Information," earlier in this chapter.

Laundry/Dry Cleaning For dry-cleaning self-service machines and a wash-and-fold service by the pound, call **All Laundry Service,** 5701 NW 7th St. (② 305/261-8175); it's open daily from 7am to 10pm. **Clean Machine Laundry,** 226 12th St., South Beach (② **305/534-9429**), is convenient to South Beach's Art Deco hotels; it's open 24 hours. **Coral Gables Laundry & Dry Cleaning,** 250 Minorca Ave., Coral Gables (② **305/446-6458**), has been dry cleaning, altering, and laundering since 1930. It offers a lifesaving same-day service and is open weekdays from 7am to 7pm and Saturday from 8am to 3pm.

Liquor Laws Only adults 21 or older may legally purchase or consume alcohol in the state of Florida. Minors are usually permitted in bars that serve food. Liquor laws are strictly enforced; if you look young, carry identification. Beer and wine are sold in most supermarkets and convenience stores. The city of Miami's liquor stores are closed on Sunday. Liquor stores in the city of Miami Beach are open all week.

Lost Property If you lost it at the airport, call the **Airport Lost and Found** office (② **305/876-7377**). If you lost it on the bus, Metrorail, or Metromover, call **Metro-Dade Transit Agency** (② **305/770-3131**). If you lost it somewhere else, phone the **Dade County Police Lost and Found** (② 305/ 375-3366). You may also want to fill out a police report for insurance purposes.

Luggage Storage/Lockers In addition to the baggage check at Miami International Airport, most hotels offer luggage storage facilities. If you are taking a cruise from the Port of Miami (see "Cruises and Other Caribbean Getaways," in chapter 7), bags can be stored in your ship's departure terminal.

Newspapers/Magazines The *Miami Herald* is the city's only English-language daily. It is especially known for its Latin American coverage and has a decent Friday "Weekend" entertainment guide. The most respected alternative weekly is the give-away tabloid called **New Times,** which contains up-to-date listings and reviews of food, films, theater, music, and whatever else is happening in town. Also free, if you can find it, is *Ocean Drive,* an oversized glossy magazine that's limited on text and heavy on ads and society photos; it's available at a number of chic South Beach boutiques and restaurants. It is also available on newsstands.

For a large selection of foreign-language newspapers and magazines, check with any of the large bookstores (see chapter 8) or try **News Café** at 800 Ocean Dr., South Beach (© **305/538-6397**), or in Coconut Grove at 2901 Florida Ave. (© **305/774-6397**). Adjacent to the **Van Dyke Café,** 846 Lincoln Rd., South Beach (© **305/534-3600**) is a fantastic newsstand with magazines and newspapers from all over the world. Also check out **Eddie's Normandy,** 1096 Normandy Dr., Miami Beach (© **305/866-2026**), and **Worldwide News,** 1629 NE 163rd St., North Miami Beach (© **305/940-4090**).

Pharmacies **Walgreens Pharmacy** has dozens of locations all over town, including 8550 Coral Way (© **305/221-9271**), in Coral Gables; 1845 Alton Rd. (© **305/531-8868**), in South Beach; and 6700 Collins Ave. (© 305/861-6742), in Miami Beach. The branch at 5731 Bird Rd. at SW 40th Street (© 305/666-0757) is open 24 hours, as is **Eckerd Drugs,** 1825 Miami Gardens Dr. NE, at 185th Street, North Miami Beach (© **305/932-5740**).

Photographic Needs **One Hour Photo,** in the Bayside Marketplace (© **305/377-FOTO**), is pricey (about $17 to develop and print a roll of 36 pictures) but they're open Monday to Saturday from 10am to 10pm and Sunday from noon to 8pm. **Coconut Grove Camera,** 3317 Virginia St. (© **305/445-0521**), features 30-minute color processing and maintains a huge selection of cameras and equipment. It rents, too. Walgreens or Eckerd will develop film for the next day for about $6 or $7.

Police For emergencies, dial © **911** from any phone. No coins are needed. For other matters, call © **305/595-6263**.

Post Office The **Main Post Office,** 2200 Milam Dairy Rd., Miami, FL 33152 (© **305/639-4280**), is located west of Miami International Airport. Letters addressed to you and marked "c/o General Delivery" can be picked up at 500 NW 2nd Ave. Conveniently located post offices include 1300 Washington Ave. in South Beach, and 3191 Grand Ave. in Coconut Grove. There is one central number for all post offices: © **800/275-8777.**

Radio On the AM dial, 610 (WIOD), 790 (WNWS), 1230 (WJNO), and 1340 (WPBR) are all talk. There is no all-news station in town, although 940 (WINZ) gives traffic updates and headline news in between its talk shows. WDBF (1420) is a good big-band station and WPBG (1290) features golden oldies. The two most popular R&B stations are WEDR or 99 Jams (99.1) and Hot 105 (105.1). The best rock stations on the FM dial are WZTA (94.9) and the progressive college station WVUM (90.5). WKIS (99.9) is the top country station. Top-40 music can be heard on WHYI (100.3) and classic disco on Mega 103 (103.5). Public radio can be heard either on WXEL (90.7) or WLRN (91.3). WGTR (97.3) plays easy listening. WDNA (88.9) has the best Latin jazz and multiethnic sounds.

Religious Services Miami houses of worship are as varied as the city's population and include St. Patrick Catholic Church, ?716 Garden Ave., Miami Beach (© **305/531-1124**); Coral Gables Baptist Church, 5501 Granada Blvd. (© **305/665-4072**); Temple Judea, 5500 Granada Blvd., Coral Gables (© **305/667-5657**); Coconut Grove United Methodist, 2850 SW 27th Ave. (© **305/443-0880**); Christ Episcopal Church, 3481 Hibiscus St. (© **305/ 442-8542**); and Plymouth Congregational Church, 3400 Devon Rd., at Main Highway (© **305/444-6521**).

Restrooms Stores rarely let customers use the rest rooms, and many restaurants offer their facilities for customers only. Most malls have bathrooms, as do many fast-food restaurants. Many public beaches and large parks provide toilets, though in some places you have to pay or tip an attendant. Most large hotels have clean rest rooms in their lobbies.

Safety As always, use your common sense and be aware of your surroundings at all times. Don't walk alone at night, and be extra wary when walking or driving though downtown Miami and surrounding areas.

Reacting to several highly publicized crimes against tourists several years ago, both local and state governments have taken steps to help protect visitors. These measures include special highly visible police units patrolling the airport and surrounding neighborhoods and better signs on the state's most tourist-traveled routes.

When driving around Miami, always keep a good map handy, keep the doors locked, and stay alert. Never stop on a highway—if you get a flat tire, drive to the nearest well-lighted, populated place. If you are renting a car, you may consider additional safety features in the car, such as cellular telephones or electronic maps.

Spas & Massage There are some great spa packages at some ritzier hotels (see "The Best Hotel Spas," in chapter 5), but those without spas often have relationships with on-call massage therapists. Ask the concierge to make an appointment for an in-room session. Popular day spas include the **Russian Turkish Baths,** 5445 Collins Ave. at the Castle Hotel (© **305/867-8316**), otherwise known as "The Schvitz," where the old guard meets the new in eucalyptus-scented Turkish steam rooms and aroma baths bolstered by marble columns. **Il Paradiso Day Spa,** 345 Alton Rd., Miami Beach (© **305/672-2600**), is the city's best-kept secret, tucked away in a house, offering massages, reflexology, facials, manicures, and the ever-popular Peppermint Twist, in which a blend of seaweed and essential oil of peppermint has been known to reduce cellulite.

Taxes A 6% state sales tax (plus 0.5% local tax, for a total of 6.5% in Miami) is added on at the register for all goods and services purchased in Florida. In addition, most municipalities levy special taxes on restaurants and hotels. In Surfside, hotel taxes total 10.5%; in Bal Harbour, 9.5%; in Miami Beach (including South Beach), 11.5%; and in the rest of Dade

County, a whopping 12.5%. In Miami Beach, Surfside, and Bal Harbour, the resort (hotel) tax also applies to hotel restaurants and restaurants with liquor licenses.

Taxis See "Getting Around," earlier in this chapter.

Television The local stations are Channel 6, WTVJ (NBC); Channel 4, WCIX (CBS); Channel 7, WSVN (Fox); Channel 10, WPLG (ABC); Channel 17, WLRN (PBS); Channel 23, WLTV (independent); and Channel 33, WBFS (independent).

Time Zone Miami, like New York, is in the Eastern Standard Time zone. Between April and October, daylight saving time is adopted, and clocks are set 1 hour ahead. America's eastern seaboard is 5 hours behind Greenwich Mean Time. To find out what time it is, call ℂ 305/324-8811.

Transit Information For Metrorail or Metromover schedule information, phone ℂ 305/770-3131 or surf over to **www.co.miami-dade.fl.us/mdta/**.

Weather Hurricane season runs from August through November. For an up-to-date recording of current weather conditions and forecast reports, call ℂ **305/229-4522.**

5

Miami Accommodations

As much a part of the landscape as the palm trees, many of Miami's hotels are on display as if they were contestants in a beauty pageant. The city's long-lasting status on the destination A-list has given rise to an ever-increasing number of upscale hotels. And no place in Miami has seen a greater increase in construction than Miami Beach. Since the renaissance that began in the late 1980s, the beach has turned what used to be a beachfront retirement home into a sand-swept hot spot for the Gucci and Prada set. Contrary to popular belief, however, the beach does not discriminate, and it's the juxtaposition of the chic elite and the hoi polloi that contributes to its allure.

While the increasing demand for rooms on South Beach means increasing costs, you can still get a decent room at a fair price. In fact, most hotels in the Art Deco District are less Ritz-Carlton than they are Holiday Inn, unless, of course, they've been renovated. Keep in mind that most hotels in this area were built in the 1930s for the middle class. Unless you plan to center your vacation entirely in and around your hotel, most of the cheaper Deco hotels are adequate and a wise choice for those who plan to use the room only to sleep. The smart vacationer can almost name his price if he's willing to live without a few luxuries, such as an oceanfront view. Ask about packages, since it's often possible to get a better deal than the published rates.

Many of the old hotels from the 1930s, 1940s, and 1950s have been totally renovated, giving way to dozens of "boutique" hotels. Keep in mind that when a hotel claims that it was just renovated, that can mean they've completely gutted the building—or just a coat of fresh paint. Always ask what specific changes were made during a renovation, and be sure to ask if a hotel will be undergoing construction while you're there. You should also find out how near your room will be to the center of the nightlife crowd; trying to sleep directly on Ocean Drive, especially during the weekend, is next to impossible, unless your lullaby of choice happens to include throbbing salsa and bass beats.

I've included the best hotel options for their price as well as those that have been fully upgraded recently. Exceptions are noted. Also, keep in mind that along South Beach's Collins Avenue are dozens of hotels and motels—in all price categories—so there's bound to be a vacancy. If you do try the walk-in routine, don't forget to ask to see one of the rooms first. A few dollars could mean all the difference.

SEASONS & RATES South Florida's tourist season is well defined, beginning in mid-November and lasting until Easter. Hotel prices escalate until about March, after which they begin to decline. During the off-season, hotel rates are typically 30% to 50% lower than their winter highs.

But timing isn't everything. In many cases, rates also depend on your hotel's proximity to the beach and how much ocean you can see from your window. Small motels a block or two from the water can be up to 40% cheaper than similar properties right on the sand.

Rates below have been broken down into two broad categories: winter (generally, Thanksgiving through Easter) and off-season (about mid-May through August). The months in between, the shoulder season, should fall somewhere in between the highs and lows. Rates always go up on holidays. Remember, too, that state and city taxes can add as much as 12.5% to your bill in some parts of Miami. Some hotels, especially those in South Beach, also tack on additional service charges. And parking is pricey.

PRICE CATEGORIES The hotels below are divided first by area, then by price, using the following guidelines: **very expensive,** over $250; **expensive,** $180 to $250; **moderate,** $90 to $180; and **inexpensive,** below $90. Prices are based on published rates (or rack rates) for a standard double room during the high season. Check with the reservations agent, since many rooms are also available above and below the category ranges listed. And always ask about packages, since it's often possible to get a better deal than these "official" rates. Most important, always call the hotel to confirm rates, which may be subject to change without notice because of special events, holidays, or blackout dates.

LONG-TERM STAYS If you plan to visit Miami for a month, a season, or more, think about renting a room in a long-term hotel or condominium apartment. Long-term accommodations exist in every price category, from budget to deluxe, and in general are extremely reasonable, especially during the off-season. Check with the reservation services below, or write a short note to the chamber of commerce in the area where you plan to stay. In addition, many local real estate agents also handle short-term rentals (meaning less than a year).

RESERVATION SERVICES Central Reservations (✆ 800/950-0232 or 305/274-6832; www.reservation-services.com) works with many of Miami's hotels and can often secure discounts of up to 40%. It also gives advice on specific locales, especially in Miami Beach and downtown.

The **South Florida Hotel Network** (✆ 800/538-3616 or 305/538-3616) lists more than 300 hotels throughout the area, from Palm Beach to Miami and down to the Keys.

For bed-and-breakfasts throughout the state, contact **Florida Bed and Breakfast Inns** (✆ 800/524-1880).

1 South Beach

Choosing a hotel on South Beach is similar to deciding whether you'd rather pay a $1.50 for french fries at Denny's or $8.50 for the same fries—but let's call them *pomme frites*—in a pricey haute cuisinerie. It's all about atmosphere. The rooms of some hotels may *look* ultrachic, but they can be as comfortable as sleeping on a concrete slab. Once you decide how much atmosphere you want, the choice will be easier. Fortunately, for every chichi hotel in South Beach—and there are many—there are just as many moderately priced, more casual options.

Prices mentioned here are rack rates—that is, the price you would be quoted if you walked up to the front desk and inquired about rates. The actual price you will end up paying will usually be less than this—especially if a travel agent makes the reservations for you. Many hotels on South Beach have stopped quoting seasonal and off-season rates and have, instead, chosen to go with a low-to-high rate representing the hotel's complete pricing range. It pays to try to negotiate the price of a room. In some of the trendier hotels, however, negotiating is highly unfashionable and not highly regarded. In other words, your attempt at negotiation will either be met with a blank stare or a snippy refusal. It never hurts to try, though.

If status is important to you, as it is to many South Beach visitors, then you will be quite pleased with the number of haute hotels in the area. As popular as nightclubs and restaurants are on South Beach, so are these sleek boutique hotels.

Art Deco hotels, while pleasing to the eye, may be a bit run-down inside. Par for the course on South Beach, appearances are at times deceiving.

VERY EXPENSIVE

Bentley Hotel ✦✦   The biggest coup the Bentley Hotel pulls off is its ability to remain unmoved by the throngs of pedestrians on the well-traveled Ocean Drive. Guests enjoy a private front entrance that leads, via elevator, to the main lobby. Inside this enclave of Old World luxury you will find a charming ambience and an overly accommodating, professional staff.

The hotel's 53 suites are similar to those of the Miami Beach's famed Alexander in that they are both hotel rooms and condos; some of them can be rented year-round. Rooms are complete with marble floors, well-stocked kitchens, and roomy bathrooms with steam showers. Try not to get a corner room, though, or you will learn more about your neighbors than you'd ever want to.

Because it is located on South Beach's bustling strip of neon and nightlife, the Bentley, despite its efforts to stand apart from the rest of its neighbors, isn't impervious to noise. However, if you want luxe in the midst of all the action, the Bentley is a great choice.

510 Ocean Dr., South Beach, FL 33139. © **800/236-8510** or 305/538-1700. Fax 305/532-4865. www.thebentleyhotel.com. 53 units. Winter $290–$1,100 double. Off-season $210–$625 double. AE, DC, DISC, MC, V. **Amenities:** Rooftop pool, concierge, 24-hour room service, dry-cleaning service. *In room:* A/C, TV/DVD player, fax, dataport, kitchen, minibar, coffeemaker, hair dryer.

Casa Grande Suite Hotel ✦✦   A touch of prim Europe clashes with the exotic at this all-suite hotel favored by the jet set and located on the busy, noisy thoroughfare of Ocean Drive. No matter how well insulated the windows may be, you're likely to hear, or feel, the thunderous bass coming from cars cruising by. Fortunately, you will have privacy, thanks to the impeccable service of the hotel's accommodating staff.

A member of record mogul–turned–hotelier Chris Blackwell's Island Outpost resort empire, the Casa Grande Suite Hotel is a visual extravaganza, with towering antique columns from Rajasthan lining the lobby and French and Italian Tagina tiles adorning the floors. Rooms are decorated in exotic fabrics and furnished with carved Balinese teak and mahogany antiques from Blackwell's Island Trading Company Store. Making up for the lack of a pool are the hotel's unrivaled in-room amenities such as a state-of-the-art sound system, plush beds, full kitchens with custom stocked refrigerators, and enormous baths.

834 Ocean Dr., South Beach, FL 33139. © **800/OUTPOST** or 305/672-7003. Fax 305/673-3669. www.islandlife.com. 34 units. Winter $310 junior suite; $340 1-bedroom suite; $525 2-bedroom suite; $1,500 3-bedroom suite. Off-season $195 junior suite; $230 1-bedroom suite; $350 2-bedroom suite; $750 3-bedroom suite. Additional person $15. AE, DC, DISC, MC, V. Limited street parking; valet parking $14. **Amenities:** Access to nearby health club, activities desk, room service, babysitting; overnight dry cleaning and laundry service. *In room:* A/C, TV/VCR, stereo with CD and cassette players, kitchen, minibar, coffeemaker, hair dryer.

South Beach Accommodations

To Central Miami Beach ↗

The Bass Museum of Art

COLLINS PARK

22nd St.
20th St.
19th St.
18th St.
17th St.

Dade Boulevard

Miami Beach Convention Center

Jackie Gleason Theater of Performing Arts

Venetian Causeway

BELLE ISLAND

Purdy Ave.
Dade Boulevard
West Ave.
Bay Rd.
Lincoln Rd.
Alton Rd.

Lincoln Road Mall

16th St.
15th St.

Española Way

14th St.
13th St.
12th St.
11th St.
10th St.
9th St.
8th St.
7th St.
6th St.
5th St.
4th St.
3rd St.
2nd St.
1st St.

Miami Beach Post Office

Biscayne Bay

FLAMINGO PARK

Lenox Ave.
Michigan Ave.
Jefferson Ave.
Meridian Ave.
Pennsylvania Ave.
Washington Ave.
Collins Ave.
James Ave.
Ocean Dr.

Beach Patrol Station

Art Deco Welcome Center

LUMMUS PARK

ATLANTIC OCEAN

West Ave.
Alton Rd.
Lenox Ave.
Michigan Ave.

Commerce St.
Biscayne St.

Government Cut

SOUTH POINTE PARK

Abbey Hotel **2**
Banana Bungalow **1**
The Beachcomber Hotel **10**
Brigham Gardens **9**
The Clevelander **15**
Crest Hotel Suites **5**
The Delano **6**
The Hotel **20**
Hotel Astor **14**
Hotel Impala **12**
Hotel Leon **19**
Park Washington Hotel **13**
The Pelican Hotel **17**
Raleigh Hotel **4**
The Ritz-Carlton **7**
Townhouse **3**
Villa Paradiso **8**
Villas at Caffé Milano **16**
Whitelaw Hotel **18**

Casa Tua   This outrageous boutique property, scheduled to open summer 2001, will provide custom-tailored amenities (from toiletries to snacks) for each of its guests, who fill out a detailed profile when booking one of Casa Tua's five suites. Styled like a glorious Mediterranean beach house, Casa Tua also promises a posh restaurant with an Italian-accented menu and a second-floor lounge for afternoon tea and evening cocktails.

1700 James Ave., Miami Beach, FL 33139. ℂ **305/673-1010.** 5 suites. $750 and up. Call for details.

The Delano ✪ *(Overrated)*   Unless your name's Madonna, Gwyneth, or the equivalent, you will definitely feel like you are paying for the privilege of staying here. The hipper-than-thou hotel is known for its extravagant decor and deco architecture in which Alice in Wonderland meets South Beach. Dolled up in the whimsically minimalist style of designer Philippe Starck, the Delano may not be the friendliest place in which to stay, but it certainly is amusing to look at—with 40-foot sheer white curtains hanging outside, mirrors everywhere, white billowing curtains, Adirondack chairs, and faux-fur-covered beds. The rooms are done up sanitarium style: sterile, yet toxically trendy, in pure white save for a perfectly crisp green Granny Smith apple in each room—the only freebie you're going to get here. A bathroom renovation is taking place in all the rooms—but they will remain small and spartan. Bathrooms in the suites and bungalows have been done up in Italian marble with oversized monolithic bathtubs. An attractive, white-clad staff look as if they were hand-picked from last month's *Vogue*. While they may sigh if you ask for something, eventually they'll get it for you. The gym here is great, but it costs $15 a day, even if you are a guest. The fantastic wading pool, thankfully, is free, but get out early to snag a chair. The Blue Door restaurant, formerly part-owned by Madonna, serves lots of attitude with its pricey haute cuisine; the lobby's Rose Bar is command central for the chic elite who don't flinch at paying in excess of $10 for a martini. The hotel's major saving grace is Agua, the rooftop spa, where, if you can afford it, an hour massage while overlooking the ocean is blissful.

1685 Collins Ave., South Beach, FL 33139. ℂ **800/555-5001** or 305/672-2000. Fax 305/532-0099. 209 units, 1 penthouse. Winter $325–$810 standard; $750–$2,000 suite; $2,000–$3,000 bungalow or 2-bedroom; $2,800–$3,000 penthouse. Off-season $245–$660 standard; $600–$2,000 suite; $940–$3,000 bungalow or 2-bedroom; $2,400–$3,000 penthouse. Additional person $35. AE, DC, DISC, MC, V. Valet parking $20. **Amenities:** 3 restaurants, bar, large outdoor pool, 24-hour state-of-the-art David Barton gym, extensive watersports equipment, children's programs, concierge, business center, room service, in-room massage, same-day dry cleaning and laundry service. *In room:* A/C, TV/VCR, CD player, minibar, hair dryer.

Fisher Island Club ✪✪✪   This exclusive island just off Miami Beach is a luxurious cross between "Fantasy Island," "Lifestyles of the Rich and Famous," and "Survivor." But you will not be roughing it on this island, which serves as a retreat for Luciano Pavarotti and Oprah Winfrey, among others. To get to the resort, visitors and residents take a private ferry, which shuttles guests to and from the mainland every 15 to 20 minutes. It can be somewhat of a hassle—especially if you need to make a quick return to the island—but it does run on a very regular schedule. Visitors should be forewarned that the ferry lets residents on first, so if there's no room after all the Rolls Royces and Ferraris roll on, you're outta luck and will have to wait for the next one. Don't worry if you are car-less—on this exclusive island, golf carts will get you anywhere you need to go.

As for location, you're only minutes from the airport, South Beach, Coral Gables, and Coconut Grove (not counting ferry time). Still, considering the pampering you'll receive in this former Vanderbilt mansion turned resort extra-ordinaire, you probably won't want to leave the seclusion of the island for the frenetic city. Rooms vary in size and shape, and cottages come with hot tubs. A world-class spa and club offer all the amenities you could imagine. And you definitely won't go hungry: The elegant Vanderbilt Club offers continental cuisine; the Beach Club and Golfer's Grill serve basic but expensive sandwiches and salads; an Italian Cafe prepares good pizza and pastas; and a gourmet general store sells everything else.

1 Fisher Island Dr., Fisher Island, FL 33190. ℂ **800/537-3708** or 305/535-6020. Fax 305/535-6003. www.fisherisland-florida.com. 60 units. Winter $385–$625 double; $750–$1,350 suite or cottage. Off-season $330–$415 double; $525–$1,200 suite or cottage. Golf, tennis, and spa packages available seasonally. 20% gratuity added to all food and beverages. AE, DC, MC, V. **Amenities:** 3 restaurants, 3 bars, P. B. Dye Golf Course, 18 tennis courts, 2 marinas, world-class spa, concierge, airport transportation, secretarial service, limited room service, babysitting, dry cleaning and laundry service. *In room:* A/C, TV/VCR, minibar, coffeemaker, hair dryer.

Loews Hotel ⟨★⟨★   The Loews Hotel is one of the largest beach hotels to arrive in South Beach in almost 30 years, consuming an unprecedented 900 feet of oceanfront, not to mention the hotel next door. This 800-room behemoth is considered an eyesore by many, an architectural triumph by others. However you perceive it, you can't miss the hotel's multitiered cone-shaped 18-story tower perched high above the rest of South Beach. Rooms are a bit boxy and nothing to rave about;

In the Swim
At 205 feet long, the National's pool is the supermodel of hotel pools, lithe and graceful and almost too sleek for splashing.

---

they're clean and a bit bland. New carpets and bedspreads were recently added to erase signs of early wear and tear due to the heavy traffic of the hotel. The Loews deserves credit for attempting to maintain the intimacy of an Art Deco hotel while still trying to accommodate business travelers who come to the nearby convention center, but because it is so large, it does tend to feel like a convention hall. You're not going to get personal doting service, but the staff does try, even if it takes them a while. If you can steer your way through all the name-tagged business people in the lobby, you can escape to the pool that is large enough to accommodate families and conventioneers alike. The hotel's lauded Argentine steak house, Gaucho Room, is superb. The landscaped entrance to the pool is more Maui than Miami and undisputedly gorgeous.

1601 Collins Ave., South Beach, FL 33139. ℂ **800/23-LOEWS** or 305/604-1601. www.loewshotels.com. 800 units. Winter from $269 double. Off-season from $169 double. AE, DC, DISC, MC, V. Valet parking $19. Pets accepted. **Amenities:** 3 restaurants, 3 bars, coffee bar, sprawling outdoor pool, health club, Jacuzzi, sauna, watersports rentals, children's programs, concierge, business center, 24-hour room service, babysitting, dry cleaning. *In room:* A/C, TV, dataport, minibar, coffeemaker, hair dryer.

National Hotel ⟨★   With its towering ceilings, sultry furnishings, and massive gilded mirrors, the elegant 1940s-style National ought to be the backdrop for a gangster flick. At 11 stories, the main building stands taller than most of its neighbors and offers grand views of the beach and ocean below. Rooms in the garden wing are slightly larger and have balconies, but all are comfortable and pretty spacious with sleek and modern bathrooms. Poolside rooms have slightly larger bathrooms, but beyond that they really are a just a step above a motel room. And speaking of the pool, the National's is a winner. It's Miami's longest pool (205 feet) and can be considered the supermodel of hotel pools, lithe and graceful and almost too sleek (rivaling even the Delano's pool) for splashing. Café Mosaic is an elegant and formal dining room offering tropical Floridian fare with a Latin twist. The nicest aspects of the hotel are the ultra-Deco lobby bar and Press Room cigar bar, which look like 1940s movie sets.

1677 Collins Ave., South Beach, FL. 33139. (C) **800/327-8370** or 305/532-2311. Fax 305/534-1426. www.nationalhotel.com. 152 units. Winter $315–$1,000 double. Off-season $255–$800 double. AE, DC, DISC, MC, V. Valet parking $16. **Amenities:** Restaurant, 3 bars, large outdoor pool, exercise room, watersports equipment rental, concierge, limited room service, babysitting, dry cleaning and laundry service. *In room:* A/C, TV/VCR, minibar, hair dryer, stereo.

Ritz-Carlton ✿✿✿ The luxe life comes to a congested and somewhat seedy corner of South Beach in the form of this beachfront, lushly landscaped Ritz-Carlton, which has restored a landmark 1950s building to its original Art Moderne style and filled it with the hotel's signature five-star service. Far from ostentatious, the Ritz-Carlton's South Beach property moves away from gilded opulence in favor of the more soothing pastel-washed touches of Deco. Though South Beach is better known for its trendy boutique hotels, the Ritz-Carlton offers comfort to those who might prefer 100% cotton sheets and goose-down pillows to high-style minimalism.

With impeccable service, an impressive stretch of sand, and a world-class 13,000-square-foot spa and wellness center, the Ritz-Carlton kicks sand in the faces of some of the smaller hotels that think they're doing *you* a favor by allowing you to sleep there.

1 Lincoln Rd., South Beach, FL 33139. (C) **800/241-3333** or 305/648-5900. Fax 305/648-1448. www. ritzcarlton.com. 375 units. Winter $450–$750 double. Off-season $275–$625 double. AE, DISC, MC, V. Valet parking $30. **Amenities:** 3 restaurants, outdoor heated pool, health club, spa, extensive watersports rentals, children's program, 24-hour business center, salon, 24-hour room service, babysitting, overnight laundry service. *In room:* A/C, TV, dataport, minibar, hair dryer, coffeemaker, iron, safe.

Shore Club Giving the Delano a run for its money, the Shore Club, scheduled to open July 2001, is already making waves within the jet set and fabulatti thanks to two things in particular: the impending opening of Nobu sushi restaurant and cocktail lounge (already a hit in New York and London), and former supermodel Christy Turlington's Sundari Spa. The Shore Club also boasts that 80% of its 325 rooms have an ocean view. Exquisite gardens draw guests toward the beach through courtyards and reflecting pools. Rooms are loaded with state-of-the-art amenities, not to mention 400-thread linen bedding, Mexican sandstone flooring in the bathroom with custom-designed glass and an enclosed "wet area" with bathtub, shower, and teak bench. Molton Brown bathroom amenities are worth bringing an extra bag for. For superluxe, a 6,000-square-foot 3-story penthouse with private elevator is up for grabs at a mere $10,000 a night.

1901 Collins Ave., Miami Beach, FL 33139. (C) **877/640-9500** or 305/695-3222. Fax 305/695-3299. www.shoreclubsouthbeach.com. 318 units; 7 cabanas. Winter $475–$775 double; $1,125 suite; $2,500 cabana. Off-season $425–$675 double; $1,025 suite; $1,500 cabana. AE, DC, MC, V. Valet parking (price unavailable at press time). **Amenities:** 2 restaurants, 2 bars, outdoor reflecting pools with poolside dataports, health club with steam room and outdoor equipment, spa, concierge, 24-hour room service. *In room:* A/C, TV, Intrigue System with digitally downloaded movies and high-speed Internet access, CD player, stereo, fax, minibar.

The Tides ✿✿✿ This 12-story Art Deco masterpiece is reminiscent of a gleaming ocean liner, with porthole windows and lots of stainless steel and frosted glass. Rooms are starkly white but much more luxurious and comfortable than those at the Delano. Also, all rooms are at least twice the size of a typical South Beach hotel room and have a view of the ocean. They feature king beds, spacious closets, large bathrooms, and even a telescope from which to view the vast ocean. The penthouses on the 9th and 10th floors are situated at the highest point on Ocean Drive, allowing for a priceless panoramic view of the ocean, the skyline, and the beach. Although small, the freshwater pool is a welcome plus for those who aren't in the mood to feel the sand between their toes; but it really doesn't fit with the rest of the hotel, lacking in ambience and view (it overlooks an alley). The hotel's restaurant, Twelve Twenty, is an elegant, excellent, and pricey eatery with seating in the lobby. The Terrace is a less expensive outdoor cafe.

1220 Ocean Dr., South Beach, FL 33139. ☎ **800/OUTPOST** or 305/604-5000. Fax 305/672-6288. www.islandoutpost.com. 45 units. Winter $475 suite; $2,500 penthouse. Off-season $350 suite; $2,000 penthouse. Additional person $15. AE, DC, DISC, MC, V. Valet parking $18. **Amenities:** 2 restaurants, lounge, bar, outdoor heated pool, small health club and discount at large nearby health club, concierge, secretarial services, 24-hour room service, in-room massage, babysitting, laundry and dry-cleaning service. *In room:* A/C, TV/VCR, stereo/CD player w/selection of music, video rentals, minibar, hair dryer.

Villas at Caffé Milano ★★   With prices like these, you could've actually gone to Milan, but nonetheless, this 11-room boutique hotel boasts enormous, luxurious oceanfront rooms with state-of-the-art industrial-style kitchen appliances, flat- or big-screen televisions, and DVD players. In addition to the fantastic in-room amenities, the service here is particularly attentive, as well it should be for these prices. The one drawback, for some, is its location on a busy stretch of Ocean Drive—the noise level is rather high here and there's nothing the hotel can do about it. But they will try to fulfill any other requests you might have.

850 Ocean Dr., South Beach, FL 33139. ☎ **888/535-5135** or 305/ 535-8879. Fax: 305/695-2942. 11 units. Year-round $600–$750 double. AE, DC, DISC, MC, V. Valet parking $18. **Amenities:** Restaurant, lounge, dry-cleaning service. *In room:* A/C, TV/VCR, DVD, kitchen, coffeemaker, hair dryer, washer and dryer; Jacuzzi in one unit.

W South Beach   The Ritz Plaza, located at 17th Street and Collins Avenue, has been resuscitated from its decrepit state into a revitalized stylish boutique hotel with a new wing of oceanview rooms. Located next door to the ever-fabulous Delano Hotel and scheduled to open in 2001, we expect this W to approximate its sister properties that cater to business travelers (and others who don't spend too much time in their rooms) with stylish yet functional guest rooms, supercomfortable beds, attentive service, and a fabulous scene at its restaurant and bar.

1701 Collins Avenue, Miami Beach ☎ **877/ Whotels.** Call for details.

EXPENSIVE

Albion Hotel ★★   An architectural masterpiece originally designed in 1939 by internationally acclaimed architect Igor Polevitzky (of Havana's legendary Hotel Nacional fame), this sleek, modern, nautical-style hotel was once the local headquarters for Abbie Hoffman and the Students for a Democratic Society during the 1972 Democratic National Convention in Miami. Though it was totally renovated under the guidance of the hip hotel family, the

> **Impressions**
>
> *The size of the hotels vary . . . rates begin at about $2 and there is one that charges $50 a day (Winter season). They are modern, architectural masterpieces.*
>
> —Highlights of Greater Miami, 1949

Rubells, the hotel still maintains a neo-hippie democratic feeling of peace, love, togetherness—albeit with a hipster twist. Despite its location 2 blocks from the beach, a large portholed pool and artificial beach are enough to keep you at the property and off the real beach. Rooms are industrial chic, and, for some people, not very warm; recent renovations have taken a little of the edge off. The staff is wonderful. Cookies at the registration desk make you feel as if you're a guest in someone's home and not a hotel. A restaurant is scheduled to open mid-2001; in the meantime, the mezzanine-level Pantry provides snacks and continental breakfast items.

1650 James Ave. (at Lincoln Rd.), South Beach, FL 33139. ℂ **888/665-0008** or 305/913-1000. Fax 305/674-0507. www.rubellhotels.com. 100 units. Winter $255–$375 double. Off-season $165–$265 double. AE, DC, DISC, MC, V. Valet parking $17. Pets accepted. **Amenities:** Snack bar, bar, large outdoor heated pool with adjacent artificial sand beach, small exercise room, concierge, airport limo service, business and secretarial services, 24-hour room service, in-room massage, babysitting, dry cleaning. *In room:* A/C, TV/VCR, stereo with CD and cassette player, dataport, minibar, hair dryer, iron.

The Hotel 🐾🐾🐾 Kitschy fashion designer Todd Oldham whimsically restored this 1939 gem (formerly the Tiffany Hotel) as he would have a vintage piece of couture. He laced it with lush, cool colors, hand-cut mirror, and glass mosaics from his ready-to-wear factory, then added artisan detailing, terrazzo floors, and porthole windows. The small, soundproof rooms are very comfortable and incredibly stylish, though the bathrooms are a bit cramped. There's no need to pay more for an oceanfront view—go up to the rooftop, where the pool is located, and you'll see the most amazing view of the Atlantic. The hotel's restaurant, Wish, is one of South Beach's best.

801 Collins Ave., South Beach, FL 33139. ℂ **877/843-4683** or 305/531-2222. Fax 305/531-2222. www.the hotelofsouthbeach.com. 52 units. Year-round $195–$345 double. AE, DC, DISC, MC, V. Valet parking $18. **Amenities:** Restaurant, bar, pool bar, small pool, health club, concierge, business center, room service. *In room:* A/C, TV/VCR, stereo system with CD and cassette players, Kiehl's products, video library, dataport, minibar, coffeemaker, hair dryer.

Hotel Astor 🐾🐾🐾 Cozy-chic best describes this diminutive Deco hotel built in 1936. A 1995 renovation greatly improved on the original design of this simple three-story property which has hosted the likes of Cameron Diaz and Madonna and continues to attract a lively local crowd to the small but sleek lobby bar. There is a small lap pool and a beautiful waterfall outside the bar area, but if you're looking to catch some sun, you may want to consider walking the 2 blocks to the beach because there are very few lounge chairs at the pool. The rooms are small but soothing in beige tones, featuring plush and luxurious details—swivel stands for the large-screen TVs, Belgian linens and towels, and

---

Hotel Dining

While travelers don't necessarily choose a hotel by their dining options, some of Miami's best restaurants can be found inside hotels. Some of the city's most hailed cuisine can be had at the Hotel Astor's **Astor Place Bar and Grill,** the Delano's **Blue Door,** The Hotel's **Wish,** and the Mandarin Oriental's **Azul. Nobu,** a New York import scheduled to open at the Shore Club, will surely join the list. *Warning:* In some cases, your tab at these restaurants may be almost as high as the price of a room. See chapter 6 for reviews of these and other hotel restaurants.

funky custom mood lighting with dimmer switches. The mattresses are incredibly plush and difficult to leave. Views are probably the worst thing about this hotel, as most rooms face the street or a neighboring seedy hotel. The hotel staff is known for its extreme attentiveness—especially Arturo, the hotel's "Cheers"-y bartender who actually knows everybody's names and their drinks of choice. Astor Place Bar and Grill in the hotel's basement is one of the city's best and most expensive.

956 Washington Ave., South Beach, FL 33139. ℂ **800/270-4981** or 305/531-8081. Fax 305/531-3193. www.hotelastor.com. 40 units. Winter $150–$800 double. Off-season $110–$500 double. Additional person $30. AE, DC, MC, V. Valet parking $20. **Amenities:** Restaurant, 2 bars, small outdoor pool, access to nearby health club, 24-hour concierge service, secretarial services, limited room service, in-room massage, babysitting, laundry and dry-cleaning service. *In room:* A/C, TV, dataport, minibar, fridge, hair dryer.

Hotel Impala ⭐⭐⭐   This renovated Mediterranean inn is one of the areas best, and it's just beautiful, from the Greco-Roman frescos and friezes to an intimate garden that is perfumed with the scents from carefully hanging lilies and gardenias. Rooms are extremely comfortable, with super-cushy sleigh beds, sisal floors, wrought iron fixtures, imported Belgian cotton linens, wood furniture, and fabulous roomy bathrooms done up in stainless steel and coral rock. Adjacent to the hotel is Spiga, an intimate, excellent Italian restaurant that is reasonably priced. Enclaves like this one are rare on South Beach.

1228 Collins Ave., South Beach, FL 33139. ℂ **800/646-7252** or 305/673-2021. Fax 305/673-5984. www. hotelimpala1@aol.com. 17 units. Winter $200–$400 double. Off-season $169–$279 double. AE, DC, MC, V. Valet parking $18. No children under 16 permitted. **Amenities:** Restaurant, concierge, room service. *In room:* A/C, TV/VCR, stereo, CD player, complimentary videos, dataport, hair dryer.

Hotel Nash ⭐⭐⭐   Bridging the gap between hypertrendy and schlocky hotels often found on South Beach, the Hotel Nash is a rarity in that it boasts both style and substance. Located a block from the beach and behind the infamous Versace mansion, the Nash is housed in a 1930s Deco structure, which received an $11 million renovation. The result is a soothing, almost therapeutic hotel in which the scents of aromatherapy seep into every room and public space on the property. An aromatic indoor garden of jasmine, bougainvillea, star anise, and cypress, three tiny yet intimate pools—freshwater, saltwater, and mineral water—and possibly the best restaurant on the beach—Mark's South Beach—are permanent fixtures in this beautiful hotel. Rooms are adorned in sage and ivory and overlook either the city or the Versace mansion observatory.

1120 Collins Ave., Miami Beach, FL 33139. ℂ **305/674-7800.** Fax 305/538-8288. www.hotelnash.com. 55 units. Winter $300–$330 double; $355–$560 suite; $825 duplex; $665–$1,700 penthouse. Off-season $180 double; $250–$480 suite; $780 duplex; $580–$1,100 penthouse. Rates change frequently. AE, DC, DISC, MC, V. Valet parking $16. **Amenities:** Restaurant, bar, 3 outdoor pools, watersports equipment rental, car service. *In room:* A/C, TV/VCR or DVD, CD player, dataport, minibar, hair dryer, iron, safe.

Hotel Ocean ⭐⭐   This Mediterranean enclave, located smack in the middle of crazy Ocean Drive, remains somehow protected from the disarray, perhaps due to the lovely French-style courtyard, on which live jazz is often performed. The European-style hotel's 27 suites are fabulous, with authentic Art Deco furniture, soundproof windows, terraces facing the ocean, massive bathrooms with French toiletries, and original fireplaces that add to the coziness even if you're not likely to use them. Once a year, the hotel changes the color scheme (and sometimes the flooring) of each suite, keeping everything fresh. The hotel's restaurant, Les Deux Fontaines, is known for its superb service, excellent seafood, and intimate Speakeasy Bar. The only drawback to this hotel is its lack of a pool, but since the beach is directly across the street, it really shouldn't stop you from staying at this excellent spot.

1230 Ocean Dr., Miami Beach, FL 33139. ✆ **800/783-1725** or 305/672-2579. Fax 305/672-7665. www. hotelocean.com. 27 units. Winter $200–$280 double; $300–$450 suite; $600 penthouse. Off-season $179–$275 double; $325–$345 suite; $515 penthouse. Rates include continental breakfast. AE, DC, DISC, MC, V. Valet parking $16. Pets accepted for $15 per day. **Amenities:** Half-price admission to nearby health club, concierge, secretarial services, limited room service, babysitting, laundry and dry-cleaning service. *In room:* A/C, TV/VCR, CD player, dataport, minibar (stocked with guests' personalized order), fridge, hair dryer.

Marlin ⭐⭐   Don't be surprised if you hear guitar riffs upon entering the Marlin. This rock-and-roll hotel, owned by Chris Blackwell, founder of Island Records, also houses South Beach Studios, a recording and mixing facility, which has been put to use by Aerosmith and U2 among others. And don't be taken aback if you see beautiful models strolling by—the Elite Modeling Agency also calls the Marlin home.

The rooms here sport a sleek, industrial Caribbean decor, with soft earth tones, custom furniture, and hardwood floors; each suite feels like a private bungalow. No two rooms are alike, and each one is distinctive enough that even Martha Stewart, a past guest, approved. The very hip but relaxed Marlin Bar attracts a sleek crowd trying to escape the overblown South Beach bar scene. The major drawbacks of this hotel are its location on a busy, highly trafficked corner of Collins Avenue and its lack of a pool. The rooftop garden/bar area provides a fantastic view of the beach and the city.

1200 Collins Ave., Miami Beach, FL 33139. ✆ **800/OUTPOST** or 305/672-5254. Fax 305/672-6288. www.islandoutpost.com. 13 units. Winter $280–$395 double. Off-season $195–$275 double. AE, DC, DISC, MC, V. Valet parking $16. **Amenities:** Bar, reduced rates at Crunch Fitness and VIP access to local clubs, concierge, secretarial services, room service provided by The Tides (see above), babysitting, laundry service. *In room:* A/C, TV/VCR, CD player, dataport, kitchenette, minibar, fridge, microwave, coffeemaker, hair dryer.

Mercury ⭐   This small boutique hotel is located in the fast-rising area known as SoFi, or South of Fifth Street, South Beach's latest recipient of a hipster takeover. The Mercury is an upscale, modern all-suite resort that combines Mediterranean charm with trendy South Beach flair. A member of Design Hotels, a worldwide collection of four-star boutique hotels, the Mercury is actually a well-kept secret that's attached to one of the beach's best restaurants, Nemo, which also provides the hotel's room service. A small outdoor heated pool and Jacuzzi are located in a courtyard that's shared with the restaurant. Accommodations are ultrastylish, with sleek light wood furnishings, Belgian cotton bedding, European kitchens, and spacious bathrooms with spa tubs. If you're looking to stay in style without the hassle of the South Beach hustle and bustle, this is the place.

100 Collins Ave., Miami Beach, FL 33139. ✆ **877/786-2732** or 305/398-3000. Fax 305/398-3001. www. mercuryresort.com. 44 units. Winter $225 double. Off-season $165 double. Rates include continental breakfast. AE, DC, DISC, MC, V. Valet parking $18. **Amenities:** Heated pool, access to fitness center behind hotel, Jacuzzi, concierge, room service, in-room massage. *In room:* TV/VCR, entertainment center with CD player and stereo, video and music library, fax, dataport, kitchen, minibar, coffeemaker, hair dryer.

Miami Beach Marriott at South Beach ⭐   This is not your father's Marriott. Located in the throbbing heart of South Beach, this mammoth oceanfront property works hard to leave its mass-market image behind, with a rain forest aviary and waterfall in the lobby, funky flower arrangements on every floor, and a punchy blue and lime room decor (a bit tacky, but a world apart from standard Marriott interiors). A fantastic beachfront pool, cabanas, and watersports

Checking into Hotel Bars

While South Beach is known for its trendy club scene, hotel bars are very much a part of the nightlife. Among the hottest hotel bars are the **Rose Bar** at the Delano, the **lobby bar at the Hotel Astor,** the **Bond St. Lounge** at the Townhouse, the **Tower Bar** at the Shore Club (scheduled to open at press time), the **lobby bar at the Whitelaw Hotel,** and the **Marlin Bar** at the Marlin Hotel. A South Beach outpost of the boutique chain of W Hotels, featuring hot watering hole Whiskey Blue, owned by Cindy Crawford's husband, Rande Gerber, is scheduled to open fall 2002 at 1701 Collins Ave. (© **305/534-3500**). See chapter 9, "Miami After Dark," for more details.

rentals are an added plus, and a rarity on Ocean Drive. Some rooms have balconies with ocean and city views.

161 Ocean Dr., Miami Beach, FL 33139. © **305/536-7700.** Fax 305/536-9900. www.marriott.com. 256 units. $219 general view; $239 city view; $279 ocean view; $299 direct oceanfront; $309 concierge level. Rates change frequently. AE, DC, DISC, MC, V. Valet parking $18. **Amenities:** Restaurant, coffee shop, lounge, pool, health club, extensive watersports rentals, bike rental, concierge, business center, 24-hour room service, laundry service. *In room:* Dataport, minibar, coffeemaker, hair dryer.

Raleigh Hotel ★★ Upon entering the lobby of this oceanfront Art Deco hotel, you will feel like you've stepped back into the 1940s. Polished wood, original terrazzo floors, and an intimate martini bar add to the fabulous atmosphere that's favored by fashion photographers and production crews, for whom the hotel's fleur-de-lis pool is the favorite subject. In fact, one look at the pool and you'll expect Esther Williams to splash up in a dramatic, aquatic plié. Should you glance quickly inside the dimly lit lobby restaurant, the constantly changing Tiger Oak Room (last we checked, it was Pan-Asian), you could swear Dorothy Parker and her fellow round-tablers took a detour from New York's Algonquin Hotel and landed here. Rooms are tidy and efficient, nothing too elaborate, but that's not why people stay here. It's the Raleigh's romantic Deco lure that has people skipping over from the chilly, antiseptic Delano a few blocks up for much needed warmth.

1775 Collins Ave., Miami Beach, FL 33139. © **800/848-1775** or 305/534-6300. Fax 305/538-8140. www.raleighhotel.com. 107 units. Winter $299–$749 double. Off-season $199–$599 double. Rates are cheaper if booked on the hotel's website. AE, DC, DISC, MV, V. Valet parking $20. **Amenities:** Restaurant, bar, coffee bar, fantastic, large outdoor pool, small open-air fitness center, concierge, business services, room service (24-hr. in winter, limited off-season), massage, overnight laundry service. *In room:* A/C, TV/VCR, CD player, dataport, minibar.

W South Beach The Ritz Plaza, located at 17th Street and Collins Avenue, has been resuscitated from its decrepit state into a revitalized stylish boutique hotel with a new wing of oceanview rooms. Located next door to the ever-fabulous Delano Hotel and scheduled to open in the fall of 2002 (along with its Away Spa), we expect this W to approximate its sister properties that cater to business travelers (and others who don't spend too much time in their rooms) with stylish yet functional guest rooms, supercomfortable beds, attentive service, and a fabulous scene at its restaurant and bar.

1701 Collins Avenue, Miami Beach © **877/Whotels.** Call for details.

The Best Hotel Spas

- **Agua Spa at the Delano,** 1685 Collins Ave., Miami Beach (© 305/ 673-2900), is sublimely situated on the rooftop of the hotel, overlooking the Atlantic, and featuring stellar treatments such as the milk-and-honey massage. Lose yourself in a tub of fragrant oils, algaes, or minerals for a 20-minute revitalization. And, to accommodate its celebrity clientele, there's also collagen, mud, and hydrating masks.
- **Sundari Spa at the Shore Club Hotel,** 1901 Collins Ave., Miami Beach (© 305/695-3100), co-owned by former supermodel Christy Turlington, is scheduled to open at press time, is located on the rooftop of the hotel (also overlooking the ocean), and will offer wet and dry treatment rooms, outdoor terraces and massage decks, Ayurvedic treatments, and Sundari skin-care products.
- **Turnberry Isle Resort & Club,** 19999 W. Country Club Dr., Aventura (© 305/932-6200), offers a sprawling 25,000-square-foot spa with a massive menu of treatments, Finnish saunas, Turkish steam rooms, turbulent whirlpools, and bracing cold plunge tubs that are sure to give you an uplifting jolt.
- **Spa Internazionale at Fisher Island,** 1 Fisher Island Dr., Fisher Island, (© 800/ 537-3708), is the city's poshest spa, known for its picturesque setting and the Guinot Paris Hydradermie facial—a 75-minute moisturizing and cleansing facial that leaves the skin silky smooth.
- **Spa of Eden at the Eden Roc Resort,** 4525 Collins Ave., Miami Beach (© 304/531-0000), offers salt glows, chamomile polishes, seaweed wraps, and Swedish and shiatsu massages in a spectacular setting overlooking the ocean.
- **Away Spa at the W South Beach,** 1701 Collins Ave., Miami Beach, (© 877-WHOTELS). At press time, we were still awaiting the grand opening of Away, but it will no doubt offer stiff competition to South Beach neighbors Agua and the new Sundari. The spa will offer eight different facials, numerous styles of massage (including Hot Stone), and three body scrubs and wraps. There are also alternative healing services like Reiki and craniosacral therapy, herbal mineral baths, and exotic body treatments such as the "Star of India" (a 90-minute facial-massage-wrap combo), and, for the truly indulgent, the nearly 2-hour "Javanese Lulur," which originated as a pre-wedding service for the princesses of Java.

MODERATE

Abbey Hotel 🏖🏖 (Finds)   This charming, off-the-beaten-path '40s revival boutique hotel is possibly the best deal on the entire beach. A haven for artists looking for quiet inspiration, the Abbey has recently undergone a $2.5 million renovation that restored its original Deco glory. Soft white-covered chairs and candles grace the lobby, and the rooftop sundeck has been restored to its 1940s glamour as a bar and grill. Rooms are furnished with oversized earth-toned chairs and chrome beds that are surprisingly comfortable. The lobby also doubles as a chic Mediterranean-style restaurant. It's extremely quiet at this hotel, as it is located in the midst of a sleepy residential neighborhood, but it's only 1 block from the beach and within walking distance of the Jackie Gleason Theater, the Convention Center, the Bass Museum of Art, and the Miami City Ballet.

300 21st St., Miami Beach, FL 33139. ℂ 305/531-0031. Fax 305/672-1663. www.abbeyhotel.com. 50 units. Winter $165–$210 double; $225 studio. Off-season $145–$190 double; $205 studio. AE, DC, DISC, MC, V. Off-site parking $15. **Amenities:** Restaurant, bar, exercise room, spa within a solarium, concierge, business center, room service, laundry and dry-cleaning service. *In room:* A/C, TV/VCR, dataport, hair dryer, iron. Studios also have stereo with CD player, minibar, safe.

Avalon Majestic Hotel 🏵 The architecture of this classic Deco hotel, located opposite the beach, is infinitely more interesting than the inside, which is clean and simple but hardly exciting. The well-priced accommodations are decorated in traditional, unremarkable 1930s style, and are comfortable but a bit on the small side. The bathrooms have all been renovated and updated. About half the rooms have partial or full ocean views. The hotel's restaurant, A Fish Called Avalon, offers excellent seafood dishes, is always crowded, and is a local's favorite. The modest lobby holds a casual restaurant, best for lunch either inside or on the breezy outdoor patio. Rooms for the disabled are available here.

700 Ocean Dr. (at 7th St.), South Beach, FL 33139. ℂ **800/933-3306** or 305/538-0133. Fax 305/534-0258. www.southbeachhotels.com. 103 units. Winter $159–$240 double. Off-season $89–$165 double. Rates include continental breakfast. 10% discount for stays of 7 days or more. AE, DC, DISC, MC, V. Valet parking $16. **Amenities:** Restaurant, bar, pool available at companion property (the South Seas), complimentary passes to nearby health club, secretarial services, room service, laundry and dry-cleaning service. *In room:* A/C, TV/VCR, dataport, iron, safe.

Cavalier 🏵 The name of this hotel is quite ironic, as there is nothing cavalier about this reasonably priced Chris Blackwell–owned Island Outpost property. It's warm and welcoming, and you can't beat its oceanfront location, which is adjacent to shops and restaurants. Palm trees brush the ceilings of the modest lobby, where young trendy guests make their way to their rooms. Funky prints, the colors of a tequila sunrise, cover the walls, and African fabrics cover cozy couches. A young, competent staff waits on guests and offers lots of good advice about local clubs, restaurants, and shopping. While there is no pool here, guests have access to the pool at the hotel's swankier sister property, The Tides.

1320 Ocean Dr., South Beach, FL 33139. ℂ **800/OUTPOST** or 305/604-5064. Fax 305/531-5543. www.islandoutpost.com. 45 units. Winter $185–$395 double. Off-season $130–$295 double. Additional person $15. AE, DC, DISC, MC, V. Valet parking $16; self-parking $6. **Amenities:** Concierge, massage, room service, babysitting, dry cleaning. *In room:* A/C, TV/VCR, minibar, fridge, hair dryer, iron, safe.

Chesterfield Hotel 🏵🏵 The Chesterfield Hotel is an oft-neglected, kitschy place, located in the heart of South Beach's Deco District, just a skip away from all the restaurants on Ocean or the nightclubs on Washington Avenue. Its Zimbabwe-meets-Baroque lobby is a far cry from its original 1930s Art Deco beginnings, but it remains an attractive place for funk-loving hipsters. The 50 rooms are finished with zebra or leopard prints and adorned with faux renditions of fabulous Euro art. The hotel's Safari Bar/Café caters to both a European and an alternative crowd. The bar turns into a spot for a quaint Euro continental breakfast in the morning. There's also a happy hour each evening from 4 to 8pm with two-for-one cocktails. The hotel's proximity to area clubs and modeling agencies, and its ability to create its own eclectic nightlife, make the Chesterfield an award-worthy locale for people watching.

855 Collins Ave., South Beach, FL 33139. ⓒ **800/244-6023** or 305/531-5831. Fax 305/672-4900. www.southbeachgroup.com. Winter $129–$249 double. Off-season $69–$179 double. Rates include complimentary breakfast. AE, MC, V. Valet parking $18. **Amenities:** Restaurant, bar, access to VIP lists at area clubs, free airport transportation, free Internet connection. *In room:* A/C, TV.

Crest Hotel Suites ⭒⭒   One of South Beach's best-kept secrets, the Crest Hotel is located next to the pricier, trendier Albion Hotel and features a quietly fashionable, contemporary, relaxed atmosphere with fantastic service. Built in 1939, the Crest was restored to preserve its Art Deco architecture, but inside the hotel is thoroughly modern with rooms resembling cosmopolitan apartments. All suites have a living room/dining room area, kitchenette, and executive workspace. An indoor/outdoor cafe with terrace and poolside dining isn't besieged with trendy locals, but does attract a younger crowd. Crest Hotel Suites is conveniently located in the heart of the Art Deco Historic District near all the major attractions. Around the corner from the hotel is Lincoln Road, with its sidewalk cafes, gourmet restaurants, theaters, and galleries.

1670 James Ave., Miami Beach, FL 33139. ⓒ **800/531-3880** or 305/531-0321. Fax 305/531-8180. www. cresthotel.com. Winter $155–$235 double. Off-season $115–$175 double. Packages available and 10% discount offered if booked on website. AE, MC, V. **Amenities:** Restaurant, cafe, pool, laundry and dry-cleaning service. *In room:* A/C, TV, dataport, kitchenette, fridge, coffeemaker.

Dorchester Hotel and Suites   Being located across the street from the overhyped Delano works to the Dorchester's advantage. Without the Delano, there would be little reason to stay on this loud, traffic-plagued stretch of Collins Avenue. With a new all-suite wing completed in 2000, the Dorchester is a great value. The private pool deck lounge and tropical patio garden serve as a great escape from blaring horns and glaring neon. A small cafe serves breakfast in the garden, and, if watersports are your thing, the hotel's sister beachfront property, the Marseilles (ⓒ 800/327-4739), will provide equipment rentals for you.

1850 Collins Ave., Miami Beach, FL 33139. ⓒ **800/327-4739** or 305/531-5745. Fax 305/673-1006. www. dorchesterhotel.com. 100 units. Winter $135–$199 double. Off-season $105–$159 double. AE, DC, MC, V. Self-parking $10. Pets under 20 lb. accepted (dogs and cats only). **Amenities:** Small cafe, outdoor pool, access to nearby health club, concierge, laundry and dry-cleaning service. *In room:* A/C, TV, fax, dataport, fridge; plus kitchen, coffeemaker, microwave, and hair dryer in suites.

Essex House Hotel and Suites ⭒⭒   The Essex House Hotel was created by Deco pioneer Henry Hohauser in 1938 and has received numerous awards for its authentic restoration. The hotel's whimsically created ship-like architecture rises from the shore with decks that are designed to take in succulent ocean breezes. The sleek Bauhaus interiors add to the distinct charm of the place. All suites feature solid oak furnishings and have a fridge, wet bar, and Jacuzzi. Although the hotel is right on the pulse of South Beach's constant activity, the new double-glazed, sound-absorbing windows provide an acoustical barrier to the street noise. A spa pool graces the south patio and gardens. In an area where the infamous Al Capone used to play cards with cronies now rests an intimate dining area where complimentary breakfast is served and evening cocktails are enjoyed.

1001 Collins Ave., Miami Beach, FL 33139. ⓒ **800/ 553-7739** or 305/534-2700. Winter $169–$379 double. Off-season $119–$300 double. Rates include breakfast. AE, DC, DISC, MC, V. **Amenities:** Bar; outdoor pool; concierge. *In room:* A/C, TV, dataport, minibar in deluxe suites, fridge, coffeemaker, hair dryer, iron.

Greenview ⭒   Art Deco takes a decidedly Parisian turn in this 1939 Hohauser hotel completely renovated in 1994 by Parisian designer Chahan

Minassian. A member of the family-run Rubell Hotels, the Greenview is located just 2 blocks from the ocean on a quiet corner that's close enough to the action, but far enough away that you'll actually feel secluded from the nearby hyperactivity. Recordings of Edith Piaf and Marlene Dietrich provide background to this elegantly understated hotel, whose jewel-box, living room–like lobby opens to a serene courtyard. Rooms feature handcrafted furnishings, original Modernist artwork, hardwood floors, sisal area rugs, and crisp white linens. Typical at Rubell Hotels is the feel-at-home factor, bolstered by the complimentary baker's breakfast and iced tea and chocolate-chip cookies in the afternoon.

1671 Washington Ave. (at Lincoln Rd.), Miami Beach, FL 33139. ✆ **877/RUBELLS** or 305/531-6588. Fax 305/531-4580. www.rubellhotels.com. 45 units. Winter $95–$175 double. Off-season $150–$230 double. AE, DC, DISC, MC, V. **Amenities:** Small business center, same-day laundry service. In room: A/C, TV.

Hotel Leon ✪ (Finds)   A fabulous hotel without the fabulous attitude, the Hotel Leon is like a reasonably priced high-fashion garment found hidden on a rack full of overpriced threads. This charismatic sliver of a property has won the loyalty of fashion industrialists and romantics alike. Built in 1929 and restored in 1996, the hotel still retains many original details such as facades, woodwork, and even fireplaces (every room has one, not that you'll need to use it). The very central location 1 block from the ocean is a plus, especially since the Leon lacks a pool. Most of the spacious and stylish rooms are immaculate and reminiscent of a loft apartment; spacious bathrooms with large, deep tubs are especially enticing. Gleaming wood floors and simple pale furnishings are appreciated in a neighborhood where many others overdo the Art Deco motif. However, some rooms have not seen such upgrades and are to be avoided; do not hesitate to ask to change rooms. In the standard rooms, there are no minibars or fridges, but you can order room service. Service is warm, friendly, and accommodating. The lobby has an informal bar and restaurant, not to mention a large communal table at which guests—production crews, fashion photographers, Europeans, and young hipsters—tend to mix and mingle. Because its entrance is not directly on pedestrian-heavy Collins Avenue, the Hotel Leon remains one of South Beach's best-kept secrets. A disabled-accessible room is available. In 2000, proprietors opened Hotel Aqua, a modern and moderately priced 50-room hotel located at 1530 Collins Ave., Miami Beach (✆ 305/538-4361).

841 Collins Ave., South Beach, FL 33139. ✆ **305/673-3767.** Fax 305/673-5866. www.hotelleon.com. 18 units. Winter $145–$245 suite; $395 penthouse. Off-season $100–$195 suite; $335 penthouse. Additional person $10. AE, DC, MC, V. Valet parking $18. "Well-behaved" pets accepted for $20 per night. **Amenities:** Restaurant and lobby bar, reduced rates at local gym, concierge, business services, room service (breakfast), massage, babysitting, laundry and dry-cleaning service. In Room: A/C, TV, hair dryer, CD players w/CDs.

The Kent ✪✪   This is an excellent value right in South Beach's active center. Even if the other Island Outpost hotels are full, you're likely to find a spot here. The prices are the same as the Cavalier, but the rooms tend to be less noisy. The staff is eager to please and the clientele comes largely from the fashion industry. Frequent photo shoots are coordinated in the lobby and conference room, where full office services are available. Thanks to a vacant lot in the backyard (for now), some rooms in the rear offer nice views of the ocean. The decor is modest but tasteful. There's no pool or sundeck, but you're only 1 block from the beach.

1131 Collins Ave., South Beach, FL 33139. ✆ **800/OUTPOST** or 305/604-5000. Fax 305/531-0720. www.islandlife.com. 54 units. Winter $160–$295 suite. Off-season $125–$250 suite. Additional person $15. AE, DC, DISC, MC, V. Valet parking $16; self-parking $6. **Amenities:** Access to concierge and massage service at The Tides (see listing above). In room: A/C, TV/VCR, CD player, minibar, safe.

Lily Guest House 🌊🌊 The Lily was built in 1936 and completely remodeled in 1999 by local interior designers who gave the place a modern look without stripping its laid-back atmosphere. The decor can best be described as eclectic, mixing Art Deco walls with European cabinetry and furniture. The all-suite property has just 21 guest rooms, all featuring wrought iron and wood furnishings, hardwood floors, and marble bathrooms. While not all rooms are decorated exactly alike, all have plush oversized furniture and gauzy white curtains; the marble bathrooms are fantastic and surprisingly large for a guesthouse. The ambience is very relaxing and homey. It's also immaculate. All guests have access to a private sundeck.

835 Collins Ave., South Beach, FL 33139. ℂ 888/742-6600 or 305/535-9900. Fax 305/535-0077. www.southbeachgroup.com. 21 units. Winter $159–$259 double. Off-season $109–$209 double. Rates include complimentary breakfast. AE, MC, V. Valet parking $18; self-parking $6; parking garage $10. Pets accepted for $10 a day. **Amenities:** Bar, access to nearby gym, concierge, free airport transportation, secretarial services, limited room service, laundry service. *In room:* A/C, TV, kitchenette, coffeemaker, hair dryer.

Mermaid Guesthouse 🌊🌊 There's something magical about this little hideaway tucked behind tropical gardens in the very heart of South Beach and less than 2 blocks from the ocean. You won't find the amenities of the larger hotels here, but the charm and hospitality at this one-story guesthouse keep people coming back. Owners Ana and Gonzalo Torres did a thorough clean-up, adding new brightly colored fretwork around the doors and windows and installing phones in each room. Also, the wood floors have been stripped or covered in straw matting, one of the many Caribbean touches that make this place so cheery. Rooms have four-poster beds with mosquito nets. There are no TVs, so guests tend to congregate in the lush garden in the evenings. The owners sometimes host free impromptu dinners for their guests and friends. Ask if they've scheduled any live Latin music during your stay; you won't want to miss it. What you also don't want to miss is a preview of your room before you put down a deposit, as some rooms tend not to be as tidy as the quaint garden.

909 Collins Ave., Miami Beach, FL 33140. ℂ 305/538-5324. Fax 305/538-2822. 8 units. Winter $115–$280 single or double. Off-season $95–$215 single or double. Additional person $10. Discounts available for longer stays. AE, MC, V. **Amenities:** Bar. *In room:* A/C, TV upon request, radio.

Nassau Suite Hotel 🌊🌊 Stylish and reasonably priced, this 1937 hotel feels more like a modern apartment building with its 22 suites (studios or one-bedroom available), featuring wood floors, rattan furniture, and fully equipped open kitchens. Beds are all king sized and rather plush, but the bed isn't the room's only place to rest. Each room also has a sitting area that's quite comfortable. Registered as a National Historic Landmark, the Nassau Suite Hotel may exist in an old building, but both rooms and lobby are fully modernized. The Nassau Suite caters to a young, hip crowd of both gay and straight guests. Continental breakfast is available for $5 per person.

1414 Collins Ave., South Beach, FL 33139. ℂ 305/532-0043. Fax 305/534-3133. 22 units. Winter $150 studio; $190 1-bedroom. Off-season $120 studio; $160 1-bedroom. AE, DC, DISC, MC, V. Parking $12. **Amenities:** Access to nearby health club, bike rental, concierge, secretarial services. *In room:* A/C, TV, fax, dataport, coffeemaker, hair dryer.

Pelican Hotel 🌊🌊 Owned by the same creative folks behind the Diesel Jeans company, the Pelican is South Beach's only self-professed "toy-hotel," in which each of its 30 rooms and suites is decorated as outrageously as some of the area's more colorful drag queens. Each room has been designed daringly and rather wittily by Swedish interior decorator Magnus Ehrland, whose countless trips to antiques markets combined with his wild imagination have turned Room 309, for instance, into the "Psychedelic(ate) Girl," Room 201 into the "Executive Fifties" suite, and Room 313 into the "Jesus Christ Megastar" room. But the most popular room is the tough-to-score Room 215, or the "Best Whorehouse," which is said to have made even former Hollywood madam Heidi Fleiss red with envy. As South Beach is known for poseurs of all types, this hotel fits right in.

826 Ocean Dr., Miami Beach, FL 33139. ✆ 800/7-PELICAN or 305/673-3373. Fax 305/673-3255. www. Pelicanhotel.com. Winter $170–$220 double; $240 oceanfront suite. Off-season $135–$155 double; $225 oceanfront suite. AE, DC, MC, V. Valet parking $16. **Amenities:** Restaurant, bar, access to area gyms, concierge, business services, same-day laundry and dry cleaning. *In room:* A/C, TV/VCR, stereo/CD player, dataport, fridge, hair dryer, iron, safe.

Townhouse 🌟🌟   New York hipster Jonathan Morr felt that Miami Beach had lost touch with the bon vivants who gave the city its original cache, so he decided to take matters into his own hands. His solution: this 67-room, five-story hotel in which standard rooms started at just $99 during its opening in the fall of 2000. The $99 rate proved too good to be true, but even the revised starting rate of $125 is still a great deal. The charm of this hotel is found in its clean and simple yet chic design with quirky details: exercise equipment that stands alone in the hallways, free laundry machines in the lobby, a water bed–lined rooftop. Comfortable, shabby chic rooms boast L-shaped couches for extra guests (for whom you aren't charged), and the hotel's basement features the hot New York import, Bond St. Lounge.

150 20th St., South Beach, FL 33139. ✆ 877/534-3800 or 305/534-3800. Fax 305/534-3811. www. townhousehotel.com. Winter $195–$225 double; $395 penthouse. Off-season $125–$155 double; $395 penthouse. Rates include Parisian-style breakfast. AE, MC, V. Valet parking $17–$18. **Amenities:** Restaurant, bar, workout stations, bike rental, free laundry. *In room:* A/C, TV/VCR, CD player, dataport, fridge, hair dryer (upon request), safe.

Whitelaw Hotel 🌟🌟   With a slogan that reads "clean sheets, hot water and stiff drinks," the Whitelaw Hotel stands apart from the other boutique hotels with a fierce sense of humor, but never compromising on its fabulous amenities. Only half a block from Ocean Drive, this hotel, like its clientele, is full of distinct personalities, pairing such disparate elements as luxurious Belgian sheets with shag carpeting to create a completely innovative setting. All-white rooms manage to be homey and plush and not antiseptic. Bathrooms are large and well stocked with just about everything you may have forgotten at home. Complimentary cocktails in the lobby every night from 8 to 10pm contribute to a very social atmosphere.

808 Collins Ave., Miami Beach, FL 33139. ✆ 305/398-7000. Fax 305/398-7010. www.whitelawhotel.com. Winter $175 double; $195 suite. Off-season $125 double; $145 suite. Rates include breakfast. AE, MC, V. Parking $12. **Amenities:** Bar. *In room:* A/C, TV/VCR, stereo, dataport, minibar, hair dryer, safe.

INEXPENSIVE

Banana Bungalow   This hostel-like hotel is cheap, campy, and quintessentially Miami Beach. Popular with the MTV set, the Banana Bungalow is a redone 1950s two-story motel where it's always Spring Break. The hotel surrounds a pool and deck complete with shuffleboard, a small alfresco cafe serving cheap meals, and a tiki bar where young European travelers hang out. The best rooms face a narrow canal where motorboats and kayaks are available for a small charge. In general, rooms are clean and well kept, despite a few rusty faucets and chipped Formica furnishings. Guests in shared rooms need to bring their own towels. This is one of the only hotels in this price range with a private pool.

2360 Collins Ave., Miami Beach, FL 33139. ✆ **800/7-HOSTEL** or 305/538-1951. Fax 305/531-3217. www.bananabungalow.com. 90 units. Winter $13–$16 per person in shared units; $95–$104 double. Off-season $12–$14 per person in shared units; $50–$60 double. MC, V. Free parking. **Amenities:** Cafe, bar, large pool, access to nearby health club, game room, coin-op laundry. *In room:* A/C, TV, fridge.

Bayliss Guest House ⍟   The Bayliss Guest House is the anti-budget budget hotel, with enormous, sparkling clean rooms, complete with sitting rooms and baths. Built in 1939 in the tropical Art Deco style, rounded corners, glass blocks, neon, and a lobby floor of fancy terrazzo give the Bayliss a definite '40s feel. The Bayliss offers hotel rooms, large efficiencies, and one-bedroom apartments. The property is a bit off the beaten path, but this quiet residential spot offers a break from the racket that defines Collins and Washington avenues. The owners of the Bayliss also own two other similar properties in South Beach: the Riviere Apart-Hotel, 1424 Collins Ave., South Beach, FL 33139 (✆ 305/531-3488), and the Mediterranee Guest House, 612 15th St., South Beach, FL 33139 (✆ 305/538-5620).

504 14th St., South Beach, FL 33139. ✆ **888/305-4863** or 305/538-5620. Fax 305/531-4440. Riviere1@aol.com. 20 units. Winter $75 double; $95 efficiency. Off-season $45 double; $60 efficiency. AE, DC, DISC, MC, V. **Amenities:** Room service (9am–7pm). *In room:* A/C, TV, kitchenette, coffeemaker, hair dryer.

Beachcomber Hotel ⍟   The Beachcomber Hotel was built in 1937 and renovated in 1997. The rooms are decorated in a colorful Art Deco style, and all have a private bathroom and shower. A Deco terrace on Collins Avenue provides the perfect place for sipping a cocktail. The hotel's restaurant serves breakfast, lunch, and dinner, but dine there only as a last resort. Check before arrival if a continental breakfast is included in your rate. The property's location couldn't be better, since it's away from the noise but near the action.

1340 Collins Ave., South Beach, FL 33139. ✆ **888/305-4683** or 305/531-3755. Fax 305/673-8609. www.beachcombermiami.com. 29 units. Winter $90–$145 double. Off-season $70–$125 double. Continental breakfast included. AE, DC, DISC, MC, V. Municipal parking $7. **Amenities:** Restaurant, bar. *In room:* A/C, TV, fridge, hair dryer.

Brigham Gardens ⍟⍟   This funky place, consisting of two buildings—Art Deco and Mediterranean—is a homey and affordable oasis run by a mother-daughter team that will make sure you feel like a member of the family. Also, the location is prime. Because most rooms have full kitchens—you can also barbecue in the garden—you'll find many people staying for longer than a weekend. When you enter the tropically landscaped garden, you'll hear macaws and parrots chirping and see cats and lizards running through the bougainvillea. The tiny but lush grounds are framed by quaint Mediterranean buildings—they're pleasant, although in need of some sprucing up. A rooftop sundeck with a view of the ocean is the hotel's newest attraction.

1411 Collins Ave., South Beach, FL 33139. ✆ **305/531-1331.** Fax 305/538-9898. www.brighamgardens. com. 23 units. Winter $100–$145 1-bedroom. Off-season $70–$110 1-bedroom. Additional person $5. 10% discount on stays of 7 days or longer. Pets accepted for $6 a night. AE, MC, V. **Amenities:** Coin-op washers and dryers. *In room:* A/C, TV, kitchen, microwave, coffeemaker.

Clay Hotel & International Hostel ⍟   A member of the International Youth Hostel Federation (IYHF), the Clay occupies a beautiful 1920s–style Spanish Mediterranean building at the corner of historic Española Way. Like other IYHF members, this hostel is open to all ages and is a great place to meet people. The usual smattering of Australians, Europeans, and other budget travelers makes it Miami's best clearinghouse of "insider" travel information. Even if you don't stay here, you might want to check out the ride board or mingle with fellow travelers over a beer at the sidewalk cafe.

Although a thorough renovation in 1996 made this hostel an incredible value and a step above any others in town, don't expect nightly turndown service or chocolates. But, for a hostel, it's full of extras. Ninety rooms have private baths and 12 "VIP" rooms have balconies overlooking quaint Española Way. You will find occasional movie nights, an outdoor weekend market, and a tour desk with car rental available. Reservations for private rooms are essential in season and recommended year-round. Don't bother with a car in this congested area.

1438 Washington Ave. (at Española Way), South Beach, FL 33139. © **800/379-2529** or 305/534-2988. Fax 305/673-0346. www.theclayhotel.com. 350 units. $45–75 double; $15–$17 dorm beds. During the off-season, pay for 6 nights in advance and get 7th night free. MC, V. Parking $10. **Amenities:** Cafe, access to nearby health club, bike rental, concierge, computer center, coin-op washers and dryers, lockers, kitchen. *In room:* A/C, TV, dataport, fridge, hair dryer.

Clevelander   A South Beach institution favored by the beer-swilling set, the Clevelander is best known for its neon- and glass-blocked poolside and bar used in countless photo shoots and Budweiser commercials. As far as its reputation as a hotel, well, it's conveniently located on Ocean Drive and it's dirt cheap considering its location. Unfortunately, the dirt doesn't stop there. It seems that the hotel is more concerned with polishing its poolside glass than its rooms. And the noise level can be deafening. Party animals don't mind at all. But if your idea of a party doesn't involve drinking challenges and wet T-shirt contests, visit the Clevelander for a cocktail and stay elsewhere.

1020 Ocean Dr., Miami Beach, FL 33139. © **305/531-3485.** Fax 305/534-4707. 57 units. Winter $140–$170 double. Off-season $99–$135 double. AE, DC, MC, V. Valet parking $6. **Amenities:** Outdoor cafe, bar, outdoor pool, health club. *In room:* A/C, TV.

Park Washington Hotel ★★   The Park Washington, designed in the 1930s by Henry Hohauser, is a large refurbished hotel just 2 blocks from the ocean that offers some of the best values in South Beach. Most of the rooms have original furnishings and well-kept interiors, and some have kitchenettes. Bathrooms are small and clean. Guests also enjoy a decent-sized outdoor heated pool with a sundeck, bikes for rent, and access to a nearby health club. The hotel attracts a large gay clientele. It offers privacy, lush landscaping, a great pool and sundeck, consistent quality, and a value-oriented philosophy.

1020 Washington Ave., South Beach, FL 33139. © **305/532-1930.** Fax 305/672-6706. www. parkwashingtonresort.com. 36 units. Winter $129–$159 double. Off-season $79–$109 double. Rates include self-serve coffee and Danish. Additional person $20. AE, MC, V. Off-site parking $6. **Amenities:** Pool. *In room:* A/C, TV, kitchenettes in some rooms, fridge.

Villa Paradiso ★★   This guesthouse, like Brigham Gardens, is more like a cozy apartment house than a hotel. There's no elegant lobby or restaurant, but the amicable hosts, Lisa and Pascal Nicolle, are happy to give you a room key and advice on what to do. The recently renovated, spacious apartments are simple but elegant—hardwood floors, French doors, and stylish wrought-iron furniture—and are remarkably quiet considering their location, a few blocks from Lincoln Road and all of South Beach's best clubs. Most have full kitchens or at least a fridge, and Murphy beds or foldout couches for extra friends. Bathrooms have recently been renovated with marble tile. All rooms overlook the hotel's pretty courtyard garden.

1415 Collins Ave., Miami Beach, FL 33139. © **305/532-0616.** Fax 305/673-5874. www.villaparadiso.com. 17 units. Winter $100–$145 apartment. Off-season $69–$105 apartment. Weekly rates are 10% cheaper.

Additional person $5–$10. AE, DC, MC, V. Parking nearby $12. Pets (including small "nonbarking" dogs) accepted for $10 with a $100 deposit. **Amenities:** Coin-op washers and dryers. *In room:* A/C, TV, kitchen, fridge, coffeemaker.

2 Miami Beach: Surfside, Bal Harbour & Sunny Isles

The area just north of South Beach encompasses Surfside, Bal Harbour, and Sunny Isles. Unrestricted by zoning codes throughout the 1950s, 1960s, and especially the 1970s, area developers went crazy, building ever-bigger and more brazen structures, especially north of 41st Street, which is now known as "Condo Canyon." Consequently, there's now a glut of medium-quality condos, with a few scattered holdouts of older hotels and motels casting shadows over the beach by afternoon.

Miami Beach, as described here, runs from 24th Street to 192nd Street, a long strip that varies slightly from end to end. Staying in the southern section, from 24th to 42nd streets, can be a good deal—it's still close to the South Beach scene, but the rates are more affordable. The North Beach area begins at 63rd Street and extends north to the city limit at 87th Terrace and west to Biscayne Bay (at Bay Drive West). The downtown area of Biscayne Bay is experiencing a slow renaissance. Bal Harbour and Bay Harbor are at the center of Miami Beach and retain their exclusivity and character. The neighborhoods north and south of here, like Surfside and Sunny Isles, have nice beaches and some shops, but are a little worn around the edges.

Just north of South Beach is the **Days Inn** (© **800/325-2525** or 305/673-1513) at 42nd Street and Collins Avenue. It's well kept and right on the ocean. Rates in season start at about $99. The **Howard Johnson** (© **800/ 446-4656** or 305/532-4411) at 4000 Alton Rd., just off the Julia Tuttle Causeway (I-95), is a generic eight-story building on a strip of land near a busy road, but it's convenient to the beach, by car or bike. Rooms, renovated in 1995, are clean and spacious, and some have pretty views of the city and the Intracoastal Waterway. Winter rates start at $100.

VERY EXPENSIVE

Alexander All-Suite Luxury Hotel ★★★   This luxury hotel is a place you'd expect to see Robin Leach shouting "champagne wishes and caviar dreams" from the balcony. Just a few miles from either happening South Beach or ritzy Bal Harbour, the Alexander is pricey, but worth it for the size of the suites and the doting attention. The Alexander features spacious one- and two-bedroom miniapartments with private balconies overlooking the Atlantic Ocean and Miami's Intracoastal Waterway. Each contains a living room, a fully equipped kitchen, *two* bathrooms—one with just a shower and the other with an extremely inviting shower/tub combo—and a balcony. The rooms are elegant without being pretentious and have every convenience you could want. The hotel itself is well decorated, with sculptures, paintings, antiques, and tapestries, most of which were garnered from the Cornelius Vanderbilt mansion. An ongoing renovation to upgrade the suites promises to keep the Alexander on the forefront of modern luxury. Two oceanfront pools are surrounded by lush vegetation; one of these "lagoons" is fed by a cascading waterfall. Shula's Steakhouse, owned by former Dolphins football coach Don Shula, is open for lunch and dinner daily, and is a favorite of both meat eaters and Dolphins fans.

5225 Collins Ave., Miami Beach, FL 33140. © **800/327-6121** or 305/865-6500. Fax 305/341-6553. www.alexanderhotel.com. 150 units. Winter $325 1-bedroom suite; $470 2-bedroom suite. Off-season $250

Miami Beach Accommodations

Alexander All-Suite
  Luxury Hotel **8**
Bay Harbor Inn and Suites **3**
Baymar Ocean Resort **5**
Beach Castle Hotel **14**
Beach House Bal Harbour **6**
Best Western Beach Resort **12**
Days Inn Oceanside **13**
Dezerland Beach Resort Hotel **7**
Eden Roc Renaissance
  Resort and Spa **9**
Fontainebleau Hilton **10**
Four Points Sheraton
  Miami Beach **11**
Indian Creek Hotel **17**
Miami Beach Ocean Resort **16**
Newport Beachside
  Hotel & Resort **2**
Ramada Miami Beach Resort **15**
Roney Plaza Resort & Spa **18**
Sheraton Bal Harbour
  Beach Resort **4**
Suez Oceanfront Resort **1**

1-bedroom suite; $370 2-bedroom suite. Additional person $35. Packages available. AE, MC, V. Valet parking $18. Very small pets accepted for a $250 nonrefundable deposit for cleaning the suite. **Amenities:** 2 restaurants, 2 bars, 2 large outdoor pools, small fitness center, Jacuzzis, sauna, watersports equipment, concierge, car rental through concierge, business center and secretarial services, salon, limited room service, in-room massage, dry cleaning and laundry service. *In room:* A/C, TV, VCR upon request, fax, dataport, kitchen, coffeemaker, hair dryer, radio.

Beach House Bal Harbour ⭑⭑⭑ The Beach House Bal Harbour is the closest thing the city has to a summer beach home—comfortable, unpretentious, and luxurious, yet decidedly low-key. In place of an elaborate hotel lobby, the public spaces of the Rubell-owned Beach House are divided into a series of intimate homey environments, from the wicker-furnished screened-in porch to the Asian-inspired Bamboo Room, with overstuffed Ralph Lauren leather couches and Japanese bric-a-brac. The 24-hour Pantry, inspired by Long Island's Sagaponack General Store, is packed with all the needs of the hotel's "unplugged" urban clientele. The ultraspacious rooms are literally brimming with the comforts of home, including whitewashed wood wainscoting and plush furnishings, also by Ralph Lauren. Cute touches such as a collecting vase for seashells found at the hotel's private beachfront and a bottle of bathing suit wash make the room seem like it's your own. If that's not homey enough, there's a bedside copy of Dr. Seuss's *Cat in the Hat* and chocolate-chip cookies at the front desk. The Atlantic Restaurant offers a little of Nantucket right here in Miami. Sheila Lukins, author of the best-selling Silver Palate cookbooks, creates some delicious feasts, such as buttermilk fried chicken with Austin baked beans and homemade cornbread. The Seahorse Bar features a giant tank of—you guessed it—seahorses. The 200-foot private beach, hammock grove, and topiary garden are so lush they're said to have caused several New York hipsters to renege on their summer shares in the Hamptons in favor of this Beach House.

9449 Collins Ave., Surfside, FL 33154. ℂ 877/782-3557 or 305/865-3551. Fax 305/861-6596. www.rubell hotels.com. 170 units. Winter $215–$315 double; $245–$305 junior suite. Off-season $180–210 double; $230–$270 junior suite. Year-round $800 1-bedroom suite. AE, DC, DISC, MC, V. Valet parking $15. **Amenities:** Restaurant, 24-hour pantry, bar, heated pool, health club & spa, watersports equipment, children's playground, business center. *In room:* A/C, TV, stereo/CD player, dataport, fridge, hair dryer, iron.

Eden Roc Renaissance Resort and Spa ⭑⭑ Just next door to the mammoth Fontainebleau, this large Morris Lapidus–designed flamboyant hotel, opened in 1956, seems almost intimate by comparison. The hotel completed a top-to-bottom $24 million renovation in late 1999 and an $11 million renovation of the beachfront in 2001. The nautical Deco decor is a bit gaudy, but nonetheless reminiscent of Miami Beach's Rat-Packed glory days of the '50s. The 55,000-square-foot modern Spa of Eden has excellent facilities and exercise classes, including yoga. The big, open, and airy lobby is often full of name-tagged conventioneers and tourists looking for a taste of Miami Beach kitsch. The rooms, uniformly outfitted with purple and aquatic-colored interiors and retouched 1930s furnishings, are unusually spacious, and the bathrooms boast Italian marble baths. Because of the hotel's size, you should be able to negotiate a good rate unless there's a big event going on. Harry's Grille specializes in seafood and steaks. From Jimmy Johnson's, the poolside sports bar, patrons can watch swimmers through an underwater "porthole" window.

4525 Collins Ave., Miami Beach, FL 33140. ℂ 800/327-8337 or 305/531-0000. Fax 305/674-5568. www.edenrocresort.com. 349 units. Winter $299–$359 double; $369 suite; $2,500 penthouse. Off-season $159–$224 double; $310 suite; $1,500 penthouse. Additional person $15. Packages available. AE, DC, DISC, MC, V. Valet parking $20–$25. Pets under 20 lb. accepted for a $75 fee. **Amenities:**. 2 restaurants, lounge, bar, 2 outdoor pools, squash courts, racquetball courts, basketball courts, rock-climbing arena, health club &

spa, watersports equipment, concierge, tour desk, car-rental desk, business center, salon, limited room service, in-room massage, babysitting, laundry and dry-cleaning service. *In room:* A/C, TV, VCRs for rent, dataport,
kitchenettes in suites and penthouses, minibar, hair dryer.

Fontainebleau Hilton *Kids*   In many ways, this is the quintessential
Miami Beach hotel. Also designed by Morris Lapidus, who oversaw an expansion in 2000, this grand monolith has symbolized Miami decadence. Since its
opening in 1954, the Fontainebleau has hosted presidents, pageants, and movie
productions, including the James Bond thriller *Goldfinger.* This is where all the
greats, including Sinatra and his pals, performed in their prime. Club Tropigala
is reminiscent of Ricky Ricardo's Tropicana and features a Las Vegas–style floor
show with dozens of performers and two orchestras. Rooms are newly luxurious
and decorated in various styles from 1950s to ultramodern; bathrooms are done
up in Italian marble a la Caesar's Palace. Adding to the Fontainebleau's opulence
is the 7,000-square-foot Octopus pool; the water slide and river raft ride bring
a bit of Disney to Deco-land.

4441 Collins Ave., Miami Beach, FL 33140. © 800/HILTONS or 305/538-2000. Fax 305/674-4607.
www.fontainebleau.hilton.com. 1,206 units. Winter $289–$459 double. Off-season $209–$329 double. Year-
round $525–$1300 suite. Additional person $30. Packages available. AE, DC, DISC, MC, V. Overnight valet
parking $13. Pets accepted at no extra cost. **Amenities:** 7 restaurants (including 2 by the pool), 5 cocktail
lounges, 2 large outdoor pools, 7 lighted tennis courts, state-of-the-art health club, 3 whirlpool baths, watersports rentals, children's programs, game rooms, concierge, tour desk, car-rental desk, business center, shopping arcade, salon, room service, in-room massage, babysitting, laundry and dry-cleaning service. *In room:*
A/C, TV, fax, dataport, minibar, coffeemaker, hair dryer, iron, safe.

Roney Palace Resort & Spa *K*   In its heyday, this luxury hotel and apartment building hosted such celebrities as Rita Hayworth, Orson Welles, and the
duke and duchess of Windsor. Fortunately, a recent $25 million renovation has
restored much of its luster. The outdated pink and green flamingo furnishings
have been replaced with an ultramodern decor and natural woods. Located
directly on the ocean, the hotel offers its guests a private beach club and an
indoor-outdoor cafe. Because of its pre-renovation reputation as a run-down
apartment building, most people don't consider the Roney Palace to be a luxe
resort, but it is once more. The location on a trafficky, tacky Collins Avenue corner doesn't help the hotel's new image, but once you're inside you'll forget about
the unsightly Lums restaurant across the street. One of the hotel's greatest attractions is the Larry North Fitness Center of South Beach, a 10,000-square-foot fitness center and spa.

2399 Collins Ave., Miami Beach, FL 33139. © 305/604-1000. Fax 305/538-7141. www.roney-palace.com.
585 units. Year-round $300–$450 executive suite; $400–$750 1-bedroom suite; $600–$800 2-bedroom suite;
$1,275–$2,950 penthouse suite. AE, DC, MC, V. Valet parking $10. **Amenities:** 24-hour restaurant, pool-
side bar and grill, in-suite spa services, game room, concierge, airport pickup and delivery service, business
center, room service, babysitting, child-care center, laundry and dry-cleaning service. *In room:* A/C, TV/ VCR,
dataport, minibar, microwave, coffeemaker, hair dryer, safe.

Sheraton Bal Harbour Beach Resort *Kids*   This hotel has the best
location in Bal Harbour, on the ocean and just across from the swanky Bal Harbour Shops. Bill and Hillary Clinton have stayed here, and Bill even jogged
along the beach with local fitness enthusiasts. It's one of the nicest Sheratons I've
seen, with a glass-enclosed two-story atrium lobby that's especially welcoming.
A spectacular staircase wraps itself around a cascading fountain full of wished-
on pennies. A lushly landscaped pool area is reminiscent of that found at an
island resort, with a water slide that will keep the kids occupied while you work
on your tan. Speaking of kids, a maximum of four children through the age of

17 stay free in existing bedding with a least one adult. Rooms are large and fairly standard as far as Sheratons are concerned, with the exception of ocean-view rooms, which have balconies. Make sure to ask for a free coupon book with over $800 in savings at the Bal Harbour Shops.

9701 Collins Ave., Bal Harbour, FL 33154. ✆ 800/999-9898 or 305/865-7511. Fax 305/864-2601. 642 units. Winter $349–$539 double. Off-season $129–$449 double. Year-round $650–$1,500 suite or villa. Additional person $25. Packages and senior discounts available. Lowest rates reflect bookings made at least 14 days in advance for rooms without ocean views. AE, DC, DISC, MC, V. Valet parking $12. **Amenities:** 4 restaurants, lounges, 2 outdoor heated pools (1 kids' pool), nearby golf course, 2 outdoor tennis courts, large state-of-the-art health club & spa, watersports equipment, children's programs, game room, concierge, tour desk, business center, shopping arcade, 24-hour room service, in-room massage, babysitting, laundry and dry-cleaning service. *In room:* A/C, TV, VCRs in some rooms, minibar, coffeemaker, hair dryer, iron, safe.

EXPENSIVE

Miami Beach Ocean Resort ✿   Popular with tour groups and Europeans, this oceanfront resort is overpriced and not the best choice for those have some extra bucks to spare. Reminiscent of an insipid chain hotel, the Miami Beach Ocean Resort *is* quiet, very quiet, and located on the ocean, which can be a plus for some. The vast lobby is done up in Mexican tile, wood fretwork, and Pier One–type furnishings. Rooms are very basic and unremarkably decorated with wicker and rattan furnishings. There is, however, new carpeting. A huge outdoor area is landscaped with palms and hibiscus and has a large heated pool as its centerpiece. It faces a popular boardwalk for runners and strollers as well as a large beach where watersports equipment is available.

3025 Collins Ave., Miami Beach, FL 33140. ✆ 800/550-0505 or 305/534-0505. Fax 305/534-0515. www.mbo.com. 243 units. Winter $220–$265 double. Off-season $180–$195 double. AE, DC, MC, V. Valet parking $8. **Amenities:** Restaurant, garden cafe, poolside bar, lounge, outdoor heated pool, bike rental, game room, concierge, tour desk, car-rental desk, salon, room service, babysitting, coin-op washers and dryers, laundry and dry-cleaning service. *In room:* A/C, TV, coffeemaker, hair dryer.

MODERATE

Bay Harbor Inn and Suites ✿✿   Under the management of Johnson & Wales University, this thoroughly renovated inn is just moments from the beach, fine restaurants, and the Bal Harbour Shops. The inn comes in two parts. The more modern section overlooks a swampy river, a heated outdoor pool, and a yacht named *Celeste* where guests eat a complimentary breakfast buffet. On the other side of the street, "townside" is the cozier, antiques-filled portion, where glass-covered bookshelves hold good beach reading. The rooms have a hodge-podge of wood furnishings (mostly Victorian replicas). Suites boast an extra half bathroom. You can often smell the aroma of cooking from the restaurant below, which is operated by students at Johnson & Wales Culinary Institute.

9660 E. Bay Harbor Dr., Bay Harbor Island, FL 33154. ✆ 305/868-4141. Fax 305/867-9094. www.bayharborinn.com. 45 units. Winter $149–$239 double; $159–$279 suite. Off-season $80–$159 double; $95–$179 suite. Additional person $35. Rates include continental breakfast. AE, MC, V. Free parking and dockage space. **Amenities:** Restaurant, brunch room, bar, exercise room, concierge, business center, limited room service. *In room:* A/C, TV, dataport, minibar, hair dryer.

Baymar Ocean Resort   Depending on what you're looking for, this hotel could be one of the beach's best buys. It's just south of Bal Harbour, in sleepy Surfside, right on the ocean, with a low-key beach that attracts few other tourists. In 2001, efficiencies were transformed into junior suites and all carpets were removed and replaced with terra-cotta tile. The location is close enough to walk to tennis courts, and some shopping and dining; it's just a few minutes' drive to larger attractions. It may not be worth it to pay more for the oceanfront rooms, since they tend to be smaller than the others. Rooms overlooking the large pool and sundeck area can get loud on busy days. The first-floor ocean-view rooms have a nice shared balcony space.

9401 Collins Ave., Miami Beach, FL 33154. ℂ **800/8-BAYMAR** or 305/866-5446. Fax 305/866-8053. www.baymar.com. 96 units. Winter $115–$125 double; $125–$235 suite. Off-season $75–$95 double; $95–$185 suite. Additional person $10. AE, DC, DISC, MC, V. Parking $5. **Amenities:** Restaurant, lounge, tiki bar, olympic-size pool. *In room:* A/C, TV, kitchen.

Dezerland Beach Resort Hotel   Designed by car enthusiast Michael Dezer, the Dezerland is where "Happy Days" meets Miami Beach, with its visible homage to hot rods and antique cars. Visitors, many of them German tourists, are welcomed by a 1959 Cadillac stationed by the front door, one of a dozen mint-condition classics around the grounds and lobby. This kitschy beachfront hotel recently underwent a $2 million renovation of its guest rooms, lobby, and public areas. The rooms are still somewhat lackluster despite the fact that the renovation added new drapes, bedspreads, furniture, and wall coverings. Though named for various fabulous cars, these, alas, are the Pintos of hotel rooms—nothing more than a typical motel room. The lovely pool, however, has its requisite Cadillac—a mosaic pink one, located at the bottom of the pool. For '50s kitsch and car fanatics, this is a fun place to stay; otherwise, you may think you were taken for a ride.

8701 Collins Ave., Miami Beach, FL 33154. ℂ **800/331-9346** in the U.S., 800/331-9347 in Canada, or 305/865-6661. Fax 305/866-2630. www.dezerhotels.com. 227 units. Winter $99–$139 double. Off-season $69–$99 double. Additional person $10. Special packages and group rates available. AE, DC, DISC, MC, V. **Amenities:** Restaurant, pool, nearby tennis courts, small spa, Jacuzzi, watersports rentals, game room, car-rental desk, tour desk, shuttle service to Aventura Mall and nearby antiques shop, coin-op washers and dryers. *In room:* A/C, TV, kitchen in some rooms, fridge on request, hair dryer, iron, safe.

Four Points Sheraton Miami Beach ⚑   Right on the Miami Beach board-walk, this chain hotel aspires to elegance with gaudy interiors inspired by the grandeur of ancient Greece. *Yikes!* A lobby of marble and rich mahogany goes against the grain of a typical South Beach hotel and only adds to this contrived, out-of-place decor. However, it's not all an eyesore. Its location right on the beach is obviously a perk, as is its spacious rooms and good Sheraton-quality service. It's not luxury, but it's not a bad choice if you're looking to be right on the beach and near the trendier, less ancient side of town.

4343 Collins Ave., Miami Beach, FL 33140. ℂ **800/525-6994** or 305/531-7494. Fax 305/532-2490. 216 units. Winter $199–$299 double. Off-season $119–$199 double. AE, DC, DISC, MC, V. Valet parking $12.50. **Amenities:** Restaurant, bar, pool, exercise room, Jacuzzi, concierge, car-rental desk, business center, room service, same-day dry cleaning. *In room:* A/C, TV, dataport, coffeemaker.

Indian Creek Hotel ⚑⚑   Located off the beaten path, the Indian Creek Hotel is a meticulously restored 1936 building featuring one of the beach's first operating elevators—and is the most charming hotel in the area. Besides that, the service is impeccable. This Because of its location facing the Indian Creek waterway and its lush landscaping, this place feels more like an old-fashioned Key West bed-and-breakfast than your typical Miami Beach Art Deco hotel. The rooms are outfitted in Art Deco furnishings, such as an antique writing desk, with pretty tropical prints and small but spotless bathrooms. As of March 2001, half the rooms were completely renovated. Just 1 short block from a good stretch of sand, the hotel is also within walking distance of shops and restaurants. A landscaped pool area is a great place to lounge in the sun. If you're looking for charm, friendly service, peace and quiet, it pays to paddle away from the South Beach hype and up to this creek.

2727 Indian Creek Dr. (1 block west of Collins Ave.), Miami Beach, FL 33140. ℂ 800/491-2772 or 305/531-2727. Fax 305/531-5651. www.indiancreekhotelmb.com. 61 units. Winter $140–$240 double. Off-season $90–$150 double. Additional person $10. Group packages and summer specials available. AE, DC, DISC, MC, V. Limited street parking. **Amenities:** Restaurant, bar, pool, concierge, car-rental desk, limited room service, laundry and dry-cleaning service. *In room:* A/C, TV/VCR, CD player, dataport, hair dryer; fridge in suites.

Newport Beachside Hotel & Resort This hotel is a great budget option, especially for young families who don't mind being away from the hustle and bustle of South Beach. The continental Newport Pub restaurant is very good and reasonably priced. The pool area is massive, which makes it great for kids. The hotel is situated directly on the beach, and for the aspiring angler, there is also a fishing pier out back. At night, by their poolside bar, a calypso band plays. Another plus is it's location directly across the street from the R. K. Centres, a destination for both tourists and residents with ample shopping and numerous restaurants from fine dining to fast food. Guest rooms are comfortable and spacious, and most have ocean views and balconies.

16701 Collins Ave., Miami, FL 33160. ℂ 800/327-5476 or 305/949-1300. Fax 305/947-5873. 300 units. Winter $129–$299 double. Off-season $95–$250 double. AE, DC, MC, V. Valet parking $5. **Amenities:** Restaurant, sports bar, massive outdoor pool, concierge, business center, babysitting. *In room:* A/C, TV, minibar, fridge, coffeemaker, hair dryer, iron, safe, microwave, radio.

Ramada Miami Beach Resort Situated in the heart of Miami Beach— within minutes of the 41st Street Shopping area, the Convention Center, the Art Deco District, and the Bal Harbour Shops—the Ramada is situated on the strip known as Millionaire's Row. But this hotel was not created for millionaires. Formerly the kosher Crowne Hotel, Ramada has revamped this lush property, making it less a tawdry chain hotel and more of a pretty nice beach resort. The rooms have been refurbished and a complimentary fitness center has been added. The outdoor pool and tiki bars are relaxing; the inside bar and cafe are quaint and intimate. This is one property that is no secret—even in the off-season it operates at 85% capacity.

4041 Collins Ave., Miami Beach, FL 33140. ℂ 305/531-5771. Fax 305/673-1612. 254 units. Winter $109–$139 double. Off-season $95–$105 double. AE, MC, V. **Amenities:** Cafe, 2 bars, outdoor pool, exercise room. *In room:* A/C, TV, dataport, fridge, iron, safe.

INEXPENSIVE

Days Inn Oceanside The Days Inn Oceanside is still home to a kosher Chinese restaurant, a throwback to the days when the area was inundated with Brooklyn's elderly Jewish population during the season. The western section of the neighborhood still maintains a religious preference, but visiting tourists, replete with Speedos and thong bikinis, from Argentina to Germany, are clearly taking over. One of the most economical choices for travelers, this hotel has been refurbished in splashy pastels and bright lavenders. It's clean and cheap, and children under 17 stay free.

4299 Collins Ave., Miami Beach, FL 33140. ℂ 800/356-3017 or 305/673-1513. Fax 305/538-0727. 143 units. Winter $99–$119 double. Off-season $79–$99 double. AE, MC, V. Valet parking $12.50. Pets accepted (deposit required). **Amenities:** 2 restaurants, lounge, pool, access to nearby watersports, concierge, room service, dry-cleaning service, laundry. *In room:* A/C, TV, dataport, fridge on request, coffeemakers in some rooms, iron, safe.

Shorehaven Hotel ★★   Sadly, what used to be a fabulous and funky hotel has become a rather shabby, not-so-chic accommodation, located in the up-and-coming (but-not-there-yet) North Beach. While the large rooms of this two-story 1950s beach motel offer full kitchens and spacious bathrooms, they are in dire need of a good scrubdown. However, each room still has its own theme, like the Lemon Twist room, which has huge murals of bright yellow lemons on the walls and wood floors painted a glossy royal blue. Other rooms have early Banana Republic decor with mosquito netting or other creative touches. There's also a holistic day spa providing aromatherapy, facials, massages, past life regression (!), and Reiki treatment. Don't expect deluxe accommodations here, but it's a bargain, just 1 block from the beach, and a short drive to South Beach.

8505 Harding Ave. (1 block west of Collins Ave.), Miami Beach, FL 33141. ℂ 888/775-0346 or 305/867-1906. Fax 305/867-1716. www.shorehaven.com. 15 units. Winter $89–$129 up to 3 people. Off-season $69–$79. Additional person $10. AE, DISC, MC, V. Free street parking. **Amenities:** Car-rental desk, room service, in-room massage, laundry service. *In room:* A/C, TV, kitchen, hair dryer, iron.

Suez Oceanfront Resort   The king of kitsch, the Las Vegas–like Suez is guarded by an undersized replica of Egypt's famed Sphinx—you can't miss it. Unfortunately, the Sphinx can't keep a quasi-seedy crowd from gathering here. The campy hotel does offer newly renovated rooms on the beach, whereas most of the other old hotels have turned condo. Its location on Collins Avenue's traf-ficky, tacky motel row is convenient if your idea of convenience includes T-shirt shops, Denny's, and Walgreen's. It is, however, right on the beach, so if you stick to the back of the hotel, you'll appreciate it more. For the price, it's a decent choice. There's a restaurant on the premises, though it's not very good.

18215 Collins Ave., Sunny Isles Beach, FL 33160. ℂ 800/327-5278 or 305/932-0661. Fax 305/937-0058. www.suezresort.com. 200 units. Winter $95–$105 double. Off-season $70–$85 double. Kitchenettes $10–$15 extra. AE, DC, MC, V. Free parking. **Amenities:** Restaurant, outdoor heated pool, tennis courts, exercise room, coin-op washers and dryers. *In room:* A/C, TV, dataport, fridge, hair dryer, irons on request; kitchenette in some rooms for additional fee.

3 Key Biscayne

Locals call it the Key, and, technically, Key Biscayne is the northernmost island in the Florida Keys even though it is located in Miami. A relatively unknown area until an impeached Richard Nixon bought a home here in the '70s, Key Biscayne is an affluent but hardly lively residential and recreational island known for its pricey homes, excellent beaches, and actor Andy Garcia, who makes his home here. The island is far enough from the mainland to make it feel semiprivate, yet close enough to downtown for guests to take advantage of everything Miami has to offer.

VERY EXPENSIVE

Ritz-Carlton Key Biscayne ★★★   Described by some as an oceanfront mansion, the Ritz-Carlton takes Key Biscayne to the height of luxury with 44 acres of tropical gardens, a 20,000-square-foot European-style spa, and a world-class tennis center under the direction of tennis pro Cliff Drysdale. Decorated in British colonial style, the Ritz-Carlton looks as if it was straight out of Bermuda with its impressive flower-laden landscaping. The Ritz Kids programs provide children ages 5 to 12 with fantastic activities, and the 1,200-foot beach-front offers everything from pure relaxation to fishing, boating, or windsurfing.

Spacious and luxuriously appointed rooms are elegantly Floridian, featuring large balconies overlooking the ocean or the lush gardens. Admirers of Key Biscayne were wondering how long it would take for the island to start puttin' on the Ritz. Now it's here, and, unlike many behemoth hotels, the Ritz-Carlton is as much a part of the aesthetic value of the island as is its natural beauty.

415 Grand Bay Dr., Key Biscayne, FL 33149. ℂ **800/241-3333** or 305/648-5900. Fax 305/648-1448. www.ritzcarlton.com. 352 units. Winter $270–$850 suite. Off-season $225–$800 suite. AE, DC, DISC, MC, V. Valet parking (call for fees). **Amenities:** 3 restaurants, 3 bars, 2 outdoor heated pools, tennis center w/lessons available, health club & spa, watersports equipment, children's programs, 24-hour room service, overnight laundry service. *In room:* A/C, TV, dataport, minibar, hair dryer, safe.

Silver Sands Beach Resort

If Key Biscayne is where you want to be and you don't want to pay the prices of the Sonesta next door, consider this quaint one-story motel. Everything is crisp and clean, and the pleasant staff will help with anything you may need, including babysitting. But despite the name, it's certainly no resort. Except for the beach and pool, you'll have to leave the premises for almost everything else, including food. The well-appointed rooms are very beachy, sporting a tropical motif and simple furnishings. Oceanfront suites have the added convenience of full kitchens with stoves and pantries. You'll sit poolside with an unpretentious set of Latin-American families and Europeans who have come for a long and simple vacation—and get it.

301 Ocean Dr., Key Biscayne, FL 33149. ℂ **305/361-5441.** Fax 305/361-5477. 56 units. Winter $149–$349 double. Off-season $129–$309 double. Additional person $30. Weekly rates available. AE, DC, MC, V. Free parking. **Amenities:** Medium-sized pool, secretarial services, coin-op washers and dryers. *In room:* A/C, TV, VCRs in some rooms, kitchenette, fridge, coffeemaker, microwave.

Sonesta Beach Resort Key Biscayne 🐸🐸 *Kids*

The Sonesta is an idyllic, secluded resort-resort in the middle of Miami—like a souped-up summer camp. Families and couples alike love this place for its oceanfront location and its many high-caliber amenities, which make it almost impossible to venture off the property. From the moment the valets, clad in tropical prints, take your car, you'll know you've entered a world of no concern. An $8 million renovation of the lobby and expansion of the spa has kept the Sonesta sparkling and at the top of the list of vacationers looking for a relaxing resort vacation. Each of the plush 292 rooms, also recently upgraded, has a private balcony or terrace. There are also 12 one- and two-bedroom suites as well as fully furnished three- and four-bedroom vacation homes with private pool adjacent to the main hotel. Known for having the best piña coladas in the entire city, the pool and beach bars are popular with locals and vacationers alike. The hotel's Two Dragons restaurant is good, featuring Chinese, Thai, and Japanese food. A fantastic, free, and fully supervised kids' program (ages 3 to 12) will actually allow parents to have a vacation of their own. Although you may not want to leave the lush grounds, Bill Baggs State Recreation Area and the area's best beaches are right at hand. If you choose to venture out, you're only about 15 minutes from Miami Beach and even closer to the mainland and Coconut Grove.

350 Ocean Dr., Key Biscayne, FL 33149. ℂ **800/SONESTA** or 305/361-2021. Fax 305/361-3096. www. sonesta.com. 292 units. Winter $295–$465 double; $875–1,475 suite; $1,750 penthouse. Off-season $195–$285 double; $650–$1,000 suite; $1,250 penthouse. 15% gratuity added to food and beverage bills. Special packages available. AE, DC, DISC, MC, V. Valet parking $12. **Amenities:** 4 restaurants, 2 bars, lounge, outdoor heated Olympic-style pool, access to nearby golf, 9 tennis courts, health club & spa, Jacuzzis, extensive watersports equipment rental, bike and moped rental, children's programs, sports court, sailing lessons, shuttle service to shopping, business center, salon, limited room service, laundry and dry-cleaning service. *In room:* A/C, TV, dataport, minibar, coffeemaker, hair dryer.

Accommodations in Coral Gables, Coconut Grove, Downtown & Key Biscayne

Biltmore Hotel **18**
Biscayne Bay Marriott **4**
The Clarion Hotel & Suites **7**
David William Hotel **17**
Don Shula's Hotel
& Golf Club **3**
Doral Golf Resort & Spa **1**
Everglades Hotel **5**
Grove Isle
Club & Resort **25**
Hampton Inn **19**
Hotel Inter-Continental **10**
Hotel Place St. Michel **14**
Hyatt Regency
Coral Gables **15**
Hyatt Regency at Miami
Convention Center **12**
JW Marriott Hotel **11**
Mandarin Oriental Miami **10**
Mayfair House Hotel **21**
Miami International
Airport Hotel **2**
Miami River Inn **6**
Miccousukee Resort
& Convention Center **13**
Mutiny Hotel **23**
The Omni Colonnade Hotel **16**
Riviera Court Motel **20**
Ritz-Carlton Coconut Grove
(opening Oct. 2001) **22**
Sheraton Biscayne Bay **9**
Wyndham Grand Bay **24**

KEY BISCAYNE
Ritz-Carlton Key Biscayne **28**
Silver Sands
Beach Resort **27**
Sonesta Beach Resort **26**

97

4 Downtown

If you've ever read Tom Wolfe's *Bonfire of the Vanities,* you may understand what downtown Miami is all about. If not, it's this simple: Take a wrong turn and you could find yourself in some serious trouble. Desolate and dangerous at night, downtown is trying to change its image, but it's a long, tedious process. Most downtown hotels cater primarily to business travelers and pre- and postcruise passengers. Although business hotels are expensive, quality and service are of a high standard. Look for discounts and packages for the weekend, when offices are closed and rooms often go empty. If you're the kind of person who digs an urban setting, you may enjoy downtown, but if you're looking for shiny, happy Miami, you're in the wrong place (for now). As of press time, the developer of the Ritz-Carlton on South Beach was about to close a deal with downtown's shoddy DuPont Plaza, located on the sketchier side of the Miami River, in which millions of dollars would be invested to revamp the decrepit property, upgrading it into a classy lower-end hotel. Keep your eyes on this area.

VERY EXPENSIVE

Hotel Inter-Continental Miami ⟨⟨⟨ This hotel presents a serious catch-22: It's got a front-row view of all of Miami Beach, Biscayne Bay, the Miami River, and the Atlantic Ocean, but it is also located in downtown Miami. It depends on what you're looking for. If it's the view, then you will want to stay here. If it's location, you may want to reconsider. However, with the decidedly threatening presence of the hyperluxurious Mandarin Oriental just over the Brickell Bridge, the Inter-Continental had no choice but to keep up with the competition. A $34 million renovation has brought it up to speed, rendering it downtown proper's swankiest hotel. It boasts more marble than the Liberace Museum (both inside and out), but it's warmed by bold colors and a fancified Florida flavor. The five-story lobby features a marble centerpiece sculpture by Henry Moore and is topped by a pleasing skylight. Plenty of plants, palm trees, and eclectic furnishings also add charm and enliven the otherwise stark space. Perfectly designed for business travelers, each room is outfitted with a desk and Internet-ready telephone lines. Some suites have fully equipped kitchenettes. Guests who stay in the Inter-Continental are big fish in the very small sea of desolate downtown Miami.

100 Chopin Plaza, Miami, FL 33131. (℃) **800/327-3005** or 305/577-1000. Fax 305/577-0384. www. interconti.com. 640 units. Winter $255–$335 double. Off-season $150–$245 double. Year-round $550–$3,000 suite. Additional person $20. Weekend and other packages available. AE, DC, DISC, MC, V. Valet parking $17. **Amenities:** 3 restaurants, 2 lounges, Olympic-size outdoor heated pool, access to nearby golf course, spa, concierge, tour desk, car-rental desk, large business center, shopping arcade, salon and barbershop, room service, coin-op washers and dryers, laundry and dry-cleaning service. *In room:* A/C, TV/VCR, CD player, mini-bar, hair dryer.

Mandarin Oriental Miami ⟨⟨⟨⟨ Corporate big shots finally have a high-end luxury hotel to stay in while wheeling and dealing their way through Miami. Catering to business travelers, conventioneers, and the occasional leisure traveler who doesn't mind spending in excess of $500 a night for a room, the swank Mandarin Oriental features a waterfront location, residential-style rooms, most with balconies, and several upscale dining and bar facilities. Much of the hotel's staff was flown in from Bangkok and Hong Kong to demonstrate the hotel's unique brand of superattentive Asian-inspired service. The hotel's two restaurants, the high-end Azul and the more casual Café Sambal, are up to Mandarin standards and are both wonderful.

500 Brickell Key Dr., Miami, FL 33131. © **305/913-8288**. Fax 305/913-8300. www.mandarinoriental.com. 329 units. $550–$740 double; $1,200–$4,000 suite. AE, DC, DISC, MC, V. Valet parking $24. **Amenities:** 2 restaurants, bar, outdoor pool, state-of-the-art health club, full-service spa, outdoor Jacuzzi, concierge, 24-hour business center. *In room:* A/C, TV, dataport, minibar, hair dryer, iron, safe.

EXPENSIVE

Hyatt Regency at Miami Convention Center ⭐⭐
The Hyatt Regency is located just off the Miami River in the heart of downtown Miami. It shares space with the Miami Convention Center, the James L. Knight Convention Center Theater, an exhibition hall, and a 5,000-seat auditorium and concert hall. The University of Miami even holds classes here. This hotel is perfect for large groups, business travelers, or basketball fanatics in town to see the Miami Heat play at the nearby American Airlines Arena. The People Mover and Metro-rail are just blocks away, and water taxis are available at the front steps. Most of the spacious guest rooms have a balcony with a view of either the city or the bay.

400 SE Second Ave., Miami, FL 33131. © **305/358-1234**. Fax 305/374-1728. 612 units. Winter $229–$254 double. Off-season $139–$179 double. AE, DC, DISC, MC, V. Valet parking $18. **Amenities:** Restaurant, outdoor pool, health club, extensive business center. *In room:* A/C, TV, dataport, coffeemaker, hair dryer, safe.

MODERATE

Biscayne Bay Marriott ⭐
Just 7 miles east of the airport, the Biscayne Bay Marriott Hotel and Marina is on the sketchy outskirts of downtown Miami, yet it manages to create its own world of tranquility and entertainment. The 603-room hotel is equipped with a 220-slip full-service marina. Watersports rentals are available nearby. There's also 24-hour on-site security and valet parking. Some rooms face the bay, and some have balconies. The views are fantastic. If you want to stay in a Marriott, however, you may want to consider the newer JW Marriott (see below) on the less-desolate Brickell Avenue a few miles south.

1633 N. Bayshore Dr., Miami, FL 33132. © **305/374-3900**. Fax 305/375-0597. www.marriott.com. 600 units. Winter $194–$250 double. Off-season $124–$204 double. AE, DC, DISC, MC, V. Valet parking $15. **Amenities:** 3 restaurants, 2 lounges, pool, health club, Jacuzzi, concierge, business center, limited room service, coin-op washers and dryers, laundry and dry-cleaning service. *In room:* A/C, TV, dataport, minibar, coffeemaker, hair dryer.

JW Marriott Hotel ⭐⭐
Located smack in the middle of the business-oriented Brickell Avenue near downtown Miami, the JW Marriott is a *really* nice Marriott catering mostly to business travelers, but located conveniently enough between Coconut Grove and South Beach that it isn't a bad choice for vacationers, either. A small but elegant lobby features the classy, appropriately named Drake's Power Bar. The buzz of business deals being sealed amidst clouds of cigar smoke contributes to the smoky, but not staid, atmosphere here. Rooms are equipped with every amenity you might need. A lovely outdoor pool, fitness center, sauna, and hot tub should become everybody's business at this hotel. Next door is the area's bustling brewery, Gordon Biersch, which attracts well-heeled, young professional types who gather for postwork revelry.

1111 Brickell Ave., Miami, FL 33131. © **800/228-9290** or 305/374-1224. Fax 305/374-4211. www.marriott.com. Winter $219 deluxe room; $319 concierge room; $450 junior suite. Off-season $189 deluxe room; $229 concierge room; $350 junior suite. AE, DC, DISC, MC, V. Valet parking $18; self-parking $16. **Amenities:** 3 restaurants, bar, outdoor pool, health club, sauna, concierge, tour desk, business center, laundry service. *In room:* A/C, TV, dataport, minibar, coffeemaker, hair dryer, iron, safe.

Miami River Inn ⭐⭐⭐
The Miami River Inn, listed on the National Register of Historic Places, is a quaint country-style hideaway consisting of four cottages smack in the middle of downtown Miami. In fact, it's so hidden that most locals don't even know it exists, which only adds to its panache. It's also Miami's

only bed-and-breakfast. Every room has hardwood floors and is uniquely furnished with antiques dating from 1908. In one room, you might find a hand-painted bathtub, a Singer sewing machine, and an armoire from the turn of the 20th century restored to perfection. Thirty-eight rooms have private baths—4 have a shower only, 6 have a tub only, and 28 have a splendid shower and tub combo. One-and two-bedroom apartments are available as well. In the foyer you can peruse a library filled with books about old Miami, with histories of this land's former owners: Julia Tuttle, William Brickell, and Henry Flagler. It's close to public transportation, restaurants, and museums, and only 5 minutes from the business district.

118 SW South River Dr., Miami, FL 33130. © **800/468-3589** or 305/325-0045. Fax 305/325-9227. www.miamiriverinn.com. 40 units. Winter $99–$229 double. Off-season $69–$109 double. Rates include continental breakfast. Additional person $15. AE, DC, DISC, MC, V. Free parking. Pets accepted for $25 per night. **Amenities:** Small, lushly landscaped swimming pool, access to nearby YMCA facilities, Jacuzzi, babysitting, coin-op washers and dryers, laundry and dry-cleaning service. *In room:* A/C, TV, dataport, hair dryer, iron, safe.

Sheraton Biscayne Bay Hotel &
This downtown hotel's waterfront location is its greatest asset. Nestled between Brickell Park and Biscayne Bay, the Sheraton is set back from the main road and surrounded by a pleasant bayfront walkway. Since a recent $14 million renovation, this Sheraton is especially recommendable. Its identical rooms are well furnished and comfortable. The hotel is popular with business travelers, but a fine choice for those who don't mind driving a few minutes to Miami's more populated areas.

495 Brickell Ave., Miami, FL 33131. © **800/284-2000** or 305/373-6000. Fax 305/374-2279. www.sheraton. com. 598 units. Winter $199–$209 double; $225–$305 suite. Off-season $149–$175 double; $200–$250 suite. Additional person $10. Senior discounts and weekend and other packages available. AE, DC, DISC, MC, V. Self-parking $18. **Amenities:** Restaurant, bar, pool, exercise room. *In room:* AC, TV, dataport, fridges available on request, coffeemaker, hair dryer, iron.

INEXPENSIVE
Clarion Hotel & Suites &
This hotel is especially designed for the seasoned business traveler. Its location in downtown Miami (right on the river) provides excellent access to the commercial world of nearby Brickell Avenue and the legal precincts in downtown. Due to its position adjoining the Hyatt, a Metromover station, and some major parking lots, this hotel does, however, lack a room with a view, which may be disheartening for some guests. The spacious and elegantly appointed guest rooms and suites offer many amenities, and the two-room apartment suites are ideal for extended stays.

100 SE 4th St., Miami, FL 33131. © **800/838-6501** or 305/374-5100. Fax 305/381-9826. www. clarionmiaconctr.com. 149 units. Year-round $99–$169 double. AE, DC, DISC, MC, V. Valet parking $15. **Amenities:** Restaurant, lounge, outdoor heated pool, exercise room, room service (7am–11:30pm), laundry service. *In room:* A/C, TV, dataport, coffeemaker, hair dryer.

Everglades Hotel
As swampy as its namesake, this hotel isn't the cleanest place, having been around almost forever on downtown's active Biscayne Boulevard. Many traveling business types and Latin American families stay here because of its low rates and many services, which include a bank in the building. It's near the highways and Metrorail, and there's shopping across the street at Bayside Marketplace. Rooms are shabby and screaming for refurbishment. It may not be the most extravagant choice, but it's definitely one of the least expensive.

244 Biscayne Blvd., Miami, FL 33132. © **800/327-5700** or 305/379-5461. Fax 305/577-8445. www. miamigate.com/everglades. 376 units. Year-round $95 double; $120 suite. Extra person $10. AE, DC, DISC, MC, V. Parking $8. **Amenities:** Restaurant, pool, business center, babysitting, coin-op washers and dryers. *In Room:* A/C, TV, hair dryer on request.

5 West Miami/Airport Area

As Miami continues to grow at a rapid pace, expansion has begun westward, where land is plentiful. Several resorts have taken advantage of the space to build world-class tennis and golf courses. While there's no sea to swim in, a plethora of facilities makes up for the lack of an ocean view.

EXPENSIVE

Doral Golf Resort and Spa ⓖ   This 650-acre golf and tennis resort is in the middle of nowhere, but with all it's got, it's really a destination in itself. While the pamperings in the spa are nothing to sneer at, the next-door golf resort hosts world-class tournaments and boasts the Great White Course—the Southeast's first desert-scape course, designed by The Shark himself, Greg Norman. The season is usually booked well in advance, often by repeat guests. The Blue Lagoon water park features two 80,000-gallon pools with cascading waterfalls, a rock facade, and the 125-foot Blue Monster water slide. Rooms here, like the hotel itself, are spacious, all with private balconies, many overlooking a golf course or garden. The hotel itself shines in a polished marble and gold decor. The spa's restaurant serves tasty, healthy fare—so good you won't realize it's health food, actually. The hotel is just moments from the Miami airport. For a spa or golf vacation, the Doral is an ideal choice. Otherwise, consider investing your money in a hotel that's better located.

4400 NW 87th Ave., Miami, FL 33178. ⓒ 800/71-DORAL or 305/592-2000. Fax 305/594-4682. www.doralresort.com. 693 units. Winter $339 double; $425 suite; $545 1-bedroom suite; $879 2-bedroom suite. Off-season $155 double; $225 suite; $305 1-bedroom suite; $405 2-bedroom suite. Additional person $35. Golf and spa packages available. AE, DC, DISC, MC, V. Valet parking $15. **Amenities:** Restaurant, sports bar, 4 pools and a 125-ft. water slide, 5 golf courses and driving range, 10 tennis courts, health club & world-class spa, bike rental, concierge, business center, room service, babysitting, laundry and dry-cleaning service. *In room:* A/C, TV, fax, dataport, minibar, coffeemaker, hair dryer, iron, safe.

Miccosukee Resort and Convention Center ⓖ   Located on the edge of the Everglades, about 30 to 40 minutes west of the airport, the Miccosukee Resort is the closest thing South Florida's got to Las Vegas, but accommodations really are just a step above a Holiday Inn. The Miccosukee tribe was originally part of the lower Creek Nation and lived in areas now known as Alabama and Georgia. Following the final Seminole War in 1858, the last of the Miccosukees settled in the Everglades. Following the lead set recently by many other Native American tribes, they built the resort to accumulate gambling revenue. Although many tourists go out to the resort solely to gamble, it also has expansive meeting and banquet facilities, spa services, great children's programs, entertainment (I saw Isaac Hayes), and excursions to the Florida Everglades. Guest rooms are standard, furnished with custom pieces made exclusively for the resort, but if you're here, you're not likely to spend that much time in your room.

500 SW 177th Ave. (at intersection with SW 8th St.), Miami, FL 33194. ⓒ 877/242-6464 or 305/221-8623. Fax 305/221-8309. www.miccosukee.com. 302 units. Winter $99 double; $135 suite. Year-round $325 presidential. All rooms sleep up to 4 people. AE, DC, DISC, MC, V. Free parking. **Amenities:** 3 restaurants, 24-hour deli, indoor heated pool, state-of-the-art health club & spa, game room, 24-hour room service, dry-cleaning and laundry service. *In room:* A/C, TV, in-room movies, dataport, minibar, coffeemaker, hair dryer; some suites have whirlpool and wet bars.

MODERATE

Don Shula's Hotel and Golf Club   Guests come to Shula's mostly for the golf, but there's plenty here to keep nongolfers busy, too. Opened in 1992 to much fanfare from the sports and business community, Shula's resort is an all-encompassing oasis in the middle of the planned residential neighborhood of Miami Lakes, complete with a Main Street and nearby shopping facilities—a good thing, since the site is more than a 20-minute drive on the highways from anything. The guest rooms, located in the main building or surrounding the golf course, are plain but pretty in typical, uninspiring Florida decor—pastels, wicker, and light wood. As expected, the hotel's Athletic Club features state-of-the-art equipment and classes, but costs hotel guests $10 per day or $35 per week. The award-winning Shula's Steak House and the more casual Steak House Two get high rankings nationwide. They serve huge Angus beef steaks and seafood, which can be worked off with a round of golf the next day.

Main St., Miami Lakes, FL 33014. ✆ 800/24-SHULA or 305/821-1150. Fax 305/820-8190. 330 units. Winter $129–$289 suite. Off-season $99–$209 suite. Additional person $10. Business packages available. AE, DC, MC, V. **Amenities:** 6 restaurants, 2 bars, 2 pools, 2 golf courses and a driving range, 9 tennis courts, health club, saunas, sporting courts. *In room:* A/C, TV/VCR.

Miami International Airport Hotel ✦   I don't know of a nicer airport hotel, and you can't beat the convenience—it's actually in the airport at Concourse E. You'll find every amenity of a first-class tourist hotel. The rooms are modern, clean, and spacious, with newly renovated furnishings, mattresses, fixtures, and carpeting. You might think you'd be deafened by the roar of the planes, but all of the rooms have been soundproof and actually allow very little noise. In addition, the hotel has modern security systems and is extremely safe.

Airport Terminal Concourse E (at the intersection of NW 20th St. and LeJeune Rd.; P.O. Box 997510), Miami, FL 33299-7510. ✆ 800/327-1276 or 305/871-4100. Fax 305/871-0800. www.miahotel.com. 260 units. Winter $179–]$650 double. Off-season $130–$270 double. Additional person $10. AE, DC, MC, V. Parking $10. **Amenities:** Restaurant, cocktail lounge, large rooftop pool, racquetball courts, well-equipped health club, Jacuzzi, sauna, concierge, tour desk, business center, limited room service, salon, laundry and dry-cleaning service. *In room:* A/C, TV, dataport, hair dryer, iron.

BARGAIN CHAINS

If you must stay near the airport, consider any of the dozens of moderately priced chain hotels. You'll find one of the cheapest and most recommendable options at either of the **Days Inn** locations at 7250 NW 11th St. or 4767 NW 36th St. (✆ 800/329-7466 or 305/888-3661), each about 2 miles from the airport. Rates range from $47 to $69.

The larger property on 36th Street offers slightly cheaper rates with singles starting as low as $49. The 11th Street locale may charge more for weekends, but prices usually start at $70. Prices include free transportation from the airport.

A more luxurious option is the **Wyndham** at 3900 NW 21st St. (✆ 800/933-1100), with rates from $100 to $225. There's also another location in downtown Miami at 1601 Biscayne Blvd. (✆ 800/WYNDHAM or 305/374-0000). Rates there run from a high of $238 in season to $158 during the summer.

6 North Dade

Turnberry Isle Resort and Club ✦✦✦   One of Miami's classiest (if not *the* classiest) resorts, this gorgeous 300-acre compound has every possible facility for active guests, particularly golfers. You'll pay a lot to stay here—but it's worth it. The main attractions are two Trent Jones courses, available only to members and guests of the hotel. A new seven-story Jasmine wing looks like a Mediterranean village surrounded by tropical gardens that are joined by covered marble walkways to the other wings. Treat yourself to a "Turnberry Retreat" at the Turnberry Spa, which has been renovated to the tune of $10 million. The spa comprises three levels of deluxe pampering and includes aerobics and fitness classes, stress reductions, massage therapy, and a juice bar designed for complete rejuvenation. Impeccable service from check-in to checkout brings loyal fans back to this resort for more. Its location in the well-manicured residential and shopping area of North Miami Beach known as Aventura means you'll find excellent shopping and some of the best dining in Miami right in the neighborhood. Unless you're into boating, the higher-priced resort rooms are where you'll want to stay; you'll be steps from the spa facilities and the renowned Veranda restaurant. The well-proportioned rooms are gorgeously tiled to match the Mediterranean-style architecture. The huge bathrooms even have a color TV mounted within reach of the whirlpool bathtubs and glass-walled showers. The only drawback to this hotel is that you'll need to take a shuttle to the beach.

19999 W. Country Club Dr., Aventura, FL 33180. ℂ **800/327-7028** or 305/936-2929. Fax 305/933-6560. www.turnberryisle.com. 395 units. Winter $395–$495 double; $605–$1,200 suite; $3,000–$4,200 penthouse. Off-season $175–$275 double; $375–$730 suite; $$2,500–$3,500 penthouse. AE, DC, DISC, MC, V. Valet parking $12; free self-parking. **Amenities:** 6 restaurants, numerous bars and lounges, 2 outdoor pools, 2 golf courses, 2 tennis complexes, state-of-the-art spa, extensive watersports equipment rental, concierge, secretarial services, 24-hour room service, babysitting. *In room:* A/C, TV/VCR, CD player, fax, dataport, minibar, fridge and coffeemaker on request, hair dryer.

7 Coral Gables

Translated appropriately as "City Beautiful," the Gables, as it's affectionately known, was one of Miami's original planned communities and is still among the city's prettiest, pedestrian-friendly, albeit preservation obsessed, neighborhoods. Pristine with a European flair, Coral Gables is best known for its wide array of excellent upscale restaurants of various ethnicity, as well as a hotly contested (the quiet city didn't want to welcome the new traffic) mega-shopping complex featuring upscale stores such as Nordstrom.

If you're looking for luxury, Coral Gables has a number of wonderful hotels, but if you're on a tight budget, you may be better off elsewhere. Coconut Grove eases into Coral Gables, which extends north toward Miami International Airport and offers a few less expensive hotels. Two popular and well-priced chain hotels in the area are a **Holiday Inn** (ℂ **800/327-5476** or 305/667-5611) at 1350 S. Dixie Hwy., with rates between $75 and $125, and a **Howard Johnson** (ℂ **800/446-4656** or 305/665-7501) at 1430 S. Dixie Hwy., with rates ranging from $65 to $95. Both are located directly across the street from the University of Miami and are popular with families and friends of students.

VERY EXPENSIVE

Biltmore Hotel ★★★ A romantic sense of old world glamour combined with a rich history permeate the Biltmore as much as the pricey perfume of the guests who stay here. Built in 1926, it's the oldest Coral Gables hotel and a National Historical Landmark—one of only two operating hotels in Florida to receive the designation. Rising above the Spanish-style estate is a majestic 300-foot copper-clad tower, modeled after the Giralda bell tower in Seville and visible throughout the city. Over the years, the Biltmore has passed through many incarnations (including a post–World War II stint as a VA hospital), but is now back to its original 1926 splendor. More intriguing than scary is the rumor that ghosts of wounded soldiers and even Al Capone, for whom the Everglades Suite is nicknamed, roam the halls here. But don't worry. The hotel is far from a haunted house. It is warm, welcoming, and extremely charming. Now under the management of the Westin Hotel group, the hotel boasts large Moorish-style

rooms decorated with tasteful period reproductions and some high-tech amenities. The enormous lobby, with its 45-foot vaulted ceilings, makes a bold state-
ment of elegance. Always a popular destination for golfers, including former
President Clinton (who stays in the Al Capone suite), the Biltmore is situated
on a lush, rolling 18-hole course that is as challenging as it is beautiful. The spa
is fantastic and the enormous winding pool is legendary—it's where a pre-
Tarzan Johnny Weismuller broke the world's swimming record.

1200 Anastasia Ave., Coral Gables, FL 33134. ℂ **800/727-1926** or 305/445-1926; Westin 800/228-3000. Fax
305/442-9496. www.biltmorehotel.com. 275 units. Winter $339–$509. Off-season $259–$479. Additional
person $20. Special packages available. AE, DC, DISC, MC, V. Valet parking $14; free self-parking. **Amenities:**
5 restaurants, 2 bars, 21,000-sq.-ft. swimming pool surrounded by arched walkways and classical sculptures,
18-hole golf course, 10 lighted tennis courts, state-of-the-art health club, full-service spa, sauna, concierge,
car rental through concierge, elaborate business center and secretarial services, salon, 24-hour room service,
babysitting, laundry and dry-cleaning service. *In room:* A/C, TV, VCR on request, fax, dataport, minibar, hair
dryer, iron, safe; kitchenette in tower suite.

Hyatt Regency Coral Gables 🎯🎯
High on style, comfort, and price, this
Hyatt is part of Coral Gables's Alhambra, an office-hotel complex with a
Mediterranean motif. The building itself is gorgeous, designed with pink stone,
arched entrances, grand courtyards, and tile roofs. Most recently, the pool and
lobby were beautifully renovated. Inside you'll find overstuffed chairs on marble
floors surrounded by opulent antiques and chandeliers. The large guest rooms
are comfortable, if uninspired. A few rooms have balconies. Though the hotel
fails to authentically mimic something much older and much farther away, it is
attractive in its newness and an excellent place from which to admire the more
historic properties in the neighborhood.

50 Alhambra Plaza, Coral Gables, FL 33134. ℂ **800/233-1234** or 305/441-1234. Fax 305/441-0520. www.
hyatt.com. 242 units. Winter $340 double. Off-season $254 double. Year-round $375–$1,800 1-bedroom
suite; $575–$2,050 2-bedroom suite. Additional person $25. Packages and senior discounts available. AE, MC,
V. Valet parking $14; self-parking $11. **Amenities:** Restaurant, bar, large outdoor heated pool, nearby golf
course, health club, Jacuzzi, 2 saunas, concierge, business center, limited room service, in-room massage,
babysitting, same-day laundry and dry-cleaning service. *In room:* A/C, TV, fax in some rooms, dataport, minibar, coffeemaker, hair dryer, iron, safe.

EXPENSIVE

David William Hotel 🎯🎯
This sister hotel to the Biltmore shares many of the
same amenities without the Biltmore's price. You can even take a shuttle to the
Biltmore to play a round of golf, enjoy the health club and spa, play tennis, or take
a dip in the pool. The luxurious one- and two-bedroom suites are extremely spacious and have eat-in kitchens for extended stays. For a spectacular view of Miami,
go up to the roof and have a drink by the pool. The hotel, which has undergone
a recent external renovation, is directly across the street from the Granada Golf
Course, less than 5 miles from the airport and only 20 minutes from Miami
Beach. Donna's Bistro, a fusion restaurant with a homey feel, is spectacular. Executive chef Donna Wynter was the Chef de Cuisine at the Biltmore Hotel and has
worked as a chef at New York's Tavern on the Green and Toscana Ristorante. If
you want luxury without the price, this is your best alternative in the Gables.

700 Biltmore Way, Coral Gables, FL 33134. ℂ **800/757-8073** or 305/445-7821. Fax 305/913-1943.
www.davidwilliamhotel.com.. 116 units. Winter $249–$489 double. Off-season $209–$269 double. AE, DISC,
MC, V. Valet parking $9. **Amenities:** Restaurant, coffee shop, lounge, gourmet market, rooftop pool, limited
room service. *In room:* A/C, TV, fax, kitchenette, minibar, coffeemaker, hair dryer, iron, safe.

Hotel Place St. Michel 🎯🎯🎯
This European-style hotel in the heart of
Coral Gables is one of the city's most romantic options. The accommodations

and hospitality are straight out of Old World Europe, complete with dark wood–paneled walls, cozy beds, beautiful antiques, and a quiet elegance that seems startlingly out of place in trendy Miami. Everything here is charming—from the brass elevator and parquet floors to the paddle fans. One-of-a-kind furnishings make each room special. All bathrooms, with the exception of two rooms, have a shower and tub and are on the smaller side but hardly cramped. Guests are treated to fresh fruit baskets upon arrival and enjoy perfect service throughout their stay. The exceptional Restaurant St. Michel is a very romantic dining choice.

162 Alcazar Ave., Coral Gables, FL 33134. ℭ **800/848-HOTEL** or 305/444-1666. Fax 305/529-0074. www.hotelplacestmichel.com. 27 units. Winter $165 double; $200 suite. Off-season $125 double; $160 suite. Additional person $10. Rates include continental breakfast. AE, DC, MC, V. Self-parking $7. **Amenities:** Restaurant, lounge, deli, access to nearby health club, concierge, room service, in-room massage, laundry and dry-cleaning service. *In room:* A/C, TV, dataport, hair dryer, iron.

Omni Colonnade Hotel ℜ   The Colonnade occupies part of a large historic building, originally built by Coral Gables's founder George Merrick in 1926. Faithful to its original style, the hotel is a successful amalgam of new and old, with an emphasis on modern conveniences. The structure stands 14 elegant stories high, although guest rooms occupy only 4 floors. It's popular with business travelers. The oversized rooms are worthy of the hotel's rates. They feature sitting areas, historic photographs, marble counters, gold-finished faucets, and solid wood furnishings. Thoughtful extras include complimentary shoe shines and champagne upon arrival. Doc Dammers Saloon and restaurant offers a good happy hour for the 30-something crowd. There's also live entertainment on weekends.

180 Aragon Ave. (at Ponce de León and Miracle Mile), Coral Gables, FL 33134. ℭ **800/THE-OMNI** or 305/441-2600. Fax 305/445-3929. 157 units. Winter $215–$425 double. Off-season $165–$365 double. Free morning coffee and tea in lobby. Packages available. AE, DC, DISC, MC, V. Valet parking $10. **Amenities:** Restaurant, heated rooftop pool, small modern rooftop health club, Jacuzzi, concierge, tour desk, car-rental desk, shopping arcade, 24-hour room service, in-room massage, babysitting, coin-op washers and dryers, same-day laundry and dry-cleaning service. *In room:* A/C, TV, VCR upon request, fax, dataport, minibar, coffeemaker, hair dryer, iron.

INEXPENSIVE

Riviera Court Motel   Besides the Holiday Inn down the road, this family-owned motel is the best discount option in the area. The comfortable and clean two-story property, dating from 1954, has a small pool and is set back from the road, so the rooms are all relatively quiet. Vending machines are the only choice for refreshments, but guests are near many great dining spots. You can also choose to stay in one of the efficiencies, which all have fully stocked kitchens. For gossip mavens, this is the place where tennis star Jennifer Capriati was busted for drug possession.

5100 Riviera Dr. (on U.S. 1), Coral Gables, FL 33146. ℭ **800/368-8602** or 305/665-3528. 30 units. Winter $75–$88 double. Off-season $68–$80 double. 10% discount for seniors and AAA members. AE, DC, DISC, MC, V. **Amenities:** Pool. *In room:* A/C, TV.

8 Coconut Grove

This waterfront village hugs the shores of Biscayne Bay, just south of U.S. 1 and about 10 minutes from the beaches. Once a haven for hippies, head shops, and arty bohemian characters, the Grove succumbed to the inevitable temptations of commercialism and has become a Gap nation, featuring a host of fun, themey restaurants, bars, a megaplex, and lots of stores. Outside of the main shopping area, however, you will find the beautiful remnants of old Miami in the form of flora, fauna, and, of course, water.

VERY EXPENSIVE

Grove Isle Club and Resort ⭐⭐⭐   Hidden away in the bougainvillea and lushness of the Grove, the Grove Isle Resort is off the beaten path on its own lushly landscaped 20-acre island just outside the heart of Coconut Grove. The isolated exclusivity of this resort contributes to a country club vibe, though, for the most part, the people here aren't snooty; they just value their privacy and precious relaxation time. Everyone dresses in white and pastels, and if they're not on their way to a set of tennis, they're not in a rush to get anywhere. You'll step into rooms that are elegantly furnished with mosquito-netted canopy beds and a patio overlooking the bay. You'll need to reserve early here—rooms go very fast. Baleen, a fantastic yet pricey haute cuisinerie, serves fresh seafood and other regional specialties in a spectacular, elegant dining room, or, better yet, outside on the water.

4 Grove Isle Dr., Coconut Grove, FL 33133. © 800/88-GROVE or 305/858-8300. Fax 305/854-6702. 49 units. Winter $350–$495 suite. Off-season $295–$475 suite. Rates include breakfast. Additional person $20. AE, DC, MC, V. Valet parking $15. **Amenities:** Large outdoor heated pool, 12 outdoor tennis courts, deluxe health club, watersports rentals, concierge, secretarial services, salon, room service, in-room massage, babysitting, laundry and dry-cleaning service. *In room:* A/C, TV/VCR, video rental delivered to room for $5, dataport, mini-bar, hair dryer, iron, safe.

Mayfair House Hotel ⭐   This Gaudi-esque hotel located within the deserted streets of Mayfair Mall certainly makes you feel removed from the mayhem in the surrounding streets of the Grove, but to me it's somewhat desolate. Each guest unit has been individually designed and was renovated in 1998. No two rooms are alike, though each room has its own Roman tub or whirlpool and private terrace. Some suites are downright opulent and include a private outdoor Japanese-style hot tub. The top-floor terraces offer good views, and all are hidden from the street by leaves and latticework. Since the lobby is in a shopping mall, recreation is confined to the roof, where you'll find a small pool, sauna, and snack bar. NBA players have been known to stay here, as has new Miami resident OJ Simpson. If you're looking for complete seclusion, the Wyndham Mayfair is fine, but, for the money, the airier Grand Bay or Mutiny hotels are better choices (see below).

3000 Florida Ave., Coconut Grove, FL 33133. © 800/433-4555 or 305/441-0000. Fax 305/441-1647. www.mayfairhousehotel.com. 179 units. Winter $289–$379 suite. Off-season $169–$379 suite. Year-round $800 penthouse. Packages available. AE, DC, DISC, MC, V. Valet parking $15; self-parking $6. **Amenities:** Restaurant, rooftop snack bar, private nightclub, outdoor pool, access to nearby health club, Jacuzzi, concierge, elaborate business center and secretarial services, 24-hour room service, dry cleaning. *In room:* A/C, TV/VCR, fax, dataport, minibar, coffeemaker, hair dryer.

Mutiny Hotel ⭐⭐   En route to the center of the Grove, docked along Sailboat Bay and marina, lies this revamped hotel best known as the hangout for the *Miami Vice* set—drug kingpins, undercover cops, and other shady characters—during the mid-80s. Now it caters to a much more legitimate clientele. Service and style are bountiful at the Mutiny, which somehow has avoided the nouveau hotel hype and managed to stand on its own quiet merits without becoming part of the scene. The newly converted condos promise to be the best-kept secret in the Grove. The suites' British Colonial motif is warmed up with soft drapes, comfortable mattresses, and regal Old English furnishings. Each suite comes with a large bathroom with shower and tub (executive and two-bedroom suites have two bathrooms), full kitchen complete with china and complimentary

coffee, and all the usual amenities associated with this class of hotel. The Mutiny is just a few blocks away from CocoWalk and the shops at Mayfair.

2951 S. Bayshore Dr., Miami, FL 33133. ℭ **888/868-8469** or 305/441-2100. Fax 305/441-2822. www.mutinyhotel.com. 120 suites. Winter $229–$799 1- and 2-bedroom suites. Off-season $179–$599 1- and 2-bedroom suites. Year-round $799–$1,799 1- and 2-bedroom penthouses. AE, DC, DISC, MC, V. Valet parking $16. **Amenities:** Restaurant, small outdoor heated pool with whirlpool spa, health club, concierge, limited room service, babysitting, laundry and dry-cleaning service. In room: A/C, TV/VCR, dataport, kitchen, coffeemaker, hair dryer.

Ritz-Carlton Coconut Grove

The third and smallest of Miami's Ritz-Carlton hotels, scheduled to open in October 2001, promises to be the most intimate of its properties, surrounded by 2 acres of tropical gardens and overlooking Biscayne Bay and the Miami skyline. Decorated as if it were a turn-of-the-19th-century mansion, the hotel's understated luxury will be a welcomed addition to an area known for its gaudiness. Expect the Ritz-Carlton standard of service and comfort.

2700 Tigertail Ave., Coconut Grove, FL 33133. ℭ **800/241-3333** or 305/648-5900. Fax 305/648-1448. www.ritzcarlton.com. 115 units. Winter $475–$750 double. Off-season $285–$550 double. AE, DC, DISC, MC, V. Valet parking. **Amenities:** 2 restaurants, cigar bar, outdoor pool, health club, concierge, business center, 24-hour room service. In room: A/C, TV, dataport, minibar, hair dryer.

Wyndham Grand Bay Hotel 🏨🏨🏨

Grand in size and stature, the Grand Bay Hotel looks like it belongs in Acapulco with its ziggurat structure and tropical landscaping, but once you see the massive bright red structure done by late Condé Nast editorial director Alexander Lieberman in the driveway, you know you're not in Mexico. Ultraluxurious, the Grand Bay is quietly elegant, and, as a result, has hosted the likes of privacy fanatics such as Michael Jackson. British singer George Michael filmed his "Careless Whisper" video here because of its sweeping views of Biscayne Bay. Rooms are superb, with views of the bay and the Coconut Grove Marina, and they're decorated in soft peach tones with a country French theme. Bathrooms are equally luxurious. Service is outstanding, and the clientele ranges from families to international jet-setters. Bice, a sublime Northern Italian restaurant, is the hotel's most popular dining option.

2669 S. Bayshore Dr. (at 27th Ave.), Coconut Grove, FL 33133. ℭ **800/327-2788** or 305/858-9600. Fax 305/858-1532. www.wyndham.com. 181 units. Winter $359–$400 suite. Off-season $279–$349 suite. Additional person $20. AE, DC, MC, V. Valet parking $16. **Amenities:** 4 restaurants, lounge serving afternoon tea, indoor heated pool and outdoor pool, 24-hour health club, Jacuzzi, sauna, concierge, business center, babysitting. In room: A/C, TV, CD player, fax, dataport, minibar, coffeemaker, hair dryer, iron, safe.

MODERATE *$109 incl paht bfast => $119 King Bed*

Hampton Inn This very standard chain hotel is a welcome reprieve in an area otherwise known for very pricey accommodations. The rooms are nothing exciting, but the freebies, like local phone calls, parking, in-room movies, breakfast buffet, and hot drinks around the clock make this a real steal. Although there is no restaurant or bar, it is close to lots of both—only about half a mile to the heart of the Grove's shopping and retail area and about as far from Coral Gables. Rooms are brand new, sparkling clean, and larger than that of a typical motel. Located at the residential end of Brickell Avenue, it's a quiet, convenient location 15 minutes from South Beach and 5 minutes from Coconut Grove. If you'd rather save your money for dining and entertainment, this is a good bet.

2800 SW 28th Terrace (at U.S. 1 and SW 27th Ave.), Coconut Grove, FL 33133. ℭ **888/287-3390** or 305/448-2800. Fax 305/442-8655. www.Hampton-inn.com. 137 units. Winter $134–$154 double. Off-season $104–$124 double. Rates include continental breakfast buffet and local calls. AE, DC, DISC, MC, V. Free parking. **Amenities:** Large outdoor pool, Jacuzzi, exercise room. In room: A/C, TV, microwave on request.

6

Miami Dining

Don't be fooled by the plethora of superlean model types you're likely to see posing throughout Miami. Contrary to popular belief, dining in this city is as much a sport as in-line skating on Ocean Drive. With over 6,000 restaurants to choose from, dining out in Miami has become a passionate pastime for locals and visitors alike. In fact, we excel when it comes to food; our star chefs have fused Californian-Asian with Caribbean and Latin elements to create a world-class flavor all its own: *Floribbean.* Think mango chutney splashed over fresh swordfish or a spicy sushi sauce served alongside Peruvian ceviche.

Formerly synonymous with early-bird specials, Miami's new-wave cuisine, 10 years in the making, now rivals that of San Francisco or even New York. Nouveau Cuban chef Douglas Rodriguez may have fled his Miami kitchen in favor of one in Manhattan, but other stellar chefs such as Mark Militello, Allen Susser, Norman van Aken, and Jonathan Eismann remain firmly planted in the city's culinary scene, fusing local ingredients into edible masterpieces. Indulging in this New World cuisine is not only high in calories, it's high in price. But if you can manage to splurge at least once, it's worth it.

Thanks to a thriving cafe society in both South Beach and Coconut Grove, you can also enjoy a moderately priced meal and linger for hours without having a waiter hover over you, waiting to "turn" your table. In Little Havana, you can chow down on a meal that serves about six for less than $10. And since seafood is plentiful, it doesn't have to cost you an arm and a leg to enjoy the appendages of a crab or lobster. Don't be put off by the looks of our recommended seafood shacks in places such as Key Biscayne—oftentimes these spots get the best and freshest catches.

Whatever you're craving, Miami's got it—with the exception of decent Chinese food and a New York–style slice of pizza. If you're craving a scene with your steak, then South Beach is the place to be. Like many cities in Europe, it is fashionable to dine late in South Beach, preferably after 9, sometimes as late as midnight. Service on South Beach is notoriously slow and arrogant, but it comes with the turf. (Of course, it is possible to find restaurants that defy the notoriety and actually pride themselves on friendly service.) On the mainland—especially in Coral Gables, and, more recently, downtown and on Brickell Avenue—you can also experience fine, creative dining without the pretense.

The biggest complaint when it comes to Miami dining isn't the haughtiness, but rather the dearth of truly moderately priced restaurants, especially in South Beach and Coral Gables. It's either really cheap or really expensive; the in-between somehow gets lost in the culinary shuffle. Quick-service diners don't really exist here as they do in other cosmopolitan areas. I've tried to cover a range of cuisines in a range of prices. But with new restaurants opening on a weekly basis, you're bound to find a savory array of dining choices on every budget.

Many restaurants keep extended hours in season (roughly December to April), and may close for lunch and/or dinner on Monday, when the traffic is slower. Always call ahead, since schedules do change. Also, always look carefully at your bill—many Miami restaurants add a 15% gratuity to your total. Feel free to adjust it if you feel your server deserves more or less. If you want to picnic on the beach or pick up some dessert, check out the gourmet food shops, green markets, and bakeries listed in chapter 8.

1 Restaurants by Cuisine

AMERICAN
Big Pink ✦ (South Beach, $, p. 125)

Biscayne Miracle Mile Cafeteria ✦ (Coral Gables, $, p. 149)

Christy's ✦✦ (Coral Gables, $$$$, p. 146)

Curry's (Miami Beach, $, p. 133)

11th Street Diner (South Beach, $, p. 125)

Forge Restaurant ✦✦✦ (Miami Beach, $$$$, p. 128)

Front Porch Café ✦ (South Beach, $, p. 126)

Gables Diner ✦ (Coral Gables, $$, p. 148)

Granny Feelgood's (Downtown, $, p. 140)

Here Comes the Sun ✦ (North Dade, $, p. 145)

Joe Allen ✦✦ (South Beach, $$, p. 122)

News Café ✦ (South Beach, $, p. 127)

News Café in the Grove ✦ (Coconut Grove, $, p. 153)

Nexxt Café ✦ (South Beach, $$, p. 124)

S&S Restaurant (Downtown, $, p. 141)

Sheldon's Drugs ✦ (Miami Beach, $, p. 134)

Shula's Steak House ✦✦ (Miami Beach, $$$, p. 131)

Soyka Restaurant & Café ✦ (Downtown, $$, p. 139)

Sundays on the Bay ✦ (Key Biscayne, $$$, p. 136)

Tobacco Road (Downtown, $, p. 141)

Wilderness Grill (South Dade, $$, p. 154)

Van Dyke Cafe ✦ (South Beach, $, p. 125)

ASIAN
Pacific Time ✦✦✦ (South Beach, $$$$, p. 117)

Spice ✦✦ (Miami Beach, $$, p. 133)

BARBECUE
Shorty's ✦(South Miami, $, p. 155)

BISTRO
Jeffrey's ✦✦ (South Beach, $$, p. 121)

CHINESE
Christine Lee's ✦✦ (North Miami Beach, $$$, p. 130)

Kon Chau ✦ (West Miami, $, 155

Red Lantern ✦ (Coconut Grove, $$, p. 152)

Tropical Chinese ✦✦ (West Miami, $$, p. 154)

COLOMBIAN
Mama Vieja ✦ (South Beach, $$, p. 132)

CONTINENTAL
Azul ✦✦✦ (Downtown, $$$$, p. 137)

Crystal Café ✦✦✦ (Miami Beach, $$$, p. 130)

Franz & Joseph's in the Grove ✦✦ (Coconut Grove, $$, p. 151)

Gordon Biersch Brewery (Downtown, $$, p. 139)

Green Street Café ✦ (Coconut Grove, $$, p. 152)

Jeffrey's ✰✰ (South Beach, $$, p. 121)

Lagoon ✰ (North Dade, $$, p. 145)

Rusty Pelican ✰ (Key Biscayne, $$$, p. 134)

CREPES

Crepe Maker Café ✰ (South Miami, $, p. 154)

CUBAN/LATIN FARE

Casa Salsa ✰ (South Beach, $$$, p. 119)

Gaucho Room ✰✰✰ (South Beach, $$$$, p. 115)

La Carreta ✰ (Little Havana, $, p. 142)

La Cibeles Café ✰ (Downtown, $, p. 140)

La Esquina de Tejas ✰✰ (Little Havana, $, p. 143)

Larios on the Beach ✰ (South Beach, $$, p. 122)

Lincoln Road Café ✰ (South Beach, $, p. 126)

Macarena ✰✰ (South Beach, $$, p. 123)

Oasis (Key Biscayne, $, p. 136)

Porcao ✰✰ (Downtown, $$$, p. 137)

Puerto Sagua ✰ (South Beach, $, p. 127)

Versailles ✰✰ (Little Havana, $, p. 143)

Yuca ✰ (South Beach, $$$$, p. 119)

DELI

Wolfie Cohen's Rascal House ✰ (Miami Beach, $$, p. 133)

DINER FARE

S&S Restaurant (Downtown, $, p. 141)

ECLECTIC

Azul ✰✰✰ (Downtown, $$$$, p. 137)

BED ✰✰ (South Beach, $$$$, p. 114)

Blue Door ✰✰ (South Beach, $$$$, p. 114)

Meza Fine Art Gallery Café ✰✰ (Coral Gables, $$, p. 149)

Poet's Café at Power Studios ✰✰ (Downtown, $, p. 141)

Tantra ✰✰✰ (South Beach, $$$$, p. 117)

Touch ✰✰ (South Beach, $$$$, p. 118)

Wish ✰✰✰ (South Beach, $$$, p. 119)

ENGLISH TEA

Tea Room ✰ (South Miami, $, p. 155)

FAST FOOD

Le Sandwicherie (South Beach, $, p. 126)

Mrs. Mendoza's Tacos al Carbon ✰ (South Beach, West Miami $, p. 126)

Pizza Rustica ✰ (South Beach, $, p. 127)

Pucci's Pizza (South Beach, $, p. 127)

San Loco Tacos ✰ (South Beach, $, p. 128)

FONDUE

Melting Pot (North Dade, $$, p. 145)

FRENCH

Brasserie Les Halles ✰✰ (Coral Gables, $$, p. 148)

Crepe Maker Cafe ✰ (South Miami, $, p. 154)

Le Bouchon du Grove ✰✰ (Coconut Grove, $$$, p. 151)

Le Festival ✰✰ (Coral Gables, $$$, p. 147)

Lemon Twist ✰✰ (Miami Beach, $$, p. 132)

L'Entrecote de Paris ✰✰ (South Beach, $$, p. 122)

Les Deux Fontaines ✰✰ (South Beach, $$, p. 123)

Provence Grill ✰✰ (Downtown, $$, p. 139)

Twelve Twenty ✰✰ (South Beach, $$$$, p. 118)

GERMAN
Daub Haus ✿ (South Beach, $, p. 126)

GREEK
Daily Bread Marketplace (Coral Gables, $, p. 149)

Greek Place (Miami Beach, $, p. 133)

HAITIAN
Tap Tap ✿ (South Beach, $$, p. 124)

HEALTH FOOD
Amos' Juice Bar (North Dade, $, p. 145)

Granny Feelgood's (Downtown, $, p. 140)

Here Comes the Sun ✿ (North Dade, $, p. 145)

Suzanne's Vegetarian Bistro ✿✿ (Downtown, $$, p. 140)

INDIAN
Anokha Fine Indian Cuisine ✿✿✿ (Coconut Grove, $$$, p. 150)

House of India ✿ (Coral Gables, $, p. 150)

INTERNATIONAL
Balan's ✿✿ (South Beach, $$, p. 120)

Cafe Tu Tu Tango ✿ (Coconut Grove, $, p. 153)

Globe (Coral Gables, $$, p. 148)

IRISH
John Martin's ✿ (Coral Gables, $$, p. 148)

ITALIAN
Bice ✿✿✿ (Coconut Grove, $$$, p. 151)

Big Fish ✿✿ (Downtown, $$, p. 138)

Cafe Prima Pasta ✿✿ (Miami Beach, $$, p. 131)

Cafe Ragazzi ✿✿ (Miami Beach, $$, p. 132)

Caffe Abbracci ✿✿ (Coral Gables, $$$, p. 147)

Carpaccio ✿ (Miami Beach, $$$, p. 130)

Coco Pazzo ✿✿ (South Miami, $$$, p. 153)

Escopazzo ✿✿✿ (South Beach, $$$$, p. 115)

Franz & Joseph's in the Grove ✿✿ (Coconut Grove, $$, p. 151)

Joia Restaurant and Bar ✿✿ (South Beach, $$$, p. 119)

Laurenzo's Cafe ✿✿ (North Dade, $, p. 146)

Macaluso's ✿✿ (South Beach, $$, p. 123)

Oggi Caffe ✿ (Miami Beach, $$, p. 132)

Osteria del Teatro ✿✿✿ (South Beach, $$$$, p. 116)

Pauloluigi's Ristorante Italiana ✿ (Coconut Grove, $$, p. 152)

Perricone's Marketplace ✿ (Downtown, $, p. 140)

Spice ✿✿ (Miami Beach, $$, p. 133)

Spiga ✿ (South Beach, $$, p. 124)

Sport Café ✿ (South Beach, $, p. 128)

Stefano's ✿ (Key Biscayne, $$$, p. 134)

Tuscan Steak ✿✿✿ (South Beach, $$$$, p. 118)

JAMAICAN
Ortanique on the Mile ✿✿ (Coral Gables, $$, p. 149)

JAPANESE
Bambu ✿ (South Beach, $$$$, p. 114)

Bond St. Lounge ✿✿ (South Beach, $$, p. 121)

Nobu (South Beach, $$$$, p. 116)

Sushi Rock Café ✿ (South Beach, $, p. 128)

Toni's New Tokyo Cuisine and Sushi Bar ✿ (South Beach, $$, p. 124)

MEDITERRANEAN
Balan's ✿✿ (South Beach, $$, p. 120)

Baleen ✿✿✿ (Coconut Grove, $$$, p. 150)

Baraboo ★★ (Miami Beach, $$$, p. 130)

Café Tabac ★ (South Beach, $$, p. 121)

Lemon Twist ★★ (Miami Beach, $$, p. 132)

Macarena ★★ (South Beach, $$, p. 123)

Mark's South Beach ★★★ (South Beach, $$$$, p. 116)

Tantra ★★★ (South Beach, $$$$, p. 117)

MEXICAN

El Rancho Grande ★★ (South Beach, $, p. 125)

El Toro Taco Family Restaurant ★★ (Homestead, $, p. 154)

Mrs. Mendoza's Tacos al Carbon ★ (South Beach, West Miami, $, p. 126)

San Loco Tacos ★ (South Beach, $, p. 128)

Señor Frogs (Coconut Grove, $$, p. 152)

NEW WORLD CUISINE

Astor Place in the Hotel Astor ★★★ (South Beach, $$$$, p. 113)

Blue Door ★★ (South Beach, $$$$, p. 114)

Chef Allen's ★★★ (North Dade, $$$$, p. 143)

Crystal Café (Miami Beach, $$$, p. 130)

Mark's South Beach ★★★ (South Beach, $$$$, p. 116)

Nemo ★★★ (South Beach, $$$, p. 120)

Norman's ★★★ (Coral Gables, $$$$, p. 146)

Ortanique on the Mile ★★ (Coral Gables, $$, p. 149)

PAN-ASIAN

Bambu ★ (South Beach, $$$$, p. 114)

China Grill ★★★ (South Beach, $$$$, p. 115)

Nemo ★★★ (South Beach, $$$, p. 120)

Pacific Time ★★★ (South Beach, $$$$, p. 117)

PIZZA

Pizza Rustica ★ (South Beach, $, p. 127)

Pucci's Pizza (South Beach, $, p. 127)

PUERTO RICAN

Casa Salsa ★ (South Beach, $$$, p. 119)

SEAFOOD

Baleen ★★★ (Coconut Grove, $$$$, p. 150)

Bayside Seafood Restaurant and Hidden Cove Bar ★ (Key Biscayne, $, p. 136)

Big Fish ★★ (Downtown, $$, p. 138)

Bubba Gump Shrimp Co. (Downtown, $$, p. 138)

East Coast Fisheries (Downtown, $$, p. 138)

Fishbone Grille ★★ (Downtown, $$, p. 139)

Grillfish ★★ (South Beach, $$, p. 121)

Jimbo's (Key Biscayne, $, p. 136)

Joe's Stone Crab Restaurant ★★ (South Beach, $$$$, p. 115)

Lagoon ★ (North Dade, $$, p. 145)

Les Deux Fontaines ★★ (South Beach, $$, p. 123)

Monty's Stone Crab/Seafood House ★ (South Beach, $$$, p. 120)

SPANISH

Cafe Tu Tu Tango ★ (Coconut Grove, $, p. 153)

Casa Juancho ★★ (Little Havana, $$, p. 141)

Gaucho Room ★★★ (South Beach, $$$$, p. 115)

Macarena ★★ (South Beach, $$, p. 123)

Puerto Sagua ★ (South Beach, $, p. 127)

STEAK

Capital Grille ★★ (Downtown, $$$, p. 137)

Christy's ★★ (Coral Gables, $$$$, p. 146)

Forge Restaurant ★★★ (Miami Beach, $$$$, p. 128)

Gaucho Room (South Beach, $$$$, p. 115)

Morton's of Chicago ★ (Downtown, North Miami Beach, $$$, p. 137)

Palm ★ (Bal Harbour, $$$, p. 131)

Shula's Steak House ★★ (Miami Beach, $$$, p. 131)

Smith & Wollensky ★ (South Beach, $$$$, p. 117)

Tuscan Steak ★★★ (South Beach, $$$, p. 118)

SUSHI

Bond St. Lounge ★★ (South Beach, $$, p. 121)

Nobu (South Beach, $$$$, p. 116)

Sushi Rock Café ★ (South Beach, $, p. 128)

Toni's New Tokyo Cuisine and Sushi Bar ★ (South Beach, $$, p. 124)

VIETNAMESE

Hy-Vong ★★ (Little Havana, $, p. 142)

Miss Saigon Bistro ★★ (Coral Gables, $, p. 150)

2 South Beach

The renaissance of South Beach has spawned dozens of first-rate restaurants. In fact, big-name restaurants from across the country have capitalized on South Beach's international appeal and opened, and continue to open, branches here with great success. A few old standbys remain from the *Miami Vice* days, but the flock of newcomers dominates the scene, with places going in and out of style as quickly as the tides. The listings below represent the restaurants that have (or should have) quickly gained national attention.

The Lincoln Road area is packed with places offering good food and great atmosphere. Since it's impossible to list them all, I recommend strolling and browsing. Most restaurants post a copy of their menu outside, and staff members are happy to chat with curious passersby.

With very few exceptions, the places on Ocean Drive are crowded with tourists and priced accordingly. You'll do better to venture a little farther into the pedestrian-friendly streets just west of Ocean Drive.

VERY EXPENSIVE

Astor Place ★★★ NEW WORLD CUISINE   Caribbean cowboy chef Johnny Vinczenz has returned Astor Place to its original chic-chuck-wagon glory, whipping his chef's lasso into an epicurean frenzy with signature dishes straight from the American-Caribbean heartland: wild mushroom pancake short stack with balsamic syrup, sautéed local yellowtail snapper, and wasabi skillet-seared tuna steak. Portions are huge and often enough for two to share. Appetizers are also generous in size, popular among the many lightweight model types who frequent the place. Desserts are glorious; chocoholics will be in heaven with the Cuarto de Chocolates featuring flourless chocolate cake, a chocolate dome, and peanut-butter chocolate bars. Sunday's Gospel Brunch is the ideal way to pay penance for your sins of the night before, but beware: The live gospel music is LOUD! Comfortable booths and soothing lighting give way to a scene that's reminiscent of a Hollywood movie premiere. Beware of whiplash-inducing situations, especially on weekend nights. Sitting in the booth next to you at any time could be Cameron Diaz, Oliver Stone or Neve Campbell, among other luminaries for whom the food is comfort enough against the scene-sucking gawkers.

In the Hotel Astor, 956 Washington Ave., South Beach. 𝄞 305/672-7217. Reservations recommended. Main courses $27–$36. AE, MC, V. Mon–Sat 7:30–11am and 11:30am–2:30pm; Sun–Thurs 7–11pm, Fri–Sat 7pm–midnight; Sunday Gospel Brunch noon–2:30pm.

Bambu ✸ PAN-ASIAN   Not just another Asian-inspired haute eatery and sushi palace, this restaurant is better known as the "Cameron Diaz restaurant," because the Hollywood "it" girl owns a share in the place. Though its ownership is infinitely more stellar than the cuisine, the restaurant's bamboo floors and woven raffia drapes create a Zen-like setting that has become a haven to the who's who of Hollywood.

The food here is overpriced and not always edible, with dishes that sound more exotic than they taste: ginger-marinated seared *hamachi* (Japanese onion, shiso leaves, and seaweed salad); dim sum with lobster, Asian mushrooms, pork, and scallops with *Haora* sauce; and noodle dishes such as grilled salmon and cellophane noodles accented with chiles, ginger, cilantro, and black beans. There's also a full sushi bar offering sometimes fresh sashimi, tartares, and yakitori skewers. The best thing about this place besides its clientele and upstairs VIP lounge are the saketinis—martinis made with sake and cucumber. Don't even try to tip the hostess if you forgot to call ahead; you won't get in without a reservation.

1661 Meridian Ave., South Beach. 𝄞 305/531-4800. Reservations required. Main courses $22–$38. AE, MC, V. Daily 7pm–midnight.

BED ✸✸ ECLECTIC   BED—that's Beverage. Entertainment. Dining—is one of the most innovative dining lounges to land in South Beach in a very long time. When you walk inside, you'll feel as if you've entered a Buddhist temple. An array of inviting mosquito-netted beds awaits diners. You'll rest your head against soft cushiony pillows. A deejay spins Euro mood music and some techno. You'll have no problem appreciating the taste and aroma of the exquisite (and exquisitely priced) cuisine, featuring dishes such as Asian spice–crusted yellowtail snapper with scallop noodles and shiitake sauce. For dessert, try a little Pillow Talk—Grand Marnier crème anglaise with meringue pillows—or take a Roll in the Hay—a tropical fruit crêpe with coconut haystacks. Beware of crumbs in the sheets, as they aren't always changed between customers, and for the agoraphobic, do not go to BED on a weekend night—it's a nightmare.

929 Washington Ave., South Beach. 𝄞 305/532-9070. Fax 305/532-7757. Reservations required. Main courses $29–$37. AE, DC, MC, V. Wed–Sun: first lay (no actual seats) 8:30pm; second lay 10:30pm. Reservations only accepted on the day you plan to dine there. Lounge 11pm–3am.

Blue Door ✸✸ ECLECTIC/NEW WORLD   It used to be that the Blue Door's greatest claim to fame was that Madonna was part owner. The food was unremarkable, but the eye candy was sickly sweet. When the maternal girl fled, so did others, leaving the Blue Door wide open for anything as long as it was as fabulous as the hotel in which it sits. The most recent incarnation of the restaurant begs for superlatives more flattering than the standard "fabulous." The eye candy is still here, but now you have good reason to focus your eyes on the food rather than who's eating it. Thanks to award-winning chef Claude Troisgros (rhymes with foie gras)—a star in his own right—the menu frowns upon the ubiquitous fusion moniker in favor of a more classic French approach to tropical spices and ingredients. Ragout of Maine lobster in coconut milk broth; sea bass with brown butter, cashews, and roasted hearts of palm; and ravioli stuffed with taro root mousseline are just a few of the Blue Door's tempting offerings.

South Beach Dining

To Central Miami Beach ↑

The Bass Museum of Art

COLLINS PARK

22nd St.

Dade Boulevard

20th St.

19th St.

Miami Beach Convention Center

18th St.

Jackie Gleason Theater of Performing Arts

17th St.

Lincoln Road Mall

16th St.

15th St.

Española Way

14th St.

Miami Beach Post Office

13th St.

12th St.

FLAMINGO PARK

11th St.

10th St.

9th St.

Beach Patrol Station

Art Deco Welcome Center

8th St.

7th St.

6th St.

5th St.

4th St.

3rd St.

2nd St.

1st St.

Commerce St.

Biscayne St.

ATLANTIC OCEAN

LUMMUS PARK

SOUTH POINTE PARK

Government Cut

Venetian Causeway

BELLE ISLAND

Purdy Ave.

West Ave.

Bay Rd.

Alton Rd.

Lincoln Rd.

Lenox Ave.

Michigan Ave.

Jefferson Ave.

Meridian Ave.

Pennsylvania Ave.

Washington Ave.

Collins Ave.

Ocean Dr.

James Ave.

Collins Ave.

Dade Boulevard

Astor Place **33**
Balan's **13**
Bambu **5**
BED **34**
Big Pink **49**
Blue Door **6**
Bond St. Lounge **1**
Café Tabac **50**
Casa Salsa **47**
China Grill **46**
Dab Haus **39**
El Rancho Grande **15**
11th Street Diner **31**
Escopazzo **24**
Front Porch Café **20**
Gaucho Room **16**
Grillfish **17**
Jeffrey's **14**
Joe Allen **3**
Joe's Stone Crab
    Restaurant **53**
Joia Restaurant & Bar **52**
Larios on the Beach **35**
Le Sandwicherie **22**
Les Deux Fontaines **28**
L'entrecote de Paris **45**
Lincoln Road Café **12**
Macaluso's **4**
Macarena **23**
Mark's South Beach **30**
Monty's Stone Crab/
    Seafood House **48**
Mrs. Mendoza's
    Tacos al Carbon **32**
Nemo **51**
News Café **38**
Nexxt Café **8**
Nobu *(opening 2001)* **2**
Osteria del Teatro **18**
Pacific Time **9**
Pizza Rustica **36**
Pucci's Pizza **42**
Puerto Sagua **40**

San Loco Tacos **21**
Smith & Wollensky **54**
Spiga **27**
Sport Café **41**
Sushi Rock Café **25**
Tantra **19**
Tap Tap **43**
Toni's **26**
Touch **11**
Tuscan Steak **44**
Twelve Twenty **29**
Van Dyke Cafe **10**
Wish **37**
Yuca **7**

Service can be snippy, but the food makes up for what the restaurant lacks in hospitality.

In the Delano Hotel, 1685 Collins Ave., South Beach. © **305/674-6400.** Reservations recommended for dinner. Main courses $19–$34. AE, DC, MC, V. Daily 7am–1am.

China Grill ✦✦✦ PAN-ASIAN　Unless your surname is Pacino, DeNiro, or Winfrey (you get the idea), you might find yourself digging a hungry hole to China Grill at the gauche hour of 6pm or the ungodly, indigestion-inducing hour of midnight. But with an incomparable albeit dizzying array of amply portioned dishes such as the outrageous crispy spinach, wasabi mashed potatoes, seared rare tuna in spicy Japanese pepper, broccoli rabe dumplings, lobster pancakes, and a sinfully delicious dessert sampler complete with sparklers, this hub of South Beach flash is well worth the wait. In fact, the wait is part of the China Grill experience. A coveted spot at the bar is headquarters for many of Miami's movers and shakers who come solely for the frenetic scene. On weekend nights, there's barely room to breathe. Keep in mind that China Grill is a family-style restaurant and that dishes are meant to be shared.

404 Washington Ave., South Beach © **305/534-2211.** Reservations strongly recommended. Main courses $15–$25. AE, DC, M, V. Mon–Thurs 11:45am–midnight, Fri 11:45am–1am, Sat 6pm–1am, Sun 6pm–midnight.

Escopazzo ✦✦✦ ITALIAN　Escopazzo means "crazy" in Italian, but the only sign of insanity in this primo Northern Italian eatery is the fact that it only seats 70. The wine bottles have it better—the restaurant's cellar holds 1,000 bottles of various vintages. Should you be so lucky to score a table at this romantic local favorite, you'll have trouble deciding between dishes that will have you swearing off the Olive Garden with your first bite. Among these, pappardelle with wild game and mushroom ragout, swordfish carpaccio, and braised leg of lamb with juniper berries, rosemary, and fennel. Eating here is like dining with a big Italian family—service is excellent and nobody's happy until you are blissfully full.

1311 Washington Ave., South Beach. © **305/674-9450.** Reservations required. Main courses $18–$28. AE, MC, V. Mon, Tues, and Thurs 6pm–midnight, Fri–Sat 6pm–1am, Sun 6–11pm.

Gaucho Room ✦✦✦ STEAK　This restaurant will set you back *mucho dinero*, but it is one of the best steak houses in the city. The Gaucho Room is a hip Argentinean dining room that serves prime aged meats with unparalleled service. Argentine rib eye is marinated in garlic, herbs, and olive oil before being grilled and served on butcher blocks. *Warning:* Those with lighter palates should probably request light seasoning on their food.

In the Loews Hotel, 1601 Collins Ave. (St. Moritz Bldg.), South Beach. © **305/604-5290.** Reservations recommended. Main courses $22–$52. AE, MC, V. Daily 7pm–1am.

Joe's Stone Crab Restaurant ✦✦ SEAFOOD　Unless you grease the palms of one of the stone-faced maitre d's with some stone-cold cash, you'll be waiting for those famous claws for up to 2 hours—if not more. As much a Miami landmark as the beaches themselves, Joe's is a microcosm of the city, attracting everyone from T-shirted locals to a bejeweled Ivana Trump. Whatever you wear, however, will be eclipsed by a kitschy, unglamorous plastic bib that your waiter will tie on you unless you say otherwise. Open only during stone-crab season (October through May), Joe's reels in the crowds with the freshest, meatiest stone crabs and their essential accoutrements: creamed spinach and excellent sweet potato fries. Start with a salad—your basic head of lettuce dressed with the requisite Joe's vinaigrette (a delicious combo of oil, spices, and hearts of palm)—and a basket of fresh onion rolls. Then come the claws: medium, large, or jumbo. Some say size doesn't matter; others swear by the jumbo (and more expensive) ones. Whatever you choose, pair them with a savory mustard sauce (a perfect mix of mayo and mustard) or hot butter. Not feeling crabby? The fried chicken and liver and onions on the regular menu are actually considered by many as far superior—they're definitely far cheaper—to the crabs. Oh yeah, and save room for dessert. The Key lime pie here is the best in town. If you don't feel like waiting, try Joe's Take Away, which is located next door to the restaurant— it's a lot quicker and just as tasty.

11 Washington Ave. (at Biscayne St., just south of 1st St.), South Beach. ℭ 305/673-0365, or 305/673-4611 for takeout. www.joesstonecrab.com. Reservations not accepted. Market price varies but averages $62.95 for a serving of jumbo crab claws, $38.95 for large claws. AE, DC, DISC, MC, V. Daily 11:30am–2:30pm; Mon–Thurs 5–10pm, Fri–Sat 5–11pm, Sun 4:45–10pm. Open mid-Oct to mid-May.

Mark's South Beach ⭐⭐⭐ NEW WORLD/MEDITERRANEAN Named after owner and chef Mark Militello, this is one of the best restaurants in all of Miami. A cozy, contemporary restaurant nestled in the basement of the quietly chic Hotel Nash, Mark's New World and Mediterranean-influenced menu changes nightly. What doesn't change is the consistency and freshness of the restaurant's exquisite cuisine. The roast garlic stuffed tenderloin of beef with polenta and a ragout of root vegetables is exceptional and worth every bit of cholesterol it may have. Cornmeal-dusted black grouper wrapped in Serrano ham and zucchini is in a school of its own. Desserts, including an impressive cheese cart, are outrageous, especially the pistachio cake with chocolate sorbet. Unlike many South Beach eating establishments, the knowledgeable servers are here because of their experience in the restaurant—not modeling—business.

In the Hotel Nash, 1120 Collins Ave., South Beach. ℭ 305/604-9050. Reservations recommended. Main courses $18–$38. AE, DC, DISC, MC, V. Daily 6–11pm.

Nobu SUSHI Despite the fact that at press time Nobu wasn't even open yet, the sushi palace, owned by star chef Nobuyuki Matsuhisa, was already taking reservations. The raw facts: Nobu has been hailed as one of the best sushi restaurants in the world, with always packed eateries in New York, London, and Los Angeles. The Omakase, or Chef's Choice—a multicourse menu entirely up to the chef for $70 per person and up—gets consistent raves. And although you won't wait long for your food to be cooked, you will wait forever to score a table here.

At the Shore Club Hotel, 1901 Collins Ave., South Beach. ℭ 305/695-3100. Reservations required. Main courses $10–$70. AE, MC, V. Daily 6pm–1am.

Osteria del Teatro ⭐⭐⭐ ITALIAN Located in an unassuming storefront beneath the ultrasceney crobar nightclub, it's hard to believe that Osteria del Teatro is the best Italian bistro on the beach. What it might be lacking in decor is certainly not absent in the elaborate cuisine. Regulars who swear by this place won't even bother looking at the menu; instead they concentrate on the enormous changing list of specials on the blackboard. You will definitely be faced with some tough choices: plump chicken breast sautéed with shallots and sun-dried tomatoes in champagne cream sauce; seafood baked with linguine, garlic, fresh tomatoes, and olive oil in parchment paper; or homemade ravioli stuffed with scallops and crab in lobster sauce. The regulars here are on a first-name basis with the waiters, who always seem to know what you're in the mood for.

1443 Washington Ave. (at Española Way), South Beach. ℭ 305/538-7850. Reservations recommended. Main courses $13–$34. AE, DC, MC, V. Mon–Sat 6pm–midnight. Closed Sept.

Pacific Time ⭐⭐⭐ PAN-ASIAN Chef and co-owner (and former model) Jonathan Eismann was awarded the Robert Mondavi Award for Culinary

Excellence in June 1994, and his restaurant, Pacific Time, has been recognized by *Bon Appétit* and *Esquire* magazines as one of America's "Best New Restaurants." Eismann's dishes are stunning hybrids of Chinese, Japanese, Korean, Vietnamese, Korean, Mongolian, and Indonesian flavors. One of the best dishes is the Mongolian lamb salad, which has a lightly sweet, earthy taste with a crunchy kick of onion. For a main course, the ever-changing menu offers many locally caught fish specialties such as Szechuan grilled local grouper served on a bed of shredded shallots and ginger with a sweet sake-infused sauce and tempura-dunked sweet potato slivers on the side. The famous chocolate bomb is every bit as decadent as they say, with hot bittersweet chocolate bursting from the cupcake-like center. The wine list is quite extensive and includes red and white wines from Italy, France, the Napa Valley, Australia, Argentina, New Zealand, and South Africa.

915 Lincoln Rd. (between Jefferson and Michigan aves.), South Beach. © **305/534-5979**. Reservations recommended. Main courses $20–$32. AE, DC, MC, V. Sun–Thurs 6–11pm, Fri–Sat 6pm–midnight.

Smith & Wollensky ☆ STEAK   This pricey New York import is a decent steak house better appreciated for its waterfront setting than its average steaks. Taking the concept of comfort food to an entirely new level, Smith & Wollensky is located in a most soothing setting with spectacular views of the Intercoastal Waterway that leads to the Port of Miami. The menu is basic, almost austere, with a few chicken and fish choices and beef served about a dozen ways. The classic is the sirloin, seared lightly and served naked. The veal chop is of Flintstonian proportion. Mediocre side dishes such as asparagus, baked potato, onion rings, creamed spinach, and hash browns are sold a la carte. Service is erratic, from highly professional to rudely aloof. Desserts are decent, but not worth the calories. You'll find much tastier steaks (at comparable prices) at the Forge or Tuscan Steak; for a less-expensive yet no less-delicious steak, check out nearby L'Entrecote de Paris. What Smith & Wollensky's got on them, however, is its fantastic waterfront location.

1 Washington Ave. (in South Pointe Park), South Beach. © **305/673-2800**. www.smithandwollensky.com. Reservations recommended. Main courses $20–$35; lobster $38. AE, DC, DISC, MC, V. Mon–Sat noon–2 am; Sunday brunch 11:30am–3pm.

Tantra ☆☆☆ ECLECTIC   Marrakesh meets Miami Beach in this truly original, outrageously priced exotic outpost devoted to the ancient Indian tantric philosophy of tempting the senses with all things pleasurable. Begin with your surroundings: a sultry interior of soft grass (yes, it's real; they resod weekly) and starry lights overhead. In the front room by the bar, there are low-lying couches and pillow-lined booths bolstered by drapes that can be closed for privacy. Belly dancers mix with cocktail waitresses singing the praises of Tantra's special aphrodisiac cocktails and offering you a puff of Turkish tobacco from the communal hookah pipe (they insist it's clean, but I'd be wary). A private VIP room off to the side features a hammock and a peaceful spiritual soundtrack.

Tantra serves a combination of Middle Eastern, Mediterranean, and Indian dishes that really are divine. Consider the Tantra Love Apple: a ripe tomato layered with Laura Chenel goat cheese and basil oil, garnished with pomegranate seeds; or perhaps Nine Jewel Indian Spiced Rack of Lamb. The $52 filet mignon is delicious, but its price tag borders on obscene.

Don't come to Tantra looking for a serene vibe to match the setting and menu. Tantra practically turns into a nightclub after dinner, attracting a crowd of celebrities and scenesters.

1445 Pennsylvania Ave. (at Española Way), South Beach. © **305/672-4765**. Reservations required. Main courses $26–$46. AE, DC, DISC, MC, V. Daily 7pm–1am. Late-night menu 1am to closing.

Jugglers, dancers and an assortment of acrobats fill the street.

She shoots you a wide-eyed look as a seven-foot cartoon character approaches.

What brought you here was wanting the kids

to see something magical while they still believed in magic.

America Online Keyword: Travel

With 700 airlines, 50,000 hotels and over 5,000 cruise and vaca-

tion getaways, you can now go places you've always dreamed of.

Travelocity.com
A S a b r e C o m p a n y
Go Virtually Anywhere.

"WORLD'S LEADING TRAVEL WEB SITE, 5 YEARS IN A ROW" WORLD TRAVEL AWARDS

I HAVE TO CALL THE TRAVEL AGENCY AGAIN. DARN, OUT TO LUNCH. NOW I HAVE TO CALL THE AIRLINE. I HATE CALLING THE AIRLINES. I GOT PUT ON HOLD AGAIN. "INSTRUMENTAL TOP-40" ... LOVELY. I HATE GETTING PUT ON HOLD. TICKET PRICES ARE ALL OVER THE MAP. HOW DO I DIAL INTERNATIONALLY? OH SHOOT, FORGOT THE RENTAL CAR. I'M STILL ON HOLD. THIS MUSIC IS GIVING ME A HEADACHE. I WONDER IF SOMEONE ELSE HAS CHEAPER FLIGHTS. FORGET IT, CAN'T TAKE IT ANYMORE ... I'M HANGING UP.

YAHOO! TRAVEL
100% MUZAK-FREE

Booking your trip online at Yahoo! Travel is simple. You compare the best prices. You click. You go have fun. Tickets, hotels, rental cars, cruises & more. Sorry, no muzak.

YAHOO!®
Travel
travel.yahoo.com

Touch ★★ ECLECTIC   Despite the presence of the ubiquitous velvet ropes out front and the loud soundtrack inside, Touch is not a nightclub. Located on busy Lincoln Road, Touch works harder to be something of a tropical supper club, complete with faux palm trees.

The food is a mod Southwestern, with dishes as dolled up as the restaurant's interior. Specialties include delicious red curry–crusted ahi mignon; pan-seared filet served with pear vegetable sauté, wasabi mashed potatoes, and candied ginger; and "Stoned in Florida," an appetizer of cracked Florida stone crab claws served on toasted walnut black rye bread with black-cherry marmalade and mango mustard. For dessert, the Menage a Mousse—layers of dark milk and white chocolate mousse accented with praline crisp—is outrageously good. Despite the air of haughtiness you may receive out front at the ropes, service is actually quite good. If the noise inside is too loud, and it often is, request a table outside, ensconced safely behind the ropes where you can watch the passersby try to put their fingers on what, exactly, Touch portends to be.

910 Lincoln Rd., South Beach. ✆ 305/532-8003. Reservations required. Main courses $25–$39. AE, DC, MC, V. Sun–Thurs 6pm–midnight, Fri–Sat 6pm–1am.

Tuscan Steak ★★★ ITALIAN/STEAK   This excellent Northern Italian restaurant, a member of the China Grill scion, is all about meat served Italian style, in large family-style portions. With a rich wood interior, the atmosphere is reminiscent of the dining room of a well-connected *family*—ornate and very loud. The house salad is a massive undertaking of the classic antipasto, filled with shredded slices of salami and pepperoni, chunks of mozzarella, and a delicate vinaigrette. Everything here is a la carte, so be sure to order the sautéed spinach with garlic and the onion mashed potatoes with whichever steak you choose. All steaks are big enough for at least three people to share. The house specialty is a delicious T-bone steak served with pungent garlic puree. On any given weekend night, reservations are secondary to being friends with the ultra-tanned host, so expect a long wait for a table. The bar is the only place to wait if you can find a spot there, and drinks are rather pricey. The background music is straight out of Studio 54 and so is the flashy crowd. Despite the long waits, after one meal here, you'll likely want to kiss the ring of the true boss of this culinary mob scene—the chef.

433 Washington Ave., South Beach. ✆ 305/534-2233. Reservations strongly recommended on weekends. Main courses $20–$65. Family-style meals are $50 per person, including appetizer and main course. AE, DISC, MC, V. Sun–Thurs 6pm–midnight, Fri–Sat 6pm–1am.

Twelve Twenty ★★★ FRENCH   Prepare to shell out a pretty penny for the very French, very haute cuisine that rolls out of this kitchen in the high and mighty Tides Hotel. The air of elegance (perhaps pickled by the scent of money) mixes with the fragrances of dishes such as the parsley risotto with fried asparagus and steamed sea bass over seaweed. Comfortable booths line the interior of the exclusive restaurant, strategically placed wide open in the hotel's minimalist lobby. Unlike the oft-harried atmospheres of other South Beach eateries, where scene serves as an aperitif, there really is no scene here other than a trickle of hotel guests who pass through the lobby from time to time. Despite its exposure, Twelve Twenty does offer a fair share of privacy. Conversations are audible even at a whisper, earning the restaurant its well-deserved status as a good place for a power dinner, which is a good thing if you can expense the meal. Portions are small and prices are big.

In the Tides Hotel, 1220 Ocean Dr., South Beach. ✆ 305/604-5130. Reservations recommended. Main courses $17–$26. AE, MC, V. Daily 7–11pm.

Wish ✸✸✸ ECLECTIC   Wish got its start as a haute vegetarian restaurant, located in the stylish Todd Oldham–designed The Hotel. It was, and still is, a terrific setting (request an outside table in the serene, umbrellaed courtyard), but the foodies couldn't bear a meal without meat. Culinary whiz Andrea Curto came on board and redirected the menu, which now features an international fusion of ingredients including imported meats, poultry, and seafood. Two of Wish's finest are pan-seared scallops with blackened corn, pecans, purple Thai sticky rice, and adzuki-bean puree; and orange buerre blanc and spicy-seared yellowfin tuna with chive potato napoleon, roasted Japanese eggplant, Chinese long bean, and soy wasabi vinaigrette.

In The Hotel, 801 Collins Ave., South Beach. ✆ **305/531-2222.** Reservations recommended. Main courses $16–$32. AE, DC, DISC, MC, V. Daily 6–10:30pm.

Yuca ✸ CUBAN   While the name, which stands for Young Upscale Cuban Americans, is correctly pronounced "*Yoo*-ka," it really should be called as it looks: "*Yuck-a.*" Overpriced with a rude staff to boot, Yuca has been hailed as Miami's premier nouveau cubano restaurant, and it was—when Douglas Rodriguez was helming the galley. When Rodriguez left, I think he took all the good stuff with him to New York's lauded Patria restaurant, but folks still flock here. The food is little more than greasy concoctions of Cuban food masking itself as nouveau under heavy beds of sauces and other foreign substances. What Yuca is good for, however, is live Latin entertainment in the upstairs lounge. There's a two-drink minimum—a small price compared to the cost of the food.

501 Lincoln Rd. (corner of Drexel), South Beach. ✆ **305/532-9822.** Reservations recommended. Main courses $22–$40. AE, DC, DISC, MC, V. Mon–Sat noon–11pm, Sun noon–10pm.

EXPENSIVE

Casa Salsa ✸ PUERTO RICAN   Superstar Ricky Martin can now list restaurateur next to heartthrob on his expanding resume. Casa Salsa pays homage to Martin's Puerto Rican culture, serving up authentic *criollo* food such as the restaurant's most popular dish, *mofongo en pilon,* green plantain dough filled with your choice of pork chunks, chicken, shrimp, or lobster, or *arroz con gandules* (rice and peas). The food's pretty good, albeit overpriced, but not nearly as popular as you'd expect for a celebrity-owned restaurant. However, should you indulge in one of the many varieties of Puerto Rican rum, you'll have a fine time.

524 Ocean Dr., South Beach. ✆ **305/604-5959.** Reservations recommended. Main courses $16–$29. AE, MC, V. Daily noon–4pm; Sun–Thurs 6–11pm, Fri–Sat 6pm–1am.

Joia Restaurant and Bar ✸✸ ITALIAN   Owned by Miami nightlife diva Ingrid Casares, famous for her friendship with Madonna, Joia exudes a cozy atmosphere of self-conscious camaraderie, with a few tables indoors and several outdoors in a large courtyard. On any given night you're bound to see celebrities such as Ben Stiller, Donald Trump, Rupert Everett, and, yes, Madonna. Without harping on the service too much (it's quite leisurely), the pasta here is among the freshest anywhere on the beach. The chef is a native Italian and he takes great pride in crafting the perfect pasta no matter who's eating it. There is a laundry list of appetizers, salads, and pastas in every conceivable shape, from penne to farfalle. Recommended dishes include the *rigatoni al funghi,* a mushroom-lover's delight, with large tube pasta filled with shiitake and porcini mushrooms; the *gnocchi di zucca,* homemade potato and pumpkin dumplings in a tomato or cheese sauce; and the *bauletti di pollo al funghi,* a folded chicken breast stuffed with Fontina cheese, mushrooms, and sage. The wine list is exquisite; there are Italian whites and robust reds from Italy, France, and California that run from $25 to $150. If you're not up for a lengthy meal here, grab a seat at the bar and witness what could only be described as a taste of *La Dolce Vita*, South Beach style. As in any club of the moment, Joia also has a private VIP room in the back, where we hear the service is a bit quicker.

140 Ocean Dr., South Beach. © **305/674-8855.** Reservations recommended. Main courses $12–$30. AE, DC, DISC, MC, V. Daily noon–4pm; Sun–Thurs 6pm–midnight, Fri–Sat 6pm–1am.

Monty's Stone Crab/Seafood House ✿ SEAFOOD   This restaurant is the antithesis of South Beach trendiness with scrappy wood floors and a very casual raw bar set outside around a large swimming pool. The best deal in town is still the all-you-can-eat stone crabs—about $40 for the large ones and $35 for the mediums. That's about the same price that Joe's, located 2 blocks away, charges for just three or four claws. (But don't order stone crabs in summer—they aren't as fresh.) Enjoy the incredible views and off-season fish specialties, including the Maryland she-crab soup, rich and creamy without too much thickener. Beware of Friday nights, when the happy-hour crowds convene around (and sometimes in) the pool for post-work revelry.

300 Alton Rd., South Beach. © **305/673-3444.** Reservations recommended. Main courses $20–$40. AE, DC, MC, V. Sun–Thurs 5:30–11pm; Fri–Sat 5:30pm–midnight.

Nemo ✿✿✿ PAN-ASIAN   What Wolfgang Puck is to foodies on the West Coast, Nemo's chef, Michael Schwartz, is to Miami. Hailing from Puck's lauded Chinois in L.A., Schwartz's Pan-Asian cuisine is masterful. Located on the quickly developing South Beach area known as SoFi (for "south of Fifth Street"), Nemo is a funky, high-style eatery with an open kitchen and an outdoor court-yard canopied by trees and lined with an eclectic mix of model types, foodies, and Schwartz groupies. Among the reasons to eat in this restaurant whose name is actually "omen" spelled backward: wok-charred salmon with roasted pumpkin seeds, crispy prawns with salsa, and an inspired dessert menu by Hedy Gold-smith that's not for the faint of calories. Seating inside is comfy cozy, but bor-ders on cramped. On Sunday mornings, the open kitchen is converted into a buffet counter for the restaurant's unparalleled brunch. Coveted tables outside surround the serene courtyard, and, most recently, the pool at the adjacent Mer-cury Hotel. Be prepared for a wait, which tends to spill out onto the street.

100 Collins Ave., South Beach. © **305/532-4550.** Reservations recommended. Main courses $22–$36; Sun brunch $26. AE, MC, V. Mon–Fri noon–3pm and 7pm–midnight, Sun 11am–3pm and 6–11pm. Valet parking $10.

MODERATE

Balan's ✿✿ MEDITERRANEAN   Balan's provides undeniable evidence that the Brits actually do know a thing or two about cuisine. A direct import from London's hip Soho area, Balan's draws inspiration from various Mediter-ranean and Asian influences, labeling its cuisine "Mediterrasian." With a brightly colored interior straight out of a mod '60s flick, Balan's is a local favorite among the gay and arty crowds. The moderately priced food is rather good here—especially the sweet-potato soufflé with leeks and roasted garlic, fried goat cheese, and portobello mushrooms, and the Chilean sea bass with roasted tomato. Adding to the ambience is the restaurant's people-watching vantage point on Lincoln Road.

1022 Lincoln Rd. (between Lenox and Michigan), South Beach. © **305/534-9191.** Reservations not accepted. Main courses $6–$16. AE, DISC, MC, V. Daily 8am–midnight.

Bond St. Lounge ✿✿ SUSHI   A New York City import, the sceney Bond St. Lounge is located in the basement of the shabby chic Townhouse Hotel and is packing in hipsters as tightly as the crab meat in a California Roll. Despite its tiny size, Bond St. Lounge's superfresh nigiri and sashimi, and funky sushi rolls such as the sun-dried tomato and avocado or the arugula crispy potato, are worth cramming in for. As the evening progresses, however, Bond St. becomes more of a bar scene than a restaurant, but sushi is always available at the bar to accompany your sake Bloody Mary.

Townhouse Hotel, 150 20th St., South Beach. © 305/534-3800. Reservations not accepted. Sushi $6–$12. AE, MC, V. Daily 6pm–2am.

Café Tabac ⭐ MEDITERRANEAN   Here's another Miami eatery where the scene is more appetizing than the food. Live deejays spin a mix of sounds guaranteed to put diners in the mood for a lively evening. The Mediterranean menu is rather ordinary with some moderately priced chicken and fresh fish dishes. In the tasty sandwich department, a Eurofavorite is the *pan bagnot* (tuna, onion, tomato, anchovies, eggs, lettuce, olives, and dressing), or, if you're not counting calories, the *croque monsieur* (grilled ham and cheese sandwich) is also good. Appetizers range from soup du jour to steamed stuffed mussels. But the real reason this place is always smokin' is not coming from the kitchen, but, rather, the packed tables of the in-crowd.

136 Collins Ave., South Beach. © 305/695-8411. Reservations highly recommended. Main courses $7–$14. AE, DC, MC, V. Daily 11am–2am.

Grillfish ⭐⭐ SEAFOOD   From the beautiful Byzantine–style mural and the gleaming oak bar, you'd think you were eating in a much more expensive restaurant, but Grillfish manages to pay the exorbitant South Beach rent with the help of a loyal local following who come for fresh, simple seafood in a relaxed but upscale atmosphere.

The servers are friendly and know the menu well. The barroom seafood chowder is full of chunks of shellfish, as well as some fresh white fish fillets in a tomato broth. The small ear of corn, included with each entree, is about as close as you'll get to any type of vegetable offering besides the pedestrian salad. Still, at these prices, it's worth a visit to try some local fare including mako shark, swordfish, tuna, marlin, and wahoo. At press time, Grillfish was preparing to dive into a meaty venture right next door, at Grillsteak (1438 Collins Ave., same hours, credit cards, price range, and reservation policy). The early buzz has Grillsteak getting along with Grillfish swimmingly. A second Grillfish location is at 2325 Galliano St., Coral Gables (© 305/445-6411).

1444 Collins Ave. (corner of Española Way), South Beach. © 305/538-9908. www.grillfish.com. Reservations for 6 or more only. Main courses $9–$16. AE, DC, DISC, MC, V. Daily 6 pm–midnight.

Jeffrey's ⭐⭐ *Finds* CONTINENTAL/BISTRO   Some say this is the most romantic restaurant on the beach; South Beach's gay crowd certainly seems to agree. Old-fashioned lace curtains and candlelight are a welcome respite from the glitz and chrome of the rest of the island. Most people don't even realize this restaurant exists. But don't think that means there are empty tables. Jeffrey's certainly has its fair share of regulars.

You can choose a succulent three-quarter-pound burger or try a hearty chicken breast marinated in balsamic sauce and served with freshly mashed sweet potatoes over spinach, on white lace tablecloths. Some of the better seafood options include the conch fritters and the meaty crab cakes. Most desserts are tasty, but the homemade tarte tatin, a caramelly deep-dish apple tart, is delicious.

1629 Michigan Ave. (half block south of Lincoln Rd.), South Beach. © 305/673-0690. Reservations highly recommended. Main courses $12–$24. AE, DC, MC, V. Tues–Sat 6–11pm, Sun 5–10pm. Closed Sept.

Joe Allen 🎭🎭 *Finds* AMERICAN   It's hard to compete in a city with haute spots everywhere you look, but Joe Allen, a restaurant that has proven itself in both New York and London, has stood up to the challenge by establishing itself off the beaten path in possibly the only area of South Beach that has managed to remain impervious to trendiness and overdevelopment. Located on the bay side of the beach, Joe Allen is nestled in an unassuming building conspicuously devoid of excess neon lights, valet parkers, and fashionable pedestrians. Inside, however, one discovers a hidden jewel: a stark yet elegant interior and no-nonsense, fairly priced, ample-portioned dishes such as meat loaf, pizza, fresh fish, and salads. The scene has a homey feel flavored by locals looking to escape the hype without compromising quality.

1787 Purdy Ave. (3 blocks west of Alton Rd.), South Beach. ℂ **305/531-7007**. Reservations recommended, especially on weekends. Main courses $13–$24. MC, V. Mon–Fri 11:30am–11:45pm.

Larios on the Beach 🎭 CUBAN   If you're a fan of singer Gloria Estefan, you will definitely want to check out this restaurant, which she and her husband Emilio co-own; if not, you may want to reconsider, as the place is an absolute mob scene, especially on weekends. The classic Cuban dishes get a so-so rating from the Cubans, but a better one from those who aren't as well versed in the cuisine. The portions here are larger than life, as are some of the restaurant's patrons, who come here for the sidewalk scenery and the well-prepared black beans and rice. Inside, the restaurant turns into a makeshift salsa club, with music blaring over the animated conversations and the sounds of English clashing with Spanish. Because of its locale on Ocean Drive, Larios is a great place to bring someone who's never experienced the Cuban culture or tasted its cuisine.

820 Ocean Dr., South Beach. ℂ **305/532-9577**. Reservations recommended. Main courses $8–$24. AE, MC, V. Sun–Thurs 11:30am–midnight, Fri–Sat 11:30am–2am.

L'Entrecote de Paris 🎭🎭 FRENCH   New York's got the Statue of Liberty and Miami's got L'Entrecote de Paris. We don't complain. Everything in this little piece of Paris, a classy little bistro, is simple. For dinner, you choose between salmon or steak, and beyond a few salads, that's it—but both are great. The salmon looks like spa cuisine, served with a pile of bald steamed potatoes and a salad with simple greens and an unmatchable vinaigrette. The steak, on the other hand, is the stuff cravings are made of, even if you're not a die-hard carnivore. Its salty sharp sauce is rich but not thick, and full of the beef's natural flavor. The slices are served on top of your own little hibachi, which also keeps the accompanying fries warm.

Most diners are very Euro and pack a petit attitude. Servers, however, are superquick and professional, and almost friendly in a French kind of way, making up for the close quarters. The short and very French wine list includes several well-priced bottles for under $20. I loved the *profiteroles au chocolat,* a perfect puff pastry filled with vanilla ice cream and topped with a dark bittersweet chocolate sauce.

413 Washington Ave., South Beach. ℂ **305/673-1002**. Reservations recommended on weekends. Fixed-price dinner $14–$21. DC, MC, V. Tues–Sat 6pm–1am.

Les Deux Fontaines 🎭🎭 SEAFOOD   Les Deux Fontaines successfully sets an example for many South Beach eateries with superb service, fresh seafood (10 different kinds of local fish), and an ambience that transports you to a chic, far-off French countryside. Attached to the elegant Hotel Ocean, Les Deux Fontaines features an expansive courtyard, which contains the two fountains for which the place is named, and is lined with tables and wicker chairs straight out of the Left Bank. On any given day or night, live music adds to the charm. Inside, it's a bona fide French bistro, awash in soothing hues and alive with the scents of seafood dishes prepared any way you'd like. The crowd here ranges from tourists to locals looking to escape the fray of Ocean Drive. In addition to romantic evening dinners, Sunday brunches are extremely popular.

1230 Ocean Dr., South Beach. ℂ 305/672-7878. Reservations recommended. Main courses $10–$20. AE, DC, MC, V. Daily 7:30am–midnight.

Macaluso's ⋒⋒ ITALIAN   At this star-studded spot, it's all about Frank (as in Sinatra), but don't be surprised to hear the groovy sounds of Lauryn Hill or Barry White as you munch on a wonderful pizza pie (perfect for two people or as appetizers for four to six). Catch the fantastic clam pie when in season—the portions are huge. Pricier items vary throughout the season, but will likely feature fresh fish handpicked by Chef Michael. Everyone will recommend perennial favorites such as the rigatoni and broccoli rabe. There are delicious desserts that range from homemade anisette cookies to Patricia Scott's pastries. The wine list is also good. The George Duboeuf Beaujolais at $22 a bottle is a steal, when you consider it comes nicely chilled with slices of luscious Georgia peaches, which make a great and affordable dessert by themselves.

1747 Alton Rd., Miami Beach. ℂ 305/604-1811. Main courses $9–$23; pizza $9–$11. AE, MC, V. Tues–Sat noon–3pm and 6pm–midnight, Sun 6–11pm. After 10:30pm only pies are served.

Macarena ⋒⋒ SPANISH/MEDITERRANEAN   This Macarena has long outlived its passé line-dance namesake and is rather hip, actually, looked after by a young crew of Spanish imports whose families own several popular restaurants in Madrid. Show up before 10pm and you're sure to get a table. After that time, especially on weekends, it's standing room only. The gorgeous Euro crowd shows up for foot-stomping flamenco (every Wednesday, Friday, and Saturday—call for show times) and an outrageous selection of tapas, as well as Miami's very best paella (order a large portion and share it among at least four people). The garlic shrimp are tasty and aromatic, and the yellow squash stuffed with seafood and cheese is especially delicious. Really, all the seafood, such as mussels in marinara sauce and clams in green sauce, is worth sampling. With such reasonable prices, you can taste lots of dishes and leave satisfied. Try some of the terrific sangria made with slices of fresh fruit and a subtle tinge of sweet soda. Sidewalk seating is available on busy Washington Avenue, but the action is more entertaining inside.

1334 Washington Ave., South Beach. ℂ 305/531-3440. Reservations recommended on weekends. Main courses $12–$20; tapas $5–$9. AE, DC, MC, V. Daily 7pm–midnight.

Nexxt Café ⋒ AMERICAN   Locals joke that this lively, always packed outdoor cafe should be called Nexxt Year to reflect the awfully slow service that has become its unfortunate trademark. Service aside, Nexxt has made quite a splash on South Beach, attracting an evening crowd looking for nighttime revelry and a morning crowd on the weekends for a standing-room-only brunch sensation. The fresh food comes in lavish portions that could easily feed two; the salads are an especially good bargain. Start your meal with the calamari fritti—they're a lot fresher here than at most other local restaurants—or the popcorn shrimp, which are larger than you might expect. The burgers and sandwiches are similarly big, and the steaks are well worth a taste. They have coffees in tall, grande, and "maxxi." There are also plenty of coffee cocktails, mixed drinks, frozen beverages, and wines, giving this place a nice bar life too.

700 Lincoln Rd. (off Euclid Ave.), South Beach. ℂ 305/532-6643. Reservations accepted (no shows will be charged $15 per seat). Main courses $12–$23. AE, MC, V. Daily 9am–1am.

Spiga ✹✹ ITALIAN   This intimate Italian restaurant is cool without being pretentious, concentrating on the food rather than the fanfare that has become central to so many South Beach eateries. Like the hotel in which it resides, Spiga's atmosphere is wonderfully low-key, making it a quiet favorite with locals and some luminaries. The complimentary bruschetta with grilled eggplant, served to you at one of the few tables inside or out, is the first of many culinary treats. The garlicky gnocchi with tomato and basil is an incredible illustration of how simple doesn't have to mean bland. The pungent Gorgonzola polenta appetizer is a meal in itself, and the risotto with bay scallops is a rousing display of culinary precision. The place is vaguely reminiscent of a Florentine trattoria, and if you stop to listen, you'll notice the prevailing language here is, in fact, Italian.

Hotel Impala, 1228 Collins Ave., South Beach. ✆ **305/534-0079.** Reservations accepted. $7–$15 main courses. AE, DC, MC, V. Daily 6pm–midnight.

Tap Tap ✹ HAITIAN   The whole place looks like an overgrown tap tap, a brightly painted jitney common in Haiti. Every inch is painted in vibrant neon hues (blue, pink, purple, and so on) and the atmosphere is always fun. It's where the Haiti-philes and Haitians, from journalists to politicians, hang out.

The *lanbi nan citron*, a tart, marinated conch salad, is perfect with a tall tropical drink and maybe some lightly grilled goat tidbits, which are served in a savory brown sauce and are less stringy than a typical goat dish. Another supersatisfying choice is the pumpkin soup, a rich brick-colored puree of subtly seasoned pumpkin with a dash of pepper. An excellent salad of avocado, mango, and watercress is a great finish. Soda junkies should definitely try the watermelon soda. For the ethnophobic, there's a rather tasty vegetable stew, but I strongly recommend the goat—it tastes just like chicken.

819 5th St. (between Jefferson and Meridian aves., next to the Shell Station), South Beach. ✆ **305/ 672-2898.** Reservations accepted. Main courses $9–$16. AE, MC, V. Sun–Thurs 6pm–midnight, Fri–Sat 6pm–2am. Closed Aug.

Toni's New Tokyo Cuisine and Sushi Bar SUSHI/JAPANESE   One of Washington Avenue's first tenants, Toni's has quizzically withstood the test of time on fickle South Beach. The quality of the food here is erratic. One night, the sushi could be really fresh, but the next night you could discover a piece of plastic, as I did, in your California Roll. The atmosphere is comfortable and even allows for quiet conversation—a rarity in this neighborhood, but you will pay for that privilege. Toni's is overpriced, overrated, and not the best place to indulge your sushi cravings.

1208 Washington Ave., South Beach. ✆ **305/673-9368.** Reservations recommended. Main courses $13–$25; rolls $3.50–$10.50. AE, MC, V. Daily 6pm–midnight, Fri–Sat 6pm–1am.

Van Dyke Cafe ✹ AMERICAN   The younger, jazzier sibling of Ocean Drive's News Café, the Van Dyke is similar in spirit and cuisine but different in attitude. Unlike the much scenier and much more touristy News Café, Van Dyke is a locals' favorite, at which people watching is also premium, but attitude is practically nonexistent. Both cafes have nearly the same menu, with decent salads, sandwiches, and omelets, but the Van Dyke's warm wood-floored interior, upstairs jazz bar, accessible parking, and intense chocolate soufflé make it a less taxing alternative. Also, unlike News, Van Dyke turns into a sizzling nightspot, featuring live jazz nearly every night of the week (a $5 cover charge is added to your bill if you sit at a table; the bar's free). Outside there's a vast tree-lined seating area.

846 Lincoln Rd., South Beach. ✆ **305/534-3600.** Reservations recommended for evenings. Main courses $8–$17. AE, DC, MC, V. Sun–Thurs 8am–1am, Fri–Sat 8am–3am.

MODERATE/INEXPENSIVE

Big Pink ✵ AMERICAN   Real Food for Real People is the motto to which this restaurant strictly adheres. Located on what used to be a gritty corner of Collins Avenue, Big Pink—owned by the folks at the higher-end Nemo—is quickly identified by a whimsical Pippi Longstocking–type mascot, whose picture is largely displayed on a sign outside. Scooters and motorcycles line the streets surrounding the place, which is a favorite among beach bums, club kids, and those craving Big Pink's comforting and hugely portioned pizzas, sandwiches, salads, and hamburgers. The fare is above average at best, and the menu is massive, but it comes with a good dose of kitsch, such as their "gourmet" spin on the classic TV dinner, which is done perfectly, right down to the compartmentalized dessert. Televisions line the bar area and family-style table arrangement (there are several booths, too) promotes camaraderie among diners. Outdoor tables are also available.

157 Collins Ave., Miami Beach. ℭ 305/532-4700. Main courses $7–$12. AE, DC, MC, V. Sun–Thurs 9am–1am, Fri–Sat 9am–2am.

11th Street Diner AMERICAN   Like many of Miami's residents, this retro-diner is a transplant from the Northeast. Uprooted from its 1948 Wilkes Barre, Pennsylvania, foundation, the actual structure was dismantled and rebuilt on a bustling corner of Washington Avenue. It's a popular round-the-clock spot that attracts a friendly yet motley crew of locals, club kids, and curious tourists and is well known for its slow service and greasy diner fare. Come in for breakfast and you'll find bleary-eyed patrons chowing down after a night of partying.

1065 Washington Ave., South Beach. ℭ 305/534-6373. Items $5–$7. AE, MC, V. Tues 8am–1am; Wed–Mon 24 hours.

El Rancho Grande ✵✵ MEXICAN   Hidden just off Lincoln Road, El Rancho Grande was once a well-kept secret among devout Mexican food fanatics. It's not such a secret anymore. With a relatively restrained decor (clay pots, sponge-painted yellow walls), El Rancho Grande doesn't hold anything back when it comes to the cuisine. The Aztec Soup, a hot and spicy blend of chicken and tortilla strips, is some of the best I've had. Fresh, spicy salsa and expertly prepared, hugely portioned enchiladas, burritos, and fajitas are sensational. The scene is young and lively without being too rowdy. Margaritas are a little weak when frozen, and better ordered on the rocks. Expect a wait at the small bar for your table, especially on weekends. Limited outdoor seating is available.

1626 Pennsylvania Ave., Miami Beach. ℭ 305/673-0480. Items $8–$12. AE, DC, MC, V. Daily 11am–11pm.

Front Porch Café ✵ AMERICAN   Located in an unassuming, rather dreary looking Art Deco hotel, the Front Porch Café is a relaxed local hangout known for cheap breakfasts. While some of the wait staff might be a bit sluggish (many are bartenders or club kids by night), it seems that nobody here is in a rush. If you are, this is *not* the place for you. Enjoy home-style French toast with bananas and walnuts, omelets, fresh fruit salads, pizzas, and classic breakfast pancakes that put IHOP to shame. Front Porch Café is also known for its daily dose of local gossip, which flows as freely as the syrup.

In the Penguin Hotel, 1418 Ocean Dr., South Beach. ℭ 305/531-8300. Main courses $5[nd$11. AE, DC, DISC, MC, V. Daily 8:30am–10:30pm.

INEXPENSIVE

Daub Haus ✵ GERMAN   This lively, often rowdy, German ale house/restaurant turned out good German fare. The honey-garlic Brie appetizer melted over hot French bread is irresistible and very pungent. A mug of one of the many Germany beers available here is the perfect accompaniment to the house specialties, which include veal bratwurst, *knodel mit pilzsauce* (bread dumplings served with a mushroom-wine sauce), and the ubiquitously wiener schnitzel. Capped off with a dessert of apple strudel or crepes, a meal here is like taking a trip to Germany, minus the jet lag.

852 Alton Rd., South Beach. ℂ305/534-9557. $6–$9 main courses. Mon–Thurs 4–11pm; Fri–Sat 4pm–midnight; Sun 4–11pm. MC, V.

Le Sandwicherie SANDWICHES   You can get mustard, mayo, or oil and vinegar on sandwiches elsewhere in town, but you'd be missing out on all the local flavor. This gourmet sandwich bar, open until the crack of dawn, caters to ravenous club kids, biker-types, and the body artists who work in the tattoo parlor next door. For many people, in fact, no night of clubbing is complete without capping it off with a turkey sub from Le Sandwicherie.

229 14th St. (behind the Amoco station), South Beach. ℂ 305/532-8934. Sandwiches and salads $5–$10. No credit cards. Daily 9:30am–5am. Delivery 9:30am–10pm.

Lincoln Road Café ⟨Value CUBAN   A local favorite, this down-to-earth Cuban-accented cafe is very popular for its cheap breakfasts. For $5, you can indulge in a hearty portion of eggs any style, with bacon, ham, sausage, Cuban toast, and coffee. Lunch and dinner specials are delicious and very cheap as well; try the ubiquitous black beans and rice or a chicken fricassee with plantains. The few tables inside are usually passed up in favor of the several outdoors, but in the evenings the house is full inside and out, as talented Latin musicians perform out front.

941 Lincoln Rd., South Beach. ℂ 305/538-8066. Items $5–$10. AE, DC, MC, V. Daily 8am–midnight.

Mrs. Mendoza's Tacos al Carbon ⟨ MEXICAN   Somehow this place manages to make Mexican food seem healthy with its flavorful, marinated charbroiled meats and fresh vegetarian selections. In addition to bountiful burritos, Mrs. Mendoza's is known for fabulous salsas, from mild to five-alarm spicy. Whereas San Loco Tacos (see below) is known for its clubby crowd, the atmospherically lacking Mrs. Mendoza's is better known for a low-frills clientele who know and want great Mexican food—not a scene. There's another location at 9739 NW 41st St. (the Doral Plaza) in West Miami (ℂ 305/477-5119).

1040 Alton Rd., South Beach. ℂ 305/535-0808. Main courses $3–$5. No credit cards. Mon–Sat 11am–10pm, Sun noon–10pm.

News Café ⟨ AMERICAN   In the late '80s, South Beach pioneer Mark Soyka opened this cafe on a depressed, decrepit Ocean Drive, sparking what some now call the South Beach renaissance. The thriving News has become part of Miami history and it still draws locals onto what has become the most tourist-ridden street in the area. Whether you come by foot, blade, Harley, or Ferrari, you should wait for an outside table, which is where you need to be to fully appreciate the experience. Service is notoriously slow and often arrogant (perhaps because the tip is included), but the menu, while not newsworthy, has some fairly good items, such as the Middle Eastern platter of hummus, tahini, tabouli, and grape leaves; hamburgers; and omelets. If it's not too busy, you can enjoy a leisurely cappuccino outside; creative types like to bring their laptops and sit here all day. There's also an extensive collection of national and international newspapers and magazines at the in-house newsstand.

800 Ocean Dr., South Beach. ℂ 305/538-6397. Items $5–$10. AE, DC, MC, V. Open 24 hours.

Pizza Rustica ⍟ PIZZA   Italians often scoff at the way Americans have mangled their recipe for pizza. But at Pizza Rustica, even the Italians marvel at these thin-crusted gourmet meals. This is the real deal—no thick, doughy, greasy concoctions here. Instead, Rustica features several delicious, huge slices of gourmet, authentically Tuscan-style pizza. Spinach and Gorgonzola cheese blend harmoniously with a brush of olive oil and garlic on a slate of the delicious, crispy dough. There's also a four-cheese, arugula, and rosemary potato slice, among others.

863 Washington Ave., South Beach. ℂ 305/674-8244. Slice $4. No credit cards. Daily 11am–4am.

Pucci's Pizza PIZZA   Pucci's was the parlor of choice for a New York–style slice long before Washington Avenue became the victim of a pizza parlor influx (there are at least 10 within 5 blocks). While no one will go on the record, rumor has it that Pucci's imports New York water to make sure the dough is authentic. Slices are slinging until the wee hours, and for the weight conscious, there's even a low-fat version.

651 Washington Ave., South Beach. ℂ 305/673-8117. About $2 slice, $12 pie. No credit cards. Daily 11am–midnight.

Puerto Sagua ⍟ CUBAN/SPANISH   This brown-walled diner is one of the only old holdouts on South Beach. Its steady stream of regulars ranges from *abuelitos* (little old grandfathers) to hipsters who stop in after clubbing. It has endured because the food is good, if a little greasy. Some of the less heavy dishes are a superchunky fish soup with pieces of whole flaky grouper, chicken and seafood paella, or marinated kingfish. Also good are most of the shrimp dishes, especially the shrimp in garlic sauce, which is served with white rice and salad.

This is one of the most reasonably priced places left on the beach for simple, hearty fare. Don't be intimidated by the hunched, older waiters in their white button shirts and black pants. Even if you don't speak Spanish, they're usually willing to do charades. Anyway, the extensive menu, which ranges from BLTs to grilled lobsters to yummy fried plantains, is translated into English. Hurry, before another boutique goes up in its place.

700 Collins Ave., South Beach. ℂ 305/673-1115. Main courses $8–$24; sandwiches and salads $5–$10. AE, DC, MC, V. Daily 7:30am–2am.

San Loco Tacos ⍟ MEXICAN   There are no talking Chihuahuas to promote this excellent fast-food Mexican joint, but word of human mouth seems to do the trick. The food is served quickly, with no frills attached, but it's done very well. The guacamole is very fresh, and the tacos, burritos, enchiladas, and a host of other Mexican munchies are zesty, not skimpy, and really cheap. Salsa is not watered down or prepackaged and comes in mild, medium, or hot. There are a few tables inside, but most people prefer to pick up their chow and take it out with them.

235 14th St., South Beach. ℂ 305/538-3009. Items $3–$7. No credit cards. Sun–Thurs 11am–5am, Fri–Sat 11am–6am.

Sport Café ⍟ ITALIAN   When Sport Café first opened, way back when South Beach was still a fledgling in the trendoid business, it had a plain interior, wooden chairs, and a view of the parking lot. Televisions inside were tuned to soccer matches at all times—hence the name. The key to Sport's success was, and still is, its good, cheap, homemade Italian food—nothing fancy. Only now the cafe has moved up the block to a large corner space complete with private outdoor garden. The restaurant might have moved on to better digs, but one thing remains the same: The food is still great and the soccer matches continue to kick the crowd into a European-style frenzy. Try the nightly specials, especially when the owners' mother is cooking her secret lasagna.

560 Washington Ave., South Beach. ℭ **305/674-9700.** Reservations accepted for 4 or more. Main courses $8–$14; sandwiches and pizzas $6–$9. AE, MC, V. Daily noon–1am.

Sushi Rock Café ⋆ SUSHI   Perhaps it has something to do with its campy name, but for some reason almost every rock star that comes to town makes a requisite stop here for a sushi fix. Aerosmith's Joe Perry and Steven Tyler ate here almost every night during their Miami-based recording sessions, and David Lee Roth has been spotted here more than once. Sushi Rock is known for a sporadically fresh assortment of sushi, hand rolls, and traditional Japanese cuisine, funky atmosphere, and hip late-night crowds.

1351 Collins Ave. (at 14th St.), South Beach. ℭ **305/532-2133.** Items $5–$15. AE, DC, MC, V. Mon–Thurs noon–midnight, Fri–Sat noon–1am, Sun noon–11pm.

3 Miami Beach: Surfside, Bal Harbour & Sunny Isles

The area north of the Art Deco District—from about 21st Street to 163rd Street—had its heyday in the 1950s when huge hotels and gambling halls blocked the view of the ocean. Now, many of the old hotels have been converted into condos or budget lodgings and the bay-front mansions have been renovated by and for wealthy entrepreneurs, families, and speculators. The area has many more residents, albeit seasonal, than visitors. On the culinary front, the result is a handful of superexpensive, traditional restaurants and a number of value-oriented spots.

VERY EXPENSIVE

Forge Restaurant ⋆⋆⋆ STEAK/AMERICAN   English oak paneling and Tiffany glass suggest high prices and haute cuisine, and that's exactly what you get at the Forge. Each elegant dining room possesses its own character and features high ceilings, ornate chandeliers, and European artwork. The atmosphere is elegant but not too stuffy. On Wednesday night, however, it's pandemonium as the who's who of Miami society gather for dinner, dancing, and schmoozing.

Like the rest of the menu, appetizers are mostly classics, from Beluga caviar to baked onion soup to shrimp cocktail and escargot. When they're in season, order the stone crabs. For the main course, any of the seafood, chicken, or veal dishes are recommendable, but the Forge is especially know for its award-winning steaks. It's wine selection is equally lauded—ask for a tour of the cellar.

432 Arthur Godfrey Rd. (41st St.), Miami Beach. ℭ **305/538-8533.** Reservations required. Main courses $21–$55. AE, DC, MC, V. Sun–Thurs 6pm–midnight, Fri–Sat 6pm–1am.

EXPENSIVE

Baraboo ⋆⋆ MEDITERRANEAN   Baraboo, a crowded eatery in up-and-coming North Beach, is named for the small Wisconsin town that served as the original winter quarters of the Ringling Brothers Circus. Strolling mimes and magicians work the room, entertaining—or harassing, at times—diners who are indulging in the Mediterranean fare. Though not necessarily a theme restaurant, if they took away the clowning around, Baraboo could be a serious restaurant, featuring excellent ravioli with spinach, ricotta, and egg yolk; potato-crusted sea bass with saffron-sage sauce; and roasted muscovy duck breast. If you prefer to remain outside the big top, there are several outdoor tables that will protect you from a wayward mime or magician.

7300 Ocean Terrace (at 73rd St. and Collins Ave.), North Beach. ℭ **305/867-4242.** Reservations recommended, required on weekends. Main courses $9.50–$22. AE, MC, V. Tues–Sun 11:30am–1am.

Carpaccio 🕊 ITALIAN   A favored spot for the ladies who lunch, Carpaccio's location in the ritzy Bal Harbour Shops is its tastiest aspect. It's definitely a place to see and be seen. Ask for specials rather than ordering off the regular menu—they're much more interesting—linguine lobster, snapper picatta, and veal chop any style—though they may be a bit pricier. Wear sunglasses to block the blinding glare of all the diamonds.

9700 Collins Ave. (97th St., in Bal Harbour Shops), Bal Harbour. ℂ **305/867-7777.** Reservations recommended. Main courses $15–$25; pastas $12–$15. AE, MC, V. Daily 11:30am–11pm.

Christine Lee's 🕊🕊 CHINESE   This Cantonese restaurant is a 35-year-old Miami staple that serves excellent but overpriced Chinese steak, shrimp and lobster sauce, and steak kew. Considering the dearth of good Chinese restaurants in Miami, this is a good choice if you absolutely *must* satisfy your cravings for Chinese, but it will definitely cost you more than it should.

17082 Collins Ave. ℂ **305/947-1717.** Reservations recommended. Main courses $6.95–$29. AE, DISC, MC, V. Daily 4–11pm; winter lunch 11am–3pm.

Crystal Café 🕊🕊🕊 CONTINENTAL/NEW WORLD   The setting is sparse, with a bottle of wine and Lucite salt and pepper grinders and as the only centerpiece on each of the 15 or so tables. I promise you won't need the seasoning. Chef Klime has done it all with the help of his affable wife and a superb wait staff. Enjoy his unique sparkle at this little-known hideaway, which attracts stars like Julio Iglesias and other in-the-know gourmands.

With approximately 30 entrees, including a few nightly specials, each is beautifully presented and perfectly prepared. The shrimp cake appetizer, for example, is the size of a bread plate and rests on top of a small mound of lightly sautéed watercress and mushrooms. Surrounding the delicately breaded disc are concentric circles of beautiful sauces. The veal Marsala is served in a luscious brown sauce thickened not with heavy cream or flour but with delicate vegetable broth and a hearty mix of mushrooms. Most main courses come with a choice of three side dishes, such as zucchini, carrots, mashed potatoes, or pasta. The osso buco is a masterpiece.

726 41st St., Miami Beach. ℂ **305/673-8266.** Reservations recommended on weekends. Main courses $11–$25. AE, DC, DISC, MC, V. Tues–Thurs 5–10pm, Fri–Sat 5–11pm.

Palm 🕊 STEAK   As sturdy as the tree that shares its name, the Palm is one of the country's most heralded steak houses, known for its Jurassic portions and no-nonsense service. Everything here is a la carte, and the prices add up quicker than the cholesterol courses through your veins. Both fish and meat are praiseworthy; the blackened swordfish steak is as hearty and massive as the filet mignon. Prime rib and New York strip are full of flavor as well, and cooked to perfection. To complicate matters further, the veal and lamb chops are absolutely divine. For those who like a little surf with their turf, the lobsters here are truly freaks of nature, weighing in at 4 pounds and up. The food is prepared simply, but needs no enhancement. Sharing is encouraged unless you're a linebacker, and even they've been known to split a steak. Side dishes include salads, potatoes, and vegetables; be sure to try the superb creamed spinach.

9650 E. Bay Harbor Dr., Bay Harbor Island (From Collins Ave., turn west onto 96th St.; at Bal Harbour Shops, go over a small bridge, and turn right onto East Bay Harbor Dr. The restaurant is half a block down on the left.). ℂ **305/868-7256.** Reservations highly recommended. Main courses $18–$29. AE, DC, MC, V. Daily 5–11pm.

Shula's Steak House 🕊🕊 AMERICAN/STEAK   Climb a sweeping staircase in the Alexander All-Suite Luxury Hotel and go through the glass hallway—

Miami Beach Dining

Baraboo **10**
Cafe Prima Pasta **13**
Cafe Ragazzi **5**
Carpaccio **4**
Christine Lee's **1**
Crystal Café **17**
Curry's **9**
The Forge Restaurant **16**
The Greek Place **6**
Here Comes the Sun **2**
Lemon Twist **11**
Mama Vieja **18**
Miami Beach Place **12**
Oggi Caffe **14**
The Palm **3**
Sheldon's Drugs **7**
Shula's Steak House **15**
Spice **8**
Wolfie Cohen's
  Rascal House **1**

designed like an atrium, so exotic flora and fauna beckon both within and without—and you'll find yourself in this magnificent restaurant that has been acclaimed as one of the greatest steak houses in all of North America. If you're feeling adventurous, try the 48-ounce club (you can get your name engraved on a gold plaque if you can finish this absolutely *huge* piece of meat) or settle for the 20-ounce Kansas City strip or the 12-ounce filet mignon. Fresh seafood abounds when in season, and the oysters Rockefeller are a particularly good choice. The entertaining staff is very knowledgeable, and there's a sizable and reasonably priced wine list. The restaurant also has the "No Name Lounge," where live piano music, premium spirits, and cigar smoking are available.

There's another branch of Shula's at 7601 NW 154th St. (in Don Shula's Golf Club off the Palmetto Expressway; ℂ 305/820-8102) in West Dade.

In the Alexander Hotel, 5225 Collins Ave., Miami Beach. ℂ 305/341-6565. Reservations recommended. Main courses $18–$58. AE, DISC, MC, V. Daily 11am–3:30pm and 6–11pm. Free valet parking.

MODERATE

Cafe Prima Pasta ⟨ℛℛ⟩ ITALIAN   Proving that good things do come in small packages, this tiny corner cafe's home cooking draws nightly hordes of carbo-craving diners who don't seem to mind waiting for a table for upward of an hour, maybe more on weekends. The scent of garlic wafting into the street is guaranteed to kill any vampire, and it makes the wait for a table a bit more torturous. Other choice ingredients include the ripest, freshest tomatoes, the finest olive oil, mozzarella that melts in your mouth, and fish that puts some seafood restaurants to shame. The spicy garlic and oil dip that comes with the bread is hard to resist and will likely linger with you for days, like the memory of this fine meal. Though tables are packed in a bit, the atmosphere still manages to be romantic.

414 71st St. (half a block east of the Byron movie theater), Miami Beach. ℂ 305/867-0106. Reservations not accepted. Main courses $9–$17; pastas $7–$9. No credit cards. Mon–Thurs noon–midnight, Fri noon–1am, Sat 1pm–1am, Sun 5pm–midnight.

Cafe Ragazzi ⟨ℛℛ⟩ ITALIAN   This diminutive Italian cafe, with its rustic decor and a swift, knowledgeable wait staff, enjoys great success for its tasty simple pastas. The spicy puttanesca sauce with a subtle hint of fish is perfectly prepared. Also recommended is the salmon with radicchio. You can choose from many decent salads and carpacci, too. Lunch specials are a real steal at $7, including soup, salad, and daily pasta. Unlike Cafe Prima Pasta, Cafe Ragazzi is light on sceniness—people come here for the food only. Expect to wait on weekend nights.

9500 Harding Ave. (on corner of 95th St.), Surfside. ℂ 305/866-4495. Reservations accepted for 4 or more. Main courses $9–$18. MC, V. Mon–Fri 11:30am–3pm and 5:30–11pm, Sat–Sun 5:30–11pm.

Lemon Twist ⟨ℛℛ⟩ MEDITERRANEAN   In addition to great Mediterranean fare, there is a twist to this place in the form of a complimentary shot of the eponymous house spirit (a lemon vodka shot). But that comes after your meal. To start, you will receive a bowl of perfectly marinated olives, which can endanger your appetite, so go easy on them. A soothing, mellow interior makes for a romantic dining experience, or, if you prefer, outdoor tables are available (though the street is hardly as scenic). In between, expect friendly service and excellent meat and pasta dishes at terrific prices. Specialties such as spinach lasagna with smoked salmon and shank of lamb caramelized with whole garlic are savored by a savvy crowd that has likely escaped South Beach for this refreshing change of scenery.

908 71st St. (on 79th St. Causeway), Miami Beach/Normandy Isle. © **305/868-2075.** Reservations recommended on weekends. Main courses $9–$18. AE, MC, V ($25 minimum). Tues–Sun 5:30pm–midnight. Closed July 4 weekend.

Mama Vieja ⋒ COLOMBIAN   This funky Colombian hangout looks like a total dive from the outside, but once inside you will want to dive right in to the supremely fresh national specialties such as *pargo rojo estofado a la mama vieja* (red snapper stuffed with a supercreamy and delicate seafood sauce in a rice base). Brightly painted walls and elevated porches look out onto a large-screen TV showing music videos from the old country. The walls and ceilings are decorated with hundreds of hats that have been donated by customers and signed in exchange for a free meal. Bring in an interesting hat and mention it to the server before placing your order so that he or she can bring you to the attention of the owner. All the dishes here are worth trying and are so reasonably priced that it's easy to order a lot. Try to save room for the milky sweet desserts and a good strong coffee—you'll need it if you want to dance it off after at Lola, the very popular, unpretentious hot spot next door.

235 23rd St. (just west of Collins Ave.), South Beach. © **305/538-2400.** Main courses $4.95–$14.95. AE, DC, DISC, MC, V. Daily noon–midnight.

Oggi Caffe ⋒ ITALIAN   Tucked away in a tiny strip mall on the 79th Street Causeway, this neighborhood favorite makes fresh pastas daily. Each one, from the agnolotti stuffed with fresh spinach and ricotta to the wire-thin spaghettini, is tender and tasty. A hearty *pasta e fagiola* is filled with beans and vegetables and could almost be a meal. I also recommend the daily soups, especially the creamy spinach soup when it's on the menu. Though you could fill up on the starters, the entrees, especially the grilled dishes, are superb.

> **You Should Have Such Luck**
>
> Since 1954, over 6.7 million stuffed cabbages, 750,000 chickens, and 26.5 million pickles have been consumed by over 100 million diners at the Rascal House.

The salmon is served on a bed of spinach with a light lemon-butter sauce. The place is small and a bit rushed, but it's worth the slight discomfort for this authentic, moderately priced food.

1740 79th St. Causeway (in the White Star shopping center next to the Bagel Cafe), North Bay Village. © **305/866-1238.** Reservations recommended. Main courses $14–$25; pastas $9–$13. AE, DC, MC, V. Mon–Fri 11:30am–2:30pm; daily 6–11pm.

Spice ⋒⋒ ITALIAN/ASIAN   The owners of Café Prima Pasta decided that their excellent Italian fare needed a little Asian spice, so they opened this interesting restaurant to prove that the Italian-Asian combination does not have to be washed down with a Pepto-Bismol cocktail. (Actually, the menu's split down the middle, so you won't find mu shu lasagna or anything like that.) Though the Italian dishes on the menu are better—the seafood linguine is top-notch—the Asian items, such as the duck with soba noodles, aren't too shabby, either. And while the food here is quite good, even better is the restaurant's loungy atmosphere, which often features live music.

928 71st St., North Beach. © **305/861-6707.** Reservations recommended. Main courses $8–$15. AE, DC, MC, V. Fri–Sat 7pm–5am, Sun–Thurs. 7pm–2am.

Wolfie Cohen's Rascal House ⋒ DELI   Open since 1954 and still going strong, this historic, nostalgic culinary extravaganza is one of Miami Beach's greatest traditions. Scooch into one of the ancient vinyl booths—which have hosted many a notorious bottom, from Frank Sinatra to mob boss Sam Giancana—and review the huge menu that's loaded with authentic Jewish staples. Consider the classic corned beef sandwich, stuffed cabbage, brisket, or potato pancakes. If you're lucky, the waitress will give you a wax-paper doggy bag to wrap up the leftover rolls and danish from your breadbasket.

17190 Collins Ave., Sunny Isles. © **305/947-4581.** Main courses $8–$30. AE, MC, V. Daily 24 hours.

INEXPENSIVE

Curry's AMERICAN   Established in 1937, this large dining room on the ocean side of Collins Avenue is one of Miami Beach's oldest, and kitschiest, restaurants. Neither the restaurant's name nor the tacky Polynesian wall decorations are indicative of its offerings, which are straightforwardly American and reminiscent of the area's heyday. Broiled and fried fish dishes are available, but the best selections, including steak, chicken, and ribs, come off the open charcoal grill perched by the front window. Prices are incredibly reasonable here, and include an appetizer, soup, or salad, as well as a potato or vegetable, dessert, and coffee or tea.

7433 Collins Ave., Miami Beach. © **305/866-1571.** Reservations accepted. Main courses (including appetizer and dessert) $9–$20. MC, V. Daily 4–10pm.

Greek Place GREEK   This little hole-in-the-wall diner with sparkling white walls and about 10 wooden stools serves fantastic Greek and American diner-style food. Daily specials like *pastitsio,* chicken *alcyone,* and roast turkey with all the fixings are big lunchtime draws for locals working in the area. Typical Greek dishes like shish kebab, souvlaki, and gyro are cooked to perfection as you wait. Even the hamburger, prime ground beef delicately spiced and freshly grilled, is wonderful.

233 95th St. (between Collins and Harding aves.), Surfside. © **305/866-9628.** Main courses $6–$7. No credit cards. Mon–Fri 10am–5:30pm, Sat 11am–3pm.

Sheldon's Drugs ⊛ AMERICAN   This typical old-fashioned drugstore counter was a favorite breakfast spot of Isaac Bashevis Singer. Consider stopping into this historic site for a good piece of pie and a side of history. According to legend, the author was sitting at Sheldon's eating a bagel and eggs when his wife got the call in 1978 that he had won the Nobel Prize for Literature. The menu hasn't changed much since then. You can get eggs and oatmeal and a good tuna melt. A blue-plate special might be generic spaghetti and meatballs or grilled frankfurters. The food is pretty basic, but you can't beat the prices.

9501 Harding Ave., Surfside. © **305/866-6251.** Main courses $4–$8; soups and sandwiches $2–$5. AE, DISC, MC, V. Mon–Sat 7am–9pm, Sun 7am–4pm.

4 Key Biscayne

Key Biscayne has some of the world's nicest beaches, hotels, and parks, yet it's not known for great food. Locals, or "Key rats" as they're known, tend to go off-island for meals or take-out, but here are some of the best on-the-island choices.

EXPENSIVE

Rusty Pelican ⊛ CONTINENTAL   The Pelican's private tropical walkway leads over a lush waterfall into one of the most romantic dining rooms in the city, located right on beautiful blue-green Biscayne Bay. The restaurant's windows look out over the water onto the sparkling stalagmites of Miami's magnificent downtown. Inside, quiet wicker paddle fans whirl overhead and saltwater fish swim in pretty tableside aquariums.

Dining in Coral Gables, Coconut Grove, Downtown & Key Biscayne

KEY BISCAYNE
Bayside Seafood Restaurant and Hidden Cove Bar **48**
Jimbo's **45**
The Oasis **50**
Rusty Pelican **46**
Stefano's **49**
Sundays on the Bay **47**

Porcao **10**
Provence Grill **11**
The Red Lantern **27**
News Cafe in the Grove **29**
Norman's **32**
S&S Restaurant **3**
Señor Frog's **28**
Soyka Restaurant & Café **1**
Pauloluigi's Ristorante Italiana **25**
Perricone's Marketplace **12**
Suzanne's Vegetarian Bistro **1**
The Poet's Café at Power Studios **2**
Tobacco Road **7**
Versailles **44**

Morton's of Chicago Steakhouse **14**

Anoka Fine Indian Cuisine **19**
Azul **9**
Baleen **22**
Bice **23**
Big Fish **4**
Biscayne Miracle Mile Cafeteria **32**
Brasserie Les Halles **32**
Bubba Gump Shrimp Co. **1**
Cafe Tu Tu Tango **24**
Caffe Abbracci **40**
The Capital Grille **8**
Casa Juancho **18**
Christy's **31**
The Daily Bread Marketplace **20**
East Coast Fisheries **5**
Fishbone Grille **16**
Franz & Joseph's in the Grove **26**
Gables Diner **35**
The Globe **41**
Gordon Biersch Brewery Restaurant **15**
Granny Feelgood's **17**
Green Street Café **30**
House of India **34**
Hy-Vong **42**
John Martin's **33**
La Carreta **43**
La Cibeles Café **6**
La Esquina de Tejas **13**
Le Bouchon du Grove **21**
Le Festival **37**
Meza Fine Art Gallery Café **38**
Miss Saigon Bistro **39**

135

The restaurant's surf-and-turf menu features conservatively prepared prime steaks, veal, shrimp, and lobster. The food is good, but the atmosphere—the reason why you're here—is even better, especially at sunset, when the view over the city is magical.

3201 Rickenbacker Causeway, Key Biscayne. © **305/361-3818.** Reservations recommended. Main courses $16–$20. AE, DC, MC, V. Daily 11:30am–4pm; Sun–Thurs 5–11pm, Fri–Sat 5pm–midnight.

Stefano's ⓖ ITALIAN   For its cheesy mid-80s ambience, Stefano's has no match. Its restaurant and disco share the same strobe-lit atmosphere. Food is traditional and reliable, if a little pricey. You'll find an older country club crowd here in the evenings, enjoying steaks, pastas, and seafood. Among the best entrees are the flavorful *risotto frutti di mare* (saffron risotto with shrimp, clams, mussels, and calamari) and the very cheesy lasagna. The best dish with meat is the surf and turf, or *mare e terra,* in which you get an Angus filet mignon and a meaty lobster tail.

After 7:30pm, the band starts playing American pop and Latin favorites. Some nights you feel as if you've accidentally happened upon your long-lost cousin's wedding, as you watch the parade of taffeta dresses and tipsy uncles.

24 Crandon Blvd., Key Biscayne. www.stefanos.net. © **305/361-7007.** Reservations recommended on weekends. Main courses $11–$29; appetizers $8–$12. AE, DC, MC, V. Sun–Thurs 5–11pm, Fri–Sat 5pm–5am. Disco open later Sun–Thurs.

Sundays on the Bay ⓖ AMERICAN   Although its food is fine, Sundays is really a fun tropical bar that features an unbeatable view of downtown, Coconut Grove, and the Sunday's marina. The menu features local favorites—grouper, tuna, snapper, and good shellfish in season. Competent renditions of such classic dishes as oysters Rockefeller, shrimp scampi, and *lobster fra diablo* are recommendable. Particularly popular is the Sunday brunch, when a buffet the size of Bimini attracts a lively, hungry crowd.

5420 Crandon Blvd., Key Biscayne. © **305/361-6777.** Reservations recommended for Sun brunch. Main courses $15–$24; Sun brunch $18.95. AE, DC, MC, V. Daily 11:30am–11:45pm; Sun brunch 11am–4pm.

INEXPENSIVE

Bayside Seafood Restaurant and Hidden Cove Bar ⓖ SEAFOOD Known by locals as "the Hut," this ramshackle restaurant and bar is a laid-back outdoor tiki hut and terrace that serves pretty good sandwiches and fish platters on paper plates. A blackboard lists the latest catches, which can be prepared blackened, fried, broiled, or in a garlic sauce. The fish dip is wonderfully smoky and moist, if a little heavy on mayonnaise. Local fishers and yachties share this rustic outpost with equal enthusiasm and loyalty. A completely new air-conditioned area for those who can't stand the heat is a welcome addition, as are the new deck and spruced-up decor. But behind it all, it's nothing fancier than a hut—if it was anything else, it wouldn't be nearly as appealing.

3501 Rickenbacker Causeway, Key Biscayne. © **305/361-0808.** Reservations accepted for 15 or more. Appetizers, salads, and sandwiches $4.50–$8; platters $7–$13. AE, MC, V. Daily 11:30am until closing (which varies).

Jimbo's ⓕⁱⁿᵈˢ SEAFOOD   Locals like to keep quiet about Jimbo's, an unassuming seafood shack that started as a gathering spot for fishermen and has since become the quintessential South Florida watering hole, snack bar, and hangout for those in the know. Grab yourself a dollar can of beer from the cooler and take in the view of the tropical lagoon where they shot *Flipper.* You may even see a manatee or two. Vacant shacks that served as backdrops for films such as *True Lies* surround this hidden enclave, which attracts everyone from shrimpers and politicians to well-oiled beach bums. Oddly enough, there's even a bocce court here, and the owner, Jimbo, may challenge you to a game. Play if you must, but word has it he never loses. The smoked fish here is the best in town.

Off the Rickenbacker Causeway at Sewerline Rd., Virginia Key. ℭ 305/361-7026. No credit cards. Daily 6am–6.30pm.

Oasis CUBAN   Everyone, from the city's mayor to the local handymen, meet for delicious paella and Cuban sandwiches at this little shack. They gather outside, around the little take-out window, or inside at the few tables for superpowerful *cafesitos* and rich *croquetas*. It's slightly dingy, but the food is good and cheap.

19 Harbor Dr. (on corner of Crandon), Key Biscayne. ℭ 305/361-5709. No credit cards. Main courses $4–$12; sandwiches $3–$4. Daily 6am–9pm.

5 Downtown

Downtown Miami is a large sprawling area divided by the Brickell bridge into two distinct areas: Brickell Avenue and the bayfront area near Biscayne Boulevard. You shouldn't walk from one to the other—it's quite a distance and unsafe at night. Convenient Metromover stops do adjoin the areas, so for a quarter it's better to hop on the scenic sky tram (closed after midnight).

VERY EXPENSIVE

Azul 🏵🏵🏵 GLOBAL FUSION   If there was an Epicurean version of the Academy Awards, this restaurant would win Best Director, hands down. Executive chef Michelle Bernstein, Miami's wunderkind in the kitchen, creates a tour de force of international cuisine, inspired by Caribbean, French, Argentine, Asian, and even American flavors. Like a stunning designer gown, the restaurant's decor, with its waterfront view, high ceilings, walls burnished in copper, and silk-covered chairs, is complemented by sparkling jewels—in this case, the food. The hamachi carpaccio appetizer is a sumptuous arrangement of yellowtail (imported from Japan), shaved fennel, mixed greens, and cucumber. Entrees, or "Plates of Resistance" as they're called here, include braised langoustine openfaced ravioli; ginger-lemongrass glazed Chilean sea bass served with black rice, kimchi, and Napa cabbage; and chicken with red Thai curry. Desserts range from fruity to chocolatey and shouldn't be skipped.

At the Mandarin Oriental Hotel, 500 Brickell Key Dr., Miami. ℭ 305/913-8258. Reservations strongly recommended. Main courses $24–$38. AE, DC, DISC, MC, V. Mon–Fri noon–3pm; Mon–Sat 7–11pm.

Morton's of Chicago 🏵 STEAK   A private club-like ambience, with dark wood, leather booths, and tablecloths, makes Morton's of Chicago the preferred spot for major business transactions and quiet, romantic dinners. A vast menu includes a wide variety of excellent steaks, namely the New York Prime, and an award-winning menu consisting of shrimp Alexander, oysters on the half shell, sea scallops with apricot chutney, swordfish medallions with béarnaise sauce, and a dense, hot Godiva chocolate cake that's out of this world. Private dining rooms are perfect in which to carry on clandestine conversations and romantic liaisons. The open kitchen is probably the only thing here that's not private. At lunchtime, the power is tangible as business deals are sliced and diced as often as the steak is. At night, the scene is more elegant, attracting older sophisticates and pre- and post-theater crowds.

1200 Brickell Ave., Miami. ℭ 305/400-9990. Reservations recommended. Main courses $20–$30. AE, DC, MC, V. Mon–Fri 11:30am–11pm, Sat 2:30–11pm, Sun 2:30–10pm.

Porcao 🕸🕸 BRAZILIAN   The name sounds eerily like "pork out," which is what you'll be doing at this exceptional Brazilian *churrascaria*. For about $30, you can feast on salads and meats *after* you sample the unlimited gourmet buffet, which includes such fillers as pickled quail eggs, marinated onions, and an entire prosciutto. Do not stuff yourself here, as the next step is the meaty part: Choose as much lamb, filet mignon, chicken hearts, and steaks as you like, grilled, skewered, and sliced right at your table. Side dishes also come with the meal, including beans and rice and fried yucca.

801 Brickell Bay Dr., Miami. ✆ 305/373-2777. Reservations accepted. Prix fixe $31.50 per person, all you can eat. AE, DC, MC, V. Daily noon–midnight.

EXPENSIVE

Capital Grille 🕸🕸 STEAK   This place reeks of power. Seated among wine cellars filled with high-end classics, the dark wood paneling, pristine white tablecloths, chandeliers, and marble floors all contribute to the clubby atmosphere. For an appetizer, start with the lobster and crab cakes. If you're not in the mood for beef or lobster, try the pan-seared red snapper and asparagus covered with Hollandaise. The wine cellars you're surrounded by are filled with about 5,000 bottles of wine—too extensive and rare to list. There are private dining rooms for large parties and smaller ones for more intimate settings. While some people prefer the more stalwart style and service of Morton's up the block, others find Capital to be a bit livelier. The food's pretty much the same between the two, though I personally find the steaks at Morton's to be a notch better; however, the atmosphere at the Capital Grille is *much* more inviting. Complimentary valet parking here as opposed to Morton's, which charges a fee, is another reason to visit this carnivorous capital.

444 Brickell Ave., Miami. ✆ 305/374-4500. Reservations recommended. Main courses $17–$32. AE, DC, DISC, MC, V. Mon–Fri 11:30am–3pm; Mon–Thurs 5–10:30pm, Fri 5–11pm, Sat 6–11pm, Sun 5–10 pm.

East Coast Fisheries SEAFOOD   East Coast Fisheries is a no-nonsense retail market and restaurant offering a terrific variety of the freshest fish available. The dozen or so plain wood tables are surrounded by refrigerated glass cases filled with snapper, salmon, mahi mahi, trout, tuna, crabs, oysters, lobsters, and the like. The absolutely huge menu features every fish imaginable, cooked the way you want it—grilled, fried, stuffed, Cajun style, Florentine, hollandaise, or blackened. However, the smell of frying grease detracts from the otherwise quaint old Miami feel right on the riverfront. Service is fast, but good prices and good food can mean long lines on weekends.

360 W. Flagler St., Miami. ✆ 305/372-1300. Reservations recommended. Main courses $17–$24. AE, MC, V. Daily 11am–10pm. From I-95 south, exit at NW 8th St. (exit 5A). Follow to NW 3rd St. and turn right. The next block is North River Dr. Turn left. The restaurant is 3 blocks down on the right side.

MODERATE

Big Fish 🕸🕸 *Finds* SEAFOOD/ITALIAN   This scenic seafood shack on the Miami River is a real catch—if you can find it. Hard to locate, but well worth the search, Big Fish's remote location keeps many people biting. In fact, Big Fish added some Italian options to its all-seafood menu in the hopes of luring more people, and that worked, too. With a spectacular riverfront setting, Big Fish has a sweeping view of the Miami skyline and some of the freshest catch around; the pasta served with it is only a starchy diversion. But the setting may be the real draw, right there on the sketchy Miami River where freighters, fishing boats, dinghies, and sometimes yachts slink by to the amusement of the faithful diners who no longer have to fish around for a charming, serene seafood restaurant.

55 SW Miami Avenue Rd. ⓒ 305/373-1770. Main courses $8–$28. AE, DC, MC, V. Daily 11am–11pm. Cross the Brickell Ave. Bridge heading south and take the first right on SW 5th St. The road narrows under a bridge. The restaurant is just on the other side.

Bubba Gump Shrimp Co. SEAFOOD   Inspired by the Tom Hanks megahit, *Forrest Gump,* the Bubba Gump Shrimp Co. likens life not to a box of chocolates, but rather to a bucket o' shrimp. Located right on the water, this place offers lots of affordable, oddly named shrimp specials. For starters, try the "Run Across America Sampler," which includes Bubba's Far Out Dip and Chips, New Orleans Peel n' Eat Shrimp, Texas Wild Wings, and Alabama Fried Shrimp for only $12.99. The "Bubba's After the Storm Bucket of Boat Trash" will trash your arteries with a deep-fried, albeit tasty, mix of shrimp, slipper lobster, and mahi mahi. "Lt. Dan's Drunken Shrimp" is a delicious concoction of shrimp in bourbon sauce with spicy sausage and garlic-mashed potatoes. A number of shrimpless salads and sandwiches are also on the menu. It's a fun place to bring the kids on a sunny afternoon. If you haven't stuffed yourself on shrimp, which is unlikely, you may want to try the overly caloric Jenny's Strawberry Dream— pound cake layered with vanilla ice cream, surrounded by Jenny's "special sauce," and topped with fresh strawberry puree and whipped cream.

In Bayside Marketplace, 401 Biscayne Blvd, Miami. ⓒ 305/379-8866. Main courses $8–$18. AE, DC, DISC, MC, V. Sun–Thurs 11am–11pm, Fri–Sat 11am–midnight. Closed Thanksgiving and Dec 25.

Fishbone Grille 🐟🐟 SEAFOOD   Fish are flying in the open kitchen of this extremely popular, reasonably priced seafood joint. Whether you take yours grilled, blackened, or sautéed, the chefs here work wonders with superfresh snapper, grouper, dolphin, tuna, sea bass, and shrimp, to name just a few. For nonfish eaters, there are delicious pizzas and an excellent New York strip steak. All meals come with salad and a fantastic slab of jalapeño cornbread. The interior is plain and simple; the only thing elaborate is the long list of daily specials.

650 S. Miami Ave. (SW 7th Ave., next to Tobacco Rd.), Miami. ⓒ 305/530-1915. Reservations recommended for 6 or more. Main courses $9–$20. AE, DC, DISC, MC, V. Mon–Thurs 11:30am–10pm, Fri 11:30am–11pm, Sat 5–11pm, Sun 5:30–9 pm.

Gordon Biersch Brewery Restaurant CONTINENTAL   Best known for its home-brewed lager beers and strict adherence to the 1516 German Purity Law (which mandates the use of only malt, hops, water, and yeast in the brewing process), Gordon Biersch is always buzzing with locals who cram into every bit of the restaurant's sprawling 10,800 square feet. The food, for a beer hall, is particularly good, but sometimes too exotic. There are the usual suspects— burgers and pizza—offset by heavier dishes such as chicken and andouille sausage gumbo and cashew chicken stir-fry. A popular lunch place for local businesspeople, Gordon Biersch is absolutely packed and oppressive on Friday night, when happy hour turns into harassment hour.

1201 Brickell Ave. (next to the JW Marriott), Miami. ⓒ 786/425-1130. Main courses $7.25–$19.95. AE, DC, MC, V. Sun–Thurs 11:30am–midnight, Fri–Sat 11:30am–2am.

Provence Grill 🐟🐟 FRENCH   This restaurant serves some of the best French meals this side of Toulouse. The brothers Cormouls-Houles use their prodigious culinary skills to assemble an affordable menu that allows the rest of us to know just how the French really live—and they do it, dare we say, with incredible panache. The grilled specialties, from chicken to salmon, are imbued with only the best seasonings and sauces. Sautéed mussels with garlic and chives are fabulous as a meal and as a dipping sauce for the crusty bread. Canard lovers will enjoy the grilled duck filet in a red port sauce. Real culinary adventurers should try the dessert menu—crème brûlée spiced with lavender (a local French favorite) is just one selection—which is truly a delight. A full bar outside brings you back from your French delusions of grandeur and returns you to a delightful downtown Miami state of mind with beautiful views of the downtown skyline.

1001 South Miami Ave., Miami. ✆ 305/373-1940. Main courses $13.95–$21.95; appetizers $4.95–$6.95. AE, MC, V. Mon–Fri 11am–3pm, Sun–Thurs 5:30–10:30pm, Fri–Sat 5:30–11pm.

Soyka Restaurant & Café ✿ AMERICAN   Brought to us by the same man who owns the News and Van Dyke cafes in South Beach, Soyka is a much-needed addition to the seedy area known as the Biscayne Corridor. The motif inside is industrial chic, reminiscent of a souped-up warehouse you might find in New York. Lunches focus on burgers, sandwiches, and wood-fired oven pizzas. Dinners include simple fare such as an excellent, massive Cobb salad, or more elaborate dishes such as the delicious turkey Salisbury steak. The bar area offers a few comfy couches and bar stools and tables on which to dine, if you prefer not to sit in the open dining room. A children's menu is available for both lunch and dinner. A lively crowd of bohemian Design District types, professionals, and singles gather here for a taste of urban life. On weekends, the place is packed and very loud. Do not expect an after-dinner stroll around the neighborhood—it's still too dangerous for pedestrian traffic. Head over the causeway to South Beach and stroll there.

5556 NE 4th Court (Design District), Miami. ✆ 305/759-3117. Reservations recommended. Main courses $10.75–$24. AE, MC, V. Daily 11am–11pm (bar open until midnight), Fri–Sat 11am–midnight (bar open until 1am). Happy hour Mon–Fri 4–7pm.

Suzanne's Vegetarian Bistro ✿✿ HEALTH FOOD   If you're in the mood to detox without compromising taste, Suzanne's Vegetarian Bistro can help you with delicious organic vegetarian fare from salads and sandwiches to a massive lotus bowl of miso soup with soba noodles and vegetables. Located in a charming house situated on a seedy stretch of Biscayne Boulevard, Suzanne's is a haven of healthy eating with excellent service and a wait staff that appears to really care about you. There's also a great selection of organic wines.

7251 Biscayne Blvd. ✆ 305/758-5859. Main courses $6.75–$12.95. AE, MC, V. Tues–Sat noon–10 pm, Sun noon–9pm.

INEXPENSIVE

Granny Feelgood's AMERICAN/HEALTH FOOD   Owner Irving Fields has been in the business of serving healthful food for more than 28 years, and his flagship store's offerings are priced right. Due to its proximity to the courthouse, there's a lot of legal eagle traffic and networking going on here. Locals love Granny's for the fresh fish and poultry specials, a line of salads that define greenery and good health, and the always-impeccable service by a family-oriented staff who likes to get to know its clientele. Tourists swinging through downtown on the Metromover or just spinning by can munch healthily on anything from a brown rice and steamed vegetable plate to Granny's famous tuna salad platter. The chef's identity is a secret, but I happen to know he was trained under local chef extraordinaire Allen Susser, and also did a stint on nearby Fisher Island's swanky members-only restaurant, so the cuisine here will most definitely please the palate. Granny Feelgood's sells its own line of vitamins and herbal products.

25 W. Flagler St., Miami. ✆ 305/377-9600. Reservations not accepted. Main courses $9–$12. AE, MC, V. Mon–Fri 7am–5pm.

La Cibeles Café ✪ CUBAN This typical Latin diner serves some of the best food in town. Just by looking at the line that runs out the door every afternoon between noon and 2pm, you can see that you're not the first to discover it. For about $5, you can have a huge and filling meal. Pay attention to the daily lunch specials and go with them. A pounded, tender chicken breast *(pechuga)* is smothered in sautéed onions and served with rice and beans and a salad. The trout and the roast pork are both very good. When available, try the *ropa vieja,* a shredded beef dish delicately spiced and served with peas and rice.

105 NE 3rd Ave. (1 block west of Biscayne Blvd.), Miami. ℂ **305/577-3454.** No credit cards. Main courses $5–$9. Mon–Sat 7:30am–7:30pm.

Perricone's Marketplace ✪ ITALIAN A large selection of groceries and wine, plus an outdoor porch and patio for dining, makes this one of the most welcoming spots downtown. Its rustic setting in the midst of downtown is a fantastic respite from city life. Sundays offer buffet brunches and all-you-can-eat dinners, too. But it's most popular weekdays at noon, when the suits show up for delectable sandwiches, quick and delicious pastas, and hearty salads.

15 SE 10th St. (corner of S. Miami Ave.), Miami. ℂ **305/374-9693.** Sandwiches $6.95–$8.25; pastas $11.50–$16.95. AE, MC, V. Sun–Mon 7:30am–10:30pm, Tues–Sat 7:30am–midnight.

Poet's Café at Power Studios ✪✪ *Finds* ECLECTIC Everything flows here in a rhythmic motion, from the tasty reasonably priced food to the sublime atmosphere. With a chef hailing from the Wolfgang Puck school of cuisine, the Poet's Café, located in the multimedia nightlife, entertainment, and production complex known as Power Studios, features delicious Puckian pizzas as well as an assortment of excellent sandwiches—peanut butter and banana is a treat, though the chicken sandwich on focaccia is best if you're looking for something substantial—appetizers (have the crab cakes), salads, and entrees. Seating is your choice—either downstairs in the main bar and restaurant area, or preferably upstairs in the rooftop garden/cinema, which overlooks the funky Design District and even projects old movies on the buildings across the street and on a big screen overlooking the tables. Weekends pack in a powerful crowd of scenesters, arty types, and even foodies.

3701 NE 2nd Ave., Miami. ℂ **305/576-1336.** $5–$15 main courses. AE, DC, MC, V. Tues–Sun 11am–3am.

S&S Restaurant AMERICAN/DINER FARE This tiny chrome-and-linoleum-counter restaurant in the middle of downtown looks like a truck stop. But locals have been coming back since it opened in 1938. Expect a wait at lunchtime while the mostly male clientele, from lawyers to linemen, wait patiently for huge quantities of old-fashioned fast food. You'll get a slice of Miami history along with your pie at S&S. Although the neighborhood has become pretty undesirable, the food—basic diner fare with some excellent stews and soups—hasn't changed in years In addition to cheap breakfasts, the diner serves up some of the best comfort food in Miami.

1757 NE 2nd Ave., Miami. ℂ **305/373-4291.** Main courses $5–$11. No credit cards. Mon–Fri 6am–4pm, Sat–Sun 6am–2 or 2:30pm (later on Heat game nights).

Tobacco Road AMERICAN Miami's oldest bar is a bluesy Route 66–inspired institution favored by barflies, professionals, and anyone else who wishes to indulge in good and greasy bar fare—chicken wings, nachos, and so on—for a reasonable price in a down-home, gritty-but-charming atmosphere. The burgers are also good—particularly the Death Burger, a deliciously unhealthy combo of choice sirloin topped with grilled onions, jalapeños, and pepper jack cheese—bring on the Tums! Also a live music venue, the Road, as it is known by locals, is well traveled, especially during Friday's happy hour and Tuesday's lobster night, when 100 1¼-pound lobsters go for only $10.99 a piece.

626 S. Miami Ave. ⓒ 305/374-1198. Main courses $7–$10. AE, DC, MC, V. Mon–Sat 11:30am–5am, Sun noon–midnight. Cover charge $5 Fri–Sat night.

6 Little Havana

The main artery of Little Havana is a busy commercial strip called Southwest 8th Street, or Calle Ocho. Auto body shops, cigar factories, and furniture stores line this street, and on every corner there seems to be a pass-through window serving superstrong Cuban coffee and snacks. In addition, many of the Cuban, Dominican, Nicaraguan, Peruvian, and other Latin American immigrants have opened full-scale restaurants ranging from intimate candlelit establishments to bustling stand-up lunch counters.

MODERATE

Casa Juancho ⓡⓡ SPANISH   A generous taste of Spain comes to Miami in the form of the cavernous Casa Juancho, which looks like it escaped from a production of *Don Quixote*. The numerous dining rooms are decorated with traditional Spanish furnishings and enlivened nightly by strolling Spanish musicians who tend to be annoying and expect tips—do not encourage them to play at your table; you'll hear them loud and clear from other tables, trust me. Try not to be frustrated with the older staff that doesn't speak English or respond quickly to your subtle glance—the food's worth the frustration. Your best bet is to order lots of *tapas,* small dishes of Spanish finger food. Some of the best include mixed seafood vinaigrette, fresh shrimp in hot garlic sauce, and fried calamari rings. A few entrees stand out, like roast suckling pig, baby eels in garlic and olive oil, and Iberian-style snapper.

2436 SW 8th St. (just east of SW 27th Ave.), Little Havana. ⓒ 305/642-2452. Reservations recommended, but not accepted Fri–Sat after 8pm. Main courses $15–$34; tapas $6–$8. AE, DC, DISC, MC, V. Sun–Thurs noon–midnight, Fri–Sat noon–1am.

INEXPENSIVE

Hy-Vong ⓡⓡ VIETNAMESE   Expect to wait hours for a table, and don't even think of mumbling a complaint. Despite the poor service, it's worth it. Vietnamese cuisine combines the best of Asian and French cooking with spectacular results. Food at Hy-Vong is elegantly simple and superspicy. Appetizers include small, tightly packed Vietnamese spring rolls and kimchi, a spicy, fermented cabbage. Star entrees include pastry-enclosed chicken with watercress cream-cheese sauce and fish in tangy mango sauce.

Enjoy the wait with a traditional Vietnamese beer and lots of company. Outside this tiny storefront restaurant, you'll meet interesting students, musicians, and foodies who come for the large delicious portions.

3458 SW 8th St. (between 34th and 35th aves.), Little Havana. ⓒ 305/446-3674. Reservations not accepted. Main courses $8–$15. No credit cards. Wed–Sun 6–11pm. Closed 2 weeks in Aug

La Carreta ⓡ CUBAN   This cavernous family-style restaurant is filled with relics of an old farm and college kids eating *medianoches* (midnight sandwiches with ham, cheese, and pickles) after partying all night. Waitresses are brusque but efficient and will help Anglos along who may not know the lingo. The menu is vast and very authentic. Try the *sopa de pollo,* a rich golden stock loaded with

Cuban Coffee

Despite the more than dozen Starbucks that dot the Miami landscape, locals still rely on the many Cuban cafeterias for their daily caffeine fix. The most popular—and most animated—Cuban cafeterias are **La Carreta** and **Versailles,** though many establishments throughout Miami serve espresso masked as Cuban coffee. These two places are the real deal.

Cuban coffee is a longstanding tradition in Miami. You'll find it served from the take-out windows of hundreds of *cafeterías* or *luncherías* around town, especially in Little Havana, Downtown, Hialeah, and the beaches. Depending on where you are and what you want, you'll spend between 40¢ and $1.50 per cup.

The best *café cubano* has a rich layer of foam on top formed when the hot espresso shoots from the machine into the sugar below. The result is the caramelly, sweet, potent concoction that's a favorite of locals of all nationalities.

To partake, you've just got to learn how to ask for it *en español.*

chunks of chicken and fresh vegetables, or the *ropa vieja,* a shredded beef stew in thick brown sauce.

Because of its immense popularity and low prices, La Carreta has opened several branches throughout Miami, including a counter in the Miami airport. Check the white pages for other locations.

3632 SW 8th St., Little Havana. ℂ 305/444-7501. Main courses $5–$22. AE, DC, DISC, MC, V. Daily 24 hours.

La Esquina de Tejas ⭐⭐ CUBAN   Best known as the diner where Ronald Reagan ate during his 1983 campaign in Miami, La Esquina de Tejas has gained a national reputation for its great food and low prices. There's a shrine dedicated to the former president in the "Presidential Quarters," and the menu even has his signed autograph and the presidential seal of approval. This is Cuban food at its best. You must try the *arroz a la marinera,* the Cuban version of Spanish paella. It's filled with clams, oysters, mussels, lobster, shrimp, squid, snapper, stone crab, and scallops cooked in fresh seafood broth. If you're not in the mood for seafood (after all, this is a Cuban joint), try the *vaca frita,* a grilled, shredded flank steak served with moro rice (black beans cooked with white rice) and *maduros* (sweet, fried plantains). Another house specialty is the *masas de puerco fritas,* a pork tenderloin cut in chunks, roasted, and then quickly deep-fried and served with mojo, grilled onions, garlic, olive oil, and bitter orange. You won't regret a trip here.

101 SW 12th Ave., Little Havana. ℂ 305/545-0337. Daily specials $4–$12; appetizers 75¢–$5.50. AE, MC, V. Daily 8am–9pm.

Versailles ⭐⭐ CUBAN   Versailles is the meeting place of Miami's Cuban power brokers, who meet daily over *café con leche* to discuss the future of the exiles' fate. A glorified diner, the place sparkles with glass, chandeliers, murals, and mirrors meant to evoke the French palace. There's nothing fancy here—nothing French, either—just straightforward food from the home country. The menu is a veritable survey of Cuban cooking and includes specialties such as *Moors and Christians* (flavorful black beans with white rice), ropa vieja, and fried whole fish. Whereas La Esquina de Tejas is known more for its food and Ronald Reagan than its atmosphere, Versailles is the place to come for mucho helpings of Cuban kitsch.

3555 SW 8th St., Little Havana. ✆ 305/444-0240. Soup and salad $2–$10; main courses $5–$8. DC, DISC, MC, V. Mon–Thurs 8am–2am, Fri 8am–3:30am, Sat 8am–4:30am, Sun 9am–2am.

7 North Dade

Although there aren't many hotels in North Dade, the population in the winter months explodes due to the onslaught of seasonal residents from the Northeast. A number of exclusive condominiums and country clubs, including William's Island, Turnberry, and the Jockey Club, breed a demanding clientele, many of whom dine out nightly. That's good news for visitors, who can find superior service and cuisine at value prices.

VERY EXPENSIVE

Chef Allen's ☺☺☺ NEW WORLD CUISINE   If anyone deserves to have a restaurant named after him, it's chef Allen Susser, winner of the esteemed James Beard Award for Best American Chef in the Southeast—the Academy Award of cuisine—and practically every other form of praise and honor awarded by the most discriminating palates. Chef Allen, the man, is royalty around here. Chef Allen, the restaurant, is his province, and foodies are his disciples. His platform? New World Cuisine and the harmony of exotic tropical fruits, spices, and vegetables. It is under Chef Allen's magic that ordinary Key limes and mangos reappear in the form of succulent salsas and sauces. A traditional antipasto is transformed into a Caribbean one, with papaya-pineapple barbeque shrimp, jerk calamari, and charred rare tuna. Whole yellowtail in coconut milk and curry sauce is a particularly spectacular entree. Unlike other restaurants where location is key, Chef Allen's, located in the rear of a strip mall, could be in the desert, and hordes of people would still make the trek.

19088 NE 29th Ave. (at Biscayne Blvd.), North Miami Beach. ✆ 305/935-2900. Reservations recommended. Main courses $26–$35. AE, DC, MC, V. Sun–Thurs 6–10:30pm, Fri–Sat 6–11pm.

MODERATE

Lagoon ☺ SEAFOOD/CONTINENTAL   This old bayfront fish house has been around since 1936. Major road construction nearby should have guaranteed its doom years ago, but the excellent view and incredible specials make it a worthwhile stop. If you can disregard the somewhat dirty bathrooms and nonchalant service, you'll find the best-priced juicy Maine lobsters around.

Yes, it's true! Lobster lovers can get two 1½ pounders for $22.95. Try them broiled with a light buttery seasoned coating. This dish is not only inexpensive but incredibly succulent, too. Side dishes include fresh vegetables, like broccoli or asparagus, as well as a huge baked potato, stuffed or plain.

488 Sunny Isles Blvd. (163rd St.), North Miami Beach. ✆ 305/947-6661. Reservations accepted. Main courses $12–$40; appetizers $6–$14. AE, MC, V. Daily 4:30–11pm. Happy hour daily 4:30–6pm.

Melting Pot FONDUE   Traditional fondue is supplemented by combination meat-and-fish dinners, which are served with one of almost a dozen different sauces. With its lace curtains and cozy booths, the Melting Pot can be quite romantic.

To satisfy health-conscious diners, the owners have introduced a more wholesome version of fondue, in which you cook vegetables and meats in a low-fat broth. It tastes good, although this version is less fun than watching drippy

From Ceviche to Picadillo: Latin Cuisine at a Glance

In Little Havana and wondering what to eat? Many restaurants list menu items in English for the benefit of *norteamericano* diners. In case you're wondering what to order, though, here are translations and suggestions for filling and delicious meals:

Arroz con pollo   Roast chicken served with saffron-seasoned yellow rice and diced vegetables.

Café cubano   Very strong black coffee, served in thimble-size cups with lots of sugar. It's a real eye-opener.

Camarones   Shrimp.

Ceviche   Raw fish seasoned with spice and vegetables and marinated in vinegar and citrus to "cook" it.

Croquetas   Golden-fried croquettes of ham, chicken, or fish.

Paella   A Spanish dish of chicken, sausage, seafood, and pork mixed with saffron rice and peas.

Palomilla   Thinly sliced beef, similar to American minute steak, usually served with onions, parsley, and a mountain of french fries.

Pan cubano   Long, white crusty Cuban bread. Ask for it *tostada* (toasted and flattened on a grill with lots of butter.

Picadillo   A rich stew of ground meat, brown gravy, peas, pimientos, raisins, and olives.

Plátano   A deep-fried, soft, mildly sweet banana.

Pollo asado   Roasted chicken with onions and a crispy skin.

Ropa vieja   A delicious shredded beef stew whose name literally means "old clothes."

Sopa de pollo   Chicken soup, usually with noodles or rice.

Tapas   A general name for Spanish-style hors d'oeuvres, served in grazing-size portions.

cheese flow from the hot pot. Best of all, perhaps, is dessert: chunks of pineapple, bananas, apples, and cherries that you dip into a creamy chocolate fondue. No liquor is served here, but the wine list is extensive, and beer is available. A second Melting Pot is located at 9835 SW 72nd St. (Sunset Drive) in Kendall (© 305/279-8816).

In Sunny Isles Plaza shopping center, 3143 NE 163rd St. (between U.S. 1 and Collins Ave.), North Miami Beach. © **305/947-2228.** www.meltingpot.net. Reservations recommended on weekends. Appetizers $7.95 for two. Fondues $11–$18. AE, DC, DISC, MC, V. Sun–Thurs 5:30–11pm, Fri–Sat 5:30pm–midnight.

INEXPENSIVE

Amos' Juice Bar HEALTH FOOD   This brightly painted stand in the middle of a busy road attracts a varied crowd, from young pony-tailed Europeans to bikers. If you don't mind a bit of car exhaust with your snapper sandwich, consider this North Dade landmark.

The food is made on the premises and includes a great tuna salad, served in a pita with tons of crisp vegetables, including alfalfa sprouts, tomato, and lettuce.

The hummus is also superb, although garlic lovers might want a hint more spark. You can also get a fresh smoothie or vegetable juice made on the spot.

18315 W. Dixie Hwy. (1 block west of Biscayne Blvd.), North Miami Beach. ☎ 305/935-9544. Sandwiches and salads $4–$6. No credit cards. Mon–Sat 8:30am–6:30pm.

Here Comes the Sun ⭐ AMERICAN/HEALTH FOOD   One of Miami's first health-food spots, this bustling grocery-store-turned-diner serves hundreds of plates a night, mostly to blue-haired locals. It's noisy and hectic but worth it. In season, all types pack the place for a $7.95 special, served between 4 and 6:30pm, which includes one of more than 20 choices of entrees, soup or salad, coffee or tea, and a small frozen yogurt. Fresh grilled fish and chicken entrees are reliable and served with a nice array of vegetables. The miso burgers with "sun sauce" are a vegetarian's dream.

2188 NE 123rd St. (west of the Broad Causeway), North Miami Beach. ☎ 305/893-5711. Reservations recommended in season. Main courses $8–$14; early-bird special $7.95; sandwiches and salads $5–$11. AE, DC, DISC, MC, V. Mon–Sat 11am–8:30pm.

Laurenzo's Café ⭐⭐ ITALIAN   This recently expanded lunch counter in the middle of a chaotic grocery store has been serving delicious buffet lunches to the *paesanos* for years. New additions include an open kitchen and wood-burning pizza oven. A meeting place for the growing Italian population in Miami, the store has been open for more than 40 years. Daily specials usually include lasagna or eggplant parmigiana and two or three salad options. Also good are the rustic pizzas. Choose a wine from the vast selection and take your meal to go, or sit in the trellis-covered area amid busy shoppers buying their evening's groceries. You'll get to eavesdrop on some great conversations over your plastic tray of real Southern Italian–style cooking.

16385 W. Dixie Hwy. (corner of 164th St.), North Miami Beach. ☎ 305/945-6381. MC, V. Main courses $4–$12; salads $2–$5. Mon–Fri 11am–7:30pm, Sat 11am–7pm, Sun 11am–4pm.

8 Coral Gables & Environs

VERY EXPENSIVE

Christy's ⭐⭐ STEAK/AMERICAN   Power is palpable at this elegant English-style restaurant where an ex-president could be sitting at one table and a rock star at another. But Christy's is the kind of place where conversations are at a hush and no one seems to care who they're sitting next to. The selling point here, rather, is the corn-fed beef and calf's liver, not to mention the broiled lamb chops, prime rib of beef with horseradish sauce, teriyaki marinated filet mignon, and perfectly tossed Caesar salad. Baked sweet potatoes and a sublime blackout cake are also yours for the taking. Just like a fine wine or the typical Christy's customer, the meat here is aged a long time. A landmark since 1978, Christy's has thrived amid the comings and goings of neighboring nouveau Coral Gables restaurants. Located on a nondescript corner, you know you've arrived at the right place if you can count the Rolls Royces parked out front.

3101 Ponce de León Blvd., Coral Gables. ☎ 305/446-1400. Reservations recommended. Main courses $19.50–$35. AE, DC, MC, V. Mon–Thurs 11:30am–4pm, Fri 4–11pm, Sat 5–11pm, Sun 5–10pm.

Norman's ⭐⭐⭐ NEW WORLD CUISINE   *Gourmet* magazine called Norman's the best restaurant in South Florida, but many disagree. They think it's the best restaurant in the entire United States. Gifted chef and cookbook author Norman van Aken takes New World Cuisine (which, along with chef Allen

---

Kids Family-Friendly Restaurants

Baraboo *(see p. 130)* While the cuisine may be a bit funky for kids' palates, the wandering magicians and mimes are guaranteed to entertain the little ones, who will likely eat anything after the magician says "abracadabra."

Big Pink *(see p. 125)* One of South Beach's only family-friendly sit-down restaurants, Big Pink is a fun, noisy restaurant with a comprehensive menu consisting of macaroni and cheese, hamburgers, and other comfort foods guaranteed to satisfy the pickiest kids.

Bubba Gump Shrimp Co. *(see p. 138)* Named after the character from the motion picture *Forrest Gump,* this is a great place to bring the entire family on a lazy Sunday afternoon. You get to eat some good moderately priced seafood, watch ships sail by on the bay, and shop at the Bayside Marketplace afterward. There's a gift shop where you can buy Forrest Gump souvenirs, T-shirts, and caps.

Wilderness Grill *(see p. 154)* Let the kids run wild in this noisy theme restaurant that serves as many sound effects as it does hamburgers.

Susser, he helped create) to another plateau with dishes that have landed him on such shows as the Discovery Channel's "Great Chefs of the South" and on the wish lists of gourmands everywhere. The open kitchen invites you to marvel at the mastery that lands on your plate in the form of pan-roasted swordfish with black-bean *muneta;* stuffed baby bell pepper in cumin-scented tomato broth with avocado *crema;* char-grilled New York strip steak with *chimichurri* sabayon, *pommes frites,* and Créole mustard–spiced caramelized red onions; plantain-crusted dolphin; or chicken and tiny shrimp paella with garbanzo beans and chorizo mojo, to name a few.

The staff is adoring and professional and the atmosphere is tasteful without being too formal. The portions are realistic, but still, be careful not to overdo it. You'll want to try some of the funky, fantastic desserts.

21 Almeria Ave. (between Douglas and Ponce de León), Coral Gables. © **305/446-6767.** Reservations highly recommended. Main courses $26–$38. AE, DC, MC, V. Mon–Thurs 6–10:30pm, Fri–Sat 6–11pm.

EXPENSIVE

Caffe Abbracci ✦✦ ITALIAN You'll understand why this restaurant's name means "hugs" in Italian the moment you enter the dark romantic enclave: Your appetite will be embraced by the savory scents of fantastic Italian cuisine wafting through the restaurant. The homemade black and red ravioli filled with lobster in pink sauce, risotto with porcini and portobello mushrooms, and the house specialty—grilled veal chop topped with tricolor salad—are irresistible and perhaps the culinary equivalent of a warm, embracing hug. A cozy bar and lounge was added recently to further encourage the warm and fuzzy feelings.

318 Aragon Ave. (between LeJeune Rd. and Miracle Mile), Coral Gables. © **305/441-0700.** Reservations recommended for dinner. Main courses $16–$25; pastas $15–$20. AE, DC, MC, V. Mon–Fri 11:30am–3pm; Sun–Thurs 6–11pm, Fri–Sat 6pm–midnight.

Le Festival ☆☆ FRENCH   Le Festival's contemporary pink awning hangs over one of Miami's most traditional Spanish-style buildings, hinting at the unusual combination of cuisine and decor that awaits inside. The modern dining rooms, enlivened with New French features and furnishings, belie the traditional highlights of a well-planned menu.

Shrimp and crab cocktails, fresh pâtés, and an unusual cheese soufflé are star starters. Both meat and fish are either simply seared with herbs and spices or doused in wine and cream sauces. Dessert can be a delight if you plan ahead: Grand Marnier and chocolate soufflés are individually prepared and must be ordered at the same time as the entrees. There's also a wide selection of other homemade sweets.

2120 Salzedo St. (5 blocks north of Miracle Mile), Coral Gables. ℂ 305/442-8545. Reservations required for dinner. Main courses $16–$25. AE, DC, DISC, MC, V. Mon–Fri 11:45am–2:30pm; Mon–Thurs 6–10:30pm, Fri–Sat 6–11pm.

MODERATE

Brasserie Les Halles ☆☆ FRENCH   Known especially for its fine steaks and delicious salads, this very welcome addition to the Coral Gables dining scene became popular as soon as it opened in 1997 and has since continued to do a brisk business. The modest and moderately priced menu is particularly welcome in an area of overpriced, stuffy restaurants. For starters, try the mussels in white wine sauce and the escargot. For a main course, the duck confit is an unusual and rich choice. Pieces of duck meat wrapped in duck fat are slow-cooked and served on salad frissé with baby potatoes with garlic. Service by the young French staff is polite but a bit slow. The tables tend to be a little too close, although there is a lovely private balcony space overlooking the long, thin dining room where large groups can gather.

2415 Ponce de León Blvd. (at Miracle Mile), Coral Gables. ℂ 305/461-1099. Reservations recommended on weekends. Main courses $12.50–$22.50. AE, DC, DISC, MC, V. Daily 11:30am–midnight.

Gables Diner ☆ AMERICAN   This upscale diner serves an eclectic mix of comfort food and nouvelle health food. From meat loaf to Chinese chicken salad, there are moderately priced options for everyone. My favorite is the chicken pot pie, a flaky homemade crust filled with big chunks of white meat, pearl onions, peas, and mushrooms. Also good are the large burgers with every imaginable condiment. Vegetarians can find a few good choices, including pastas, bean soups, pizzas, vegetable stir-fry, and some hearty salads. All the ingredients are fresh and crisp. No need to dress up here, although the clean, almost romantic setting is as appropriate for first dates as it is for families.

2320 Galiano Dr. (between Ponce de León Blvd. and 37th Ave.), Coral Gables. ℂ 305/567-0330. Main courses $9–$16; pastas $10–$12; burgers and sandwiches $7–$9; salads $8–$10. AE, DC, DISC, MC, V. Daily 8am–10pm, Fri–Sat 8am–10:30pm.

Globe INTERNATIONAL   The Globe used to be the Gables' premier happy hour centerpiece, a yuppy hot spot, packing in crowds until the fire marshals came to rescue them from suffocation. Now that the happy hour has moved up the road to Satchmo's, the intimate pub-like Globe can focus on its food, which is a notch above average bar fare. Your best bets are the salads and pizzas, particularly the chicken and blue cheese pizza, my favorite. In addition to an extensive list of wines and specialty beers, there are many interesting nonalcoholic choices. There's excellent live music every weekend.

377 Alhambra Circle (just off Le Jeune Rd.), Coral Gables. ☎ **305/445-3555.** Reservations accepted for 6 or more. Main courses $10–$22; salads $6–$10; pizzas and sandwiches $7–$11. AE, DISC, MC, V. Mon–Fri 11:30am–midnight, Sat 6:30pm–2am, Sun 10:30am–10:30pm.

John Martin's 🍴 IRISH PUB   Forest green and dark wood give way to a very intimate pub-like atmosphere in which local businesspeople and barflies alike come to hoist a pint or two. The menu offers some tasty British specialties (not necessarily an oxymoron!), such as bangers and mash and shepherd's pie, as well as Irish lamb stew and corned beef and cabbage.

Of course, to wash it down, you'll want to try one of the ales on tap or one of the more than 20 single-malt scotches. The crowd is upscale and chatty, as is the young wait staff. Check out happy hour on weeknights, plus the Sunday brunch with loads of hand-carved meats and seafood.

253 Miracle Mile, Coral Gables. ☎ **305/445-3777.** Reservations recommended on weekends. Main courses $9–$20; sandwiches and salads $5–$16. AE, DC, DISC, MC, V. Mon–Thurs 11:30am–midnight, Fri–Sat 11:30am–1am, Sun noon–10pm.

Meza Fine Art Gallery Café 🍴🍴 ECLECTIC   This unique restaurant is located in a sleek, arty atmosphere featuring paintings, performance artists, and a multimedia array of talent—very Warhol. As eclectic as the art and artists who convene here, the menu is varied, featuring well-priced, well-prepared dishes such as pan-seared tuna with sesame crust and balsamic vinegar reduction and a delicious grilled churrasco skirt steak with chimichurri. Live music nightly from jazz and Latin to electronica brings out a motley crew of youngsters who look as if they stepped out of a Gap ad. A lively bar scene attracts a 30s-and-under crowd on late weekend nights. Earlier in the evenings, Meza caters to an older, more sophisticated dining crowd.

275 Giralda Ave., Coral Gables. ☎ **305/461-2723.** Reservations accepted. Main courses $6.95–$13.95. Three-course twilight dinner served Mon–Sat 6–8pm for $15.95 per person, including glass of wine. AE, DC, DISC, MC, V. Daily noon–3pm; Mon–Thurs 6–10:30pm, Fri–Sun 6pm–2am.

Ortanique on the Mile 🍴🍴 NEW WORLD CARIBBEAN   Ortanique is as unique to the Gables as the orange-like fruit is to Jamaica. You'll be greeted as you walk in by soft spider-like lights and canopied mosquito netting that will make you wonder whether you're on a secluded island or inside one of King Tut's temples. A friendly host greets you at the door and glides you past simple canvas oils hanging from papaya- and mango-colored walls, and hand-painted columns laced with ortaniques.

Chef Cindy Hutson has truly perfected her tantalizing New World Caribbean menu. For starters, an absolute must is the pumpkin bisque with a hint of pepper sherry. Afterward, move on to the tropical mango salad with fresh marinated Sable hearts of palm, julienne mango, baby field greens, toasted Caribbean candied pecans, and passion fruit vinaigrette. For an entree, I recommend the pan-sautéed Bahamian black grouper marinated in teriyaki and sesame oil. It's served with an ortanique orange liqueur sauce and topped with steamed seasoned chayote, zucchini, and carrots on a lemon-orange *boniato*–sweet plantain mash. For dessert, try the chocolate mango tower—layers of brownie, chocolate mango mousse, meringue, and sponge cake, accompanied by mango sorbet and tropical fruit salsa. Entrees may not be cheap, but they're a lot less than airfare to the islands, from where most, if not all, the ingredients used here hail.

278 Miracle Mile (next to Actor's Playhouse), Coral Gables. ☎ **305/446-7710.** Reservations requested. Main courses $11–$29. AE, DC, MC, V. Mon–Tues 6–10pm, Wed–Sat 6–11pm, Sun 5:30–9:30pm.

INEXPENSIVE

Biscayne Miracle Mile Cafeteria ⭐ AMERICAN   Here you'll find no bar, no music, and no flowers on the tables—just great Southern-style cooking at unbelievably low prices. The menu changes, but roast beef, baked fish, and barbecued ribs are typical entrees, few of which exceed $5.

Food is picked up cafeteria style and brought to one of the many unadorned Formica tables. The restaurant is always busy. The kitschy 1950s decor is an asset in this last of the old-fashioned cafeterias, where the gold-clad staff is proud and attentive. Enjoy it while it lasts.

147 Miracle Mile, Coral Gables. ✆ **305/444-9005.** Main courses $3.50–$4.50. MC, V. Daily 11am–8:30pm.

Daily Bread Marketplace GREEK   This place is great for take-out food and homemade breads. The falafel and gyro sandwiches are large, fresh, and filling. The spinach pie for less than $1 is also recommended, though it's short on spinach and heavy on pastry. Salads, including luscious tabouli, hummus, and eggplant, are also worth a go. To take in or eat out, the Middle Eastern fare here is a real treat, especially in an area so filled with fancy French and Cuban fare. Plus, you can pick up hard-to-find groceries such as grape leaves, fresh olives, couscous, fresh nuts, and pita bread.

2400 SW 27th St. (off U.S. 1 under the monorail), Coral Gables. ✆ **305/856-0363** or 305/856-0366. Sandwiches and salads $3–$6. MC, V. Mon–Sat 8am–8pm, Sun 11am–5pm.

House of India ⭐ INDIAN   House of India's curries, kormas, and kabobs are very good, but the restaurant's well-priced all-you-can-eat lunch buffet is unsurpassed. All the favorites are on display, including tandoori chicken, naan, various meat and vegetarian curries, as well as rice and dal (lentils). This place isn't fancy and could use a good scrub-down (in fact, I've heard it described as a "greasy spoon"), but the service is excellent and the food is good enough to keep you from staring at your surroundings.

22 Merrick Way (near Douglas and Coral Way, a block north of Miracle Mile), Coral Gables. ✆ **305/444-2348.** Reservations recommended. Main courses $8–$17. AE, DC, DISC, MC, V. Daily 11:30am–3pm; Sun–Thurs 5–10pm, Fri–Sat 5–11pm.

Miss Saigon Bistro ⭐⭐ VIETNAMESE   Unlike Andrew Lloyd Webber's bombastic Broadway show, this Miss Saigon is small, quiet, and not at all flashy. Servers at this family-run restaurant—among them, the owners' son—will graciously offer to recommend dishes or even to custom-make something for you. The menu is varied and reasonably priced and the portions are huge—large enough to share. Noodle dishes and soup bowls are hearty and flavorful; caramelized prawns are fantastic, as is the whole snapper with lemongrass and ginger sauce. Despite the fact that there are few tables inside and a hungry crowd usually gathers outside in the street, they will not at all rush you through your meal, which is worth savoring.

146 Giralda Ave., Coral Gables. ✆ **305/446-8006.** Main courses $10–$16.95. AE, DC, DISC, MC, V. Mon–Thurs 11am–3pm and 5:30–10pm, Fri–Sat 5:30–11pm, Sun 5:30–10pm.

9 Coconut Grove

Coconut Grove was long known as the artists' haven of Miami, but the rush of developers trying to cash in on the laid-back charm of this old settlement has turned it into something of an overgrown mall. Still, there are several great dining spots both in and out of the confines of Mayfair or CocoWalk.

EXPENSIVE

Anokha Fine Indian Cuisine ✿✿✿ INDIAN   This is the best Indian restaurant in Miami. Anokha's motto is "a guest is equal to God and should be treated as such," and they do stick to it. The food here is from the gods, with fantastic tandooris, curries, and stews. The restaurant's location at the end of a quiet stretch of Coconut Grove is especially enticing because it prevents the throngs of pedestrians from overtaking what some people consider a diamond in the rough.

3195 Commodore Plaza, Coconut Grove. ✆ **786/552-1030.** AE, DC, MC, V. Main courses $13–$21. Tues–Sun 11:30am–10:30pm.

Baleen ✿✿✿ SEAFOOD/MEDITERRANEAN   While the prices aren't lean, the cuisine here is worth every pricey, precious penny. Oversized crab cakes, oak-smoked diver scallops, and steak house–quality meats are among Baleen's excellent offerings. The lobster bisque is the best on Biscayne Bay. Everything here is a la carte, so order wisely, as it tends to add up quicker than you can put your fork down. The restaurant's spectacular waterfront setting makes Baleen a true knockout. Brunch is particularly noteworthy as well.

4 Grove Isle Dr. (in the Grove Isle Hotel), Coconut Grove. ✆ **305/858-8300.** Reservations recommended. Main courses $17–$36. AE, DC, MC, V. Daily 7am–11pm.

Bice ✿✿✿ ITALIAN   Located in the ritzy Grand Bay Hotel, it is not surprising that Bice is a first-class establishment. As you exit the elevator on the hotel's mezzanine level, an ornate glass chandelier lights the way into the beautiful, expansive bar area with dim lighting and a sleek, rich wood floor. To the left of the maitre d' stand is the restaurant's private wine room, with an impressive collection encased in wall-to-wall glass, and a banquet table that comfortably seats six. Upon entering the dining room, you feel as if you're sailing on a grand ocean liner, with several cozy tables and booths, high ceilings, and a glorious view of the hotel's sprawling waterfall and pool area. Knowledgeable and friendly servers rush a fresh basket of warm assorted breads—focaccia, breadsticks—to the table as you begin to peruse the comprehensive Italian menu. Every appetizer sounds so good that it's almost impossible to decide. Beef carpaccio is a delight on the palate with hearts of palm and Reggiano cheese; a colorful grilled vegetable pyramid consists of gargantuan portions of meaty portobello mushrooms, fresh asparagus, and peppers with bursts of mouthwatering goat cheese lying within; Maryland crab cakes with the perfect hint of lemon are exceptional. For main courses, the pastas, homemade and extremely fresh, are eclipsed by a heavenly slab of Nebraska filet mignon with peppercorn sauce and a tower of french fries and onion rings. The veal chop is also sublime. For dessert, the crème brûlée and coffee gelato are delicious. Unlike many chichi restaurants, especially those found within swanky hotels, all dishes at Bice are generous in portion—huge actually—and the only thing stuffy about dining here is how you'll feel after indulging.

2669 S. Bayshore Dr. (in the Grand Bay Hotel), Coconut Grove. ✆ **305/860-0960.** Reservations recommended. Main courses $13–$34. AE, MC, V. Daily 7–11am, 11:30am–3pm, and 6–11pm.

Le Bouchon du Grove ✿✿ FRENCH   Planet Hollywood came and went in Coconut Grove, but the marks of commercialism still remain. Thankfully, there's a haven from the Disneyfied madness of the Grove in the form of this very authentic, exceptional French bistro. An excellent starter is the wonderful *gratinée Lyonnaise* (traditional French onion soup). Fish is brought in fresh daily; try the Chilean sea bass when in season *(filet de loup poele)*. Though it is slightly heavy on the oil, it is delivered with succulent artichokes, tomato confit, and seasoned roasted garlic that is a gastronomic triumph. The *carre d'agneau roti* (roasted rack of lamb with Provence herbs) is served warm and tender, with an excellent amount of seasoning. There is an excellent selection of pricey but doable French and American red and white wines. Try the St. Emilion 1996 Baron Rothschild ($34, or $7 per glass), which compliments nearly the entire menu.

3430 Main Highway, Coconut Grove. © 305/448-6060. Reservations recommended. Main courses $16–$24. AE, MC, V. Mon–Thurs 9:30am–11pm, Fri–Sun 8am–midnight.

MODERATE

Franz & Joseph's in the Grove ✶✶ CONTINENTAL/ITALIAN   This is a favorite restaurant of theatergoers and actors—Kathleen Turner and Jean Stapleton to name two—alike. Franz or Joseph, the gracious owners of this romantic restaurant that is chock full of Old-World charm, will personally greet you at the door. Before you sit down to dine, enjoy a glass of wine at the intimate, atmospheric bar and begin to give in to the European ambience here. A few starters are recommended: the escargot in Roquefort butter with grilled herb bread is wonderful as is the stuffed avocado with marinated sea scallops, mussels, and shrimp—a local favorite and absolutely fresh. I also recommend the soup du jour, whatever it is. Don't be afraid to order pasta, either. The penne with spicy grilled chicken, plum tomatoes, spinach, and feta cheese is wonderful. But if you've come to Florida for the seafood, you can't go wrong with the restaurant's filet of snapper, pan-seared with mango chutney and glazed banana over rice. Well-prepared steaks and exotic chicken dishes are a specialty here, too. Their delicious desserts are made on premises. The kitchen is small, so the food is consistently fresh and cooked to order. The last thing the chef does each night before going home, is order for the next day's menu.

3145 Commodore Plaza, Coconut Grove. © 305/448-2282. Reservations highly recommended. Main courses $15–$20. AE, MC, V. Tues–Sun 11:30am–2:30pm and 6–10:30pm.

Green Street Café ✶ CONTINENTAL   The location and the loads of outdoor seating (great for people-watching) relieve Green Street of the pressure to turn out fine meals, but the food is still well above average. Continental-style breakfasts include fresh croissants and rolls, cinnamon toast, and cereal. Heartier American-style offerings include eggs and omelets, pancakes, waffles, and French toast. Soup, salad, and sandwich lunches are overstuffed chicken-, turkey-, and tuna-based meals. Dinners are more elaborate, with several decent pasta entrees as well as fresh fish, chicken, and burgers, including one made of lamb.

3110 Commodore Plaza, Coconut Grove. © 305/567-0662. Reservations not accepted. Main courses $10–$15. AE, MC, V. Sun–Thurs 7am–11:30pm, Fri–Sat 7am–1am.

Pauloluigi's Ristorante Italiana ✶ ITALIAN   Pauloluigi's serves rich dishes that include cold and hot appetizers, homemade soups and salads, pastas, and pizzas. Owners Paul and Lola Shalaj, restaurant entrepreneurs for the past 27 years, have gained and kept a large devoted clientele with their tasty light Italian cuisine, generous portions, and friendly environment that has served as the perfect fine-dining hideaway for both local and national customers alike.

A favorite is the *jumbo rigatti rubino,* a chicken dish with a side of sausages, asparagus, and portobello mushrooms in light marinara sauce. There's also *chicken Marsala, linguine al fruitti di mare* (for poultry and seafood lovers), and a special children's menu. Sample a wine from their excellent list.

3324 Virginia St., Coconut Grove. © 305/445-9000. Reservations recommended. Main courses $9–$17. AE, MC, V. Daily noon–4pm and 5–11pm, Fri–Sat 5pm–1am.

Red Lantern 🐸 CANTONESE   Miami is not known for having good Chinese food. This popular Chinese spot is better than most. Specialties include shark's fin with chicken, and steamed whole snapper with black-bean sauce. There's also an assortment of vegetarian dishes and some excellent soups. My favorite is the clay-pot stew of chicken in ginger broth. Although the atmosphere is nothing to speak of, the varied menu and interesting preparation keep locals happy and make a meal here worthwhile.

3176 Commodore Plaza (Grand Ave.), Coconut Grove. 🏦 305/529-9998. Main courses $8–$20. AE, MC, V. Mon–Thurs 11:30am–11pm, Fri 11:30am–midnight, Sat 4pm–midnight, Sun 4–11pm.

Señor Frogs MEXICAN   Filled with a collegiate crowd, this restaurant is known for a raucous good time, a mariachi band, and powerful margaritas. The food at this rocking cantina is a bit too cheesy, but it's tasty, if not exactly authentic. The mole enchiladas, with 14 different kinds of mild chiles mixed with chocolate, is as flavorful as any I've tasted. Almost everything is served with rice and beans in quantities so large that few diners are able to finish.

3480 Main Hwy., Coconut Grove. 🏦 305/448-0999. Reservations not accepted. Main courses $12–$17. AE, DC, DISC, MC, V. Mon–Sat 11:30am–2am, Sun 11:30am–1am.

INEXPENSIVE

Cafe Tu Tu Tango 🐸 SPANISH/INTERNATIONAL   This second-floor restaurant in the bustling CocoWalk is designed to look like a disheveled artist's loft. Dozens of original paintings—some only half-finished—hang on the walls and on studio easels. Seating at sturdy wooden tables and chairs is either inside, on wooden floors among the clutter, or outdoors, overlooking the Grove's main drag.

Flamenco and other Latin-inspired tunes complement a menu with a decidedly Spanish flare. Hummus spread on rosemary flat bread and baked goat cheese in marinara sauce are two good starters. Entrees include roast duck with dried cranberries, toasted pine nuts, and goat cheese, plus Cajun chicken egg rolls filled with corn, cheddar cheese, and tomato salsa. Pastas, ribs, fish, and pizzas round out the eclectic offerings, and several visits have proved each consistently good. Try the sweet, potent sangria and enjoy the warm, lively atmosphere from a seat with a view.

3015 Grand Ave. (on the second floor of CocoWalk), Coconut Grove. 🏦 305/529-2222. Reservations not accepted. Main courses $4–$10. AE, MC, V. Sun–Wed 11:30am–midnight, Thurs 11:30am–1am, Fri–Sat 11:30am–2am.

News Café in the Grove 🐸 AMERICAN   Like its predecessor in South Beach, this big modern diner offers everything from Caesar salads to hummus to burgers to omelets to ice cream sundaes. The food is predictably good and the service lively and pleasant. The best part is that it's open around the clock to serve the after-movie crowd from CocoWalk and Mayfair, as well as the real late-night club-goers.

2901 Florida Ave. (behind Mayfair), Coconut Grove. 🏦 305/774-6397. Main courses $12–$19. AE, DC, MC, V. Daily 24 hours.

10 South Miami & West Miami

Mostly residential, these areas have several eating establishments worth the drive.

MODERATE

Coco Pazzo 🐸🐸 ITALIAN   The atmosphere here depends on where you choose to sit: the outside cafe, with a full view of all the shopping frenzy and active children, or the more serene, airy lushness of the Tuscan dining room inside. The hand-painted murals of the ocean and the wide-open kitchen invite you into the dining area. Owner Pino Luongo, who owns 14 other Coco Pazzos nationwide, strives to combine the best of Tuscan cuisine with accents of Latin and Caribbean favorites. One of the restaurant's signature dishes is the *focaccia alla robiola,* a thin-crusted focaccia stuffed with robiola cheese and drizzled with white truffle oil. Another great choice is the *calamari alla griglia,* or grilled calamari stuffed with oxtails in red wine sauce. My favorite is the *salmone con insalata estiva,* which is grilled salmon with mesclun lettuce, asparagus, mango, and balsamic reduction. For dessert try the tiramisù with mascarpone cream and ladyfingers soaked in espresso. While service here isn't up to par with the Coco Pazzo in New York, it'll do. Remember, you are in a shopping mall—would you rather be in the food court?

Inside the Shops at Sunset, 5701 Sunset Dr., South Miami. ℂ **305/665-6055.** Reservations accepted weekdays only. Main courses $14–$25; lunch menu $4.50–$14. AE, DC, MC, V. Sun–Thurs 11:30am–10pm, Fri–Sat 11:30am–midnight.

Tropical Chinese ᴿᴿ CHINESE   This strip mall restaurant way out there in West Miami Dade is hailed as the best Chinese restaurant in the city. While the food is indeed very good—certainly more interesting than at your typical beef-and-broccoli shop—it still seems somewhat overpriced. Garlic spinach and prawns in a clay pot is delicious with the perfect mix of garlic cloves, mushrooms, and fresh spinach, but it's not cheap at $16.99. And unlike most Chinese restaurants, the dishes here are not large enough to share. Sunday afternoon dim sum is extremely popular and lines often snake around the shopping center.

7991 Bird Rd., West Miami. ℂ **305/262-7576.** Reservations highly recommended. Main courses $10–$25. AE, DC, MC, V. Mon–Fri 11:30am–10:30pm, Sat 11am–10:30pm, Sun 10:30am–10pm.

Wilderness Grill AMERICAN   A cross between Outback Steakhouse and the Rainforest Café, this theme restaurant caters to kids, with sound effects, rolling lights simulating lightning in the outback, and aquariums and terrariums that abound with exotic flora and fauna. The varied menu has everything from salads to emu steak. It's all okay, not great. Try the Adelaide BBQ chicken; it's slow roasted in a tasty sauce and a bargain at $12.95. Children's menus, which double as coloring books, are also available. *Note:* If you are an adult and attend without children, don't be surprised to find them a part of the wilderness wildlife.

Shops at Sunset (57th and U.S. 1), 5701 Sunset Dr., #114, South Miami. ℂ **305/740-3033.** Main courses $8–$21. AE, MC, V. Daily 11:30am–midnight. Bar open until 1am on weekends

INEXPENSIVE

Crepe Maker Café ᴿ CREPES/FRENCH   Create your own delicious crepes at this little French cafe. You can choose from ham, tuna, black olives, red peppers, capers, artichoke hearts, and pine nuts. Some of the best combinations include a Philly cheese steak with mushrooms and a classic cordon bleu. Delicious dessert crepes have ice cream, strawberries, peaches, walnuts, and pineapples. Enjoy your crepe fresh off the griddle at the counter or on a bar stool. The soups are also delicious. Kids can run around in a small play area, too.

8269 SW 124th St., South Miami. ℂ **305/233-4458** or 305/233-1113. Crepes $3–$7.50. No credit cards. Sun and Tues–Thurs 10:30am–8:30pm, Fri–Sat 10:30am–10:30pm. Crepe cart in CocoWalk Tues–Wed 4–10pm, Thurs 11am–11pm, Fri–Sat 11am–1am, Sun 11am–11pm.

El Toro Taco Family Restaurant ★★ *Finds* MEXICAN   Until I discovered this Mexican oasis in the midst of South Florida farmland, I'd never had good enough reason to leave my quasi-cosmopolitan confines in Miami for rural Homestead way down south. This 96-seat family-run restaurant has put major miles on my car since I first stumbled upon it a few years ago when I was lost and very hungry. Fabulous, and I mean fabulous, Mexican fare, from the usual tacos, enchiladas, and burritos drenched with the freshest and zestiest salsa this side of Baja, is what you'll find here in abundance. It may sound odd to travel from a big city with tons of restaurants to farm country for Mexican food, but trust me, it's so cheap and delicious, it's worth the trip.

1 S. Krome Ave., Homestead © **305/245-8182**. Main courses $1.39–$8.75. DISC, MC, V. Tues–Sun 11am–9pm.

Kon Chau ★ CHINESE/DIM SUM   Don't be put off by the rather unappealing shopping center in which this cheap dim sum palace is located. If you want fancy plastic chopsticks and fancy prices, go up the block to Tropical Chinese. If you want delicious dim sum at ridiculously low prices, Kon Chau is where you'll find it. A simple checklist allows you to choose as much of whatever you want, from savory steamed shrimp dumplings to airy pork buns, for as little as $1 a piece.

8376 Bird Rd., West Miami. © **305/553-7799**. Items $1 and up. MC, V. Mon–Sat 11am–10pm, Sun 10am–10pm.

Shorty's ★ BARBECUE   A Miami tradition since 1951, this honky-tonk of a log cabin is still serving some of the best ribs and chicken in South Florida. People line up for the smoke-flavored, slow-cooked meat that's so tender it seems to fall off the bone. The secret, however, is to ask for your order with sweet sauce. The regular stuff tastes bland and bottled. All the side dishes, including the coleslaw, corn on the cob, and baked beans, look commercial, but are necessary to complete the experience. This is a jeans and T-shirt kind of place, but you may want to wear an elastic waistband as overeating is not uncommon.

A second Shorty's is located in Davie at 5989 S. University Dr. (© 305/944-0348).

9200 S. Dixie Hwy. (between U.S. 1 and Dadeland Blvd.), South Miami. © **305/670-7732**. Main courses $5–$9. DISC, MC, V. Mon–Thurs 11am–10pm, Fri–Sat 11am–11pm.

Tea Room ★ ENGLISH TEA   Do stop in for a spot of tea at this recently rebuilt tearoom in historic Cauley Square off U.S. 1. The little lace-curtained room is an unusual site in this heavily industrial area better known for its warehouses than its doilies.

Try one of the simple sandwiches, such as the turkey club with potato salad and a small lettuce garnish or onion soup full of rich brown broth and stringy cheese. Daily specials, such as spinach and mushroom quiche, and delectable desserts are a must before beginning your explorations of the old antiques and art shops in this little enclave of civility down south.

12310 SW 224th St. (at Cauley Square), South Miami. © **305/258-0044**. Sandwiches and salads $7–$12; soups $3–$4. AE, DISC, MC, V. Mon–Sat 11am–4pm.

7

What to See & Do in Miami

If there's one thing Miami doesn't have, it's an identity crisis. In fact, it's the city's vibrant, multifaceted personality that attracts millions each year, from all over the world. South Beach may be on the top of many Miami to-do lists, but the rest of the city, a fascinating assemblage of multicultural neighborhoods, should not be neglected. Once considered "God's Waiting Room," the Magic City now attracts an eclectic mix of old and young, celebs and plebes, American and international, and geek and chic with an equally varied roster of activities.

For starters, Miami boasts some of the most natural beauty there is, with blinding blue waters, fine, sandy beaches, and lush tropical parks. The city's human-made brilliance, in the form of Crayola-colored architecture, never seems to fade in Miami's unique Art Deco District. For cultural variation, you can experience the taste, sounds, and rhythms of Cuba in Little Havana.

Lose yourself in the city's nature and its neighborhoods, and, best of all, its people—a sassy collection of artists and intellectuals, beach bums and international transplants, dolled-up drag queens and bodies beautiful. No wonder celebrities love to vacation here—the spotlight is on the city and its residents. And unlike most stars, Miami is always ready for its close-up. With so much to do and see, Miami is a virtual amusement park that's bound to entertain all those who pass through its palm-lined gates.

1 Miami's Beaches

Perhaps Miami's most popular attraction is its incredible 35-mile stretch of beachfront, which runs from the tip of South Beach north to Sunny Isles and circles Key Biscayne and the numerous other pristine islands dotting the Atlantic. The characteristics of Miami's many beaches are as varied as the city's population: There are beaches for swimming, socializing, or serenity; for family, seniors, or gay singles; some to make you forget you're in the city, others darkened by huge condominiums. But for whatever beach vacation you're looking for, you'll find it in one of Miami's two distinct beach areas: Miami Beach and Key Biscayne.

MIAMI BEACH'S BEACHES Collins Avenue fronts more than a dozen miles of white-sand beach and blue-green waters from 1st to 192nd streets. Although most of this stretch is lined with a solid wall of hotels and condos, beach access is plentiful. There are lots of public beaches here, wide and well maintained, complete with lifeguards, toilet facilities, concession stands, and metered parking (bring lots of quarters). Except for a thin strip close to the water, most of the sand is hard-packed—the result of a $10 million Army Corps of Engineers Beach Rebuilding Project meant to protect buildings from the effects of eroding sand.

Miami Area Attractions & Beaches

Amelia Earhart Park **3**
American Police Hall of
  Fame and Museum **5**
The Barnacle State
  Historic Site **23**
Bayside Marketplace
  & Bayfront Park **15**
CocoWalk **22**
Diaspora Vibe Art Gallery **9**
Hialeah Park **7**
Hialeah Racetrack **6**
Latin American Art Museum **16**
Marjory Stoneman Douglas
  Biscayne Nature Park **25**
Miami-Dade Cultural Center
  (Miami Art Museum &
  The Historical Museum
  of Southern Florida) **14**

Miami Herald **11**
Miami Jai Alai Fronton **8**
Miami Museum of Science
  and Space Transit
  Planetarium **18**
Miami Seaquarium **24**
Miami Youth Museum **17**
Museum of
  Contemporary Art **4**

Orange Bowl **13**
Pro Player Stadium **1**
Rubell Family Collection **10**
Scott Rakow Youth Center **12**
Spanish Monastery Cloisters **2**
University of Miami **19**
Venetian Pool **20**
Villa Vizcaya **21**

> **Impressions**
> *Miami was like paradise. We had never been anywhere where there*
> *were palm trees. . . . We'd never seen a policeman with a gun, and those*
> *Miami cops did look pretty groovy.*
> —Paul McCartney in *The Beatles Anthology*

In general, the beaches on this barrier island become less crowded the farther north you go. A wooden boardwalk runs along the hotel side of the beach from 21st to 46th streets—about 1½ miles—offering a terrific sun-and-surf experience without getting sand in your shoes. Aside from "The Best Beaches," listed below, Miami's lifeguard-protected public beaches include 21st Street, at the beginning of the boardwalk; 35th Street, popular with an older crowd; 46th Street, next to the Fontainebleau Hilton; 53rd Street, a narrower, more sedate beach; 64th Street, one of the quietest strips around; and 72nd Street, a local old-timers' spot.

KEY BISCAYNE'S BEACHES   If Miami Beach doesn't provide the privacy you're looking for, try Virginia Key and Key Biscayne. Crossing the Ricken-backer Causeway ($1 toll), however, can be a lengthy process, especially on weekends, when beach bums and tan-o-rexics flock to the Key. The 5 miles of public beach here are blessed with softer sand and are less developed and more laid-back than the hotel-laden strips to the north.

THE BEST BEACHES
Here are my picks:
- **Best Party Beach:** In Key Biscayne, **Crandon Park Beach,** on Crandon Boulevard, is National Lampoon's *Vacation* on the sand. It's got a diverse crowd consisting of dedicated beach bums and lots of leisure-seeking families, set to a soundtrack of salsa, disco, and reggae music blaring from a number of competing stereos. With 3 miles of oceanfront beach, 493 acres of park, 75 grills, three parking lots, several soccer and softball fields, and a public 18-hole championship golf course, Crandon is like a theme park on the sand. Admission is $2 per vehicle. It's open daily from 8am to sunset.
- **Best Beach for People-Watching: Lummus Park Beach,** a.k.a. Glitter Beach, runs along Ocean Drive from about 6th to 14th streets on South Beach. It's the best place to go if you're seeking entertainment as well as a great tan. On any day of the week, you might spy models primping for a photo shoot, nearly naked (topless is legal here) sun-worshippers avoiding tan lines, and an assembly line of washboard abs off of which you could (but shouldn't) bounce your bottle of sunscreen. Pop star Sisquo's "The Thong Song" was inspired by this beach.
- **Best Swimming Beach:** The **85th Street Beach,** along Collins Avenue, is the best place to swim away from the maddening crowds. It's one of Miami's only stretches of sand with no condos or hotels looming over sunbathers. Lifeguards patrol the area throughout the day.
- **Best Windsurfing Beach: Hobie Beach,** on the right side of the causeway leading to Key Biscayne, is not really a beach, but an inlet with predictable winds and a number of places where you can rent Windsurfers.
- **Best Shell-Hunting Beach:** You'll find plenty of colorful shells at **Bal Harbour Beach,** Collins Avenue at 96th Street, just a few yards north of Surfside Beach. There's also an exercise course and good shade—but no lifeguards.

- **Best (Ahem) All-Around Tanning Beach:** For that all-over tan, head to **Haulover Beach,** just north of the Bal Harbour border, and join nudists from around the world in a top-to-bottom tanning session.
- **Best Surfing Beach: Haulover Beach/Harbor House,** just north of Miami Beach, seems to get Miami's biggest swells. Go early to avoid getting mauled by the aggressive young locals prepping for Maui.
- **Best Scenic Beach: Matheson Hammock Park Beach** is the epitome of tranquility, tucked away off of scenic Old Cutler Road in South Miami. And while it's scenic, it's not too much of a scene. It's a great beach for those seeking "alone time."
- **Best Family Beach:** Because of its man-made lagoon, which is fed naturally by the tidal movement of the adjacent Biscayne Bay, the waters of **Matheson Hammock Park Beach** are extremely calm, not to mention safe and secluded enough for families to keep an eye on the kids.

2 The Art Deco District

"You know what they used to say?" recalls Art Deco revivalist Dona Zemo, "Who's Art?" "You'd say, 'This is an Art Deco building,' and they'd say, 'Really, who is Art?' These people thought 'Art Deco' was some guy's name."

How things have changed. This guy Art has become one of the most popular Florida attractions since, well, that mouse Mickey. The district is roughly bounded by the Atlantic Ocean on the east, Alton Road on the west, 6th Street to the south, and Dade Boulevard (along the Collins Canal) to the north.

Most of the finest examples of the whimsical Art Deco style are concentrated along three parallel streets—Ocean Drive, Collins Avenue, and Washington Avenue—from about 6th to 23rd streets.

After years of neglect and calls for the wholesale demolition of its buildings, South Beach got a new lease on life in 1979. Under the leadership of Barbara Baer Capitman, a dedicated crusader for the Art Deco region, and the Miami Design Preservation League, founded by Baer Capitman and five friends, an area made up of an estimated 800 buildings was granted a listing on the National Register of Historic Places. Designers then began highlighting long-lost architectural details with soft sherbet shades of peach, periwinkle, turquoise, and purple. Developers soon moved in, and the full-scale refurbishment of the area's hotels was under way.

(Fun Fact From Desert Island to Fantasy Island

Miami Beach wasn't always a beachfront playground. In fact, it was a deserted island until the late 1800s, when a developer started a coconut farm there. That action sparked an interest in many other developers, including John Collins (for whom Collins Avenue is named), who began growing avocados. Other visionaries admired Collins's success and eventually joined him, establishing a ferry service and dredging parts of the bay to make the island more accessible. In 1921, Collins built a 2½-mile bridge linking downtown Miami to Miami Beach, creating excellent accessibility *and* the longest wooden bridge in the world. Today Miami Beach has six links to the mainland.

Not everyone was pleased, though. Former Miami Beach commissioner Abe Resnick said, "I love old buildings. But these Art Deco buildings are 40, 50 years old. They aren't historic. They aren't special. We shouldn't be forced to keep them." But Miami Beach kept those buildings, and Resnick lost his seat on the commission.

Today, hundreds of new hotels, restaurants, and nightclubs have been renovated or are in the process, and South Beach is on the cutting edge of Miami's cultural and nightlife scene.

EXPLORING THE AREA

If you're touring this unique neighborhood on your own, start at the **Art Deco Welcome Center,** 1001 Ocean Dr. (© **305/531-3484**), the only beachside building across from the Clevelander Hotel and bar. They give away lots of informational material including maps and pamphlets. Art Deco books (including *The Art Deco Guide,* an informative compendium of all the buildings here), T-shirts, postcards, mugs, and other paraphernalia are for sale. It's open Monday to Saturday from 9am to 6pm, sometimes later.

Take a stroll along **Ocean Drive** for the best view of sidewalk cafes, bars, colorful hotels, and even more colorful people. Another great place for a walk is **Lincoln Road,** which is lined with galleries, cafes, and funky art and antiques stores. The Community Church, at the corner of Lincoln Road and Drexel Avenue, is the neighborhood's first church and one of its oldest surviving buildings, dating from 1921.

For details on guided tours, see "Sightseeing Cruises & Organized Tours," later in this chapter.

3 Animal Parks

For a tropical climate, Miami's got a lot of nontropical animals to see, and we're not talking about the motorists on I -95. Everything from dolphins and alligators to lions, tigers, and bears call Miami home (most in parks, some in nature). Call to inquire about discount packages or coupons, which may be offered at area retail stores or in local papers.

Butterfly Mystique ✸ *Finds* Possibly Miami's wackiest attraction, Butterfly Mystique is a family-owned and -operated 5-acre butterfly farm that raises and sells the bugs in masses for various occasions. Recently opened to the public, the farm is crawling with insect lovers who marvel at the working farm and state-of-the-art mobile insect exhibit. Witness the hatching of cocoons, and, best of all, enter the farm's enclosure and feel your heart flutter as hundreds of free-flying butterflies occupy your air space. Make sure to bring an anti-itch cream before you head into the Creepy Crawly exhibit and do take the free guided tours on the hour for a bit more insect—er, insight. As far as souvenirs are concerned, butterflies are actually sold by the dozen at a pricey $75.

22601 SW 152nd Ave., Miami (a half-mile from Monkey Jungle). © **305/242-2847.** www.butterflyinmiami. com. Admission $5 adults, $ 4 children 3–12. Daily 9am–4pm.

Miami Metrozoo ✸✸ *Kids* This 290-acre complex is quite a distance from Miami proper and the beaches—about 45 minutes—but worth the trip. Isolated and never really crowded, it's also completely cageless—animals are kept at bay by cleverly designed moats. This is a fantastic spot to take the kids; there's a wonderful petting zoo and play area, and the zoo offers several daily programs designed to educate and entertain. Mufasa and Simba (of Disney fame) were modeled on a couple of Metrozoo's lions. Other residents include two rare white Bengal tigers, a Komodo dragon, rare koala bears, a number of kangaroos, and an African meerkat. The air-conditioned Zoofari Monorail tour offers visitors a nice overview of the park. An Andean Condor exhibit opened in 2000, and the zoo is always upgrading its facilities, including the impressive aviary. *Note:* The distance between animal habitats can be great, so you'll be doing *a lot* of walking here. Young children and the elderly, especially in summer, should take several rest breaks during the day (there are benches and shaded gazebos strategically positioned throughout the zoo). Also, because the zoo can be miserably hot during summer months, plan these visits in the early morning or late afternoon.

12400 SW 152nd St., South Miami. ℂ **305/251-0400.** www.miamimetrozoo.org. Admission $8 adults, $4 children 3–12. Daily 9:30am–5:30pm (ticket booth closes at 4pm). Free parking. From U.S. 1 south, turn right on SW 152nd St. and follow signs about 3 miles to the entrance.

Miami Seaquarium ★★ *Overrated*   If you've been to Orlando's SeaWorld, you may be disappointed with Miami's version, which is considerably smaller and not as well maintained. It's hardly a sprawling seaquarium, but you will want to arrive early to enjoy the effects of its mild splash. You'll need at least 3 hours to tour the 35-acre oceanarium and see all four daily shows starring a number of showy ocean mammals. You can cut your visit to 2 hours if you limit your shows to the better, albeit corny, Flipper Show and Killer Whale Show. The highly regarded Water and Dolphin Exploration Program (WADE) allows visitors to touch and swim with dolphins in the Flipper Lagoon. The program costs $125 per person and is offered twice daily, Wednesday through Sunday. Children must be at least 52 inches tall to participate. Reservations are necessary for this program. Call ℂ **305/365-2501** in advance for reservations.

4400 Rickenbacker Causeway (south side), en route to Key Biscayne. ℂ **305/361-5705.** www.miamiseaquarium.com. Admission $23 adults, $18 children 3–9, free for children under 3. Daily 9:30am–6pm (ticket booth closes at 4:30pm).

Monkey Jungle ★ *Overrated*   Personally, I think this place is disgusting. It reeks, the monkeys are either sleeping or in heat, and it's really far from the city, even farther than the zoo. But if primates are your thing and you'd rather pass on the zoo, you'll be in paradise. You'll see rare Brazilian golden lion tamarins and Asian macaques. There are no cages to restrain the antics of the monkeys as they swing, chatter, and play their way into your heart. Screened-in trails wind through acres of "jungle," and daily shows feature the talents of the park's most progressive pupils. People who go here are not monkeying around—many of the park's frequent visitors are scientists and anthropologists. Despite the smell, however, I must admit that I found myself thoroughly amused by the animal antics at the Orangutans' Asiatic Ape Exhibit. New exhibits in 2001 included the Cameroon Jungle and the Lemurs of Madagascar.

14805 SW 216th St., South Miami. ℂ **305/235-1611.** www.monkeyjungle.com. Admission $13.50 adults, $10.50 seniors and active-duty military, $8 children 4–12. Daily 9:30am–5pm (tickets sold until 4pm). Take U.S. 1 south to SW 216th St., or from Florida Turnpike, take exit 11 and follow the signs.

Parrot Jungle and Gardens ★★ *Kids*   This Miami institution will take flight from its current location in South Miami and head north in 2003 to a new $46 million home on Watson Island, along the McArthur Causeway near Miami Beach. While the island will double as a protected bird sanctuary, the jungle's soon-to-be former digs in the heart of South Miami in a circa 1900 coral rock structure are a lot more charming and kitschier. The new 18.6-acre park will feature an Everglades exhibit, a petting zoo, and several theaters, jungle trails, and aviaries. Watch your heads because flying above are hundreds of parrots, macaws, peacocks, cockatoos, and flamingos. Continuous cheesy shows star roller-skating cockatoos, card-playing macaws, and numerous stunt-happy parrots. There are also tortoises, iguanas, and a rare albino alligator on exhibit. The park's website sometimes offers downloadable discount coupons, so if you have Internet access, take a look before you visit. In its current locale, a suggested 4 hours is enough to make sure you see all the sites and shows.

11000 SW 57th Ave., Southern Miami–Dade County. ℂ 305/666-7834. www.parrotjungle.com. Admission $15.95 adults, $13.95 seniors, $10.95 children 3–10. Daily 9:30am–6pm. Cafe opens at 8am. Take U.S. 1 south and turn left at SW 57th Ave., or exit Kendall Dr. from the Florida Turnpike and turn right on SW 57th Ave.

Sea Grass Adventures 🔎 *Value*   Even better than the Seaquarium is Sea Grass Adventures, in which a naturalist from the Marjory Stoneman Douglas Biscayne Nature Center will introduce kids and adults to an amazing variety of creatures that live in the sea grass beds of the Bear Cut Nature Preserve near Crandon Beach on Key Biscayne. Not just a walking tour, you will be able to wade in the water with your guide and catch an assortment of sea life in nets provided by the guides. At the end of the program, participants gather on the beach while the guide explains what everyone's just caught, passing the creatures around in miniature viewing tanks. A real bargain at just $10 per person. Call for available dates and reservations.

Marjory Stoneman Biscayne Nature Center, 6767 Crandon Blvd., Key Biscayne. ℂ 305/361-6767.

4 Miami's Museum & Art Scene

Miami has never been known as a cultural mecca as far as museums are concerned. Though several exhibition spaces have made forays into collecting nationally acclaimed work, limited support and political infighting have made it a difficult proposition. Recently, with the reinvention of the Wolfsonian, the reincarnation of MOCA, and the increased daring of the Miami Art Museum, the scene has improved dramatically. It's now safe to say that world-class exhibitions start here. Listed below is a cross-section of the valuable treasures that have become a part of the city's cultural heritage, and as such, are as diverse as the city itself.

For gallery lovers, see "Specialized Tours," below, for scheduled gallery walks.

IN SOUTH BEACH

Work continues to proceed on the **Miami Beach Cultural Park,** which comprises a trio of arts buildings on Collins Park and Park Avenue (off Collins Avenue), bounded by 21st to 23rd streets—the newly expanded Bass Museum of Art (see below), the new Arquitectonica-designed home of the Miami City Ballet, and the Miami Beach Regional Library, which broke ground in January 2001 and will have a special focus on the arts. Collins Park, the former site of the Miami Beach Library, will return to its original incarnation as an open space extending to the Atlantic, but it will also be the site of large sculpture installations and cultural activities planned jointly by the organizations that share the space.

Art Center/South Florida 🔎   Not exactly a museum in the classic sense of the word, Art Center/South Florida is a multichambered space where local artists display their works in all mediums—from photography and sculpture to

South Beach Attractions

To Central Miami Beach ↗ ↑ **1**

2

The Bass Museum of Art **3**

4 22nd St.
COLLINS PARK

Dade Boulevard

20th St.

19th St.

5 **6** Miami Beach Convention Center

18th St.

7

17th St. **8**

Venetian Causeway

Dade Boulevard

BELLE ISLAND

Lincoln Road Mall **9**

10 **11** Lincoln Rd. **12**

Purdy Ave.

Bay Rd.

West Ave.

Alton Rd.

HISTORIC ART DECO DISTRICT

16th St.

15th St.

Collins Ave.

James Ave.

13 Española Way

14th St. Miami Beach Post Office

Biscayne Bay

Lenox Ave.

Michigan Ave.

Jefferson Ave.

Meridian Ave.

13th St.

12th St. **14**

FLAMINGO PARK

Washington Ave.

Ocean Dr.

West Ave.

11th St.

15 Beach Patrol Station

16

10th St.

Pennsylvania Ave.

Art Deco Welcome Center

9th St.

Michigan Ave.

8th St.

LUMMUS PARK

7th St.

6th St.

17

18 5th St.

4th St.

3rd St.

2nd St.

Washington Ave.

19

Collins Ave.

Ocean Dr.

ATLANTIC OCEAN

1st St.

Commerce St.

Biscayne St.

SOUTH POINTE PARK

Government Cut

ART & ATTRACTIONS
Art Center/South Florida **13**
Bass Museum of Art **3**
Bayshore Golf Course **2**
Estefan Enterprises **18**
Holocaust Memorial **6**
Mermaid Sculpture **8**
Miami Beach Botanical Garden **7**
Morris Lapidus sculpture **12**
Oleta River State
   Recreational Area **1**
Sanford L. Ziff Jewish Museum **19**
Versace Mansion **15**
The Wolfsonian **16**

BIKE & BLADE RENTALS
Fritz's Skate Shop **11**
Miami Beach Bicycle Center **17**

GYM
Crunch **14**

PERFORMANCE SPACES
Colony Theater **10**
Jackie Gleason Theater of the
   Performing Arts **8**
Lincoln Theater **9**
Ophelia & Juan Jr. Roca Center **4**

INFORMATION
Miami Beach Chamber
   of Commerce **5**

0   1/4 mi
0   0.25 km

N

Roadside Attractions

The following examples of public art and prized architecture are great photo opportunities and worth visiting if you're in the area.

- **Versace Mansion (Amsterdam Palace):** Morbid curiosity has led hordes of people—tourists and locals—to this, the only private home on Ocean Drive, better known as the Versace mansion. If you can get past the fact that the late designer was murdered on the steps of this palatial estate, you should definitely observe the intricate Italian architecture that makes this house stand out from its streamlined Deco neighbors. Built in the 1930s as a replica of Christopher Columbus's son's palace in Santo Domingo, the house was originally called Casa Casuarina (House of the Pine), but was rechristened the Amsterdam Palace in 1935 when George Amsterdam purchased it. While there were rumors that the mansion was to be turned into a Versace museum, it was purchased by a private citizen from Texas. Located at the northwest corner of Ocean Drive and 11th Street, South Beach.

- **Estefan Enterprises:** Miami's royal family—Gloria and Emilio Estefan—may reside on private Star Island, but the headquarters of their musical empire is located in a whimsical building designed by the world-famous Arquitectonica architecture company. Its facade is carved with color-lined waves and fanciful shapes. But don't get caught up in the design, as you may miss an opportunity to run into the next Ricky Martin or even Gloria herself. The address is 420 Jefferson Ave. (at 5th Street), Miami Beach.

- **Miami Beach Post Office:** Usually known for long lines and surly people, post offices are rarely considered a must-see, but this one's an

video and just about anything else that might exemplify their artistic nature. Admission is free and it's quite fun to wander through the space viewing the various artists at work in their studios. Of course, all the art is for sale, but there's no pressure to buy. Ask for a guided tour of the gallery for extra insight into particular exhibits.

924 Lincoln Rd. (at Meridian Ave.), South Beach. (✆) **305/674-8278.** Free admission. Daily 11am–11pm.

Bass Museum of Art ✹✹✹   The Bass Museum of Art has expanded and received a dramatically new look. World-renowned Japanese architect Arata Isozaki designed the magnificent new facility, which has triple the former exhibition space, and added an outdoor sculpture terrace, a museum cafe and courtyard, and a museum shop, among other improvements. In addition to providing space in which to show the permanent collection, exhibitions of a scale and quality not presently seen in Miami will now be featured at the Bass. The museum's permanent collection includes European paintings from the 15th through the early 20th centuries with special emphasis on Northern European art of the Renaissance and Baroque periods, including Dutch and Flemish masters such as Bol, Flinck, Rubens, and Jordaens.

2121 Park Ave. (1 block west of Collins Ave.), South Beach. (✆) **305/673-7530.** www.bassmuseum.org. Admission $5 adults, $3 students and seniors, free for children 6 and under; second and fourth Wed of the exception. Built in 1937, this historic Depression modern-style building features a fabulous rotunda. Utterly Floridian are the coral steps that lead to the entrance. In addition to the requisite mailboxes, stamp machines, and Wanted posters, inside an intricate sun motif surrounds a lantern hanging from the ceiling, which illuminates the epic mural. One glimpse of this magnificent building and you'll rethink the meaning of "going postal." Find it at at 1300 Washington Ave., Miami Beach.

- **Mermaid Sculpture:** A pop art masterpiece designed by Roy Lichtenstein, this sculpture captures the buoyant spirit of Miami Beach and its environs. It's in front of the Jackie Gleason Theater of the Performing Arts, 1700 Washington Ave., Miami Beach.

- **Morris Lapidus on Lincoln Road:** Famed designer/architect, the late Morris Lapidus—the "high priest of high kitsch"—who is best known for the Fountainebleau Hotel, created a series of sculptures that are angular, whimsical, and quirky, competing with the equally amusing mix of pedestrians who flock to Lincoln Road. In addition to the sculptures on Lincoln Road (at Washington Avenue), which you can't miss, Lapidus also created the Colony Theater, 1040 Lincoln Rd., which was built by Paramount in 1943; the 1928 Sterling Building, 927 Lincoln Rd., whose glass blocks and blue neon are required evening viewing; and the Lincoln Theater, 555 Lincoln Rd., which features remarkable tropical bas-relief.

month by donation from 5–9pm. Tues–Sat 10am–5pm, Sun 1–5pm (every second and fourth Wed open 1–9pm). Closed major holidays.

Holocaust Memorial 𝕲𝕲𝕲 This heart-wrenching memorial is hard to miss and would be a shame to overlook. The powerful centerpiece, Kenneth Triester's *Sculpture of Love & Anguish,* depicts victims of the concentration camps crawling up a giant, yearning hand, stretching up to the sky, marked with an Auschwitz number tattoo. Along the reflecting pool is the story of the Holocaust, told in cut marble slabs. Inside the center of the memorial is a tableau that is one of the most solemn and moving tributes to the millions of Jews who lost their lives in the Holocaust I've seen. You can walk through an open hallway lined with photographs and the names of concentration camps and their victims. From the street, you'll see the outstretched arm, but do stop and tour the sculpture at ground level.

1933 Meridian Ave. (at Dade Blvd.), South Beach. 𝕮 **305/538-1663.** Free admission. Daily 9am–9pm.

Sanford L. Ziff Jewish Museum 𝕲 Chronicling over 230 years of Jewish heritage and experiences in Florida, the Jewish Museum presents a fascinating look at religion and culture through films, lectures, and exhibits such as "Passages: An Immigrant's Journey," featuring memorabilia, photos, and documents tracing the immigration to the United States of 24 families of various ethnic and religious backgrounds. The museum is housed in a former synagogue.

301 Washington Ave., South Beach. © **305/672-5044**. www.jewishmuseum.com. $5 adults, $4 seniors and students, $10 families. Free admission Sat. Tues–Sun 10am–5pm.

Wolfsonian ★★★ *Finds* Mitchell Wolfson Jr., heir to a family fortune built on movie theaters, was known as an eccentric, but I'd call him a pack rat. A premier collector of propaganda and advertising art, Wolfson was spending so much money storing his booty that he decided to buy the warehouse that was housing it. It ultimately held more than 70,000 of his items from Nazi propaganda to King Farouk of Egypt's match collection. Thrown in the eclectic mix are also zany works from great modernists such as Charles Eames and Marcel Duchamp. He then gave this incredibly diverse and controversial collection to Florida International University. The former storage facility has been retrofitted with such painstaking detail that it's the envy of curators around the world. The museum is unquestionably fascinating and even hosts lectures and rather swinging events surrounding particular exhibits.

1001 Washington Ave., South Beach. © **305/531-1001**. Admission $5 adults; $3.50 seniors, students, and children 6–12; $5 tour-group members. Free admission Thurs evenings. Free admission for members, children under 6, and students or faculty of Florida Universities. Mon–Tues and Fri–Sat 11am–6pm, Thurs 11am–9pm, Sun noon–5pm.

IN & NEAR DOWNTOWN

American Police Hall of Fame and Museum This strange museum appeals mostly to those fascinated by police and their gadgetry. Once inside, you'll find a combination of reality and fantasy that's part thoughtful tribute, part Hollywood-style drama. Just past the car featured in the motion picture *Blade Runner* is a mock prison cell, in which visitors can take pictures of themselves pretending they're doing 5 to 10. Also on hand are execution devices, including a guillotine and an electric chair (whose controversial use was recently abolished in Florida). In the entry is a touching memorial to the more than 3,000 police officers who have lost their lives in the line of duty. Even if you don't go inside, you can't miss the museum, which has a real police car attached to its facade. Try not to speed by—you never know what sort of radar the car's got.

3801 Biscayne Blvd., Miami. © **305/573-0070**. www.aphf.org. Admission $6 adults, $4 seniors over 61, $3 children 11 and under, $1 police officers. 50% off coupons often available from hotel racks. Daily 10am–5:30pm. Go north on U.S. 1 from downtown; it's the building with police car affixed to its side.

Diaspora Vibe Art Gallery ★★ This art complex housed in an old bakery is a funky artist hangout and home to some of the greatest artworks of Miami's diverse Caribbean, Latin American, and African-American cultures. The gallery has two seasons of shows, often focusing on emerging artists. During the winter, three artists are selected by the gallery to travel to and exhibit their work in Paris.

On the last Friday of every month from May through October is the gallery's fabulous "Final Fridays." A new artist's work is spotlighted inside, while outside in the courtyard are live music performances and readings of poetry and folk tales. Delicious Caribbean cuisine is also served. The who's who of Miami's cognoscenti gather here to recharge their cultural batteries.

561 NW 32nd St., Studio 48 (Bakehouse Art Complex), Miami. © **305/759-1110**. www.diasporavibe.com. "Final Fridays" admission $15. Mon–Fri by appointment; Sat–Sun 1–6pm; May–Oct last Fri of the month 7–11pm.

Latin American Art Museum   In addition to the permanent collection of contemporary artists from Spain and Latin America, this 3,500-square-foot museum hosts monthly exhibitions of works from Latin America and the Caribbean Basin. Usually, the exhibitions focus on a theme, such as international women or surrealism. It's not a major attraction, but worth a stop if you're interested in Latin American art. On the same block, you'll find great design stores and a few other galleries.

2206 SW 8th St., Little Havana. ℭ 305/644-1127. hispmuseum@aol.com. Free admission. Tues–Fri 11am–5pm, Sat 11am–4pm. Closed Aug and major holidays.

Miami Art Museum at the Miami–Dade Cultural Center ★★★   The Miami Art Museum (MAM) features an eclectic mix of modern and contemporary works by such artists as Eric Fischl, Max Beckmann, Jim Dine, and Stuart Davis. Rotating exhibitions span the ages and styles, and often focus on Latin American or Caribbean artists. There are also fantastic themed exhibits such as the Andy Warhol exhibit, which featured all-night films by the artist, make-your-own pop art, cocktail hours, and parties with local deejays. JAM at MAM is the museum's popular happy hour, which takes place the second Thursday of the month and is tied in to a particular exhibit. Almost as artistic as the works inside the museum is the composite sketch of the people—young and old—who attend these events.

The Miami–Dade Cultural Center, where the museum is housed, is a fortress-like complex designed by Phillip Johnson. In addition to the acclaimed Miami Art Museum, the center houses the main branch of the Miami–Dade Public Library, which sometimes features art and cultural exhibits, and the Historical Museum of Southern Florida, which highlights the fascinating history of the area. Unfortunately, the plaza onto which the complex opens is home to many of downtown Miami's homeless population.

101 W. Flagler St., Miami. ℭ 305/375-3000. Admission $5 adults, $2.50 seniors and students, free for children under 12; by contribution on Tues. Tues–Fri 10am–5pm; third Thurs of each month 10am–9pm; Sat–Sun noon–5pm. Closed major holidays. From I-95 south, exit at Orange Bowl–NW 8th St. and continue south to NW 2nd St.; turn left at NW 2nd St. and go 1½ blocks to NW 2nd Ave.; turn right.

Museum of Contemporary Art (MOCA) ★★★   MOCA boasts an impressive collection of internationally acclaimed art with a local flavor. A high-tech screening facility allows for film presentations to complement the exhibitions. You can see works by Jasper Johns, Roy Lichtenstein, Larry Rivers, Duane Michaels, and Claes Oldenberg, plus there are special exhibitions by such artists as Yoko Ono, Sigmar Polke, John Baldessari, and Goya. Guided tours are offered in English, Spanish, French, Creole, Portuguese, German, and Italian.

770 NE 125th St., North Miami. ℭ 305/893-6211. Fax 305/891-1472. www.mocanomi.org. Admission $5 adults, $3 seniors and students with ID, free for children 12 and under. Tues–Sat 11am–5pm, Sun noon–5pm. Closed major holidays.

Rubell Family Art Collection ★★★ *Finds*   This impressive collection owned by the Miami hotelier family, the Rubells, is housed in a two-story 40,000-square-foot former Drug Enforcement Agency warehouse in a sketchy area north of downtown Miami. The building looks like a fortress, which is fitting: Inside is a priceless collection of more than a thousand works of contemporary art, by the likes of Keith Haring, Damien Hirst, Julian Schnabel, Jean-Michel Basquiat, Paul McCarthy, Charles Ray, and Cindy Sherman. But be forewarned: Some of the art is extremely graphic and may be off-putting to some. The gallery changes exhibitions twice yearly and there is a seasonal program of lectures, artists' talks, and performances by prominent artists.

95 NW 29th St. (on the corner of NW 1st Ave. near the Design District), Miami. 🕻 **305/573-6090.** Free admission. Thurs–Sat 11am–4pm and by appointment.

IN CORAL GABLES & COCONUT GROVE

Lowe Art Museum 🕿🕿 Located on the University of Miami campus, the Lowe Art Museum has a dazzling collection of 8,000 works that include American paintings, Latin American art, Navajo and Pueblo Indian textiles, and Renaissance and Baroque art. Traveling exhibits such as *Rolling Stone* magazine's photo collection also stop here.

University of Miami, 1301 Stanford Dr. (at Ponce de León Blvd.), Coral Gables. 🕻 **305/284-3603.** Admission $5 adults, $3 seniors, $2 students with ID. Tues, Wed, Fri, and Sat 10am–5pm, Thurs noon–7pm.

Miami Museum of Science and Space Transit Planetarium 🕿🕿 *Kids* The Museum of Science features more than 140 hands-on exhibits that explore the mysteries of the universe. Live demonstrations and collections of rare natural history specimens make a visit here fun and informative. Many of the demos involve audience participation, which can be lots of fun for willing and able kids and adults alike. There is also a Wildlife Center with more than 175 live reptiles and birds of prey. The adjacent Space Transit Planetarium projects astronomy and laser shows as well as interactive demonstrations of upcoming computer technology and cyberspace features. Call, or visit their website, for a listing of upcoming exhibits and laser shows.

3280 S. Miami Ave. (just south of the Rickenbacker Causeway), Coconut Grove. 🕻 **305/646-4200** for general information, or 305/854-2222 for planetarium show times. www.miamisci.org. $10 adults, $8 seniors and students, $6 children 3–12, free for children 2 and under; laser shows $6 adults, $3 seniors and children 3–12. Half price 4:30–6pm weekdays; 25% discount for AAA members. Museum of Science, daily 10am–6pm; call for planetarium show times (last show is at 4pm).

Weeks Air Museum This well-maintained museum is a must-see for aeronautic buffs, who will enjoy talking to the thoroughly dedicated staff who are always eager to answer questions from fellow enthusiasts. Exhibitions include a dramatic portrait of the Tuskegee Airmen, who share their experiences on video. Also on display are dozens of airplanes dating from the turn of the 20th century and an intriguing display of planes damaged by Hurricane Andrew in 1992. Other highlights include a collection of propellers throughout the ages, a J47 jet engine, an aerobatic plane, the "Little Stinker" Soviet bombers, and lots of war memorabilia.

14710 SW 28th St. (south of 120th St. and west of the Florida Turnpike at the Kendall–Tamiami Airport), Miami. 🕻 **305/233-5197.** Admission $6.95 adults, $5.95 seniors, $4.95 children under 12. Daily 10am–5pm.

5 Historic Homes & Sites

South Beach's well-touted Deco District is but one of many colorful neighborhoods that can boast dazzling architecture. The rediscovery of the entire Biscayne Corridor (from downtown to the 80s) has given light to a host of ancillary neighborhoods on either side that are filled with Mediterranean-style homes and Frank Lloyd Wright gems. Coral Gables is home to many large and beautiful homes, mansions, and churches that reflect architecture from the 1920s, '30s, and '40s. Some of the homes, or portions of their structure, have been created from coral rock and shells. Even if you don't stay at the Biltmore Hotel, definitely take a tour of it. Call 🕻 **305/445-1926** for more information.

Barnacle State Historic Site ⭐⭐ The former home of naval architect and early settler Ralph Middleton Munroe is now a museum in the heart of Coconut Grove. It's the oldest house in Miami and rests on its original foundation, which sits on 5 acres of hardwood and landscaped lawns. The house's quiet surroundings, wide porches, and period furnishings illustrate how Miami's first snowbird lived in the days before condo-mania and luxury hotels. Enthusiastic and knowledgeable state park employees offer a wealth of historical information to those interested in quiet, low-tech attractions like this one. Call for details on the fabulous monthly moonlight concerts during which folk, blues, or classical music is presented and picnicking is encouraged.

3485 Main Hwy. (1 block south of Commodore Plaza), Coconut Grove. ☎ **305/448-9445.** Fax 305/448-7484. Admission $1. Concerts $5, free for children under 10. Fri–Mon 9am–4pm. Tours Fri–Sun at 10am, 11:30am, 1pm, and 2:30pm. Group tours Mon–Thurs with 2-week advance reservations. From downtown Miami, take U.S. 1 south to 27th Ave., make a left, and continue to S. Bayshore Dr.; then make a right, follow to the intersection of Main Hwy., and turn left.

Coral Castle ⭐⭐ *(Finds)* There's plenty of competition, but Coral Castle is probably the strangest attraction in Florida. In 1923, the story goes, a 26-year-old crazed Latvian, suffering from unrequited love of a 16-year old who left him at the altar, immigrated to South Miami and spent the next 25 years of his life carving huge boulders into a prehistoric-looking roofless "castle." It seems impossible that one rather short man could have done all this, but there are scores of affidavits on display from neighbors who swear it happened. Apparently, experts have studied this phenomenon to help figure out how the Great Pyramids and Stonehenge were built. Rocker Billy Idol was said to have been inspired by this place to write his song "Sweet Sixteen." An interesting 25-minute audio tour guides you through the spot, now in the National Register of Historic Places. Although Coral Castle is overpriced and undermaintained, it's worth a visit when in the area.

28655 S. Dixie Hwy., Homestead. ☎ **305/248-6345.** www.coralcastle.com. Admission $7.75 adults, $6.50 seniors, $5 children 7–12. Mon–Sat 9am–7pm, Sun 9am–6pm. Take U.S. 1 south to SW 286th St.

Spanish Monastery Cloisters ⭐⭐⭐ *(Finds)* Did you know that the alleged oldest building in the Western Hemisphere dates from 1133 and is located in Miami? The Spanish Monastery Cloisters were first erected in Segovia, Spain. Centuries later, newspaper magnate William Randolph Hearst purchased and brought them to America in pieces. The carefully numbered stones were quarantined for years until they were finally reassembled on the present site in 1954. It has often been used as a backdrop for movies and commercials and is a very popular tourist attraction.

16711 W. Dixie Hwy. (at NE 167th St.), North Miami Beach. ☎ **305/945-1461.** monastery@earthlink.net. Admission $5 adults, $2.50 seniors, $2 children 3–12. Mon–Sat 10am–4pm, Sun 1–5pm.

Venetian Pool ⭐⭐⭐ *(Kids)* Miami's most beautiful and unusual swimming pool, dating from 1924, is hidden behind pastel stucco walls and is honored with a listing in the National Register of Historic Places. Underground artesian wells feed the free-form lagoon, which is shaded by three-story Spanish porticos and features both fountains and waterfalls. It can be cold in the winter months. During summer, the pool's 800,000 gallons of water are drained and refilled nightly, ensuring a cool, *clean* swim. Visitors are free to swim and sunbathe here, just as Esther Williams and Johnny Weissmuller did decades ago. For a modest fee, you or your children can learn to swim during special summer programs.

2701 DeSoto Blvd. (at Toledo St.), Coral Gables. © 305/460-5356. www.venetianpool.com. Admission and hours vary seasonally. Nov–Mar, $5 for those 13 and older, $2 children under 13; April–Oct, $8 for those 13 and older, $4 children under 13. Children must be 3 years old or 38 inches tall to enter or provide proof of 3 years of age with birth certificate.

Villa Vizcaya ✿✿✿   Sometimes referred to as the "Hearst Castle of the East," this magnificent villa is more Gatsby-esque than anything you'll find in Miami. It was built in 1916 as a winter retreat for James Deering, cofounder and former vice president of International Harvester. The industrialist was fascinated by 16th-century art and architecture, and his ornate mansion, which took 1,000 artisans 5 years to build, became a celebration of that period. Most of the original furnishings, including dishes and paintings, are still intact. A free guided tour of the 34 furnished rooms takes about 45 minutes. The spectacularly opulent villa wraps itself around a central courtyard. Outside, lush formal gardens, accented with statuary, balustrades, and decorative urns, front an enormous swath of Biscayne Bay. While Vizcaya is a premier venue for society events and weddings, there are several events that are open to the public such as the Renaissance Fair; definitely take the tour of the rooms, but immediately thereafter, you will want to wander and get lost in the resplendent gardens.

3251 S. Miami Ave. (just south of Rickenbacker Causeway), North Coconut Grove. © 305/250-9133. Admission $10 adults, $5 children 6–12, free for children 5 and under. Villa daily 9:30am–5pm (ticket booth closes at 4:30pm); gardens daily 9:30am–5:30pm.

6 Nature Preserves, Parks & Gardens

The Miami area is a great place for outdoors types, with beaches, parks, and gardens galore. Plus, South Florida has two national parks; see chapter 10, "South Florida Side Trips," for coverage of the Everglades and Biscayne National Park.

BOTANICAL GARDENS & A SPICE PARK

Fairchild Tropical Garden ✿✿✿   This garden at 10901 Old Cutler Rd. (© 305/667-1651; www.ftg.org), is the largest of its kind in the continental United States. A veritable rain forest of both rare and exotic plants, as well as 11 lakes and countless meadows, are spread across 83 acres. Palmettos, vine pergola, palm glades, and other unique species create a scenic, lush environment. More than 100 species of bird have been spotted at the garden (ask for a checklist at the front gate), and it's home to a variety of animals. You should not miss the 30-minute narrated tram tour (tours leave on the hour from 10am to 3pm weekdays and 10am to 4pm on weekends) to learn about the various flowers and trees on the grounds. There is also a museum, a cafe, a picnic area, and a gift shop with fantastic books on gardening and cooking and edible gifts. A new 2-acre rain-forest exhibit will save you a trip to the Amazon.

Admission is $8 for adults, and free for children 12 and under accompanied by an adult. Open daily, except December 25, from 9:30am to 4:30pm. Take I-95 south to U.S. 1, turn left onto Le Jeune Road, and follow it straight to the traffic circle; from there, take Old Cutler Road 2 miles to the park.

Although an ocean and a continent apart, Hawaii and Florida share similar climates because both lie near the Tropic of Cancer. As a result, the organization known as the National Tropical Botanical Gardens has four gardens and three preserves in Hawaii and one in South Florida—**The Kampong** ✿. Located on Biscayne Bay in Coconut Grove (4013 Douglas Rd.), the Kampong contains a stunning array of flowering trees and tropical fruit trees including mango, avocado, and pomelos. In the early 1900s, noted plant explorer David Fairchild (for whom the Fairchild Tropical Gardens are named) traveled the world seeking rare plants of economic and aesthetic value that might be culti-vated in the United States. In 1928, he and his wife, Marian (daughter of Alexander Graham Bell), built a two-story residence here (listed on the National Register of Historic Places) amid some of his collections, borrowing the Malaysian word *kampong* for his home in a garden. In the 1960s, the Fairchilds sold the Kampong to Catherine Hauberg Sweeney, who donated the property to the National Tropical Botanical Garden to promote and preserve this South Florida treasure. It's a must-see. Tours are by appointment only, from Monday to Friday. For tour information, call ✆ **305/442-7169.**

A testament to Miami's unusual climate, the **Preston B. Bird and Mary Heinlein Fruit and Spice Park** ✮, 24801 SW 187th Ave., Homestead (✆ **305/ 247-5727**), harbors rare fruit trees that cannot survive elsewhere in the country. If a volunteer is available, you'll learn some fascinating things about this 30-acre living plant museum, where the most exotic varieties of fruits and spices—ackee, mango, Ugli fruits, carambola, and breadfruit—grow on strange-looking trees with unpronounceable names.

The best part? You're free to take anything that *naturally* falls to the ground. You'll also find samples of interesting fruits and jellies made from the park's bounty in the gift store. Cooks who like to experiment should visit the park store, which carries a number of exotic ingredients and cookbooks.

Admission to the spice park is $3.50 for adults and $1 for children under 12. It's open daily from 10am to 5pm; closed major holidays. Tours are included in the price of admission and are offered 11am, 1pm, and 2:30pm. Take U.S. 1 south, turn right on SW 248th Street, and go straight for 5 miles to SW 187th Avenue. Hours are 10am to 5pm daily.

MORE MIAMI PARKS

Because so many people are so focused on the beach itself, the **Miami Beach Botanical Garden,** 2000 Convention Center Dr., Miami Beach (✆ **305/ 673-7256**), remains, for the most part, a secret garden. The lush, tropical 4½-acre garden is a fabulous, all-natural retreat from the hustle and bustle of the silicone-enhanced city. Open Monday through Friday from 8:30am to 5pm, Saturday and Sunday from 9:30am to 5pm. Free admission.

The **Amelia Earhart Park,** 401 E. 65th St., Hialeah (✆ **305/685-8389**), is the only real reason to travel to industrial, traffic-riddled Hialeah. There are five lakes stocked with bass and bream for fishing; playgrounds; picnic facilities; and a big red barn that houses cows, sheep, and goats for petting, and ponies for rid-ing. There's also a country store and dozens of old-time farm activities like horse-shoeing, sugarcane processing, and more. Parking is free on weekdays and $3.50 per car on weekends. Open daily from 9am to sunset. To drive here, take I-95 north to the NW 103rd Street exit, go west to East 4th Avenue, and then turn right. Parking is 1½ miles down the street.

At the historic **Bill Baggs Cape Florida State Recreation Area,** 1200 Cran-don Blvd. (✆ **305/361-5811**), at the southern tip of Key Biscayne, you can explore the unfettered wilds and enjoy some of the most secluded beaches in Miami. There's also a recently reopened lighthouse. A rental shack rents bikes, hydrobikes, kayaks, and many more water toys. It's a great place to picnic, and a newly constructed restaurant serves homemade Latin food, including great fish soups and sandwiches. Just be careful that the raccoons don't get your lunch—

the furry black-eyed beasts are everywhere. Admission is $4 per car with up to eight people. Open daily from 8am to sunset. Tours of the lighthouse are available every Thursday through Monday at 10am and 1pm. Arrive at least half an hour early to sign up—there is only room for 10 people on each.

Tropical Park, 7900 SW 40th St. (℗ 305/226-8315), has it all. Enjoy a game of tennis and racquetball for a minimal fee, or swim and sun yourself on the secluded little lake. You can use the fishing pond for free, and they'll even supply you with the rods and bait. If you catch anything, however, you're on your own. Open daily from sunrise to sunset.

Named after the late champion of the Everglades, the **Marjory Stoneman Douglas Biscayne Nature Center,** 6767 Crandon Blvd., Key Biscayne (℗ 305/361-6767), has just moved into a brand-new $4 million facility and offers hands-on marine exploration, hikes through coastal hammocks, bike trips, and beach walks. Local environmentalists and historians lead intriguing trips through the local habitat. Be sure to wear comfortable closed-toe shoes for hikes through wet or rocky terrain. Open daily 10am–7pm Memorial Day–Labor Day; daily 10am–4pm rest of year. Admission to park is $4 per person; admission to nature center free. Call for weekend programs.

The **Oleta River State Recreation Area,** 3400 NE 163rd St., North Miami (℗ 305/919-1846), consists of 993 acres—the largest urban park in the state—on Biscayne Bay. The beauty of the Oleta River combined with the fact that you're essentially in the middle of a city makes this park especially worth visiting. With miles of bicycle and canoe trails, a sandy swimming beach, shaded picnic pavilions, and a fishing pier, Oleta River State Recreation Area offers visitors an outstanding outdoor recreational experience cloistered from the confines of the big city. Open daily 8am–sunset. Admission for pedestrians and cyclists is $1 per person. By car: driver plus car $2; driver plus 1 to 7 passengers and car $4.

7 Especially for Kids

The **Scott Rakow Youth Center,** 2700 Sheridan Ave. (℗ 305/673-7767), is a hidden treasure on Miami Beach. This two-story facility boasts an ice-skating rink, bowling alleys, a basketball court, gymnasium equipment, and full-time supervision for kids. Call for a complete schedule of organized events. The only drag is that it's not open to adults (except on Sunday, which is family day). Admission is $1.50 per day for visiting children 9 to 17. Open daily from 2 to 8:30pm.

The following is a roundup of other attractions that kids will especially enjoy. Details on each one can be found earlier in the chapter. Also, see "Video Arcades & Entertainment Centers," later in this chapter.

AMELIA EARHART PARK *(see p. 171)*   This is the best park in Miami for kids. They'll like the petting zoos, pony rides, and a private island with hidden tunnels.

MARJORY STONEMAN DOUGLAS BISCAYNE NATURE CENTER *(see p. 172)*   Kids seem to enjoy touching slimy marine animals and spotting unusual creatures out at sea. This brand-new exhibit and tour center offers lots of educational and fun programs.

MIAMI METROZOO *(see p. 160)*   This completely cageless zoo offers such star attractions as a monorail "safari" and a petting zoo. Kids can take a ride on an elephant.

MIAMI MUSEUM OF SCIENCE & SPACE TRANSIT PLANETARIUM *(see p. 168)* Kids can learn about space and science by watching entertaining films and cosmic shows. The space museum also offers child-friendly explanations for natural occurrences.

MIAMI SEAQUARIUM *(see p. 161)* Kids can touch, swim with, or kiss a dolphin and watch exciting performances.

PARROT JUNGLE *(see p. 161)* Kids just love these well-trained feathered friends.

8 Video Arcades & Entertainment Centers

GameWorks ☆ *Kids* Steven Spielberg's SEGA GameWorks in the Shops at Sunset Place has become the hottest place for young adults to play. You'll see kids, gen-Xers, and baby boomers fighting off dinosaurs from *Jurassic Park,* racing in the Indy 500, swooshing down a snowy ski trail, throwing darts, and shooting pool in this sleek multilevel playground. The young at heart will find the perfect combination of vintage arcade games, high-tech videos, virtual-reality arenas, pool tables, food, and cocktails in this playground occupying more than 33,000 square feet. The GameWorks Grill serves up everything from gourmet salads to pizzas and burgers. Bring lots—and we mean lots—of change.

5701 Sunset Dr. South Miami. ℂ 305/667-4263. Mon–Fri 11am–2am, Sat 10am–2am, Sun 10am–midnight. Games 50¢–$5.

IMAX Theatre at Sunset Place ☆ *Kids* Utilizing high-tech film techniques, six-story-high screens, and wraparound digital sound, this unique movie experience really makes you feel like you're part of the action. Films tend to be on the more educational side, but kids won't mind because the effects are outstanding. Also available is a 3-D theater that really tempts you to reach out and touch the images.

5701 Sunset Dr., South Miami. ℂ 305/663-4629. www.imax.com/miami. IMAX, $9 adults, $8 seniors and students, $7 children under 12. Shows daily 11am–11pm. Call for schedule.

9 Sightseeing Cruises & Organized Tours

BOAT & CRUISE-SHIP TOURS

Celebration ☆ This 1-hour air-conditioned cruise will take you past Millionaires' Row and the Venetian Islands for just $10. There's also a food stand and cash bar. The tours are bilingual.

Bayside Marketplace Marina, 401 Biscayne Blvd., Downtown. ℂ 305/373-7001. Tickets $10 adults, children sail free. Millionaire's Row tour daily 1, 3, 5, and 7pm. Evening party cruise Fri–Sat 9–11pm.

Heritage Miami II Topsail Schooner This relaxing ride aboard Miami's only tall ship is a fun way to see the city. The 2-hour cruise passes by Villa Vizcaya, Coconut Grove, and Key Biscayne and puts you in sight of Miami's spectacular skyline and island homes. Call to make sure the ship is running on schedule. On Friday, Saturday, and Sunday evenings, there are 1-hour tours to see the lights of the city, leaving at 6:30pm, for $10 per person.

Bayside Marketplace Marina, 401 Biscayne Blvd., Downtown. ℂ 305/442-9697. Fax 305/442-0119. Tickets $15 adults, $10 children 12 and under. Sept–May only. Tours leave daily at 1:30, 4, and 6:30pm, and Fri–Sun also at 9, 10, and 11pm.

Water Taxi ☆☆☆ *Value* Not exactly a tour, per se, the Water Taxi is a cheap and fantastic way to see the city via local waterways. The two major routes run

Venice in Miami

You don't have to endure jet lag and time zone differences to enjoy the beauty of Italy. Located just off Miami Beach, Florida's own Venetian Islands (NE 15th Street and Dade Boulevard) were joined together in 1926 by a bascule bridge known as the Venetian Causeway. A series of 12 bridges connecting the Venetian Islands and stretching between Miami and Miami Beach feature octagonal concrete entrance towers. The oldest causeway in metropolitan Miami, the Venetian is rickety in a charming way, featuring fantastic views of the city and the mammoth cruise ships docked at the port, not to mention a glimpse of some of Miami's most beautiful waterfront homes. Bikers and joggers especially love the Venetian because of limited traffic and beautiful scenery.

between Bayside Marketplace and the 5th Street Marina on South Beach; the second is basically a downtown water shuttle service between the various hotels in downtown as well as the Port of Miami, the Hard Rock Cafe at Bayside, East Coast Fisheries, and Fisher Island. Cost is $7 one-way, $12 round-trip, and $15 for an all-day pass. The Bayside/South Beach trip is the best one to take because there aren't as many stops.

© 305/467-6677. www.watertaxi.com.

A SIGHTSEEING TOUR

While there are several sightseeing tour operators in Miami, most unfortunately either don't speak English or are just plain shoddy. The following is the one we'd recommend:

Miami Nice Excursion Travel and Service (★)   Pick your destination. The Miami Nice tours will take you to the Everglades, Fort Lauderdale, South Beach, the Seaquarium, Key West, Cape Canaveral, or wherever you desire. The best trip for first-timers is the City Tour, a comprehensive tour of the entire city and its various neighborhoods. If you've got the time, you will definitely want to add on a side trip to the Everglades and/or Key West. Included in most Miami trips is a fairly comprehensive city tour narrated by a knowledgeable guide. The company is one of the oldest in town.

18430 Collins Ave., Miami Beach. © 305/949-9180. Tours are $29–$55 adults, $25 children. Daily 7am–10pm. Call ahead for directions to various pickup areas.

SPECIALIZED TOURS

In addition to those listed below, a great option for seeing the city is to take a tour led by **Dr. Paul George.** Dr. George is a history teacher at Miami–Dade Community College and a historian at the Historical Museum of Southern Florida. He also happens to be "Mr. Miami." There's a set calendar of tours, but all of them are fascinating to South Florida buffs. Tours focus on neighborhoods, such as Little Havana, Brickell Avenue, or Key Biscayne, and on themes, such as Miami cemeteries and the Miami River. The often long-winded discussions can be a bit much for those who just want a quick look around, but Dr. George certainly knows his stuff. The cost is $15 to $25; reservations are required (© **305/ 375-1621**). Tours leave from the Historical Museum at 101 W. Flagler St., Downtown.

Art Deco Biking Tour 🏕️🏕️   If you'd rather bike than walk, catch this fun and interesting morning tour on the third Sunday of every month. The bicycle is the most efficient mode of transportation through the streets of South Beach, and one of the best ways to see the historic Art Deco District. Call to reserve a spot.

601 5th St., South Beach. ℭ 305/674-0150. mbbicycle@aol.com. $10 per person, plus $10 for bike rental. Tours depart the third Sun of every month at 10am from the Miami Beach Bicycle Center.

Biltmore Hotel Tour 🏕️🏕️🏕️ *Value*   Take advantage of these free Sunday walking tours to enjoy the hotel's beautiful grounds. The Biltmore is chock-full of history and mystery, including a few ghosts; go out there and see for yourself. In addition, there are also free weekly fireside sessions that are open to the public and presented by Miami Storytellers. Learn about the hotel's early days and rich stories of the city's past. These wonderful sessions are held in the main lobby by the fireplace and are accompanied by a glass of champagne.

1200 Anastasia Ave., Coral Gables. ℭ 305/445-1926. www.biltmorehotel.com. Free admission. Tours depart on Sun at 1:30, 2:30, and 3:30pm. Call for times of storytelling sessions.

Coral Gables Art and Gallery Tour 🏕️🏕️🏕️ *Value*   This is a fabulous and *free* event that draws art aficionados and the generally curious to sip wine and analyze the various works of art displayed in the many galleries of Coral Gables featuring American folk art, African, Native American, and Latin art, and photography. On the first Friday of every month, art lovers are shuttled to more than 20 galleries that participate in Gables Night. Most galleries are on Ponce de León Boulevard, between SW 40th and SW 24th streets. The vans run continuously from 7 to 10pm.

Various locations in Coral Gables. For more information, call Elite Fine Art (ℭ 305/448-3800), or stop by any of the galleries in the area. Free. First Fri of the month 7–10pm.

Miami Design Preservation League 🏕️🏕️   On Thursday evenings and Saturday mornings, the Design Preservation League sponsors walking tours that offer a fascinating inside look at the city's historic Art Deco District. Tour-goers meet for a 1½-hour walk through some of America's most exuberantly "architectured" buildings. The league led the fight to designate this area a National Historic District and is proud to share the splendid locale with visitors.

Art Deco Welcome Center, 1001 Ocean Dr., South Beach. ℭ 305/672-2014. www.mdpl.org. Walking tours $10 per person. Tours leave Sat at 10:30am and Thurs at 6:30pm. Self-guided audio tours also available daily for $10. No reservations necessary. Call ahead for updated schedules.

Murder, Mystery and Mayhem Bus Tour 🏕️🏕️🏕️   Visit the past by video and bus to Miami–Dade's most celebrated crimes and criminals from the 1800s to the present. From the murder spree of the Ashley Gang to the most notorious murders and crimes of our century, including the murder of designer Gianni Versace, historian Paul George conducts a most fascinating tour of scandalous proportions.

Leaves Sat at 10pm from the Dade Cultural Center, 101 W. Flagler St., Miami. Tickets $35. Advance reservations required; call ℭ 305/375-1621.

Second Thursdays: Miami Beach Arts Night 🏕️🏕️🏕️ *Value*   The artistic equivalent of a triathlon, this free cultural open house in Miami Beach takes place on the second Thursday of every month at various venues throughout the city. Hear a string quartet at an area church and then hop on the shuttle for a Haitian dance performance at the Miami Beach Recreation Center. A celebration of the arts, Second Thursdays are a wonderful way to explore the rich and diverse cultures that make the city such a fascinating melting pot.

Various venues. (© 305/673-7600. www.2ndthursdays.com. Free. Second Thurs of every month 6–9pm.

10 Watersports

BOATING

Private rental outfits include **Boat Rental Plus,** 2400 Collins Ave., Miami Beach (© **305/534-4307**), where 50-horsepower 18-foot powerboats rent for some of the best prices on the beach. There's a 2-hour minimum and rates go from $99 to $449. There are great specials on Sunday. All rates include taxes and gas. A $250 cash or credit-card deposit is required. Cruising is permitted only in and around Biscayne Bay. Ocean access is prohibited. Renters must be over 21. The rental office is at 23rd Street, on the inland waterway in Miami Beach. It's open daily from 10am to sunset.

Club Nautico of Coconut Grove, 2560 S. Bayshore Dr. (© **305/858-6258**), rents high-quality powerboats for fishing, water-skiing, diving, and cruising in the bay or ocean. All boats are Coast Guard equipped, with VHF radios and safety gear. Rates range from $199 for 4 hours and $299 for 8 hours, to as much as $419 on weekends. Club Nautico is open daily from 9am to 5pm (weather permitting). Other locations include the Crandon Park Marina, 4000 Crandon Blvd., Key Biscayne (© **305/361-9217**), with the same rates and hours as the Coconut Grove location; and the Miami Beach Marina, Pier E, 300 Alton Rd., South Beach (© **305/673-2502**), where rates are $229 for 4 hours and $299 for 8 hours for a 20-foot boat, and $259 for 4 hours and $359 for 8 hours for a 24-footer. Nautico on Miami Beach is open daily from 9am to 5pm.

JET SKIS/WAVERUNNERS

Don't miss a chance to tour the islands on the back of your own powerful watercraft. Bravery is, however, a prerequisite, as Miami's waterways are full of speeding jet skiers and boaters who think they're in the Indy 500. Many beachfront concessionaires rent a variety of these popular (and loud) water scooters. The latest models are fast and smooth. Try **Tony's Jet Ski Rentals,** 3601 Rickenbacker Causeway, Key Biscayne (© **305/361-8280**), one of the city's largest rental shops, located on a private beach in the Miami Marine Stadium lagoon. There are three models available accommodating up to three people. Rates range from $45 for a half hour to $80 for a full hour, depending on the number of riders. Tony's is open daily from 10:30am to 6:30pm.

KAYAKING

The laid-back **Urban Trails Kayak Company** rents boats at 10800 Collins Ave. (© **305/947-1302**). It offers scenic routes through rivers with mangroves and islands as your destination. Most of the kayaks are sit-on-tops, and most are plastic, although there are some fiberglass models available. Rates are $8 an hour, $20 for up to 4 hours, and $25 for over 4 hours. Tandems are $12 an hour, $30 for up to 4 hours, and $35 for the day. Open daily from 9am to 5pm.

The outfitters here give interested explorers a map to take with them and quick instructions on how to work the paddles and boats. If you have at least four people, you can get a guided half-day tour for $35 per person. This is a fun way to experience some of Miami's unspoiled wildlife, and it's good exercise, too.

SAILING

You can rent sailboats and catamarans through the beachfront concessions desk of several top resorts, such as the Doral Golf Resort, Sheraton Bal Harbour Beach Resort, and Dezerland Beach Resort Hotel (see chapter 5, "Miami Accommodations").

Sailboats of Key Biscayne Rentals and Sailing School, in the Crandon Marina (next to Sundays on the Bay), 4000 Crandon Blvd., Key Biscayne (© **305/361-0328** days, 305/279-7424 evenings), can also get you out on the water. A 22-foot sailboat rents for $27 an hour, or $81 for a half day. A Cat-25 or J24 is available for $35 an hour or $110 for a half day. If you've always had a dream to win the America's Cup but can't sail, the able teachers at Sailboats will get you started. It offers a 10-hour course over 5 days for $300 for one person or $400 for you and a buddy.

Shake-a-Leg, 2600 Bayshore Dr., Coconut Grove (© **305/858-5550**), is a unique sailing program for disabled and able-bodied people alike. The program pairs up sailors for day and evening cruises and offers sailing lessons as well. Consider a moonlight cruise (offered monthly) or a race clinic. Shake-a-Leg members also welcome able-bodied volunteers for activities on and off the water. It costs $60 for nonmembers to rent a boat for 3 hours; free for volunteers. Open Wednesday through Sunday from 9am to 5pm.

SCUBA DIVING

In 1981, the government began a wide-scale project designed to increase the number of habitats available to marine organisms. One of the program's major accomplishments has been the creation of nearby artificial reefs, which have attracted all kinds of tropical plants, fish, and animals. In addition, Biscayne National Park (see "Biscayne National Park," in chapter 10) offers a protected marine environment just south of downtown.

Several dive shops around the city offer organized weekend outings, either to the reefs or to one of over a dozen old shipwrecks around Miami's shores. Check "Divers" in the Yellow Pages for rental equipment and for a full list of undersea tour operators.

Divers Paradise of Key Biscayne, 4000 Crandon Blvd. (© **305/361-3483**), offers two dive expeditions daily to the more than 30 wrecks and artificial reefs off the coast of Miami Beach and Key Biscayne. You can take a 3-day certification course for $399, which includes all the dives and gear. If you already have your C-card, a dive trip costs about $90 if you need equipment and only $35 if you bring your own gear. It's open Monday to Friday from 10am to 6pm and Saturday and Sunday from 8am to 6pm. Call ahead for times and locations of dives.

WINDSURFING

Many hotels rent Windsurfers to their guests, but if yours doesn't have a watersports concession stand, head for Key Biscayne.

Sailboards Miami, Rickenbacker Causeway, Key Biscayne (© **305/361-SAIL**), operates out of big yellow trucks on Hobie Beach, the most popular windsurfing spot in the city. For those who've never ridden a board but want to try it, they offer a 2-hour lesson for $69 that's guaranteed to turn you into a wave warrior or you get your money back. After that, you can rent a board for $20 an hour or $38 for 2 hours. If you want to make a day of it, a 10-hour card costs $150. Open daily from 10am to 5:30pm. Make your first right after the toll booth to find the outfitters.

11 More Ways to Play, Indoors & Out

BIKING

The cement promenade on the southern tip of the island is a great place to ride. Biking up the beach is great for surf, sun, sand, exercise, and people watching—just be sure to keep your eyes on the road as the scenery can be most distracting. Most of the big beach hotels rent bicycles, as does the **Miami Beach Bicycle Center,** 601 5th St., South Beach (© **305/674-0150**), which charges $5 per hour or $14 per day. It's open Monday to Saturday from 10am to 7pm, Sunday from 10am to 5pm.

Bikers can also enjoy more than 130 miles of paved paths throughout Miami. The beautiful and quiet streets of Coral Gables and Coconut Grove are great for bicyclists. Old trees form canopies over wide, flat roads lined with grand homes and quaint street markers. Several bike trails are spread throughout these neighborhoods, including one that begins at the doorstep of **Grove Cycle,** 3216 Grand Ave., Coconut Grove (© **305/444-5415**). Open Tuesday to Saturday from 11am to 5:30pm, Sunday from 11am to 6pm.

The terrain in Key Biscayne is perfect for biking, especially along the park and beach roads. If you don't mind the sound of cars whooshing by, **Rickenbacker Causeway** is also fantastic, since it is one of the only bikeable inclines in Miami from which you get fantastic elevated views of the city and waterways. **Key Biking,** 61 Harbor Dr., Key Biscayne (© **305/361-0061**), rents mountain bikes for $5 an hour or $15 a day. It's open Monday through Friday from 10am to 7pm, Saturday from 10am to 6pm, and Sunday from 11am to 4pm.

If you want to avoid the traffic altogether, head out to **Shark Valley** in the Everglades National Park—one of South Florida's most scenic bicycle trails and a favorite haunt of city-weary locals. For more information, see chapter 10.

Biking note: Children under the age of 16 are required by Florida law to wear a helmet, which can be purchased at any bike store or retail outlet selling biking supplies.

FISHING

Some of the best surf casting in the city can be had at **Haulover Beach Park** at Collins Avenue and 105th Street, where there's a bait-and-tackle shop right on the pier. **South Pointe Park,** at the southern tip of Miami Beach, is another popular fishing spot and features a long pier, comfortable benches, and a great view of the ships passing through Government Cut.

You can also do some deep-sea fishing. One bargain outfitter, the **Kelley Fishing Fleet,** at the Haulover Marina, 10800 Collins Ave. (at 108th Street), Miami Beach (© **305/945-3801**), has half-day, full-day, and night fishing aboard diesel-powered "party boats." The fleet's emphasis on drifting is geared toward trolling and bottom fishing for snapper, sailfish, and mackerel, but it also schedules 2- and 3-day trips to the Bahamas. Half-day and night fishing trips are $29 for adults and $20 for children; full-day trips are $36 for adults and $18 for children; rod and reel rental is $5. Daily departures are scheduled at 9am, 1:45pm, and 8pm; reservations are recommended.

Also at the Haulover Marina is the charter boat *Helen C* (10800 Collins Ave., Haulover; © **305/947-4081**). Although there's no shortage of private charter boats here, Capt. Dawn Mergelsberg is a good pick, since she puts individuals together to get a full boat. Her *Helen* is a twin-engine 55-footer, equipped for big-game "monster" fish like marlin, tuna, dolphin, shark, and sailfish. The cost is $85 per person. Full-day trips are available and cost $800. Group rates and

A Berry Good Time

South Florida's farming region has been steadily shrinking in the face of industrial expansion, but you'll still find several spots where you can get back to nature while indulging in a local gastronomic delight—picking your own produce at the "U-Pic-'Em" farms that dot South Dade's landscape. Depending on what's in season, you can get everything from fresh herbs and vegetables to a mélange of citrus and berries. During berry season—January to April—it's not uncommon to see hardy pickers leaving the groves with hands and faces that are stained a tale-telling crimson and garnished with happy smiles. On your way through South Dade, keep an eye out for the bright red "U-Pic" signs.

There are also a number of fantastic fruit stands in the region. **Burr's Berry Farms,** 12741 SW 216th St. (© **305/251-0145**), located in the township of Goulds, has created a sensation with their fabulous fruit milk shakes. To get there, go south on U.S. 1 and turn right on SW 216th Street. The fruit stand is about 1 mile west and on the same road as Monkey Jungle. Open daily from 9am to 5:30pm.

For fresh fruit in a yummy pastry or tart, head over to **Knaus Berry Farm** at 15980 SW 248th St. (© **305/247-0668**), in an area known as the Redlands. Some people erroneously call this farm an Amish farm, but in actuality it's run by a sect of German Baptists. The stand offers items ranging from fresh flowers to ice cream, but be sure to indulge in one of their famous homemade cinnamon buns. Be prepared to wait on a long line to stock up—people flock here from as far away as Palm Beach. Head south on U.S. 1 and turn right on 248th Street. The stand is 2½ miles farther on the left-hand side. Open Monday through Saturday from 8am to 5:30pm.

specials are also available. Sailings are scheduled for 8am to noon and 1 to 5pm daily; call for reservations. Private charters and transportation are also available. Children are welcome.

Key Biscayne offers deep-sea fishing to those willing to get their hands dirty and pay a bundle. The competition among the boats is fierce, but the prices are basically the same no matter which you choose. The going rate is about $400 to $450 for a half day and $600 to $700 for a full day of fishing. These rates are usually for a party of up to six, and the boats supply you with rods and bait as well as instruction for first-timers. Some will take you out to Key Biscayne and even out to the Upper Keys if the fish aren't biting in Miami.

You might consider the following boats, all of which sail out of the Key Biscayne marina: *Sunny Boy III* (© **305/361-2217**), *Queen B* (© **305/361-2528**), and *L & H* (© **305/361-9318**). Call for reservations.

Bridge fishing is also popular in Miami; you'll see people with poles over almost every waterway. But look carefully for signs telling you whether it's legal to do so wherever you are. Some bridges forbid fishing. The Biscayne Bay area is prime tarpon fishing country and a pretty good spot for a lot of other trophy sportfish: snook, bonefish, dolphin, and sailfish.

Tips **A Fisherman's Friend**

The Biscayne Bay area is prime tarpon fishing country and a pretty good spot for a lot of other trophy sportfish: snook, bonefish, dolphin, and sailfish. For a fee, local guides are happy to show you the hot spots and make sure you hook up. One such guide is **Capt. David Parsons** (© 305/968-9603), who owns a 28-foot boat, *Hakuna Matada*. He will take you from Biscayne Bay to the Atlantic Ocean in search of the best catch of the day.

GAMBLING

Although gambling is technically illegal in Miami, there are plenty of loopholes that allow all kinds of wagering. Gamblers can try their luck at offshore casinos, bingo, jai alai, card rooms, horse tracks, and dog races.

Especially popular is **Miccosukee Indian Gaming,** 500 SW 177th Ave. (off S.R. 41; © **800/741-4600** or 305/222-4600), where a touch of Vegas meets west Miami. This tacky casino isn't Caesar's Palace, but you can play tab slots, high-speed bingo (watch out for the serious blue-haired players who will scoff if you make too much noise or if you win before they do), and even poker (with a $10 maximum pot). With more than 85,000 square feet of playing space, the complex even offers overnight accommodations for those who can't get enough of the thrill.

One of the most popular gambling "cruises to nowhere" is the **Europa Sea Kruz.** It departs every afternoon and evening from Dock A at 1280 5th St., South Beach (© **800/688-PLAY** or 305/538-8300). Tickets cost $10 to $15. A reasonably priced a la carte menu offers basic American fare, from hamburgers to grilled chicken and salads. Most evenings, you'll hear live music on board. You and a few hundred other passengers can play blackjack or the slots. The biggest drawback—if you're losing big or just get bored, you're stuck at sea for 4½ hours.

A newer and more elegant option is the *Casino Princesa,* which docks behind the Hard Rock Cafe in Bayside Marketplace. This 200-foot $15 million yacht has more than 200 slot machines, 32 tables, a restaurant, and four lounges in 10,000 square feet of gaming space on two decks. A major bargain (unless, of course, you lose) at $5.95 per person. Ships sail for 4½ hours from 12:30 to 5pm on weekdays and weekends and also from 7:30pm to midnight on weekend nights. Call © **305/379-5825** for updated schedules.

GOLF

There are more than 50 private and public golf courses in the greater Miami area. Contact the **Greater Miami Convention and Visitors Bureau** (© **800/283-2707** or 305/539-3063) for a list of more courses and costs.

The best hotel courses in Miami are found at the **Doral Resort and Spa** (see chapter 5), home of the legendary Blue Monster course as well as the Gold Course designed by Raymond Floyd, the Great White Shark Course and the Silver Course, refinished by Jerry Pate.

Other hotels with excellent golf courses include the **Biltmore Hotel,** with modest greens fees and an 18-hole par-71 course located on the hotel's spectacular grounds, and the **Turnberry Isle Resort and Spa,** with two Robert Trent

Jones–designed courses for guests and members. For more information, see chapter 5, "Miami Accommodations."

Otherwise, the following represent some of the area's best public courses. **Crandon Park Golf Course,** formerly known as the Links, 6700 Crandon Blvd., Key Biscayne (© **305/361-9129**), is the no. 1 ranked municipal course in the state and one of the top five in the country. The park is situated on 200 bayfront acres and offers a pro shop, rentals, lessons, carts, and a lighted driving range. The course is open daily from dawn to dusk; greens fees (including cart) are $86 per person during the winter and $45 per person during the summer. Special twilight rates are available.

One of the most popular courses among real enthusiasts is the **Doral Park Golf and Country Club,** 5001 NW 104th Ave., West Miami (© **305/ 591-8800**); it's not related to the Doral Hotel or spa. Call to book in advance, since this challenging 18-holer is popular with locals. The course is open from 6:30am to 6pm during the winter and until 7pm during the summer. Cart and greens fees vary, so call © **305/594-0954** for information.

Known as one of the best in the city, the **Golf Club of Miami,** 6801 Miami Gardens Dr., at NW 68th Avenue (© **305/829-8456**), has three 18-hole courses of varying degrees of difficulty. You'll encounter lush fairways, rolling greens, and some history to boot. The west course, designed in 1961 by Robert Trent Jones and updated in the 1990s by the PGA, was where Jack Nicklaus played his first professional tournament and Lee Trevino won his first professional championship. The course is open daily from 6:30am to sunset. Cart and greens fees are $45 to $75 per person during the winter, and $20 to $34 per person during the summer. Special twilight rates are available.

Golfers looking for some cheap practice time will appreciate **Haulover Park,** 10800 Collins Ave., Miami Beach (© **305/940-6719**), in a pretty bayside location. The longest hole on this par-27 course is 125 yards. It's open daily from 7:30am to 5:30pm during the winter, and until 7:30pm during the summer. Greens fees are $5 per person during the winter and $4 per person during the summer. Handcarts cost $1.40.

HEALTH CLUBS

Being situated in a very body-conscious city, many of Miami's hotels have state-of-the-art gyms. The **David Barton Gym** at the Delano Hotel, 1685 Collins Ave., South Beach (© **305/673-2900**), boasts an advanced free-weight system, life cycles, treadmills, a celebrity clientele, and wall-to-wall mirrors for the buff to admire themselves and others. A warning, however: Even hotel guests have to pay a $15 fee to sweat. The **Spa of Eden** at the Eden Roc Hotel, 4525 Collins Ave., South Beach (© **305/531-0000**), is a sports complex that has state-of-the-art equipment and one of the city's only rock-climbing walls. It's free to hotel guests but $35 for everyone else. The fitness center at the **Biltmore Hotel** (1200

ⓘ Tips Par for the Course

You can get information about most Florida courses, including current greens fees, and reserve tee times through **Tee Times USA,** P.O. Box 641, Flagler Beach, FL 32136 (© **800/374-8633,** 888/465-3567, or 904/439-0001; fax 904/439-0099). This company also publishes a vacation guide that includes many stay-and-play golf packages.

Anastasia Ave., Coral Gables; (℗ **305/445-1926**) is also impressive, with 15,000 square feet of cardio and weight machines. There is no charge for hotel guests, but a $15 fee for visitors. If you don't mind competing with Oprah Winfrey, the Spa Internazionale at **Fisher Island Club** (One Fisher Island Dr., Fisher Island; (℗ **800/537-3708** or 305/535-6020) is probably the swankiest private gym in the city, open only to its guests, with one-on-one trainers, an assortment of cardio and weight equipment, and a sublime waterfall in which to submerge your sweaty body after a grueling workout

Although many of Miami's full-service hotels have fitness centers, you can't count on them in less upscale establishments or in the small Art Deco District hotels. Several health clubs around the city will take in nonmembers on a daily basis. If you're already a member at the megaclub chain **Bally's Total Fitness,** dial (℗ **800/777-1117** to find the clubs in the area. There are no outlets on the beaches; most are in South Miami.

One of the most popular clubs, which welcomes walk-in guests, is **Crunch,** 1253 Washington Ave., South Beach (℗ **305/674-8222**), where you might work out with Cindy Crawford, Madonna, or any of a number of supermodels when they're in town. This club offers star appeal and top-of-the-line equipment. Use of the facility is $18 daily or $65 weekly. It keeps late hours, especially in season, when it's often open until midnight.

IN-LINE SKATING

Miami's consistently flat terrain makes in-line skating easy. Lincoln Road, for example, is a virtual skating rink as bladers compete with bikers and walkers for a slab of slate. But the city's heavy traffic and construction make it tough to find long routes. Remember to keep a pair of sandals or sneakers with you, since many area shops won't allow you inside with skates on.

Because of the popularity of blading and skateboarding, the city has passed a law prohibiting skating on the west side (the cafe-lined strip) of Ocean Drive in the evenings. In addition, the city has passed a law that all bladers must skate slowly and safely. You wouldn't want to mow down an elderly stroller.

You can still have fun, though, and the following rental outfit can help chart an interesting course for you and supply you with all the necessary gear. In South Beach, **Fritz's Skate Shop,** 726 Lincoln Rd. Mall (℗ **305/532-1954**), rents top-quality skates, including safety pads, for $8 per hour, $24 per day, and $34 overnight. If you're an in-line skater newbie, an instructor will hold your hand for $25 an hour. The shop also stocks lots of gear and clothing.

SWIMMING

There is no shortage of water here. See "The Best Beaches" and also the Venetian Pool under "Historic Homes & Sites," earlier in this chapter, for descriptions of good swimming options.

TENNIS

Hundreds of tennis courts in South Florida are open to the public for a minimal fee. Most courts operate on a first-come, first-served basis, and are open from sunrise to sunset. For information and directions, call the **City of Miami Beach Recreation, Culture, and Parks Department** (℗ **305/673-7730**), or the **City of Miami Parks and Recreation Department** (℗ **305/575-5256**).

The three hard courts and seven clay courts at the **Key Biscayne Tennis Association,** 6702 Crandon Blvd. (℗ **305/361-5263**), get crowded on weekends, since they're some of Miami's most beautiful. You'll play on the same courts as Lendl, Graf, Evert, McEnroe, and other greats; this is the venue for one of the world's biggest annual tennis events, the Ericsson Open (see "South Florida Calendar of Events," in chapter 2). There's a pleasant, if limited, pro shop, plus many good pros. Only four courts are lit at night, but if you reserve at least 48 hours in advance, you can usually take your pick. They cost $6 per person per hour. The courts are open daily from 8am to 9pm.

Hotels with the best tennis facilities are the Biltmore, Turnberry Isle Resort and Spa, the Doral Resort and Spa, and the Inn and Spa at Fisher Island. See chapter 5 for information about these accommodations.

12 Spectator Sports

Check the *Miami Herald*'s sports section for a daily listing of local events and the paper's Friday "Weekend" section for comprehensive coverage and in-depth reports. For last-minute tickets, call the venue directly, since many season ticket holders sell singles and return unused tickets. Expensive tickets are available from brokers or individuals, listed in the classified sections of the local papers. Some tickets are also available through **TicketMaster** (© **305/358-5885**).

BASEBALL

The **Florida Marlins** shocked the sports world in 1997 when they became the youngest expansion team to win a World Series, but then floundered as their star players were sold off by former owner Wayne Huizenga. If you're interested in catching a game, be warned: The summer heat in Miami can be unbearable, even in the evenings. As long as the rebuilding process continues and the Marlins continue to struggle, tickets are easy to come by.

Home games are held at the **Pro Player Stadium,** 2267 NW 199th St., North Miami Beach (© **305/626-7426**). Tickets are $4 to $30. Box office hours are Monday to Friday from 8:30am to 6pm, Saturday from 8:30am to 4pm, and before games; tickets are also available through TicketMaster. The team currently holds spring training in Melbourne, Florida.

BASKETBALL

The **Miami Heat** (© **305/577-HEAT** or 305/835-7000), now led by celebrity coach Pat Riley, made its NBA debut in November 1988 and their games remain one of Miami's hottest tickets. Courtside seats are full of visiting celebrities from Puff Daddy to Madonna. The season lasts from October to April, with most games beginning at 7:30pm. They'll now play in the brand-new waterfront **American Airlines Arena** located downtown on Biscayne Boulevard. Tickets are $14 to $50. Box office hours are Monday to Friday from 10am to 4pm (until 8pm on game nights); tickets are also available through TicketMaster.

FOOTBALL

Miami's golden boys are the **Miami Dolphins,** the city's most recognizable team, followed by thousands of "dolfans." The team plays at least eight home games during the season, between September and December, at **Pro Player Stadium,** 2267 NW 199th St., North Miami Beach (© **305/620-2578**). Tickets cost between $20 and $40. The box office is open Monday to Friday from 8:30am to 5:30pm; tickets are also available through **TicketMaster** (© **305/350-5050**).

HORSE RACING

Wrapped around an artificial lake, **Gulfstream Park,** at U.S. 1 and Hallandale Beach Boulevard, Hallandale (𝄐 **305/931-7223**), is both pretty and popular. Large purses and important races are commonplace at this suburban course, and the track is often crowded. Call for schedules. Admission is $3 to the grandstand and $3 to the clubhouse; free parking. From January through March, post times are Wednesday to Monday at 1pm. Many weekends feature live concerts by musicians well past their heyday, from Peter Frampton to Air Supply.

You might remember the pink flamingos at **Hialeah Park,** 2200 E. 4th Ave., Hialeah (𝄐 305/885-8000), from *Miami Vice.* This famous colony is the largest of its kind. The track, listed on the National Register of Historic Places, is one of the most beautiful in the world, featuring old-fashioned stands and acres of immaculately manicured grounds. Admission is $1 to the grandstand and $2 to the clubhouse on weekdays, and $2 and $4, respectively, on weekends. Children 17 and under enter free with an adult. Parking starts at $2. Races are held mid-March to mid-May, but the course is open year-round for sightseeing Monday to Saturday from 9am to 5pm. Call for post times.

ICE HOCKEY

The young **Florida Panthers** (𝄐 954/835-7000) have already made history. In the 1994–95 season, they played in the Stanley Cup finals, and they have amassed a legion of fans who love them. Much to the disappointment of

 On Location in Miami

Warm weather, picturesque skylines, perfect sunsets—Miami is the perfect setting for making movies.

Since the earliest days of the film industry, Miami has had a starring role in some of America's most celebrated celluloid classics, from the Marx Brothers' first feature, *The Cocoanuts* (1929), to the 1941 classic, *Citizen Kane,* which used the spectacular South Florida coastline as the setting for Kane's own Hearst Castle, Xanadu. As the film industry evolved and productions became more elaborate, Miami was thrice seized by a suave international man of intrigue known as Bond, James Bond, in *Dr. No, Live and Let Die,* and *Goldfinger.* In the past 5 years, there were over 60 major motion pictures filmed in Miami–Dade County, from action flicks like *True Lies* and *On Any Given Sunday* to comedies such as *There's Something About Mary* and dramas such as *Random Hearts.*

At any given time of day—or night—actors, directors, and film crews can be spotted on the sands and streets of Miami working on what may be the next blockbuster to hit the big screen. Watching a film being shot is fun, free entertainment; of course, it could be boring, if actors can't get the scene right and you have to suffer through take after take. Unfortunately, filming schedules are not publicized, so keep an eye out for CREW signs posted throughout the city and check with hotel personnel, who are usually up-to-date on who's in town shooting what. Who's knows? You could be discovered.

Miamians, they moved to a new venue in Sunrise, the next county north of Miami–Dade. Call for directions and ticket information.

JAI ALAI

Jai alai, sort of a Spanish-style indoor lacrosse, was introduced to Miami in 1924 and is regularly played in two Miami-area frontons. Although the sport has roots stemming from ancient Egypt, the game as it's now played was invented by Basque peasants in the Pyrenees Mountains during the 17th century.

Players use woven baskets, called *cestas,* to hurl balls, called pelotas, at speeds that sometimes exceed 170 miles per hour. Spectators, who are protected behind a wall of glass, place bets on the evening's players.

The **Miami Jai Alai Fronton,** 3500 NW 37th Ave., at NW 35th Street (© **305/633-6400**), is America's oldest fronton, dating from 1926. It schedules 13 games per night. Admission is $1 to the grandstand, $5 to the clubhouse. It's open year-round. There are games Monday and Wednesday to Saturday at 7pm and matinees on Monday, Wednesday, and Saturday at noon.

13 Cruises & Other Caribbean Getaways

Cruising has come a long way since the days of bingo, shuffleboard, and even the delusional *Love Boat.* Whether you prefer megaships with rock-climbing walls or a smaller, less elaborate ship that just sails you to your destination, a floating vacation can be a very enticing option for people traveling to South Florida. The proximity to the Caribbean makes a 3-, 4- or 7-day cruise an excellent diversion from the hustle and bustle of the big city.

If you want to catch a weekend in the Caribbean while you're in South Florida but aren't enthralled with the idea of boat travel, there are a number of air packages available as well. Travel to Cuba is strictly prohibited from Miami (or anywhere in the United States) for all but those who have obtained licenses from the U.S. State Department, although many people choose to go there from Mexico, Jamaica, or the Bahamas.

The following sections aren't intended to be detailed descriptions of the cruising and package options available out of Miami and the Keys—that would fill up an entire book on its own—but they will give you a good overview of the cruising and package picture.

CRUISES

The Port of Miami is the world's busiest cruise-ship port, with a passenger load of close to 3 million annually. The popularity of these cruises shows no sign of tapering off, and the trend in ships is toward bigger, more luxurious liners. Usually all-inclusive, cruises offer value and simplicity compared to other vacation options. Most of the Caribbean-bound cruise ships sail weekly out of the Port of Miami. They are relatively inexpensive, can be booked without advance notice, and make for an excellent excursion.

All the shorter cruises are well equipped for gambling. Their casinos open as soon as the ship clears U.S. waters—typically 45 minutes after leaving port. Usually, four full-size meals are served daily, with portions so huge they're impossible to finish. Games, movies, and other onboard activities ensure you're always busy. Passengers can board up to 2 hours before departure for meals, games, and cocktails.

There are dozens of cruises from which to choose—from a 1-day excursion to a trip around the world. You can get a full list of options from the **Metro–Dade**

Seaport Department, 1015 North America Way, Miami, FL 33132 (© 305/ 371-7678). It's open Monday through Friday from 8am to 5pm.

The cruise lines and ships listed below offer 2- and 3-day excursions to the Caribbean, Key West, and other longer itineraries that change often. If you want more information, contact the individual line, or, for Bahamas cruises, call the **Bahamas Tourist Office,** 19495 Biscayne Blvd., Suite 809, Aventura, FL 33180 (© 305/932-0051). All passengers must travel with a passport or proof of citizenship for reentry into the United States.

For detailed information on Caribbean cruises, pick up copies of *Frommer's Caribbean Cruises* and *Frommer's Caribbean Ports of Call.*

Carnival Cruise Lines (© 800/327-9501 or 305/599-2200; www.carnival. com) has 3- and 4-day cruises to Key West and the Caribbean as well as 7-day excursions that include stops in Mexico, Jamaica, and the Cayman Islands. Carnival's ships are appropriately known as Fun Ships, catering to a young party-hearty crowd. There's also a smoke-free ship called the *Paradise.* Cruises usually depart from Miami Friday through Monday. Prices range from $400 to $3,000, not including port charges, which can be as high as $100 per person.

Cunard (© 800/528-6273 or 305/463-3000; www.cunardline.com), which moved here in late 1997, is known for its old-world elegance. If you're looking for Internet cafes and ice-skating rinks, Cunard isn't for you. It caters to an older, sophisticated crowd. Its Miami ships include the legendary throwback from the halcyon days of the mighty luxe ocean liner, *Queen Elizabeth 2,* as well as the *Caronia* and the *Queen Mary 2.* Itineraries are usually at least 10 days long, though there are some that last 6 days, such as the jazz, fine arts, and big-band cruises. Prices start at $3,300 per person.

Norwegian Cruise Line (© 800/327-7030 or 305/436-0866; www.ncl. com) has four ships based in Miami during the winter months and usually one in the summer. NCL is known for its excellent theme cruises—mostly sports oriented. A mixture of young and older crowds can be found on their ships. Ships go to Key West, the Bahamas, and the Western Caribbean. Its shortest cruises are 3 days; the longest—from Miami to France—is 15 days. Rates range from $349 per person for an inside cabin on the shortest cruises to $4,500 per person for the very best cabin on the transcontinental journey.

Royal Caribbean International (© 800/327-6700 or 305/539-6000; www. rccl.com), one of the premier lines in Miami, has about half a dozen ships departing Miami at any given time. The Port of Miami actually had to renovate three cruise terminals in 1999—at a price of $60 million—to accommodate Royal Caribbean's 142,000-ton ship *Voyager of the Seas,* which boasts an ice-skating rink and a rock-climbing wall, among other theme-park-like diversions. *Explorer of the Seas* is the line's second, newer, theme park at sea, also featuring extreme sports and an assortment of high-tech activities. As a result, RCI caters to a young, active crowd as well as families with children. The line mostly offers Caribbean cruises and some Bahamas destinations. The *Legend of the Seas* and the *Splendor of the Seas* offer 3- and 4-night Bahamas trips starting at $400. Longer trips can range from $1,600 per person to $7,500 for an 11-night cruise through the Caribbean.

FLIGHTS & WEEKEND PACKAGES

For those who want a quick getaway to the Caribbean without the experience of cruising, many airlines and hotels team up to offer extremely affordable weekend packages.

For example, the Bahamas' most entertaining and family-friendly resort, the **Atlantis** on Paradise Island (© **888-528-7155;** www.atlantis.com), is a tropical theme park offering extensive watersports plus an active casino. Reasonably priced 3-day packages start at about $390, depending on departure date. It's generally cheaper to fly midweek. Flights on **Continental Airlines** (© **800/ 786-7202**) or **Paradise Airlines** (© **800/231-0856**) depart at least twice daily from Miami International. You can also choose to stay in the company's other luxurious resorts: the Paradise Beach Resort or the Ocean Club. Book package deals through **Paradise Island Vacations** (© **800/722-7466**).

Other groups that arrange competitively priced packages include **American Flyaway Vacations,** operated by American Airlines (© **800/321-2121**); **Bahamas Air** (© **800/222-4262** or 305/593-1910); **Chalks Ocean Airways** (© **305/371-8628**); and the slightly run-down **Princess Casino** in Freeport (© **305/359-9898**). Call for rates, since they vary dramatically throughout the year and also depend on what type of accommodations you choose.

8

Miami Shopping

Miami is one of the world's premier shopping cities; more than 10 million visitors came here last year and they spent in excess of $13 billion. Visitors come to Miami from all over—from Latin America to Hong Kong—in search of something all-American. So if you're not into sunbathing and outdoor activities, or you just can't take the heat, you'll be in good company in one of Miami's many malls—and you are not likely to emerge empty-handed. In addition to the strip malls, Miami offers a choice of megamalls, from the upscale Shops at Sunset to the mammoth Aventura to the ritzy Shops at Bal Harbour (just to name a few). Miami also offers more unique shopping spots, such as Bayside's Marketplace, where you can buy such eclectic items as handcrafted tropical birds or jewelry made of precious stones. In Little Havana, you can buy hand-rolled cigars, and in Little Haiti, you'll find one-of-a-kind paintings by young artists starving to get their names and work recognized.

You may want to order the Greater Miami Convention and Visitors Bureau's "Shop Miami: A Guide to a Tropical Shopping Adventure." Although it is limited to details on the bureau's paying members, it provides some good advice and otherwise unpublished discount offers. The glossy little pamphlet is printed in English, Spanish, and Portuguese and provides information about transportation from hotels, translation services, and shipping. Call © **800/ 283-2707** or 305/539-3034.

1 The Shopping Scene

Below, you'll find descriptions of some of the more popular retail areas, where many stores are conveniently clustered together to make browsing easier.

As a general rule, shop hours are Monday through Saturday from 10am to 6pm and Sunday from noon to 5pm. Many stores stay open late (until 9pm or so) one night of the week (usually Thursday). Shops in Coconut Grove are open until 9pm Sunday through Thursday, and even later on Friday and Saturday nights. South Beach's stores stay open later—as late as midnight. Department stores and shopping malls also keep longer hours, with most staying open from 10am to 9 or 10pm Monday through Saturday, and noon to 6pm on Sunday.

The 6.5% state and local sales tax is added to the price of all nonfood purchases.

Most Miami stores can wrap your purchase and ship it anywhere in the world via United Parcel Service (UPS). If they can't, you can send it yourself, either through UPS (© **800/742-5877**) or through the U.S. Mail (see "Fast Facts: Miami," in chapter 4).

SHOPPING AREAS

Most of Miami's shopping happens at the many megamalls scattered from one end of the county to the other; however, there is also some excellent boutique shopping and browsing to be done in the following areas: See "City Layout," in chapter 4 for more information about these areas.

AVENTURA   On Biscayne Boulevard between Miami Gardens Drive and the county line is a 2-mile stretch of major retail stores including Best Buys, Borders, Circuit City, Linens N' Things, Marshall's, Sports Authority, and more. Also here is the mammoth Aventura Mall, housing a fabulous collection of shops and restaurants; and Loehmann's Plaza, a small shopping village anchored around Loehmann's, the discount clothing store (see "Fashion," below).

> **Impressions**
> Someday . . . Miami will become the great center of South American trade.
> —Julia Tuttle, Miami's founder, 1896

CALLE OCHO   For a taste of "Little Havana," take a walk down 8th Street between SW 27th Avenue and 12th Avenue, where you'll find some lively street life and many shops selling cigars, baked goods, shoes, furniture, and record stores specializing in Latin music. Be sure to take your Spanish dictionary if you need it.

COCONUT GROVE   Downtown Coconut Grove, centered on Main Highway and Grand Avenue and branching onto the adjoining streets, is one of Miami's most pedestrian-friendly zones. The Grove's wide sidewalks, lined with cafes and boutiques, provide hours of browsing pleasure. Coconut Grove is best known for its chain stores (Gap, Banana Republic) and some funky holdovers from the days when the Grove was a bit more bohemian, plus excellent sidewalk cafes centered around CocoWalk and the Streets of Mayfair.

CORAL GABLES—MIRACLE MILE   Actually only a half-mile long, this central shopping street was an integral part of George Merrick's original city plan. Today, the strip still enjoys popularity, especially for its bridal stores, ladies' shops, haberdashers, and gift shops. Recently, newer chain stores, like Barnes and Noble, Old Navy, and Starbucks, have been appearing on the Mile. At press time, **Merrick Park,** a mammoth upscale shopping center between Ponce de León Boulevard and Le Jeune Road, and slated to feature Armani, Yves St. Laurent, Dean & DeLuca, the Palm, and the Greenhouse Spa, among others, was in construction, set to open September 2002. The Gables also features several excellent restaurants before it terminates at the City Hall rotunda.

DOWNTOWN MIAMI   If you're looking for discounts on all types of goods—especially watches, fabric, buttons, lace, shoes, luggage, and leather—Flagler Street just west of Biscayne Boulevard is the best place to start. I wouldn't necessarily recommend buying expensive items here as many stores are on the shady side. They do not understand the word *warranty.* Be prepared for some hustling and haggling. Most signs are printed in English, Spanish, and Portuguese; however, many shopkeepers may not be entirely fluent in English.

SOUTH BEACH—LINCOLN ROAD   This luxurious pedestrian mall, originally designed in 1957 by Morris Lapidus, recently underwent a multimillion-dollar renovation restoring it to its former glory. Here, shoppers find an array of clothing and art and a menagerie of South Beach's finest sidewalk cafes flanked on one end by a multiplex movie theater, and at the other, the Atlantic Ocean.

+ Bayside Marketplace (UL p 29A)

COLLINS & WASHINGTON AVENUES (between 6th Street & 9th Street)
This is the Madison Avenue of Miami. For the hippest clothing boutiques including Armani, Versace, Benetton, Agnes B, Guess?, Club Monaco, Kenneth Cole, and Nicole Miller, among others, stroll along this pretty strip of the Deco District.

2 Shopping A to Z
ANTIQUES/COLLECTIBLES

Miami's antiques shops are scattered in small pockets around the city. Many that feature lower-priced furniture can be found in North Miami, in the 1600 block of Northeast 123rd Street near West Dixie Highway. About a dozen shops sell china, silver, glass, furniture, and paintings. But you'll find the bulk of the better antiques in Coral Gables and in Southwest Miami along Bird Road between 64th and 66th avenues and between 72nd and 74th avenues. There are dozens of shops with eclectic offerings. For international collections from Bali to France, check out the burgeoning scene in the Design District centered on Northeast 40th Street west of 1st Avenue. Miami also hosts several large antiques shows each year. In October and November, the most prestigious one—the **Antique Show**—hits the Miami Beach Convention Center (© **305/754-4931**). Exhibitors from all over come to display their wares, including jewelry. There's also a decent monthly show at the **Coconut Grove Convention Center** (© **305/444-8454**). Miami's huge concentration of Deco buildings from the '20s and '30s makes this the place to find the best selections of Deco furnishings and decorations.

Architectural Antiques   A great place to browse—if you don't mind a little dust—this huge warehouse has an impressive stash of ironwork, bronzes, paintings, lamps, furniture, and sculptures, which have been salvaged from estates worldwide. Don't be surprised to find odd items too, like an old British phone booth or a pair of gargoyles off an ancient church. 2500 SW 28th Lane (just west of U.S. 1), Miami. © **305/285-1330.** archantique@earthlink.net.

Dietel's Antiques   An active trade business here means that lots of different styles are revolving constantly. You'll find baubles of every assortment in this stocked shop located near Coral Gables' quaint antiques district. 6572 Bird Rd., South Miami. © **305/666-0724.**

Fine Antiques William Limited   This is a collector's treasure chest: a showroom offering a huge range of authentic period pieces (the Ming Dynasty, among others!) including furniture, clocks, silver, and porcelains. 91 NE 40th St., Design District. © **305/868-8889.**

Miami Twice   While they are not technically antiques yet, the Old Florida furniture and decorations from the '30s, '40s, and '50s are great fun (and collectible). In addition to loads of Deco memorabilia, there are vintage clothes, shoes, and jewelry. 6562 SW 40th St., South Miami. © **305/666-0127.** Fax 305/661-1142. www.miamitwice.com.

Modernism Gallery   Specializing in 20th-century furnishings from Gilbert Rohde, Noguchi, and Heywood Wakefield, this shop has some of the most beautiful examples of Deco goods from France and the United States. If they don't have what you're looking for, ask. They possess the amazing ability to find the rarest items. 1622 Ponce de León Blvd., Coral Gables. © **305/442-8743.**

Senzatempo *(Finds)*   If the names Charles Eames, George Nelso, or Gio Ponti mean anything to you, then this is where you'll want to visit. There's retro, Euro fabulous designer furniture and decorative arts from 1930 to 1960, as well as collectible watches, timepieces, and clocks. 1655 Meridian Ave. (at Lincoln Rd.), South Beach. (C) 305/534-5588.

ART GALLERIES

Miami's finest art galleries are located within walking distance of one another in Coral Gables along Ponce de León Boulevard, extending from U.S. 1 to Bird Road. Still others are clustered in Bal Harbour's ritzy shopping district. South Beach's Lincoln Road, which once had dozens of galleries, now has only a few—a result of soaring rents.

Also, check out the burgeoning art scene in the Design District north of downtown just west of Biscayne Boulevard around 40th Street. Listed below is a selection of galleries both in and out of these areas.

If you happen to be in town on the first Friday of the month, you should take the free trolley tour of the Coral Gables Art District. The tour runs from 7 to 10pm; meet at Elite (listed below) or at any of the other participating galleries in the area. See chapter 7, "What to See & Do in Miami," for more details on this tour and others.

Ambrosino Gallery   This well-respected gallery shows works by contemporary artists and stages performance art and installations. 769 NE 125th St. North Miami (across from the Museum of Contemporary Art). (C) 305/891-5577. www.ambrosinogallery.com. Closed for Christmas holidays.

Barbara Gillman Gallery   This gallery's ongoing exhibit of jazz photographer Herman Leonard's fantastic black and white photographs of legends such as Billie Holiday and Frank Sinatra has been so popular it hasn't changed in years. In addition to the works of Leonard and other renowned artists such as Andres Serrano, Andy Warhol, and James Rosenquist, the gallery displays the work of new local talent. 5582 NE 4th Court #5, Miami. (C) 305/759-9155.

Britto Central   Some people liken local Brazilian artist Romero Britto to Andy Warhol because of his colorful, whimsical paintings of young children and animals, among other things. Serious art lovers, however, consider Britto's cartoonish works more along the lines of a second-rate Walt Disney. You decide. 818 Lincoln Rd., South Beach. (C) 305/531-8821.

Elite Fine Art   Touted as one of the finest galleries in Miami, Elite features modern and contemporary Latin American painters and sculptors such as Angel Hurtado, Olga Sinclair, and Gina Pellon, among others. 3140 Ponce de León Blvd., Coral Gables. (C) 305/448-3800.

Evelyn S. Poole Ltd.   Known as the finest of the fine antiques collections, the Poole assortment of European 17th-, 18th-, and 19th-century decorative furniture and accessories is housed in 5,000 square feet of space in the newly revived Decorator's Row. 3925 N. Miami Ave., Miami. (C) 305/573-7463. www.evelynpoolettd.com.

Meza Fine Art Gallery Café *(Finds)*   Dine amidst fine works of art in this funky gallery and cafe that specializes in Latin American artists, including Carlos Betancourt, Javier Marin, and Gloria Lorenzo (see also chapter 6). 275 Giralda Ave., Coral Gables. (C) 305/461-2723.

Tower Theater   This renovated movie theater in Little Havana features highly regarded Cuban art such as Carlos Navarro's *Cosas Cubanas (Cuban Things)*. 1508 SW 8th St., Little Havana. (C) 305/443-5415.

Wallflower Gallery *(finds* Funky, eclectic, and reminiscent of Andy Warhol's Factory, the Wallflower Gallery features an assortment of exhibits from local artists from erotica to exotica and everything in between. Performance art and live music are also featured here. 10 NE 3rd St., Miami. (℃ 305/579-0069.

BOOKS

Barnes & Noble Booksellers With half a dozen outlets in the area and more on the way, this huge chain offers anything readers could ask for, including a comfortable cafe, a large children's section, and tons of magazines. Plus, you'll get a 10% discount on all best-sellers and incredible close-out specials. They often schedule readings with noted authors, too. There are more than six locations in Miami. There's a nice little scene at this branch of B&N, featuring local intellectuals, students, and professors from nearby University of Miami. 152 Miracle Mile, Coral Gables. (℃ 305/446-4152. www.bn.com.

Books & Books A dedicated following turns out to browse at this warm and wonderful little independent shop. Enjoy the upstairs antiquarian room, which specializes in art books and first editions. If that's not enough intellectual stimulation for you, the shop hosts free lectures from noted authors and experts almost nightly, from Monica Lewinsky to Martin Amis. 265 Aragon Ave., Coral Gables. (℃ 305/442-4408. www.booksandbooks.com.

At another location (933 Lincoln Rd., South Beach; (℃ **305/532-3222**), you'll rub elbows with tanned and buffed South Beach bookworms sipping cappuccinos at the Russian Bear Cafe inside the store. They stock a large selection of gay literature and also feature lectures.

Kafka's Cyberkafe Check your e-mail and surf the Web while you sip a latte or snack on a sandwich or pastry with friendly neighborhood regulars. This popular used bookstore also stocks a wide range of foreign and domestic magazines and caters to an international youth hostel–type crowd. 1464 Washington Ave., South Beach. (℃ 305/673-9669.

CIGARS

Although it is illegal to bring Cuban cigars into this country, somehow forbidden Cohibas show up at every dinner party and nightclub in town. Not that I condone it, but if you hang around the cigar smokers in town, no doubt one will be able to tell you where you can get some of the highly prized contraband. Be careful, however, of counterfeits.

The stores listed below sell excellent hand-rolled cigars made with domestic and foreign-grown tobacco. Many of the *viejos* (old men) got their training in Cuba working for the government-owned factories in the heyday of Cuban cigars.

La Gloria Cubana This tiny storefront shop employs about 45 veteran Cuban rollers who sit all day rolling the very popular torpedoes and other critically acclaimed blends. They've got backorders until next Christmas, but it's worth stopping in. They will sell you a box and show you around. 1106 SW 8th St., Little Havana. (℃ 305/858-4162.

Mike's Cigars *(finds* Mike's recently moved to this location, but it's one of the oldest and best smoke shops in town. Since 1950, Mike's has been selling the best from Honduras, the Dominican Republic, and Jamaica, as well as the very hot local brand, La Gloria Cubana. Many say it has the best prices, too. 1030 Kane Concourse (at 96th St.), Bay Harbor Island. (℃ 305/866-2277. www.mikescigars.com.

COSMETICS, FRAGRANCES & BEAUTY PRODUCTS

Brownes & Co. *Finds* Designed to look like an old-fashioned apothecary, this beauty emporium combines the best selection of makeup and hair products— MAC, Shu Uemura, Kiehl's, Stila, and Dr. Hauschka, just to name a few—with lots of delicious-smelling bath and body stuff, plus a full-service beauty salon. Feel free to browse and sample here, as you won't be bothered by perfume-spritzing salespeople. If you do need help, the staff is a collection of experts when it comes to beauty and hair products. Upstairs is the store's renowned salon, Some Like It Hot, in which you can get fabulously coiffed, colored, buffed, and waxed. If you do want to get waxed, make sure to ask for the city's best waxer, Latecia. 841 Lincoln Rd., South Beach. ℂ 305-532-8703. www.brownesbeauty.com.

Sephora The Disneyworld of makeup, Sephora offers a dizzying array of cosmetics, perfumes, and styling products. Unlike Brownes & Co., however, personal service and attentiveness is at a minimum. Because there are so many products, shopping here can be a harrowing experience. Two locations: 721 Collins Ave., South Beach. ℂ 305/532-0728; 2982 Grand Ave., Coconut Grove. ℂ 305/448-3003.

FASHION

Miami didn't become a fashion capital until—believe it or not—the pastel-hued, Armani-clad cops on *Miami Vice* had their close-ups on the tube. Before that, Miami was all about old men in white patent leather shoes and well-tanned women in bikinis. How things have changed. Miami is now a fashion mecca in its own right, with the some of the same high-end stores you'd find on Rue de Fauborg St. Honore in Paris or Bond Street in London. You'll find all of it, including Prada and Gucci, right here at the posh Bal Harbour Shops. For funkier frocks, South Beach is the place, where designers such as Cynthia Rowley, Betsey Johnson, and Giorgio Armani compete for window shoppers with local up-and-coming designers and those who design for drag queens and club kids only. The strip on Collins Avenue between 7th and 10th streets has become quite upscale, including such shops as Armani Exchange and Nicole Miller, along with the inescapable Gap and Banana Republic. Of course, there's also more mainstream shopping in the plethora of malls and outdoor shopping and entertainment complexes.

UNISEX

Agnes B This fabulous French import features unique women's, men's, and children's high fashion at high prices. If you don't have carte blanche, however, the best buy in the store is the one-of-a-kind Agnes B perfume, in a lovely heart bottle, for just $20. 640 Collins Ave., South Beach. ℂ 305/604-8705.

Base A beautiful store featuring one-of-a-kind clothing made in St. Vincent that's light, breezy, fashionable, and, of course, pricey. Keep on the lookout for excellent sales. 939 Lincoln Rd., South Beach. ℂ 305/531-4982.

Glitzy Tartz The name alone says it all. This outlandish boutique features everything you'd want if you were a go-go boy or girl, in vinyl, mesh, and lamé—all in several sizes way too tight to accentuate the, uh, positive. 1251 Washington Ave., South Beach. ℂ 305/535-0068.

Island Trading One more part of music mogul Chris Blackwell's empire, Island sells everything you'll need to wear in a tropical resort town: batik sarongs, sandals, sundresses, bathing suits, cropped tops, and more. Many of the unique styles are created on the premises by a team of young, innovative designers. 1332 Ocean Dr., South Beach. ℂ 305/673-6300.

Laundry Industry If you're color blind, from New York, or just can't be bothered with coordinating your colors, Laundry Industry is for you, with the chicest (and priciest) black-and-white–only threads for men and women this side of SoHo. 666 Collins Ave., South Beach. ℂ **305/531-2277.**

Urban Outfitters It took a while for this urban outpost to hit Miami, but once it did, it became a favorite for the young hipster set who favors T-shirts that say "Princess" instead of Prada. Cheapish, utilitarian, and funky, Urban Outfitters is an excellent place to pick up a pair of used jeans or some funky tchotchkes for your apartment. Two locations: 653 Collins Ave., South Beach. ℂ **305/535-9726;** Shops at Sunset, 5701 SW 72nd St., South Miami. ℂ **305/663-1536.**

WOMEN'S

Alice's Day Off For beachwear, Alice's is the place. Season after season, you'll find pretty and flattering floral patterns and many flashy bikinis. If an itsy-bitsy bikini is not your style, Alice's also has a range of more modest cuts. Three locations: Miami International Mall, 1455 NW 107th Ave, Miami. ℂ **305/477-0393;** Dadeland Mall, 7223 SW 88th St. Miami. ℂ **305/663-7299;** 5900 SW 72nd St., South Miami. ℂ **305/284-0301.** www.alicesdayoff.com.

Betsey Johnson Wacky, spirited New York designer Betsey Johnson offers outrageous, funky, and very loud clothes for young women. 805 Washington Ave., South Beach. ℂ **305/673-0023.** www.betseyjohnson.com.

Intermix Pretty young things get all dolled up thanks to Intermix's fun assortment of hip women's fashions, from Stella McCartney's pricey rhinestone T-shirts to the latest jeans worn by everyone at the MTV Awards. 634 Collins Ave., South Beach. ℂ **305/531-5950.**

Place Vendome For cheap and funky club clothes from zebra print pants to bright, shiny tops. Two locations: 934 Lincoln Rd., South Beach. ℂ **305/673-4005;** Aventura Mall, North Miami Beach. ℂ **305/932-8931.**

Therapy Opened by Ellen Lansburgh, who ran successful shops in Aspen and New York that catered to a famous clientele, including Cher and Goldie Hawn, this intimate boutique offers one-of-a-kind pieces. The clothes, made of luxurious fabrics such as silk, taffeta, and tulle, are elegant and comfortable. 1065 Kane Concourse, Bay Harbor Islands. ℂ **305/861-6900.**

MEN'S

Giorgio's One of the finest custom men's stores, Giorgio's features an extensive line of Italian suits and all the latest by Canelli. 208 Miracle Mile, Coral Gables. ℂ **305/448-4302.**

La Casa de las Guayaberas *Finds* Miami's premier purveyor of the traditional yet retro-hip Cuban shirt known as the *guayabera*—a loose-fitting, pleated, button-down shirt—was founded by Ramon Puig, who emigrated to Miami over 40 years ago. He still uses the same scissors he did back then, only now he's joined by a team of seamstresses who hand-sew 20 shirts a day in all colors and styles. Prices range from $15 to $375. 5840 SW 8th St., Little Havana. ℂ **305/266-9683.**

Wilke Rodriguez Miami designer Eddie Rodriguez is a Latin Hugo Boss, with high-fashion suits in linens and light wool blends made especially for warmer climates. Cool T-shirts, shorts, and jackets are also part of this line, which is a local status symbol for many of Miami's fashion-conscious males.

Prices range from the high $50s for T-shirts to $275 and up for jackets. 801 Washington Ave., South Beach. © 305/534-4030.

ACCESSORIES

SEE   This fantastic eyewear store features an enormous selection of stylish specs all priced at $169, including your prescription. The staff is patient and knowledgeable. 921 Lincoln Rd., South Beach. © 305/672-6622.

Simons and Green   Fantastic sterling silver jewelry, leather goods, and other assorted high-end tchotchkes and gift items are what you'll find in this quaint mainstay on South Miami's Sunset Drive. 5842 Sunset Dr., South Miami. © 305/667-1692.

CHILDREN'S

Most department stores have extensive children's sections. But if you can't find what you are looking for, consider one of the many Baby Gaps or Gap Kids outlets around town or try one of the specialty boutiques listed here.

French Kids Inc.   This fashionable boutique imports beautiful (and expensive) clothes for newborns to teenagers. 5829 Sunset Dr., South Miami. © 305/667-5880.

Roland Children's Wear   You'll find a unique assortment of kid's clothes for dress-up or playtime. They specialize in cute, funky stuff. 450 41st St., Miami Beach. © 305/531-0130.

LINGERIE

Belinda's   This German designer makes some of the most beautiful and intricate teddies, nightgowns, and wedding dresses. The styles are a little too Stevie Nicks for me, but the creations are absolutely worth admiring. The prices are appropriately up there. 827 Washington Ave., South Beach. © 305/532-0068.

Corset Corner   As the name suggests, this little old store on Miracle Mile sells the basic, good old-fashioned gear. 300 Miracle Mile, Coral Gables. © 305/444-6643.

La Perla   The only store in Florida that specializes in this superluxurious Italian intimate apparel. Of course, you could fly to Milan for the price of a few bras and a nightgown, but you can't find better quality. Also in Bal Harbour, see Flash Lingerie (© 305/868-7732), which carries a diverse selection of imports. 9700 Collins Ave. (in the Bal Harbour Shops), Bal Harbour. © 305/864-2070.

FOOD

There are dozens of ethnic markets in Miami, from Cuban bodegas to Jamaican import shops and Guyanese produce stands. Check the phone book under grocers for listings. I've listed a few of the biggest and best markets in town that sell prepared foods as well as staple items. On Saturday mornings, vendors set up stands loaded with papayas, melons, tomatoes, and citrus, as well as cookies, ice creams, and sandwiches on South Beach's Lincoln Road.

Biga Bakery   You'll be happy to pay upward of $6 a loaf when you sink your teeth into these inimitable Old-World–style breads. Also, most of the locations have a to-die-for prepared food counter serving up everything from chicken curry salad to hummus and pot pies. Pastries and cakes are as gorgeous as they are delicious. Several locations include 1080 Alton Rd., South Beach. © 305/535-1008; 305 Alcazar, Coral Gables. © 305/446-2111. Check directory for other locations.

East Coast Fisheries   This retail market and restaurant (see the review in chapter 6) has shipped millions of pounds of seafood worldwide from its own fishing fleet. Order 5- or 10-pound packages of stone-crab claws, Florida lobsters, Florida Bay pompano, fresh Key West shrimp, and a variety of other local delicacies to be shipped via overnight delivery. 330 W. Flagler St., Downtown. © 305/ 577-3000.

Epicure   This is the closest thing Miami Beach has got to the famed Balducci's or Dean & DeLuca. Here, you'll find not only fine wines, cheeses, meats, fish, and juices, but some of the best produce, such as portobello mushrooms the size of a yarmulke. This neighborhood landmark is best known for supplying the Jewish residents of the beach with all the Jewish favorites, such as matzo ball soup, gefilte fish, and deli items. Prices are steep, but generally worth it. The cakes in particular are rich and decadent, and a rather large one doesn't cost more than $10. 1656 Alton Rd., Miami Beach. © 305/672-1861.

Gardner's Market   Anything a gourmet or novice cook could desire can be found here. One of the oldest and best grocery stores in Miami, Gardner's now has three locations, all of which offer great take-out and the freshest produce. 7301 Red Rd., South Miami. © 305/667-9953; 8287 SW 124th St., Pinecrest. © 305/255-2468; 651 Brickell Key Drive, Downtown. ©305/371-3701.

Joe's Stone Crab   If you don't want to wait 2 hours to get your paws on Joe's meaty claws, let Joe's, Miami's stone crab institution (see the review in chapter 6), ship you stone crabs anywhere in the country, but only during the season, which runs from mid-October through mid-May. 227 Biscayne St., South Beach. © 800/780-CRAB or 305/673-0365.

La Brioche Doree   This tiny storefront off 41st Street is packed most mornings with French expatriates and visitors who crave the real thing. There are luscious pastries and breads, plus soup and sandwiches at lunch. No one makes a better croissant. 4017 Prairie Ave., Miami Beach. © 305/538-4770.

Laurenzo's Italian Supermarket and Farmer's Market   Anything Italian you want—homemade ravioli, hand-cut imported Romano cheese, plus fresh fish and meats—can be found here. Laurenzo's also offers one of the most comprehensive wine selections in the city. Be sure to see the neighboring store full of just-picked herbs, salad greens, and vegetables from around the world. A daily Farmer's Market is open from 7am to 6pm. Incredible daily specials lure thrifty shoppers from all over the city (see the review of the cafe in chapter 6). 16385 and 16445 W. Dixie Hwy., North Miami Beach. © 305/945-6381 or 305/944-5052.

JEWELRY

For name designers like Gucci and Tiffany & Co., go to the Bal Harbour Shops (see "Malls," below).

International Jeweler's Exchange   At least 50 jewelers hustle their wares from individual counters at one of the city's most active jewelry centers. Haggle your brains out for excellent prices on timeless antiques from Tiffany's, Cartier, or Bulgari, or on unique designs you can create yourself. 18861 Biscayne Blvd. (in the Fashion Island), North Miami Beach. © 305/931-7032.

Seybold Building   Jewelers of every assortment gather here daily to sell diamonds and gold. With 300 jewelry stores located inside this independently owned and operated multilevel treasure chest, the glare is blinding as you enter. You'll see handsome and up-to-date designs, but not too many bargains. 36 NE 1st St., Downtown. © 305/374-7922. www.seyboldbldg.com.

MALLS

There are so many malls in Miami and more being built that it would be impossible to mention them all. What follows is a list of the biggest and most popular.

You can find any number of nationally known department stores including Saks Fifth Avenue, Macy's, Lord & Taylor, Sears, and JCPenney in the Miami malls listed below, but Miami's own is **Burdines**, at 22 E. Flagler St., Downtown (© **305/835-5151**), and 1675 Meridian Ave. (just off Lincoln Rd.) in South Beach (© **305/674-6311**). One of the oldest and largest department stores in Florida, Burdines specializes in good-quality home furnishings and fashions.

Aventura Mall   A multimillion-dollar makeover has made this spot one of the premier places to shop in South Florida. With more than 2.3 million square feet of space, this airy, Mediterranean-style mall has a 24-screen movie theater and more than 250 stores, including megastores JCPenney, Lord & Taylor, Macy's, Bloomingdale's, Sears, and Burdines. The mall offers moderate to high-priced merchandise and is extremely popular with families. A large indoor playground, Adventurer's Cove, is a great spot for kids, and the mall frequently offers activities and entertainment for children. There are numerous theme restaurants and a food court that eschews the usual suspects in favor of local operations. The mall provides free shuttle service to and from the top downtown and Miami Beach hotels. 19501 Biscayne Blvd. (at 197th St. near the Dade–Broward County line), Aventura. © 305/935-1110. www.shopaventuramall.com.

Bal Harbour Shops   One of the most prestigious fashion meccas in the country, Bal Harbour offers the best-quality goods from the finest names. Giorgio Armani, Dolce & Gabbana, Christian Dior, Fendi, Joan & David, Krizia, Rodier, Gucci, Brooks Brothers, Waterford, Cartier, H. Stern, Tourneau, and many others are sandwiched between Neiman-Marcus and a newly expanded Saks Fifth Avenue. Well-dressed shoppers stroll in a pleasant open-air emporium, featuring several good cafes, covered walkways, and lush greenery. Parking costs $1 an hour with a validated ticket. You can stamp your own at the entrance to Saks Fifth Avenue even if you don't make a purchase. 9700 Collins Ave. (on 97th St., opposite the Sheraton Bal Harbour Hotel), Bal Harbour. © 305/866-0311. www.balharbourshops.com.

Bayside Marketplace   A popular stop for cruise-ship passengers, this touristy waterfront marketplace is filled with the usual suspects of chain stores as well as a slew of tacky gift shops and carts hawking assorted junk in the heart of downtown Miami. The second-floor food court is stocked with dozens of fast-food choices and bars. Most of the restaurants and bars stay open later than the stores. There's Lomardi's Conga Bar, Dick's Last Resort, Hard Rock Cafe, Fat Tuesday, Sharkey's, and Let's Make a Daiquiri. Parking is $1 per hour. While we wouldn't recommend you necessarily drop big money at Bayside, you should go by just for the view alone. In June you can watch the Opsail show, and in February, the Miami Sailboat Show. Beware of the adjacent amphitheater known as Bayfront Park, which usually hosts large-scale concerts and festivals, causing major pedestrian and vehicle traffic jams. 401 Biscayne Blvd., Downtown. © 305/577-3344. www.baysidemarketplace.com.

Dadeland Mall   One of the county's first malls, Dadeland features more than 175 specialty shops, anchored by four large department stores: Burdines, JCPenney, Lord & Taylor, and Saks Fifth Avenue. Sixteen restaurants serve from the adjacent Treats Food Court. New retail stores are constantly springing up around this centerpiece of South Miami suburbia. If you're not in the area, however, the mall is not worth the trek. Additionally, many non-Spanish-speaking people are put off by Dadeland because of the predominance of Spanish-speaking store employees. 7535 N. Kendall Dr. (intersection of U.S. 1 and SW 88th St., 15 minutes south of Downtown), Kendall. ✆ 305/665-6226.

Dolphin Mall   As if Miami needed another mall, this $250 million megamall and amusement park rivals Broward County's monstrous Sawgrass Mills outlet. The 1.4-million-square-foot mall features outlets such as Off Saks Fifth Avenue, plus shops, a 28-screen movie theater, and, not to be outdone by the Mall of the Americas, a roller coaster. Florida Turnpike at S.R. 836, West Miami. ✆ 305/365-7446.

Falls Shopping Center   Traffic to this mall borders on brutal, but once you get there, you'll feel a slight sense of serenity. Tropical waterfalls are the setting for this outdoor shopping center with dozens of moderately priced and slightly upscale shops. Miami's first Bloomingdale's is here, as are Polo, Ralph Lauren, Caswell-Massey, and more than 60 other specialty shops. A recent renovation added Macy's, Crate & Barrel, Brooks Brothers, and Pottery Barn, among others. If you are planning to visit any of the nearby attractions, which include Metro Zoo and Monkey Jungle, check with customer service for information on discount packages. 8888 Howard Dr. (at the intersection of U.S. 1 and 136th St., about 3 miles south of Dadeland Mall), Kendall. ✆ 305/255-4570. www.shopthefalls.com.

Miami International Mall   Housing more than 150 specialty stores and several well-known department stores, including Burdines, JCPenney, and Sears, this popular mall is close to Miami International Airport and is filled with foreign shoppers. 1455 NW 107th Ave., Miami. ✆ 305/593-1775.

Sawgrass Mills   Just as some people need to take a tranquilizer to fly, others need one to traipse through this mammoth mall—the largest outlet mall in the country. Depending on what type of shopper you are, this experience can either be blissful or overwhelming. If you've got the patience, it is worth setting aside a day to do the entire place. Though it's located in Broward County, it is a phenomenon that attracts thousands of tourists and locals sniffing out bargains. 12801 W. Sunrise Blvd., Sunrise. ✆ 800/ FL-MILLS. (See chapter 13, "The Treasure Coast," for more details.)

From Miami, buses run three times daily; the trip takes just under an hour. Call **Coach USA** (✆ 305/887-6223) for exact pick-up points at major hotels. The price is $10 for a round-trip ticket. If you are driving, take I-95 north to 595 west to Flamingo Road. Exit and turn right, driving 2 miles to Sunrise Boulevard. You can't miss this monster on the left. Parking is free, but don't forget where you parked your car or you might spend a day looking for it. 12801 W. Sunrise Blvd., Sunrise (west of Fort Lauderdale). ✆ 954/846-2300.

Shops at Sunset Place   Completed in early 1999 at a cost of over $140 million, this sprawling outdoor shopping complex offers more than just shopping. Visitors experience high-tech special effects, such as daily tropical storms (minus the rain) and the electronic chatter of birds and crickets. In addition to a 24-screen movie complex and an IMAX theater, there's a GameWorks—Steven Spielberg's Disneyesque playground for adults—a Virgin Records store, and a NikeTown. 5701 Sunset Dr. (at 57th Ave. and U.S. 1, near Red Rd.), South Miami. ✆ 305/663-0482.

Streets of Mayfair This sleepy, labyrinthine complex conceals a movie theater, several top-quality shops, restaurants, art galleries, and nightclubs. It also seems to conceal a crowd, as this complex pales in comparison to the more populated, open-air CocoWalk complex just up the road. 2911 Grand Ave. (just east of Commodore Plaza), Coconut Grove. ✆ **305/448-1700.**

MUSIC & MUSICAL EQUIPMENT

Blue Note Records *(Finds* Here for more than 15 years, Blue Note is music to the ears of music fanatics with hard-to-find progressive and underground music. There are new, used, and discounted CDs and old vinyl, too. Call to find out about performances. Some great names show up occasionally. A second location features jazz and LPs only. 16401 NE 15th Ave., North Miami Beach. ✆ **305/940-3394.** Fax 305/948-3583. For jazz/LPs: 2299 NE 164th St., North Miami Beach ✆ **305/354-4563.** www. bluenoterecords.com.

Casino Records Inc. The young, hip salespeople here speak English and tend to be music buffs. You'll find the largest selection of Latin music in Miami, including pop icons such as Willy Chirino, Gloria Estefan, Albita, and local boy Nil Lara. Their slogan translates to "If we don't have it, forget it." Believe me, they've got it. 1208 SW 8th St., Little Havana. ✆ **305/856-6888.**

Esperanto Music *(Finds* According to the experts, this independently owned record store boasts the city's best collection of Cuban and Latin music. 513 Lincoln Rd, Miami Beach. ✆ **305/ 534-2003.**

Mars (Music and Recording Superstore) You could spend a week here. With 35,000 square feet of space, Mars offers everything from musical instruments to sheet music, plus a recording studio, live stage, and repair center. 12115 Biscayne Blvd., North Miami. ✆ **305/893-0191.** www.marsmusic.com.

Revolution Records and CDs Here you'll find a quaint and fairly well-organized collection of CDs, from hard-to-find jazz to original recordings of Buddy Rich. They'll search for anything and let you hear whatever you like. 1620 Alton Rd., Miami Beach. ✆ **305/673-6464.**

Specs Music Don't buy CDs here unless you absolutely must have them right away; this place is way overpriced. The good news is that you can spend all day listening to music here, as most of the CDs are available at listening stations. Oftentimes, there is a deejay spinning music in hopes of enticing you to buy CDs. There are two locations: 501 Collins Ave., South Beach. ✆ **305/534-3667;** 12451 Biscayne Blvd., North Miami Beach. ✆ **305/899-0994.**

Virgin Records This enormous music store is the best place to buy import CDs at reasonable prices. It also indulges shoppers with listening booths and an "in-store radio station." There's a huge collection of CDs, cassettes, and videos. 5701 Sunset Place (Shops at Sunset), South Miami. ✆ **305/665-4445.**

Yesterday and Today Records *(Finds* This is Miami's most unique and well-stocked store for vinyl—you know, the audio dinosaur that went out with the Victrola? Y & T, as it's known, is a collector's heaven, featuring every genre of music imaginable on every format. Chances are, you could find some eight-track tapes, too. 7902 NW 36th St., Miami. ✆ **305/468-0311.**

SPORTS EQUIPMENT

People watching seems to be the number-one sport in South Florida, but for the more athletic pursuits consider these shops. One of the area's largest chains is the

Sports Authority, with at least six locations throughout the county. Check the white pages for details.

Alf's Golf Shop   This is the best pro shop around. The knowledgeable staff can help you with equipment for golfers of every level, and the neighboring golf course offers discounts to Alf's clients. 524 Arthur Godfrey Rd., Miami Beach. ✆ 305/ 673-6568; 15369 S. Dixie Hwy., Miami. ✆ 305/378-6086.

Bass Pro Shops Outdoor World   Fishing and sports enthusiasts must head north to Broward County to see this huge retail complex, which offers demonstrations in such sports as fly-fishing and archery, classes in marine safety, and every conceivable gadget you could ask for (see chapter 13 for more details). 200 Gulf Stream Way (west side of I-95), Dania Beach. ✆ 954/929-7710.

Bird's Surf Shop   If you're a hard-core surfer or just want to look like one, head to Bird's Surf Shop. Although Miami doesn't regularly get huge swells, if you're here during the winter and one should happen to hit, you'll be ready. The shop carries more than 150 boards. Call its surf line (✆ **305/947-7170**) to find the best waves from South Beach to Cape Hatteras and even the Bahamas and Florida's West Coast. 250 Sunny Isles Blvd., North Miami Beach. ✆ **305/940-0929.** www.birdsurfshop.com.

Edwin Watts Golf Shops   One of 30 Edwin Watts shops throughout the Southeast, this full-service golf retail shop is one of the most popular in Miami. You can find it all, including clothing, pro-line equipment, gloves, bags, balls, videos, and books. Plus, you can get coupons for discounted greens fees on many courses. 15100 N. Biscayne Blvd., North Miami Beach. ✆ 305/944-2925.

Island Water Sports   You'll find everything from booties to gloves to baggies and tanks. Check in here before you rent that WaveRunner or windsurfer. 16231 Biscayne Blvd., North Miami. ✆ 305/944-0104.

Golf Headquarters (Finds)   This chain store guarantees the lowest prices on golf equipment and accessories. There's more than 6,000 square feet of store here; you can even practice your swing at an indoor driving range, where a radar gun will clock your speed. 7930 NW 36th Ave. (near the airport), Miami. ✆ 305/593-2999.

X-Isle Surf Shop   Prices are slightly higher at this beach location, but you'll find the hottest styles and equipment. They also offer surfboard rental. Free surf report at ✆ **305/534-7873.** 437 Washington Ave., South Beach. ✆ **305/673-5900.**

THRIFT STORES/RESALE SHOPS

Children's Exchange   Selling everything from layettes to overalls, this pleasant little shop is chock-full of good Florida-style stuff for kids to wear to the beach and in the heat. 1415 Sunset Dr., Coral Gables. ✆ 305/666-6235.

Douglas Gardens Jewish Home and Hospital Thrift Shops   Prices here are no longer the major bargain they once were, but for housewares and books, you can do all right. Call to see if they are offering any specials for seniors or students. 5713 NW 27th Ave., North Miami Beach. ✆ 305/638-1900.

Rags to Riches   This is an old-time consignment shop in the thrift-store row. You might find some decent rags, and maybe even some riches. Not as upscale as it used to be, this place is still a good spot for costume jewelry and shoes. 12577 Biscayne Blvd., North Miami. ✆ 305/891-8981.

Red White & Blue   Miami's best-kept secret is this mammoth thrift store that is meticulously organized and well stocked. You've got to search for great stuff, but it is there. There are especially good deals on children's clothes and house-wares. 12640 NE 6th Ave., North Miami. © **305/893-1104.**

WINES & SPIRITS

Most gourmet stores carry wines and beers. See "Food," above.

Crown Wine and Spirits   This liquor store offers one of the most diverse selections in Miami. Its ever-rotating stock comes from estate sales around the country and worldwide distributors. And since there are several stores in the chain, the owners get to buy in bulk, which results in lower prices for oenophiles. If you want one of the tastiest and most affordable champagnes ever, try its exclusive import, Billecarte Salmon. There are two locations: 6751 Red Rd., Coral Gables. © **305/669-0225;** 1255 Biscayne Blvd., North Miami. © **305/892-WINE.**

Estate Wines & Gourmet Foods   This exceedingly friendly storefront in the middle of Coral Gables' main shopping street offers a small but well-chosen selection of vintages from around the world. It also sells a great array of gourmet cheeses, patés, salads, and sandwiches. 92 Miracle Mile (at Douglas and Galiano), Coral Gables. © **305/442-9915.**

Laurenzo's *(Finds*   Laurenzo's dedicates a few small aisles to its superb wine collection. A full-time expert can help you choose a bottle. *A word of warning:* You'll get an attitude from them if you're a novice. 16385 and 16445 W. Dixie Hwy., North Miami Beach. © **305/945-6381** or 305/944-5052.

Sunny Isles Liquors   This well-located store stocks hundreds of brands of imported beer and hard-to-find liquor. It will also search and find decanters and minis for your collection. There's also a selection of imported cigarettes and cigars. 18180 Collins Ave., Sunny Isles Beach. © **305/932-5782.**

9

Miami After Dark

With all the hype, you'd have expected Miami to have long outlived its 15 minutes of fame by now. But you'd be wrong. Miami's nightlife, especially in South Beach, is hotter than ever. Practically every club has installed closely guarded velvet ropes to create an air of exclusivity. Don't be fooled or intimidated by them—you can go clubbing in the magic city; throughout this chapter, I've provided tips to ensure entry. South Beach is certainly Miami's uncontested nocturnal nucleus, but more and more suburban areas, such as the Design District, South Miami, and even Little Havana, are providing fun alternatives without the ludicrous cover charges and drink prices. And while South Beach dances to a more electronic beat, other parts of Miami dance to a Latin beat—from salsa and merenge to tango and cha cha. However, if you're looking for a less frenetic good time, Miami's bar scene offers something for everyone, from haute hotel bars to sleek, loungey watering holes.

If the possibility of a celebrity sighting doesn't fulfill your cultural needs, Miami also offers a variety of first-rate diversions in theater, music, and dance, including a world-class ballet under the aegis of Edward Villella, a recognized symphony, and a talented opera company.

For up-to-date listing information, and to make sure time hasn't elapsed for the club of the moment, check the *Miami Herald*'s "Weekend" section, which runs on Friday, or the more comprehensive listings in *New Times*, Miami's free alternative weekly, available each Wednesday, or visit www.miamicitysearch.com online.

1 Bars & Lounges

There are countless bars in and around Miami with the highest concentration on trendy South Beach. The selection listed here is a mere sample. Keep in mind that many of the popular bars—and the easiest to get into—are in hotels. For a clubbier scene, if you don't mind making your way through hordes of inebriated club kids, a stroll on Washington Avenue will provide you with ample insight into what's hot and what's not. Just hold onto your bags. It's not dangerous, but occasionally a few shady types manage to slip into the crowd. Another very important tip when in a club: Never put your drink down out of your sight—there have been unfortunate incidents in which drinks have been spiked with illegal chemical substances. For a less hard-core, collegiate nightlife, head to Coconut Grove. Unless mentioned, the bars listed below generally don't charge a cover. Most require proof that you are over 21 to enter.

> ### Impresssions
> *Miami is where neon goes to die.*
> —Lenny Bruce

Ground Rules: Stepping Out in Miami

First things first: Nightlife on South Beach doesn't really get going until after 11pm. As a result, you may want to consider taking what is known as a disco nap so that you'll be fully charged until the wee hours. Second: If you're unsure of what to wear out on South Beach, your safest bet will be anything black. Third: Do *not* try to tip the door-men manning the velvet ropes. That will only make you look desperate and you'll find yourself standing outside for what will seem like an ungodly amount of time. Instead, try to land your name on the ever-present guest lists by calling the club early in the day yourself, or, better yet, having the concierge at your hotel do it for you. Concierges have connections. If you don't have connections and you find yourself without a concierge, then act assertive, not surly, at the velvet rope, and your patience will usually be rewarded with admittance. If all else fails—for men, especially—surround yourself with a few leggy model types and you'll be noticed quicker. Finally, have fun. It may look like serious business when you're on the outside, but once you're in, it's another story. Attacking clubland with a sense of humor is the best approach to a successful, memorable evening out.

Blue   A very laid-back, very locals scene set to a sultry soundtrack of deep soul and deep house music has Miami's hipsters feeling the blues on a nightly basis from 10pm to 5am. Before you whip out the St. John's Wort, reconsider your mood and dive into this so-not-trendy-it's-trendy lounge, in which the pervasive color blue will actually heighten your spirits as an eclectic haze of models, locals, and lounge lizards gather to commiserate in their dreaded trendy status. 222 Española Way (between Washington and Collins aves.), South Beach. ☎ **305/534-1009.** No cover.

Clevelander   If wet T-shirt contests and a fraternity party atmosphere are your thing, then this Ocean Drive mainstay is your kind of place. Popular with tourists and locals who like to pretend they're tourists, the Clevelander attracts a lively, sporty, adults-only crowd (the burly bouncers *will* confiscate fake IDs) who have no interest in being part of a scene, but, rather, taking in the very revealing scenery. A great time to check the Clevelander out is on a weekend afternoon, when beach Barbies and Kens line the bar for a post-tanning beer or frozen cocktail. 1020 Ocean Dr., South Beach. ☎ **305/531-3485.** www.clevelanderhotel.com. No cover.

Forge   This Forge lounge hosts an unusual mix of the uptight and those who wear their clothes too tight. It's also where surgically altered ladies look for their cigar-chomping sugar daddies. Call well in advance if you want to watch the parade of characters from your dinner table (see chapter 6). As if that's not enough, a ritzier nightclub reminiscent of a cruise-ship lounge, called Jimmy'z, is adjacent. They say it's a private club, but if you dine at the restaurant or know someone, you can get in. A popular Latin hot spot, Cafe Nostalgia, an offshoot of the original in Little Havana, has recently opened next door and is a show-case of recent Arthur Murray dance school grads. 432 41st St., Miami Beach. ☎ **305/538-8533.** No cover (though door policy tends to be a bit exclusive; dress up and you should have no problem).

Fox's Sherron Inn *(Finds* The spirit of Frank Sinatra is alive and well at this dark and smoky watering hole that dates back to 1946. Everything down to the vinyl booths and the red lights make Fox's a retro fabulous dive bar. Cheap drinks, couples cozily huddling in booths, and a seasoned staff of bartenders and barflies make Fox's the perfect place to retreat from the trenches of trendiness. Oh, and the food's actually good here, too. 6030 S. Dixie Hwy. (at 62nd Ave.), South Miami. ⓒ 305/661-9201. No cover.

Laundry Bar The only place in Miami where it's okay to let friends drink and dry. Laundry Bar features working washers, dryers, a fully stocked bar, and several other distractions to help make doing your laundry a fun rather than a dreaded chore. It's also one of the only bars on South Beach open from 7am to 5am daily. Thursdays seem to be laundry night on South Beach, when a deejay spins the best in house music. And although it's most popular with the gay community, Laundry Bar draws a mixed crowd; on weekends, the place is packed like an overloaded washing machine. 721 Lincoln Lane (behind Burdines off Lincoln Rd.), South Beach. ⓒ 305/531-7700. www.laundrybar.com. No cover.

Lola *(Finds* Lola redefines the neighborhood bar, striking the perfect balance between chill and chic. This bar, located away from the South Beach mayhem, is a showgirl in her own right—a swank, sultry lounge where people are encouraged to come as they are, leaving the attitude at home. Attracting a mixed crowd of gay, straight, young, and old(er), Lola reinvents itself each night with deejays spinning everything from retro '80s music to hard rock and classic oldies. Tuesday night is the bar's most popular—and populated—so be prepared to wait a while until they start cramming people in. A warning to the budget conscious: Lola's cocktails are among the most expensive on the beach, charging upward of $14 for a martini. 247 23rd St., South Beach. ⓒ 305/695-8697. No cover.

> **Impressions**
>
> *There are two shifts in South Beach. There's nine to five. And then there's nine to five.*
>
> —South Beach artist Stewart Stewart

Mac's Club Deuce Standing on its own amidst an oasis of trendiness, Mac's Club Deuce is the quintessential dive bar, with cheap drinks and a cast of characters ranging from your typical barfly to your atypical drag queen. It's got a well-stocked juke box, friendly bartenders, a pool table, and best of all, it's an insomniac's dream, open daily from 8am to 5am. 222 14th St., South Beach. ⓒ 305/673-9537. No cover.

Murphy's Law Irish Pub This wood- and brass-decorated Irish pub is a decent choice for those who want to feel like they're back in college again. Weekends offer live music, Irish or otherwise, and a big-screen TV shows sports events. But this place is really about sharing a pint or two at the bar with the young professionals who call Murphy's their "Cheers." On Thursday night, the place is packed with party-hearty collegiate types. 2977 McFarlane Dr., Coconut Grove. ⓒ 305/446-9956. No cover.

Piccadilly Garden Lounge Hardly anyone in Miami knows that this completely off-the-beaten-path Design District lounge exists, which makes it that much cooler. A young, alternative crowd (bordering on Gothic) gathers in this garden every Saturday night for what is known as Pop Life, a musical homage to

South Beach After Dark

To Central Miami Beach

The Bass Museum of Art

Miami Beach Convention Center

Lincoln Road Mall

HISTORIC
ART DECO
DISTRICT

Española Way

Miami Beach Post Office

FLAMINGO PARK

Biscayne Bay

BELLE ISLAND

Venetian Causeway

Beach Patrol Station

Art Deco Welcome Center

ATLANTIC OCEAN

LUMMUS PARK

SOUTH POINTE PARK

Government Cut

COLLINS PARK

0   1/4 mi
0   0.25 km

Star Gazing

While it may not be a big deal to spot a celebrity in, say, Los Angeles, no matter how many stars fall on Miami's shores, it's still a thrill. Should you come into contact with a celebrity, use your best judgment as far as whether or not to approach them. Although they may be out in public, it's not an invitation for people to swarm them. The most popular places for celebrity sightings include Cameron Diaz's Bambu restaurant, Tantra, the lobby bar at the Hotel Astor, poolside at the Delano, Level nightclub, and crobar nightclub. Miami Heat games are also star magnets.

the sounds of British pop and alternative music. While the dank interior resembles a stuffy old Holiday Inn lounge, the music and the crowd is very mod. 35 NE 40th St., Miami. ℂ 305/573-8221. Cover $5 Sat.

Purdy Lounge   With the exception of a wall of lava lamps, Purdy is not unlike your best friend's basement, featuring a pool table and a slew of board games such as Operation to keep the attention deficit disordered from getting bored. Because it's a no-nonsense bar with relatively cheap cocktails (by South Beach standards), Purdy gets away with not having a star deejay or fancy bass-heavy Bose sound system. A CD player somehow does the trick. With no cover and no attitude, a line is inevitable, so be prepared to wait. Saturday night has become the preferred night for locals, while Friday night happy hour draws a young professional crowd on the prowl. 1811 Purdy Ave., Miami Beach. ℂ 305/531-4622. No cover.

Rose Bar at the Delano   If every rose has its thorn, the thorn at this painfully chic hotel bar is the excruciatingly high-priced cocktails. Otherwise, the crowd here is full of the so-called glitterati, fabulati, and other assorted poseurs who view life through (Italian-made) rose-colored glasses. 1685 Collins Ave., South Beach. ℂ 305/672-2000. No cover.

Wet Willie's   With such telling drinks as "Call a Cab," this beachfront oasis is not the place to go if you have a long drive ahead of you. A popular pre-and post-beach hangout, Wet Willie's inspires serious drinking. Popular with the Harley Davidson set, tourists, and beachcombers, this bar is best known for its rooftop patio (get there early if you plan to get a seat) and its half-nude bikini beauties. 760 Ocean Dr., South Beach. ℂ 305/532-5650. No cover. There's another Wet Willie's in Coconut Grove at 3390 Mary St., but it's not as fun (ℂ 305/443-5060), on the third level of Mayfair.

2 The Club & Music Scene

LIVE MUSIC

Surprisingly, Miami's live music scene is not thriving. More thriving than local bands are local deejays who skyrocket to fame thanks to the city's lauded dance club scene. However, there are several places that strive to bring Miami up to speed as far as live music is concerned. You just have to look—and listen—for it a bit more carefully.

Churchill's Hideaway *(Finds*   British expatriate Dave Daniels couldn't live in Miami without a true English-style pub, so he opened Churchill's Hideaway, the city's premier space for live rock music. Filthy and located in a rather unsavory neighborhood, Churchill's is committed to promoting and extending the lifeline of the lagging local music scene. A fun no-frills crowd hangs out here. Bring

Haute Hotel Bars

Long gone are the days of the Holiday Inn lounges. In fact, some hotels seem to spend more money on their bars than they do on their bedding. That aside, hotel bar hopping is very popular in Miami. Here's my list of the best:

Rose Bar at the Delano (see earlier), for seeing and being seen.

Lobby bar at the Hotel Astor, 956 Washington Ave., South Beach (✆ 305/ 672-1402), to bask in a flattering light with a sophisticated, not snobby, crowd.

Marlin Bar at the Marlin Hotel, 1200 Collins Ave., South Beach (✆ 305/ 673-8373), to experience what is known as Caribbean chic.

Bond St. Lounge at the Townhouse Hotel, 150 20th St., South Beach (✆ 305/534-3800), a New York import known for excellent sushi and a hip, cheap, chic jet-set crowd.

Harry's American Bar at the Eden Roc Resort, 4525 Collins Ave., Miami Beach (✆ 305/674-5568), a throwback to the days of Miami Beach kitsch, when Liza, Sammy, and Frank were splashing around at the pool.

earplugs with you, as it is deafening once the music starts. 5501 NE 2nd Ave., Miami. ✆ 305/757-1807. Cover $0–$5.

Jazid *(Finds* Smoky, sultry, and illuminated by flickering candelabras, Jazid is the kind of place where you'd expect to hear Sade's "Smooth Operator" on constant rotation. Instead, however, you'll hear live jazz—sometimes on acid—soul and funk. Past surprise performers at Jazid include former Smashing Pumpkin's front man Billy Corgan. An eclectic mix of mellow folk convene here for a much necessary respite from the surrounding Washington Avenue mayhem. 1342 Washington Ave., South Beach. ✆ 305/673-9372. No cover.

Power Studios *(Finds* A nocturnal funhouse for the Ritalin generation, Power Studios takes the concept of multimedia to new heights with several performance spaces, an art gallery, a disco, an outdoor Latin-Caribbean patio, and a rooftop restaurant and cinema. Local bands—good ones, at that—clamor for a spot in the limelight, as many as four or five performing on a nightly basis. 3701 NE 2nd Ave., Miami. ✆ 305/573-8042. Cover $0–$10.

Satchmo Blues This is a very popular happy-hour hangout. In fact, it's a restaurant, club, and bar all rolled into one. Every Friday night it's packed by locals and curious visitors—spilling over the sidewalks and into the streets— looking for an exciting night out. If you're lucky enough to get inside, you can listen to a live jazz, blues, or rock band playing everything from Chuck Berry to Miles Davis. Black and white photos of the great ones—Dizzie Gillespie, Louis Armstrong, Billie Holiday, Duke Ellington, John Coltrane, and Sam Cooke— adorn the walls. There's an American menu with Cajun fare and a full-service bar. The bartenders will gladly mix anything you ask them to. The happy-hour crowd dies down after 9pm, but another nightly crowd strolls right in its place. You can park in a huge lot next door for $1.50 an hour. 60 Merrick Way, Coral Gables (1 block from Coral Way and Douglas Rd). ✆ 305/774-1883. www.miamiblues. Cover $5–$10. Fri–Sat.

Tobacco Road   Al Capone used to hang out here when it was a speakeasy. Now, locals flock here to see local bands perform, as well as national acts such as George Clinton and the P-Funk All-Stars, Koko Taylor, and the Radiators. It's small and gritty, and meant to be that way. This place is the proud owner of Miami's very first liquor license. Escape the smoke and sweat in the backyard patio, where air is a welcome commodity. The downright cheap nightly specials, such as the $11 lobster on Tuesday, are quite good and are served until 2am; the bar is open until 5am. 626 S. Miami Ave. (over the Miami Ave. Bridge near Brickell Ave.), Downtown. (C) 305/374-1198. Cover $5 Fri–Sat.

Upstairs at the Van Dyke Café *(Finds)*   The cafe's jazz bar, located on the second floor, resembles a classy speakeasy in which local jazz performers play to an intimate, enthusiastic crowd of mostly adults and sophisticated young things, who huddle at the small tables often until the wee hours. 846 Lincoln Rd., Miami Beach. (C) 305/534-3600. Cover $3–$6 for a seat; no cover at the bar.

DANCE CLUBS

Anyone who's ever salvaged a disastrous party knows the rescue effort usually boils down to one thing: good music. Fortunately, the club music found on Miami's ever-evolving social circuit is good enough to get even the most rhythmically challenged wallflowers dancing. *Note:* As with anything on Miami's nocturnal circuit, call in advance to make sure that the dance club you're planning to go to hasn't become a video arcade.

To keep things fresh in clubland, local promoters throw one-nighters, which are essentially parties with various themes or motifs, from funk to fashion. Because these change so often, we can't possibly list them here. Word of mouth, local advertising, and listings in the free weekly *New Times,* miami.citysearch. com, or the Weekend section of the *Miami Herald* are the best ways to find out about these ever-changing events.

320   The second coming of the haute spot formerly known as Bar Room (which closed abruptly after its twentysomething owner was thrown in prison for dealing in "family" business), 320 imitates its predecessor in that it aims to create itself in the likeness of Studio 54. Unfortunately, it falls flat because it tries too hard. Aging glitterati types try to relive the glory days of 15 minutes ago, when seeing and being seen at Bar Room actually mattered. Still, 320 offers an excellent sound system, a VIP area you can rent for a cool $3,000, and the occasional appearance by Sean "Puffy" Combs. 320 Lincoln Rd., South Beach. (C) 305 /672-2882. Cover $15 and up, unless you're on the guest list (see "Ground Rules," above).

Bermuda Bar and Grill   This North Miami Beach spot is a sanctuary for those who'd rather not deal with the hustle, bustle, and hassle of driving and parking in South Beach or Coconut Grove. Bermuda Bar is a mega–dance club that is often frequented by young suburban professionals. Good pizzas and

---

Rock 'n' Bowl

Inspired by the alcohol-free rave dance parties of the '90s, Rave Bowling at **Cloverleaf Lanes,** 17601 NW 2nd Ave., North Dade ((C) **305/652-4197**), keeps teens off the streets, but in the gutters. Low lighting, glow-in-the-dark pins, and loud music keep things rolling every Friday and Saturday night from 8:30pm until 3am. Games are $4.50 each; shoes and balls are an extra $2.

grilled foods are available, too. It's usually open until the sun comes up. Wednesday's ladies nights are particularly popular, when women drink free and men are at their mercy. 3509 NE 163rd St., North Miami Beach. © 305/945-0196. www.bermudabar.com. Cover $0–$10. No cover before 9pm. Open Wed–Sat.

Bongos Cuban Café   Gloria Estefan's latest hit in the restaurant business pays homage to the sites, sounds, and cuisine of pre-Castro Cuba, Bongo's is a mammoth restaurant attached to the American Airlines Arena in downtown Miami. On Friday and Saturday after 11:30pm, Bongos is transformed from a friendly family restaurant into the city's hottest 21-and-over salsa nightclub. Cover charge at that time is a hefty $20, but consider it your ticket to what happens to be an astounding show of some of the best salsa dancers in the city. Prepare yourself for standing room only. At the American Airlines Arena, 601 Biscayne Blvd. © 786/777-2100. Cover $20.

> **Impresssions**
>
> *Working the door teaches you a lot about human nature.*
> —A former South Beach doorman

Club Space   Clubland hits the mainland with this cavernous downtown warehouse of a club. With over 30,000 square feet of dance space, you can spin around a la Stevie Nicks (albeit to a techno beat) without having to worry about banging into someone. However, after hours, Club Space packs them in. While Saturday caters to a more homogeneous crowd, Friday is a free-for-all. Conveniently, the club often runs shuttles from the beach. 142 NE 11th St., Miami. © 305/577-1007. Cover $0–$20.

crobar *(Finds)*   Still haunted by the ghost of clubs past, the space formerly known as the Cameo Theatre is now possessed by the mod, millennial, industrial spirit that is crobar. With its intense, dance-heavy sound system, an industrially chic ambience, and crowds big enough to scare away any memories of a sadly abandoned Cameo, this Chicago import has raised the bar on South Beach nightlife with crazy theme nights (the monthly Sex is particularly, uh, stimulating), top-name deejays, and the occasional celebrity appearance. On Sunday, the club hosts an extremely popular gay night known as Anthem. (See "The Gay & Lesbian Scene," later in this chapter.) 1445 Washington Ave., South Beach. © 305/531-8225. www.crobarmiami.com. Cover $25.

Krave   After countless incarnations and one failed ownership by actor Mickey Rourke, this large space has come into its own as a respected member of South Beach clubland, offering the ubiquitous fashion shows, dance deejays, and an assortment of colorful club kids. 817 Washington Ave., South Beach. © 305/532-5632. Cover $10–$20.

Level   Overdone and some say overhyped, Level takes the notion of South Beach excess even further with its outlet mall–sized, 40,000-square-foot space featuring four dance floors, three levels, five rooms, and nine bars. Like a video game, your status here is determined by which level you can land on. If you befriend one of the club's owners, you may end up at the top. Leveling out the competition, this club has cornered the market on parties and events, throwing one nearly every night. Because it is the largest club on the beach, the velvet rope scene can be quite harassing, but if you call in advance, the accommodating staff will usually put you on the guest list. Friday night is a very popular gay night, while the rest of the week attracts a mixed crowd of straight, gay, and somewhere in between. Celebs love Level because it has so many VIP rooms. 1235 Washington Ave., South Beach. © 305/532-1525. www.levelnightclub.com. Cover $20–$30.

Living Room at the Strand   What you'll find in this model-decorated Living Room is a blanket of beautiful people lazing about, sipping the finest champagne, and waxing philosophical on the ways of the fabulous world. Beware of the often nasty, so-called Door Nazis, who get their thrills from rejecting the sea of people that only parts for six-foot Amazonian model types or Eurotrash who wouldn't be caught dead anywhere else. 671 Washington Ave., South Beach. © 305/532-2340. www.livingroom2000.com. Cover $15–$20.

N   Owned by the same team that owns Level, N is an intimate, exclusive club with several luxury VIP suites big enough to accommodate even the largest of egos. Resurrecting the spirit of South Beach past, N prides itself on a rigid velvet rope policy and an Ibiza-style patio with open-air suites and a dance floor. While we're not sure what N stands for exactly, we think it could stand for "narcissistic" judging by the clientele. 743 Washington Ave., South Beach. © 305/695-9299. Cover $10–$20.

Nikki Beach Club *(Finds*   What the Playboy Mansion is to Hollywood, the Nikki Beach Club is to South Beach. It's the product of local nightlife royalty—Tommy Pooch and Eric Omores. Bare-naked ladies and men actually venture into the daylight (around 4pm) to see, be seen, and, at times, be obscene. At night, it's very sexy in a tiki hut sort of way. The Sunday afternoon beach party is almost legendary and worth a glimpse—that is, if you can get in. This is not your equal opportunity beach club. Egos have been shattered as surly doormen are known to reject those who don't drive up in a Ferrari. Also located within this bastion of hedonism is the superhot **Pearl,** a mod-ish, 380-seat, orange hued restaurant and lounge that features a Continental menu created by Nikki chef Brian Rutherford. Forget the food and go for the eye candy. 101 Ocean Dr., South Beach. © 305/538-1111. Cover $10–$20.

Rumi   Named after a 13th-century Sufi mystic, South Beach's first upscale supper club was, at press time, scheduled to open summer 2001. Designed by hot NYC designers Nancy Mah and Scott Kester, Rumi will be an urbane oasis of reds, tans, and chocolates, reminiscent of the golden age of supper clubs of the '30s and '40s. This massive space features intimate lounge areas as well as private and public dining rooms, in which haute Florida-Caribbean cuisine will be served until the tables conspicuously disappear and give way to a neo-Zen-like stomping ground for South Beach's chic elite. Make sure to check out the queen-sized Murphy bed that snaps down from the wall to make room for late-night lounging. 330 Lincoln Rd., South Beach. © 305/672-4353. www.rumimiami.com. No cover.

THE GAY & LESBIAN SCENE

Miami and the beaches have long been host to what is called a "first-tier" gay community. Similar to the Big Apple, the Bay Area, or LaLa land, Miami has had a large alternative community since the days when Anita Bryant used her citrus power to boycott the rise in political activism in the early '70s. Well, things have changed and Miami–Dade now has a gay rights ordinance.

Newcomers intending to party in any bar, whether downtown or certainly on the beach, will want to check ahead for the schedule, as all clubs must have a gay or lesbian night to pay their rent. Miami Beach, in fact, is the capital of the gay circuit party scene, rivaling San Francisco, Palm Springs, and even the mighty Sydney, Australia, for tourist dollars.

Cactus Bar & Grill   Somewhere, over the causeway, there is life beyond South Beach—that is, for Miami's gay society. Housed in a large two-story space, Cactus attracts a mix of unpretentious, professional, and also very attractive men and women. There's something for everyone here, whether it's the indoor pool tables, the outdoor swimming pool, or drinks that are considerably cheaper than on South Beach. Friday evening happy hours and Sunday afternoon Tea Dances are a virtual cattle call, attracting hordes of folks looking to quench their thirst for fun at Miami's sprawling urban oasis. 2401 Biscayne Blvd., Downtown. ℂ 305/ 438-0662. No cover.

crobar   Sunday nights at crobar sing the gay anthem with this hyperpopular one-nighter featuring Miami's own superstar deejay Abel. 1445 Washington Ave., South Beach. ℂ 877/CRO-SOBE or 305/531-5027. Cover $25.

Eagle   Miami's Levi-leather emporium features beer and handcuffs. It's not for first-timers or the faint of heart. 1252 Coral Way, South Miami. ℂ 305/860-0056. Cover $15.

Federation 1235   Hordes of gay men (and some women) join the Federation at Level every Friday, when the dance floor is packed with wall-to-wall hard bodies. 1235 Washington Ave., South Beach. ℂ 305/532-1525. Cover $20–$30.

Friends   This is Miami's only boy strip club. It's open every night with video monitors screening movies and all kinds of other stuff. 17032 Collins Ave., Sunny Isles/Aventura. ℂ 305/949-4112. Cover $10–$15.

Loading Zone   A leather and Levi bar known for its cruisability, pool tables, movies, and pitchers of beer. There's an in-house leather store for the kinky shopper. 1426 Alton Rd., South Beach. ℂ 305/531-5623. Cover $15–$20.

O-Zone   This is the zone of choice for gay men with an aversion to South Beach's cruisy, scene-heavy vibes. It's known for a heavily Latin crowd (mixed with a few college boys from nearby University of Miami) and fantastic, outlandish drag shows. 6620 SW 57th Ave. (Red Rd.), South Miami. ℂ 305/667-2888. No cover for men on Sat; other nights $5–$10.

Salvation   For those seeking liberation from the cookie-cutter mold of run-of-the-mill Saturday night dance clubs, Salvation is where you'll find it. Housed in an old warehouse, Salvation is spacious but always filled to capacity with shirtless, sweaty circuit boys dancing themselves into oblivion. Major deejays spin here, and, at times, divas sing here, such as Bette Midler, who did a rare and ribald cabaret performance to an SRO audience. You can't blame the owners for charging $20 to get in when you see this bevy of beautiful boys. 1771 West Ave., Miami Beach. ℂ 305/673-6508. Cover $20.

Score   There's a reason this Lincoln Road hotbed of gay social activity is called Score. In addition to the huge pick-up scene, Score offers a multitude of bars, dance floors, lounge-like areas, and outdoor tables in case you need to come up for air. Sunday afternoon Tea Dances are legendary here. 727 Lincoln Rd., South Beach. ℂ 305/535-1111. No cover.

Twist   One of the of the most popular bars (and hideaways) on South Beach (and literally across the street from the police station), this recently expanded bar has a casual yet lively local atmosphere. It's open from 1pm to 5am. 1057 Washington Ave., South Beach. ℂ 305/538-9478. No cover.

LATIN CLUBS

Considering that Hispanics make up a large part of Miami's population and that there's a huge influx of Spanish-speaking visitors, it's no surprise that there are some great Latin nightclubs in the city.

Plus, with the meteoric rise of the international music scene based in Miami, many international stars come through the offices of MTV Latino, SONY International, and a multitude of Latin TV studios based in Miami—and they're all looking for a good club scene on weekends. Most of the Anglo clubs reserve at least 1 night a week for Latin rhythms.

Añoranzas   You've heard of *son?* Hear it here—along with salsa, cumbia, merengue, vallenato, and house music. This neighborhood Latin disco and nightclub gets going after hours with a wild strobe-lit atmosphere. If you don't know how to do it, just wait. You'll have plenty of willing teachers on hand. Open Friday to Sunday from 8pm to 5am. 241 23rd St. (1 block west of Collins Ave.), South Beach. ℂ 305/538-1196. No cover.

Cafe Nostalgia   As the name implies, Cafe Nostalgia is dedicated to reminiscing about old Cuba. After watching a Celia Cruz film, you can dance to the hot sounds of Afro-Cuban jazz. With pictures of old and young Cuban stars smiling down on you and a live band celebrating Cuban heritage, Cafe Nostalgia sounds like a bit much, and it is. Be prepared—it's packed after midnight and dance space is mostly between the tables. Open Thursday to Sunday from 9pm to 4am. Films are shown from 10pm to midnight, followed by live music. Another location is on Miami Beach next to the Forge restaurant. 2212 SW 8th St. (Calle Ocho), Miami. ℂ 305/541-2631. Cover $10 Thurs–Sun.

Casa Panza *Finds*   This *casa* is one of Little Havana's liveliest and most popular nightspots. Every Tuesday, Thursday, and Saturday night, Casa Panza, in the heart of Little Havana, becomes the House of Flamenco, with shows at 8 and 11pm. You can either enjoy a flamenco show or strap on your own dancing shoes and participate in the celebration. Enjoy a fantastic Spanish meal before the show, or just a glass of sangria before you start stomping. Open until 4am, Casa Panza is a hot spot for young Latin club kids, and, occasionally, a few older folks who are so taken by the music and the scene that they've failed to realize it's well past bedtime. 1620 SW 8th St. (Calle Ocho), Miami. ℂ 305/643-5343. No cover.

La Covacha *Finds*   Forget about the love shack and get thee to the Latin shack that is La Covacha. This hut, located virtually in the middle of nowhere (West Miami), is the hottest Latin joint in the entire city. Sunday features the best in Latin rock, with local and international acts. But the shack is really jumping on weekend nights when the place is open until 5am. Do not wear silk here, as you will sweat. Friday is *the* night here, so much that the owners had to place a red velvet rope out front to maintain some semblance of order. An amusing sight—a velvet rope guarding a shack—but once you get in, you'll understand the need for it. 10730 NW 25th St. (at NW 107th Ave.), Miami. ℂ 305/594-3717. Cover $0–$10.

Mango's Tropical Café   Claustrophobic types do not want to go near Mango's. Ever. One of the most popular spots on Ocean Drive, this outdoor enclave of Latin liveliness shakes with the intensity of a Richter-busting earthquake. Welcome and *bienvenido,* Mango's is *Cabaret,* Latin style. Nightly live

Rhythm Is Gonna Get You

Are you feeling shy about hitting a Latin club because you fear your two left feet will stand out? Then take a few lessons from one of the following dance companies and dance teachers. They offer individual and group lessons to dancers of any origin who are willing to learn. These folks have made it their mission to teach merengue and flamenco to non-Latinos and Latino left-foots.

At **Ballet Flamenco La Rosa,** in the PAN building, 555 17th St., South Beach (✆ **305/672-0552**), you can learn to flamenco, salsa, or merengue with the best of them. They are the only professional flamenco company in the area, so you'll hear those castanets going. If you're feeling shy, $50 will buy you a private lesson; otherwise, it's $10 for a group lesson.

Nobody salsas like **Luz Pinto** (✆ **305/868-9418**), and she also knows how to teach the basics with patience and humor. She charges between $40 and $55 for a private lesson for up to four people and $10 per person for a group lesson. A good introduction is her multi-level group class at 7pm Sunday evenings at the PAN building. Although she teaches everything from ballroom to merengue, her specialty is Casino-style salsa, popularized in the 1950s in Cuba, Luz's homeland. A mix between disco and country square dancing, Casino-style salsa is all the rage in Latin clubs in town. Good students may be able to convince Luz to chaperone a trip to a nightclub to show off their moves. She'll work out a fee based on the number of participants and their ability.

Angel Arroya has been teaching salsa to the clueless out of his home at 16467 NE 27th Ave., North Miami Beach (✆ **305/949-7799**), for the past 10 years. Just $10 will buy you an hour's time in his "school." He traditionally teaches Monday and Wednesday nights, but call ahead to check for any schedule changes.

Brazilian and other Latin music, not to mention scantily clad male and female dancers, draw huge gawking crowds in from the sidewalk from 11am to 5am. But pay attention to the music if you can: Incognito international musicians often lose their anonymity and jam with the house band on stage. 900 Ocean Dr., South Beach. ✆ 305/673-4422. Cover $5–$15; varies by performer.

3 The Performing Arts

THEATER

Highbrows and culture vultures complain that there is a dearth of decent cultural offerings in Miami. What do locals tell them? Go back to New York! In all seriousness, however, in recent years, the performing arts scene has improved greatly. The city's Broadway Series features Tony Award–winning shows (the touring version, of course). The performances aren't always Broadway caliber, but they are usually pretty good and not nearly as pricey! Local arts groups such as the Miami Light Project, a not-for-profit cultural organization that presents live performances by innovative dance, music, and theater artists, have had huge success in attracting big-name artists such as Nina Simone and Philip Glass to Miami. In addition, a burgeoning bohemian movement in Little Havana has given way to performance spaces that have become nightclubs in their own right.

The **Actors' Playhouse,** at the newly restored Miracle Theater at 280 Miracle Mile, Coral Gables (© **305/444-9293**), is a grand 1948 Art Deco movie palace with a 600-seat main theater and a smaller theater/rehearsal hall that hosts a number of excellent musicals for children throughout the year. In addition to these two rooms, the Playhouse recently added a 300-seat children's balcony theater. Tickets run from $26 to $50.

The **Coconut Grove Playhouse,** 3500 Main Hwy., Coconut Grove (© **305/442-4000**), was also a former movie house, built in 1927 in an ornate Spanish rococo style. Today, this respected venue is known for its original and innovative staging of both international and local dramas and musicals. The house's second, more intimate Encore Room is well suited to alternative and experimental productions. Tickets run from $37 to $42.

The **Gables Stage** at the Biltmore Hotel, Anastasia Avenue, Coral Gables (© **305/445-1119**), stages at least one Shakespearean play, one classic, and one contemporary piece a year. This well-regarded theater usually tries to secure the rights to a national or local premiere as well. Tickets cost $22 and $28; $10 and $17 for students and seniors.

The **Jerry Herman Ring Theatre** is on the main campus of the University of Miami in Coral Gables (© **305/284-3355**). The University's Department of Theater Arts uses this stage for advanced-student productions of comedies, dramas, and musicals. Faculty and guest actors are regularly featured, as are contemporary works by local playwrights. Performances are usually scheduled Tuesday through Saturday during the academic year. In the summer, don't miss "Summer Shorts," a selection of superb one-acts. Tickets sell for $5 to $20.

The **New Theater,** 65 Almeria Ave., Coral Gables (© **305/443-5909**), prides itself on showing world-renowned works from America and Europe. As the name implies, you'll find mostly contemporary plays, with a few classics thrown in for variety. Performances are staged Thursday to Sunday year-round. Tickets are $20 on weekdays, $25 weekends. If tickets are available on the day of the performance—and they usually are—students pay half price.

CLASSICAL MUSIC

In addition to a number of local orchestras and operas, which regularly offer quality music and world-renowned guest artists, each year brings a slew of special events and touring artists. One of the most important and longest-running series is produced by the **Concert Association of Florida (CAF),** 555 17th St., South Beach (© **305/532-3491**). Known for more than a quarter of a century for its high-caliber, star-packed schedules, CAF regularly arranges the best "serious" music concerts for the city. Season after season, the schedules are punctuated by world-renowned dance companies and seasoned virtuosi like Itzhak Perlman, Andre Watts, and Kathleen Battle. Since CAF does not have its own space, performances are usually scheduled in the Dade County Auditorium or the Jackie Gleason Theater of the Performing Arts (see later in this chapter). The season lasts from October through April, and ticket prices range from $20 to $70.

Florida Philharmonic Orchestra   South Florida's premier symphony orchestra, under the direction of James Judd, presents a full season of classical and pops programs interspersed with several children's and contemporary popular music performances. The Philharmonic performs downtown in the Gusman Center for the Performing Arts and at the Dade County Auditorium. 1243 University Dr., Miami. ℭ 800/226-1812 or 305/476-1234. Tickets $15–$60. When extra tickets are available, students are admitted free on day of performance.

Miami Chamber Symphony   This professional orchestra is an inexpensive alternative to the high-priced classical venues. Renowned international soloists perform regularly. The season runs October to May, and most concerts are held in the Gusman Concert Hall, on the University of Miami campus. 5690 N. Kendall Dr., Kendall. ℭ 305/858-3500. Tickets $12–$30.

New World Symphony   This organization, led by artistic director Michael Tilson Thomas, is a stepping stone for gifted young musicians seeking professional careers. The orchestra specializes in ambitious, innovative, energetic performances and often features renowned guest soloists and conductors. The symphony's season lasts from October to May during which time there are many free concerts. 541 Lincoln Rd., South Beach. ℭ 305/673-3331. www.nws.org. Tickets free–$58. Rush tickets (remaining tickets sold 1 hour before performance) $20. Students $10 (1 hour before concerts limited seating).

OPERA

Florida Grand Opera   Around for over 60 years, this company regularly features singers from top houses in both America and Europe. All productions are sung in their original language and staged with projected English supertitles. Tickets become scarce when Placido Domingo or Luciano Pavarotti (who made his American debut here in 1965) comes to town. The opera's season runs roughly from November to April, with five performances each week. A new multimillion-dollar headquarters for the opera is scheduled to open in late 2002; until then, performances take place at the Miami–Dade Auditorium and the Broward Center for the Performing Arts. Box office: 1200 Coral Way, Miami. ℭ 800/741-1010 or 305/854-1643; 305/854-7890 for box office. www.fgo.org. Tickets $19–$145. Student discounts available.

DANCE

Several local dance companies train and perform in the Greater Miami area. In addition, top traveling troupes regularly stop at the venues listed above. Keep your eyes open for special events and guest artists.

Ballet Flamenco La Rosa   For a taste of local Latin flavor, see this lively troupe perform impressive flamenco and other styles of dance on Miami stages. ℭ 305/672-0552 or 305/757-8475. Tickets $25 at door, $20 in advance, $18 for students and seniors.

Miami City Ballet   This artistically acclaimed and innovative company, directed by Edward Villella, features a repertoire of more than 60 ballets, many by George Balanchine, and more than 20 world premieres. The company moved into a new $7.5 million headquarters in January 2000—the Ophelia and Juan Jr. Roca Center at the Collins Park Cultural Center in Miami Beach. The three-story center features eight rehearsal rooms, a ballet school, a boutique, and ticket offices. The City Ballet season runs from September to April. Ophelia and Juan Jr. Roca Center, Collins Ave. and 22nd St., Miami Beach. ℭ 305/532-4880 or 305/532-7713 for box office. Tickets $17–$50.

MAJOR VENUES

After a much-needed $1 million face-lift, the **Colony Theater,** on Lincoln Road in South Beach (© 305/674-1026), has become an architectural showpiece of the Art Deco District. This multipurpose 465-seat theater stages performances by the Miami City Ballet and the Ballet Flamenco La Rosa, as well as off-Broadway shows and other special events.

At the **Miami–Dade Auditorium,** West Flagler Street at 29th Avenue, Miami (© 305/547-5414), performers gripe about the lack of space, but for patrons, this 2,430-seat auditorium is the only Miami space in which you can hear the opera—for now. A multimillion-dollar performing arts center downtown has been in the works for years. For now, the Dade County Auditorium is home to the city's Florida Grand Opera, and it also stages productions by the Concert Association of Florida, many Spanish programs, and a variety of other shows.

At the 1,700-seat **Gusman Center for the Performing Arts,** 174 E. Flagler St., Downtown Miami (© 305/372-0925), seating is tight, and so is funding, but the sound is superb. In addition to producing a regular stage for the Philharmonic Orchestra of Florida and the Miami Film Festival, the elegant Gusman Center features pop concerts, plays, film festival screenings, and special events. The auditorium was built as the Olympia Theater in 1926, and its ornate palace interior is typical of that era, complete with fancy columns, a huge pipe organ, and twinkling "stars" on the ceiling.

Not to be confused with the Gusman Center (above), the **Gusman Concert Hall,** 1314 Miller Dr., at 14th Street, Coral Gables (© 305/284-6477), is a roomy 600-seat hall that gives a stage to the Miami Chamber Symphony and a varied program of university recitals.

The elegant **Jackie Gleason Theater of the Performing Arts (TOPA),** located at Washington Avenue at 17th Street, South Beach (© 305/673-7300), is the home of the Miami Beach Broadway Series, which recently presented *Rent, Phantom of the Opera,* and *Les Misérables.* This 2,705-seat hall also hosts other big-budget Broadway shows, classical music concerts, opera, and dance performances.

At press time, the city granted a budget in excess of $200 million for its official performing arts center. Planned are a 2,400-seat ballet/opera house and a 2,000-seat concert hall for the Florida Philharmonic, Florida Grand Opera, New World Symphony, and Miami City Ballet, and a major concert series. Designed by world-renowned architect Cesar Pelli, the center will be the focal point of a planned Arts, Media and Entertainment District in mid-Miami. The complex will be wrapped in limestone, slate, decorative stone, stainless steel, glass curtain walls, and tropical landscaping. A major new destination point for the community, more than 500,000 people, including 100,000 schoolchildren, will attend the center's year-round schedule of performances and activities. Millions more will participate in related events and will visit the site annually.

4 Movies & More

CINEMAS

In addition to the annual Miami Film Festival in February and other, smaller film events (See "South Florida Calendar of Events," in chapter 2), Miami is lucky to have some wonderful art cinemas showing a range of films from *Fresa y Chocolate* to *Crumb.*

Absinthe Cinemateque, 235 Alcazar Ave., Coral Gables (© 305/446-7144), is a small one-screen theater that shows good movies, often Spanish-language

Warhol Redux?
While all the world may indeed be a stage, Miami's Artemis Performance Network has been setting the stage for the city's creative types with eclectic venues and events dedicated to and showcasing the local arts community. A network of performing artists, visual artists, musicians, presenters, educators, and administrators, Artemis is backed by the support of the Miami–Dade County Cultural Affairs Council, among others. Responsible for turning Little Havana into a bohemian hangout, Artemis sponsors events at a loft-like performance space simply known as PS 742, 742 SW 16th Ave., Little Havana (© 305/643-6611), in which events such as Surreal Saturdays (first Saturday of every month) feature a funky roster of spoken word, multimedia, and musical artists. Locals have compared the scene at PS 742 to that of New York City's East Village, circa 1980.

films, without the hustle and bustle of the crowded multiplexes. The Alcazar shows the more artsy of the major films as well as some obscure independents. Tickets are $6.

Astor Art Cinema, 4120 Laguna St. (© 305/443-6777), is an oasis in the midst of a desert of Cineplex Odeons and AMCs in Coral Gables. This quaint double theater hosts foreign, classic, independent, and art films and serves decent popcorn, too. Tickets are $5, $3 for seniors.

The **Bill Cosford Cinema** at the University of Miami, located on the second floor of the memorial building off Campo Sano Avenue (© 305/284-4861), is named after the deceased *Herald* film critic. This well-endowed little theater was recently revamped and boasts high-tech projectors, new air-conditioning, and new decor. It sponsors independent films as well as lectures by visiting filmmakers and movie stars. Andy Garcia and Antonio Banderas are a few of the big names this theater has attracted. It also hosts the African American Film Festival and a Student Film Festival, plus collaborations with the Fort Lauderdale Festival. Admission is $5.

The **Mercury Theatre,** Biscayne Boulevard at 55th Street, Miami (© 305/759-8809), is the city's newest art house cinema, showing classic and contemporary films from all over the world.

THE LITERARY SCENE
Books & Books, in Coral Gables at 296 Aragon Ave., and in Miami Beach at 933 Lincoln Rd., hosts readings almost every night and is known for attracting such top authors as Colleen McCullough, Jamaica Kincaid, and Martin Amis. For details on the free readings, call © 305/442-4408.

To hear more about what's happening on Miami's literary scene, tune into the "Cover to Cover" show, broadcast at 8pm on Monday on public radio station WLRN (91.3 FM).

5 Late-Night Bites
Although some dining spots in Miami stop serving at 10pm, many are open very late or even around the clock—especially on weekends. So, if it's 4am and you need a quick bite after clubbing, don't fret. There are a vast number of pizza places lining Washington Avenue in South Beach that are open past 6am. Especially good is **Pucci's,** with several locations, including one at 651 Washington Ave. **La Sandwicherie,** 229 14th St. (behind the Amoco station;

© 305/532-8934), serves up a great late-night sandwich until 5am. Another place of note for night owls is the **News Café,** 800 Ocean Dr. (© **305/ 538-6397**), a trendy and well-priced cafe that has an enormous menu offering great all-day breakfasts, Middle Eastern platters, fruit bowls, or steak and potatoes—and everything is served 24 hours a day. In Coconut Grove, there's another crowded News Café, 2901 Florida Ave. (behind Mayfair; © **305/ 774-6397**), serving up the same fresh food around the clock.

If your night out was at one of the Latin clubs around town, stop in at **Versailles,** 3555 SW 8th St. (© **305/444-0240**), in Little Havana. What else but a Cuban *medianoche* (midnight sandwich) will do? It's not open all night, but its hours extend well past midnight—usually until 3 or 4am on weekends—to cater to gangs of revelers, young and old.

10

South Florida Side Trips: The Everglades & Biscayne National Park

Miami has been called the "gateway to the world," because its port leads the pack in passengers heading to the Caribbean and to Latin America. But many tourists also take some time out to see the wild plant and animal life in the swampy Everglades, and the underwater treasures of Biscayne National Park.

1 A Glimpse of Everglades National Park— The Southeast Portion

35 miles SW of Miami

Marjory Stoneman Douglas, who fought tirelessly to save this fragile resource until her death in 1998 at the age of 108, might well be called the Mother of the Everglades. This vast and unusual ecosystem is actually a shallow, 40-mile-wide, slow-moving river. Rarely more than knee-deep, the water is the lifeblood of this wilderness. Subtle shifts in water level dictate the life cycle of the native plants and animals. Most folks viewed it as a worthless swamp until Douglas focused attention on the area with her moving and insightful book *The Everglades: River of Grass,* published in 1947.

In that same year, 1.5 million acres—less than 20% of Everglades wilderness—were established as Everglades National Park. At that time, few lawmakers understood how neighboring ecosystems relate to each other: You can't just chop off a chunk of a much larger wilderness and expect it to survive. The park is heavily affected by surrounding territories and is at the butt end of every environmental insult that occurs upstream in Miami.

Recently, environmental activists have succeeded in persuading politicians to enact legislation to clean up the pollution that has threatened this unusual ecosystem ever since the days when heavy industry—most notably the sugar industry—first moved into the area. There has been a marked decrease in the indigenous wildlife here, but Everglades National Park nevertheless remains one of the few places where you can see dozens of endangered species in their natural habitat, including the swallowtail butterfly, American crocodile, leatherback turtle, southern bald eagle, West Indian manatee, and Florida panther.

Take your time on the trails, and a hypnotic beauty begins to unfold. Follow the rustling of a bush, and you might see a small green tree frog or tiny brown anole lizard, with its bright-red spotted throat. Crane your neck to see around a bend and discover a delicate, brightly painted mule-ear orchid.

Everglades National Park

Tamiami Trail

(41)

Miccosukee
Indian
Village

Shark Valley
Information Center

Tram Tour

Chekika

Richmond Dr.

Krome Ave.

(997)

(27)

(997)

(826)

(836)

(112)

(95)

MIAMI

Florida's Turnpike

(874)

(1)

BISCAYNE
NATIONAL
PARK

ELLIOTT KEY

Pay-Hay-Okee
Overlook

Homestead

Florida City

SW 137th
Ave.

North Canal Dr.

SW 328th St.

Dante Fascell
Visitor Center

9336

Main Visitor
Center

Long Pine Key

Palm Dr.

Card Sound Rd.

Royal Palm
Visitor Center

(1)

Old
Ingraham

Ernest Coe

Hell's Bay
Canoe Trail

Nine Mile Pond
Canoe Trail

Noble Hammock
Canoe Trail

North Nest Key

KEY LARGO

JOHN PENNEKAMP
CORAL REEF STATE PARK

THE FLORIDA KEYS

(1)

Florida Bay

ATLANTIC OCEAN

221

The slow and subtle splendor of this exotic land may not be immediately appealing to kids raised on video games and rapid-fire commercials, but they'll certainly remember the experience and thank you for it later. Meanwhile, you'll find plenty of dramatic fun around the park, such as airboat rides, alligator wrestling, and biking to keep the kids satisfied for at least a day.

In the 1800s, before the southern Everglades were designated a national park, the only inhabited piece of this wilderness was a quiet fishing village called Flamingo. Accessible only by boat and leveled every few years by hurricanes, the mosquito-infested town never grew very popular. When the 38-mile-long road from Florida City was completed in 1922, many of those who did live here fled to someplace either more or less remote. Today, Flamingo is a center for visitor activities and the main jumping-off point for backcountry camping and exploration. Flamingo is now home to National Park Service and concessionaire employees and their families.

Lazy River

It takes a month for 1 gallon of water to move through Everglades National Park.

Some 1,400 residents still live in the small enclave in the eastern section of the park, though the local agency governing the area has recently begun a buy-out program to remove them so that the area can be returned to its original state.

Everglades National Park's northern Shark Valley entrance and the eastern approaches described below are the most accessible from Miami and the rest of Florida's east coast. You'll stumble upon interesting and entertaining diversions along the way, like Indian villages, alligator farms, and boat rides. An excellent tram tour goes deep into the park along a trail that's also terrific for biking. This is also the best way to reach the park's only accommodation (and full-service outfitters), the Flamingo Lodge.

JUST THE FACTS

GETTING THERE & ACCESS POINTS   Everglades National Park has four entrances. If you want to take the more scenic route, then skip the speedier turnpike and head west on the Tamiami Trail, on which you may actually see alligators tanning on the roadside. The following three are the most popular entrances and the ones most convenient to visitors from Florida's east coast, including Miami. No matter which part of Miami you are starting from, the drive should take no longer than an hour (unless of course you are traveling during rush hour: between 8 and 9:30am or from 4 until 6pm. Then, the roads, especially State Route 836, will be backed up, and your driving time could be doubled).

The main entrance, in Homestead on the park's east side, is located 10 miles southwest of Florida City. From Miami, take State Route 836 west to the Florida Turnpike south until it ends in Florida City. Signs will point you southwest onto the road that leads into the park, State Route 9336. The Park Ranger Station at the main entrance is open 24 hours.

The Shark Valley entrance, on the park's north side, is located on the Tamiami Trail (U.S. 41), about 35 miles west of downtown Miami. From Miami, take State Route 836 west to the Florida Turnpike south; exit on Tamiami Trail (U.S. 41) and go west for approximately 30 miles. The park will be on the left. Shark Valley is known for its 15-mile trail loop that's used for bicycling and walking and for an excellent interpretive tram tour. This entrance is open daily from 8:30am to 5:30pm, with some seasonal variation. Call ahead.

Chekika, popular with day visitors, picnickers, and campers, is located halfway between the two entrances mentioned above, in the northeast section of the park. Chekika can be reached from Miami as if going to Shark Valley (see above). After exiting on Tamiami Trail (Highway 41), head west 5 miles to Krome Avenue (177th Avenue) and turn left. Then proceed to Southwest 168th Street (Richmond Avenue) and head west (left) until you reach a stop sign. Turn right; the entrance will be on the left. There are picnic facilities and a 20-site campground. You can enter Chekika from 8:30am until sundown.

VISITOR CENTERS & INFORMATION   General inquiries and specific questions should be directed to **Everglades National Park Headquarters,** 40001 S.R. 9336, Homestead, FL 33034 (© **305/242-7700**). Ask for a copy of *Parks and Preserves,* a free newspaper that's filled with up-to-date information about goings-on in the Everglades. Headquarters is staffed by helpful phone operators daily from 8:30am until 4:30pm. You can also try the park's website at **www.nps.gov/ever/**.

Note that all hours listed are for the high season, generally November through May. During the slow summer months, many offices and outfitters keep abbreviated hours.

The **Flamingo Lodge, Marina and Outpost Resort,** in Flamingo (© **800/ 600-3813** or 941/695-3101), is the one-stop clearinghouse—and the only option—for in-park accommodations, equipment rentals, and tours.

Especially since its recent expansion, the **Ernest F. Coe Visitor Center,** located at the park's main entrance, is the best place for gathering information for your trip. In addition to information on tours and boat rentals, and free brochures outlining trails, wildlife, and activities, you will also find state-of-the-art educational displays, films, and interactive exhibits. A gift shop sells postcards, film, unusual gift items, the best selection of books about the Everglades, and a supply of your most important gear: insect repellent. The shop is open from 8am until 5pm daily.

The **Royal Palm Visitor Center,** a small nature museum located 3 miles past the park's main entrance, is a smaller information center at the head of the popular Anhinga and Gumbo-Limbo Trails and is open daily from 8am until 4pm.

The Shark Valley Information Center at the park's northern entrance and the Flamingo Visitor Center are also staffed by knowledgeable rangers who provide brochures and personal insight into the park's activities. They are open from 8:30am until 5pm.

Impressions

There are no other Everglades in the world. They are, they have always been, one of the unique regions of the earth, remote, never wholly known. Nothing anywhere else is like them: their vast glittering openness, wider than the enormous visible round of the horizon, the racing free saltiness and sweetness of their massive winds, under the dazzling blue heights of space.

—Marjory Stoneman Douglas,
The Everglades: River of Grass, 1947

ENTRANCE FEES, PERMITS & REGULATIONS   Permits and passes can be purchased either at the main park entrance, the Chekika entrance, or the Shark Valley entrance stations only.

Even if you are just visiting the park for an afternoon, you'll need to buy a 7-day permit, which costs $10 per vehicle. Pedestrians and cyclists are charged $5 each and $4 at Shark Valley.

An Everglades Park Pass, valid for a year's worth of unlimited admissions, is available for $20. U.S. citizens may purchase a 12-month Golden Eagle Passport for $65, which is valid for entrance into any U.S. national park. U.S. citizens aged 62 and older pay only $10 for a Golden Age Passport—that's valid for life. A Golden Access Passport is available free to U.S. citizens with disabilities.

Permits are required for campers to stay overnight either in the backcountry or in primitive campsites. See Camping, in "Where to Stay," below.

Those who want to fish without a charter captain must obtain a standard State of Florida saltwater fishing license. These are available in the park at Flamingo Lodge or any tackle shop or sporting goods store nearby. Nonresidents will pay $17 for a 7-day license or $7 for 3 days. Florida residents can get a fishing license good for the whole year for $14. Snook and crawfish licenses must be purchased separately at a cost of $2.

Charter captains carry vessel licenses that cover all paying passengers, but ask to be sure. Freshwater fishing licenses are available at various bait and tackle shops outside the park at the same rates. A good one nearby is **Don's Bait & Tackle** located at 30710 S. Federal Hwy., in Homestead right on U.S. 1 (© **305/247-6616**). Most of the area's freshwater fishing, limited to murky canals and artificial lakes near housing developments, is hardly worth the trouble when so much good saltwater fishing is available.

Firearms are not allowed anywhere in the park.

SEASONS   There are two distinct seasons in the Everglades: high season and mosquito season. High season is also dry season and lasts from late November to May. Despite the bizarre cold and wet weather patterns that El Niño brought in 1998, most winters here are warm, sunny, and breezy—a good combination for keeping the bugs away. This is the best time to visit because low water levels attract the largest variety of wading birds and their predators. As the dry season wanes, wildlife follows the receding water; and by the end of May, the only living things you are sure to spot will cause you to itch. The worst, called "no-see-ums," are not even swattable. If you choose to visit during the buggy season, be vigilant in applying bug spray.

Also, realize that many establishments and operators either close or curtail offerings in the summer, so always call ahead to check schedules.

RANGER PROGRAMS   More than 50 ranger programs, free with admission, are offered each month during high season and give visitors an opportunity to gain an expert's perspective. Ranger-led walks and talks are offered year-round from the Royal Palm Visitor Center west of the main entrance, and at Flamingo, Shark Valley, and Gulf Coast during the winter months. Some programs occur regularly, such as Glade Glimpses, a walking tour during which rangers point out flora and fauna and discuss issues affecting the Everglade's survival. These tours are scheduled at 10:15am, noon, and 3:30pm daily. The Anhinga Ambles, a similar program that takes place on the Anhinga Trail, starts at 10:30am, 1:30pm, and 4pm.

Park rangers tend to be helpful, well informed, and good-humored. Since times, programs, and locations vary from month to month, check a schedule, available at any of the visitor centers (see above).

SAFETY There are dangers inherent in this vast wilderness area. Always let someone know your itinerary before you set out on an extended hike. It's mandatory that you file an itinerary when camping overnight in the backcountry. When you're on the water, watch for weather changes; severe thunderstorms and high winds often develop rapidly. Swimming is not recommended because of the presence of alligators, sharks, and barracudas. Watch out for the region's four indigenous poisonous snakes: diamondback and pygmy rattlesnakes, coral snakes (identifiable by their colorful rings), and water moccasins (which swim on the surface of the water). Again, bring insect repellent to ward off mosquitoes and biting flies.

First aid is available from park rangers. The nearest hospital is in Homestead, 10 miles from the park's main entrance.

SEEING THE HIGHLIGHTS

Shark Valley provides a fine introduction to the wonder of the Everglades, but don't plan on spending more than a few hours here. Bicycling or taking a guided tram tour are fantastic ways to see the park's highlights.

If you want to see a greater array of plant and animal life, make sure that you venture into the park through the main entrance, pick up a trail map, and dedicate at least a day to exploring from there.

Stop first along the Anhinga and Gumbo-Limbo Trails, which start right next to one another, 3 miles from the park's main entrance. These trails provide a thorough introduction to Everglades flora and fauna and are highly recommended to first-time visitors. Each of them is 0.5 mile round-trip. **Anhinga Trail** is one of the most popular trails in the park because of its abundance of wildlife. **Gumbo-Limbo Trail** meanders through a shaded, junglelike hammock of gumbo limbo trees, royal palms, ferns, and air plants. Both trails are wheelchair accessible. There's more water and wildlife here than in most parts of the Everglades, especially during dry season. Alligators, turtles, river otters, herons, egrets, and other animals abound, making this one of the best trails for seeing wildlife. Arrive early to spot the widest selection of exotic birds; like the Anhinga Trail's namesake, a large black fishing bird so used to humans that many of these birds build their nests in plain view. Others travel deeper into the park during daylight hours. Take your time—at least an hour is recommended. If you treat the trails and modern boardwalk as pathways to get through quickly, rather than destinations to experience and savor slowly, you'll miss out on the still beauty and hidden treasures that await.

Also, it's worth climbing the observation tower at the end of the quarter-mile-long Pa-hay-okee Trail for sweeping vistas of the river of grass. The panoramic view of undulating grass and seemingly endless expanses gives the impression of a semiaquatic Serengeti. Flocks of tropical and semitropical birds traverse the landscape, alligators and fish stir the surface of the water, small grottoes of trees thrust up from the sea of grass marking higher ground, and the vastness of the hidden world you've entered seems unparalleled.

If you want to get closer to nature, a few hours in a canoe along any of the trails allows paddlers the chance to sense the park's fluid motion and to become a part of the ecosphere. Visitors who choose this option end up feeling more like explorers than merely observers. (See "Sports & Outdoor Activities," below.)

Island Hopping

Beginning at Marco Island and heading south into the Everglades, there are a whopping 10,000 islands, whose primary residents are the same red mangrove trees that can be found throughout the Everglades. Often called "walking trees" because of their roots, mangrove trees arch above the ground like crouched legs.

No matter which option you choose (and there are many), I strongly recommend staying for the 7pm program, available during high season at the Long Pine Key Amphitheater. This talk and slide show given by one of the park's rangers will give you a detailed overview of the park's history, natural resources, wildlife, and threats to its survival.

SPORTS & OUTDOOR ACTIVITIES

BIKING   The relatively flat 38-mile-long paved Main Park Road is great for biking because of the multitude of hardwood hammocks and a dwarf cypress forest, but Shark Valley is the best biking trail by far. Expect to spend 2 to 3 hours along either.

If the park isn't flooded from excess rain (which it often is, especially in spring), Shark Valley in Everglades National Park is South Florida's most scenic bicycle trail. Many locals haul their bikes out to the Glades for a relaxing day of wilderness-trail riding. You can ride the 15-mile loop with no other traffic in sight. Instead, you'll share the flat paved road only with other bikers and a menagerie of wildlife. Don't be surprised to see a gator lounging in the sun or a deer munching on some grass. Otters, turtles, alligators, and snakes are common companions in the Shark Valley area. There are no shortcuts, so if you become tired or are unable to complete the entire 15-mile trip, turn around and return on the same road.

Those who love to mountain bike, and who prefer solitude, might check out the **Southern Glades Trail,** a 14-mile-long unpaved trail opened in late 1998 that is lined with native trees and teeming with wildlife such as deer, alligators, and the occasional snake. The remote trail runs along the C-111 canal, off State Route 9336 and Southwest 217th Street.

You can rent bikes at the Flamingo Lodge, Marina and Outpost Resort (see "Where to Stay," below) for $17 per 24 hours, $14 per full day, $8.50 per half day (any 4-hr. period), and $3 per hour. A $50 deposit is required for each rental. Bicycles are also available from Shark Valley Tram Tours, at the park's Shark Valley entrance (© **305/221-8455**), for $3.25 per hour; rentals can be picked up anytime after 8:30am and must be returned by 4pm.

BIRD WATCHING   More than 350 species of birds make their homes in the Everglades. Tropical birds from the Caribbean and temperate species from North America can be found here, along with exotics that have blown in from more distant regions. Eco and Mrazek Ponds, located near Flamingo, are two of the best places for birding, especially in early morning or late afternoon in the dry winter months. Pick up a free birding checklist from a visitor center (see "Just the Facts," above), and ask a park ranger what's been spotted in recent days.

BOATING   Motorboating around the Everglades seems like a great way to see plants and animals in remote habitats. However, environmentalists are taking stock of the damage motorboats (especially airboats) inflict on the delicate ecosystem. If you choose to motor, remember that most of the areas near land are "no wake" zones and that, for the protection of nesting birds, landing is prohibited on most of the little mangrove islands. There's a long list of restrictions and restricted areas, so get a copy of the park's boating rules from National Park Headquarters before setting out (see "Just the Facts," above).

The Everglades' only marina—accommodating about 50 boats with electric and water hookups—is the Flamingo Lodge Marina and Outpost Resort, located in Flamingo. The well-marked channel to the Flamingo is accessible to boats with a maximum 4-foot draft and is open year-round. Reservations can be made through the marina store (© **941/695-3101, ext. 304**). Skiffs with 15-horsepower motors are available for rent. These low-power boats cost $90 per day, $65 per half day (any 5-hr. period), and $22 per hour. A $125 deposit is required.

CANOEING   Canoeing through the Everglades may be one of the most serene, suprisingly diverse adventures you'll have. From a canoe, your vantage point is priceless—it's the one place in the state where you realize just how flat and close to the water level you are. Canoers in the Glades can co-exist with the gators and birds there in a way no one else can; they behave as if you are part of the ecosystem—something that can't happen on an airboat.

Everglades National Park's longest "trails" are designed for boat and canoe travel, and many are marked as clearly as walking trails. The Noble Hammock Trail, a 2-mile loop, takes 1 to 2 hours and is recommended for beginning canoers. The Hell's Bay Trail, a 3- to 6-mile course for hardier paddlers, takes 2 to 6 hours, depending on how far you choose to go. Park rangers can recommend other trails that best suit your abilities, time limitations, and interests.

You can rent a canoe at the Flamingo Lodge, Marina and Outpost Resort (see "Where to Stay," below) for $40 for 24 hours, $32 per full day, $22 per half day (any 4-hr. period), and $8 per hour. They also have family canoes that rent for $12, $30, $40, and $50, respectively. A deposit is required. Skiffs, kayaks, and tandem kayaks are also available. The concessionaire will shuttle your party to the trailhead of your choice and pick you up afterward. Rental facilities are open daily from 6am to 8pm.

You can also take a canoe tour from the Parks Docks on Chokoloskee Causeway on Route 29, a half-mile south of the traffic circle at the ranger station in Everglades City. Call Everglades National Park Boat Tours at © **800/445-7724.**

FISHING   About one-third of Everglades National Park is open water. Freshwater fishing is popular in brackish Nine-Mile Pond (25 miles from the main entrance) and other spots along the Main Park Road, but because of the high mercury levels found in the Everglades, freshwater fishers are warned not to eat their catch. Before casting, check in at a visitor center, as many of the park's lakes are preserved for observation only. Fishing licenses are required. See "Just the Facts," earlier in this chapter.

Saltwater anglers will find snapper and sea trout plentiful. Charter boats and guides are available at Flamingo Lodge, Marina and Outpost Resort (see "Where to Stay," later in this chapter). Phone for information and reservations.

ORGANIZED TOURS
AIRBOAT TOURS   Shallow-draft, fan-powered airboats were invented in the Everglades by frog hunters who were tired of poling through the brushes. And even though airboats are the most efficient way to get around, they are not

At Home in the Everglades

The Everglades offers a protective area in which an eclectic mix of mammals and reptiles flourishes. One such mammal is the endangered sea cow, or manatee, which typically inhabits saltwater except during winter months when they migrate to the rivers and springs for warmth. It is an amorphous-looking, grey-toned creature with no distinct shape; it can grow to 13 feet in length and 1,300 pounds. Although their size is intimidating, they are extremely timid mammals.

Also sharing space among the mangroves, and found in most bodies of water in the Everglades, are the ubiquitous alligators, reminiscent of a half-submerged log. The alligator is a protected species in the state, but a designated alligator hunting season done on a lottery system exists to control the population.

---

permitted in the park. Just outside the boundaries, however, you'll find a number of outfitters offering rides. These shallow-bottom runabouts tend to inflict severe damage on the animals and plants there. If you choose to ride on one, you should consider bringing earplugs; these high-speed boats are loud. Airboat rides are offered at the **Miccosukee Indian Village,** just west of the Shark Valley entrance on U.S. 41, on the Tamiami Trail (© **305/223-8380**). Native American guides will take you through the reserve's rushes at high speed and stop along the way to point out alligators, native plants, and exotic birds. The price is $7.

The **Everglades Alligator Farm,** 4 miles south of Palm Drive/State Route 9336 and on Southwest 192nd Avenue (© **305/247-2628**), offers half-hour guided airboat tours from 9am until 6pm daily. The price, which includes admission to the park, is $12 for adults, $6 for children.

MOTORBOAT TOURS   Both Florida Bay and backcountry tours are offered at the **Flamingo Lodge, Marina and Outpost Resort** (see "Where to Stay," later in this chapter). Both are available in 1½ - and 2-hour versions that cost an average of $16 for adults, $8 for children, under 6 free. There are also charter-fishing and sightseeing boats that can be booked through the main reservation number (© **941/695-3101**). Florida Bay tours cruise nearby estuaries and sandbars, while six-passenger backcountry boats visit smaller sloughs. Tours depart throughout the day, and reservations are recommended.

TRAM TOURS   At the park's Shark Valley entrance, open-air tram buses take visitors on 2-hour naturalist-led tours that delve 7½ miles into the wilderness. At the trail's midsection, passengers can disembark and climb a 65-foot observation tower that offers good views of the Glades. Visitors will see plenty of wildlife and endless acres of sawgrass. Tours run November to April only, daily from 9am to 4pm, and are sometimes stalled by flooding or particularly heavy mosquito infestation. Reservations are recommended from December to March. The cost is $9.30 for adults, $5.15 for children 12 and under, and $8.25 for seniors. For further information, contact the **Shark Valley Tram Tours** at © **305/221-8455**.

SHOPPING

You won't find big malls or lots of boutiques in this area, although there is an outlet center nearby, the **Keys Factory Shops** (© **305/248-4727**), at 250 E. Palm Drive (where the Florida Turnpike meets U.S. 1), in Florida City, with more than

60 stores, including Nike Factory Store, Bass Co. Store, Levi's, OshKosh, and Izod. You can pick up a free coupon booklet from the Customer Service Center called the Come Back Pack, which includes coupons good for discounts at the outlet center. It's open Monday to Saturday until 9pm, Sunday until 6pm.

A necessary stop and good place for a refreshment is one of Florida's best-known fruit stands, **Robert Is Here** (© 305/246-1592). Robert has been selling home-grown treats for nearly 40 years at the corner of Southwest 344th Street (Palm Drive) and Southwest 192nd Avenue. You'll find the freshest pineapples, bananas, papayas, mangos, and melons anywhere, as well as his famous shakes in unusual flavors like key lime, coconut, orange, and cantaloupe. Exotic fruits, bottled jellies, hot sauces, and salad dressings are also available. This is a great place to pick up culinary souvenirs and sample otherwise unavailable goodies. Open daily 8am until 7pm.

Along Tamiami Trail, there are several roadside shops hawking Native American handicrafts, including one at the **Miccosukee Indian Village** (© 305/223-8380), just west of the Shark Valley entrance. At nearly every one of these shops, you'll find the same stock of feathered dreamcatchers, stuffed alligator heads and claws, turquoise jewelry, and other trinkets. Be sure to take note of the unique, colorful, handmade cloth Miccosukee dolls.

WHERE TO STAY

The only lodging in the park proper is the Flamingo Lodge, a fairly priced and very recommendable option. However, there are a few hotels just outside the park that are even cheaper. A $45 million casino hotel was recently built adjacent to the Miccosukee bingo and gaming hall on the northern edge of the park.

Although bugs can be a major nuisance, especially in the warm months, camping is really the way to go in this very primitive environment. Tenters have dozens of campsites and chickee platforms (see below for details) from which to choose. The best places for camping are found within the Everglades National Park, which consists of three campgrounds for tenters and RVs; Long Pine Key offers 108 drive-up sites; Flamingo has 234 drive-up sites and 64 walk-in-sites; and Cheeka has 20 sites. For campsite reservations in any of the aforementioned, call © 800/365-2267.

IN & AROUND EVERGLADES NATIONAL PARK

Flamingo Lodge, Marina and Outpost Resort ⋆⋆ The Flamingo Lodge is the only lodging actually located within the boundaries of Everglades National Park. This woodsy, sprawling complex offers rooms overlooking the Florida Bay in either a two-story simple motel or the lodge. Either option feels very much like being at summer camp, with a few more amenities. More interesting than the actual motel, however, are the visitors who crop up on the lawn—alligators, raccoons, and other nomadic creatures. The hotel is open year-round although the restaurant closes in the summer.

1 Flamingo Lodge Hwy., Flamingo, FL 33034. © 800/600-3813 or 941/695-3101. Fax 941/695-3921. www.flamingolodge.com. 127 units. Winter from $95 double, from $135 cottage, $135–$150 suite. Off-season $65–$80 double, $89–$100 cottage, $99–$110 suite. Rates for cottages or suites are for 1 to 4 people. Children under 18 stay free. Continental breakfast included in rates from May to October. AE, DC, DISC, MC. Take Florida Tpk. south to Florida City; exit on U.S. 1. At 4-way intersection, turn right onto Palm Drive; continue for 3 miles and turn left at Robert Is Here fruit stand. Turn right at the 3-way intersection. The park entrance is 3 miles ahead. Continue for about 38 more miles to reach lodge. **Amenities:** Waterside bar and restaurant; freshwater swimming pool; convenience store; coin-op washers and dryers, bike, canoe, and kayak rentals; marina with boat tours; boat rentals; houseboat and fishing charters. *In room:* A/C, TV/VCR in standard rooms or suites but not in cottages, kitchen in cottages only.

LODGING IN EVERGLADES CITY

Since Everglades City is 35 miles southeast of Naples and 83 miles west of Miami, many people choose to explore this western entrance to Everglades National Park, located right off the Tamiami Trail. An annual seafood festival held the first weekend in February is a major event that draws hordes of people.

Ivey House B&B 𝕬𝕬 *(Finds)*   Housed in what used to be a recreational center for the men who built the Tamiami Trail, the Ivey House is named after Earl W. Ivey, who was in charge of creating the trail's roadbed. Today, the Ivey House offers three types of accommodations. In the original house are 10 small rooms that share communal bathrooms (one each for women and men). The Ivey's new inn (opened in 2001) adds 17 rooms (with private bathrooms) that face a courtyard with a beautifully landscaped shallow "conversation" pool. One private cottage consists of two bedrooms, a full kitchen, private bath, and a screened-in porch.

Owners Sandee and David are extremely knowledgeable about the Everglades, and usually the guests are as well. A living room area offers guests the opportunity to mingle. A typical continental breakfast is available from 7 to 9am only. Boxed lunches, stored in a cooler so you can bring it along for your Everglades excursions, are offered for $9.50 each. Dinners weren't available at press time but will be available in 2002. The Ivey House is closed in September. No smoking in any of the buildings.

107 Camellia St., Everglades City, Florida 34139 ℂ 941/695-3299. Fax 941/695-4155. www.iveyhouse.com. 27 units. Winter $60–$85 main house (older rooms); $125–$155 (cottage, 2-night minimum); $100 and up for one of the newer rooms. Off-season $50–$70 main house; $90–$105 cottage; $90 and up for newer rooms. MC, V. **Amenities:** Restaurant; small pool, free use of bikes. Everglades excursions available. *In room:* AC (all rooms), TV, telephone, fridge (inn and cottage), kitchen (cottage only).

CAMPING & HOUSEBOATING IN THE EVERGLADES

Campgrounds are available in Flamingo and Long Pine Key, where there are more than 300 sites designed for tents and RVs. They have level parking pads, tables, and charcoal grills. There are no electrical hookups, and showers are cold water. Private ground fires are not permitted, but supervised campfire programs are conducted during winter months. Reservations may be made in advance through The National Park Reservations Service at ℂ **800/365-CAMP.** Campsites are $14 per night with a 14-day consecutive stay limit, 30 days a year maximum.

Camping is also available in the backcountry year-round on a first-come, first-served basis and is only accessible by boat, on foot, or by bicycle. Campers must register in person or by telephone no more than 24 hours before the start of their trip. Permits must be obtained at ranger stations in either Flamingo or Everglades City. Campers can use only designated campsites, which are plentiful and well marked on visitor maps.

Many backcountry sites are *chickee huts*—covered wooden platforms on stilts. They're accessible only by canoe and can accommodate free-standing tents (without stakes). Ground sites are located along interior bays and rivers, and beach camping is also popular. In summer especially, mosquito repellent is necessary gear.

Houseboat rentals are one of the park's best-kept secrets. Available through the Flamingo Lodge, Marina and Outpost Resort, motorized houseboats make it possible to explore some of the park's more remote regions without having to worry about being back by nightfall. You can choose from two different types of houseboats. The first, a 40-foot pontoon boat, sleeps six to eight people in a single large room that's separated by a central head (bathroom) and shower. There's a small galley (kitchen) that contains a stove, oven, and charcoal grill. Prices aren't cheap unless you are with a good-sized group. It rents for between $340 and $475 for 2 nights (with a 2-night minimum in high season).

The newer, sleeker Gibson fiberglass boats sleep six, have toilets and showers, air-conditioning, and electric stoves. There's also a full rooftop sundeck. These rent for $575 for 2 nights (with a 2-night minimum). With either boat, the seventh night is free when renting for a full week.

Boating experience is helpful but not mandatory, as the boats only cruise up to 6 miles per hour and are surprisingly easy to use. In-season, reservations should be made months in advance; call ℂ **800/600-3813** or 941/695-3101.

NEARBY IN HOMESTEAD & FLORIDA CITY

Homestead and Florida City, two adjacent towns that were almost blown off the map by Hurricane Andrew in 1992, have come back better than before. Located about 10 miles from the park's main entrance, along U.S. 1, 35 miles south of Miami, these somewhat rural towns offer several budget lodging options, including a handful of chain hotels. There is a very recommendable **Days Inn** (ℂ **305/245-1260**) in Homestead and a **Hampton Inn** (ℂ **800/426-7866** or 305/247-8833) right off the turnpike in Florida City. The best option is the Best Western Gateway to the Keys.

Best Western Gateway to the Keys   This two-story, pink-and-white standard motel offers contemporary style and comfort about 10 miles from the park's main entrance. A decent-sized pool and a small spa are especially attractive. Each identical standard room has bright, tropical bedspreads and oversized picture windows. The suites offer convenient extras like a microwave, coffeemaker, an extra sink, and a small fridge. Clean and conveniently located if you're en route to the Keys, the only drawback is that in season there is often a 3-day minimum stay requirement. You'd do best to call the local reservation line (ℂ **305/246-5100**) instead of the toll-free number—on several occasions, the hotel made an exception to the rule while the central reservation line was not able to.

411 S. Krome Ave. (U.S. 1), Florida City, FL 33034. ℂ 800/528-1234 or 305/246-5100. Fax 305/242-0056. www.bestwestern.com. 114 units. Winter from $91–$109; off-season from $71–$89. Rates include continental breakfast. During races and very high season, there may be a 3-night minimum. AE, DC, DISC, MC, V. **Amenities:** Pool; laundry and dry-cleaning. *In room:* A/C, TV, dataport, fridge, coffeemaker, hair dryer.

WHERE TO DINE IN & AROUND THE PARK

You won't find fancy nouvelle cuisine in this suburbanized farm country, but there are plenty of fast-food chains along U.S. 1 and a few old favorites worth a taste.

Here for nearly a quarter of a century, **El Toro Taco** (see chapter 6, "Miami Dining") at 1 S. Krome Ave. (near Mowry Drive and Campbell Drive; ℂ **305/ 245-8182**) opens daily at 9:30am and stays crowded until at least 9pm most days. The fresh grilled meats, tacos, burritos, salsas, guacamole, and stews are mild and delicious. No matter how big your appetite, it's hard to spend more than $12 per person at this Mexican outpost. Bring your own beer or wine.

Housed in a squat, one-story, windowless stone building that looks something like a medieval fort, the **Capri Restaurant,** 935 N. Krome Ave., Florida City (ℂ **305/247-1542**), has been serving hearty Italian American fare since 1958. Great pastas and salads complement a full menu of meat and fish dishes. Portions are big. They serve lunch and dinner every day (except Sunday) until 11pm.

The **Miccosukee Restaurant** (© 305/223-8380), just west of the Shark Valley entrance on the Tamiami Trail (U.S. 41), serves authentic pumpkin bread, fry bread, fish, and not-so-authentic Native American interpretations of tacos and fried chicken. This interesting spot is worth a stop for brunch, lunch, or dinner.

In Everglades City, **The Oyster House** (© 941/695-2073) on Chokoloskee Causeway, Highway 29 South, is a large, but homey, seafood restaurant with modest prices, excellent service, and a fantastic view of the 10,000 islands. Try the hush puppies.

Once inside the Everglades, you'll want to eat at the only restaurant within the boundaries of this huge park, **The Flamingo Restaurant** (© 941/695-3101). Located in the Flamingo Lodge (see "Where to Stay," earlier in this chapter), this is a very civilized and affordable restaurant. Besides the spectacular view of Florida Bay and numerous Keys from the large, airy dining room, you'll also find fresh fish, including my very favorite, mahi mahi. Fish are grilled, blackened, or deep-fried; and dinner entrees come with salad or conch chowder, and steamed vegetables, black beans, and rice or baked potato. The large menu has something for everyone, including basic and very tasty sandwiches, pastas, burgers, and salads. A kids' menu offers standard choices like hot dogs, grilled cheese, or fried shrimp for less than $6. Prices are surprisingly moderate, with full meals starting at about $11 and going no higher than $22. You may need reservations for dinner, especially in season.

2 Biscayne National Park

35 miles S. of Miami, 21 miles E. of Everglades National Park

With only about 500,000 visitors each year (mostly boaters and divers), the unusual Biscayne National Park is one of the least-crowded parks in the country. Perhaps that's because the park is a little more difficult than most to access—more than 95% of its 182,00 acres are underwater.

The park's significance was first formally acknowledged in 1968 when, in an unprecedented move and against intense pressure from developers, President Lyndon Johnson signed a bill to conserve the barrier islands off South Florida's east coast as a national monument, a protected status that's a rung below national park. After being twice enlarged, once in 1974 and again in 1980, the waters and land surrounding the northernmost coral reef in North America became a full-fledged national park—the largest of its kind in the country.

To be fully appreciated, Biscayne National Park should be thought of more as a preserve than a destination. I suggest using your time here to explore underwater life—but most of all, to relax.

The park consists of 44 islands, but you can visit only a few of them. The most popular one is **Elliott Key,** which has campsites and a visitor center plus freshwater showers (cold water only), and restrooms. It's located about 9 miles from Convoy Point. There are trails and a buoyed swim area. During Columbus Day weekend, there is a very popular regatta in which a lively crowd of party people gather—sometimes in the nude—to celebrate a long weekend. If you'd prefer to rough it a little more, the 29-acre island known as **Boca Chita Key,** once an exclusive haven for yachters, has now become a popular spot for all manner of boaters. Visitors can tour the island's restored historic buildings, including the county's second-largest lighthouse and a tiny chapel. Facilities include showers, solar-powered restrooms, and drinking fountains, as well as barbecue grills, and picnic tables.

The park's small mainland mangrove shoreline and keys are best explored by boat. Its extensive reef system is renowned by divers and snorkelers worldwide.

JUST THE FACTS

GETTING THERE & ACCESS POINTS   The park's mainland entrance is Convoy Point, located 9 miles east of Homestead. To reach the park from Miami, take the Florida Turnpike to the Speedway Boulevard (Exit 6). Turn left, heading south 4½ miles. Then turn left again at North Canal Drive (Southwest 328th Street), and follow signs to the park. If you're coming from U.S. 1, whether you're heading north or south, turn east at North Canal Drive (Southwest 328th Street).

As I mentioned earlier, most of Biscayne National Park is accessible only to boaters. Mooring buoys abound, since it's illegal to anchor on coral. When no buoys are available, boaters must anchor on sand or on the new docks surrounding the small harbor off Boca Chita. Boats can dock overnight for $15. Even the most experienced boaters should carry updated nautical charts of the area, which are available at Convoy Point. The waters are often murky, making the abundant reefs and sandbars difficult to detect—and there are more-interesting ways to spend a day than waiting for the tide to rise. There's a boat launch at adjacent Homestead Bayfront Park, and 66 slips on Elliott Key, available free on a first-come, first-served basis.

Transportation to and from the visitor center to the island costs $21 per person. Call for seasonal schedule (✆ **305/230-1100**).

VISITOR CENTERS & INFORMATION   The **Convoy Point Visitor Center,** 9700 SW 328th St., at the park's main entrance (✆ **305/230-7275;** fax 305/230-1190), is the natural starting point for any venture into the park without a boat. In addition to providing comprehensive information about the park, rangers will show you a short video on request. Open Monday to Friday from 8:30am to 4:30pm and Saturday and Sunday from 8:30am to 5pm.

For information on transportation, glass-bottom boat tours, and snorkeling and scuba diving expeditions, contact the park concessionaire, **Biscayne National Underwater Park, Inc.,** P.O. Box 1270, Homestead, FL 33030 (✆ **305/230-1100;** fax 305/230-1120; captsaw@bellsouth.net). The company is open daily from 8:30am to 5pm and later in winter.

For more information contact **Biscayne National Park,** 9700 SW 328th St., Homestead, FL 33033-5634 (✆ **305/230-7275;** www.nps.gov/bisc/).

ENTRANCE FEES & PERMITS   Entering Biscayne National Park is free. There is a $15 per night overnight docking fee at Boca Chita Key Harbor and Elliott Key Harbor ($7.50 per night for holders of Golden Age or Golden Access Passports).

SEEING THE HIGHLIGHTS

Since Biscayne National Park is primarily underwater, the only way to truly experience it is with snorkel or scuba gear. You can rent a speedboat in Miami and cruise south for about an hour and a half, but a better idea would be to take one of the organized tours offered every day from the main visitor center. Beneath the surface, the aquatic universe pulses with multicolored life: Bright parrot fish and angelfish, gently rocking sea fans, and coral labyrinths abound. Before entering the water, be sure to apply waterproof sunblock—once you begin to explore, it's easy to lose track of time, and the Florida sun is brutal, even during winter.

Afterward, take a picnic out to Elliott Key and taste the crisp salt air blowing off the Atlantic. Or, head to Boca Chita, an intriguing island that was once the private playground of wealthy yachters.

SPORTS & OUTDOOR ACTIVITIES

CANOEING & KAYAKING   Biscayne National Park offers excellent canoeing, both along the coast and across open water to nearby mangroves and artificial islands that dot the longest uninterrupted shoreline in the state of Florida. Since tides can be strong, only experienced canoeists should attempt to paddle far from shore. If you plan to go far, first obtain a tide table from the visitor center (see "Just the Facts," earlier in this chapter) and paddle with the current. Free ranger-led canoe tours are scheduled for most weekend mornings; phone for information. You can rent a canoe at the park; rates are $8 an hour or $22 for 4 hours. Kayakers will have to bring their own boats but are welcome to explore the same quiet routes.

FISHING   Ocean fishing is excellent year-round; many people cast their lines right from the breakwater jetty at Convoy Point. A fishing license is required (see "Entrance Fees, Permits & Regulations," under "Just the Facts," in section 1, for complete information). Bait is not available in Biscayne but is sold in adjacent Homestead Bayfront Park. Stone crabs and Florida lobsters can be found here, but you're allowed to catch these only on the ocean side when they're in season. There are strict limitations on size, season, number, and method of take (including spear fishing) for both fresh- and saltwater fishing. The latest regulations are available at most marinas, bait and tackle shops, and at the park's visitor centers. Or you can contact the **Florida Game and Fresh Water Fish Commission,** Bryant Building, 620 S. Meridian St., Tallahassee, FL 32399-1600 (✆ **904/488-1960**).

HIKING & EXPLORING   Since the majority of this park is underwater, hiking is not the main attraction here, but there are some interesting sights and trails. At Convoy Point you can walk along the 370-foot boardwalk, and along the half-mile jetty that serves as a breakwater for the park's harbor. From there you can usually see brown pelicans, little blue herons, snowy egrets, and a few exotic fish.

Elliott Key is accessible only by boat, but once you're there, you have two good trail options. True to its name, the Loop Trail makes a 1½-mile circle from the bay-side visitor center, through a hardwood hammock and mangroves, to an elevated ocean-side boardwalk. It's likely that you'll see purple and orange land crabs scurrying around the mangrove roots.

Reopened in 1998, Boca Chita Key was once the playground for wealthy tycoons; it still offers the peaceful beauty that attracted elite anglers from cold climates. Many of the historical buildings are still intact, including an ornamental lighthouse, which was thankfully never put into use. Since it was built on the western side of the island in the path of shallow reefs, boaters would have followed the beacon only to go aground.

Take advantage of the tours, usually led by an interpretative park ranger and available every Sunday at 1pm. The tour, including the boat trip, takes about 3 hours. The price for adults is $19.95 and $9.95 for children. However, call in advance to see if the sea is calm enough for the boat trip—the boats won't run in rough seas.

SNORKELING & SCUBA DIVING   The clear, warm waters of Biscayne National Park are packed with colorful tropical fish that swim in the offshore reefs. If you don't have your own gear, or don't want to lug it the park, you can rent or buy snorkeling and scuba gear at the full-service dive shop at Convoy Point. Rates are in line with dive shops on the mainland.

The best way to see the park from underwater is to take a snorkeling or scuba diving tour operated by **Biscayne National Underwater Park, Inc.** (© **305/ 230-1100**). Tours depart at 1:30pm daily, last about 4 hours, and cost $27.95 per person including equipment. They also run two-tank dives for certified divers and provide instruction for beginners. The price is $35.50 per person. Dives depart at 9am Monday to Friday, at 8:30am weekends. Make your reservations in advance. The shop is open daily from 9am to 5pm.

SWIMMING   You can swim at the protected beaches of Elliott Key, Boca Chita Key, and adjacent Homestead Bayfront Park, but none of these beaches matches the width or softness of other South Florida beaches. Check the water conditions before heading into the sea. The strong currents that make this a popular destination for windsurfers and sailors can be dangerous even for strong swimmers.

WINDSURFING & SURFING   Strong and steady winds provide an excellent venue for windsurfers. Feel free to bring your own board and take on some of South Florida's most beautiful surf.

GLASS-BOTTOM BOAT TOURS

If you prefer not to dive, the best way to see the sites without getting wet is on the glass-bottom boat tour. **Biscayne National Underwater Park, Inc.** (© **305/ 230-1100**) offers daily trips to view some of the country's most beautiful coral reefs and tropical fish. Boats depart year-round from Convoy Point at 10am and stay out for about 3 hours. At $19.95 for adults, $17.95 for seniors, and $9.95 for children 12 and under, the scenic and informative tours are well worth the price. Boats carry fewer than 50 passengers; therefore, reservations are almost always necessary. The company also offers guided canoe, scuba, and snorkeling reef trips led by underwater naturalists.

WHERE TO STAY

There are no facilities available for overnight guests to this watery park. Most noncamping visitors come for an afternoon on their way to the Keys and stay overnight in nearby Homestead, where there are many national chain hotels and other affordable lodgings. See "Where to Stay," in section 1 of this chapter.

CAMPING

Although you won't find hotels or lodges in Biscayne National Park, it does have some of the state's most pristine campsites. Since they are inaccessible by motor vehicle, you'll be sure to avoid the mass of RVs so prevalent in many of the state's other campgrounds. Sites are on Elliott Key and Boca Chita, and can be reached only by boat. If you don't have your own, call © **305/230-1100** to arrange a drop-off. Transportation to and from the visitor center costs $21 per person. The best facilities are on the northeast side of newly reopened Boca Chita, where there are brand-new showers, solar-powered restrooms, and drinking fountains, as well as barbecue grills and picnic tables. With a backcountry permit, available from the ranger station, you can pitch your tent somewhere even more private. Ask for a map at the visitor center, and be sure to bring plenty of bug spray. Sites cost $10 a night for up to six persons staying in one or two tents. Reservations are not accepted.

11

The Keys

The drive from Miami to the Keys is a slow descent into an unusual but breathtaking American ecosystem: On either side of you, for miles ahead, lies nothing but emerald waters. (On weekends, however, also for miles ahead on a narrow highway, is plenty of traffic.) Strung out across the Atlantic Ocean like loose strands of cultured pearls are more than 400 islands that make up this 150-mile-long chain of the Keys. Of course you want to go for the peaceful waters and the year-round warmth, but don't forget to explore the amazing sea life. Countless species of brilliantly colored fish can be found swimming above the ocean's floor. You'll also discover a stunning abundance of tropical and exotic plants, birds, and reptiles.

Despite the usually calm landscape, these rocky islands can be treacherous, as a series of tropical storms, hurricanes, and tornadoes reminded residents in the summer and fall of 1998 when millions of dollars of damage was inflicted. The exposed coast has always posed dangers to those on land as well as at sea.

When Spanish explorers Juan Ponce de León and Antonio de Herrera sailed amid these craggy, dangerous rocks in 1513, they and their men dubbed the string of islands "Los Martires" (The Martyrs) because they thought the rocks looked like men suffering in the surf. It wasn't until the early 1800s that the larger islands were settled by rugged and ambitious pioneers, who amassed great wealth by salvaging cargo from ships sunk nearby. Actually, legend has it that these shipwrecks were sometimes caused by the "wreckers," who occasionally removed navigational markers from the shallows to lure unwitting captains aground. At the height of the salvaging mania (in the 1830s), Key West boasted the highest per capita income in the country.

However, wars, fires, hurricanes, mosquitoes, and the Depression took their toll on these resilient islands in the early part of this century, causing wild swings between fortune and poverty. In 1938, the spectacular Overseas Highway (U.S. 1) was finally completed atop the ruins of Henry Flagler's railroad, opening the region to tourists, who had never before been able to drive to this seabound destination. These days, the highway connects more than 30 of the populated islands in the Keys. The hundreds of small, undeveloped islands that surround these "mainline" keys are known locally as the "backcountry" and are home to dozens of exotic animals and plants. Therein lie some of the most renowned outdoor sporting opportunities, from bone fishing to spear fishing and—at appropriate times of the year—diving for lobsters. To get to the backcountry, you must take to the water—a vital part of any trip to the Keys. Whether you fish, snorkel, dive, or just cruise, include some time on a boat in your itinerary; otherwise, you haven't truly seen the Keys.

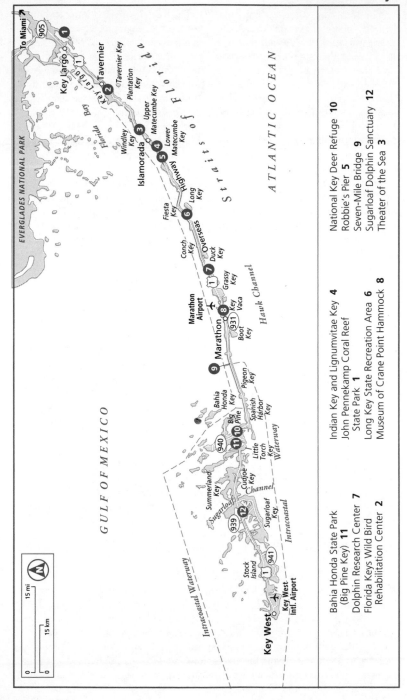

Bahia Honda State Park
(Big Pine Key) **11**
Dolphin Research Center **7**
Florida Keys Wild Bird
Rehabilitation Center **2**

Indian Key and Lignumvitae Key **4**
John Pennekamp Coral Reef
State Park **1**
Long Key State Recreation Area **6**
Museum of Crane Point Hammock **8**

National Key Deer Refuge **10**
Robbie's Pier **5**
Seven-Mile Bridge **9**
Sugarloaf Dolphin Sanctuary **12**
Theater of the Sea **3**

The sea and the teeming life beneath it are the main attractions here. Warm, shallow waters nurture living coral that supports a complex delicate ecosystem of plants and animals—sponges, anemones, jellyfish, crabs, rays, sharks, turtles, snails, lobsters, and thousands of types of fish. This vibrant underwater habitat thrives on one of only two living tropical reefs in the entire North American continent (the other is off the coast of Belize). As a result, anglers, divers, snorkelers, and watersports enthusiasts of all kinds come to explore. Keen observers and sportsmen have begun to differentiate between the shallow waters of the western (Gulf) side of the island chain and the deeper and rougher waters of the eastern (Atlantic) side.

Heavy traffic has taken its toll on this fragile ecoscape, but conservation efforts are underway. In fact, environmental efforts in the Keys exceed those in many high-traffic visitor destinations.

Although the atmosphere throughout the Keys is that of a laid-back beach town, don't expect to find many impressive beaches here, especially after the damaging effects of the tropical storms and hurricanes in 1998. Beaches are mostly found in a few private resorts and some small, sandy beaches in John Pennekamp State Park, Bahia Honda State Park, and in Key West. One great exception is Sombrero Beach in Marathon.

The Keys are divided into three sections, both geographically and in this chapter. The Upper and Middle Keys are closest to the Florida mainland, so they are popular with weekend warriors who come by boat or car to fish, drink, or relax in towns like Key Largo, Islamorada, and Marathon. Further on, just beyond the impressive 7-mile bridge (which actually measures only 6.4 miles), are the Lower Keys, a small, unspoiled swath of islands teeming with wildlife. Here, in the protected regions of the Lower Keys is where you're most likely to catch sight of the area's many endangered animals. With patience, you may spot the rare eagle, egret, or Key deer. Also, keep an eye out for alligators, turtles, rabbits, and a huge variety of birds.

The last section of this chapter is devoted to the renowned island called Key West, literally at the end of the road. Made famous by the Nobel Prize–winning rogue Ernest Hemingway, this tiny island is the most popular destination in the Florida Keys, overrun with cruise-ship passengers and day-trippers, as well as franchises and T-shirt shops. More than 1.6 million visitors pass through each year. Still, you'll find in this "Conch Republic" a tightly knit community of permanent residents who cling fiercely to their live-and-let-live attitude—an atmosphere that has made Key West famously popular with painters, writers, and free spirits.

EXPLORING THE KEYS BY CAR

After you have gotten off the Florida Turnpike and landed on U.S. 1, which is also known as the Overseas Highway (see "Getting There," under "Essentials," below), you'll have no trouble negotiating these narrow islands.

The Overseas Highway is the only main road connecting the Keys. The scenic, lazy drive from Miami to Key West can be very enjoyable if you have the patience to linger and explore the diverse towns and islands along the way. If you have the time, I recommend allowing at least 2 days to work your way down to Key West and 3 or more days once there.

Most of U.S. 1 is a narrow, two-lane highway, with some wider passing zones along the way. The speed limit is usually 55 miles per hour (35 to 45 m.p.h. on

Big Pine Key and in some commercial areas). Despite the protestations of island residents, there has been talk of expanding the highway, but plans have not been finalized. Even on the narrow road, you can usually get from downtown Miami to Key Largo in just over an hour. If you're determined to drive straight through to Key West, allow at least 3½ hours. Weekend travel is another matter entirely: When the roads are jammed with travelers from the mainland, the trip could take upward of 5 to 6 hours. If at all possible, I strongly urge you to avoid driving anywhere in the Keys on Friday afternoons or Sunday evenings.

To find an address in the Keys, don't bother looking for building numbers; most addresses (except in Key West and parts of Marathon) are delineated by mile markers (MM), small green signs on the roadside, which announce the distance from Key West. The markers start at number 127, just south of the Florida mainland. The zero marker is in Key West, at the corner of Whitehead and Fleming streets. Addresses in this chapter are accompanied by a mile marker (MM) designation when appropriate.

1 The Upper & Middle Keys: Key Largo ⍟ to Marathon ⍟

58 miles SW of Miami

The Upper Keys are a popular, year-round refuge for South Floridians who take advantage of the islands' proximity to the mainland. This is the fishing and diving capital of America, and the swarms of outfitters and billboards never let you forget it.

Key Largo, once called Rock Harbor but renamed to capitalize on the success of the 1948 Humphrey Bogart film (which wasn't actually filmed there), is the largest key and is more developed than its neighbors to the south. Dozens of chain hotels, restaurants, and tourist information centers service the many water enthusiasts who come to explore the nation's first underwater state park, **John Pennekamp Coral Reef State Park,** and its adjacent marine sanctuary. **Islamorada,** the unofficial capital of the Upper Keys, offers the area's best atmosphere, food, fishing, entertainment, and lodging. It's an unofficial "party capital" for mainlanders seeking a quick tropical excursion. In these "purple isles," nature lovers can enjoy walking trails, historic explorations, and big-purse fishing tournaments. **Marathon,** smack in the middle of the chain of islands, is one of the most populated keys. It is part fishing village, part tourist center, part nature preserve. This area's highly developed infrastructure includes resort hotels, a commercial airport, and a highway that expands to four lanes.

ESSENTIALS

GETTING THERE   From Miami International Airport, take Le Jeune Road (Northwest 42nd Avenue) to Route 836 west. Follow signs to the Florida Turnpike South (about 7 miles). The turnpike extension connects with U.S. 1 in Florida City. Continue south on U.S. 1. For a scenic option, weather permitting, take Card Sound Road south of Florida City, a backcountry drive that reconnects with U.S. 1 in upper Key Largo. The view from the Card Sound Bridge is spectacular and well worth the dollar toll.

If you're coming from Florida's west coast, take Alligator Alley to the Miami exit and then turn south onto the turnpike extension. Have plenty of quarters for the tolls.

American Eagle (© **800/433-7300**) has daily nonstop flights from Miami to Marathon, which is near the midpoint of the chain of keys and at the very

---

Moments **No Place like Homestead**

On its own, there's not much to the waterfront shack that is Alabama Jack's. The bar serves beer and wine only, and the restaurant specializes in greasy bar fare. But this quintessential Old Floridian dive, located between Homestead and Key Largo, is a colorful must on the drive south. Hordes of Harley Davidson bikers, local Miamians, barflies, and anglers flock here with much devotion, and the views of the mangroves are spectacular. Pull up a barstool, order a cold one, and take in the sights—at the bar and in the bay. To get there, pick up Card Sound Road (the old Route 1) a few miles after you pass Homestead, heading toward Key Largo. Alabama Jack's is on the right-hand side and can't be missed. 5800 Card Sound Rd., Homestead. (€ 305/ 248-8741.

---

southern end of the area referred to here as the Upper and Middle Keys. Fares range from $88 to $336 round-trip, depending on the season.

Greyhound (€ **800/231-2222;** www.greyhound.com) has buses leaving Miami for Key Largo every day. Prices range up to $20. Seats fill quickly in season, so come early. It's first come, first served.

VISITOR INFORMATION   Avoid the many "Tourist Information Centers" that dot the main highway. Most are private companies hired to lure visitors to specific lodgings or outfitters. You're better off sticking with the official, not-for-profit centers that are extremely well located and staffed. In particular, the **Key Largo Chamber of Commerce,** U.S. 1 at MM 106, Key Largo, FL 33037 (€ **800/822-1088** or 305/451-1414; fax 305/451-4726; www.keylargo.org) runs an excellent facility, with free direct-dial phones and plenty of brochures. Headquartered in a handsome clapboard house, the chamber operates as an information clearinghouse for all of the Keys and is open daily from 9am to 6pm.

The **Islamorada Chamber of Commerce,** in the Little Red Caboose, U.S. 1 at MM 82.5, P.O. Box 915, Islamorada, FL 33036 (€ **800/322-5397** or 305/ 664-4503; fax 305/664-4289; www.islamoradachamber.com), also offers maps and literature on the Upper Keys.

You can't miss the big blue Visitors Center at MM 53.5, the **Greater Marathon Chamber of Commerce,** 12222 Overseas Hwy., Marathon, FL 33050 (€ **800/ 842-9580** or 305/743-5417; fax 305/289-0183; www.floridakeysmarathon.com).

OUTDOOR SIGHTS & ACTIVITIES

Anne's Beach (at MM 73.5) is really more of a picnic spot than a full-fledged beach, but die-hard suntanners still congregate on this tiny strip of coarse sand that was damaged beyond recognition during the series of storms in 1998. Plans are in place to reconstruct the boardwalk and huts, but at press time, work had not yet started.

A better choice for real beaching is **Sombrero Beach** 𝒶𝒶 in Marathon at the end of Sombrero Beach Road (near MM 50). This wide swath of uncluttered beachfront actually benefited from Hurricane George in September 1998 with generous deposits of extra sand and a facelift courtesy of the Monroe County Tourist Development Council. More than 90 feet of sand is dotted with stands of palms, Australian Pines, and Royal Poincianas. There are barbecue grills, clean bathrooms, and some brand new tiki huts. Admission and parking at this little-known spot is free.

If you are interested in seeing the Keys in their natural state, before modern development, you must venture off the highway and take to the water. Two backcountry islands that offer a glimpse of the "real" Keys are **Indian Key and Lignumvitae Key** ✦✦✦. Visitors come here to relax and enjoy the islands' colorful birds and lush hammocks (elevated pieces of land above a marsh).

Named for the lignum vitae ("wood of life") trees found there, **Lignumvitae Key** supports a virgin tropical forest, the kind that once thrived on most of the Upper Keys. Over the years, human settlers imported "exotic" plants and animals to the Keys, irrevocably changing the botanical makeup of many backcountry islands and threatening much of the indigenous wildlife. Over the past 25 years, the Florida Department of Natural Resources has successfully removed most of the exotic vegetation, leaving this 280-acre site much as it existed in the 18th century. The island also holds a historic house built in 1919 that has survived numerous hurricanes. **Indian Key,** a much smaller island on the Atlantic side of Islamorada, was occupied by Native Americans for thousands of years before European settlers arrived. The 10-acre historic site was also the original seat of Dade County before the Civil War. You can see the ruins of the previous settlement and tour the lush grounds on well-marked trails. Off Indian Key Fill, Overseas Hwy., MM 79. ✆ **305/664-4815.**

If you want to see both islands, plan to spend at least half a day. To get there, you can rent your own power boat at **Robbie's Rent-A-Boat** (U.S. 1 at MM 77.5 on the bay side). Rates range from $70 for a 15-foot boat for half a day to $175 for an 18-foot boat for a full day. It's then a $1 admission fee to each island, which includes an informative hour-long guided tour by park rangers. This is a good option if you are a confident boater.

However, I also recommend taking Robbie's **ferry service.** A visit to one island costs $15, $10 for kids 12 and under, which includes the $1 park admission; trips to both islands cost $25 per person. (If you have time for only one island, make it Lignumvitae.) Not only is the ferry more economical, but it's easier to enjoy the natural beauty of the islands when you aren't negotiating the shallow reefs along the way. The runabouts, which carry up to six people, depart from Robbie's Pier Thursday to Monday at 9am and 1pm for Indian Key, and at 10am and 2pm for Lignumvitae Key. In the busy season, you may need to book as early as 2 days before departure. Call ✆ **305/664-4815** for information from the park service or ✆ **305/664-9814** for Robbie's.

Pigeon Key ✦✦   At the curve of the old bridge on Pigeon Key is an intriguing historical site that has been under renovation since late 1993. This 5-mile-long island was once the camp for the crew that built the old railway in the early part of the century and later served as housing for the bridge builders. From here, your vista includes both bridges, many old wooden cottages, and a truly tranquil stretch of lush foliage and sea. If you miss the shuttle tour or would rather walk or bike to the key, it's about 2.5 miles. Either way, you may want to bring a picnic to enjoy after a brief self-guided walking tour and museum visit. There is also an informative 28-minute video of the island's history offered every hour starting at 10am. Parking is available at the Knight's Key end of the bridge, at MM 48, or at the Visitors Center at the old train car across the highway on the ocean side.

East end of the 7-Mile Bridge near MM 47, Marathon. ✆ **305/743-5999.** Open 9am–5pm; shuttle tours run every hour 10am–3pm. Admission $7.50, $5 for children under 13. Price includes shuttle transportation from the Visitors Center.

Seven-Mile Bridge 𝘬𝘬𝘬 A stop at the Seven-Mile Bridge is a rewarding and relaxing break from the drive south. Built alongside the ruins of oil magnate Henry Flagler's incredible Overseas Railroad, the "new" bridge (between MM 40 and 47) is still considered an architectural feat. The wide arched span, completed in 1982 at a cost of more than $45 million, is impressive, its apex being the highest point in the Keys. The new bridge and its now-defunct neighbor provide an excellent vantage point from which to view the stunning waters of the Keys. In the daytime, you may want to walk, jog, or bike along the scenic 4-mile stretch of old bridge, or join local anglers, who catch barracuda, yellowtail, and dolphin (the fish, not the mammal) on what is known as "the longest fishing pier in the world."

Between MM 40 and 47 on U.S. 1. ℂ 305/289-0025.

Tropical Crane Point Hammock 𝘬𝘬 Crane Point Hammock is a little-known but worthwhile stop, especially for those interested in the rich botanical and archaeological history of the Keys. This privately owned 64-acre nature area is considered one of the most important historical sites in the Keys. It contains what is probably the last virgin thatch palm hammock in North America. It also has an archaeological dig site with pre-Columbian and prehistoric Bahamian artifacts.

Also headquarters for the Florida Keys Land and Sea Trust, the hammock's impressive nature museum has simple, informative displays of the Keys' wildlife, including a walk-through replica of a coral-reef cave and life-size dioramas with tropical birds and Key deer. Kids can participate in art projects, see 6-foot-long iguanas, climb through a scaled-down pirate ship, and touch a variety of indigenous aquatic and landlubbing creatures.

5550 Overseas Hwy. (MM 50), Marathon. ℂ **305/743-9100.** Admission $7.50 for adults, $6 for seniors over 64, $4 for students, and free for children under 6. Mon–Sat 9am–5pm; Sun noon–5pm.

VISITING WITH THE ANIMALS

Dolphin Research Center 𝘬𝘬𝘬 *Kids* If you've always wanted to touch, swim, or play with dolphins, this is the place to do it. Of the three such centers in the continental United States (all located in the Keys), the Dolphin Research Center is the most organized and informative. Although some people argue that training dolphins is cruel and selfish, this is one of the most respected institutions that study and protect the mammals. Knowledgeable trainers at the Dolphin Research Center will also tell you that the dolphins need stimulation and enjoy human contact. They certainly seem to. They nuzzle and seem to smile

---

⟮ Fun Fact **Bridge Mix**

The Seven-Mile Bridge is the longest fragmented bridge in the world. And it's not that old, either. Completed in 1985, the bridge was constructed parallel to the original bridge, which was part of Henry Flagler's Florida East Coast Railroad and served as the original link to the Lower Keys. Some people may recognize the remnants of the old bridge from the Arnold Schwarzenegger film *True Lies*. Others fearfully contemplate whether a wrong turn would lead them to the old bridge instead of the new one. Not to worry: The old bridge is closed to cars and has been transformed into the world's longest fishing pier.

The 10 "Keymandments"

The Keys have always attracted independent spirits, from Ernest Hemingway and Tennessee Williams to Jimmy Buffett, Zane Grey, and local hero Mel Fisher. Writers, artists, and free thinkers have long drifted down here to escape.

Although you'll generally find a very laid-back and tolerant code of behavior in the Keys, some rules do exist. Be sure to respect the 10 "Keymandments" while you're here, or suffer the consequences.

- Don't anchor on a reef. (Reefs are alive.)
- Don't feed the animals. (They'll want to follow you home, and you can't keep them.)
- Don't trash our place (or we'll send Bubba to trash yours).
- Don't touch the coral. (After all, you don't even know them. Some pose a mild risk of injury as well.)
- Don't speed (especially on Big Pine Key, where deer reside and tar-and-feathering is still practiced).
- Don't catch more fish than you can eat. (Better yet, let them go. Some of them support schools.)
- Don't collect conch. (This species is protected by Bubba.)
- Don't disturb the bird nests. (They find it very annoying.)
- Don't damage the sea grass. (And don't even think about making a skirt out of it.)
- Don't drink and drive on land or sea. (There's absolutely nothing funny about it.)

and kiss the lucky few that get to swim with them in the daily program. The "family" of 15 dolphins swims in a 90,000-square-foot natural saltwater pool carved out of the shoreline.

If you can't get into the swim program, you can still take the interesting hour-long walking tour of the facilities or sign up for a class in hand signals or feed the dolphins from docks. Because the Dolphin Encounter swimming program is the most popular, reservations must be made at least one month in advance. The cost is $125 per person. If you're not brave enough to swim with the dolphins or you have a child under 12 (not permitted to swim with dolphins), try the Dolphin Splash program, in which participants stand on an elevated platform from which to "meet and greet" the dolphins. A height requirement of 44 inches is enforced, and children under the required height must be held up by an adult. Cost for this program is $70 per person; free for children under 3.

U.S. 1 at MM 59 (on the bay side), Marathon. ☎ **305/289-1121.** Swim with the Dolphins, $125 per person. Call on the first day of the month to book for the following month. Educational walking tours five times daily: 10am, 11am, 12:30pm, 2pm, and 3:30pm. Admission $12.50 adults, $10 seniors, $7.50 children 4–12, free for children 3 and under. Daily 9:30am–4pm.

Florida Keys Wild Bird Center 🐦 Wander through lush canopies of mangroves on narrow wooden walkways to see some of the Keys' most famous residents—the large variety of native birds, including broad-wing hawks, great blue and white herons, roseate spoonbills, white ibis, cattle egrets, and a number of pelicans. This not-for-profit center operates as a hospital for the many birds that have been injured. Visit at feeding time, usually about 2pm, when you can watch the dedicated staff feed the hundreds of hungry beaks.

U.S. 1 at MM 93.6 Bayside, Tavernier. ⓒ 305/852-4486. fkwbc@reefnet.com. Donations suggested. Daily 8:30am–6pm.

Robbie's Pier 🐟🐟🐟 *Value*   One of the best and definitely one of the cheapest attractions in the Upper Keys is the famed Robbie's Pier. Here, the fierce steely tarpons, a prized catch for backcountry anglers, have been gathering for the past 20 years. You may recognize these prehistoric-looking giants that grow up to 200 pounds; many are displayed as trophies and mounted on local restaurant walls. To see them live, head to Robbie's Pier, where tens and sometimes hundreds of these behemoths circle the shallow waters waiting for you to feed them. Kayak tours promise an even closer glimpse.

U.S. 1 at MM 77.5, Islamorada. ⓒ 305/664-9814. Admission $1. Bucket of fish $2. Daily 8am–5pm. Look for the Hungry Tarpon restaurant sign on the right after the Indian Key channel.

Theater of the Sea 🐟   Established in 1946, the Theater of the Sea is one of the world's oldest marine zoos. Although the facilities could use some sprucing up, the dolphin and sea lion shows are entertaining and informative, especially for children who can also see sharks, sea turtles, and tropical fish. If you want to swim with dolphins and you haven't booked well in advance, this is the place you may be able to get into with just a few hours, or days, notice as opposed to the more rigid Dolphin Research Center in Marathon (see above). A 30-minute orientation will prepare you for your swim. Children under 5 are not permitted to participate. Other programs allow visitors to swim with sea lions or stingrays. The facility also serves as a haven for dozens of stray cats that have free run of the grounds and gift shop.

U.S. 1 at MM 84.5, Islamorada. ⓒ 305/664-2431. www.theaterofthesea.com. Admission $17.25 adults, $10.75 children 3–12. Dolphin swim $110; sea lion swim $75; stingray swim $35 per person. Reservations a must. Daily 9:30am–5:45pm (ticket office closes at 4 pm).

TWO EXCEPTIONAL STATE PARKS

One of the best places to discover the diverse ecosystem of the Upper Keys is in its most famous park, **John Pennekamp Coral Reef State Park** 🐟🐟🐟, located on U.S. 1 at MM 102.5, in Key Largo (ⓒ **305/451-1202**). Named for a former *Miami Herald* editor and conservationist, the 188-square-mile park is the nation's first undersea preserve. It's a sanctuary for part of the only living coral reef in the continental United States. The original plans for Everglades National Park included this part of the reef within its boundaries, but opposition from local homeowners made its inclusion politically impossible.

Because the water is extremely shallow, the 40 species of coral and more than 650 species of fish here are particularly accessible to divers, snorkelers, and glass-bottomed-boat passengers. To experience this park, visitors must get in the water—you can't see the reef from the shore. Your first stop should be the Visitors Center, which is full of educational fish tanks and a mammoth 30,000-gallon saltwater aquarium that re-creates a reef ecosystem. At the adjacent dive shop, you can rent snorkeling and diving equipment and join one of the boat trips that depart for the reef throughout the day. Visitors can also rent motorboats, sailboats, Windsurfers, and canoes. The 2-hour glass-bottomed-boat tour is the best way to see the coral reefs if you refuse to get wet. Inexperienced but certified scuba divers can rent gear here, too, and an off-the-shore dive excursion is nonthreatening and educational. Watch for the lobsters and other sea life residing in the fairly shallow ridge walls beneath the coastal waters. But remember: These are protected waters.

Canoeing around the park's narrow mangrove channels and tidal creeks is also popular. You can go on your own in a rented canoe or, in winter, sign up for a tour led by a local naturalist. Hikers have two short trails from which to choose: a boardwalk through the mangroves and a dirt trail through a tropical hardwood hammock. Ranger-led walks are usually scheduled daily from the end of November to April. Phone for schedule information and reservations.

Park admission is $2.50 per vehicle for one occupant; for two or more, it is $4 per vehicle, plus 50¢ per passenger; $1.50 per pedestrian or bicyclist. On busy weekend days, there's often a line of cars to get into the park. Call ⓒ 305/451-1621 for information. On your way into the park, ask the ranger for a map. Glass-bottomed-boat tours cost $18 for adults and $10 for children 11 and under. Snorkeling tours are $25.95 for adults and $19.95 for children 17 and under, including equipment. Sailing and snorkeling tours are $31.95 for adults, $26.95 for children 17 and under, including equipment but not tax. Canoes rent for $10 per hour. For experienced boaters only, four different-sized Reef boats (powerboats) rent for $27.50 to $50 per hour; cheaper half-day and full-day rates available, call ⓒ 305/451-6325. A $300 deposit (and up depending on boat size) is required. Open daily from 8am to 5pm; phone for tour and dive times. Reservations are recommended for all of the above. Also, see below for more options on diving, fishing, and snorkeling these reefs.

Long Key State Recreation Area 🦘🦘🦘, U.S. 1 at MM 68, Long Key (ⓒ 305/664-4815), is one of the best places in the Middle Keys for hiking, camping, snorkeling, and canoeing. This 965-acre site is situated atop the remains of an ancient coral reef. At the entrance gate, ask for a free flyer describing the local trails and wildlife.

There are two nature trails here perfect for hiking. The Golden Orb Trail is a 1-mile loop around a lagoon that attracts a large variety of birds. Rich in West Indian vegetation, this trail leads to an observation tower that offers good views of the mangroves. Layton Trail, the only part of the park that doesn't require an admission fee, is a quarter-mile shaded loop that goes through tropical hammocks before opening onto Florida Bay. The trail is well marked with interpretive signs; you can easily walk it in about 20 minutes.

The park's excellent 1½-mile canoe trail is also short and sweet, allowing visitors to loop around the mangroves in about an hour. You can rent canoes at the trailhead for about $4 per hour. Long Key is also a great spot to stop for a picnic if you get hungry on your way to Key West.

Railroad builder Henry Flagler created the Long Key Fishing Club here in 1906, and the waters surrounding the park are still popular with game fishers. In summer, sea turtles lumber onto the protected coast to lay their eggs.

Admission is $3.25 per car plus 50¢ per person (except for the Layton Trail, which is free). Open daily from 8am to sunset.

WATERSPORTS FROM A TO Z

There are literally hundreds of outfitters in the Keys who will arrange all kinds of water activities, from cave dives to parasailing. If those recommended below are booked up or unreachable, ask the local chamber of commerce for a list of qualified members.

BOATING   In addition to the rental shops in the state parks, you will find dozens of outfitters along U.S. 1 offering a range of runabouts and skiffs for boaters of any experience level. **Captain Pip's,** U.S. 1 at MM 47.5, Marathon (© 800/707-1692 or 305/743-4403), rents 18- to 24-foot motorboats with 90- to 225-horsepower engines for $130 to $225 per day. Overnight accommodations are available and include a free boat rental; 2-night minimum $220 to $255; weekly $1190 to $1890.

Robbie's Rent-a-Boat, U.S. 1 at MM 77.5, Islamorada (© 305/664-9814), rents 14- to 27-foot motorboats with engines ranging from 15 to 200 horsepower. Boat rentals are $70 to $205 for a half day and $90 to $295 for a full day.

CANOEING & KAYAKING   I can think of no better way to explore the uninhabited, shallow backcountry on the Gulf side than by kayak or canoe. You can reach places big boats just can't get to because of their large draft. Sometimes manatees will cuddle up to the boats, thinking them another friendly species.

For a more enjoyable time, ask for a sit-inside boat—you'll stay drier. Also, a fiberglass (as opposed to plastic) boat with a rudder is generally more stable and easier to maneuver. Many area hotels rent kayaks and canoes to guests, as do the outfitters listed here. **Florida Bay Outfitters,** U.S. 1 at MM 104, Key Largo (© 305/451-3018), rents canoes and sea kayaks for use in and around John Pennekamp Coral Reef State Park for $25 to $30 for a half day and $35 to $50 for a whole day. Canoes cost $25 for a half day and $35 for a whole day. At **Coral Reef Park Co.,** on U.S. 1 at MM 102.5, Key Largo (© 305/451-1621), you can rent canoes and kayaks for $8 per hour, $28 for a half day; most canoes are sit-on-tops.

DIVING & SNORKELING   The **Florida Keys Dive Center,** on U.S. 1 at MM 90.5, Tavernier (© 305/852-4599), takes snorkelers and divers to the reefs of John Pennekamp Coral Reef State Park and environs every day. PADI (Professional Association of Diving Instructors) training courses are also available for the uninitiated. Tours leave at 8am and 12:30pm and cost $25 per person to snorkel (plus $8 rental fee for mask, snorkel, and fins) and $59 per person to dive (plus an extra $20 if you need to rent all the gear).

At **Hall's Dive Center & Career Institute,** U.S. 1 at MM 48.5, Marathon (© 305/743-5929), snorkelers and divers can choose to dive at Looe Key, Sombrero Reef, Delta Shoal, Content Key, and Coffins Patch. Tours are scheduled daily at 9am and 1pm. You will spend 1 hour at each of two sites per tour. If you mention this book, you will get a special discounted rate of $30 per person to snorkel (additional gear is $11) and $40 per person to dive (tanks are $8.50 each). Choose from an impressive array of equipment.

With **SNUBA Tours of Key Largo** (© 305/451-6391; www.pennekamp. com/sw/snuba.htm), you can dive down to 20 feet attached to a comfortable breathing apparatus that really gives you the feeling of scuba diving without having to be certified. You can tour shallow coral reefs teeming with hundreds of colorful fish and plant life, from sea turtles to moray eels. Reservations are required; call to find out where and when to meet. A 2- to 3-hour underwater tour (typically 1pm to 4pm) costs $75, including all equipment. If you have never dived before, you may require a 1-hour lesson in the pool, which costs an additional $45.

FISHING   Robbie's Partyboats & Charters, on U.S. 1 at MM 84.5, Islamorada (© 305/664-8070 or 305/664-4196), located at the south end of the Holiday Isle Docks (see the Holiday Isle Resort in "Where to Stay," below), offers day and night deep-sea and reef fishing trips aboard a 65-foot party boat. Big-game fishing charters are also available, and "splits" are arranged for solo fishers. Party-boat fishing costs $25 for a half-day morning tour (rod and reel rental $3); it's $15 extra if you want to go back out on an afternoon tour. Charters run $400 for a half day, $600 for a full day; splits begin at $65 per person. Phone for information and reservations.

Bud n' Mary's Fishing Marina, on U.S. 1 at MM 79.8, Islamorada (© 800/742-7945 or 305/664-2461), one of the largest marinas between Miami and Key West, is packed with sailors offering guided backcountry fishing charters. This is the place to go if you want to stalk tarpon, bonefish, and snapper. If the seas are not too rough, deep-sea and coral fishing trips can be arranged. Charters cost $500 to $550 for a half day, $750 to $800 for a full day, and splits begin at $125 per person.

The Bounty Hunter, 15th Street, Marathon (© 305/743-2446), offers full- and half-day outings. For years, Captain Brock Hook's huge sign has boasted no fish, no pay. You're guaranteed to catch something. Choose your prey from shark, barracuda, sailfish, or whatever else is running. Prices are $350 for a half day, $375 for three-fourths day, and $450 for a full day. Rates are for groups of no more than six people.

SHOPPING

On your way to the Keys, you'll find an outlet center, the **Prime Outlets at Florida City** (© 305/248-4727), at 250 E. Palm Dr. (where the Florida Turnpike meets U.S. Hwy. 1), in Florida City. The center holds more than 60 stores, including Nike Factory Store, Bass Co. Store, Levi's, OshKosh, and Izod. Travelers can pick up a free discount coupon booklet called the Come Back Pack from the Customer Service Center. The outlet is open Monday to Saturday, from 10am to 9pm, Sunday from 11am to 6pm.

The Upper and Middle Keys have no shortage of tacky tourist shops selling shells and T-shirts (the ubiquitous "beads and trinkets") and other hokey souvenirs, but for real Keys-style shopping, check out the **weekend flea markets.** One of the best is held every Saturday and Sunday bay side at MM 103.5 (© 305/451-0677). Dozens of vendors open their stalls from 9am until 4 or 5pm, selling every imaginable sort of antiques, T-shirts, plants, shoes, books, toys, and games, as well as a hearty dose of good old-fashioned junk.

A mecca for fishing and sports enthusiasts, **The World Wide Sportsman** (© 305/664-4615) at MM 81.5, is not only the largest fishing store in the Keys, but also a meeting place for anglers from all over the world. Every possible gizmo and gadget, plus hundreds of T-shirts, hats, books, and gift items are displayed in its more than 25,000 square feet. The salespeople are knowledgeable and eager to help. Travel specialists can even arrange for charter trips and backcountry tours. The store is open daily from 7am until 8:30pm.

WHERE TO STAY

U.S. 1 is lined with chain hotels in all price ranges. In the Upper Keys, the best moderately priced options are the **Holiday Inn Key Largo Resort & Marina,** U.S. 1 at MM 99.7 (© 800/THE-KEYS or 305/451-2121), and right next door, at MM 100, the **Ramada Limited Resort & Casino** (© 800/THE-KEYS or 305/451-3939). Both hotels share three pools and a casino boat; however, the Ramada is cozier and offers slightly cheaper rates. Also, the **Best Western Suites at Key Largo,** 201 Ocean Dr., MM 100 (© 800/462-6079 or 305/451-5081), is just 3 miles from John Pennekamp Coral Reef State Park. Another good option in the Upper Keys is **Islamorada Days Inn,** U.S. 1 at MM 82.5 (© 800/DAYS-INN or 305/664-3681). In the Middle Keys, the **Howard Johnson** at

13351 Overseas Hwy., MM 54 in Marathon (© **800/321-3496** or 305/743-8550), also offers reasonably priced ocean-side rooms.

Since the real beauty of the Keys lies mostly beyond the highways, there is no better way to see this area than by boat. Why not stay in a floating hotel? Especially if traveling with a group, houseboats can be economical. To rent a houseboat, call Ruth and Michael Sullivan at **Smilin' Island Houseboat Rentals** (MM 99.5), Key Largo (© **305/451-1930**). Rates are from $750 to $1,350 for 3 nights. Boats accommodate up to six people.

For land options, consider these recommendations, grouped first by price and then geographically from north to south.

VERY EXPENSIVE

Cheeca Lodge ★★★   One of the better places to stay in the Upper Keys, Cheeca has been hosting celebrities, royalty, and politicians since its opening in 1949. Guests now enjoy the luxury of the Cheeca's freshly renovated and remodeled rooms. All of the 203 units offer all the amenities of a world-class resort in a very laid-back setting. You may not feel compelled to leave the sprawling grounds, but it's good to know the hotel is conveniently situated near the best restaurants and nightlife. Located on 27 acres of beachfront property, this rambling resort is known for its excellent sports facilities, including one of the only golf courses in the Upper Keys. All rooms are spacious and have small balconies. The nicer ones overlook the ocean and have large marble bathrooms. The Atlantic's Edge restaurant is one of the best in the Upper Keys (see "Where to Dine," below).

U.S. 1 at MM 82 (P.O. Box 527), Islamorada, FL 33036. © **800/327-2888** or 305/664-4651. Fax 305/664-2893. www.cheeca.com. 203 units. Winter $295–$650 double; $400 suite. Off-season $195–$430 double; $285 suite. AE, DC, DISC, MC, V. **Amenities:** 2 restaurants, 2 lounges (1 pool side), 3 outdoor heated pools, kids' pool, 9-hole, par-3 golf course, 6 lighted tennis courts, Jacuzzi, 5 hot tubs, access to nearby health club, nature trails, watersports equipment rental, bike rental, children's nature programs, concierge, tour desk, car-rental desk, room service, in-room massage, babysitting, dry-cleaning and laundry services. *In room:* A/C, TV/VCR, CD player, dataport, kitchenette (in suites), minibar, coffeemaker, hair dryer.

Hawk's Cay Resort ★★★ (Kids   Located on its own 60-acre island in the Middle Keys, this resort has a relaxed and casual island atmosphere and is also great for kids. If it's recreation you're looking for, Hawk's Cay is far superior to the more luxurious Cheeca Lodge. It offers an impressive array of activities—sailing, fishing, snorkeling, and water-skiing to name a few—and the unique opportunity to have your own dolphin encounter in a special pool. (You'll need to reserve a spot well in advance for the dolphins—there's a waiting list.) The rooms are large and newly renovated with island-style furniture and bright tropical bedspreads and curtains. Every room opens onto a private balcony with ocean or tropical views (pricing varies depending on the view). The large bathrooms are well appointed and have granite countertops. The clubhouse has an exercise room, whirlpool, and steam room. In addition to a lagoon and several pools for families, the resort boasts a secluded pool for adults only. Organized children's activities, including special marine- and ecologically inspired programs, will keep your little ones busy while you relax.

61 Hawk's Cay Blvd. at MM 61, Duck Key, Fl 33050. © **888/814-9104** or 305/743-7000. Fax 305/743-5215. www.hawkscay.com. 176 units. Winter $230–$385 double, $435–$875 suite; off-season $190–$260 double, $335–$775 suite. Packages available. AE, DC, DISC, MC, V. **Amenities:** 3 restaurants, lounge, outdoor heated pool, adults-only private pool, nearby golf course (transportation available), 8 tennis courts (2 lighted), small exercise room, Jacuzzi, watersports equipment, bike rental, children's programs ($25–$35 per child), game room, concierge, limited room service, in-room massage. *In room:* A/C, TV, fridge, coffeemaker.

Westin Beach Resort ⟨★★⟩   In addition to a $3 million overhaul, the resort distinguishes itself by its secluded yet convenient location—it's set back on 12 private acres of gumbo-limbo and hardwood trees, making it invisible from the busy highway. Despite its hideaway location, the sprawling pink-and-blue four-story complex is surprisingly large. A three-story atrium lobby is flanked by two wings that face 1,200 feet of the Florida Bay. The large guest rooms have tasteful tropical decor and private balconies. The suites are twice the size of standard rooms with double-size balconies and better-quality wicker furnishings. Ten suites feature private spa tubs and particularly luxurious bathrooms with adjustable showerheads, bidets, and lots of room for toiletries. The Fun Factory offers fantastic activities for the kids.

U.S. 1 at MM 97, Key Largo, FL 33037. ℭ **800/728-2738**, 800/539-5274, or 305/852-5553. Fax 305/852-8669. www.keylargoresort.com. 200 units. Winter $189–$389; Jacuzzi suites start at $279. Off-season $109–$369; Jacuzzi suites start at $369. AE, DC, DISC, MC, V. **Amenities:** 2 restaurants, snack bar, 2 outdoor heated swimming pools, 2 lighted tennis courts, exercise room, Jacuzzi, watersports equipment/rentals, bike rental, children's programs, concierge, secretarial services, 24-hour room service, dry-cleaning and laundry service, in-room massage, babysitting, nature trails. *In room:* A/C, TV, dataport, minibar, coffeemaker, hair dryer, iron.

EXPENSIVE

Jules' Undersea Lodge ⟨★★★⟩   Staying here is certainly an experience of a lifetime—if you're brave enough to take the plunge. Originally built as a research lab in the 1970s, this small underwater compartment now operates as a single-room hotel. As expensive as it is unusual, Jules' is most popular with diving honeymooners. The lodge rests on pillars on the ocean floor. To get inside, guests swim 21 feet under the structure and pop up into the unit through a 4-by-6-foot "moon pool" that gurgles soothingly all night long. The 30-foot-deep underwater suite consists of a bedroom and galley and sleeps up to six. Room service will deliver your meals, daily newspapers, even a late-night pizza in waterproof containers at no extra charge.

51 Shoreland Dr., Key Largo, FL 33037. ℭ **305/451-2353.** Fax 305/451-4789. www.jul.com. 2 units. $250–$350 per person. Rates include breakfast and dinner as well as all equipment and unlimited scuba diving in the lagoon for certified divers. Packages available. AE, DISC, MC, V. From U.S. 1 S., at MM 103.2, turn left onto Transylvania Ave., across from the Central Plaza shopping mall. **Amenities:** Entertainment center, dining area. *In room:* A/C, telephone, kitchenette.

Marriott Key Largo Bay Beach Resort ⟨★★⟩   While hardly quaint, this amenities-laden 17-acre complex has everything an active or resting traveler could want, including a private beach. Guests enjoy the new European health spa, a nine-hole minigolf course, and tennis courts. All guests are welcome to sail for free on a gambling cruise ship that anchors in international waters from 2pm until 2am daily. Rooms are decorated in a pleasant, if generic, tropical style, and most have balconies overlooking the stunning Florida Bay. For real pampering, consider the enormous suites, which can easily sleep a family of five. All have large wraparound terraces and large sitting areas. With its rates being slightly cheaper than the nearby Westin and Cheeca Lodge, you'll find it a good value.

103800 Overseas Hwy. at MM 103, Key Largo, FL 33037. ℭ **800/932-9332** or 305/453-0000. Fax 305/453-0093. www.marriottkeylargo.com. 153 units. Winter $289–$649; off-season $209–$449. AE, DC, MC, V. **Amenities:** restaurant, snack bar, large outdoor pool, access to nearby tennis and racquetball courts, health center & spa, Jacuzzi, watersports equipment/rentals, nature trail, bike rental, children's programs, game room, concierge, business center, limited room service, in-room massage, babysitting, dry-cleaning and laundry services. *In room:* A/C, TV, VCR on request, dataport, minibar, coffeemaker, hair dryer, iron, safe.

The Moorings ✹✹✹   Staying at The Moorings is more like staying at a secluded beach house than at a hotel. You'll never see another soul on this 18-acre resort if you choose not to. There isn't even maid service unless you request it. The romantic whitewashed units, from cozy cottages to three-bedroom houses, are spacious and modestly decorated with funky island prints, bamboo, and tropical motifs. All have full kitchens, and most have washers and dryers. Some have CD players and VCRs; ask when you book. The real reason to come to this cool resort is to relax on the more than 1,000-foot beach (one of the only real beaches around). There is a hard tennis court, a few kayaks and windsurfers, but absolutely no motorized water vehicles. There is no room service or restaurant (although Morada Bay across the street is excellent). This is a place for people who like each other a lot. Leave the kids at home unless they are extremely well behaved and not easily bored.

123 Beach Rd. near MM 81.5 on the ocean side, Islamorada, FL 33036. ℂ **305/664-4708.** Fax 305/664-4242. www.themooringsvillage.com. 18 cottages. Winter daily $200–$250 small cottages; $475 1-bedroom house; $3,325–$7,875 weekly oceanfront house. Off-season $150–$275, $1,900–$4,500 weekly. 2-night minimum for smaller cottages; 1-week minimum for larger cottages. MC, V. **Amenities:** 3 restaurants, large outdoor heated pool, tennis court, watersports equipment rental. *In room:* A/C, TV, kitchen, coffeemaker, hair dryer.

MODERATE

Banana Bay Resort & Marina ✹   It doesn't look like much from the sign-cluttered Overseas Highway, but when you enter the lush grounds of Banana Bay, you will realize you're in one of the most bucolic and best-run properties in the Upper Keys. Built in the early 1950s as a fishing camp, the resort is a beachfront maze of pink-and-white two-story buildings hidden among banyans and palms. Guest rooms are very similar, but those with better views are more expensive. The rooms are moderately sized, and many have private balconies where you can enjoy your complimentary coffee and newspaper every morning. The hotel's kitschy restaurant serves three meals a day, indoors or poolside.

U.S. 1 at MM 49.5, Marathon, FL 33050. ℂ **800/BANANA-1** or 305/743-3500. Fax 305/743-2670. www.bananabay.com. 60 units. Winter $115–$210 double; off-season $85–$160 double. Rates include continental breakfast. Weekend and 3- and 7-night packages available. AE, DC, DISC, MC, V. **Amenities:** Restaurant, bar; pool, fitness center, Jacuzzi, watersports equipment rental, free use of bikes, game room, self-service laundromat. *In room:* A/C, TV, fax, dataport, fridge, hair dryer.

Conch Key Cottages ✹✹   Here's your chance to play castaway in the Keys. Occupying its own private microisland just off U.S. 1, Conch Key Cottages is a unique and comfortable hideaway run by live-in owners Ron Wilson and Wayne Byrnes, who are constantly fixing and adding to their unique property. This is a place to get away from it all; the cottages aren't located close to much else, except maybe one or two interesting eateries. The cabins, which were built at different times over the past 40 years, overlook their own stretch of natural, but very small, private beach and have screened-in porches, cozy bedrooms, and bathrooms. Each has a hammock, a barbecue grill, and a two-person kayak. Request one of the two-bedroom cottages—especially if you are traveling with the family. They are the most spacious and well designed, practically tailor-made for couples or families. On the other side of the pool are a handful of efficiency apartments that are similarly outfitted, but enjoy no beach frontage. All have fully equipped kitchens. There's also a small heated freshwater pool.

Near U.S. 1 at MM 62.3, Marathon, FL 33050. ℂ **800/330-1577** or 305/289-1377. Fax 305/743-8207. www.conchkeycottages.com. 12 cottages. Dec 15–Sept 8 $110–$274; Sept 9–Dec 14 $74–$215. DISC, MC, V. **Amenities:** 2 pools. *In room:* A/C, TV, no telephone.

Faro Blanco Marine Resort ⊛   Spanning both sides of the Overseas Highway and all on waterfront property, this huge, two-shore marina and hotel complex offers something for every taste. Free-standing, camp-style cottages with a small bedroom are the resort's least-expensive accommodations, but they are in dire need of rehabilitation. Old appliances and a musty odor also make them the least-desirable units on the property. The houseboats are the best choice and value. Permanently tethered in a tranquil marina, these white rectangular boats look like floating mobile homes and are uniformly clean, fresh, and recommendable. They have colonial American-style furnishings, fully equipped kitchenettes, front and back porches, and water, water everywhere. The boats are so tightly moored, you hardly move at all, even in the roughest weather. Finally, there are two unusual rental units located in a lighthouse on the pier. Circular staircases, unusually shaped rooms and showers, and nautical decor make it a unique place to stay, but some guests might find it claustrophobic.

1996 Overseas Hwy., U.S. 1 at MM 48.5, Marathon, FL 33050. ☎ **800/759-3276** or 305/743-9018. Fax 305/866-5235. www.usahotelguide.com/states/florida/floridakeys/middlekeys/faroblanco.html. 123 units. 31 houseboats with 4 units each. Winter $89–$150 cottage; $109–$200 houseboat; $185 lighthouse; $267–$327 condo. Off-season $79–$119 cottage; $99–$178 houseboat; $145 lighthouse; $215–$263 condo. AE, DISC, MC, V. **Amenities:** 4 restaurants, 2 lounges, Olympic-size pool, fully equipped dive shop, barbecue and picnic areas, playground. *In room:* A/C, TV.

Holiday Isle Resort ⊛   A huge resort complex encompassing five restaurants, several lounges, tiki huts, a large marina, many retail shops, and four distinct (if not distinctive) hotels, the Holiday Isle is one of the biggest resorts in the Keys. It attracts a spring-break kind of crowd year-round. Its Tiki Bar claims to have invented the rum runner drink (151-proof rum, blackberry brandy, banana liqueur, grenadine, and lime juice), and there's no reason to doubt it. Hordes of partiers are attracted to the resort's nonstop merrymaking, live music, and beachfront bars. As a result, some of the accommodations can be noisy. Rooms can be bare-bones budget to oceanfront luxury, as the broad range of prices reflects. Even the nicest rooms could use a good cleaning. El Captain and Harbor Lights, two of the least-expensive hotels on the property, are both austere. Like the other hotels here, rooms could use a thorough rehab. Howard Johnson's, another Holiday Isle property, is a little farther from the action and a tad more civilized. If you plan to be here for a few days, choose an efficiency or a suite; both have kitchenettes.

U.S. 1 at MM 84, Islamorada, FL 33036. ☎ **800/327-7070** or 305/664-2321. Fax 305/664-2703. www. holidayisle.com. 199 units. Winter $85–$425 double. Off-season $65–$350 double. AE, DISC, MC, V. **Amenities:** 8 restaurants, 12 bars, 2 outdoor heated pools, kids' pool, watersports equipment/rentals. *In room:* A/C, TV.

Kona Kai Resort & Gallery ⊛⊛   Unique to the Upper Keys, this little haven, with just 11 units, is both casual and elegant. Quaint rooms and complete suites dot the lushly landscaped 2-acre property, which boasts a large variety of native vegetation like palms, bougainvillea, and ferns, plus an impressive collection of fruit-bearing trees, such as carambola, passion fruit, banana, Key lime, guava, and coconut. An orchid house has over 250 beautiful flowers. Lounge chairs, hammocks, a Jacuzzi, and a compact beach are available for those who just want to relax, while a slew of activities are available for the more active set. For the adventurous, owners Ronnie and Joe Harris will organize excursions to the Everglades, the backcountry, or wherever. No phones in the rooms and a 3-day minimum stay requirement in the winter make relaxing imperative (2-night minimum in summer). All the rooms are very private and simply furnished; bathroom amenities are fabulous, with lotions, soaps, and shampoos made from tropical fruits. CDs from local musicians are there for your in-room listening pleasure. Home-grown tropical fruits from the hotel's garden are there for guests to sample. For more substantial meals, you'll need to visit a nearby restaurant—there are three within walking distance and several more a short drive away. Smoking is not permitted in the rooms. An art gallery featuring work by American and international painters, photographers, and sculptors doubles as the property's office and lobby. Even if you are not staying here, stop in to see the artwork.

97802 Overseas Hwy. (U.S. 1 at MM 97.8), Key Largo, FL 33037. ℂ 800/365-7829 or 305/852-7200. Fax 305/852-4629. www.konakairesort.com. 11 units. Winter $196–$233 double, $257–$658 1- to 2-bedroom suite. Off-season $108–$129 double, $143–$433 1- to 2-bedroom suite, 3-night minimum stay in winter; 2-night minimum off-season. AE, DISC, MC, V. Children under 16 not permitted. Closed September. **Amenities:** Heated pool, tennis court, spa, Jacuzzi, watersports equipment/rentals, boat ramp/dockage, concierge, in-room massage and facials. *In room:* A/C, TV, fridge, hair dryer; kitchen, VCR, CD player (suites only).

Lime Tree Bay Resort Motel   The Lime Tree Bay Resort is the only hotel in the tiny town of Layton (population 183). Midway between Islamorada and Marathon, the hotel is only steps from Long Key State Recreation Area. It's situated on a very pretty piece of waterfront graced with hundreds of mature palm trees and lots of other tropical foliage. Motel rooms and efficiencies have tiny bathrooms with standing showers but are clean and well maintained. The best deal is the two-bedroom bay-view cottage. The large living area with new fixtures and furnishings leads out to a large private deck where you can enjoy a view of the Gulf from your hammock. A full kitchen and two full bathrooms make it a comfortable space for six people. Fifteen efficiencies and suites have kitchenettes.

U.S. 1 at MM 68.5 in Layton, Long Key, FL 33001. ℂ 800/723-4519 or 305/664-4740. Fax 305/664-0750. www.limetreebayresort.com. 30 units. Winter $107–$247 double; off-season $84–$189 double. AE, DC, DISC, MC, V. **Amenities:** Restaurant, small outdoor pool, tennis court, Jacuzzi, watersports equipment/rental. *In room:* A/C, TV, kitchenette (in some units), dataport.

INEXPENSIVE

Bay Harbor Lodge 🐟   A small, simple retreat that's big on charm, the Bay Harbor Lodge is an extraordinarily welcoming place. The lodge is far from fancy, though it features new windows and paint, and the widely ranging accommodations are not created equal. The motel rooms are small and ordinary in decor, but even the least expensive is recommendable. The efficiencies are larger motel rooms with fully equipped kitchenettes. The oceanfront cottages are larger still, have full kitchens, and represent one of the best values in the Keys. The vinyl-covered furnishings and old-fashioned wallpapers won't win any design awards, but elegance isn't what the "real" Keys are about. The 1½ lush acres of grounds are planted with banana trees and have an outdoor heated pool and several small barbecue grills. A small beach is ideal for some quiet sunning and relaxation. Guests are free to use the rowboats, paddleboats, canoes, kayaks, and snorkeling equipment. Bring your own beach towels.

97702 Overseas Hwy., U.S. 1 at MM 97.7 (off the southbound lane of U.S. 1), Key Largo, FL 33037. ℂ 800/385-0986 or 305/852-5695. www.thefloridakeys.com/bayharborlodge. 16 units. Winter $75–$165 double. Off-season $65–$95 efficiency; $85–$125 double. MC, V. **Amenities:** Freshwater pool; watersports equipment/rental. *In room:* A/C, TV, fridge, microwave, coffeemaker, hair dryer.

Ragged Edge Resort 🐟🐟   This small oceanfront property's 11 units are spread out along more than half a dozen gorgeous, grassy waterfront acres. All are immaculately clean and comfortable, and most are outfitted with full kitchens and tasteful furnishings. There's no bar, restaurant, or staff to speak of, but the retreat's affable owner, Jackie Barnes, is happy to lend you bicycles or good advice on the area's offerings. A large dock attracts boaters and a good variety of local and migratory birds.

243 Treasure Harbor Rd. (near MM 86.5), Islamorada, FL 33036. © **800/436-2023** or 305/852-5389. www.ragged-edge.com. 11 units. Winter $69–$189; off-season $48–$125. AE, MC, V. **Amenities:** Outdoor pool, free use of bikes, laundromat. *In room:* A/C, kitchen (most units), fridge, coffeemaker.

CAMPING

John Pennekamp Coral Reef State Park 🐾🐾   One of Florida's best parks (see above), Pennekamp offers 47 well-separated campsites, half of which are available by advance reservation, the rest distributed on a first-come, first-served basis. The car-camping sites are small but well equipped with bathrooms and showers. Note that the local environment provides fertile breeding grounds for insects, particularly in the late summer. Two man-made beaches and a small lagoon nearby attract many large wading birds. Reservations are held until 5pm, and the park must be notified of late arrival by phone on the check-in date. Pennekamp opens at 8am and closes around sundown.

U.S. 1 at MM 102.5 (P.O. Box 487), Key Largo, FL 33037. © **305/451-1202.** 47 campsites. Reservations can be made in advance. $24–$26 per site for camping. Park entry $4 per vehicle (50¢ for each additional person). Yearly permits and passes available. AE, DISC, MC, V. No pets.

Long Key State Park 🐾   The Upper Keys' other main state park is more secluded than its northern neighbor—and more popular. All sites are located ocean side and surrounded by narrow rows of trees and nearby toilet and bathroom facilities. Reserve well in advance, especially in winter. If you prefer not to stay overnight, the park is available for daytime picnicking for $3.25 per vehicle plus 50¢ per person.

U.S. 1 at MM 67.5 (P.O. Box 776), Long Key, FL 33001. © **305/664-4815.** 60 oceanfront sites. $24–$26 per site for 1–4 people. $3.25 per vehicle. Special permits and passes available. AE, DISC, MC, V. No pets.

WHERE TO DINE

Although not known as a culinary hot spot, the Upper and Middle Keys do offer some excellent restaurants, most of which specialize in seafood. And dining opportunities are always improving. Often, visitors (especially those who fish) take advantage of accommodations that have kitchen facilities and cook their own meals. Some restaurants will even clean and cook your catch, for a fee.

VERY EXPENSIVE

Atlantic's Edge 🐾🐾🐾 SEAFOOD/REGIONAL   Ask for a table by the oceanfront window to feel really privileged at this restaurant, the most elegant in the Keys. Although the service and food are generally first rate, don't get dressed up—a sports coat for men will be fine but isn't necessary. You can choose from an innovative, varied menu, which offers several choices of fresh fish, steak, chicken, and pastas. The crab cakes, made with stone crab when in season, are the very best in the Keys; served on a warm salad of baby greens with a mild sauce of red peppers, they're the stuff cravings are made of. Other excellent dishes include a Thai-spiced fresh baby snapper and the vegetarian angel-hair pasta with mushrooms, asparagus, and peppers in a rich broth. Service can sometimes be less than efficient but is always courteous and professional.

In the Cheeca Lodge, U.S. 1 at MM 82, Islamorada. © **305/664-4651.** Reservations recommended. Main courses $20–$36. AE, DC, DISC, MC, V. Daily 6 pm–10pm.

EXPENSIVE

Barracuda Grill 🐟🐟 SEAFOOD   Owned by Lance Hill and his wife, Jan (a former sous chef at Little Palm Island), this small, casual spot serves excellent seafood, steaks, and chops. It's too bad it's open only for dinner. Some of the favorite dishes are the Caicos Gold Conch and Mangrove Snapper and Mango. Try the Tipsy Olives appetizer, marinated in gin or vodka, to kick-start your meal. Decorated with barracuda-themed art, the restaurant also features a well-priced American wine list with lots of California vintages.

U.S. 1 at MM 49.5 (bay side), Marathon. 🕿 **305/743-3314.** Main courses $10–$32. AE, MC, V. Mon–Sat 6–10pm.

Marker 88 🐟🐟🐟 SEAFOOD/REGIONAL   An institution in the Upper Keys, Marker 88 has been pleasing locals and visitors since it opened in the early 1970s. Chef-owner Andre Mueller fuses tropical fruit and fish with such items as crabmeat stuffing, asparagus, tomatoes, lemons, olives, capers, and mushrooms to make the most delectable and innovative seafood dishes around. Taking full advantage of his island location, Andre offers dozens of seafood selections, including Keys lobster, Bahamas conch, Florida Bay stone crabs, Gulf Coast shrimp, and an impressive variety of fish from around the country. After you've figured out what kind of seafood to have, you can choose from a dozen styles of preparation. The Keys' standard is meunière, which is a subtle, tasty sauce of lemon and parsley. Although everything looks tempting, don't overorder—portions are huge. The waitresses, who are pleasant enough, require a bit of patience, but the food is worth it.

U.S. 1 at MM 88 (bay side), Islamorada. 🕿 **305/852-9315.** Reservations suggested. Main courses $14–$33. AE, DC, DISC, MC, V. Tues–Sun 5–11pm. Closed in September.

Morada Bay 🐟🐟 CARIBBEAN/AMERICAN   This lovely bay-side bistro offers superfresh, innovative seafood as well as more basic offerings, such as chicken fajitas, hamburgers, and salads. Salads such as the Sunshine Salad are large and lavished with slices of avocado, mango, and tomato. When in season, delicious raw oysters are imported from Long Island. Fish dishes are always fresh and served in a number of styles; I like mine jerked with a peppery coating and nearly black finish. If you can't decide, share a few items from the tapas menu: jumbo shrimp cocktails, fried calamari, conch fritters, smoked fish dip, or a charcuterie of sausage and ham on country bread.

U.S. 1 at MM 81.6, Islamorada. 🕿 **305/664-0604.** Reservations recommended for large groups. Main courses $17–$28. AE, MC, V. Daily 11:30am–10pm.

MODERATE

Green Turtle Inn 🐟🐟 SEAFOOD   The Green Turtle Inn was established in 1947 as a place where anglers and travelers to and from Key West could stop for local delicacies made from sea turtles harvested in local waters. It has become the quintessential Keys eatery, with a friendly, local flavor and delicious and *different* fare, such as turtle steaks, soups, and chowders. Alligator steak is also popular and, yes, it does taste like chicken. Campy house pianist Tina Martin has become somewhat of a local celebrity, but it's really the Turtle Chowder for which the Inn has become best known. The restaurant also has a cannery so you can take some of the chowder to your friends who won't believe how good it is until they taste it for themselves.

U.S. 1 at MM 81.5, Islamorada. 🕿 **305/664-9031.** Main courses $13.50–$21.95. AE, DISC, MC, V. Tues–Sun Noon–10pm.

Lazy Days Oceanfront Bar and Seafood Grill 🌟 SEAFOOD/AMERICAN
Opened in 1992, the Lazy Days quickly became one of the most popular restaurants around, mostly because of its large portions and lively atmosphere. Dining
on the oceanfront outdoor veranda is highly recommended. Meals are pricier
than the casual dining room would suggest, but the food is good enough and
the menu varied. Steamed clams with garlic and bell peppers make a tempting
appetizer. The menu focuses on—what else?—seafood, but you can also find
good pasta dishes such as linguine with littleneck clams. Most main courses
come with baked potato, vegetables, a tossed salad, and French bread, making
appetizers redundant.

U.S. 1 at MM 79.9, Islamorada. ℂ **305/664-5256.** Main courses $11–$24. AE, DISC, MC, V. Wed–Sun
11:30am–10pm.

Lorelei Restaurant and Cabana Bar 🌟🌟 SEAFOOD/BAR FOOD   Don't
resist the siren call of the enormous, sparkling roadside mermaid—you won't be
dashed onto the rocks. This big old fish house and bar is a great place for a
snack, a meal, or a beer. Inside, a good-value menu focuses mainly on seafood.
When in season, lobsters are the way to go. For $20, you can get a good-sized
tail—at least a 1 pounder—prepared any way you like. Other fare includes the
standard clam chowder, fried shrimp, and doughy conch fritters. Salads and
soups are hearty and satisfying. For those tired of fish, the menu also offers a few
beef selections. The outside bar has live music every evening, and you can order
snacks and light meals from a limited menu that is satisfying and well priced.

U.S. 1 at MM 82, Islamorada. ℂ **305/664-4656.** Reservations not usually required. Main courses $12–$24.
AE, DC, DISC, MC, V. Daily 7am–10:30pm. Outside bar serves breakfast 7–11am; lunch/appetizer menu
11am–9pm. Bar closes at midnight.

INEXPENSIVE

Calypso's 🌟 SEAFOOD/PASTA   The awning still bears the name of the former restaurant, Demar's, but the food here is all Todd Lollis's. Even though he
looks like he might be more comfortable at a Grateful Dead concert than in a
kitchen, this inspired young chef turns out inventive seafood dishes in a casual
and rustic waterside setting. If it's available, try the butter pecan sauce over whatever fish is freshest. Don't miss the white wine sangria, full of tangy oranges and
limes and topped with a dash of cinnamon. The prices are surprisingly reasonable, but the service can be a little more laid-back than you're used to. The
toughest part is finding the place. From the south, turn right at the blinking yellow lights near MM 99.5 to Ocean Bay Drive; turn right. Look for the blue
vinyl-sided building on the left.

1 Seagate Blvd. (near MM 99.5), Key Largo. ℂ **305/451-0600.** Main courses $8–$16. MC, V. Wed–Mon
11:30am–10pm; Fri until 11pm.

Islamorada Fish Company 🌟🌟 SEAFOOD   The original Islamorada Fish
Company has been selling seafood out of its roadside shack since 1948. It's still
the best place to pick up a cooler of stone crab claws in season (mid-October
through April). Also great are the fried-fish sandwiches, served with melted
American cheese, fried onions, and coleslaw. A few hundred yards up the road
(at MM 81.6) is Islamorada Fish Company Restaurant & Bakery, the newer
establishment, which looks like an average diner, but has a selection of fantastic
seafood and pastas. It's also the place for breakfast. Locals gather for politics
and gossip as well as delicious grits, oatmeal, omelettes, and homemade pastries.
ℂ 305/664-8363; open Thursday to Tuesday 6am to 9pm, Wednesday 6am to
2pm. Discover, MasterCard, and Visa are accepted.

U.S. 1 at MM 81.5 (up the street from Cheeca Lodge), Islamorada. ℂ **800/258-2559** or 305/664-9271. www.islamoradafishco.com. Reservations not accepted. Main courses $8–$27; appetizers $4–$7. DISC, MC, V. Sun–Thurs, 11am–9 pm; Fri–Sat, 11am–10pm.

Key Largo's Crack'd Conch SEAFOOD   This colorful little shack looks appealing from the road and isn't a bad place to stop for a beer— more than 100 imported and domestic flavors to choose from—and a decent basket of fried clams, shrimp, chicken, and, of course, conch. Prices are higher than they ought to be, considering the quality and atmosphere, but they won't bust your budget.

U.S. 1 at MM 105.5 (ocean side). ℂ **305/451-0732.** Reservations not accepted. Main courses $9–$15; sandwiches $3.25–$7. AE, DC, DISC, MC, V. Thurs–Tues noon–10pm.

Time Out Barbecue ⭐⭐ BARBECUE   This barbecue joint serves up hot and hearty old-fashioned barbecue that is among the best around. According to management, the secret is in the slow-cooking—more than 10 hours for the melt-in-your-mouth soft pork sandwich. Topped off with delicious, not-too-creamy coleslaw and sweet baked beans, any of the many offerings are worth a stop. You can grab a seat at the picnic table on the grassy lawn next to the Trading Post.

U.S. 1 at MM 81.5 (ocean side). ℂ **305/664-8911.** Sandwiches $4.25–$6; rib and chicken platters to share $7–$15. MC, V. Daily 11am–10pm.

THE UPPER & MIDDLE KEYS AFTER DARK

Nightlife in the Upper Keys tends to start before the sun goes down, often at noon, since most people—visitors and locals alike—are on vacation. Also, many anglers and sports-minded folk go to bed early.

Hog Heaven opened in the early 1990s, the joint venture of some young locals tired of tourist traps. Located at MM 85.3 just off the main road on the ocean side in Islamorada (ℂ **305/664-9669**), it's a welcome respite from the neon-colored cocktail circuit. This whitewashed biker bar offers a waterside view and diversions that include big-screen TVs and video games. The food isn't bad, either. The atmosphere is cliquish since most patrons are regulars, so start up a game of pool or skeet to break the ice.

No trip is complete without a stop at the **Tiki Bar at the Holiday Isle Resort,** U.S. 1 at MM 84, Islamorada (ℂ **800/327-7070** or 305/664-2321). Hundreds of revelers visit this ocean-side spot for drinks and dancing at any time of day, but the live rock music starts at 8:30pm. (See "Where to Stay," above.) The thatched-roof Tiki Bar draws a high-energy but laid-back mix of thirsty people, all in pursuit of a good time. In the afternoon and early evening (when everyone is either sunburned, drunk, or just happy to be dancing to live reggae), head for **Kokomo's,** just next door. Kokomo's often closes at 7:30pm on weekends, so get there early. For information, call the Holiday Isle Resort.

Locals and tourists mingle at the outdoor cabana bar at **Lorelei** (see "Where to Dine," above). Most evenings after 5pm, you'll find local bands playing on a thatched-roof stage—mainly rock and roll, reggae and sometimes blues.

Woody's Saloon and Restaurant, on U.S. 1 at MM 82, Islamorada (ℂ **305/664-4335**), is a lively, wacky, raunchy place serving up mediocre pizzas and live bands almost every night. The house band, Big Dick and the Extenders, showcases a 300-pound Native American who does a lewd, rude, and crude routine of jokes and songs starting at 9pm, Tuesday through Sunday. He is a legend. By the way, don't think you're lucky if you are offered the front table: It's the target seat for Big Dick's haranguing. Avoid the lame karaoke performance on Sunday and Monday evenings. There's a small cover charge most nights. Drink specials, contests, and the legendary Big Dick keep this place packed until 4am almost every night.

For a more subdued atmosphere, try the handsome wood bar at **Zane Grey's** (on the second floor of World Wide Sportsman at MM 81.5). Outside, enjoy a view of the calm waters of the bay; inside, soak up the history of some real old anglers. You'll feel like a real swell in this stained-glass, mahogany-decked club. It is open from 11am to 11pm, and later on weekends. Call to find out who is playing on weekends (© **305/664-4244**), when there is live entertainment and no cover charge.

2 The Lower Keys: Big Pine Key to Coppitt Key

128 miles SW of Miami

Unlike their neighbors to the north and south, the Lower Keys (including Big Pine, Sugarloaf, and Summerland) are devoid of rowdy spring-break crowds, boast few T-shirt and trinket shops, and have almost no late-night bars. What they do offer are the very best opportunities to enjoy the vast natural resources on land and water that make the area so rich. Stay overnight in the Lower Keys, rent a boat, and explore the reefs—it might be the most memorable part of your trip.

ESSENTIALS
GETTING THERE   See "Essentials," for the Upper and Middle Keys. Continue south on U.S. 1. The Lower Keys start at the end of the Seven-Mile Bridge.

VISITOR INFORMATION   The **Big Pine and Lower Keys Chamber of Commerce,** ocean side of U.S. 1 at MM 31 (P.O. Box 430511), Big Pine Key, FL 33043 (© **800/872-3722** or 305/872-2411; fax 305/872-0752; www. lowerkeyschamber.com), is open Monday through Friday from 9am to 5pm and Saturday from 9am to 3pm. The pleasant staff will help with anything a traveler may need. Call, write, or stop in for a comprehensive, detailed information packet.

WHAT TO SEE & DO
Once the centerpiece of the Lower Keys and still a great asset is **Bahia Honda State Park** 𝕬, U.S. 1 at MM 37.5, Big Pine Key (© **305/872-2353**), which, even after the violent storms of 1998, has one of the most beautiful coastlines in South Florida. Bahia Honda (pronounced *Bah*-ya) is a great place for hiking, bird watching, swimming, snorkeling, and fishing. The 524-acre park encompasses a wide variety of ecosystems, including coastal mangroves, beach dunes, and tropical hammocks. There are miles of trails packed with unusual plants and animals and a small white beach. Shaded seaside picnic areas are fitted with tables and grills. Although the beach is never wider than 5 feet even at low tide, this is the Lower Keys' best beach area.

True to its name (Spanish for "deep bay"), the park has relatively deep waters close to shore, and they are perfect for snorkeling and diving. Easy offshore snorkeling here gives even novices a chance to lie suspended in warm water and simply observe diverse marine life passing by. Or else head to the stunning reefs at Looe Key, where the coral and fish are more vibrant than anywhere else in the United States. Snorkeling trips depart daily from March through September and cost $25.95 for adults, $20.95 for youths 6 to 14, and free for children 5 and under. Call © **305/872-3210** for a schedule.

Admission to the park is $4 per vehicle (plus 50¢ per person), $1.50 per pedestrian or bicyclist, free for children 5 and under. If you are alone in a car, you'll pay only $2.50. Open daily from 8am to sunset.

The most famous residents of the Lower Keys are the tiny Key deer. Of the estimated 300 existing in the world, two-thirds live on Big Pine Key's **National Key Deer Refuge** . To get your bearings, stop by the rangers' office at the Winn-Dixie Shopping Plaza near MM 30.5 off U.S. 1. They'll give you an informative brochure and map of the area. The refuge is open Monday through Friday from 8am to 5pm.

If the office is closed, head out to the Blue Hole, a former rock quarry now filled with the fresh water that's vital to the deer's survival. To get there, turn right at Big Pine Key's only traffic light onto Key Deer Boulevard (take the left fork immediately after the turn) and continue 1½ miles to the observation-site parking lot, on your left. The half-mile **Watson Hammock Trail,** about a third of a mile past the Blue Hole, is the refuge's only marked footpath. Try coming out here in the early morning or late evening to catch a glimpse of these gentle, dog-sized deer. They are more active in cool hours and in cooler times of the year. Refuge lands are open daily from half an hour before sunrise to half an hour after sunset. Don't be surprised to see a lazy alligator warming itself in the sun, particularly in outlying areas around the Blue Hole. Whatever you do, do not feed the deer—it will threaten their survival. Call the **park office** (© **305/872-2239**) to find out about the infrequent free tours of the refuge, scheduled throughout the year.

The only man-made attraction in the Lower Keys is the **Sugarloaf Bat Tower,** off U.S. 1 at MM 17 (next to Sugarloaf Airport on the bay side). In a vain effort to battle the ubiquitous troublesome mosquitoes in the Lower Keys, developer Clyde Perkey built this odd structure to lure bug-eating bats. Despite his alluring design and a pungent bat aphrodisiac, his guests never showed. Since 1929, this wooden, flat-topped, 45-foot-high pyramid has stood empty and deserted, except for the occasional tourist who stops to wonder what it is. There is no sign or marker to commemorate this odd remnant of ingenuity. It's worth a 5-minute detour to see it. To get there, turn right at the Sugarloaf Airport sign and then right again onto the dirt road that begins just before the airport gate; the tower is about 100 yards ahead.

OUTDOOR PURSUITS

BICYCLING   If you have your own bike, or your lodging offers a rental (many do), the Lower Keys is a great place to get off busy U.S. 1 to explore the beautiful back roads. On Big Pine Key, cruise along Key Deer Boulevard (at MM 30). Those with fat tires can ride into the National Key Deer Refuge.

BIRD WATCHING   Bring your birding books. A stopping point for migratory birds on the Eastern Flyway, the Lower Keys are populated with many West Indian bird species, especially during spring and fall. The small vegetated islands of the Keys are the only nesting sites in the United States for the great white heron and the white-crowned pigeon. They're also some of the very few breeding places for the reddish egret, the roseate spoonbill, the mangrove cuckoo, and the black-whiskered vireo. Look for them on Bahia Honda and the many uninhabited islands nearby.

BOATING   Dozens of shops rent powerboats for fishing and reef exploring. Most also rent tackle, sell bait, and have charter captains available. **Bud Boats,**

at the Old Wooden Bride Fishing Camp and Marina, MM 30 in Big Pine Key (© **305/872-9165**), has a wide selection of well-maintained boats. Depending on the size, rentals cost between $70 and $250 for a day, between $50 and $130 for a half day. Another good option is **Jaybird's Powerboats,** U.S. 1 at MM 33, Big Pine Key (© **305/872-8500**). They rent for full days only. Prices start at $155 for a 19-footer.

CANOEING & KAYAKING   The Overseas Highway (U.S. 1) touches on only a few dozen of the many hundreds of islands that make up the Keys. To really see the Lower Keys, rent a kayak or canoe—perfect for these shallow waters. **Reflections Kayak Nature Tours,** operating out of Parmer's Resort, on U.S. 1 at MM 28.5, Little Torch Key (© **305/872-2896**), offers fully outfitted backcountry wildlife tours, either on your own or with an expert. A former U.S. Forest Service guide, Mike Wedeking, keeps up an engaging discussion describing the area's fish, sponges, coral, osprey, hawks, eagles, alligators, raccoons, and deer. The 3-hour tours cost $49 per person and include spring water, fresh fruit, granola bars, and use of binoculars. Bring a towel and sea sandals or sneakers.

DIVING & FISHING   A day spent fishing, either in the shallow backcountry or in the deep sea, is a great way to ensure yourself a fresh fish dinner, or you can release your catch and just appreciate the challenge. Whichever you choose, **Larry Threlkeld's Strike Zone Charters,** U.S. 1 at MM 29.5, Big Pine Key (© **305/872-9863**), is the charter service to call. Prices for fishing boats start at $450 for a half day and $595 for a full day. If you have enough anglers to share the price, it isn't too steep. They may be able to match you with other interested visitors.

Especially since the *Adolphus Busch Sr.* was sunk off Looe Key in 100 feet of water, the lower Keys also offers some prime diving. To get to the 210-foot island freighter on your own boat, head to coordinates 24.31.819 N, 81.27.643W, between Looe Key and American Shoals. Strike Zone will take you for $50 without equipment.

HIKING   You can hike throughout the flat marshy Keys, on both marked trails and meandering coastlines. The best places to trek through nature are **Bahia Honda State Park** at MM 29.5 and **National Key Deer Refuge** at MM 30 (for more information on both, see "What to See & Do," above). Bahia Honda Park has a free brochure describing an excellent self-guided tour along the Silver Palm Nature Trail. You'll traverse hammocks, mangroves, and sand dunes and cross a lagoon. You can do the walk (which is less than a mile) in under half an hour and explore a great cross-section of the natural habitat in the Lower Keys.

SNORKELING & DIVING   Snorkelers and divers should not miss the Keys' most dramatic reefs at the **Looe Key National Marine Sanctuary.** Here, you'll see more than 150 varieties of hard and soft coral—some, centuries old—as well as every type of tropical fish, including the gold and blue parrot fish, moray eels, barracudas, French angels, and tarpon. **Looe Key Dive Center,** U.S. 1 at MM 27.5, Ramrod Key (© **305/872-2215**), offers a mind-blowing 5-hour tour aboard a 45-foot catamaran with two shallow 1-hour dives for snorkelers and scuba divers. Snorkelers pay $25, and divers with their own equipment pay $40; on Wednesdays and Saturdays you can do a fascinating dive to a wreck for $45. Good-quality rentals are available. (See "What to See & Do," above, for other diving options.)

SHOPPING

Certainly not known for great shopping, the Lower Keys do happen to be home to many talented visual artists, particularly those who specialize in depicting their natural surroundings. The **Artists in Paradise Gallery,** on Big Pine Key in the Winn-Dixie Shopping Plaza, near MM 30.5, 1 block north of U.S. 1 at the traffic light (© **305/872-1828**), displays a changing selection of watercolors, oils, photos, and sculptures. This cooperative gallery displays the work of more than a dozen artists who share the task of watching the store. Hours are usually daily from 10am to 6pm.

WHERE TO STAY

There are a number of cheap, fairly gross fish shacks along the highway for those who want bare-bones accommodations. So far, there are no national hotel chains in the Lower Keys. For information on lodging in cabins or trailers at local campgrounds, see "Camping," below.

VERY EXPENSIVE

Little Palm Island ⟨⟨★★★⟩   This exclusive island escape—host to presidents and royalty—is not just a place to stay while in the Lower Keys; it is a destination all its own. Built on a private 5-acre island, it's accessible only by boat. Guests stay in thatched-roof duplexes amid lush foliage and flowering tropical plants. Many villas have ocean views and private sundecks with rope hammocks. Inside, the romantic suites have all the comforts and conveniences of a luxurious contemporary beach cottage, but without telephones, TVs, or alarm clocks. As if its location weren't idyllic enough, a new full-service spa opened on the island. Note that on the breezeless south side of the island, you may get invaded by mosquitoes, even in the winter. (So bring spray and lightweight long-sleeved clothing.) Known for its innovative and pricey food, Little Palm also hosts visitors just for dinner or lunch. If you are staying on the island, opt for the full American plan, which includes three meals a day for about $140 per person. If you pay a la carte, you could spend that much just on dinner. At these prices, Little Palm appeals to those who aren't keeping track.

Launch is at the ocean side of U.S. 1 at MM 28.5, Little Torch Key, FL 33042. © **800/343-8567** or 305/872-2524. Fax 305/872-4843. www.littlepalmisland.com. 28 bungalows, 2 deluxe suites. Winter $795–$1,695 per couple. Off-season $695–$1,595. Rates include transportation to and from the island and unlimited (nonmotorized) watersports. Meal plans include 2 meals daily for $125 per person per day, 3 meals at $140 per person. AE, DC, DISC, MC, V. No children under 16. **Amenities:** Restaurant, bar, 2 pools (1 outdoor with small waterfall, 1 indoor), health club and spa, jogging trail, extensive watersports equipment/rental, concierge, courtesy van from Key West or Marathon airport, ferry service to and from the mainland, limited room service, in-room massage, dry-cleaning and laundry services. *In room:* A/C, dataport, Jacuzzi, minibar, coffeemaker, hair dryer.

MODERATE

Deer Run Bed and Breakfast ⟨⟨★★⟩ *(finds)*   Located directly on the beach, Sue Abbott's small, homey, smoke-free B&B is a real find. One upstairs and two downstairs guest rooms are comfortably furnished with queen-size beds, good closets, and touch-sensitive lamps. Rattan and 1970s-style chairs and couches furnish the living room, along with 13 birds and three cats. Breakfast, which is served on a pretty, fenced-in porch, is cooked to order by Sue herself. The wooded area around the property is full of deer, which are often spotted on the beach as well. Ask to use one of the bikes to explore nearby nature trails. The owner prefers adults and mature children only.

Long Beach Dr. (P.O. Box 431), Big Pine Key, FL 33043. (C) **305/872-2015**. Fax 305/872-2842. www. deerrunbb@aol.com. 3 units. Winter from $165 double; off-season from $95 double. Rates include full American breakfast. No credit cards. From U.S. 1 S., turn left at the Big Pine Fishing Lodge (MM 33); continue for about 2 miles. No children under 16. **Amenities:** Jacuzzi; free use of bikes. *In room:* A/C, TV.

INEXPENSIVE

Parmer's Resort *(R)(R)*   Parmer's, a fixture here for more than 20 years, is well known for its charming hospitality and helpful staff. This downscale resort offers modest but comfortable cottages, each one of them unique. Some are waterfront, many have kitchenettes, and others are just a bedroom. Room 26, a one-bedroom efficiency, is especially nice, with a small sitting area that faces the water. Room 6, a small efficiency, has a kitchenette and an especially large bathroom. The rooms all have linoleum floors, dated painted rattan furnishings, fake flowers, and thrift-store art—but they're very clean. Many can be combined to accommodate large families. The hotel's waterfront location almost makes up for the fact that you must pay extra for maid service.

Barry Ave. (P.O. Box 430665), near MM 28.5, Little Torch Key, FL 33043. (C) **305/872-2157**. Fax 305/872-2014. www.parmersresort.com. 45 units. Winter and summer, from $69 double; from $95 efficiency. Fall $55–$65 double; from $75 efficiency. Rates include continental breakfast. AE, DISC, MC, V. Turn right onto Barry Ave. Resort is a half-mile down on the right. **Amenities:** Heated pool, boat ramp, bike rental, Laundromat. *In room:* A/C, TV.

CAMPING

Bahia Honda State Park *(R)(R)(R)* ((C) **305/872-2353;** www8.myflorida.com/ communities/learn/stateparks/district5) offers some of the best camping in the Keys, even after the devastating storms of 1998. It is as loaded with facilities and activities as it is with campers. However, don't be discouraged by its popularity— this park encompasses more than 500 acres of land. There are 80 campsites and six spacious and comfortable cabin units that were reconstructed between 2000 and 2001. Cabins hold up to eight guests and come complete with linens, kitchenettes, and utensils. You'll enjoy the wraparound terrace, barbecue pit, and rocking chairs.

For one to four people, camping here costs about $25 per site without electricity and $26 with electricity. Depending on the season, cabin prices change: Prices range from $50 to $110. Additional people (over four) cost $6 each. MasterCard and Visa are accepted.

Another excellent value can be found at the **KOA Sugarloaf Key Resort** *(R)(R)*, near MM 20. This ocean-side facility has 200 fully equipped sites, with water, electricity, and sewer, that rent for about $70 a night (no-hook-up sites cost about $38). Or pitch a tent on the 5 acres of lush waterfront property. The resort also rents travel trailers. The 22-foot Dutchman sleeps six and is equipped with eating and cooking utensils. It costs about $100 a day. More luxurious trailers go for $160 a day. All major credit cards are accepted. For details, write them at P.O. Box 420469, Summerland Key, FL 33042 ((C) **800/562-7731** or 305/745-3549; fax 305/745-9889; sugarloaf@koa.net).

WHERE TO DINE

There aren't many fine dining options in the Lower Keys, but the following are worth a stop for those passing through.

MODERATE

Mangrove Mama's Restaurant SEAFOOD/CARIBBEAN   As the dedicated locals who come daily for happy hour will tell you, this is a true Lower

Keys institution and a dive in the best sense of the word. The restaurant is a shack that used to have a gas pump as well as a grill. Now, guests share the property with some miniature horses (out back) and stray cats. A handful of simple tables, inside and out, are shaded by banana trees and palm fronds. Fish is the menu's mainstay, although soups, salads, sandwiches, and omelets are also good. Grilled teriyaki chicken and club sandwiches are tasty alternatives to fish, as are meatless chef's salads and spicy barbecued baby back ribs.

U.S. 1 at MM 20, Sugarloaf Key. © **305/745-3030.** Main courses $10–$20; lunch $6–$9; brunch $5–$7. MC, V. Daily 11:30am–10pm (11am in season).

Monte's SEAFOOD   Monte's has survived for more than 20 years because the food is very good and incredibly fresh. Certainly nobody goes to this restaurant/fish market for its atmosphere: Plastic place settings rest on plastic-covered picnic-style tables in a screen-enclosed dining patio. The day's catch may include shark, tuna, lobsters, stone crabs, or shrimp.

U.S. 1 at MM 25, Summerland Key. © **305/745-3731.** Main courses $13–$17; lunch $6–$10. No credit cards. Mon–Sat 9am–10pm; Sun 10am–9pm.

INEXPENSIVE

Coco's Kitchen ⊛ CUBAN/AMERICAN   This tiny storefront has been dishing out black beans, rice, and shredded beef to fans of Cuban cuisine for more than 10 years. The owners, who are actually from Nicaragua, cook not only superior Cuban food but also some local specialties, Italian food, and Caribbean food. Specialties include fried shrimp, whole fried yellowtail, and Cuban-style roast pork (available only on Saturdays). The best bet is the daily special, which may be roasted pork or fresh grouper, served with rice and beans or salad and crispy fries. Top off the huge, cheap meal with a rich caramel-soaked flan.

283 Key Deer Blvd. (in the Winn-Dixie Shopping Center), Big Pine Key. © **305/872-4495.** Main courses $4.79–$11.95; breakfast $2–$4.50. No credit cards. Mon–Sat 7am–7:30pm. Turn right at the traffic light near MM 30.5. Stay in the left lane.

No Name Pub PUB FOOD/PIZZA   This funky old bar out in the boonies serves snacks and sandwiches until 11pm on most nights, and drinks until midnight. Pizzas are tasty—thick-crusted and supercheesy. Try one topped with local shrimps, or consider a bowl of chili with all the fixings—hearty and cheap. Also decent is the smoked fish dip. Everything is served on paper plates. Locals hang out at the rustic bar, one of the Florida Keys' oldest, drinking beer and listening to a jukebox heavy with 1980s selections. The decor, if you can call it that, is basic—the walls and ceilings are plastered with thousands of autographed dollar bills.

¼ mile south of No Name Bridge on N. Watson Blvd., Big Pine Key. © **305/872-9115.** Pizzas $6–$18; subs $5. MC, V. 11am–11pm. Turn right at Big Pine's only traffic light (near MM 30.5) onto Key Deer Blvd. Turn right on Watson Blvd. At stop sign, turn left. Look for a small wooden sign on the left marking the spot.

THE LOWER KEYS AFTER DARK

Although the mellow islands of the lower Keys aren't exactly known for wild nightlife, there are some friendly bars and restaurants where locals and tourists gather to hang out and drink.

One of the most scenic is **Sandbar** (© **305/872-9989**), a wide-open breezy wooden house built on slender stilts and overlooking a wide channel on Barry Avenue (near MM 28.5). It attracts an odd mix of bikers and blue-hairs daily from 11am until 10pm and is a great place to overhear local gossip and colorful

The Truth About Keys Cuisine

There are few world-class chefs in the Florida Keys, but that's not to say the food isn't great. Restaurants here serve very fresh fish and a few local specialties—most notably conch fritters and chowder, Key lime pie, and stone crab claws and lobster when they're in season.

Although a commercial net-fishing ban has diminished the stock of once-abundant fish in these parts, even the humblest of restaurants can be counted on to take full advantage of the gastronomic treasures of their own backyard. The Keys have everything a cook could want: the Atlantic and the Gulf of Mexico for impeccably fresh seafood; a tropical climate for year-round farm stand produce, including great tomatoes, beans, berries, and citrus fruit; and a freshwater swamp for rustic delicacies such as alligator, frog legs, and hearts of palm.

Conch fritters and chowder are mainstays on most tourist-oriented menus. Because the queen conch was listed as an endangered species by the U.S. government in 1985, however, the conch in your dish was most likely shipped fresh-frozen from the Bahamas or the Caribbean.

Key lime pie consists of the juice of tiny yellow Key limes (a fruit unique to South Florida), along with condensed milk, all in a graham cracker crust. Experts debate whether the true Key lime pie should have a whipped cream or a meringue topping, but all agree that the filling should be yellow, *never* green.

Another unique offering, the **Florida lobster** is an entirely different species from the more common Maine variety and has a sweeter meat. It's also known as the "Spiney" lobster because of all the bumps on its shell. You'll see only the tails on the menu because the Florida lobster has no claws.

Stone crabs are even better—succulent, sweet, tender, and very meaty. They've been written about and talked about by kings, presidents, and poets. Although you'll find them on nearly every menu in season (from October until May), consider buying a few pounds of jumbos at the fish store to take to the beach in a cooler. Don't forget to ask to have them cracked for you, and get a cup of creamy mustard sauce. Topped off with a cold bottle of champagne, there is no better meal. You'll be glad to know that after their claws are harvested, the crabs grow new ones, thus ensuring a long-lasting supply of these unique delicacies.

metaphors. Pool tables are the main attraction, but there's also live music some nights. The drinks are reasonably priced, and the food isn't too bad, either. For another fun bar scene, see **No Name Pub,** listed above in "Where to Dine."

3 Key West ★★★

159 miles SW of Miami

The locals, or "conchs" (pronounced *conks*), and the developers here have been at odds for years. This once low-key island has been thoroughly commercialized—there's a Hard Rock Cafe smack in the middle of Duval Street and thousands of cruise ship passengers descending on Mallory Square each day. It's definitely not the seedy town Hemingway and his cronies once called their own.

Laid-back Key West still exists, but it's now found in different places: the backyard of a popular guest house, for example, or an art gallery, or a secret garden, or the hip hangouts of Bahama Village. Fortunately there are plenty of these, and Key West's greatest historic charm is found just off the beaten path. Don't be afraid to explore these residential areas, as conchs are notoriously friendly. Of course, there are always the calm waters of the Atlantic and the Gulf of Mexico all around.

The heart of town offers party people a good time. Here, you'll find good restaurants, fun bars, live music, rickshaw rides, and lots of shopping. Don't bother with a watch or tie—this is the home of the perennial vacation.

ESSENTIALS

GETTING THERE   For directions by car, see "Essentials," for the Upper and Middle Keys, above. Continue south on U.S. 1. When entering Key West, stay in the far-right lane onto North Roosevelt Boulevard, which becomes Truman Avenue in Old Town. Continue for a few blocks, and you will find yourself on Duval Street ⋆, in the heart of the city. If you stay to the left, you'll also reach the city center after passing the airport and the remnants of historic houseboat row, where a motley collection of boats once made up one of Key West's most interesting neighborhoods.

Several regional airlines fly nonstop from Miami to Key West; fares are about $120 to $300 round-trip. **American Eagle** (© 800/443-7300; www.aa.com) and **US Airways Express** (© 800/428-4322; www.usairways.com) land at **Key West International Airport,** South Roosevelt Boulevard (© 305/296-5439), on the southeastern corner of the island.

Greyhound (© 800/231-2222; www.greyhound.com) has buses leaving Miami for Key West every day for about $30 to $32 one-way and $57 to $60 round-trip. Seats fill up in season, so come early. The ride takes about 4½ hours.

GETTING AROUND   With limited parking, narrow streets, and congested traffic, driving in Old Town Key West is more of a pain than a convenience. Unless you're staying in one of the more remote accommodations, consider trading in the car for a bicycle. The island is small and as flat as a board, which makes it easy to negotiate, especially away from the crowded downtown. Many tourists also choose to cruise by moped, an option that can make navigating the streets risky, especially since there are no helmet laws in Key West. So be careful and spend the extra few bucks to rent a helmet; hundreds of visitors are seriously injured each year.

Rates for simple one-speed cruisers start at about $8 per day (from $40 per week). Mopeds start at about $12 for 2 hours, $25 per day, and $100 per week. The best shops include **The Bicycle Center** at 523 Truman Ave. (© 305/294-4556); the **Moped Hospital,** 601 Truman Ave. (© 305/296-3344); and **Tropical Bicycles & Scooter Rentals** at 1300 Duval St. (© 305/294-8136). **The Bike Shop,** 1110 Truman Ave. (© 305/294-1073), rents mountain bikes for $12 per day ($60 per week). Cruisers go for $8 per day and $40 per week. A $150 deposit is required for cruisers, $250 for mountain bikes.

PARKING   Parking in Key West's Old Town is particularly limited. There is a well-placed **municipal parking lot** at Simonton and Angela streets just behind the firehouse and police station. If you have brought a car, you may want to stash it here while you enjoy the very walkable downtown section of Key West.

Key West

ACCOMMODATIONS

Abaco Inn **30**
Angelina Guest House **27**
The Brass Key **3**
Chelsea House **10**
The Grand **4**
Island City House Hotel **6**
Key West Hilton Resort & Marina **21**
Key West International Hostel **11**
La Pensione **9**
Marquesa Hotel **14**
Oasis **7**
Ocean Key Resort **18**
Pier House Resort & Caribbean Spa **17**
Rainbow House **15**
South Beach Oceanfront Motel **32**
Southernmost Point Guest House **31**
Weatherstation Inn **12**
Wyndam Beach Resort **16**

ATTRACTIONS

Aquarium **19**
Audubon House & Tropical Gardens **26**
Cemetery **8**
Chamber of Commerce **22**
East Martello Museum and Gallery **1**
Ernest Hemingway Home and Museum **28**
Fort Zachary Beach **33**
Harry S. Truman
    Little White House Museum **13**
Higgs Beach **5**
Lighthouse Museum **29**
Mallory Square **20**
Mel Fisher Maritime Heritage Museum **24**
Memorial Sculpture Garden **23**
Oldest House/Wrecker's Museum **25**
Smathers Beach **2**

VISITOR INFORMATION The **Florida Keys and Key West Visitors Bureau,** P.O. Box 1147, Key West, FL 33041 (© **800/FLA-KEYS;** www. keywest.com), offers a free vacation kit packed with visitor information. The **Key West Chamber of Commerce,** 402 Wall St., Key West, FL 33040 (© **800/ 527-8539** or 305/294-2587; www.keywestchamber.com), also offers both general and specialized information. The lobby is open daily from 8:30am to 6pm; phones are answered from 8am to 8pm. The **Key West Visitors Center** also provides information on accommodations, goings-on, and restaurants; the number is © **800/LAST-KEY.** It's open weekdays from 8am to 5:30pm and weekends from 8:30am to 5pm. Gay travelers will want to call the **Key West Business Guild** (© **305/294-4603**), which represents more than 50 guest houses and B&Bs in town, as well as many other gay-owned businesses. Ask for its color brochure. Or try **Good Times Travel** (© **305/294-0980**), which will set up lodging and package tours on the island.

ORIENTATION A mere 2-by-4-mile island, Key West is simple to navigate, even though there is no real order to the arrangement of streets and avenues. As you enter town on U.S. 1 (also called Roosevelt Boulevard), you will see most of the moderately priced chain hotels and fast-food restaurants. The better restaurants, shops, and outfitters are crammed onto Duval Street, the main thoroughfare of Key West's Old Town. On surrounding streets are the many inns and lodges in picturesque Victorian/Bahamian homes. On the southern side of the island is the coral beach area and some of the larger resort hotels.

The area called Bahama Village has only recently become known to tourists. With several cool restaurants and guest houses opened over the years, this hippie-ish neighborhood, complete with street-roaming chickens and cats, is the most urban and rough you'll find in the Keys. You might see a few seedy drug dealings on street corners, but it's nothing to be overly concerned with. Resident business owners tend to keep a vigilant eye on the neighborhood. It looks worse than it is. It's actually quite funky and a welcome diversion from the Duvalian mainstream.

SEEING THE SIGHTS

Before shelling out big bucks for any of the dozens of worthwhile attractions in Key West, I recommend getting an overview on either of the two comprehensive island tours, **The Conch Tour Train** or the **Old Town Trolley** (see "Organized Tours," below). There are simply too many attractions to list (including a Ripley's Believe It or Not! on Duval Street) and a number of historic houses. I've highlighted my favorites below but encourage you to seek out others.

Audubon House & Tropical Gardens 🐱🐱 This well-preserved home, dating from the early 19th century, stands as a prime example of early Key West architecture. Named after renowned painter and bird expert John James Audubon, who was said to have visited the house in 1832, the graceful two-story home is a peaceful retreat from the bustle of Old Town. Included in the price of admission is a self-guided audio tour that lasts about half an hour. With voices of several characters from the house's past, the tour never gets boring—although it is at times a bit hokey. See rare Audubon prints, gorgeous antiques, historical photos, and lush tropical gardens. Even if you don't want to spend the time and money to explore the grounds and home, check out the impressive gift shop, which sells a variety of fine mementos at reasonable prices.

205 Whitehead St. (between Greene and Caroline sts.) 🕿 **305/294-2116.** Admission $8.50 adults, $3.50 children 6–12. Daily 9:30am–5pm (last admission at 4:45pm). Discounts for students and AAA and AARP members.

Ernest Hemingway Home and Museum 🐱🐱🐱 Hemingway's particularly handsome stone Spanish Colonial house, built in 1851, was one of the first on the island to be fitted with indoor plumbing and a built-in fireplace, and it contains the first swimming pool built on Key West. The author owned the home from 1931 until his death in 1961, and he lived there with about 50 cats, whose descendants, including the famed six-toed cats, still roam the premises. It was during those years that the Nobel Prize winner wrote some of his most famous works, including *For Whom the Bell Tolls, A Farewell to Arms,* and *The Snows of Kilimanjaro.* Fans may want to take the optional half-hour tour. It's interesting and included in the price of admission. If you're feline phobic, however, beware: There are cats everywhere.

907 Whitehead St. (between Truman Ave. and Olivia St.) 🕿 **305/294-1575** or 305/294-1136. Fax 305/294-2755. www.hemingwayhome.com. Admission $9 adults, $5 children. Daily 9am–5pm. Limited parking.

Harry S. Truman Little White House Museum ☆☆ President Harry Truman used to refer to the White House as the "Great White Jail." On temporary leave from the big house, Truman discovered the serenity of Key West and made his escape to what became known as the Little White House, which is open to the public for touring. The house is fully restored, and the exhibits document Truman's time in the Keys. Tours are every 20 minutes.

111 Front St., Key West. ℂ305/294-9911. www.trumanlittlewhitehouse.com. Admission $8 adults, $4 children under 12. Daily 9am–5pm.

Key West Cemetery ☆☆☆ *Finds* This funky, picturesque cemetery is the epitome of the quirky Key West image, as irreverent as it is humorous. Many tombs are stacked several high, condominium style—the rocky soil made digging 6 feet under nearly impossible for early settlers. Headstones reflect residents' lighthearted attitudes toward life and death. I TOLD YOU I WAS SICK is one of the more famous epitaphs, as is the tongue-in-cheek widow's inscription AT LEAST I KNOW WHERE HE'S SLEEPING TONIGHT.

Entrance at Margaret and Angela sts. ℂ 305/294-WALK for tour reservations. Free admission. Daily dawn to dusk.

East Martello Museum and Gallery Adjacent to the airport, the East Martello Museum is located in a Civil War–era brick fort that itself is worth a visit. The museum contains a bizarre variety of exhibits that collectively do a thorough job of interpreting the city's intriguing past. Historical artifacts include model ships, a deep-sea diver's wooden air pump, a crude raft from a Cuban "boat lift," a supposedly haunted doll, a Key West–style children's playhouse from 1918, and a horse-drawn hearse. Exhibits illustrate the Keys' history of salvaging, sponging, and cigar making. After seeing the galleries, climb a steep spiral staircase to the top of a lookout tower for good views over the island and ocean.

> **Impressions**
>
> *I've a notion to move the Capitol to Key West and just stay.*
> —President Harry S. Truman

3501 S. Roosevelt Blvd. ℂ 305/296-3913. Admission $6 adults, $4 seniors, $3 children 8–12, free for children 7 and under. Daily 9:30am–5pm (last admission is at 4pm).

Key West Aquarium ☆☆ *Kids* The oldest attraction on the island, the Key West Aquarium is a modest but fascinating exhibit. A long hallway of eye-level displays showcase dozens of varieties of fish and crustaceans. See delicate sea horses swaying in the backlit tanks. Kids can touch sea cucumbers and sea anemones in a shallow tank in the entryway. If you can, catch one of the free guided tours where you can witness the dramatic feeding frenzy of the sharks, tarpon, barracudas, stingrays, and turtles.

1 Whitehead St. (at Mallory Sq.) ℂ 305/296-2051. www.keywestaquarium.com. Admission $8 adults, $4 children 4–12, free for children under 4. Tickets are good for 2 consecutive days. Look for discount coupons at local hotels, at Duval St. kiosks, and from trolley and train tours. Daily 10am–6pm; tours at 11am, 1pm, 3pm, and 4pm.

Key West Lighthouse Museum ☆ When the Key West Lighthouse opened in 1848, many locals mourned. Its bright warning to ships signaled the end of a profitable era for wreckers, the pirate salvagers who looted reef-stricken ships. The story of this and other Keys lighthouses is illustrated in a small museum

Going, Going, Gone: Where to Catch the Famous Key West Sunset

A tradition in Key West, the Sunset Celebration can be relaxing or overwhelming, depending on your vantage point. If you're in town, you must check out this ritual at least once. Every evening, locals and visitors gather at the docks behind Mallory Square (at the westernmost end of Whitehead Street) to celebrate the day gone by. Secure a spot on the docks early to experience the carnival of portrait artists, acrobats, food vendors, animal acts, and other performers trading on the island's Bohemian image. But the carnival atmosphere isn't for everyone: Hold onto your bags and wallets as the tight crowds make Mallory Square at sunset prime pick-pocketing territory. In season, the crowd can be overwhelming, especially when the cruise ships are in port.

A better choice is the Hilton's **Sunset Deck** (© 305/294-4000), a luxurious bar on top of its restaurant at the intersection of Front and Greene streets. From the civilized calm of a casual bar, you can look down on the mayhem with a drink in hand.

Also near the Mallory madness is the **Ocean Key House's** bar. This long open-air pier serves up drinks and decent bar food against a dramatic pink- and yellow-streaked sky. It's located at the very tip of Duval Street (© **800/328-9815** or 305/296-7701).

For the very best potent cocktails and great bar food on an outside patio or enclosed lounge, try **Pier House's Havana Docks** at 1 Duval St. (© **305/296-4600**). There's usually live music and a lively gathering of visitors enjoying this island's bounty.

---

that was formerly the keeper's quarters. When radar and sonar made the lighthouse obsolete, it was opened to visitors as a tourist attraction. It's worth mustering the energy to climb the 88 claustrophobic steps to the top, where you'll be rewarded with magnificent panoramic views of Key West and the ocean.

938 Whitehead St. © **305/294-0012.** Admission $6 adults, $2 children 7–12, free for children 6 and under. Daily 9:30am–5pm (last admission at 4:30pm).

Key West's Shipwreck Historeum   You'll see more-impressive artifacts at nearby Mel Fisher's museum, but the dramatic reenactments of the old shipwrecking days at this place are unique and entertaining. The interactive show is best for teens and adults and includes scenes starring Key West's wealthiest wrecker Asa Tift, plus lots of intriguing video clips and stories of the area's heyday.

1 Whitehead St. (at Mallory Sq.) © **305/292-8990.** Fax 305/292-5536. Admission $8 adults, $4 children 4–12. Shows daily every half-hour 9:45am–4:45pm.

Mel Fisher Maritime Heritage Museum ★★★   This museum honors local hero Mel Fisher, whose death in 1998 was mourned throughout South Florida, and who, along with a crew of other salvagers, found a multimillion-dollar treasure trove in 1985 aboard the wreck of the Spanish galleon *Nuestra Señora de Atocha*. The admission price is somewhat steep, but if you're into diving, pirates, and sunken treasures, check out this small informative museum, full of doubloons, pieces of eight, emeralds, and solid-gold bars. A 1700 English merchant slave ship, the only tangible evidence of the transatlantic slave trade, is on view on the museum's second floor. A dated but informative film provides a good background for Fisher's incredible story.

200 Greene St. ℂ **305/294-2633.** Admission $6.50 adults, $2 children 6–12, free for children 5 and under. Daily 9:30am–5pm. Take U.S. 1 to Whitehead St. and turn left on Greene.

Memorial Sculpture Garden 𝄢   Installed in 1997, this impressive sculpture garden contains a large monument to the wreckers who made Key West rich more than a century ago. Also on display are 36 bronze busts of the island's most colorful leaders and characters. There's Harry Truman, Henry Flagler, and, of course, Ernest Hemingway, all mounted on elegant coral columns.

Mallory Sq. between Whitehead and Wall sts. Free admission.

Oldest House/Wrecker's Museum 𝄢   Dating from 1829, this old New England Bahama House has survived pirates, hurricanes, fires, warfare, and economic ups and downs—it gives witness to a slower, easier time in the island's life. The 1½-story home was designed by a ship's carpenter and incorporates many features from maritime architecture, including portholes and a ship's hatch designed for ventilation before the advent of air-conditioning. Especially interesting is the detached kitchen building outfitted with a brick "beehive" oven and vintage cooking utensils. Although not a must-see on the Key West tour, history and architecture buffs will appreciate the finely preserved details.

322 Duval St. ℂ **305/294-9502.** Admission $5 adults; $1 children 6–12; free for children 5 and under. Daily 10am–4pm.

ORGANIZED TOURS

BY TROLLEY-BUS & TRAM   Yes, it's more than a bit hokey to sit on this 60-foot tram of yellow cars, but it's worth it—at least once. The city's whole story is packed into a neat, 90-minute package on the **Conch Tour Train,** which covers the island and all its rich, raunchy history. Operating since 1958, the trains are open-air, which can make the ride uncomfortable in bad weather. The "train's" engine is a propane-powered Jeep disguised as a locomotive. Tours depart from both Mallory Square and the Welcome Center, near where U.S. 1 becomes North Roosevelt Boulevard, on the other side of the island. For more

---

⌒ *Moments* **A Great Escape**

Many people complain that Key West's quirky, quaint panache has been lost to the vulture of capitalism, evidenced in the glut of T-shirt shops and tacky bars. But that's not entirely so. For a quiet respite, visit the Key West Botanical Gardens, a little-known slice of serenity tucked between the Aqueduct Authority plant and the Key West Golf Course. The 11-acre gardens—maintained by volunteers and funded by donations—contain the last hardwood hammock in Key West, plus a colorful representation of wildflowers, butterflies, and birds. A genetically cloned tree is the latest addition to the gardens. Although the gardens received a terrible blow from the storms of 1998, the calm remains within them. Botanical Garden Way and College Rd., Stock Island. Free admission. Daily 8am–sunset. Follow College Rd.; then turn right just past Bayshore Manor.

---

information, contact the **Conch** at (© **305/294-5161**). The cost is $18 for adults, $9 for children 4 to 12, and free for children 3 and under. Daily departures are every half-hour from 9am to 4:30pm.

The **Old Town Trolley** is the choice in bad weather or if you are staying at one of the many hotels on its route. Humorous drivers maintain a running commentary as the enclosed tram loops around the island's streets past all the major sights. Trolleys depart from Mallory Square and other points around the island, including many area hotels. For details, call © **305/296-6688.** Tours are $18 for adults, $9 for children 4 to 12, and free for children 3 and under. Departures are daily every half-hour (though not always on the half-hour) from 9am to 4:45pm. Whichever you choose, these historic trivia-packed tours are well worth the price of admission.

BY AIR   Proclaimed by the mayor as "the official air force of the Conch Republic," **Island Airplane Tours,** at Key West Airport, 3469 S. Roosevelt Blvd. (© **305/294-8687**), offers windy rides in its open-cockpit 1940 Waco biplanes that take you over the reefs and around the islands. Thrill seekers—and only they—will also enjoy a spin in the company's S2-B aerobatics airplane, which does loops, rolls, and sideways figure-eights. Company owner Fred Cabanas was "decorated" in 1991, after he spotted a Cuban airman defecting to the United States in a Russian-built MIG fighter. Sightseeing flights cost $50 to $200, depending on the duration.

BY BOAT   The Pride of Key West, *Fireball,* at Zero Duval St. (© **305/296-6293;** fax 305/294-8704), is a 58-foot glass-bottomed catamaran that goes on both day and evening coral-reef tours and sunset cruises. Reef trips cost $20 per person; sunset cruises (4:30pm) are $25 per person and include snacks, sodas, and a glass of champagne. Kids sail for half-price.

The Wolf, at Schooner Wharf, Key West Seaport (© **305/296-9653;** fax 305/294-8388), is a 44-passenger topsail schooner, equipped with a cannon, that sets sail daily for daytime and sunset cruises around the Keys. Key West Seaport is located at the end of Greene Street. Day tours cost $35 per person (six people or more only); sunset sails cost $40 per person and include free champagne, wine, beer, soda, and live music.

Schooner Western Union (© **305/292-9830**) was built in 1939 and served as a cable-repair vessel until it was designated the flagship of the city of Key West

---

Parrotheads on Parade

For Jimmy Buffett fans, or Parrotheads as they're also known, there's a fabulous tour that shouldn't be missed. **Trails of Margaritaville (© 305/292-2040)** is an amusing 90-minute walking tour providing fans with an officially sanctioned peek at the stomping grounds of Buffett's carefree days in Key West back in the 1970s. Decked out in full Parrothead regalia—Hawaiian shirts and parrot hats—the informative and often hilarious guides lead you past the hangouts and other highpoints of Buffett's Key West, spinning yarns about the musician, and Key West in general. The tour departs daily at 4pm from **Captain Tony's Saloon** (428 Greene St.), where Buffett used to hang out and perform, and ends at, you guessed it, Margaritaville Cafe on Duval Street. Tour tickets are $18 for adults, $15 for locals with ID, and $10 for children. Bring cash or traveler's checks; no credit cards accepted. Reservations are required.

and began day, sunset, and charter sailings. Sunset sailings are especially memorable and include entertainment, cocktails, and a cannon fire. Prices vary.

OTHER TOURS   For a lively look at Key West, try a 2-hour tour of the island's five **most famous pubs.** It starts daily at 2:30pm, lasts 1½ hours, costs $21, and includes four drinks. Another fun tour is the 1-mile, 90-minute **nightly ghost tour,** leaving at 8pm from the Holiday Inn La Concha, 430 Duval St. Cost is $18 for adults and $10 for children under 12. This spooky and interesting tour gives participants insight into the many old island legends. Both tours are offered by the Key West Tour Association. Finally, there's a cemetery tour, which leaves daily at 10:30am (© **305/294-WALK**).

OUTDOOR PURSUITS

BICYCLING & MOPEDING   A popular mode of transportation for locals and visitors, bikes and mopeds are available at many rental outlets in the city (see "Getting Around," above). Escape the hectic downtown scene and explore the island's scenic side streets. Head away from Duval Street to South Roosevelt Boulevard and the beachside enclaves along the way.

BEACHES   Unlike the rest of the Keys, you'll actually find a few small beaches here, although they don't compare with the state's wide natural wonders up the coast. A narrow rocky beach is typical of the Key's beaches. Here are your options: **Smathers Beach,** off South Roosevelt Boulevard west of the airport; **Higgs Beach,** along Atlantic Boulevard between White Street and Reynolds Road; and **Fort Zachary Beach,** located off the western end of Southard Boulevard.

A magnet for partying teenagers, Smathers Beach is Key West's largest and most overpopulated beach. It was renovated in the spring of 2000 due to erosion and hurricane damage. It looks lovely. Despite the number of rowdy teens, the beach is actually quite clean. If you go early enough in the morning, you may notice some people sleeping on the beach from the night before.

Higgs Beach is a favorite among Key West's gay crowds, but what many people don't know is that beneath the sand is an unmarked cemetery of African slaves who died while waiting for freedom. Higgs has a playground and tennis courts and is near the minute Rest Beach, which is actually hidden by the White Street Pier.

Although there is an entrance fee ($3.75 per car, plus more for each passenger), I recommend Fort Zachary, since it also includes a great historical fort, a Civil War museum, and a large picnic area with tables, barbecue grills, bathrooms, and showers. Plus, large trees scattered across 87 acres provide shade for those who are reluctant to bake in the sun. The vulnerable point was damaged by Hurricane George in 1998, but replanting of native vegetation has made it better than before.

DIVING   One of the area's largest scuba schools, **Dive Key West Inc.,** 3128 N. Roosevelt Blvd. (© **800/426-0707** or 305/296-3823; fax 305/296-0609; www.divekeywest.com), offers instruction on all levels. Its dive boats take participants to scuba and snorkel sites on nearby reefs.

Wreck dives and night dives are two of the special offerings of **Lost Reef Adventures,** 261 Margaret St. (© **800/952-2749** or 305/296-9737). Regularly scheduled runs and private charters can be arranged. Phone for departure information.

FISHING   As any angler will tell you, there's no fishing like Keys fishing. Key West has it all: bonefish, tarpon, dolphin, tuna, grouper, cobia, and more. Sharks, too.

Tips **Reel Deals**

When looking for the best deals on fishing excursions, know that the bookers from the kiosks in town generally take 20% of a captain's fee in addition to an extra monthly fee. You can usually save yourself money by booking directly with a captain or going straight to one of the docks.

Step aboard a small exposed skiff for an incredibly diverse day of fishing. In the morning, you can head offshore for sailfish or dolphin (the fish, not the mammal), and then by afternoon, get closer to land for a shot at tarpon, permit, grouper, or snapper. Here in Key West, you can probably pick up more cobia—one of the best fighting and eating fish around—than anywhere else in the world. For a real fight, ask your skipper to go for the tarpon—the greatest fighting fish there is, famous for its dramatic "tail walk" on the water after it's hooked. Shark fishing is also popular.

You'll find plenty of competition among the charter fishing boats in and around Mallory Square. You can negotiate a good deal at **Charter Boat Row,** 1801 N. Roosevelt Ave. (across from the Shell station), home to more than 30 charter fishing and party boats. Just show up to arrange your outing, or call **Garrison Bite Marina** (© 305/292-8167) for details.

The advantage of the smaller, more expensive charter boats is that you can call the shots. They'll take you where you want to go, to fish for what you want to catch. These "light tackles" are also easier to maneuver, which means you can go to backcountry spots for tarpon and bonefish, as well as out to the open ocean for tuna and dolphin. You'll really be able to feel the fish, and you'll get some good fights. Larger boats, for up to six or seven people, are cheaper and best for kingfish, billfish, and sailfish. Consider Captain Vinnie Argiro's **Heavy Hitters Charters** (© 305/745-6665) if you want a light-tackle experience. For a larger boat, try Captain Henry Otto's 44-foot *Sunday,* docked at the Hyatt in Key West (© 305/294-7052).

The huge commercial party boats are more for sightseeing than serious angling, though you can get lucky and get a few bites at one of the fishing holes. One especially good deal is the *Gulfstream III* (© 305/296-8494), an all-day charter that goes out daily from 9:30am until 4pm. You'll pay $35, plus $3 for a rod and reel. This 65-foot party boat usually has at least 30 other anglers. Bring your own cooler or buy snacks on the boat. Beer and wine are allowed.

For serious anglers, nothing compares to the light-tackle boats that leave from **Oceanside Marina** (© 305/294-4676) on Stock Island, at 5950 Peninsula Ave., 1½ miles off U.S. 1. It's a 20-minute drive from Old Town on the Atlantic side. There are more than 30 light-tackle guides, which range from flatbed, backcountry skiffs to 28-foot open boats. There are also a few larger charters and a head or party boat that goes to the Dry Tortugas. Call the dockmaster for details.

For the light-tackle experience of your life, call **Captain Bruce Cronin** at © 305/294-4929 or **Captain Kenny Harris** at © 305/294-8843, two of the more famous (and pricey) captains still working these docks for over 20 years. You'll pay from $550 for a full day, usually about 8am until 4pm, and from $400 for half a day.

GOLF A relative newcomer in terms of local recreation, golf is gaining in popularity here as it is in many visitor destinations. One of the area's only courses is **Key West Golf Club** (© 305/294-5232), an 18-hole course located just north of the island of Key West at MM 4.5 (turn onto College Road to the course entrance). Designed by Rees Jones, the course has plenty of mangroves and water hazards on its 6,526 yards. It's open to the public and has a new pro shop. Call ahead for tee-time reservations. $125 per player, including cart.

KAYAKING   Mosquito Coast Outfitters, housed in a woodsy wine bar at 1017 Duval St. (© **305/294-7178**), operates a first-rate kayaking and snorkeling tour every day as long as the weather is mild. The tours depart at 9am sharp and cost $45 per person. Included in the price are snacks, soft drinks, and a guided tour of the mangrove-studded islands of Sugar Key or Geiger Key just north of Key West. You'll be back by about 3pm.

SHOPPING

You'll find all kinds of unique gifts and souvenirs in Key West, from coconut postcards to Key lime pies. On Duval Street, T-shirt shops outnumber almost any other business. If you must get a wearable memento, be careful of unscrupulous salespeople. Despite efforts to curtail the practice, many shops have been known to rip off unwitting shoppers. It pays to check the prices and the exchange rate before signing any sales slips. You are entitled to a written estimate of any T-shirt work before you pay for it.

At Mallory Square is the **Clinton Street Market,** an overly air-conditioned mall of kiosks and stalls designed for the many cruise-ship passengers who never venture beyond this supercommercial zone. Amid the dreck are some delicious coffee and candy shops and some high-priced hats and shoes. There's also a free and clean restroom.

Once the main industry of Key West, cigar making is enjoying renewed success at the handful of factories that survived the slow years. Stroll through **"Cigar Alley,"** between Front and Greene streets, where you will find *viejitos* (little old men) rolling fat stogies just as they used to do in their homeland across the Florida Straits. Stop at the **Key West Cigar Factory,** at 308 Front St. (© **305/294-3470**), for an excellent selection of imported and locally rolled smokes, including the famous El Hemingway. Remember, buying or selling Cuban-made cigars is illegal. Shops advertising "Cuban Cigars" are usually referring to domestic cigars made from tobacco grown from seeds that were brought from Cuba decades ago. To be fair, though, many premium cigars today are grown from Cuban seed tobacco—only it is grown in Latin America and the Caribbean, not Cuba.

If you are looking for local or Caribbean art, you will find nearly a dozen galleries and shops clustered on Duval Street between Catherine and Fleming streets. You'll also find some excellent shops scattered on the side streets. One

---

⌒ Fun Fact Conch If You Love Key West

Ever wonder how Key West got the nickname The Conch Republic? In 1982, the U.S. Border Patrol set up a roadblock on U.S. 1 to search for illegal aliens and drugs. This maneuver effectively slowed passage from the Keys to the mainland and damaged the economy (albeit temporarily). In response, Key West mayor Dennis Wardlow collaborated with five businessmen and established the so-called Conch Republic, declaring Key West's independence from—and war on—the U.S. The roadblock was removed, but the moniker stuck.

worth seeking out is the **Haitian Art Co.,** 600 Frances St. (© **305/296-8932**), where you can browse through room upon room of original paintings from well-known and obscure Haitian artists in a range of prices from a few dollars to a few thousand. Also, check out **Cuba, Cuba!** at 814 Duval St. (© **305/295-9442**). Here, you will find paintings, sculpture, and photos by Cuban artists, and books and art from the island.

A favorite stop in the Keys is the deliciously fragrant **Key West Aloe** at 524 Front St., between Simonton and Duval streets (© **305/294-5592**). Since 1971, this shop has been selling a simple line of bath products, including lotions, shampoos, and soothing balms for those who want a reminder of the tropical breezes once they're back home. At the main shop (open until 8pm), you can find great gift baskets, tropical perfumes, and candies and cookies, too. In addition to frangipani, vanilla, and hibiscus scents, sample Key West for Men, a unique and alluringly musky bestseller.

Literature and music buffs will appreciate the many bookshops and record stores on the island. **Key West Island Bookstore** (© **305/294-2904**) at 513 Fleming St. carries new, used, and rare books and specializes in fiction by residents of the Keys, including Hemingway, Tennessee Williams, Shel Silverstein, Ann Beattie, Richard Wilbur, and John Hersey. **Flaming Maggie's** (© **305/294-3931**) at 830 Fleming St. carries a wide selection of gay books. Both shops are open daily.

One of the area's newer and funkier shops is the combination museum and gift shop called **Reworx** just behind the quirky gift gallery **Pandemonium** and the mosaic car at 825 Duval St. (© **305/294-0351.** Actually, this is Pandemonium's number, but the owners are friends. For Reworx, ask for Valerie.) Mammoth functional art made from salvaged metal parts is on display, and smaller works from recycled material are on sale. Admission to the adjacent museum of industrial art from recycled items is $7 for adults, $5 for children aged 5 to 12, and well worth it.

Also worth checking out in the newly revitalized Bahama Village section of town are the shops along Petronia Street between Thomas and Whitehead streets. Especially interesting is **Maskerville** (© **305/293-6937**), which sells a variety of feather-laden artwork from masks to lampshades. Just next door is **Hello Gorgeous,** at 315 Petronia (© **305/294-1770**), which carries unique clothing, shoes, and jewelry for women and impersonators (the name comes from one of Barbra Streisand's more memorable lines).

Off the beaten track at 814 Fleming St. (© **305/294-7901**) is the **Helio Gallery Store,** featuring locally made crafts and fine art.

For anything else, from bed linens to candlesticks to clothing, go to downtown's oldest and most renowned department store, **Fast Buck Freddie's,** at 500 Duval St. (© **305/294-2007**). For the same merchandise at reduced prices, try **Half Buck Freddie's** ⊕, 726 Caroline St. (© **305/294-6799**). Here you can shop for out-of-season bargains and "rejects" from the main store.

WHERE TO STAY

You'll find a wide variety of places to stay in Key West, from resorts with all the amenities to seaside motels, quaint bed-and-breakfasts, and clothing-optional guest houses. Unless you're in town during Key West's most popular holidays—Fantasy Fest (around Halloween) where Mardi Gras meets South Florida for the NC-17 set, Hemingway Days (in July) where Papa is seemingly and eerily alive and well, and Christmas and New Year's—or for a big fishing tournament (many are held from October to December) or boat-racing tourney, you can almost always find a place to stay at the last minute. However, you may want to book early, especially in the winter, when prime properties fill up and many require 2- or 3-night minimums. Prices at these times are also extremely high. Finding a decent room for under $100 a night is a real trick.

Another suggestion is to call **Vacation Key West** (© **800/595-5397** or 305/295-9500; www.flakeysol.com/vkw). The phones are answered weekdays from 9am to 6pm and Saturday from 11am to 2pm. This wholesaler offers discounts of 20% to 30% and can usually find last-minute deals. They represent mostly larger hotels and motels but also can place visitors in guest houses. The **Key West Innkeepers Association,** P.O. Box 6172, Key West, FL 33041 (© **800/492-1911** or 305/292-3600), can also help find lodging in any price range from its dozens of members and affiliates.

Most major hotel chains have at least one location in Key West; most are clustered on North Roosevelt Boulevard (U.S. 1). Moderately priced options include **Howard Johnson,** 3031 N. Roosevelt Blvd. (© **800/942-0913** or 305/296-6595); the **Ramada Inn,** 3420 N. Roosevelt Blvd. (© **800/330-5541** or 305/294-5541); the **Econo Lodge,** 3820 N. Roosevelt Blvd. (© **800/ 553-2666** or 305294-5511); the **Holiday Inn Beachside,** 3841 N. Roosevelt Blvd. (© **800/292-7706** or 305/294-2571); and the **Quality Inn,** 3850 N. Roosevelt Blvd. (© **800/228-5151** or 305/294-6681). The Howard Johnson and the Holiday Inn are the only hotels with Gulf-view rooms; the other hotels listed are just across the street. Duval Street is less than 5 minutes away by car or taxi.

A last resort should be the **Holiday Inn La Concha Hotel** at 430 Duval St. (© **800/745-2191**). It is centrally located but has few amenities for the price.

Gay travelers will want to call the **Key West Business Guild** (© **305/ 294-4603**), which represents more than 50 guest houses and B&Bs in town, as well as many other gay-owned businesses. Be advised that most gay guest houses have a clothing-optional policy. One of the most elegant and popular ones is **Big Ruby's** (© **800/477-7829** or 305/296-2323) at 409 Applerouth Lane (a little alley just off Duval Street). A low cluster of buildings surrounds a lushly landscaped courtyard where a hearty breakfast is served each morning and wine is poured at dusk. The mostly male guests hang out by a good-sized pool, tanning in the buff. Also popular is **Oasis** at 823 Fleming St. (© **305/296-2131**), which is superclean and friendly, and you can enjoy the central location and a 14-seat hot tub.

Another luxurious property is **The Brass Key** at 412 Frances St. (© **305/ 296-4719**), which is more romantic and traditionally decorated and welcomes many lesbian travelers as well. *Out and About* gave it a five-star rating. For women only, the **Rainbow House,** 525 United St. (© **800/74-WOMYN** or 305/292-1450) is a large, fairly well-maintained guest house with lots of privacy and amenities, including two pools and two hot tubs. Rates in season range from $109 to $229.

VERY EXPENSIVE

Hilton Key West Resort and Marina 🐦🐦 Completed in fall 1996, this Hilton, which saw a light room renovation in 2001, is a truly luxurious addition to downtown's hotel scene, situated at the very end of Duval Street in the middle of all of Old Town's action. The sparkling rooms are large and well appointed, with tropical decor and all the modern conveniences. Choose a suite in the main building if you want a large Jacuzzi in your living room. Otherwise, the marina building has great views. The secluded beach is great for an escape from the Duval Street frenzy. This giant is very popular with corporate and convention visitors. Flagler's, the elegant indoor dining room, offers ample breakfasts and a huge Sunday brunch.

Hilton's gorgeous **Sunset Key Guest Cottages** ☆☆☆—whitewashed interiors, picture windows, fabulous views—are located 100 yards offshore on Sunset Key and are accessible only by private launch. Check in at the Hilton and take a 10-minute cruise to the island, where there are no cars, only a gourmet grocery, restaurant, bar, and free-form tropical pool with whirlpool jets. Sunset guests also have access to all watersports at the Hilton marina. Cottages are equipped with full kitchens, high-tech entertainment centers, and one, two, or three massive bedrooms. For true luxe, consider hiring a private chef for a meal or two.

245 Front St. (at the end of Duval St.), Key West, FL 33040. (C) **800/221-2424** or 305/294-4000. Fax 305/294-4086. www.keywestresort.hilton.com. 215 units. Winter $299–$525 double; $375–$800 suite. Off-season $195–$425 double; $300–$800 suite. 37 Sunset Key Cottages, up to 5 people: winter $575–$1,825; off-season $325–$1,095. Private chef: $75 per person plus add'l chef/hotel fees, tax, and gratuities. AE, DC, DISC, MC, V. Self parking $7, valet parking $10. **Amenities:** 2 restaurants, pool bar, outdoor heated pool, health club, Jacuzzi, watersports equipment/rental, full-service marina, bike rental, game room, concierge, business center, limited room service; in-room massage; dry-cleaning service, self-service laundry. *In room:* A/C, TV, dataport, minibar, coffeemaker, hair dryer, iron.

Pier House Resort and Caribbean Spa ☆☆☆

Pier House is one of the area's best resort choices, offering luxurious rooms, top-notch service, and a full-service spa. If you're looking for something a bit more intimate than the Wyndham Reach, Pier House is an ideal choice. Its location—at the foot of Duval Street and just steps from Mallory Docks—is the envy of every hotel on the island. Set back from the busy street, on a short strip of beach, this hotel is a welcome oasis of calm. The accommodations here vary tremendously, from relatively simple business-style rooms to romantic guest quarters complete with integrated stereo systems and whirlpool tubs. Their best waterfront suites and rooms have recently been renovated. Although every accommodation has either a balcony or a patio, not all overlook the water. My favorites, in the two-story spa building, don't have any view at all. But what they lack in scenery, they make up for in opulence; each well-appointed spa room has a sitting area and a huge Jacuzzi bathroom.

1 Duval St. (near Mallory Docks), Key West, FL 33040. (C) **800/327-8340** or 305/296-4600. Fax 305/296-9085. www.pierhouse.com. 142 units. Winter $290–$460 double; off-season $200–$355 double. AE, DC, DISC, MC, V. **Amenities:** 3 restaurants, 4 bars; heated swimming pool; health club ($10 per day) and spa treatments; 2 Jacuzzis; sauna; watersports equipment/rentals; bike rental; concierge; limited room service; in-room massage; babysitting; laundry services. *In room:* A/C, TV, dataport, minibar, coffeemaker, hair dryer.

Wyndham Casa Marina Resort ☆☆ (Kids)

Located on Kokomo Beach, Key West's largest private beach, the Casa Marina Resort is one of the island's most desirable. La Casa Marina (as it was called before it became a Wyndham property) was built in 1921 at the very end of the now defunct Florida East Coast Railway Line by the heirs of railroad tycoon Henry Flagler. The setting couldn't be more idyllic, and to further complement its surroundings, the hotel itself is luxurious with beamed ceilings, polished pine floors, and French Provincial furniture. Rooms are comfortable and soothing in Caribbean decor; the best ones are those with oceanfront balconies or French doors overlooking the oceanfront lawn. The pools are gorgeous with stunning views of the Atlantic. Families love the Casa Marina for its Kid's Retreat, which runs Thursday through Sunday and offers full- and half-day programs ($35 full day; $25 half-day). Evening activities are available for the whole family.

1500 Reynolds St., Key West, FL 33040 ✆800/626-0777 or 305/296-3535. www.casamarinakeywest.com. 311 units. Winter $199–$749; off-season $169–$669. AE, MC, DC, DISC, MC, V. From Key West International Airport, go west on Roosevelt Blvd. 1 mile to Atlantic Blvd. and turn left. Go 1 mile to Reynolds St. and turn right. Hotel is on left. **Amenities:** 2 restaurants, 2 outdoor pools, lighted tennis court, exercise room, sauna, watersports equipment/rental, bike/moped rental, children's programs, concierge, tour desk, courtesy airport transportation, massage, babysitting. *In room:* A/C, TV, coffeemaker, hair dryer.

Wyndham Reach Resort 🐦🐦 Unlike Wyndham's Casa Marina resort, the Reach is better suited to adults only and not families. The location here can be either a highlight or a drawback; it's a 5-minute walk away from the center of the Duval Street action. Supported by stilts that leave the entire ground floor for car parking, the hotel offers four floors of rooms designed around atriums. The wonderful guest rooms are large and feature tile floors, sturdy wicker furnishings, and tropical colors. Each has a vanity area separate from the bathroom. The rooms are so nice you can easily forgive the small closets and diminutive dressers. All have sliding glass doors that open onto balconies, and some have ocean views. The grounds are amply planted with palms and surround a small pool area. There's also a private pier for fishing and tanning. The protected waters are tame and shallow.

1435 Simonton St., Key West, FL 33040. ✆ 800/626-0777. For reservations ✆ 800/996-3426. Fax 305/296-4633. www.wyndham.com/reachresort. 150 units. Winter $259–$709 single or double. Off-season $149–$589 single or double. AE, DC, DISC, MC, V. Valet parking: $9.50. **Amenities:** 2 restaurants, bar, outdoor heated swimming pool, nearby tennis and golf, health club and spa, watersports equipment/rental, bike rental, concierge, tour desk, business center, salon, room service, in-room massage, babysitting, dry cleaning. *In room:* A/C, TV, minibar, fridge, coffeemaker.

EXPENSIVE

Island City House Hotel 🐦🐦 A small resort unto itself, the Island City House consists of three separate and unique buildings that share a common junglelike patio and pool. The first building, unimaginatively called the Island City House building, is a historic three-story wooden structure with wraparound verandas that allow guests to walk around the entire edifice on any floor. The warmly dressed old-fashioned interiors here include wood floors and many antique furnishings. Many rooms have full-size kitchens, queen-size beds, and sumptuous floral window treatments. The tile bathrooms could use more counter space, and the room lighting isn't always perfect, but eccentricities are part of this hotel's charm.

The unpainted wooden Cigar House has particularly large bedrooms, similar in ambience to those in the Island City House. Most rooms are furnished with wicker chairs and king-size beds and have big bathrooms (although lacking in counter space). The Arch House is the least appealing of the three buildings, but still recommended. Built of Dade County pine, the Arch House's cozy bedrooms are furnished in wicker and rattan and come with small kitchens and bathrooms.

411 William St., Key West, FL 33040. ✆ 800/634-8230 or 305/294-5702. Fax 305/294-1289. www. islandcityhouse.com. 24 units. Winter $175–$315; off-season $115–$210. Rates include breakfast. AE, DC, DISC, MC, V. **Amenities:** Outdoor heated pool, Jacuzzi, access to nearby health club, bike rental, concierge, in-room massage, babysitting, dry-cleaning and laundry services, self-service laundromat. *In room:* A/C, TV, coffeemaker, hair dryer.

Marquesa Hotel ☆☆☆ *Finds* The Marquesa offers the charm of a small historic hotel coupled with the amenities of a large resort. It encompasses four buildings, two swimming pools, and a three-stage waterfall that cascades into a lily pond. Two of the hotel's houses are luxuriously restored Victorian homes whose rooms are outfitted with extraplush antiques and oversize contemporary furniture. The rooms in the two other, newly constructed, buildings are even richer; many have four-poster wrought-iron beds with bright floral spreads. The green marble bathrooms are lush and spacious. The decor is simple, elegant, and spotless. These are the only hotel rooms I have ever seen that I would love to have in my own home. The hotel also boasts one of Key West's most elegant restaurants, The Cafe Marquesa.

600 Fleming St. (at Simonton St.), Key West, FL 33040. ℂ 800/869-4631 or 305/292-1919. Fax 305/294-2121. www.marquesa.com. 27 units. Winter $260–$395 double; off-season $170–$285 double. No children under 12. AE, DC, MC, V. **Amenities:** Restaurant, 2 outdoor swimming pools (1 is heated), access to nearby health club, bike rental, concierge, limited room service. *In room:* A/C, TV, dataport, minibar, hair dryer.

Ocean Key Resort ☆ You can't get much more central than this modern hotel, located across from the Pier House at the foot of Duval Street. Beyond its location, however, it's rather lackluster. Most of the guest rooms here are suites, ample-sized accommodations fitted with built-in couches. However, some of the rooms are closetlike, so ask to see your accommodations first. Many rooms have sliding glass doors that open onto small balconies, some of which enjoy unobstructed water views. All suites have Jacuzzi tubs in either the master bedroom or living room.

Zero Duval St., Key West, FL 33040. ℂ 800/328-9815 or 305/296-7701. Fax 305/292-7685. www. oceankeyhouse.com. 99 units. Winter from $289–$549 2-bedroom suite; off-season $199–$449 2-bedroom suite. AE, DC, DISC, MC, V. **Amenities:** 2 restaurants, outdoor heated pool, access to nearby health club, watersports equipment/rental, concierge, tour desk, room service, dry-cleaning and laundry services. *In room:* A/C, TV, VCRs and video rentals available upon request, minibar.

Weatherstation Inn ☆ Originally built in 1912 as a weather station, this beautifully restored and meticulously maintained two-story, Renaissance-style inn is located just 2 blocks from Duval Street. It's situated on the tropical grounds of the former Old Navy Yard, now an exclusive and very private gated community. Harry Truman, Eisenhower, and J.F.K. have all visited the station. Spacious and uncluttered, each room is uniquely furnished to complement the interior architecture: hardwood floors, tall sash windows, and high ceilings. The large modern bathrooms are especially appealing. Enjoy a complimentary continental breakfast by the pool among the flowers. The staff is friendly and accommodating.

57 Front St., Key West, FL 33040. ℂ 800/815-2707 or 305/294-7277. Fax 305/294-0544. www. weatherstationinn.com. 8 units. Winter $195–$315 double; off-season $150–$215 double. Rates include continental breakfast. AE, MC, V. **Amenities:** Outdoor pool, concierge. *In room:* A/C, TV, dataport, hair dryer.

MODERATE

Chelsea House ☆ Despite its decidedly English name, the Chelsea House is "all American," a term that in Key West isn't code for "conservative." Chelsea House caters to a mixed gay/straight clientele and displays its liberal philosophy most prominently on the clothing-optional sundeck. One of only a few guest houses in Key West that offer TVs, VCRs, private bathrooms, and kitchenettes in each guest room, Chelsea House has a large number of repeat visitors. The apartments come with full kitchens and separate living areas, as well as palm-shaded balconies in back. The bathrooms and closets could be bigger, but both are adequate and serviceable. When weather permits, which is almost always, breakfast is served outside by the pool.

707 Truman Ave., Key West, FL 33040. (© **800/845-8859** or 305/296-2211. Fax 305/296-4822. www. chelseahousekw.com. 20 units. Winter $130–$229 double; off-season $85–$135 double. Rates include breakfast. AE, DC, DISC, MC, V. Private parking. Children 14 and under not accepted. Pets accepted; $15 per night. **Amenities:** Outdoor pool, access to nearby health club, bike rental, concierge, *In room:* A/C, TV/VCR, fax, kitchenette, coffeemaker, hair dryer.

La Pensione ★★ This classic bed-and-breakfast, located in the 1891 home of a former cigar executive, distinguishes itself from other similar inns by its extreme attention to details. The friendly and knowledgeable staff treats the stunning home and its guests with extraordinary care. The comfortable rooms all have air-conditioning, ceiling fans, king-size beds, and private bathrooms. Many have French doors opening onto spacious verandas. Although the rooms have no phones or televisions, the distractions of Duval Street, only steps away, should keep you adequately occupied during your visit. Breakfast, which includes made-to-order Belgian waffles, fresh fruit, and a variety of breads or muffins, can be taken on the wraparound porch or at the communal dining table.

809 Truman Ave. (between Windsor and Margaret sts.), Key West, FL 33040. (© **800/893-1193** or 305/292-9923. Fax 305/296-6509. www.lapension.com. 9 units. Winter from $168 double; off-season from $98 double. Rates include breakfast. No children accepted. There's a 10% discount for readers who mention this book. AE, DC, DISC, MC, V. **Amenities:** Outdoor pool, access to nearby health club, bike rental. *In room:* A/C.

South Beach Oceanfront Motel   This standard two-story motel is located directly on the ocean, with a private pier and within walking distance of Duval Street. It underwent a multimillion-dollar renovation in which rooms were gutted and completely redone. Because the structure is perpendicular to the water, most of the rooms overlook a pretty Olympic-size swimming pool rather than a wide swath of beach. The best, and by far most expensive, are the lucky pair of beachfront rooms on the end (nos. 115 and 215). Three rooms have kitchenettes and private balconies that overlook the pool and ocean. When making reservations, ask for a room that's as close to the beach (and as far from the road) as possible.

508 South St. (at the Atlantic Ocean), Key West, FL 33040. (© **800/354-4455** or 305/296-5611. Fax 305/294-8272. www.oldtownresorts.com. 47 units. Winter $230–$300; off-season $155–$200. AE, MC, V. **Amenities:** Outdoor pool, Jacuzzi, bike rental, concierge, self-service laundry. *In room:* A/C, TV, coffeemaker, hair dryer.

Southernmost Point Guest House ★★ *Finds*   One of the few inns that actually welcome children and pets, this romantic and historic guest house is a real find. The antiseptically clean rooms are not as fancy as the house's ornate 1885 exterior, but each is unique and includes some combination of basic beds and couches and a hodgepodge of furnishings, including futon couches, high-back wicker chairs, and plenty of mismatched throw rugs. Each room is different. Room 5 is best; situated upstairs, it has a private porch, an ocean view, and windows that let in lots of light. Every room has a refrigerator and a full decanter of sherry. Mona Santiago, the hotel's kind, laid-back owner, provides chairs and towels that can be brought to the beach, which is just a block away. Plus, guests can help themselves to wine as they soak in the new 14-seat hot tub. Kids will enjoy the swings in the backyard and the pet rabbits.

1327 Duval St., Key West, FL 33040. (© **305/294-0715.** Fax 305/296-0641. www.southernmostpoint.com. 6 units. Winter $105–$250; off-season $65–$$95. Rates include breakfast. AE, MC, V. **Amenities:** Hot tub. *In room:* A/C, fridge.

INEXPENSIVE

Abaco Inn ⭐   This tidy little guest house is situated on a secluded lane just off Duval Street. Although there is no pool or view, the three simple but comfortable rooms are well stocked, immaculate, and charming. Each room has a sizeable private bath, queen bed, and a twin-size Murphy bed. Once the home of a cigar maker, the house dates from the early 1900s. Now, it is owned and operated by George Fontana, a friendly and knowledgeable tour guide and writer. Look for his column on local characters in the *Key West Citizen*. You can't beat the price in this superconvenient location. No smoking is allowed on the property.

415 Julia St. (between Truman Ave. and Virginia St.), Key West, FL 33040. © **800/358-6307** or 305/296-2212. Fax 305/295-0349. www.abaco-inn.com. 3 units. Winter from $99 double; off-season from $69 double. 3-day minimum stay in season. Additional person $15 extra. AE, DISC, MC, V. **Amenities:** Bike rental, concierge. *In room:* A/C, TV, microwave, fridge, coffeemaker, hair dryer.

Angelina Guest House ⭐⭐   This youth hostel–type guest house is about the cheapest in town and conveniently located near a hot, hippie restaurant called Blue Heaven (see "Where to Dine," below). It is generally safe and full of character. The rooms are all furnished differently in a modest style, recently upgraded with new decor. Only three rooms do not have private baths. Two rooms have full kitchens, and one has a microwave and small refrigerator; there are no televisions or telephones. A new pool with waterfall and tropical landscaping was an excellent addition. Even though the Angelina is sparse, it's a good place to crash if you are on the cheap. Many repeat guests consider "this old house" their home away from home.

302 Angela St. (at the corner of Thomas St.), Key West, FL 33040. ©305/294-4480. Fax 305/272-0681. www.angelinaguesthouse.com. 13 units. Winter $75–$195; off-season $49–$125. Rates include continental breakfast. DISC, MC, V. **Amenities:** Concierge, outdoor pool. *In room:* A/C.

Blue Lagoon Motel   More than half of the rooms at this funky ocean-side resort rent for less than $100 year-round—an all-too-unusual occurrence in Key West, especially for full-service resorts. The rooms, furnished in heavy cedar wood, are basic and a bit run-down but still decent—along the lines of a Howard Johnson or other budget accommodation. Second-floor rooms are generally quieter. The pricier waterfront rooms aren't really worth the extra money (although some include a jet-ski ride). Guests tend to be young college-aged kids out for a wild time. Although pretty far from Old Town, the resort is convenient by scooter and car, and it is literally surrounded by WaveRunners, boats, parasailing, and diving fun.

3101 N. Roosevelt Blvd., Key West, FL 33040-4118. © 305/296-1043. Fax 305/296-6499. 72 units. Winter $80–$240 double; off-season $50–$110 double. MC, V. *In-room:* A/C, TV.

The Grand ⭐⭐ *(Finds*   Don't expect cabbies or locals to know about this well-kept secret, located in a modest residential section of Old Town, about 5 blocks from Duval Street. It's got almost everything you could want, including a very moderate price tag. Proprietor Elizabeth Rose goes out of her way to provide any and all services for her appreciative guests. All rooms have private bathrooms, air-conditioning, telephones, and private entrances. The four two-room efficiencies have new bathrooms. The floors are painted in bright colors, and beds are dressed in light tropical prints. Room no. 2 on the back side of the house is the best deal; it's small, but it has a porch and the most privacy. Suites are a real steal, too. The large two-room units come with a complete kitchen. This place is undoubtedly the best bargain in town.

1116 Grinnell St. (between Virginia and Catherine sts.), Key West, FL 33040. © 888/947-2630 or 305/294-0590. Fax 305/294-0477. www.keywest.com/the grand. 10 units. Winter $98–$158; off-season $88–$128. Rates include continental breakfast. AE, DISC, MC, V. **Amenities:** Concierge. *In room:* A/C, TV, fridge.

Key West International Hostel   This well-run affordable hostel is a 3-minute walk to the beach and to Old Town. Very busy with European backpackers, this is a great place to meet people. The dorm rooms are dark and sparse, but clean enough. The higher-priced motel rooms are a good deal, especially those equipped with full kitchens. The common area room has been upgraded, and a two-bedroom suite has been added for those looking to upgrade a bit. Amenities include a pool table under a tiki roof, and bicycle rentals for $8 per day. There's also cheap food available for breakfast, lunch, and dinner. They also have discounted prices for snorkeling, diving, and sunset cruises.

718 South St., Key West, FL 33040. © 800/51-HOSTEL or 305/296-5719. Fax 305/296-0672. www. keywesthostel@aol.com. 100 units. Year-round members $18.50, nonmembers $21.50. Motel units $75–$105 in season; $55–$85 off-season. MC, V. **Amenities:** Kitchen, bike rental. *In room:* A/C, TV, fridge, coffeemaker, hair dryer.

WHERE TO DINE

You'll find many cuisines represented in Key West: Thai, Cuban, Bahamian, Japanese, and barbecue. Like many cities with sizable visitor populations year-round, there is plenty of poor dining to be found here. There are the usual drive-through fast-food franchises (mostly up on Roosevelt Boulevard), and Duval Street even succumbed to the lure of a Hard Rock Cafe. But over the years, an upscale and high-quality dining scene has begun to thrive. Wander Old Town or the newly spruced up Bahama Village and browse menus after you have exhausted the list of my picks below.

If you don't feel like venturing out, call **We Deliver** (© **305/293-0078**), a service that will bring you anything you want from any of the area's restaurants or stores for a small fee (between $3 and $6). We Deliver operates between 3 and 11pm. If you are staying in a condominium or efficiency, you may want to stock your refrigerator with groceries, beer, wine, and snacks from the area's oldest grocer, **Fausto's Food Palace.** Open since 1926, there are now two locations: 1105 White St. and 522 Fleming St. The Fleming Street location will deliver (© **305/294-5221** or 305/296-5663). Fausto's has a $25 minimum.

VERY EXPENSIVE

Cafe des Artistes ⋨⋨⋨ FRENCH   Open for nearly 2 decades, the Cafe des Artistes' impressive longevity is the result of its winning combination of food and atmosphere. The fact that it was once part of a hotel built in 1935 by Al Capone's bookkeeper adds to its allure, but it's really the food that people come for. Traditional French meals benefit from a subtle tropical twist. The food is served by uniformed waiters well versed in the virtues of fine food. Start with the duck-liver pâté made with fresh truffles and old cognac, or Maryland crabmeat served with an artichoke heart and herbed tomato confit. And ask about the escargot du jour. Nouvelle and traditional French entrees include lobster flambé with mango and basil and wine-basted lamb chops rubbed with rosemary and ginger.

1007 Simonton St. (near Truman Ave.). © **305/294-7100.** Reservations recommended. Main courses $25–$38. AE, MC, V. Daily 6–11pm.

Café Marquesa ★★★ CONTEMPORARY AMERICAN   This superb restaurant is one of Key West's best. The intimate 50-seat restaurant has a theater-kitchen set cleverly behind a *trompe l'oeil* of a kitchen, with large mahogany-framed mirrors, giving diners a view of the entire restaurant. But it's the food you'll really want to admire. Specialties include peppercorn-dusted, seared yellowfin tuna with saffron risotto; grilled Florida lobster tail and diver sea scallops with Thai basil sauce, black Thai rice, and Asian vegetables; and an almost perfect feta and pinenut-crusted rack of lamb with rosemary demi-glace, creamy polenta, and eggplant caponata. If you're looking to splurge, financially and gastronomically, this is the place.

The Marquesa Hotel, 600 Fleming St. ✆ 305/292-1919. Reservations highly recommended. Main courses $20–$36. AE, DC, MC, V. No smoking. Daily 7–11pm summer; 6–11pm winter.

Louie's Backyard ★★ CARIBBEAN   Nestled amid blooming bougainvillea on a lush slice of the Gulf, Louie's remains one of the most romantic restaurants on earth. Famed chef Norman Van Aiken of Norman's in Miami brought his talents farther south and started what has become one of the finest dining spots in the Keys. After dinner, sit at the dockside bar and watch the waves crash, almost touching your feet, while enjoying a cocktail at sunset. You can't go wrong with the fresh catch of the day or any seafood dish for that matter. The weekend brunches are also great. Even if you can't stay for dinner, go for lunch; this is one dining experience you won't want to miss.

700 Waddell Ave. ✆ 305/294-1061. Reservations highly recommended. Main courses $25–$30; lunch $8–$15. AE, DC, MC, V. Daily 11:30am–3pm and 6–10:30pm.

EXPENSIVE

Antonia's ★★ REGIONAL ITALIAN   The food is great, but the atmosphere is a bit fussy for Key West. If you don't have a reservation in season, don't bother. Still, if you are organized and don't mind paying high prices for dishes that go for much less elsewhere, try this old favorite. From the perfectly seasoned home-made focaccia to an exemplary crème brûlée, this elegant little standout is amazingly consistent. The menu includes a small selection of classics, such as *zuppa di pesce,* rack of lamb in a rosemary sauce, and veal Marsala. However, the way to go is with the nightly specials. You can't go wrong with any of the handmade pastas.

615 Duval St. ✆ 305/294-6565. Fax 305/294-2743. Reservations suggested. Main courses $18–$26; pastas $12–$15. AE, DC, MC, V. Daily 6–11pm.

Bagatelle ★★★ SEAFOOD/TROPICAL   Reserve a seat at the elegant second-floor veranda overlooking Duval Street's mayhem. From the calm above, you may want to start your meal with the excellent herb-and-garlic stuffed whole artichoke or the sashimi-like seared tuna rolled in black peppercorns. Also recommended is a lightly creamy garlic-herb pasta topped with Gulf shrimp, Florida lobster, and mushrooms. The best chicken and beef dishes are given a tropical treatment: grilled with papaya, ginger, and soy.

115 Duval St. ✆ 305/296-6609. Reservations recommended. Main courses $14–$21; lunch $5–$10. AE, DISC, MC, V. Sun–Thurs 11:30am–10pm; Fri–Sat 11:30am–11pm.

La Trattoria ★ ITALIAN   Have a true Italian feast in a relaxed atmosphere. Each dish here is prepared and presented according to old, Italian tradition and is cooked to order. The antipasti are scrumptious. Try the delicious baked bread-crumb-stuffed mushroom caps; they're firm yet tender. The stuffed eggplant with ricotta and roasted peppers is light and flavorful. Or have the seafood salad of shrimp, calamari, and mussels, fish-market fresh and tasty. The pasta dishes here are also great. Try the *penne Venezia,* with mushrooms, sun-dried tomatoes, and crabmeat, or the cannelloni stuffed with veal and spinach. For dessert, don't skip the homemade tiramisu; it's light yet full-flavored. The dining room is spacious but still intimate, and the waiters are friendly and informative. Before you leave, be sure to visit Virgilio's, the restaurant's very own cocktail lounge with live jazz until 2am.

524 Duval St. ⓒ **305/296-1075.** Pasta $10–$17; main courses $17–$22. AE, DC, DISC, MC, V. Daily 5:30–11pm.

Mangoes ★★★ FLORIBBEAN This restaurant's large brick patio, shaded by overgrown banyan trees, is so alluring to passersby that it's packed almost every night of the week. Many people don't realize how pricey the meals can be here because, upon first glance, it looks like a casual Duval Street cafe. Both prices and cuisine are a notch above casual. Appetizers include conch chowder laced with sherry, lobster dumplings with tangy Key lime sauce, and grilled shrimp cocktail with spicy mango chutney. Spicy sausage with black beans and rice, crispy curried chicken, and local snapper with passion fruit sauce are typical among the entrees, but Mangoes' outstanding individual-size designer pizzas are the best menu items by far. They're baked in a Neapolitan-style oven fired by buttonwood. Even though it is right on tourist-laden Duval Street, Mangoes enjoys a good reputation among locals.

700 Duval St. (at Angela St.) ⓒ **305/292-4606.** Reservations recommended for parties of 6 or more. Main courses $12–$24; pizzas $10–$12; lunch $7–$14. AE, DC, DISC, MC, V. Daily 11am–midnight; pizza until 1am.

MODERATE

Alonzo's Oyster Bar ★ SEAFOOD Alonzo's Oyster Bar offers good seafood in a Key West casual setting. It's located on the ground floor of the A&B Lobster House at the end of Front Street in the marina. To start off your meal, try the steamed beer shrimp—tantalizingly fresh jumbo shrimp in a garlic, Old Bay, beer, and cayenne pepper sauce. Don't forget to dunk your bread. A house specialty is white clam chili, a delicious mix of tender clams, white beans, and potatoes served with a dollop of sour cream. An excellent entree is the pan-fried lobster cakes, served with sweet corn mashed potatoes, chipotle gravy, and roasted corn salsa. Alonzo's is the casual section of the A&B Lobster House; if you want to dress up, go upstairs for their "fine dining." The staff is cheerful and informative, and the service is very good.

231 Margaret St. ⓒ **305/294-5880.** Appetizers $5–$8; main courses $11–$17. MC, V. Daily 11am–11pm.

Blue Heaven ★★ *Finds* SEAFOOD/AMERICAN/NATURAL This little hippie-run gallery and restaurant has become the place to be in Key West—and with good reason. Be prepared to wait in line. The food here is some of the best in town, especially for breakfast. You can enjoy homemade granola, huge tropical fruit pancakes, and seafood Benedict. Dinners are just as good and run the gamut from fresh-caught fish dishes to Jamaican-style jerk chicken, curried soups, and vegetarian stews. But if you're a neat freak, don't bother. Some people are put off by the dirt floors and roaming cats and birds. The building used to be a bordello, where Hemingway was said to hang out watching cockfights.

729 Thomas St. (at the corner of Petronia St.) ⓒ **305/296-8666.** Main courses $9–$24; lunch $5–$13; breakfast $3–$8.50. DISC, MC, V. Mon–Tues 6–10:30pm; Wed–Sat 8am–3pm and 6–10:30pm; Sun brunch 8am–1pm and 6–10:30pm.

Mangia, Mangia ⊛ (Value) ITALIAN/AMERICAN   Locals appreciate that they can get good, inexpensive food here in a town filled with tourist traps. Off the beaten track, in a little corner storefront, this great Chicago-style pasta place serves some of the best Italian food in the Keys. The family-run restaurant offers superb homemade pastas of every description, including one of the tastiest marinaras around. The simple grilled chicken breast brushed with olive oil and sprinkled with pepper is another good choice. You wouldn't know it from the glossy glass front room, but there's a fantastic little outdoor patio dotted with twinkling pepper lights and lots of plants. You can relax out back with a glass of one of their excellent wines—they're said to have the largest selection in the Keys—or homemade beer while you wait for your table.

900 Southard St. (at Margaret St.) ⓒ 305/294-2469. Reservations not accepted. Main courses $9–$15. AE, MC, V. Daily 5:30–10pm.

Pepe's (Finds) AMERICAN   This old dive has been serving good, basic food for nearly a century. Steaks and Apalachicola Bay oysters are the big draw for regulars who appreciate the rustic barroom setting and historic photos on the walls. Look for original scenes of Key West in 1909, when Pepe's first opened. If the weather is nice, choose a seat on the patio under a stunning mahogany tree. Burgers, fish sandwiches, and standard chili satisfy hearty eaters. Buttery sautéed mushrooms and rich mashed potatoes are the best comfort food in Key West. Stop by early for breakfast when you can get old-fashioned chipped beef on toast and all the usual egg dishes. In the evening, there are reasonably priced cocktails on the deck.

806 Caroline St. (between Margaret and Williams sts.) ⓒ 305/294-7192. Main courses $13–$22; breakfast $2–$9; lunch $5–$9. DISC, MC, V. Daily 6:30am–10:30pm.

Turtle Kraals Wildlife Grill ⊛ (Finds) SOUTHWESTERN/SEAFOOD   You'll join lots of locals in this out-of-the-way converted warehouse with indoor and dockside seating that serves innovative seafood at great prices. Try the twin lobster tails stuffed with mango and crabmeat or any of the big quesadillas or fajitas. Kids will like the wildlife exhibits and the very cheesy menu. Blues bands play most nights.

213 Margaret St. (corner of Caroline St.) ⓒ 305/294-2640. Main courses $10–$20. DISC, MC, V. Mon–Thurs 11am–10:30pm; Fri–Sat 11am–11pm. Sun noon–10:30pm. Bar closes at midnight.

INEXPENSIVE

Anthony's Cafe ⊛ ITALIAN DELI/ROTISSERIE   Although owned and operated by a Greek import, this rustic Italian-style trattoria is a welcome addition to an area crowded with more expensive and less delicious options. Fragrant roasted chicken and overstuffed sandwiches on fresh baked bread are the best choices. Also good are the many salads and daily specials.

1111 Duval St. (at Amelia St.). ⓒ 305/296-8899. Breakfast $2–$5; sandwiches and salads $5.50–$7 with a side; hot plates $8–$13. Cash only. Daily 8am–10pm.

Bahama Mama's Kitchen ⊛⊛ BAHAMIAN   Sit outside under an umbrella and enjoy the authentic Bahamian dishes made from recipes that have been handed down through owner Corey's family for the past 150 years. Prepared fresh daily, all dishes are created with their special "Bahamian" seasonings. Try the coconut shrimp butterflied, soaked in coconut oil, battered with egg, and then rolled in fresh shredded coconut and deep-fried. The fresh catch of the day comes blackened, broiled, or fried and is served with island plantains, shrimp hash cakes, and crab rice. The service is good and the staff is friendly.

In the Bahama Village Market, 324 Petronia St. © **305/294-3355.** Appetizers $4–$7; main courses $9–$13. MC, V. Daily 11am–10pm.

The Deli DINER/AMERICAN   In operation since 1950, this family-owned corner eatery has kept up with the times. It's really more of a diner than a deli and has a vast menu with all kinds of hearty options, from meatloaf to yellowtail snapper. The seafood options are pretty good. A daily selection of more than a dozen vegetables includes the usual diner choices of beets, corn, and coleslaw with some distinctly Caribbean additions, such as rice and beans and fried plantains. Most dinners include a choice of two vegetables and homemade biscuits or corn bread. Breakfasts are made to order and attract a loyal following of locals. The Deli also offers ice cream sundaes and gourmet coffees.

531 Truman Ave. (corner of Truman Ave. and Simonton St.). © **305/294-1464.** Full meals $7–$23; sandwiches $3–$8. DISC, MC, V. Daily 7:30am–10pm.

El Siboney Restaurant *Value* CUBAN   For good, cheap Cuban food, stop at this corner dive that looks more like a gas station than a diner. Be prepared, however, to wait like the locals for succulent roast pork, Cuban sandwiches, grilled chicken, and *ropa vieja* (a stew-like dish of beef, onion, garlic, and tomatoes), all served with heaps of rice and beans.

900 Catherine St. (at Margaret St.). © **305/296-4184.** Main courses $5–$13. No credit cards. Mon–Sat 11am–9:30pm.

PT's Late Night *Finds* AMERICAN   This place is worth knowing about not only because it's one of the only places in town serving food past 10pm, but also because it happens to serve good food at extremely reasonable prices. Enjoy heaping plates of nachos, sizzling fajitas served with all the trimmings, and superfresh salads—so big they can be a meal in themselves. PT's is more like a sports bar than a restaurant, and service can be a bit slow and brusque.

920 Caroline St. (at the corner of Margaret St.). © **305/296-4245.** Main courses $5–$14; DISC, MC, V. Daily 11am–4am.

KEY WEST AFTER DARK

Duval Street is the Bourbon Street of Florida. Amid the T-shirt shops and clothing boutiques, you'll find bar after bar serving neon-colored frozen drinks to revelers who bounce from one to the next from noon till dawn. Bands and crowds vary from night to night and season to season. Your best bet is to start at Truman Avenue and head up Duval to check them out for yourself. Cover charges are rare, except in gay clubs (see below), so stop into a dozen and see which you like.

Captain Tony's Saloon   Just around the corner from Duval's beaten path, this smoky old wooden bar is about as authentic as you'll find. It comes complete with old-time regulars who remember the island before cruise ships docked here; they say Hemingway drank, caroused, and even wrote here. The owner, Captain Tony Tarracino, a former controversial Key West mayor—"immortalized" in Jimmy Buffett's "Last Mango in Paradise"—has recently capitalized on the success of this once-quaint tavern by franchising the place. 428 Greene St. © **305/294-1838.**

Durty Harry's   This large entertainment complex features live rock bands almost every night. You can wander to one of the many outdoor bars or head up to Upstairs at Rick's, an indoor/outdoor dance club that gets going late. For the more racy singles or couples, there is the Red Garter, a pocket-sized strip club popular with bachelor and divorce parties. The hawker outside reminds couples, in case they've forgotten, that "the family that strips together sticks together." 208 Duval St. ℂ 305/296-4890.

Epoch   Until an arsonist put an end to the former legend in 1995, this former gay club was the place to dance to everything from techno to house and disco to reggae. Now expanded to include seven bars, an even bigger dance floor, a huge outside deck overlooking Duval Street, and a new state-of-the-art sound system, this is a better-than-ever choice for people of any orientation who can appreciate a good time. 623 Duval St. ℂ 305/296-8521.

Jimmy Buffett's Margaritaville Cafe   This cafe, named after another Key West legend, is a worthwhile stop. Although Mr. Buffett moved to glitzy Palm Beach years ago, his name is still attracting large crowds. This kitschy restaurant/ bar/gift shop features live bands every night—from rock to blues to reggae and everything in between. The touristy cafe is furnished with plenty of Buffett memorabilia, including gold records, photos, and drawings. The margaritas are high priced but tasty. The cheeseburgers aren't worth singing about. 500 Duval St. ℂ 305/292-1435.

Sloppy Joe's   You'll have to stop in here just to say you did. Scholars and drunks debate whether this is the same Sloppy Joe's that Hemingway wrote about, but there's no argument that this classic bar's turn-of-the-century wooden ceiling and cracked tile floors are Key West originals. There's live music nightly as well as a cigar room and martini bar. 201 Duval St. ℂ 305/294-5717, ext. 10.

THE GAY SCENE

Key West's Bohemian live-and-let live atmosphere extends to its thriving and quirky gay community. Since Tennessee Williams and before, Key West has provided the perfect backdrop to a gay scene unlike that of many large urban areas. Seamlessly blended with the prevailing culture, there is no "gay ghetto" in Key West, where alternative lifestyles are embraced and even celebrated.

Although restaurants and businesses welcome visitors without discrimination, nightlife *is* inevitably nightlife. In Key West, the best music and dancing can be found at the predominantly gay clubs. While many of the area's other hot spots are geared toward tourists who like to imbibe, the gay clubs are for those who want to rave, gay or not. Cover varies, but is rarely more than $10.

Two adjacent popular late-night spots are the **801 Bourbon Bar/Number One Saloon** (801 Duval St. and 514 Petronia St. ℂ 305/294-9349 for both), featuring great drag and lots more disco. A mostly male clientele frequents this hot spot from 9pm until 4am. Another Duval Street favorite is **Diva's** at 711 Duval St. (ℂ 305/292-8500), where you might catch drag queens belting out torch songs or judges voting on the best package in the wet jockey shorts contest.

Sunday nights are fun at two local spots. **Tea by the Sea,** on the pier at the Atlantic Shores Motel (510 South St.; ℂ 800/520-3559), attracts a faithful following of regulars and visitors alike. The clothing-optional pool is always an attraction. Show up after 7:30pm. Better known around town as La-Te-Da, **La Terraza de Marti,** the former Key West home of Cuban exile Jose Marti, at 1125 Duval St. (ℂ 305/296-6706), is a great spot to gather poolside for the best martini in town—but don't bother with the food. Just upstairs from there is **The Crystal Room** (ℂ 305/296-6706), with a high-caliber cabaret performance featuring the popular Randy Roberts in the winter.

Literary Key West

Counting Ernest Hemingway and Tennessee Williams among your denizens would give any city the right to call itself a literary mecca. But over the years, tiny Key West has been home—or at least home away from home—to dozens of literary types who are drawn to some combination of its gentle pace, tropical atmosphere, and lighthearted mood (not to mention its lingering reputation for an oft-ribald lifestyle). Writers have long known that more than a few muses prowl the tree-laden streets of Key West.

Robert Frost first visited Key West in 1934 and stayed here for the remainder of his life. In the early 20th century, writers like John Dewey, Archibald MacLeish, John Dos Passos, Wallace Stevens, and S. J. Perelman were drawn to the island. Later, Ernest Hemingway's affection for Key West attracted even more writers.

Even as Key West boomed and busted and boomed again, and despite the island's growing popularity with world travelers, writers continued to move to Key West or visit with such regularity that they were deemed honorary "conchs." Novelists Phil Caputo, Tom McGuane, Jim Harrison, John Hershey, Alison Lurie, and Robert Stone were among these.

Of course, one Key West's favorite sons also earned a spot in the annals of local literary history. Famous for his good-time, tropical-laced music, Jimmy Buffett was also a surprisingly well-received novelist in the 1990s. Although Buffett now makes the infinitely ritzier Palm Beach his Florida home, his presence is still felt in virtually every corner of Key West.

But it is Nobel Prize–winner and avid outdoorsman Ernest Hemingway who is most identified with Key West. Much of the island has changed since he lived here from 1931 to 1961. Even the famous Sloppy Joe's bar, which Hemingway frequented mostly from 1933 to 1937, changed locations. Fortunately, the Ernest Hemingway House & Museum on Whitehead Street has been lovingly preserved. But perhaps to get the best feel for what Hemingway loved most about Key West, visit the docks at Garrison Bight. It is from there that Hemingway and his many famous (and infamous) friends and contemporaries departed for Caribbean ports of call and for sport upon the sea.

Key West pays homage to its literary legacy with the annual January Key West Literary Seminar. For information, call ✆ **888/293-9291** or visit www.keywestliteraryseminar.org.

4 The Dry Tortugas ★★

70 miles W. of Key West

Few people realize that the Florida Keys don't end at Key West. About 70 miles west is a chain of seven small islands known as the Dry Tortugas. As long as you have come this far, you might wish to visit them, especially if you're into bird watching, which is their primary draw.

Ponce de León, who discovered this far-flung cluster of coral keys in 1513, named them "Las Tortugas" because of the many sea turtles, which still flock to the area during the nesting season in the warm summer months. Oceanic charts later carried the preface "dry" to warn mariners that fresh water was unavailable here. Modern intervention has made drinking water available, but little else.

These undeveloped islands make a great day trip for travelers interested in seeing the truly natural anomalies of the Florida Keys—especially the birds. The Dry Tortugas are nesting grounds and roosting sites for thousands of tropical and subtropical oceanic birds. Visitors will also find a historical fort, good fishing, and terrific snorkeling around shallow reefs.

GETTING THERE

BY BOAT   The **Yankee Fleet,** based in Key West (© **800/634-0939** or 305/294-7009), offers day trips from Key West for sightseeing, snorkeling, or both. Cruises leave daily at 7:30am from the Land's End Marina at Margaret Street. Breakfast is served on board. The journey takes 3 hours. Once on the island, called Garden Key, you can join a guided tour or explore it on your own. Boats return to Key West by 7pm. Tours cost $98 per person, including breakfast; $63 for children 16 and under; $75 for seniors, students, and military personnel. Snorkeling equipment rental is free. Phone for reservations.

The **Sunny Days Catamaran's "Fast Cat"** (© **800/ 236-7937;** 305/ 292-6100) is faster than the loud Yankee fleet and a better value. Included in the $85 round-trip adult fare and $55 for children is a continental breakfast and a buffet lunch with cold cuts, fresh veggies, fruits, and salads, plus a snorkeling excursion to a wreck in 5 to 20 feet of water. The high-speed power cat leaves Key West at 8am and returns by 6pm.

BY PLANE   **Seaplanes of Key West,** based at Key West Airport (© **800/ 950-2-FLY** or 305/294-0709), offers daily excursions. Weather permitting, flights depart at 8am, 10am, noon, and 2pm. The 40-minute trip at about 500 feet offers a great introduction to these little-known islets. Fares, which include snorkeling equipment and a cooler for use on the island, start at $179 for adults, $129 for kids 12 and under, $99 for kids 6 and under for a half-day; and $305 for adults, $225 for kids 12 and under, and $170 for kids 6 and under for a full day. Bring a bathing suit, snorkeling equipment, and some snacks to enjoy on these remote and beautiful islands. Overnight camping at Fort Jefferson costs $329 for adults, $235 for kids 12 and under, and $179 for kids 6 and under.

EXPLORING THE DRY TORTUGAS

Fort Jefferson, a huge six-sided 19th-century fortress, is built almost at the water's edge of Garden Key, giving the appearance that it floats in the middle of the sea. The monumental structure is surrounded by formidable 8-foot-thick walls that rise up from the sand to a height of nearly 50 feet. Impressive archways, stonework, and parapets make this 150-year-old monument a grand sight. With the invention of the rifled cannon, the fort's masonry construction became obsolete, and the building was never completed. For 10 years, from 1863 to 1873, Fort Jefferson served as a prison, a kind of "Alcatraz East." Among its prisoners were four of the "Lincoln Conspirators," including Samuel A. Mudd, the doctor who set the broken leg of fugitive assassin John Wilkes Booth. In 1935, Fort Jefferson became a national monument administered by the National Park Service. For more information about Fort Jefferson and the Dry Tortugas, call the **Everglades National Park Service** at © **305/242-7700.**

OUTDOOR PURSUITS

BIRD WATCHING   Bring your binoculars and your bird books. Bird watching is *the* reason to visit this little cluster of tropical islands. The islands, uniquely situated in the middle of the migration flyway between North and South America, serve as an important rest stop for the more than 200 winged varieties that pass through here annually. The season peaks from mid-March to mid-May, when thousands of birds—including thrushes, orioles, boobies, swallows, black noddys, and snooty terns—show up. Many other species from the West Indies can be found year-round.

DIVING & SNORKELING   The warm, clear, shallow waters of the Dry Tortugas combine to produce optimum conditions for snorkeling and scuba diving. Four endangered species of sea turtles—the green, leatherback, Atlantic ridley, and hawksbill—can be found here, along with a myriad of marine species. The region just outside the seawall of Garden Key's Fort Jefferson is excellent for underwater touring; an abundant variety of fish, coral, and more live in just 3 or 4 feet of water.

FISHING   Fishing for snapper, tarpon, grouper, and other fish is popular. The mandatory saltwater fishing permit costs $7 for 3 days and $17 for 7 days. No bait or boating services are available in the Tortugas, but there are day docks on Garden Key as well as a cleaning table. The water is roughest in winter, but the fishing is excellent year-round. Outfitters from Key West can arrange day charters (see "Sports & Outdoor Activities," above).

CAMPING

The rustic beauty of tiny Garden Key is a camper's dream. Don't worry about sharing your site with noisy RVs or motor homes; they can't get here. The abundance of birds doesn't make it quiet, but camping here—a stone's throw from the water—is as picturesque as it gets. Campers are allowed to pitch tents only on Garden Key. Picnic tables, cooking grills, and toilets are provided, but there are no showers. All supplies must be packed in and out. Sites are $3 per person per night and are available on a first-come, first-served basis. With only 10 sites, they book up fast. For more information, call the **National Park Service** (✆ **305/242-7700**).

12

The Gold Coast: Hallandale to the Palm Beaches

Named not for the sun-kissed skin of the area's residents but for the gold salvaged from shipwrecks off its coastline, the Gold Coast embraces more than 60 miles of beautiful Atlantic shoreline—from the pristine sands of Jupiter in northern Palm Beach County to the legendary strip in Fort Lauderdale.

If you haven't visited the cities along Florida's southeastern coast in the last few years, you'll be amazed at how much has changed. Miles of sprawling grassland and empty lots have been replaced with luxurious resorts and high-rise condominiums. Taking advantage of their close proximity to Miami, the cities that make up the Gold Coast have attracted millions looking to escape crowded sidewalks, traffic jams, and the everyday routines of life.

Fortunately, amid all the building, much of the natural treasure of the Gold Coast remains. There are 300 miles of Intracoastal Waterway, not to mention Fort Lauderdale's Venetian–inspired canals. And, just a few miles inland, is the unspoiled splendor of the Everglades.

The most popular areas in the Gold Coast are Fort Lauderdale, Boca Raton, and Palm Beach. While Fort Lauderdale is a favored beachfront destination, Boca Raton and Palm Beach are better known for their country-club lifestyles and excellent shopping. Further north is the quietly popular Jupiter, best known for spring training at the Roger Dean Stadium and for its former resident Burt Reynolds. In between these better-traveled destinations are a few things worth stopping for, but not much. The drive north along the coastline is one of the best ways to fully appreciate what the Gold Coast is all about—it's a perspective you won't find in a shopping mall.

But tourists aren't the only people coming here; thousands of transplants, fleeing the increasing population influx in Miami and the frigid winters up North, have made this area their home. As a result, there has been a construction boom in the existing cities and westward into the swampy areas of the Everglades. More than 20 homes per day are being built in Broward County alone. There has also been a great revitalization of several downtown areas, including Hollywood, Fort Lauderdale, and West Palm Beach. These once-desolate urban centers have been spruced up and now attract more young travelers and families than ever before.

Unfortunately, like its neighbors to the south, the Gold Coast can be prohibitively hot and buggy in the summer. The good news is that bargains are plentiful in the summer months (between May and October), when many locals take advantage of package deals and uncrowded resorts.

For the purposes of this chapter, the Gold Coast will consist of the towns of Hallandale, Hollywood, Pompano Beach, Fort Lauderdale, Dania, Deerfield, Boca Raton, Delray Beach, Boyton Beach, and the Palm Beaches.

EXPLORING THE GOLD COAST BY CAR

Like most of South Florida, the Gold Coast consists of a mainland and an adjacent strip of barrier islands. You'll have to check the maps to keep track of the many bridges that allow access to the islands where most of the tourist activity is centered. Interstate 95, which runs north-south, is the area's main highway. Farther west is the Florida Turnpike, a toll road that can be worth the expense since the speed limit is higher and it is often less congested than I-95. Also on the mainland is U.S. 1, which generally runs parallel to I-95 (to the east) and is a narrower thoroughfare mostly crowded with strip malls and seedy hotels.

I recommend taking Fla. A1A, a slow ocean-side road that connects the long, thin islands of Florida's whole east coast. Although the road is narrow, it is the most scenic and forces you into the relaxed atmosphere of these resort towns.

1 Broward County: Hallandale & Hollywood to Fort Lauderdale

23 miles N. of Miami

Until the 2000 election fiasco, most people had never heard of Broward County. Less exposed than the highly hyped Miami, Broward County is a lot calmer and, according to some, a lot friendlier than the magic city. In fact, a friendly rivalry exists between residents of Miami-Dade County and Broward County. Miamians consider themselves more sophisticated and cosmopolitan than their northern neighbors who, in turn, dismiss the alleged sophistication as snobbery and actually prefer their own county's gentler pace.

With more than 23 miles of beachfront and 300 miles of navigable waterways, Broward County is also a great outdoor destination. Scattered amid the shopping malls, condominiums, and tourist traps is a beautiful landscape lined with hundreds of parks, golf courses, tennis courts, and, of course, beaches.

Like many other small American towns, the South Florida's city of Hollywood has been working on redeveloping its downtown area for years. Once a sleepy community wedged between Fort Lauderdale and Miami, Hollywood is now a bustling area of 1.5 million people belonging to an array of ethnic and racial identities: from white and African American, to people of Jamaican, Chinese, and Dominican descent. *Money* magazine trumpeted the self-described "City of the Future" as having an ethnic makeup that mirrors what America will look like by the year 2022. A spate of redevelopment has made the pedestrian-friendly center along Hollywood Boulevard and Harrison Street east of Dixie Highway a popular destination for travelers and locals alike. Some predict Hollywood will be South Florida's next big destination—South Beach without the attitude, traffic jams, and parking nightmares. While the prediction is a dubious one, Hollywood is definitely awakening from its long slumber. Prices are a fraction of other tourist areas, and a quasi-bohemian vibe is apparent in the galleries, clubs, and restaurants that dot the new "strip." Its gritty undercurrent, however, prevents it from becoming too trendy.

Fort Lauderdale and its well-known strip of beaches, restaurants, bars, and souvenir shops have also undergone a major transformation. Once famous (or infamous) for the annual mayhem it hosted during Spring Break, this area is now attracting a more affluent, better-behaved yachting crowd.

In addition to beautiful wide beaches, the city, also known as the Venice of America, has more than 300 miles of navigable waterways and innumerable canals, which permit thousands of residents to anchor boats in their backyards.

Boating is not just a hobby here; it's a lifestyle. Visitors can easily get on the water, too, by renting a boat or simply by hailing a moderately priced water taxi.

Huge cruise ships also take advantage of Florida's deepest harbor, Port Everglades. It is the second-busiest cruise-ship base in Florida after Miami and one of the top five in the world. For further information on cruises, see chapter 7 ("What to See & Do in Miami") and consult *Frommer's Caribbean Cruises* or *Frommer's Caribbean Ports of Call.*

ESSENTIALS

GETTING THERE   If you're driving north from Miami, it's a straight shot to Hollywood or Fort Lauderdale. Visitors on their way to or from Orlando should take the Florida Turnpike to Exit 53, 54, 58, or 62, depending on the location of your accommodations.

The **Fort Lauderdale/Hollywood International Airport** is small, easy to negotiate, and located just 15 minutes from both of the downtown areas it services.

Amtrak (© **800/USA-RAIL**) stations are at 200 SW 21st Terrace (Broward Boulevard and I-95), Fort Lauderdale (© **954/587-6692**), and 3001 Hollywood Blvd., Hollywood (© **954/921-4517**).

VISITOR INFORMATION   The **Greater Fort Lauderdale Convention & Visitors Bureau,** 1850 Eller Dr., Suite 303 (off I-95 and I-595 east), Fort Lauderdale, FL 33316 (© **954/765-4466;** fax 954/765-4467; www.sunny.org), is an excellent resource in English, Spanish, and French. I highly recommend calling them in advance to request a free comprehensive guide covering events, accommodations, and sightseeing in Broward County. In addition, once you are in town, you can call an **information line** (© **954/527-5600**) to get easy-to-follow directions, travel advice, and assistance from multilingual operators who staff a round-the-clock help line. Also available 24 hours a day are operators who can book discount scuba, cruise, or cultural packages. Call © **800/22-SUNNY** for information.

The **Greater Hollywood Chamber of Commerce,** 330 N. Federal Hwy. (on the corner of U.S. 1 and Taylor Street), Hollywood, FL 33020 (© **954/923-4000;** fax 954/923-8737), is open Monday through Friday from 8:30am to 5pm.

HITTING THE BEACH

The southern part of the Gold Coast, Broward County, has the region's most popular and amenities-laden beaches, which stretch for more than 23 miles. Most do not charge for access, though all are well maintained. Here's a selection of some of the county's best from south to north.

Hollywood Beach, stretching from Sheridan Street to Georgia Street, is a major attraction in the city of Hollywood, a virtual carnival with a motley assortment of young hipsters, big families, and sunburned French Canadians who dodge bicyclers and skaters along the rows of tacky souvenir shops, T-shirt shops, game rooms, snack bars, beer stands, hotels, and even miniature golf courses. The 3-mile-long Hollywood Beach **Broadwalk** is notable as one of the area's only beach paths where diversions are right on the beach separated from the sand and sea by only a thin paved strip instead of a busy highway and tall buildings. Popular with runners, skaters, and cruisers, the broadwalk is also renowned as a hangout for thousands of retirement-age snowbirds who get together for

Fort Lauderdale Attractions & Accommodations

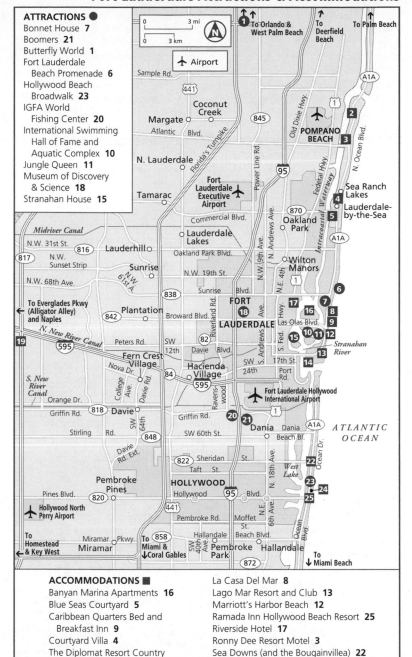

ATTRACTIONS ●
Bonnet House **7**
Boomers **21**
Butterfly World **1**
Fort Lauderdale
  Beach Promenade **6**
Hollywood Beach
  Broadwalk **23**
IGFA World
  Fishing Center **20**
International Swimming
  Hall of Fame and
  Aquatic Complex **10**
Jungle Queen **11**
Museum of Discovery
  & Science **18**
Stranahan House **15**

ACCOMMODATIONS ■
Banyan Marina Apartments **16**
Blue Seas Courtyard **5**
Caribbean Quarters Bed and
  Breakfast Inn **9**
Courtyard Villa **4**
The Diplomat Resort Country
  Club & Spa **24**
Hyatt Regency Pier Sixty-Six **14**
La Casa Del Mar **8**
Lago Mar Resort and Club **13**
Marriott's Harbor Beach **12**
Ramada Inn Hollywood Beach Resort **25**
Riverside Hotel **17**
Ronny Dee Resort Motel **3**
Sea Downs (and the Bougainvillea) **22**
Traders Ocean Resort **2**
Wyndham Resort and Spa **19**

frequent dances and shows at a faded outdoor amphitheater. Despite efforts to clear out a seedy element, the area remains a haven for drunks and scammers, so keep alert.

If you tire of the hectic diversity that defines Hollywood's broadwalk, enjoy the natural beauty of the beach itself, which is wide and clean. There are life-guards, showers, bathroom facilities, and public areas for picnics and parties.

The **Fort Lauderdale Beach Promenade** underwent a $26 million renovation, and it looks fantastic. It's especially peaceful in the mornings when there's just a smattering of joggers and walkers, but even at its most crowded on the weekend, the expansive promenade provides room for everyone. Note, however, that the beach is hardly pristine; it is across the street from an uninterrupted stretch of hotels, bars, and retail outlets. Also nearby is a mega-retail and dining complex, Beach Place, on Fla. A1A, midway between Las Olas Boulevard and Sunrise Boulevard (see "Shopping & Browsing," below).

Just across the road, on the sand, most days you will find hard-core volley-ballers, who always welcome anyone with a good spike, and an inviting ocean welcoming swimmers of any level. The unusually clear waters are under the care-ful watch of some of Florida's best-looking lifeguards. Freshen up afterward in any of the clean showers and restrooms conveniently located along the strip. Pets have been banned from most of the beach in order to maintain the impressive cleanliness not commonly associated with such highly trafficked public beaches; a designated area for pets exists away from the main sunbathing areas.

Especially on weekends, parking along the ocean-side meters is nearly impos-sible to find. Try biking, skating, or hitching a ride on the water taxi instead. The strip is located on Fla. A1A, between SE 17th Street and Sunrise Boulevard.

Dania Beach's **John U. Lloyd Beach State Park,** 6503 N. Ocean Dr., Dania (© **954/923-2833**) is 251 acres of barrier island between the Atlantic Ocean and the Intracoastal Waterway, from Port Everglades on the north to Dania on the south. Its natural setting contrasts sharply with the urban development of Fort Lauderdale. Lloyd Beach, one of Broward County's most important nesting beaches for sea turtles, produces some 10,000 hatchlings a year. The park's broad, flat beach is popular for swimming and sunning. Self-guided nature trails are great for those who are too restless to sunbathe.

ACTIVE PURSUITS

BOATING   Often called the "yachting capital of the world," Fort Lauderdale provides ample opportunity for visitors to get out on the water, either along the Intracoastal Waterway or out on the open ocean. If your hotel doesn't rent boats, try **Bill's Sunrise Watersports,** 2025 E. Sunrise Blvd., Fort Lauderdale (© **954/462-8962**). They will outfit you with a variety of craft, including jet skis, WaveRunners, 13-foot Cigarette boats, 15-foot jet boats, and 8-foot power-boats, year-round. Bill's is open daily from 9am to 6pm. Rates start at $50 per half-hour for WaveRunners, $75 to $85 for boats (2-hr. minimum), and $60 for parasailing.

CRUISES   The **Jungle Queen,** 801 Sea Breeze Blvd. (3 blocks south of Las Olas Boulevard on Fla. A1A), in the Bahia Mar Yacht Center, Fort Lauderdale (© **954/462-5596**), a Mississippi River–style steamer, is one of Fort Laud-erdale's best-known attractions, cruising up and down the New River. All-you-can-eat dinner cruises and 3-hour sightseeing tours take visitors past Millionaires' Row, Old Fort Lauderdale, and the new downtown. Cruises depart nightly at 7pm and cost $29 for adults and $15 for children 12 and under.

Turtle Trail

In June and July, the John U. Lloyd beach is crawling with nature lovers who come for the spectacular Sea Turtle Awareness Program. Park rangers begin the evening with a lecture and slide show while scouts search the beach for nesting loggerhead sea turtles. If a turtle is located—plenty of them usually are—a beach walk is conducted. The program begins at 9:00pm. Call (954/923-2833 for reservations. Comfortable walking shoes and insect repellent are recommended. The park entrance fee of $2 to $4 per carload applies.

Sightseeing tours are scheduled daily at 10am and 2pm and cost $13.25 for adults and $8.75 for children 10 and under.

If you're interested in gambling, several casino boat companies operate day cruises out of Port Everglades and offer blackjack, slots, and poker. **Discovery Cruise Lines** ((800/937-4477) has daily cruises to the Bahamas, where you can gamble, eat, and party for 5 to 6 hours for about $120. The price includes breakfast, lunch, and dinner, but drinks cost extra.

Sea Escape ((800/327-2005 or 954/453-3333) also launches daily casino cruises. But theirs don't travel more than a few miles offshore. These trips "to nowhere" depart from Monday to Thursday from 11am to 4:30pm and 7:30pm to 12:30am. The party cruises offer buffet meals and full casinos for $33 to $38 a person. I'd recommend spending an additional $20 for a cabin (do not expect *Love Boat* luxe here) so you can stretch out and relax in between hands. Even though the cruises don't go far from the coast, 5 or 6 hours is a long time to spend at sea, especially if the weather is rough. Evening cruises, which return at 1:30am on weekends, cost $48 and offer full buffet dinners and a Las Vegas–style show. Port charges are included, although you must pay a $3 departure tax and $2.65 passenger charge. This is one of the best deals you'll find. Sea Escape also has a new 2- and 3-night cruise option, where visitors can go to Nassau, the Bahamas, for as little as $199 per person with all meals included.

FISHING   Completed in 1999 at a cost of more than $32 million, the **IGFA World Fishing Center** at 300 Gulf Stream Way ((954/922-4212) in Dania Beach is an angler's paradise. One of the highlights of this museum, library, and park is the virtual reality fishing simulator, which allows visitors to actually reel in their own computer-generated catch. Also included in the 3-acre park are displays of antique fishing gear, record catches, famous anglers, various vessels, and a wetlands lab. To get a list of local captains and guides, call **IGFA headquarters** ((954/927-2628) and ask for the librarian. Admission is $5 for adults, $4 for children between 3 and 12, and free for children under 3. On the grounds is also **Bass Pro Shops Outdoor World,** a huge multifloor retail complex situated on a 3-acre lake.

GAME PARKS   **Boomers,** at 1801 NW 1st St., east of I-95 between Griffin and Sterling road exits, in Dania, is good for kids during the day—at night the park attracts a rowdy bunch of teenagers. The newest addition to the park is a 100-foot high, 3,200-foot long wooden roller coaster (the thrills are high, but the lines are long). With a massive 24-hour video arcade, five challenging miniature-golf greens, go-carts and NASCAR racing, batting cages, and a huge sky coaster, this place provides exhaustive entertainment. Plan to spend all day or night. Call for prices and hours ((954/921-1411). Rides average $6.

Kids　Wild Things

Deerfield Island Park, surrounded by the Intracoastal Waterway and two canals, is an urban wilderness area that is accessible only by boat. The heavily wooded 56-acre site includes an 8½ -acre mangrove swamp and is home to the gopher tortoise. The park also serves as a nesting place for squirrels, raccoons, and armadillos. Visitors can hike the park's two main trails. Picnic areas with grills and tables are available on a first-come, first-served basis, and there is also a small playground. A free boat shuttle transports visitors to the island hourly, but book early as the shuttle fills up quickly. Call for times and reservations. Open Wednesday to Sunday from 9am to 5pm. 1720 Deerfield Island Park, Deerfield Beach, © 954/360-1320.

For adults who love video games but can't deal with hordes of kids, there's **Dave & Busters** at 3000 Oakwood Blvd. in Hollywood, just off the Sheridan Street exit of I-95 (© **954/923-5505**). This 50,000-square-foot complex features a full bar and sit-down restaurant, as well as a more casual spot with table service. On weekends this place is packed with young adults on dates and rowdy groups of guys of all ages. An admission of $3 is charged only on Friday and Saturday after 10pm. D&B's opens weekdays at 11am and weekends at 11:30am and usually closes by 1am.

GameWorks, the mega-arcade of Hollywood movie mogul Steven Spielberg is located in the Sawgrass Mills outlet center (See "Shopping & Browsing," below) and features high-tech interactive games, plus a restaurant and bar.

GOLF　More than 50 golf courses in all price ranges compete for players. Some of the best include **Emerald Hills** at 4100 North Hills Dr., Hollywood, just west of I-95 between Sterling Road and Sheridan Street. This beauty consistently lands on the "best of" lists of golf writers throughout the country. The 18th hole on a two-tier green is the challenging course's signature; it's surrounded by water and is more than a bit rough. It's also pricey. Greens fees start at $125. Call © **954/961-4000** for tee times. For one of Broward's best municipal challenges, try the 18-holer at the **Orangebrook Golf Course** at 400 Entrada Dr. in Hollywood (© **954/967-GOLF**). Built in 1937, this is one of the state's oldest courses and one of the area's best bargains. Morning and noon rates range from $27 to $33. After 2pm, you can play for less than $20, including a cart. Men must wear collared shirts to play here, and no spikes are allowed.

SCUBA DIVING　In Broward County, the best wreck dive is the *Mercedes I,* a 197-foot freighter that washed up in the backyard of a Palm Beach socialite in 1984 and was sunk for divers the following year off Pompano Beach. The artificial reef, filled with colorful sponges, spiny lobsters, and barracudas, is located 97 feet below the surface, a mile offshore between Oakland Park Boulevard and Sunrise Boulevard. Dozens of reputable dive shops line the beach. Ask at your hotel for a nearby recommendation or contact **Lauderdale Undersea Adventures,** 1525 S. Andrews Ave., Fort Lauderdale (© **954/462-3400**).

SPECTATOR SPORTS　Baseball fans can get their fix at the **Fort Lauderdale Stadium,** 5301 NW 12th Ave. (© **954/938-4980**), where the Baltimore Orioles play Spring Training exhibition games starting in early March; call © **954/776-1921** for tickets. General admission is $6, a spot in the grandstand

$9, kids 14 and under $3, and box seats $12. During the season, the Florida Marlins play just south of Hallandale at the Pro Player Stadium near the Dade–Broward County line. Call TicketMaster for tickets (✆ **305/358-5885**), which range from $2 to $40. Tickets go on sale in January.

Pompano Park Racing, 1800 SW 3rd St., Pompano Beach (✆ **954/ 972-2000**), features parimutuel harness racing from October to early August. Grandstand admission is free; clubhouse admission is $2.

A sort of Spanish-style indoor lacrosse, jai alai was introduced to Florida in 1924 and still draws big crowds, who bet on the fast-paced action. Broward's only fronton, **Dania Jai Alai,** 301 E. Dania Beach Blvd. at the intersection of Fla. A1A and U.S. 1 (✆ **954/920-1511** or 954/426-4330), is a great place to spend an afternoon or evening.

Wrapped around an artificial lake, **Gulfstream Park,** at U.S. 1 and Hallandale Beach Boulevard, Hallandale (✆ **305/931-7223**), is pretty and popular. Large purses and important races are commonplace at this recently refurbished suburban course, and the track is often crowded. It hosts the Florida Derby each year. Call for schedules. Admission is $3 to the grandstand, and $3 to the clubhouse. Parking is free. From January 3 to March 15, post times are Wednesday to Monday at 1pm, and the doors open at 11am. Many weekends feature live concerts by well-known musicians.

In the sport of ice hockey, the young Florida Panthers (✆ **954/835-7000**) have already made history. In the 1994–95 season, they played in the Stanley Cup finals, and the fans love them. They play in Sunrise at the National Car Rental Center at 2555 NW 137th Way. Tickets range from $14 to $100. Call for directions and ticket information.

TENNIS There are hundreds of courts in Broward County, and plenty are accessible to the public. Many are at resorts and hotels. If not at yours, try one of these.

Famous as the spot where Chris Evert got in her early serves, the **Jimmy Evert Tennis Center,** 701 NE 12th Ave. (off Sunrise Boulevard), Fort Lauderdale (✆ **954/761-5378**), has 18 clay and 3 hard courts (15 lighted). Her coach and father, James Evert, still teaches young players here, though he is very picky about whom he'll accept. Nonresidents of Fort Lauderdale pay $3.50 (singles) to $4.50 (doubles) per hour. Reservations are accepted after 2pm for the following day but cost an extra $3. Lights are also an extra $3 per hour and are available only for the clay courts.

At the **Marina Bay Resort,** 2175 S.R. 84, west of I-95 and just behind the Ramada Inn, Fort Lauderdale (✆ **954/791-7600**), visitors can play free on any one of nine hard courts on a first-come, first-served basis. Three are lighted at night.

SEEING THE SIGHTS

For an overview of Fort Lauderdale, you may want to take an informative spin around the downtown area with **South Florida Trolley Tours** (✆ **954/ 946-7320**). Drivers narrate the history of the area as they loop around the city's streets past all the major (and many minor) sights. The charge for the 90-minute tour is $12 for adults, free for children 11 and under. The trolleys pick up passengers from most major hotels for six tours daily, starting at 9am. Call for current schedule.

For a tour by water, see the box below.

Museum of Discovery & Science 🕻🕻 (Kids) This museum's high-tech, interactive approach to education proves unquestionably that science equals fun. Adults won't feel as if they're in a kiddie museum, either. During the week, school groups meander through the cavernous two-story modern building. Kids 7 and under enjoy navigating their way through the excellent explorations in the "Discovery Center." Florida Ecoscapes is particularly interesting, with a living coral reef, bees, bats, frogs, turtles, and alligators. However, most weekend nights you'll find a diverse crowd ranging from hip high-school kids to thirty-somethings enjoying a rock film in the IMAX 3-D theater, which also shows short, science-related, supersize films daily. Out front, see the 52-foot-tall "Great Gravity Clock," located in the museum's atrium, the largest kinetic-energy sculpture in the state. Call for changing exhibits.

401 SW 2nd St., Fort Lauderdale. (✆) **954/467-6637**. www.mods.org. Museum admission (includes admission to 1 IMAX film) $12.50 adults, $11.50 seniors, $10.50 children 3–12. Mon–Sat 10am–5pm; Sun noon–6pm. From I-95, exit on Broward Blvd. E. Continue to SW 5th Ave.; turn right, garage on right.

Billie Swamp Safari 🕻 Catch a glimpse of how Florida looked *before* developers went wild. Skimming across the shallow swamps in an airboat with Native American guides, you may spot alligators and rare birds. Swamp buggy rides are especially amusing, and if you're lucky you'll see what seems to be strategically placed deer, buffalo, wild pigs, and ornery ostriches. A stop at an alligator farm reeks of Disney, but the kids won't care. Swamp buggy rides leave every hour on the hour until 5pm. You can also stay overnight in a native tiki hut if you're really looking to immerse yourself in the culture.

Big Cypress Reservation, 1½-hr. drive west of Fort Lauderdale. (✆) **800/949-6101**. Free admission. Boat tours $10–$20. Daily 8am–8pm. Airboats depart every 30 min.; last ride at 4:30pm.

Bonnet House 🕻🕻🕻 This historic 35-acre plantation home and estate, accessible by guided tour only, will provide you with a fantastic glimpse of old South Florida. Built in 1921, the sprawling two-story waterfront home surrounded with formal tropical gardens is really the backdrop of a love story, which the very chatty volunteer guides will share with you if you ask. Some have actually lunched with the former resident of the house, the late Evelyn Bartlett, the wife of world-acclaimed artist Frederic Clay Bartlett. The worthwhile 1¼ - hour tour brings you quirky people, whimsical artwork, lush grounds, and interesting design. Inquire about literary walks and science workshops offered regularly on the grounds.

900 N. Birch Rd. (1 block west of the ocean, south of Sunrise Blvd.), Fort Lauderdale. (✆) **954/563-5393**. www.bonnethouse.com. Admission $9 adults, $8 seniors, $7 students under 18, free for children 6 and under. Tours Wed–Fri 10am–1:30pm; Sat–Sun 12:30pm–2:30pm.

Butterfly World One of the world's largest butterfly breeders, Butterfly World cultivates more than 150 species of these colorful and delicate insects. In the park's walk-through, screened-in laboratory, visitors can see thousands of caterpillars and watch newborn butterflies emerge from their cocoons and flutter around as they learn to fly. Depending on how interested you are in these winged beauties, you may want to allow from 1 to 2 hours to tour the gardens and the well-stocked gift shop. There's a new lorikeet aviary that offers visitors the opportunity to hand-feed the butterflies, too.

Tradewinds Park S., 3600 W. Sample Rd., Coconut Creek (west of the Florida Tpk.). (✆) **954/977-4400**. www.butterflyworld.com. Admission $12.95 adults, $7.95 children 4–12, free for children 3 and under. Mon–Sat 9am–5pm; Sun 1–5pm; last admission at 4pm.

One If by Land, Taxi If by Sea

Plan to spend at least an afternoon or evening cruising Fort Lauderdale's 300 miles of waterways in the only way you can: by boat. The **Water Taxi of Fort Lauderdale (𝄢 954/467-6677)** is one of the greatest innovations for water lovers since those cool Velcro sandals. A trusty fleet of older port boats serves the dual purpose of transporting and entertaining visitors as they cruise through "The Venice of America."

Taxis operate on demand and also along a fairly regular route, carrying up to 48 passengers. If you stay at a hotel on the route, you can be picked up at your hotel, usually within 15 minutes of calling, and then be shuttled to any of the dozens of restaurants, bars, and attractions on or near the waterfront. If you aren't sure where you want to go, ask one of the personable captains who can point out historic and fun spots along the way.

For a day cruise with the kids, make a stop at the Museum of Discovery & Science, where you can catch an IMAX film or just enjoy the current educational exhibits. Then, if you are up for a walk, head across the 3-mile-long Riverwalk, a scenic palm-lined walkway along the New River where you can enjoy your picnic lunch; or try one of the restaurants dotting the way to Las Olas Boulevard and the Las Olas Riverfront. When you are ready for some shopping or a sit-down meal, reboard and head to Beach Place at Las Olas Boulevard and Cortez Street in the heart of Fort Lauderdale's most famous "strip." Stop for refreshments at Casablanca Cafe and then hit the beach.

In the evening, the water taxi is ideal for bar-hopping—no worrying about parking or choosing a designated driver. Make your first stop at Shooters, where professionals, boaters, and tourists share the large lively patio for a popular happy hour from 5 to 7pm on weekdays. Right next door is Bootlegger's, featuring more than 70 beers at an outside bar. Later debark at O'Hara's, in the downtown section of Las Olas Boulevard (see "The Hollywood & Fort Lauderdale Area After Dark"), where you'll hear a great mix of live jazz and blues.

Starting daily from 10am, boats usually run until midnight, and until 2am on weekends, depending on the weather. The cost is $7.50 per person per trip, $14 round-trip, and $16 for a full day. Children under 12 ride for half-price and free on Sunday. Opt for the all-day pass; it's worth it.

International Swimming Hall of Fame and Aquatic Complex ⍟
Olympic diver Greg Louganis dove here, and you will want to do the same when you see the two 10-lane, 50-meter pools. Fortunately you can, for just $3, so bring your bathing suit. For inspiration, take in a swim flick (featuring Esther Williams and other aquatic stars) at the complex's theater or visit the comprehensive exhibition of medals, photos, and other memorabilia of swimming contests past.

1 Hall of Fame Dr., Fort Lauderdale. 𝄢 954/462-6536 or 954/468-1580 for the pool. $3 for museum, $3 for pool. Family rate $5. Museum open daily from 9am–7pm. Pool weekdays from 8am– 4pm; weekends from 8am–4pm; closed late December to mid-January.

Stranahan House 🎭🎭🎭   In a town whose history is younger than many of its residents, visitors may want to take a minute to see Fort Lauderdale's very oldest standing structure and a prime example of classic "Florida Frontier" architecture. Built in 1901 by the "father of Fort Lauderdale," Frank Stranahan, this house once served as a trading post for Seminole trappers who came here to sell pelts. It's been a post office, town hall, and general store and now is a worthwhile little museum of South Florida pioneer life, containing turn-of-the-last-century furnishings and historical photos of the area. It is also the site of occasional concerts and social functions. Call for details.

335 SE 6th Ave. (Las Olas Blvd. at the New River Tunnel), Fort Lauderdale. ℂ **954/524-4736.** www. stranahanhouse.com. Admission $5 adults, $2 students and children. Wed–Sat 10am–4pm; Sun 1–4pm. Tours are on the hour; last tour at 3pm. Also accessible by water taxi.

SHOPPING & BROWSING

It's all about malls in Broward County. And while most of the best shopping is located within Fort Lauderdale proper, there are other areas in the county worth browsing.

Dania is known as the **Antique Capital of the South** because it is within 1 square mile of Federal Highway that the city has over a hundred dealers selling everything from small collectibles to the finest antiques. **R. Cook & Co.,** 44 N. Federal Hwy. (ℂ **954/922-1118**), for instance, deals in vintage Louis Vuitton, plus exotic skins from Ernest Hemingway and antique scientific instruments, among other things. **Louis Kleinman Collectibles,** 60 N. Federal Hwy. (ℂ **954/920-2801**), boasts a large collection of china, including Limoges porcelain pillboxes. **Iris Fields of Dania,** 60 N. Federal Hwy. (ℂ **954/926-5658**), features a fabulous collection of antique perfume bottles. **Daddy's Inc.,** 19 N. Federal Hwy. (ℂ **954/920-4001**) has a huge selection of Tiffany lamps, furniture, watercolors, silver, and gold.

For bargain mavens, there's a strip of "fashion" stores on **Hallandale Beach Boulevard's "Schmatta Row,"** east of Dixie Highway and the railroad tracks, where off-brand shoes, bags, and jewelry are sold at deep discounts. Hollywood Boulevard also offers some interesting shops with everything from Indonesian artifacts to used and rare books to leather bustiers to handmade hats. Dozens of shops line the pedestrian-friendly strip just west of Young Circle. The art galleries are clustered along Harrison Street just east of Dixie Highway.

The area's only beachfront mall, **Beach Place,** is in Fort Lauderdale on Fla. A1A just north of Las Olas Boulevard. Completed in 1997 at a cost of $23 million, this 100,000-square-foot giant sports the usual chains like Sunglass Hut, Limited Express, Banana Republic, and The Gap, as well as lots of popular bars and restaurants.

Other more traditional malls include the upscale **Galleria,** at Sunrise Boulevard near the Fort Lauderdale Beach, and Broward Mall, west of I-95 on Broward Boulevard, in Plantation.

If you are looking for unusual boutiques, especially art galleries, head to trendy **Las Olas Boulevard** 🎭, where there are hundreds of shops with alluring window decorations (like kitchen utensils posing as modern art sculptures) and intriguing merchandise such as mural-size oil paintings.

On the edge of the Arts and Science District is **Las Olas Riverfront,** a retail complex with 260,000 square feet of restaurants, clothing stores, arcades, and a multiplex movie theater.

Lord & Taylor has a little-known clearance center where discounts on new clothing for women, kids, and men can be as much as 75% off. If you can handle open dressing rooms, overstuffed racks, and surly sales help, it's a great find at 6820 N. University Dr. in Tamarac. You may want to call ☎ **954/720-1915** to find out about specials.

The Fort Lauderdale Swap Shop, 3291 W. Sunrise Blvd. (☎ **954/791-SWAP**), is one of the world's largest flea markets. I think it's rather schlocky, actually. In addition to endless acres of vendors, there's a miniature amusement park, a 13-screen drive-in movie theater, weekend concerts, and even a free circus complete with elephants, horse shows, high-wire acts, and clowns.

The monster of all outlet malls is **Sawgrass Mills,** 12801 W. Sunrise Blvd., Sunrise (☎ **800-FL-MILLS** or 954/846-2350; fax 954/846-2312). Since the most recent expansion completed in mid-1999, which added more than 30 new designer outlet stores, this behemoth (shaped like a Florida alligator) now holds more than 300 shops, kiosks, a 24-screen movie theater, and many restaurants and bars including a Hard Rock Cafe. Make sure you note which section you parked in, as it is nearly impossible to locate your car in the equally mammoth, labyrinthine parking lot. The enclosed area covers nearly 2.5 million square feet over 50 acres. There's no way to see it all in a day. Wear your most comfortable shoes, or buy an extra pair while you're there. Stores include Donna Karan Company Store, Levi's Outlet, Sunglass Hut, Ann Taylor Loft, and Barney's New York, all selling goods at between 20% and 80% below retail. Label-conscious shoppers are especially impressed with Off Fifth, the Saks Fifth Avenue outlet store, and Last Call, the Neiman-Marcus clearance center. You may want to invest in a coupon booklet ($5), which entitles you to even greater discounts at many of the mall's stores and restaurants as well as area attractions. A booklet is good for up to a year and can be turned in for an updated booklet at no charge. To get there, take I-95 to I-595 west to the Flamingo Road exit, turn right, and drive 2 miles to Sunrise Boulevard; you will see the large complex on the left. From the Florida Turnpike, exit Sunrise Boulevard west.

Fishing enthusiasts won't want to miss **Bass Pro Shops Outdoor World** (200 Gulfstream Way, Dania Beach; ☎ **954/929-7710**), a sprawling retail complex just west of I-95 where you can buy anything from yachts to lures (see "Active Pursuits," above).

WHERE TO STAY

The Fort Lauderdale beach has a hotel or motel on nearly every block, and they range from the run-down to the luxurious. Both the **Howard Johnson** (☎ **800/327-8578** or 954/563-2451), at 700 N. Atlantic Blvd. (on Fla. A1A, south of Sunrise Boulevard), and the **Days Inn** (☎ **800/329-7466** or 954/462-0444), at 435 N. Atlantic Blvd. (Fla. A1A), offer clean ocean-side rooms starting at about $150.

In Hollywood, where prices are generally cheaper, the **Holiday Inn** at 101 N. Ocean Blvd. (☎ **954/921-0990**) operates a full-service hotel right on the ocean. With prices starting at around $110 in season and discounts for AAA members, it's a great deal. **Howard Johnson** (☎ **800/423-9867** or 954/925-1411) has a good location right on the beach at 2501 N. Ocean Dr. (I-95 to Sheridan Street east to Fla. A1A south).

Extended Stay America/Crossland Economy Studios (☎ **800/398-7829**) has four superclean properties in Fort Lauderdale and offers year-round rates as low as $49 a night and $159 per week. The studios are designed with business travelers in mind. Each includes free local calls, a dataport, a kitchenette, a recliner, and a well-lit desk.

Especially for rentals for a few weeks or months, call **Florida Sunbreak** (© **800-SUNBREAK**). Or call the **South Florida Hotel Network** (© **800/538-3616**) for help in finding small inns and lodges in any price range. Also, check out the annual list of small lodgings compiled by the **Fort Lauderdale Convention & Visitors Bureau** (© **954/765-4466**). It is especially helpful for those looking for privately owned, charming, and affordable lodgings.

VERY EXPENSIVE

The Diplomat Resort Country Club & Spa In its day, the Hollywood Diplomat was a swanky affair, an oceanfront playground attending to a host of celebs that included Sinatra and Co. The new Diplomat, scheduled to open in early 2002, is being built on the site of the original to the tune of $600 million and, at press time, was considered the largest and priciest beach resort project currently being developed in the U.S.

When complete, expect a 1,060-room full-service beach resort that's loaded with amenities. The hotel's main building is a 39-story oceanfront tower (with adjacent conference center) surrounded by 8 acres of man-made lakes. A gorgeous bridged, glass-bottomed swimming pool with cascading waterfalls, private cabanas, and a slew of watersports and activities adds a tropical touch.

The Diplomat's Country Club opened in March 2000 and is modeled after an Italian villa, with 60 luxurious guest rooms, yacht slips, a 155-acre golf course, and a world-class spa and tennis club. Rooms are spacious and comfortable, done up in Art Deco style; over 70% of them feature balconies with an ocean or Intracoastal view. Bathrooms are luxurious, too, with large tubs and bidets. In addition to the clubby Marty's restaurant, a 24-hour restaurant and airy cafe will ensure that you never go hungry. The Celebrity Lounge is a throwback to the hotel's glory days, with nightly 50s-style entertainment.

3555 S. Ocean Dr. (A1A), Hollywood, FL 33019 © 800/327-1212 or 954/457-2000. www.diplomatresort. com. 1,060 units. Winter $285–$370; off-season $195–$315. AE, DC, DISC, MC, V. Valet parking $16. **Amenities:** 8 restaurants, 3 lounges, golf course, 10 clay tennis courts, health club & spa, watersports equipment/rental. *In room:* A/C, TV, fax, dataport, Web TV, minibar, coffeemaker, hair dryer.

Hyatt Regency Pier Sixty-Six ✦✦ Located on 22 tropical acres on the Intracoastal Waterway, this resort is best known for its world-class marina and its rooftop lounge that spins every 66 minutes. If you experience vertigo after sitting in the revolving lounge, a treatment at the hotel's exquisite Spa LXVI will help relocate your sense of balance. An intimate, private European spa features a host of invigorating body and skin care treatments. Equally invigorating are the hotel's recreational amenities, which include a sprawling three-pool complex with a 40-person hydrotherapy pool, tennis courts, and an aquatic center complete with every water sport imaginable. The hotel's California Cafe is a popular, eclectic eatery. After a recent renovation, the tropical-style rooms are spruced up with cherry-wood furnishings and bathrooms with marble floors and granite vanities. All rooms have balconies with views of the Intracoastal and the hotel's lushly landscaped gardens. Designer suites come with Jacuzzi, wet bar, living room, dining room, and exceptional views.

2301 SE 17th St. Causeway, Fort Lauderdale, FL 33316. © 800/233-1234 or 954/525-6666. Fax 954/728-3541. www.hyatt.com. 380 units. Winter $289 double; off-season $229 double. Year-round from $1,000 suite. AE, DC, DISC, MC, V. Valet parking $10; self-parking $8 a day. **Amenities:** 3 restaurants, 3 bars,

2 swimming pools, 2 lighted clay tennis courts, spa, watersports equipment/rental, bike rental, children's center/ programs, concierge, tour desk, courtesy car, business center, shopping arcade, salon, 24-hr. room service, babysitting, dry-cleaning and laundry services, self-service laundry. *In room:* A/C, TV, dataport, minibar, coffeemaker, hair dryer.

Marriott's Harbor Beach 松松松 This resort is loaded with the same amenities as Pier Sixty-Six but with a more secluded setting, located on 16 oceanfront acres just south of Fort Lauderdale's "strip." Everything in this place is huge—from the guest rooms and suites to the 8,000-square-foot swimming pool to the $8 million 24,000-square-foot European spa. A huge 1999 renovation added a bit more personality to the formerly stale guest rooms and suites. Accommodations now feature marble, deep crown molding, and all new bathrooms with granite vanities, Italian marble flooring, and wrap-around mirrors. A revamped lobby affords sweeping ocean views. All rooms open onto private balconies overlooking either the ocean or the Intracoastal Waterway. The hotel's 3030 Ocean is an excellent seafood restaurant and raw bar; Riva, a Mediterranean-style, oceanfront eatery is also top-notch. Return guests include many convention groups and families who enjoy the space and the great location off the beaten strip.

3030 Holiday Dr., Fort Lauderdale, FL 33316. ℭ **800/222-6543** or 954/525-4000. Fax 954/766-6193. www.marriottharborbeach.com. 659 units. Winter $259–$429 double; off-season $99–$279 double. Year-round from $600 suite. AE, DC, DISC, MC, V. Valet parking $10. From I-95, exit on I-595 east to U.S. 1 N.; proceed to SE 17th St.; make a right and go over the Intracoastal bridge past 3 traffic lights to Holiday Dr.; turn right. **Amenities:** 4 restaurants, 2 bars, outdoor heated pool, 5 clay tennis courts, health club, European-style spa, extensive watersports equipment, bike rental, children's center and programs, game room, concierge, tour desk, courtesy car, business center, salon, 24-hr. room service, in-room massage, babysitting, laundry services and self-service. *In room:* A/C, TV, dataport, minibar, coffeemaker, hair dryer.

Wyndham Resort and Spa 松 This resort couldn't be any more remote, not to mention a long way from any water or beaches; but if you're looking for a purely spa and/or golf vacation—for which there are many packages available—it's not a bad choice. Located in an unoriginal planned community known as Weston, the resort is located on a man-made lake and golf course. Rooms are spacious and bathrooms are huge, all overlooking the lake or golf course.

250 Racquet Club Rd., Fort Lauderdale, FL 33326. ℭ **800/996-3426** or 954/389-3300. Fax 954/384-6878. www.wyndham.com. 496 units. Winter from $209–$289; off-season $134–$249. Golf and spa packages (with or without meals) $265–$305 per person based on double occupancy. AE, DC, DISC, MC, V. Valet parking $8. From I-95, exit at I-595, driving west to 136th Ave., S.R. 84; turn left to Bonaventure Blvd. Make a right to Racquet Club Rd. From W. I-75, exit 12 (Arvida Parkway), continue west to Weston Blvd.; turn right and proceed to Saddle Club Rd. Turn left to Bonaventure Blvd.; make a right to Racquet Club Rd. **Amenities:** 4 restaurants (nutritionist services available), 2 bars, 5 swimming pools, concierge, 24-hr. room service, dry-cleaning and laundry service, in-room massage, courtesy car. spa, Jacuzzi, sauna, 2 championship golf courses, 15 lighted tennis courts, children's programs, business center, tour desk. *In room:* A/C, TV, dataport, kitchenette in some suites, minibar, coffeemaker, hair dryer.

EXPENSIVE

Lago Mar Resort and Club 松松松 A charming lobby with a rock fireplace and saltwater aquarium sets the tone of this utterly inviting resort, a casually elegant piece of Old Florida that occupies its own little island between Lake Mayan and the Atlantic. Lago Mar guests have access to the broadest and best strip of beach in the entire city, not to mention the wonderful bougainvillea-lined, 9,000-square-foot swimming lagoon. Lago Mar is very family oriented, with lots of facilities and supervised activities for children, especially during Spring Break and Christmas vacations. Service is spectacular. The rooms and suites have

Mediterranean or Key West influences and are well appointed—but it's likely you won't be spending much time inside. The hotel's Northern Italian restaurant, Acquario, is worth a visit even if you don't stay here.

1700 S. Ocean Lane, Fort Lauderdale, FL 33316. © 800/524-6627 or 954/523-6511. Fax 954/524-6627. www.lagomar.com. 212 units. Winter $195 double, from $295 suite; off-season $100–$135 double, from $135 suite. AE, DC, MC, V. Free valet parking. From Federal Hwy. (U.S. 1), turn east onto SE 17th St. Causeway; turn right onto Mayan Dr.; turn right again onto S. Ocean Dr.; turn left onto Grace Dr.; then left again onto S. Ocean Lane to the hotel. **Amenities:** 4 restaurants, cocktail lounge, wine room, outdoor pool and lagoon, 4 tennis courts, exercise room, watersports equipment rental, children's programs during holiday periods, game room, concierge, tour desk, business center, 24-hr. room service, dry-cleaning and laundry services. *In room:* A/C, TV, dataport, hair dryer; kitchenette, coffeemaker in some units.

Riverside Hotel ⭒⭒   A touch of New Orleans hits Fort Lauderdale's popular Las Olas Boulevard in the form of this six-story 1936 hotel. There's no beach here, but the hotel is located on the sleepy and scenic New River, capturing the essence of that ever-elusive Old Florida. On weekends, the hotel is often packed with wedding guests who attend poolside ceremonies at the hotel, but it's definitely manageable. Guest rooms are a bit nicer than the public areas (outfitted in Mexican tile and wicker furnishings) and are spacious and well maintained. Details like intricately tiled bathrooms and old-style furniture enhance the charm of the otherwise stark building. The best rooms face the New River, but it's hard to see the water past the parking lot and trees. Twelve rooms offer king-size beds with mirrored canopies and flowing drapes. There are also seven elegantly decorated suites with wet bars and French doors that lead to private balconies. As of press time, the hotel had plans to nearly double its capacity by February 2002. The hotel has two restaurants worth trying: Indigo, a fantastic Asian/Indonesian restaurant in the hotel lobby (see "Where to Dine," below), and the Grill Room, for Old World elegance.

620 E. Las Olas Blvd., Fort Lauderdale, FL 33301. © 800/325-3280 or 954/467-0671. Fax 954/462-2148. www.riversidehotel.com. 116 units. Winter $179–$369 suite; off-season $124–$339 suite. Special packages are available; discount for online bookings. AE, DC, MC, V. Valet parking $8–$10. From I-95, exit onto Broward Blvd.; turn right onto Federal Hwy. (U.S. 1). Then left onto Las Olas Blvd. **Amenities:** 2 restaurants, outdoor pool, concierge, secretarial services, limited room service, babysitting, dry-cleaning and laundry services. *In room:* A/C, TV, dataport, minibar, fridge, coffeemaker, hair dryer.

MODERATE
Banyan Marina Apartments ⭒⭒   These fabulous waterfront apartments located on a beautifully landscaped residential island may have you vowing never to stay in a hotel again. They're intimate, charming, *and* reasonably priced. Built around a stunning 75-year-old banyan tree, the Banyan Marina Apartments are located directly on the active canals halfway between Fort Lauderdale's downtown and the beach. When available, you'll choose between one- and two-bedroom apartments. Apartments have been recently renovated and all are comfortable and spacious, with French doors, full kitchens, and living rooms. The best part of staying here, besides your gracious and knowledgeable hosts, Dagmar and Peter Neufeldt, is that the water taxi will find you here and take you anywhere you want to be day or night. There is also a small outdoor heated pool and a marina for those with boats in tow. In 1998, the Neufeldts were honored by a local campaign to enhance the area, Broward Beautiful, winning First Place in the category of small multifamily dwellings.

111 Isle of Venice, Fort Lauderdale, FL 33301. © 954/524-4430. Fax 954/764-4870. www.banyanmarina.com. 10 units. Winter $95–$225 apt.; off-season $60–$160 apt. Weekly and monthly rates available. MC, V. Free parking. To get there from I-95, exit Broward Blvd. E.; cross U.S. 1 and turn right

on SE 15th Ave. At the first traffic light (Las Olas Blvd.), turn left. Turn left at the third island (Isle of Venice). **Amenities:** Restaurant, pool, dock. *In room:* A/C, TV, dataport, kitchen, coffeemaker, hair dryer.

Blue Seas Courtyard 𝔾 *Value*   This 1940s motel will take you back to the days of Old Florida, thanks to a careful restoration and renovation. Rooms are large and bright, with full kitchens, huge bathrooms, terra-cotta tiles, Haitian and Peruvian art, and Southwest and Danish furnishings. Outside are a brick pool, flowing fountains, and lounges and tables facing the gardens or even the ocean, which is just a block away. Run by Cristie and Marc Furth, the Blue Seas is a wonderful discovery—like a unique shell you might find on the beach.

4525 El Mar Dr., Lauderdale-by-the-Sea, FL 33308 [tel **877/225-8373** or 954/772-6337. Fax 954/772-6337. www.blueseascourtyard.com. 12 units. Winter $64–$94; off-season $60–$69. Free parking. MC, V. **Amenities:** Heated pool, access to nearby tennis court, nearby children's playground, coin laundry. *In room:* A/C, TV.

Caribbean Quarters Bed and Breakfast Inn 𝔾𝔾   Built in 1939, this wonderful three-story bed and breakfast (a rarity in these parts) surrounds a lush courtyard tiered with Caribbean influenced, plantation-style wooden verandas and louvered doors opening from the spacious guest quarters. Most rooms have a private bedroom and a pullout couch in the living room, accommodating up to four people. The original cypress wood floors set off the plantation-style white wicker furniture and the colorful bedspreads. All have private baths and most come with a well-stocked kitchenette, making this place especially good for long stays and families. The inn is located a half-block from the beach and a number of shops and restaurants.

3012 Granada St., Fort Lauderdale, FL 33304. ℭ **888/414-3226** or 954/523-3226. Fax 954/523-7541. www.caribbeanquarters.com. 12 units. Winter $95–$220 double; off-season $75–$175 double. Rates include continental breakfast. AE, MC, V, DISC. *In-room:* A/C, TV/VCR, kitchenette or full kitchen, coffeemaker.

Courtyard Villa 𝔾𝔾   Nestled between a bunch of larger hotels, this small, eight-room historic hotel offers a romantic getaway right on the beach. It recently underwent a complete renovation, adding 19th-century antique reproduction furnishings to its charmed setting. Courtyard Villa offers spacious oceanfront efficiencies with private balconies, larger suites overlooking the pool, and full 2-bedroom apartments. Rooms are plush with chenille bedspreads and carved four-poster beds; fully equipped kitchenettes are an added convenience. The tiled bathrooms have strong hot showers to wash off the beach sand. Relax in the hotel's unique heated pool/spa or on the second floor sundeck. You can also swim off the beach to a living reef just 50 feet offshore. Scuba diving instruction is available on premises.

4312 El Mar Dr., Lauderdale-by-the-Sea, FL 33308. ℭ **800/291-3560** or 954/776-1164. Fax 954/491-0768. www.courtyardvilla.com. 8 units. Winter $150 double; off-season $105 double. Rates include full breakfast. AE, DC, MC, V. Pets are accepted with a $200 deposit, must be caged while outside; no pit bulls, Dobermans, or Rottweilers. **Amenities:** Outdoor heated pool, Jacuzzi, scuba instruction, free use of bikes, limited room service. *In room:* A/C, TV/VCR , kitchenette, coffeemaker, hair dryer.

Fun Fact **To Dive For**

The tiny, oceanfront enclave of Lauderdale-by-the-Sea is known as the Shore Diving Capital of Florida, with its own living reef just a hundred yards offshore. Only 15 feet deep and right off the beach, the reef lets you experience the underwater world of manta rays, sea turtles, octopus, coral reefs, and other sea life.

La Casa Del Mar 🏨🏨 *Finds*   The 10 rooms in this Spanish-Mediterranean B&B, situated right on the beach, are splendid, with private baths, each decorated in a motif inspired by an artist (such as Monet) or a regional style (such as Southwestern). Enjoy exquisite personal service by the English- and German-speaking co-owners. A delicious, home-cooked buffet-style breakfast is served in the main house but can be enjoyed outdoors under a mango tree in the resplendent garden. The swimming pool is large for such a small accommodation and is a great place to mingle at a late afternoon wine and cheese party with the other guests, who range from young couples to savvy European travelers. Best of all, it's a deal and a pretty well-kept secret.

3003 Granada St., Fort Lauderdale, FL 33304. ℂ 954/467-2037. Fax 954/467-7439. www.lacasadelmar. com. 10 units. Winter $110–$145; off-season $80–$100. Rates include breakfast. AE, MC, V. **Amenities:** Outdoor pool. *In room:* A/C, TV/VCR, fridge.

Ramada Inn Hollywood Beach Resort   There is nothing cozy or quaint about this sprawling 1920s beachfront hotel, but it couldn't be better located— on the ocean, halfway between Miami and Fort Lauderdale—or better priced. This eight-story building actually operates as a privately held condominium where owners can elect to put their units on a rental program. There's no telling how rooms may be outfitted, but management does maintain certain standards— and you're always guaranteed a full kitchen. On the premises is a large outdoor pool, tiki bar, and Jacuzzi; a 4-mile boardwalk makes for a great early-morning power walk. Nearby is burgeoning downtown Hollywood, which offers restaurants, bars, and shops.

101 N. Ocean Dr. (at Fla. A1A and Hollywood Blvd.), Hollywood, FL 33019. ℂ 954/921-0990. Fax 954/920-9480. 400 units (approximately 200 on rental program). Winter $127–$245; off-season $79–$159. AE, MC, V. Valet parking $9 per day. **Amenities:** Pool, Jacuzzi, laundry facilities. *In room:* A/C, TV, kitchen.

Traders Ocean Resort 🏨   Located directly on the beach, this recently renovated hotel is not luxurious; but its service is superb, amenities are plentiful, and its atmosphere is completely conducive to a most relaxing vacation. Rooms are large and comfortable, and many feature ocean views. An outdoor tiki bar, often with live entertainment, provides further encouragement to unwind. The hotel attracts a more mature crowd. However, if it's a tranquil vacation you're after, Traders may make a loyal customer out of you regardless of your age.

1600 S. Ocean Blvd., Pompano Beach, FL 33062. ℂ 800/325-5220 or 954/941-8400. Fax 954/941-1024. www.tradersresort.com. 93 units. Winter $95–$239; off-season $79–$139. AE, DC, DISC, MC, V. **Amenities:** Restaurant, lounge, tiki bar, freshwater heated outdoor pool, extensive watersports equipment/rental, shuffleboard, volleyball, concierge, massage. *In room:* A/C, TV.

INEXPENSIVE

Ronny Dee Resort Motel 🏨   The good news is that this family-owned motel is just 100 yards from the beach and extremely affordable. The bad news is that it's located on busy Fla. A1A. Popular with European guests, this two-story yellow motel is wrapped around a central swimming pool; its guest rooms are wood-paneled (suburban style) and filled with an eclectic mix of furniture. A new coat of paint and new flooring helped to spruce up the place recently. It's clean but not overflowing with all the creature comforts of other chain motels.

717 S. Ocean Blvd., Pompano Beach, FL 33062. ℂ 954/943-3020. Fax 954/783-5112. 35 units. Winter $49–$72 double, from $390 efficiency; off-season $35–$41 double, from $249 efficiency. AE, MC, V. From I-95, exit Atlantic Blvd. E. to Fla. A1A N. **Amenities:** Outdoor heated pool, game room. *In room:* A/C, TV, dataport, fridge.

Sea Downs (and the Bougainvillea) ✿✿ This bargain accommodation is often booked months in advance by returning guests who want to be directly on the beach without paying a fortune. The hosts of this superclean 1950s motel, Claudia and Karl Herzog, live on the premises and keep things running smoothly. Renovations completed in 1997 have replaced bathroom fixtures, and many rooms have been redecorated here and at the Herzogs' other even less expensive property next door, the Bougainvillea. Guests at both hotels share the Sea Downs pool.

2900 N. Surf Rd., Hollywood, FL 33019. ☎ **954/923-4968.** Fax 954/923-8747. www.seadowns.com or www.bougainvilleahollywood.com. 14 units. Winter $75–$126 daily, $301–$595 weekly; off-season $46–$91 daily; $280–$574 weekly. No credit cards accepted. From I-95, exit Sheridan St. E. to Fla. A1A S.; drive ½ mile to Coolidge St.; turn left. **Amenities:** Freshwater outdoor pool, concierge, laundry facilities. *In room:* A/C, TV, dataport, kitchen, fridge, coffeemaker.

A HOSTEL

Floyd's Youth Hostel/Crew House It's hard to imagine that crew members from the zillion-dollar yachts that ply these waters would want to stay at this no-frills, dirt-cheap hostel—but they come here in droves. While it is a few miles inland from the beach, this well-kept lodging offers what every backpacker and international traveler wants—safety and pleasant fellow travelers, not to mention a very social atmosphere. Floyd himself takes care of the guests, many of whom have come looking for work on the area's yachts. In fact, we have agreed not to list the address since Floyd insists on interviewing each prospective guest by phone before booking. Rest assured, you've found one of the area's best and safest hostels, with extras like a cupboard full of complimentary staples—milk, cereal, and generic-brand macaroni and cheese.

Call for address and directions. ☎ **954/462-0631.** Fax 954/462-6881. FECreamer@aol.com. 20-plus beds. $17 per person for a dorm bed; 4 nights for $64.60. No credit cards. Free daytime pickup.

WHERE TO DINE

It took a while for a more sophisticated, varied Epicurean scene to reach these shores, but Fort Lauderdale, and to some extent Hollywood, finally have several fine restaurants. Increasingly, ethnic options are joining the legions of surf-and-turferies that have dominated the area for so long. **Las Olas Boulevard** has so many eateries that the city has put a moratorium on the opening of new restaurants on the 2-mile-long street.

VERY EXPENSIVE

Darrel & Oliver's Cafe Maxx ✿✿ FLORIDIAN/NEW WORLD Despite its bleak location in an unassuming storefront, Darrel & Oliver's Cafe Maxx is one of the best restaurants in Broward County. When it opened in 1984, it was the first restaurant to have an open kitchen and what a stir that caused! Now, instead of focusing on the kitchen, it's what comes out of it that's a marvel. Consider duck and smoked mozzarella ravioli with brown butter, basil, and sun-dried tomatoes; sweet onion-crusted yellowtail snapper with Madeira sauce; or a macadamia-pesto–crusted veal chop.

2601 E. Atlantic Blvd., Pompano Beach. ☎ **954/782-0606.** Fax 954/782-0648. Reservations recommended. Main courses $18–$37. AE, DC, DISC, MC, V. Mon–Thurs 5:30–10:30pm, Fri–Sat 5:30–11pm, Sun 5:30–10pm. From I-95, exit at Atlantic Blvd. E. The restaurant is 3 lights east of Federal Hwy.

Left Bank ✮✮✮ FRENCH   Regulars complain that the usually brilliant provençal cuisine at the Left Bank has suffered now that Jean-Pierre Brehier has joined the celebrity-chef bandwagon. I think they just miss him. Brehier's sous-chefs handle his menu like pros. Compared with other chefs who flee the galley for the Food Network, Brehier is still very much devoted to his own kitchen. The Left Bank provides an elegant, romantic atmosphere that's bolstered by dark woods and large murals—perfect for Valentine's Day or an anniversary.

214 SE Sixth Ave. (north of Las Olas Blvd.), Fort Lauderdale. ✆ 954/462-5376. Reservations strongly recommended. Main courses $22.95–$34.95. AE, DC, MC, V. Sun–Thurs 5:30–9:30pm, Fri–Sat 5:30–10pm.

Mark's Las Olas ✮✮✮ NEW WORLD CUISINE   Before star chef Mark Militello hit Las Olas Boulevard, there was really no reason to dine here. Once he opened the doors to his sleek, modern Las Olas, he opened the eyes and mouths of discriminating Fort Lauderdale gourmands to his excellent new world cuisine. Grilled spiny lobster, with applewood smoked bacon-conch sauce, sweet plantain mash, and conch fritters, is possibly the best item on the menu. If the kitchen is out of it—they tend to run out quickly—everything else on the menu, from the tuna pizza to the wood-oven–roasted salmon, is delicious. Save room for a chocolate dessert—any one will do.

1032 E. Las Olas Blvd., Fort Lauderdale. ✆ 954/463-1000. Reservations suggested. Main courses $14–$30. Mon–Fri 11:30am–2:30pm; Mon–Thurs 6–10:30pm; Fri–Sat 6–11pm; Sun 6–10pm. AE, DC, MC, V.

EXPENSIVE

Armadillo Cafe ✮✮✮ SOUTHWESTERN   The city of Davie may be best known for farmland and rodeos, but it's also celebrated for this outstanding Southwestern restaurant, which attracts city slickers from all over South Florida. The Armadillo recently expanded its strip-mall digs to accommodate all the foodies who flock here in search of porcini-dusted sea bass and lobster quesadillas, among other things. At press time, a more casual offshoot, Armadillo Cafe 2.0, was slated to open, offering light meals, lunch, and dinner.

4630 SW 64th Ave. (Griffin Rd.), Davie. ✆ 954/791-5104. Reservations essential. AE, MC, DC, DISC, V. $16.95–$28.95. Mon–Thurs 5–10pm; Fri–Sun 5–11pm.

Burt and Jack's ✮ SEAFOOD/STEAKS   Burt—as in Reynolds—may not know how to pick a good script, but he sure can scout a great location. Located at Port Everglades in plain view of the mammoth cruise ships pulling in and out, Burt and Jack's serves adequate, albeit overpriced, surf 'n' turf to expense-account types and couples celebrating special occasions.

Berth 23 (South Terminal), Port Everglades. ✆ 954/522-5225. Reservations strongly recommended. Jacket required for men. Main courses $14.95–$37.95. AE, DC, DISC, MC, V. Sun–Thurs 4:30–9:30pm, Fri–Sat 4:30–10:30pm.

East City Grill ✮✮ AMERICAN/SEAFOOD   This happening spot on the beach, owned by the same folks who own the pricier Cafe Maxx (see above), offers an ocean-side location and a comprehensive and eclectic menu. For starters consider steamed crab and goat-cheese dumplings, innovative sushi dishes, or Jamaican beer-steamed prawns. A steamer bar allows you to create your own dinner with a choice of steaming broths, sauces, and sides. If you must, a printed menu also exists. Wait for your table at the elegant oak bar, from which you can observe the open kitchen. Try to score a seat on the covered patio overlooking the beach.

505 N. Fort Lauderdale Beach Blvd. (Fla. A1A between Las Olas and Sunrise blvds.), Fort Lauderdale. ✆ 954/565-5569. Fax 954/565-5582. Reservations recommended well in advance. Main courses $17–$28.

AE, DC, DISC, MC, V. Mon–Thurs 6pm–midnight, Fri 11:30am–3pm and 6pm–midnight; Sat brunch 11:30am–3pm, Sun brunch 8am–3pm; Sat–Sun dinner 5:30–10:30pm.

Gibby's Steaks and Seafood STEAKS/SEAFOOD
Gibby's brings you back to South Florida's days of early-bird specials and blue-haired ladies; it's as though time stopped, circa 1974. Loud, tacky, and mobbed with families, Gibby's is an institution that serves surf 'n' turf that's a step above cafeteria food. Early-bird specials are actually excellent deals, as are the summer lobster specials.

2900 NE 12th Terrace (1 block east of Dixie Hwy.), Fort Lauderdale. © 954/565-2929. Reservations suggested. Main courses $15.95–$29.95. AE, DC, DISC, MC, V. Mon–Fri 5–10pm, Sat–Sun 4:30–10pm.

Himmarshee Bar & Grille ᴳ AMERICAN
Located on a popular street of bars frequented by Fort Lauderdale's young professionals, Himmarshee Bar & Grille is better known for its cool scene than its cuisine. A mezzanine bar upstairs is ideal for people watching; outdoor tables, if you can score one, are tight but strategically situated in front of all the street's action. On Friday and Saturday nights, in particular, it's difficult to get a table here. However, if you can deal with cramming into the bar, it's worth a cocktail or two. The wine list is particularly impressive, and the grilled sirloin burger with creamy basil Gorgonzola is a delicious meal in itself for only $7.50.

210 SW Second St. (south of Broward Blvd., west of U.S. 1), Fort Lauderdale. © 954/524-1818. Reservations recommended. Main courses $12–$24. AE, MC, V. Mon–Fri 11:30am–2:30pm, Sun–Thurs 6–10:30pm, Fri–Sat 6–11:30pm.

Hobo's Fish Joint ᴳᴳ SEAFOOD
Huge portions of extremely fresh fish are prepared in more than a dozen ways at this steakhouse-style restaurant with wood floors and white tablecloths. Despite the fact that it's located away from the ocean in the utterly suburban enclave of Coral Springs, this joint is worth the trip for littleneck clams in garlic bouillon or Chilean sea bass oreganato on a bed of orzo.

10317 Royal Palm Blvd. (at Coral Springs Dr.), Coral Springs. © 954/346-5484. Reservations for 6 or more. Main courses $17–$27. AE, MC, V. Mon–Thurs 5:30–9:30pm, Fri–Sat 5:30–10:30pm, Sun 5:30–9pm.

Mai Kai ᴳᴳᴳ CHINESE/POLYNESIAN
Forget you're in the middle of a tacky stretch of Fort Lauderdale and immerse yourself in this fabulous vestige of Polynesian kitsch: hula dancers, fire-eaters, potent (and sickly sweet) drinks served in coconuts. The food, which draws an ambiguous line between Chinese, Polynesian, and other forms of Asian cuisine, is tasty enough but definitely overpriced. No matter, it's bound to get cold as you watch the hilarious show, which includes everything from Tahitian classics to Polynesian versions of American hits. Trippy and undeniably fun, a trip to Mai Kai is a must even if you just go for cocktails, which cost almost as much as a meal.

3599 N. Federal Hwy. (between Commercial and Oakland Park blvds.), Fort Lauderdale. © 954/563-3272. www.maikai.com. Reservations required. Main courses $14.50–$34. Shows (2 nightly) are $9.95 for adults; children 12 and under free. AE, DC, DISC, MC, V. Daily 5pm–midnight.

MODERATE
Aruba Beach Café CARIBBEAN
A local favorite, Aruba Beach Café is quintessential South Florida, located directly on the beach with a spectacular view of the ocean. As for the food, it's good for the proverbial "quick bite" or some drinks after beaching it all day. Enjoy safe bets like salads, pastas, and hamburgers; trying-too-hard-to-be-creative dishes such as Caribbean bamboo chicken and Pacific crab nachos may sound tasty, but they're better left on the

menu. A lively, friendly atmosphere of singles, boaters, and assorted beach bums contributes to Aruba's enormous popularity. Although the restaurant stops serving food at 11pm, the bar scene is alive and well until at least 2am.

1 E. Commercial Blvd. (east of A1A), Lauderdale-by-the-Sea. ℂ 954/776-0001. Main courses $7.95–$15.95. AE, DC, DISC, MC, V. Mon–Fri 11am–11pm, Sat–Sun 8:30am–11pm. Bar until 2am.

Calypso ℱ CARIBBEAN   A small strip-mall restaurant, Calypso has its pulse on the beat of Caribbean cuisine, serving delicious, spicy Caribbean dishes such as Jamaican jerk wings, barbecued shrimp, and smoked pork.

460 S. Cypress Rd., Pompano Beach ℂ]954/942-1633. Main courses $8–$15. AE, MC, V. Mon–Thurs 11am–10pm; Fri–Sat 11am–10:30pm; Sun noon–9:30pm.

Conca'D'Oro ℱ ITALIAN   This family-oriented Italian restaurant is always busy. It's not that the food is so extraordinary, but that the portions are large, service is quick, and the attitude is straight from Brooklyn. The pizzas, served Neapolitan (thin crust) or Sicilian style, are large and topped with lots of cheese and a tangy tomato sauce. Don't expect more than iceberg lettuce in the salads, but do take advantage of the huge hero sandwiches and palatable house wines. If you are with a group, order one or two entrees to share. You will have leftovers. Ask for fresh mussels if they're in season (they're not always on the menu). Although other appetizers are battered and fried, the young black mussels are done to perfection in a red or white sauce. Also good is the hearty lasagna that is full of chunks of garlicky meatballs and mild sausage.

1833 Tyler St. (on Young Circle), Hollywood. ℂ 954/927-6704. Reservations not accepted. Pizzas $7–$12.50. Main courses $10–$28. MC, V. Mon–Thurs 11am–11pm; Fri–Sat 11am–midnight; Sun 4–11pm.

Creolina's ℱℱ CREOLE   You'll find authentic Louisiana Creole cuisine at this small but very popular restaurant, situated along the River Walk in old town. Try the shrimp jambalaya with shrimp sausage and vegetables in a rich brown Cajun sauce served over rice, or the crayfish étouffée with crayfish tail simmered in a mellow Cajun sauce served over rice. The mashed potatoes are homemade, and the delicious fresh-squeezed lemonade is made daily. There is also a terrific New Orleans Sunday brunch. Ask to sit in sassy Rosie's section.

209 SW 2nd St., Fort Lauderdale. ℂ 954/524-2003. Appetizers $4–$9; main courses $13–$18. AE, MC, V. Mon–Fri 11am–2:30pm and 5–10pm; Fri–Sat 5–11pm; Sun brunch 11am–2:30pm.

Indigo ℱℱ SOUTHEAST ASIAN/ECLECTIC   It seems a little strange to chow down on southeast Asian food in an utterly New Orleans–style hotel, but this is South Florida—the wackier, the better. This not-so-traditional meal begins with a basket of pappadoms, puffy naan bread, and shrimp puff bread. Next might be a superrich grilled vegetable cassoulet au gratin and a fried rice dish with shallots, corn, and asparagus; or pizzas baked on top of nan covered with such toppings as onions, shiitake mushrooms, goat cheese, spinach, eggplant, garlic, curried tomato, and pine nuts. Particularly good is the meaty soy and portobello mushroom combination wrapped in fluffy puff pastry and served with a delicate broccoli sauce. Sounds like a lot of activity going on in one dish, but, like the restaurant itself, somehow it all works.

In the Riverside Hotel, 620 E. Las Olas Blvd., Fort Lauderdale. ℂ 954/467-0671. Reservations only for groups of 6 or more. Main courses $12–$22. AE, DC, DISC, MC, V. Daily 7am–9:45pm.

Sugar Reef ℱℱ FRENCH VIETNAMESE   I could go on about the restaurant's priceless, unobstructed ocean view, but the menu of Mediterranean,

Caribbean, and French-Vietnamese dishes is just as outstanding. A pleasant tropical decor is bolstered by the fresh air wafting in from the Atlantic through the open windows. Seafood bouillabaisse in green curry and coconut broth and pork loin Benedict—layers of jerk-spiced pork and hollandaise sauce—are among the restaurant's most popular dishes. The restaurant puts a savory spin on duck, roasted and topped with sweet chile and papaya salsa. This is not a restaurant you'd expect to find on a beach boardwalk, which makes it all the more delightful.

600 N. Surf Rd. (on the boardwalk just north of Hollywood Blvd.), Hollywood. © 954/922-1119. Reservations for 6 or more. Main courses $10–$24; sandwiches and salads $4–$9. AE, DISC, MC, V. Mon 4–10:30pm; Tues–Thurs 11am–10:30pm; Fri–Sun 11am–11pm (sometimes later in winter).

Sushi Blues Cafe JAPANESE   Live loud blues and jazz combine with good sushi to make an unusual pair at this slightly grungy, small storefront eatery located on Hollywood's largest traffic circle. About 12 tables and a dozen counter stools make up this relatively straightforward and unadorned sushi room. In addition to raw fish, the cafe offers some inventive specials like salmon carpaccio with caper sauce, fried soft-shell crab drizzled with a spicy sesame sauce, miso-broiled eggplant, and grilled smoked sausage with Japanese mustard. The restaurant is popular with a 20-something crowd that doesn't seem to be bothered by the fact that there are petrified rice grains on the floor. Live music packs them in on Friday and Saturday nights.

1836 S. Young Circle (east on Hollywood Blvd.), Hollywood. © 954/929-9560. Reservations recommended on weekends. Main courses $11–$20; sushi $1.75–$2.75 per piece. AE, MC, V. Mon–Thurs 6pm–midnight; Fri–Sat 6pm–2am.

Tarpon Bend 🐟🐟 SEAFOOD/AMERICAN   This restaurant is one of the few places where the fishermen still bring the fish to the back door. The oysters from the raw bar are shucked to order and out of sight. Try the house specialty "smoked fish dip"—a king fish smoked on premises. The steamed clambake, with half a Maine lobster, clams, potatoes, mussels, and corn on the cob is scrumptious and served in its own pot. Also try some of the homemade side dishes. For chocolate lovers, the chocolate brownie sundae is a must. There's live entertainment Wednesday through Saturday, and a full bar.

200 SW 2nd St., Fort Lauderdale. © 954/523-3233. Reservations available for parties of 6 or more. Main courses $12–$15. AE, M, V. Mon–Thurs 11:30am–1am; Fri–Sat 11:30am–3am.

Tuscan Today Trattoria 🐟🐟 *Finds* ITALIAN   For classic Tuscan food in a charming atmosphere, Tuscan Today is something you should not put off until tomorrow. Inspired by the peasant origins of the original trattoria, the restaurant consistently turns out outstanding pizzas and flavorful meat and fish from a customized wood-burning brick oven imported from Tuscany. A reasonable and excellent wine list provides you with a difficult choice in two affordable price ranges: $18.75 and $22.50. Artichokes steamed in white wine broth provide a flavorful balance between garlic and sun-dried tomatoes. Grilled thin-crusted pizzas are prepared as the Italians prefer them—light on sauce and cheese but heavy on flavor. For pasta lovers, the powerful but surprisingly light gnocchi with spinach is a good way to go. And if you order a meat or fish entree, be sure to try the rosemary roasted potatoes.

1161 N. Federal Hwy., Fort Lauderdale. © 954/566-1716. Reservations for 6 or more. Main courses $8.95–$14.95. AE, DC, DISC, MC, V. Sun–Thurs 11am–10pm; Fri–Sat 11am–11pm.

INEXPENSIVE

Carlos & Pepe ⋒ MEXICAN   Tucked away in yet another strip mall, Carlos & Pepe is a restaurant that doesn't need fancy digs to convince you that its authentic homemade Mexican cuisine is worth eating. The salsa, in particular, is excellent, not the watery bottled version you find in many Mexican establishments. The food is extremely fresh and flavorful and typical of what you'd find on a Mexican menu: fajitas, burritos, quesadillas, and enchiladas. The margaritas are also quite good, but beware—they do not skimp on the tequila. A low-key local crowd tends to frequent this very casual restaurant.

1302 SE 17th St. (south of Broward Blvd.), Fort Lauderdale. ⓒ 954/467-7192. Reservations not necessary. Main courses $8–$16. AE, DC, DISC, MC, V. Mon–Thurs 11:30am–11pm; Fri–Sat 11:30am–midnight; Sun noon–10pm.

Deli Den ⋒ JEWISH-STYLE DELI   Catering to Broward's New York crowd for nearly 3 decades, this warehouse-sized deli serves the area's finest cheese blintzes, red cabbage soup, and matzo balls. Breakfast selections include superthick French toast with bacon, sausage, or ham, plus dozens of egg specialties like minced lox, eggs and onions, or corned beef hash and eggs. All baking is done on the premises. And the owners are proud to say that absolutely everything else, from coleslaw to blintzes, is also homemade. Kids under 12 eat free every Monday and Thursday.

2889 Stirling Rd. (west of I-95), Hollywood. ⓒ 954/961-4070. Lunch $4.95–$6.95; main courses $9–$13; bagel sandwiches $1–$7.50. AE, MC, V. Daily 8am–10pm.

The Floridian Restaurant ⋒ *Value* AMERICAN/DINER   The Floridian has been filling South Florida's diner void for over 63 years, serving breakfast, lunch, and dinner, 24/7. It's especially busy on weekend mornings when locals and tourists come in for huge omelets, fresh oatmeal, sausage, and biscuits.

1410 E. Las Olas Blvd., Fort Lauderdale. ⓒ 954/463-4041. Fax 954/761-3930. Sandwiches $3–$7; breakfast combos $3.50–$8; hot platters $7–$14. No credit cards. Open 24 hours.

Jaxon's ⋒ *Kids* ICE CREAM   South Florida's best and only authentic old-fashioned ice cream parlor and country store attracts sweet teeth from all over the area looking to satisfy their cravings with an unabridged assortment of homemade ice cream served any which way. Kids love the place because of the candy store in the front of the restaurant, and adults love it for its pre–Ben and Jerry's authenticity. For the calorie-conscious, the sugar-free and fat-free versions are pretty good. Jaxon's most famous everything-but-the-kitchen-sink sundae features countless scoops and endless toppings.

128 S. Federal Hwy., Dania Beach. ⓒ 954/923-4445. Sundaes $2.75–$7.95. AE, DISC, MC, V. Mon–Thurs 11:30am–11pm, Fri–Sat 11:30am–midnight; Sun noon–11pm.

Lester's Diner ⋒ AMERICAN   Since 1968, Lester's Diner has been serving swarms of hungry South Floridians large portions of great greasy- spoon fare until the wee hours. Try the Eggs Benedict and the 14-ounce "cup" of classic coffee, or sample one of Lester's many homemade desserts. The place serves breakfast 24 hours a day and is a Fort Lauderdale institution that attracts locals, after-club crowds, city officials, and a generally motley, friendly crew of hungry people craving no-nonsense food served by seasoned waitresses, whose beehive hairdos only contribute to the campy atmosphere.

250 State Rd. 84, Fort Lauderdale. ⓒ 954/525-5641. AE, MC, V. Main courses $5–$12. Open 24 hours.

Thai Spice ⭐⭐ THAI   This could be the best Thai in Fort Lauderdale, but you'd never guess it from the tacky decor. Regular menu items include a slightly sweet and almost buttery pad Thai with a generous serving of shrimp, chicken chunks, and scallions. Lunch specials are incredibly cheap and include all the favorites.

1514 E. Commercial Blvd. (east of I-95), Fort Lauderdale. ℂ 954/771-4535. Fax 954/771-5678. Reservations recommended. Main courses $9.95–$26. AE, DC, DISC, MC, V. Lunch Mon–Fri 11am–3pm; dinner Sun–Thurs 5–10pm; Fri–Sat 5–11pm.

Taverna Opa ⭐⭐ *Value* GREEK   Don't get nervous if you hear plates breaking when you enter this raucous, authentic Greek taverna situated directly on the Intracoastal Waterway—it's just the restaurant's lively staff making sure your experience here is 100% Greek. Delicious *meze* (appetizers), including a large Greek salad with hunks of fresh feta cheese, moist and savory stuffed grape leaves, and grilled calamari, are offered at ridiculously cheap prices. If you've had enough ouzo, you may want to consider hopping up on one of the tables and dancing to the jacked-up Greek music. If not, don't worry; the waiters usually wind up on the tabletop, encouraging diners to shout the restaurant's name, "Opa!" making sure you don't forget it. You won't.

410 N. Ocean Dr., Hollywood. ℂ 954/929-4010. Reservations accepted weekdays only. Meze (appetizers) $2.95–$10. AE, DC, DISC, MC, V. Open daily from 4pm "until the ouzo runs out."

THE HOLLYWOOD & FORT LAUDERDALE AREA AFTER DARK

Fort Lauderdale no longer mimics the raucous antics of *Animal House* as far as nightlife and partying are concerned. It has gotten hip to the fact that an active nightlife is vital to the city's desires to distract sophisticated, savvy visitors from the magnetic lure of South Beach. And while Fort Lauderdale is no South Beach, it has vastly improved the quality of nightlife throughout the city by welcoming places that wouldn't dare host wet T-shirt and beer-chugging contests. It also lacks the South Beach attitude, which is part of the attraction.

Hollywood's nightlife seems to be in the throes of an identity crisis, touting itself as the next South Beach, while at the same time hyping its image as an attitude-free nocturnal playground. Here's the real deal: At press time, Hollywood nightlife was barely awake, with the exception of a few bars and one struggling dance club. If you're looking for quiet night out, it's probably your best bet. But don't come too late—after midnight, the city is absolutely deserted.

For information on clubs and events, pick up a free copy of Fort Lauderdale's weekly newspaper *City Link* or the Fort Lauderdale edition of the *New Times*.

Beach Place   This outdoor shopping and entertainment complex, modeled after Coconut Grove's hugely successful Cocowalk, landed on the legendary "strip" with several franchised bars and restaurants. It's popular with a young, rowdy set. The view overlooking the ocean makes it worth a stop for a drink. 17 S. Atlantic Blvd., Fort Lauderdale. ℂ 954/760-9570.

Chili Pepper   David Bowie, who rarely gives concerts anymore, played here: not on South Beach, but right in the heart of downtown Fort Lauderdale. And what a coup that was. Since Bowie, there've been tons of Billboard-charting, mostly alternative musicians who have made Chili Pepper a requisite stop on touring itineraries. 200 W. Broward Blvd., east of I-95. ℂ 954/525-0094. Wed–Sat 10pm to 3am. Cover varies from $0 to $20.

The Culture Room   If you consider rock and heavy metal to be culture visit the Culture Room and bang your head to local bands. 3045 N. Federal Hwy. (at the corner of Oakland Park Blvd.), Fort Lauderdale. ℂ **954/564-1074.** Daily 8pm–3am. Cover varies.

Deco Drive   While its name suggests South Beach, this 15,000-square-foot, three-story dance club tries too hard to be something it isn't. In fact, the only thing remotely South Beachy about Deco Drive is the number of silicone-enhanced women who seem to frequent the place. As for the men, can you say *Miami Vice* throwbacks? It's a decent place if you *must* dance, but remember: A 20-minute drive south to the real Deco Drive can make all the difference. 2031 Harrison St., Hollywood. ℂ **954/925-3326.** Fri and Sat 10pm till closing. No cover before midnight, $5 after midnight.

Elbo Room   Formerly Spring Break central, the Elbo Room has actually managed to maintain its rowdy and divey reputation by serving up frequent drink specials and live bands. 241 S. Atlantic Blvd. on the corner of Las Olas Boulevard and Fla. A1A. ℂ **954/463-4615.** Daily 10am–2am. No cover.

Nick's   With an idyllic location on Hollywood's broadwalk, Nick's is the best place to enjoy cocktails with an unobstructed view of the ocean. 1214 N. Broadwalk, Hollywood. ℂ **954/920-2800.** Open from 10am–4am. No cover.

O'Hara's   What used to be a mediocre jazz club has turned into a premier venue for excellent, live R&B, pop, and funk music. The club has two locations: at 1905 Hollywood Blvd., Hollywood (ℂ **954/925-2555** or the 24-hr. Jazz & Blues Hotline ℂ 954/524-2801); and 722 E. Las Olas Blvd., Fort Lauderdale (ℂ **954/524-1764**).

The Parrot   Fort Lauderdale's most famous—and fun—dive bar, The Parrot is a local's and out-of-towner's choice for an evening of beer (16 kinds on tap), bonding, and browsing of the bar's virtual gallery of photos of almost everyone who's ever imbibed here since its opening in 1970. 911 Sunrise Lane, Fort Lauderdale. ℂ **954/563-1493.** Sun–Thurs 11am–2am, Fri–Sat 11am–3am. No cover.

The Poor House   Despite its unfortunate name, the Poor House is rich in live blues music and is a good spot for a couple of drinks and conversation. 110 SW 3rd Ave., Fort Lauderdale. ℂ **954/522-5145.** Daily 8pm–4am. No cover.

Riverwalk   You'll find this outdoor shopping and entertainment complex located in the heart of downtown Fort Lauderdale on the sleepy yet scenic New River—as a result of its river site, it's got more charm than most such complexes. In fact, if you've got a boat, you can sail here and anchor away until you're ready to move on. A host of bars, restaurants, and shops, not to mention a high-tech virtual reality arcade, The Escape, and a multiplex cinema, are enough to keep you occupied for at least a few hours. On weekends, this place is packed. 400 SW 2nd St. (along the New River from NE 6th Avenue to SW 6th Avenue), Fort Lauderdale.

Rush Street   Known for its ice-cream flavors of martinis, from chocolate to Key lime, Rush Street is a sleek bar, with two dance floors, that attracts a young professional crowd. 220 SW 2nd St., Fort Lauderdale. ℂ **954/522-6900.** No cover.

Shooters   This waterfront bar is quintessential Fort Lauderdale. Inside, you'll find nautical types, families, and young professionals mixed in with a good dose of sunburned tourists enjoying the live reggae, jazz, or Jimmy Buffett–style tunes with the gorgeous backdrop of the bay and marinas all around. 3033 NE 32nd Ave., Fort Lauderdale. ℂ **954/566-2855.** Mon–Fri 11:30am–2am; Sat 11:30am–3am; Sun 10am–2am. No cover.

Where the Boys Are: Gay Fort Lauderdale

While South Beach is a magnet for the so-called circuit boys—gay men who party on a continual, ritualistic basis—Fort Lauderdale has more of a low-key, small-town scene similar to, say, Provincetown. Here, local gay-owned and -operated bars, clubs, and restaurants are the places of choice for those who find South Beach's scene too pretentious, superficial, and drug infested. The Fort Lauderdale neighborhood of Wilton Manors is the hub of gay life, but there is a smattering of gay establishments throughout the city.

The Copa, located at 2800 S. Federal Hwy. (east on I-595, near the airport; ⓒ **954/463-1507)** is the hottest gay spot north of South Beach—the granddaddy of Fort Lauderdale's gay club scene. Patrons of **Cathode Ray** call this bar their "Cheers." It's located at 1105 E. Las Olas Blvd. (ⓒ **954/462-8611). Georgie's Alibi** is Wilton Manors' most popular gay bar. Find it at 2266 Wilton Dr., Wilton Manors (ⓒ **954/565-2526).** Two great dance clubs are the **Coliseum** (2520 S. Miami Rd.; ⓒ **954/832-0100)** and **The Saint** (1000 W. S.R. 84; (ⓒ **954/525-7883).**

The Velvet Lounge   This lounge and dance club comes closest to the South Beach vibe with a (sometimes) chic crowd, pretty good DJs, and very little attitude. (The two times I was there, however, two people were arrested for fighting.) 2975 N. Federal Hwy. ⓒ 954/563-4331. Tues, Fri, and Sat 10pm–3am. Cover $0 to $10.

Warehaus 57   This is the place that gives Hollywood the right to boast about its burgeoning arty and bohemian scene. A funky cafe, bookstore, and clothing store, Warehaus 57 is the city's best (and only) acoustic club, in which the storefront window doubles as a stage for poets, singers, and other creative types. Despite the place's popularity, it doesn't stay open as late as it should and closes at 6pm on weeknights, at midnight on weekends. 1904-B Hollywood Blvd., Hollywood. ⓒ 954/926-6633.

2 Boca Raton ⭐⭐ & Delray Beach ⭐

26 miles S. of Palm Beach, 40 miles N. of Miami

Boca Raton is one of South Florida's most expensive, well-maintained cities—home to ladies who lunch and SUV-driving yuppies. The city's name literally translates as "rat's mouth," but you'd be hard-pressed to find rodents in this area's fancy digs. Instead, you might check out the International Museum of Cartoon Art (see below) for rodents of the Disney kind.

If you're looking for funky, wacky, and eclectic, look elsewhere. Boca is a luxurious resort community and, for some, the only place in South Florida worth staying in. Although Jerry Seinfeld's TV parents retired to the fictional Del Boca Vista, Boca's just too pricey to be a retirement community. With minimal nightlife, entertainment in Boca is restricted to leisure sports, excellent dining, and upscale shopping. The city's residents and vacationers happily comply.

Delray, named after a suburb of Detroit, grew up completely separate from its southern neighbor. This community was founded in 1894 by a Midwestern postmaster who sold off 5-acre lots through Michigan newspaper ads. Because of their close proximity, Boca and Delray can easily be explored together. Budget-conscious travelers would do well to eat and sleep in Delray and dip into Boca for sightseeing and beaching only.

ESSENTIALS

GETTING THERE   Like the rest of the cities on the Gold Coast, Boca Raton and Delray are easily reached from I-95 or the turnpike. Both the Fort Lauderdale/Hollywood International Airport and the Palm Beach International Airport (at Congress Avenue and Belvedere Road) are convenient. Amtrak (© **800/USA-RAIL;** www.amtrak.com) trains make stops in Delray Beach at an unattended station at 345 S. Congress Ave.

VISITOR INFORMATION   Before your trip, call or write the **Palm Beach County Convention and Visitors Bureau,** 1555 Palm Beach Lakes Blvd., Suite 204, West Palm Beach, FL 33401 (© **800/554-PALM** or 561/233-3000; fax 561/471-3990; www.palmbeachfl.com). On weekdays from 8:30am until at least 4pm, stop by the **Boca Raton Chamber of Commerce** at 1800 N. Dixie Hwy., 4 blocks north of Glades Road (© **561/395-4433;** fax 561/392-3780; www.bocaratonchamber.com), Boca Raton, FL 33432, for information on attractions, accommodations, and events in the area. Also, try the **Delray Beach Chamber of Commerce** (© **561/278-0424;** fax 561/278-0555; www.delraybeach.com), at 64 SE 5th Ave., half a block south of Atlantic Avenue on U.S. 1, Delray Beach, FL 33483.

WHERE TO PLAY, ON & OFF THE BEACH

BEACHES   Thankfully, Florida had the foresight to set aside some of its most beautiful coastal areas for the public's enjoyment. Many of the area's best beaches are located in state parks and are free to pedestrians and bikers. Most do charge for parking.

The **Delray Beach Public Beach,** on Ocean Boulevard at the east end of Atlantic Avenue, is one of the area's most popular hangouts. Weekends especially attract a young and good-looking crowd of active locals and tourists. Regular volleyball, Frisbee, and paddleball games make for good entertainment. For refreshments, snack shops, bars, and restaurants are just across the street. Families enjoy the protection of lifeguards on the clean, wide beach. Gentle waters make it a good swimming beach, too. There's limited parking at meters along Ocean Boulevard.

Spanish River Park, on North Ocean Boulevard (Fla. A1A), 2 miles north of Palmetto Park Road in Boca Raton, is a huge oceanfront park with a large grassy area, making it one of the best choices for picnicking. Facilities include picnic tables, grills, restrooms, and a bilevel 40-foot observation tower. You can walk through tunnels under the highway to access nature trails that wind through fertile grasslands. Volleyball nets are ocean-side and always have at least one serious game going on. The park is open from 8am until 8pm. Also, read below about Red Reef Park.

GOLF   This area has plenty of good courses. The best ones that are not located in a gated community are found at the **Boca Raton Resort & Club** (see below) and the **Inn at Boca Teeca** (see below). Another great place to swing your clubs is at the **Deer Creek Golf Club** in Deerfield Beach (© **954/421-5550**), a 300-plus-yard driving range where a large bucket of balls costs $7, and a small one costs $4. However, from May to October or November, about a dozen private courses open their greens to visitors staying in Palm Beach County hotels. This

"Golf-A-Round" program is free or severely discounted (carts are additional), and reservations can be made through most major hotels. Ask at your hotel, or contact the **Palm Beach County Convention and Visitors Bureau** (© 561/ 471-3995) for information on which clubs are available for play.

The semiprivate, 18-hole, par-61 course at the **Boca Raton Executive Country Club,** 7601 E. Country Club Blvd. (© 561/997-9410), is usually open to the public. A driving range is on the property as well as a pro shop, where you can rent clubs, and a restaurant. If you like, take lessons from a PGA pro. From Yamato Road East, turn left onto Old Dixie Highway; after about a mile, turn left onto Hidden Valley Boulevard and continue straight to the club. Greens fees are $11 to $27.

The **Boca Raton Municipal Golf Course,** 8111 Golf Course Rd. (© 561/ 483-6100), is located just north of Glades Road, half a mile west of the Florida Turnpike. This public 18-hole, par-72 course covers approximately 6,200 yards. There's a snack bar and a pro shop where clubs can be rented. Greens fees are $11 to $14 for 9 holes and $19 to $25 for 18 holes. Ask for special summer discount fees.

SCUBA DIVING & SNORKELING   **Moray Bend,** a 58-foot dive spot located about ¾ mile off Boca Inlet, is the area's most popular. It's home to three moray eels that are used to being fed by scuba divers. The reef is accessible by boat from **Force E Dive Center,** 877 E. Palmetto Park Rd., Boca Raton (© 561/368-0555). Phone for dive times. Dives cost $40 to $45 per person.

Red Reef Park, 1400 N. Ocean Park Blvd. (© 561/393-7974), a fully developed 67-acre oceanfront park in Boca Raton, has good swimming and year-round lifeguard protection. There's snorkeling for beginners around the rocks and reefs that lie just off the beach in 2 to 6 feet of water. The park also has restrooms and a small picnic area with grills and tables. Located a half-mile north of Palmetto Park Road, it is open daily from 8am to 10pm. You pay only if you drive in. It's $8 per car during the week or $10 on weekends.

TENNIS   The snazzy **Delray Beach Tennis Center,** 201 W. Atlantic Ave. (© 561/243-7360; www.delraytennis.com), has 14 lighted clay courts and 5 hard courts available by the hour. Phone for rates and reservations.

The 17 public lighted hard courts at **Patch Reef Park,** 2000 NW 51st St. (© 561/997-0881; www.tennistwist.com/patchreefpark.htm), are available by reservation. The fee for nonresidents is $5.75 per person per hour. Courts are available Monday to Saturday from 7:30am to 10pm and Sunday from 7:30am to dusk; you can phone ahead to see if a court is available. To reach the park from I-95, exit at Yamato Road West and continue past Military Trail to the park.

The Man Who Built Boca

Self-taught architect Addison Mizner was so impressed with the Palm Beach lifestyle when he visited in 1918 that he set about designing the community's mansions, country clubs, and most of exclusive Worth Avenue. In 1925 he focused his talents on Boca Raton, joining with his brother in bringing his visions of a Mediterranean-style resort city to fruition. When the stock market plunged in 1926, Mizner's plans came to a halt. However, his legacy is visible throughout the city of Boca Raton, whose houses, strip malls, and various buildings maintain Spanish barrel-tile roofs, arches, and columns.

SEEING THE SIGHTS

Boca Raton Museum of Art ✫✫   In addition to a relatively small but well-chosen permanent collection that's strongest in 19th-century European oils, the museum stages a wide variety of temporary exhibitions by local and international artists. Lectures and films are offered on a fairly regular basis, so call ahead for details. Additional fees may apply for special exhibits and performances.

Mizner Park, 501 Plaza Real, Boca Raton. © **561/392-2500.** Admission $3 adults, $2 seniors, $1 students, children under 12 free. Free on Wed. Tues, Thurs, Sat 10am–5pm; Wed, Fri 10am–9pm; Sun noon–5pm.

Dagger Wing Nature Center ✫✫✫   Seen enough snowbirds? Head over to this 39-acre swampy splendor where birds of another feather reside, including herons, egrets, woodpeckers, and warblers. The park's trails come complete with a soundtrack provided by songbirds hovering above (watch your head).

South County Regional Park, 11200 Park Access Rd., Boca Raton. © **561/488-9953.** Free admission. Tues–Fri 1–4:30pm, Sat 9am–4:30pm. Call for tour and activity schedule.

Gumbo Limbo Environmental Complex ✫✫✫   If manicured lawns and golf courses aren't your idea of communing with nature, then head to Gumbo Limbo. Named for an indigenous hardwood tree with continuously shedding bronze bark, the 20-acre complex protects one of the few surviving coastal hammocks, or forest islands, in South Florida. Visitors can walk through the hammock on a ½-mile-long elevated boardwalk that ends at a 40-foot observation tower, from which you can see the Atlantic Ocean, the Intracoastal Waterway, and much of Boca Raton. From mid-April to September, sea turtles come ashore here to lay their eggs.

1801 N. Ocean Blvd. (on Fla. A1A between Spanish River Blvd. and Palmetto Park), Boca Raton. © **561/338-1473.** Fax 561/338-1483. Free admission. Mon–Sat 9am–4pm, Sun noon–4pm.

International Museum of Cartoon Art ✫✫ *(Kids*   This extensive collection of cartoon art spans the decades and styles in its glitzy home in Mizner Park. In a gorgeous 52,000-square-foot gallery space, cartoon fans can see prints, frames, moving pictures, and books by some of the world's greatest cartoonists, including many by the museum's late founder, Mort Walker (of *Beetle Bailey* fame). A fantastic gift shop offers posters, books, and lots of memorabilia.

201 Plaza Real at Mizner Park, Boca Raton. © **561/391-2200.** www.cartoon.org. Admission $6 adults, $5 seniors, $4 students, $3 children 6–12 years old, members and ages 5 and under free. Tues–Sat 10am–6pm, Sun noon–6pm.

Morikami Museum and Japanese Gardens ✫✫✫   Slip off your shoes and enter into a serene Japanese garden community that dates from 1905, when an entrepreneurial farmer, Jo Sakai, came to Boca Raton to build a tropical agricultural community. The Yamato Colony, as it was known, was short-lived; by the 1920s only one tenacious colonist remained: George Sukeji Morikami. But Morikami was quite successful, eventually holding one of the largest pineapple plantations in the area. The 200-acre Morikami Museum and Japanese Gardens (a stroll through the garden is actually ⅞ mile), which opened to the public in 1977, was Morikami's gift to Palm Beach County and the State of Florida. The park section, dedicated to the preservation of Japanese culture, is constructed to appeal to all the senses. An artificial waterfall that cascades into a koi- and carp-filled moat; a small rock garden for meditation; and a large bonsai collection that includes miniature maple, buttonwood, juniper, and Australian pine trees are all worth contemplation. The Gardens have been expanded, and there's also a cafe with a Japanese- and Asian-inspired menu if you want to stay for lunch.

4000 Morikami Park Rd., Delray Beach. © 561/495-0233. Museum $7 adults, $6 seniors, $4 children 6–18, free for members and children 5 and under. Museum Tues–Sun 10am–5pm; gardens Tues–Sat 10am–5pm. Closed major holidays.

SHOPPING & BROWSING

Even if you don't plan to buy anything, a trip to Boca Raton's **Mizner Park** is essential for capturing the essence of the city. Like Main Street in a small town, Mizner is the place to see and be seen, where Rolls Royces and Ferraris are parked curbside, freshly coifed women sit amidst shopping bags at outdoor cafes, and young movers and shakers make evening plans on their constantly buzzing cell phones. Beyond the human scenery, however, Mizner Park is scenic in its own right with beautiful landscaping. It's really an outdoor mall, with 45 specialty shops, seven good restaurants, and a multiplex. Each shop front faces a grassy island with blue and green gazebos, potted plants, and garden benches. Mizner Park is located on Federal Highway (between Palmetto Park Road and Glades Road; © **561/362-0606**).

Boca's **Town Center Mall,** located on the south side of Glades Road, just west of I-95, has seven huge department stores, including the state's only Nordstrom as well as Bloomingdale's, Burdines, Lord & Taylor, and Saks Fifth Avenue. Add to that the hundreds of specialty shops, an extensive food court, and a range of other restaurants, and you have the area's most comprehensive shopping center.

A lifeless, overrated area, but good enough for a quick stroll, is the more artsy community of **Delray Beach,** known by many as Pineapple Grove. Here, along Atlantic Avenue, especially east of Swinton Avenue, you'll find a few antique shops, clothing stores, and art galleries shaded by palm trees and colorful awnings. Pick up the "Downtown Delray Beach" map and guide at almost any of the stores on this strip, or call © **561/278-0424** for more information.

WHERE TO STAY

If you choose to stay in Boca Raton or the surrounding areas, you will find some very luxurious lodgings, epitomized by the famous and often photographed pink **Boca Raton Resort and Club,** where Boca's country-club lifestyle is alive and well.

A number of national chain hotels worth considering include a moderately priced **Holiday Inn Highland Beach Oceanside** at 2809 S. Ocean Blvd., on Fla. A1A southeast of Linton Boulevard (© **800/234-6835** or 561/278-6241). **The Radisson Bridge Resort** (see review below), at 999 E. Camino Real (© **800/333-3333** or 561/368-9500), operates a particularly popular and affordable resort on the Intracoastal Waterway just a few blocks from the Boca Raton Resort. Beware: It books up well in advance.

Although you won't find rows of cheap hotels as in Fort Lauderdale and Hollywood, a handful of mom-and-pop motels have survived along Fla. A1A between the towering condominiums of Delray Beach. Look along the beach just south of Atlantic Boulevard. Especially noteworthy is the pleasant little two-story, shingle-roofed **Bermuda Inn** at 64 S. Ocean Blvd. (© **561/276-5288**).

Even more economical options can be found in Deerfield Beach, Boca's neighbor, south of the county line. A number of beachfront efficiencies offer great deals, even in the winter months. Try the **Panther Motel and Apartments,** at 715 S. A1A (© **954/427-0700**). This clean and convenient motel has rates starting as low as $40, although in season you may have to book for a week at a time. Weekly rates in season start at $457.

If you are looking for something more private or for longer than just a few days, you may want to call a reservations service for help. **Palm Beach Accommodations** (© **800/543-SWIM**) handles rentals for a few weeks or months.

VERY EXPENSIVE

Boca Raton Resort and Club 🎔🎔   Built in 1926 as the Cloister Inn by Addison Mizner, the posh Boca Raton Resort now comprises three oddly matched buildings: the original, more traditional Cloister building; the somewhat drab, pink 27-story Tower; and the more modern, airier Beach Club, which is accessible by a water shuttle. Everything at this resort, which straddles the Intracoastal and encompasses over 350 acres of land, is fully at your fingertips but may sometimes require a little effort to reach it. The amenities here cannot be beat. The resort features two 18-hole championship golf courses as well as 60 golf villas located directly on the course, a $10 million Tennis and Fitness Center, indoor basketball and racquetball courts, a 25-slip marina with full fishing and boating facilities, and a private beach with various watersports equipment for rent. With a choice of 10 places to dine, including Lucca, a grand waterfront Tuscan-style restaurant designed by David Rockwell and run by Drew Nieporent's Myriad Restaurant Group; and 27 Ocean Blue, an eclectic restaurant combining the flavors of the Pacific Rim, Caribbean, Deep South, Hawaii, and Florida's "New World" cuisine; plus five pools to swim in and an excellent children's program, the resort is ideal for families. Malone's Magic Bar features table-side magic tricks, while Bar Luna offers an elegant and inviting wine library. Upon check in, see if Harry the bellman is available to take you to your room—he's been at the resort for over 46 years and has a photographic memory of the hotel's previous guests, from Joseph Cotton and Charlton Heston to Bill Gates, who became a partner in the hotel after spending enough time there.

501 E. Camino Real (P.O. Box 5025), Boca Raton, FL 33431. © **800/327-0101** or 561/395-3000. Fax 561/447-3183. www.bocaresort.com. 963 units, 120 golf villas. Winter $260–$625 double; off-season $160–$370. Reasonable seasonal packages available. AE, DC, DISC, MC, V. From I-95 N., exit onto Palmetto Park Rd. E. Turn right onto Federal Hwy. (U.S. 1), and then left onto Camino Real to the resort. **Amenities:** 10 restaurants, 6 bars, 5 pools, 2 18-hole championship golf courses, 34 tennis courts, 3 health clubs, indoor basketball court, 4 indoor racquetball courts, 25-slip marina with full fishing and boating, watersports equipment/rental, extensive children's programs, concierge, business center, 24-hr. room service, laundry. *In room:* A/C, TV, minibar, hair dryer.

MODERATE

Colony Hotel & Cabana Club 🎔🎔   The Colony was recently added to the National Trust for Historic Preservation's prestigious list of 150 hotels, resorts, and inns that combine history and architectural significance. The hotel is definitely up to speed with modern amenities but remains steeped in the Old Florida tradition of the seasonal resort, and is open only from November 1 to May 1. This three-story hotel is 2 miles from the Cabana Club, its meticulously maintained private beach and club with 250 feet of beach and a heated pool. Shuttles are available, but the walk is a pleasant one if you're not in a hurry. The guest rooms are modest in size and style but comfortable and clean with wood floors and antique John Wanamaker furniture dating back to the hotel's inception. All rooms are nonsmoking. Service is friendly, not overbearing,

Boca Raton & Delray Beach Accommodations & Dining

ACCOMMODATIONS ■
Boca Raton
Resort and Club **20**
Colony Hotel &
Cabana Club **2**
Delray Beach Marriott **5**
The Inn at Boca Teeca **8**
Ocean Lodge **16**
Radisson Bridge Resort
of Boca Raton **19**
Seagate Hotel &
Beach Club **6**
Shore Edge Motel **15**
Spanish River Resort **4**

DINING ◆
Baja Cafe **14**
Bistro Zenith **9**
Gigi's Tavern **13**
La Vieille Maison **17**
Mark's at the Park **13**
Mario's of Boca **11**
Max's Grille **13**
New York Prime **10**
Splendid Blendeds **3**
The Tin Muffin Cafe **18**
32 East **1**
Tom's Place **7**
Uncle Tai's **12**

0 ___ 1 mi
0 ___ 1 km

Lake Ida Rd.
Lake Ida
Military Trail
Barwick Rd.
Swinton Ave.
NE 5th Ave.
NE 6th Ave.
NE 2nd Ave.
Ocean Blvd
W. Atlantic Ave.
DELRAY BEACH
Lowson Blvd.
SW 10th St.
Linton Blvd.
A1A
Old Dixie Hwy.
N. Federal Hwy.
Congress Ave.
Clint Moore Rd.
Yamato Rd.
NW 51st St.
NW Spanish River Blvd.
Boca Raton Airport
BOCA RATON
FLORIDA ATLANTIC UNIVERSITY
St. Andrews Blvd.
Military Trail
Powerline Rd.
Glades Rd.
NW 20th St.
Old Dixie Hwy.
Federal Hwy.
NE 5th Ave.
Ocean Blvd
A1A
W. Palmetto Park Rd.
W. Camino Real
Lake Boca Raton
Intracoastal Waterway
ATLANTIC OCEAN

contributing to the feeling that you're staying at someone's plush beach house in, say, Kennebunkport, Maine, where the hotel's sister property is located.

525 E. Atlantic Ave. (P.O. Box 970), Delray Beach, FL 33483. ✆ **800/552-2363** or 561/276-4123. Fax 561/276-0123. www.thecolonyhotel.com. 66 units. Winter $165–$205 double; off-season $75–$135 double. AE, MC, V. **Amenities:** Restaurant, bar, heated pool, music room, putting green, weight room, afternoon tea. *In room:* A/C, TV, dataport, hair dryer.

Delray Beach Marriott ☽

Delray Beach may be a sleepy beach town, but those looking for a bit more excitement will find it in this Marriott, which features a host of activities and amenities that may almost convince you that Delray is an exciting, lively place! The hotel, decked out in a typical, yet charming, Marriott-Florida decor, offers the best of both worlds: It's located directly across the street from the slumberous beach, but on premises it has an enormous, active outdoor pool and a lively lounge. Children under 18 stay free with an adult.

10 N. Ocean Blvd., Delray Beach, FL 33483. ✆ **800/228-9290** or 561/274-3200. Fax 561/274-3202. 268 units. Winter $245–$269; Off-season $119–$139. AE, DC, DISC, MC, V. **Amenities:** Restaurant, lounge, large outdoor pool, health club, concierge. *In room:* A/C, TV, dataport, hair dryer, coffeemaker.

The Inn at Boca Teeca ☽☽☽

For over three decades, this inn has been attracting golf fanatics who could care less about the small, but comfortable, rooms because they're too busy out on the superb 27-hole golf course at the Inn's Boca Teeca Country Club, open only to members and guests of the Inn. For the golf widow(er)s, however, most of the rooms in this three-story building have balconies or patios from which to watch or signal their significant others that it's time for dinner.

5800 NW 2nd Ave., Boca Raton, FL 33487. ✆ **561/994-0400.** Fax 561/998-8279. 46 units. Winter $140 and up; off-season $80–$120. AE, DC, MC, V. **Amenities:** Restaurant; small pool, golf course, 6 tennis courts, fitness center. *In room:* A/C, TV.

Radisson Bridge Resort of Boca Raton ☽☽

Not as pricey as the Boca Raton Resort, this resort nevertheless does feature priceless water views and is an excellent choice for the money. All guest rooms have balconies with views of the Intracoastal or the Atlantic, and some corner suites have both. Its popular outdoor waterfront restaurant, Watercolors, is the only place in the city to dine on the water. The restaurant and lounge at the top of the hotel behold gorgeous panoramic views. Just a 5-minute walk to the beach, this Radisson bridges the gap between ultra-pricey and ultra-schlocky area hotels.

999 E. Camino Real, Boca Raton, FL 33432. ✆ **800/333-3333** or 561/368-9500. Fax 561/362-0492. www.radisson.com. 121 units. Winter $209–$299; off-season $109–$189. Some rates include breakfast. AE, DC, MC, V. **Amenities:** 2 restaurants, outdoor heated pool, health club & spa, watersports equipment/rental, bike rental, concierge. *In room:* A/C, TV, hair dryer, coffeemaker.

Seagate Hotel & Beach Club ☽

This modest hotel is better known for its beach club than for its "apartment suites." Recent renovations replaced the quaint Old Florida furnishings with industrial Formica, plain blond wood, and commercial-grade carpeting, stripping it of most, if not all, of its charm. The bathrooms remain tiny with little or no counter space, but the kitchens are a plus. Escape to the hotel's Beach Club, which is much more spacious with 400 feet of private beach and special programs for children.

400 S. Ocean Blvd., Delray Beach, FL 33483. ✆ **800/233-3581** or 561/276-2421. Fax 561/243-4714. www.hudsonhotels.com. 70 units. Winter $194–$349 suite; $398–$419 2-bedroom suite. Off-season $74–$305 suite; $136–$375 2-bedroom suite. AE, DC, MC, V. From I-95, exit onto Atlantic Ave. E. Turn right onto Ocean Blvd. (Fla. A1A), and continue ½ mile to the hotel. **Amenities:** Poolside grill, 2 heated pools. *In room:* A/C, TV, kitchen, hair dryer, coffeemaker.

Spanish River Resort ⭐⭐⭐   An especially good value for those staying longer than a few days, this pleasant family-oriented property offers fully furnished condominiums half a block from a popular beach and within walking distance of Delray's best shops, restaurants, and galleries. The 11-story Mediterranean-style building has lighted tennis courts, a large outdoor pool, and lovely ocean-view balconies from the fourth floor and above. Apartments are spacious and outfitted with fully equipped kitchens. All units also have pullout queen-size sofa beds and, incredibly, there is no additional charge for extra guests. A one-bedroom unit can comfortably fit four or five people; a two-bedroom unit can easily accommodate six. Cots and rollaway beds are available at a minimum charge. Compared with many of the run-down 1950s motels in the area, this moderately priced, well-maintained tower is a real find.

1111 E. Atlantic Ave., Delray Beach, FL 33483. ✆ 800/543-SWIM or 561/243-7946. Fax 561/276-9634. 75 units. Winter $150 studio; $350 2-bedroom. Off-season from $98 studio; $228 2-bedroom. Free 6th and 7th nights with weekly booking. AE, DISC, MC, V. **Amenities:** Restaurant, outdoor pool, lighted tennis courts. *In room:* A/C, TV.

INEXPENSIVE

Ocean Lodge ⭐   Situated around a small heated pool and sundeck, this two-story motel is a particularly well-kept accommodation in an area of run-down or overpriced options. The large rooms offer furnishings and decor that are clean but a bit impersonal. A recent renovation that added modern Formica and floral wallpaper lifts this a notch above a basic motel. Ask for a room in the back since the street noise can be a bit loud, especially in season. The bonus is that you are across the street from the ocean and in one of Florida's most upscale resort towns.

531 N. Ocean Blvd. (just north of Palmetto Park Rd. on Fla. A1A), Boca Raton, FL 33432. ✆ 800/STAY-BOCA or 561/395-7772. Fax 561/395-0554. 18 units. Winter $99–$125 double; off-season $75–$99 double. AE, MC, V. **Amenities:** Pool. *In room:* A/C, TV.

Shore Edge Motel   Another relic of the 1950s recently spiffed up with new landscaping and some redecorating, this motel is a good choice, especially because of its location—across the street from a public beach, just north of downtown Boca Raton. It's the quintessential South Florida motel: a small, pink, single-story structure surrounding a modest swimming pool and courtyard. Although the rooms are on the small side, they're very neat and clean. The higher-priced accommodations are larger and come with full kitchens.

425 N. Ocean Blvd. (on Fla. A1A, north of Palmetto Park Rd.), Boca Raton, FL 33432. ✆ 561/395-4491. Fax 561/347-8759. 16 units. Winter $85–$99 double; off-season $55–$65 double. AE, MC, V. **Amenities:** Pool. *In room:* A/C, TV.

WHERE TO DINE

Boca Raton, and its surrounding area, is the kind of place where you discuss dinner plans at the breakfast table. Nightlife in Boca means going out to a restaurant. But who cares? These are some of the best restaurants in South Florida.

VERY EXPENSIVE

La Vieille Maison ⭐⭐⭐ FRENCH   The luxurious setting, a Mediterranean-inspired home filled with a variety of antique French furnishings and paintings, gives you the feeling of walking into a small chateau. Culinarily speaking, this place is a castle. Begin with lobster bisque, gratin of escargots with fennel and pistachio nuts, or pan-seared foie gras—each is equally delectable. It's difficult to choose from the many enticing entrees, which range from red snapper in black- and green-olive potato crust to medallions of beef, lamb, and venison over three sauces. You'll surely have to try at least a few of the gorgeous cheeses the server offers after your main course—the most extensive selection I've seen in this country. The lemon crepe soufflé with raspberry sauce is the dessert of choice—remember to order it early.

770 E. Palmetto Park Rd., Boca Raton. (℃ **561/391-6701** or 561/737-5677. Reservations recommended. Main courses $18–$50; fixed-price dinners $42 and $68. AE, DC, DISC, MC, V. Daily 6–9:30pm (call for seating times).

New York Prime ★★★ STEAKHOUSE   Forget Morton's and Smith & Wollensky. This South Florida outpost of a South Carolina–based chain is the prime spot for carnivores looking to satisfy their cravings for big, succulent steaks. Fish dishes are also available, including lobsters ranging from 3 to 13 pounds. But the price of excess does not come cheap. In fact, the restaurant brazenly states its case on the menu: "We strive to be the Mercedes of steakhouses by offering the very best . . . but you can't drive a Mercedes for the same price as a Buick." To me, this is more like the DeLorean of steakhouses—a rare find.

2350 Executive Center Dr., Boca Raton. (℃ **561/998-3881**. Reservations recommended. Main courses $22.50–$64. AE, MC, V. Daily 5–11pm.

EXPENSIVE

32 East ★★ NEW AMERICAN   The menu changes every day at this very popular people-watching outpost of tasty, contemporary American food that has finally added a little hip to the Delray Beach dining scene. Delicious items have included rigatoni with braised lamb shank and oregano; hanger steak on roasted-garlic polenta; and grilled salmon with arugula purée and olive tapenade.

32 E. Atlantic Ave., Delray Beach. (℃ **561/276-7868**. Reservations recommended. Main courses $10–$16. AE, DC, MC, V. Sun–Thurs 5:30–10pm, Fri–Sat 5:30–11pm; bar until 2am.

Bistro Zenith ★ NEW AMERICAN   At the height of innovative cuisine, Bistro Zenith's consistently changing menu keeps local foodies coming back for its tasty offerings of traditional American dishes graced with Oriental, Mediterranean, or Southwestern influences served in a high-tech atmosphere. During its Southwestern phase, Zenith hit a new high with a fantastic Grand Canyon chicken with red beans, ancho chili sauce, rice, corn tortillas, and Tex-Mex corn and cilantro oil.

Regency Court, 3011 Yamato Rd., Boca Raton. (℃ **561/997-2570**. Reservations recommended. Main courses $9–$15. AE, MC, V. Lunch Mon–Fri 11:30am–2:30pm. Dinner Sun–Thurs 5:30–10pm, Fri–Sat 5:30–11pm.

Gigi's Tavern AMERICAN   Gigi's is a nightclub in the guise of a restaurant. Noisy and jam packed, especially on weekends, Gigi's makes it hard for diners to focus on their plates, nearly impossible to converse with their fellow diners. Not surprisingly, service is as rushed as the latest dance remix. Oysters and other appetizers are your best bets. Just make sure to let your food digest before you start spinning on the small dance floor.

346 Plaza Real, in Mizner Park, Boca Raton. (℃ **561/368-4488**. Reservations suggested. Main courses $15–$20. AE, DC, MC, V. Mon–Thurs 11:30am–11pm, Fri–Sat 11:30am–midnight, Sun 11:30am–10:30pm.

Mark's at the Park ★★ MEDITERRANEAN   Star chef Mark Militello's contribution to Boca Raton's restaurant scene attracts a well-toned, sleek crowd that seems only to pick at the restaurant's excellent thin-crusted pizzas, grilled meats, and seafood. Indoor seating is loud and bustling, and outdoor tables are coveted for their views of Mizner Park pedestrian traffic. Sunday brunch here is a fabulous all-you-can-eat affair of pizzas, salads, pastas, and assorted gourmet breakfast foods.

In Mizner Park, 344 Plaza Real, Boca Raton. ℂ 561/395-0770. Reservations suggested. $11–$28. AE, DC, MC, V. Sun–Thurs 5:30–11pm, Fri–Sat 5:30pm–midnight.

Max's Grille ★★ AMERICAN   Max's Grille is a very popular, very good option in Mizner Park, but you will inevitably wait to be seated. With a large exhibition kitchen that occupies the entire back wall of the restaurant, those lucky enough to score a table can watch as their yellowfin tuna steak or filet mignon is seared on a flaming oak grill. There's also a large selection of chicken, meatloaf, pastas, and main-course salads.

404 Plaza Real, in Mizner Park, Boca Raton. ℂ 561/368-0080. Reservations accepted for 6 or more. Main courses $14–$26; pastas $10.95–$16.95. AE , DC, DISC, MC, V. Lunch Mon–Sat 11:30am–3pm. Dinner Mon–Thurs 5–10:30pm, Fri–Sat 5–11pm. Sun brunch/dinner 11:30am–10pm.

Uncle Tai's ★★★ CHINESE   Not your average egg roll and lo-mein kind of place, Uncle Tai's, Boca's best upscale Chinese restaurant, offers a savory spin on classics such as garlic chicken and duck with plum sauce. A family-run restaurant, Uncle Tai's is the product of Wen Dah Tai, a man who studied with the master chefs in China, Japan, and the Phillippines. Like your favorite uncle, Tai wants to make sure you will emerge from his restaurant fully satisfied and will even go the extra mile to discourage you from ordering a dish that's less suited to Western palates, having been created for the restaurant's many Chinese diners (always a good sign).

5250 Town Center Circle (between Glades and Palmetto Park rds.), Boca Raton. ℂ 561/368-8806. Reservations suggested. Main courses $12–$32. AE, DISC, MC, V. Daily 11:30am–2:30pm and 5–10pm.

MODERATE

Mario's of Boca ★ ITALIAN   This extremely popular, bustling Italian bistro keeps Boca's biggest mouths busy with massive portions of great homemade Italian food. The garlic rolls and the pizza are especially worth piping down for. If you're really hungry, there's an all-you-can-eat buffet 7 days a week.

2200 Glades Rd. (between 19th St. and Sheridan Way), Boca Raton. ℂ 561/392-5595. Reservations not accepted. Main courses under $15. AE, MC, V. Mon–Thurs 11:30am–10pm, Fri–Sat 11:30am–11pm, Sun noon–9:30pm.

Splendid Blendeds ★★ (Finds ECLECTIC   Loyal regulars would like to keep this storefront bistro a secret so that the lines won't get even longer on weekends. The draw here is fresh, uncomplicated seafood and pastas that are interesting without being overly ambitious. The Southwestern-inspired chicken Santa Cruz is tender and juicy, served with a black-bean sauce and tangy pico de gallo. Many seafood specialties, like tuna, snapper, and shrimp dishes, are slight departures from classic recipes and work most of the time. The only drawback of this otherwise superb spot, aside from the name, is the well-meaning but easily flustered staff.

432 E. Atlantic Ave., Delray. ℂ 561/265-1035. Reservations recommended. Main courses $10.95–$21.95; sandwiches and salads $3.50–$8.95. AE, DC, MC, V. Mon–Fri 11:30am–2:30pm, Mon–Sat 5:30–10pm. Closed Aug.

INEXPENSIVE

Baja Cafe ⭐ MEXICAN   A jeans and T-shirt kind of place with wooden tables, Baja Cafe serves fantastic Mexican food at even better prices. It's located right by the Florida East Coast Railway tracks, so don't be surprised if you feel a little rattling. Live music and entertainment in the evening make this place a hot spot for an unpretentious crowd.

201 NW First Ave., Boca Raton. ✆ 561/ 394-5449. No reservations. Main courses $6–$10. No credit cards. Mon–Thurs 11:30am–10:30pm, Fri–Sat 11:30am–11pm, Sun 5–10pm.

The Tin Muffin Cafe ⭐ BAKERY/SANDWICH SHOP   Popular with the downtown lunch crowd, this excellent storefront bakery keeps them lining up for big fresh sandwiches on fresh bread, plus muffins, quiches, and good home-made soups like split pea or lentil. The curried chicken sandwich is stuffed with oversized chunks of only white meat doused in a creamy curry dressing and fruit. There are a few cafe tables inside and even one outside on a tiny patio. Be warned, however, that service is forgivably slow and parking is a nightmare. Try parking a few blocks away at a meter on the street.

364 E. Palmetto Park Rd. (between Federal Hwy. and the Intracoastal Bridge), Boca Raton. ✆ 561/ 392-9446. Sandwiches and salads $6.50–$10.95. No credit cards. Mon–Fri 11am–5pm, Sat 11am–4pm.

Tom's Place ⭐⭐ *Finds* BARBECUE   There are two important factors in a suc-cessful barbecue: the cooking and the sauce. Tom and Helen Wright's no-nonsense shack wins on both counts, offering flawlessly grilled meats paired with well-spiced sauces. Beef, chicken, pork, and fish are served soul-food style, with your choice of two sides such as rice with gravy, collard greens, black-eyed peas, coleslaw, or mashed potatoes. Signed celebrity photographs decorate the walls.

7251 N. Federal Hwy., Boca Raton. ✆ 561/997-0920. Reservations not accepted. Main courses $8–$15; sandwiches $5–$6; early bird special $7.95. AE, MC, V. Tues–Thurs 11:30am–9:30pm, Fri 11:30am–10; Sat noon–10pm.

BOCA RATON & DELRAY AFTER DARK
THE BAR, CLUB & MUSIC SCENE

South Ocean Boulevard and Atlantic Avenue in Delray Beach are slowly but surely getting hip to nightlife—though still a far cry from the Fort Lauderdale "strip." In Boca Raton, Mizner Park is the nucleus of a makeshift nightlife, with restaurant-bars and restaurants disguising themselves as nightclubs (see Gigi's Tavern, above).

Boston's on the Beach is a family restaurant with a somewhat lively bar scene. It's a good choice for post-sunbathing, supercasual happy hours on Monday to Friday from 4 to 8pm, or for live reggae on Monday. With two decks overlook-ing the ocean, Boston's is an ideal place to mellow out and take in the scenery. 40 S. Ocean Blvd., Delray Beach. ✆ 561/278-3364. Daily 7am–2am. No cover.

Dakotah 624 Creative cocktails such as the Kissing Cousin (Southern Com-fort, Fris vodka, lime juice, and triple sec) and its own line of cigars attract a hip, young clientele to this vaguely Southwestern-style bar on the beach. 270 E. Atlantic Ave., Delray Beach. ✆ 561/274-6244. Mon–Wed 4pm–1am, Thurs–Sat 4pm–2am, Sun 4–11pm. No cover.

Gatsby's This always-busy bar is singles central, featuring big-screen TVs, microbrews, and martinis. Thursday-night college nights are especially popular, as are Friday happy hours. 5970 SW 18th St., Boca Raton. ✆ 561/393-3900. Mon–Fri 4pm–2am, Sat–Sun 6pm–4am. No cover.

Mezzanotte   The Mezzanotte on South Beach's Washington Avenue used to be the place for a bacchanalian funfest. Then the place went from crazy to closed. The good times have traveled north to this Boca offshoot, where a well-tanned, glitzy crowd of young and old let their hair (or toupees) down, especially on weekends. 150 E. Palmetto Park Rd., Boca Raton. ✆ 561/361-0111. Sun–Thurs 5–10pm, Fri–Sat 5pm–2am. No cover.

Radius   This big, noisy techno-trance warehouse west of the highway attracts a range of big-haired girls and macho guys with gold chains. It's Boca's only attempt at a clubby nightlife and, if you don't mind dancing with a really young crowd, it can be amusing depending on your sense of humor. If you can, try to have your hotel concierge put you on the "list" so you won't have to shell out $20 or more for this nocturnal gamble. 7000 W. Palmetto Park Rd. (at the SW corner of Powerline Rd. in the Bank of America building). ✆ 561/392-3747. Thurs–Sun 9pm–5am. Cover varies $5–$20.

THE PERFORMING ARTS

For details on upcoming events, check the *Boca News* or the *Sun-Sentinel,* or call the **Palm Beach County Cultural Council** information line at ✆ 800/882-ARTS. During business hours, a staffer can give details on current performances. After hours, a recorded message describes the week's events. The *Sun-Sentinel* also hosts a comprehensive "Source Line" for information on everything from weather to garage sales. Detailed arts information is included.

The **Florida Symphonic Pops,** a 70-piece professional orchestra, performs jazz, swing, rock, big band, and classical music throughout Boca Raton. For nearly 50 years, this ever-growing musical force has entertained audiences of every age. Call ✆ 561/393-7677 for a schedule of concerts.

Boca's best theater company is the **Caldwell Theatre,** and it's worth checking out. Located in a strip shopping center at 7873 N. Federal Hwy., this equity showcase does well-known dramas, comedies, classics, off-Broadway hits, and new works throughout the year. Prices are reasonable (usually between $29 and $38). Full-time students will be especially interested in the little-advertised "Student Rush." When available, tickets are sold for $5 to those who arrive at least an hour in advance. Call ✆ 561/241-7432 for details.

3 Palm Beach ⍟ & West Palm Beach ⍟

65 miles N. of Miami, 193 miles E. of Tampa

Palm Beach County encompasses cities from Boca Raton in the south to Jupiter and Tequesta in the north. But it is Palm Beach, the small island town across the Intracoastal Waterway, that has been the traditional winter home of America's aristocracy—the Kennedys, the Rockefellers, the Pulitzers, the Trumps, titled socialites, and plenty of CEOs.

The island holds the distinction of being the only continental destination with three resorts that have earned the AAA five-diamonds rating. And beyond the upscale resorts and chic boutiques, it holds some surprises too, from a world-class art museum to one of the top bird-watching areas in the state.

Over the bridge from Palm Beach proper, or the "island" as locals call it, is downtown West Palm Beach, which is where everybody else lives. Clematis Street is the area's nightlife hub, with a great selection of bars, clubs, and restaurants. City Place is West Palm's version of Mizner Park; shops, restaurants, and other entertainment options liven up this once-dead area of West Palm. In addition to good beaching, boating, and diving, you'll find great golf and tennis throughout the county.

> **(Fun Fact** See Them All Standing in a Row
>
> In 1878 the Spanish brigantine *Providencia,* bound from Trinidad to Cadiz
> with a cargo of coconuts, washed ashore on an unknown island. The
> strewn coconuts propagated and caused a wild growth of palm trees. That
> island, of course, was Palm Beach.

ESSENTIALS

GETTING THERE   If you're driving up or down the Florida coast, you'll probably reach the Palm Beach area by way of I-95. Exit at Belvedere Road or Okeechobee Boulevard and head east to reach the most central part of Palm Beach.

Visitors on their way to or from Orlando or Miami should take the Florida Turnpike, a toll road with a speed limit of 65 miles per hour. Tolls are pricey, though; you may pay upward of $9 from Orlando and $4 from Miami. If you're coming from Florida's west coast, you can take either State Route 70, which runs north of Lake Okeechobee to Fort Pierce, or State Route 80, which runs south of the lake to Palm Beach.

Among the airlines serving Palm Beach International Airport, at Congress Avenue and Belvedere Road (© **561/471-7400**), are **American** (© **800/ 433-7300**), **Continental** (© **800/525-0280**), **Delta** (© **800/221-1212**), **Kiwi** (© **800/538-5494**), **Northwest** (© **800/225-2525**), **TWA** (© **800/ 221-2000**), **United** (© **800/241-6522**), and **US Airways** (© **800/428-4322**).

Amtrak (© **800/USA-RAIL;** www.amtrak.com) has a terminal in West Palm Beach, at 201 S. Tamarind Ave. (© **561/832-6169**).

GETTING AROUND   Although a car is almost a necessity in this area, a recently revamped public transportation system is extremely convenient for getting to some attractions. Palm Tran underwent a major expansion in late 1996, increasing service to 32 routes and more than 140 buses. The fare is $1 for adults and 50¢ for children ages 3 to 18, seniors, and riders with disabilities. Free route maps are available by calling © **561/233-4-BUS.** Information operators are available from 6am to 7pm, except Sunday.

In downtown West Palm, free shuttles operate Monday through Friday from 9am until 4pm, with plans to expand operations to evenings and weekends too. Look for the bubble-gum–pink minibuses throughout downtown. Call © **561/833-8873** for more details.

For a more nostalgic route, consider the stately wicker chariots that run in the downtown area especially on weekends and during special events. Rates vary according to the time of day but average $1 to $2 per block, plus a per person charge of $1. Call © **561/835-8922** for pickup or information.

VISITOR INFORMATION   The **Palm Beach County Convention and Visitors Bureau,** 1555 Palm Beach Lakes Blvd., Suite 204, West Palm Beach, FL 33401 (© **800/554-PALM** or 561/471-3995; www.palmbeach.com), distributes an informative brochure and will answer questions about visiting the Palm Beaches. Ask for a map as well as a copy of its Arts and Attractions Calendar, a day-to-day guide to art, music, stage, and other events in the county.

FUN ON & OFF THE BEACH

BEACHES   Public beaches are a rare commodity here in Palm Beach. Most of the island's best beaches are fronted by private estates and inaccessible to the general public. However, there are a few notable exceptions, including **Midtown Beach** on Ocean Boulevard, between Royal Palm Way and Gulfstream Road, which boasts more than 100 feet of undeveloped beach. There are no restrooms or concessions here, although a lifeguard is on duty until sundown. This newly widened sandy coast is now a centerpiece and a natural oasis in a town dominated by commercial glitz. Also, about 1½ miles north **near Dunbar Street** is a popular hangout for locals, who enjoy the relaxed atmosphere. Parking is available at meters along Fla. A1A. To the south is a less popular but better-equipped beach at

Tips Winter Advisory

Palm Beach's population swells from 20,000 in the summer to 40,000 in the winter. Book early if you plan to visit during the winter months!

Phipps Ocean Park. On Ocean Boulevard, between the Southern Boulevard and Lake Avenue causeways, is a large and lively public beach encompassing more than 1,300 feet of groomed and guarded oceanfront. With picnic and recreation areas, as well as plenty of parking, the area is especially good for families.

BIKING   Rent anything from an English single-speed to a full-tilt mountain bike at the **Palm Beach Bicycle Trail Shop,** 223 Sunrise Ave. (© 561/659-4583). The rates are —$7 an hour, $18 a half day (9am to 5pm), or $24 for 24 hours—and include a basket and lock (not that a lock is necessary in this fortress of a town). The most scenic route is called the Lake Trail, running the length of the island along the Intracoastal Waterway. On it you'll see some of the most magnificent mansions and grounds. Enjoy the views of downtown West Palm Beach and some great wildlife.

CRUISES   The *Palm Beach Princess* (© 800/841-7447 or 561/845-7447), is a small cruise ship (421 feet) offering reasonably priced casino gambling cruises out of the Port of Palm Beach (U.S. 1 between 45th Street and Blue Heron Boulevard) every day and evening. Choose from craps, roulette, poker, blackjack, and slots. Cruises include a large buffet with average food like spaghetti and meatballs, chicken, Greek salad, and vegetables; best is the prime rib at the carving board. Five-hour cruises sail daily at 12:30pm (returning at 5:30pm) and 7pm (returning at 12:30am). Friday and Saturday evening cruises leave at 7pm and return at 1am. Sunday cruises sail from 11am to 5pm and 6 to11pm. Prices during the week are $40 per person; on weekends, it's $45 per person. If your birthday is in the month you plan to sail, pay $20. AAA discounts are available.

GOLF   There's good golfing here, but many of the private club courses are maintained exclusively for the use of their members. Ask at your hotel, or contact the **Palm Beach County Convention and Visitors Bureau** (© 561/471-3995) for information on which clubs are currently available for play. In the off-season, some private courses open their greens to visitors staying in a Palm Beach County hotel. This "Golf-A-Round" program offers free greens fees (carts are additional); reservations can be made through most major hotels.

The best hotel for golf in the area is the **PGA National Resort and Spa** (see below, © 800/633-9150), which features a whopping 90 holes of golf.

One of the state's best courses that is open to the public is **Emerald Dunes Golf Course** ❀, 2100 Emerald Dunes Dr. in West Palm Beach (© 561/687-1700). Courses are also found in Delray Beach and Boynton Beach.

Designed by Tom Fazio, this dramatic 7,006-yard, par-72 course was voted "One of the Best 10 You Can Play" by *Golf* magazine. It is located just off the Florida Turnpike at Okeechobee Boulevard. Bookings are taken up to 30 days ahead. Fees start at $125, including carts.

The **Palm Beach Public Golf Course,** 2345 S. Ocean Blvd. (© **561/547-0598**), a popular public 18-hole course, is a par-54. The course opens at 8am and runs on a first-come, first-served basis. Club rentals are available. Greens fees start at $20 per person.

POLO   What's Palm Beach without polo? See the "Sport of Kings" (below) for details.

SCUBA DIVING   Year-round warm waters, barrier reefs, and plenty of wrecks make South Florida one of the world's most popular places for diving. One of the best-known artificial reefs in this area is a vintage Rolls-Royce Silver Shadow, which was sunk offshore in 1985. Mother Nature has taken her toll, however, and divers can no longer sit in the car, which has been ravaged by time and saltwater.

Call either of the following outfitters for gear and excursions: **Dixie Divers,** 1401 S. Military Trail, West Palm Beach (© **561/969-6688**); and **Ocean Sports Scuba Center,** 1736 S. Congress Ave., West Palm Beach (© **561/641-1144**).

TENNIS   There are hundreds of tennis courts in Palm Beach County. Wherever you are staying, you are bound to be within walking distance of one. In addition to the many hotel tennis courts (see "Where to Stay," below), you can play at **Currie Park,** 2400 N. Flagler Dr., West Palm Beach (© **561/835-7025**), a public park with three lighted hard courts. They are free and available on a first-come, first-served basis.

WATERSPORTS   Call the **Seaside Activities Station** (© **561/835-8922**) to arrange sailboat, jet-ski, bicycle, kayak, water-ski, and parasail rentals.

SEEING THE SIGHTS
Flagler Museum ☆☆☆   The Gilded Age is preserved in this luxurious mansion commissioned by Standard Oil tycoon Henry Flagler as a wedding present to his third wife. *Whitehall,* also known as the "Taj Mahal of North America," is a classically columned Edwardian-style mansion containing 55 rooms, including a Louis XIV music room and art gallery, a Louis XV ballroom, and 14 guest suites outfitted with original antique European furnishings. Out back, climb aboard "The Rambler," Mr. Flagler's private, restored railroad car. Allow at least 1½ hours to tour the stunning grounds and interior. School and group tours are available, but, for the most part, this is a self-guided museum.

1 Whitehall Way (at Cocoanut Row and Whitehall Way), Palm Beach. © 561/655-2833. www.flagler.org. Admission $8 adults, $3 children ages 6–12. Tues–Sat 10am–5pm, Sun noon–5pm.

Saluting Flagler

It was Henry Morrison Flagler's dream to build a grand hotel for the passengers of his Florida East Coast Railroad, and he selected Palm Beach. In 1894 his Royal Poinciana Hotel became the largest resort hotel in the world and reputedly the largest wooden structure ever built. In 1896 Flagler built a smaller oceanfront hotel called the Palm Beach Inn. He later enlarged it and renamed it the Breakers. Flagler's own marble mansion, "Whitehall" (1901), is now a museum bearing his name; it is open to the public for a fascinating look at turn-of-the-century life in the tropics.

The Sport of Kings

The annual ritual of the ponies is played out each season at the posh Palm Beach Polo and Country Club. It is one of the world's premier polo grounds and hosts some of the sport's top-rated players.

Even if you're not a sports fan, you must attend a match. Although the field is actually on the mainland in an area called Wellington, rest assured that the spectators, and many of the players, are pure Palm Beach. After all, a day at the pony grounds is one of the only good reasons to leave Palm Beach proper.

Don't worry, though—you need not be a Vanderbilt or a Kennedy to attend. Matches are open to the public and are surprisingly affordable.

Even if you haven't a clue to how the game is played, you can spend your time people-watching. Stargazers have spotted Prince Charles, Sylvester Stallone, Tommy Lee Jones, Bo Derek, and Ivana Trump in recent years, among others. Dozens of lesser-known royalty, and just plain old characters, keep box seats or chalets right on the grounds.

Incidentally, the point of polo is to keep the other team from getting the ball through your goal. The fast-paced game is divided into six chukkers—like an inning in baseball—each 7 minutes long. There are 3-minute breaks between chukkers except at half time, which lasts 10 minutes. The whole thing is narrated by a British chap who sounds as though he walked off a Monty Python set.

Dress is casual; a navy or tweed blazer over jeans or khakis is a standard for men, while neat-looking jeans or a pantsuit is the norm for women. On warmer days, shorts and, of course, a polo shirt are fine, too.

General admission is $6 to $10; box seats cost $10 to $36. Matches are held throughout the week. Schedules vary, but the big names usually compete on Sunday at 3:30pm from January to April.

The fields are located at 11809 Polo Club Rd., Wellington, 10 miles west of the Forest Hill Boulevard exit of I-95. Call © **561/793-1440** for tickets and a detailed schedule of events.

Norton Museum of Art ★★★   Since a 1997 expansion doubled the Norton's space, the museum has gained even more prominence in the art world. It is world famous for its prestigious permanent collection and top temporary exhibitions. The museum's major collections are divided geographically. The American galleries contain major works by Edward Hopper, Georgia O'Keeffe, and Jackson Pollock. The French collection contains Impressionist and post-Impressionist paintings by Cézanne, Degas, Gauguin, Matisse, Monet, Picasso, Pissarro, and Renoir. And the Chinese collection contains more then 200 bronzes, jades, and ceramics, as well as a collection of monumental Buddhist sculptures.

1451 S. Olive Ave., West Palm Beach. © **561/832-5196**. Fax 561/659-4689. www.norton.org. Admission $6 adults, $2 students, free for children 12 and under. Mon–Sat 10am–5pm, Sun noon–5pm. Free admission Wed from 1:30pm–5pm. From I-95, take Belvedere Rd. (Exit 51) east to the end; then turn left onto S. Olive Ave. to the museum.

Unreal Estate

No trip to Palm Beach is complete without at least a glimpse of Mar-A-Lago, the stately residence of Donald Trump, the 21st century's answer to Jay Gatsby. In 1985, Trump purchased Mar-A-Lago, the former estate of cereal heiress Marjorie Merriweather Post, for what was considered a meager $8 million (for a fully furnished beachfront property of this stature, it was a relative bargain, actually) to the great consternation of locals who feared that he would turn the place into a casino. Instead, Trump, who resides in a portion of the palace, opened the house to the public—for a price, of course—as a tony country club (membership fee: $100,000). Infinitely more interesting than any of Trump's real estate acquisitions, Mar-A-Lago, Spanish for "from lake to sea," has a history that's priceless.

Built as Post's vacation home in 1923, Mar-A-Lago eventually became the heiress's primary residence, which she shared with second husband, E.F. Hutton. Together they lived in utter opulence, throwing gala events and lavish dinner parties on a nightly basis. The dining room, with 27 different china patterns and at least 4,000 pieces of silver, was modeled after the Chigi Palace in Rome. Other rooms captured various styles, including Venetian and Norwegian. The exterior, done in a Hispano-Moresque style, featured a massive collection of Spanish tile for the rooftops.

When Post died in 1973 she bequeathed Mar-a-Lago to the U.S. government for use in housing presidents and travelling dignitaries. Because the maintenance was in excess of $1 million a year, the government eventually returned the estate to the Post Foundation. Enter the Donald, who, to everyone's surprise, restored the home to its original glory, saying, "Some people collect artworks . . . I collect great homes."

While there are currently no tours open to the public, you can glimpse the gorgeous manse as you cross the bridge from West Palm Beach into Palm Beach. Its website, at www.pbol.com/maralago/tour.html, offers photos, a calendar of events, and more details than you'd ever care to know. 1100 S. Ocean Blvd., Palm Beach. ⓒ561/833-2466.

Playmobil Fun Park 🏃🏃 *Kids*   In a child's mind, it doesn't get any better than this. The 17,000-square-foot Playmobil Fun Park is housed in a replica castle and loaded with themed areas for imaginative play: a medieval village, a western town, a fantasy doll house, and more. Plus, there are two water-filled tables on which kids can play with the Playmobil boats. Tech-minded kids could get bored, but toddlers (and up to age 5 or so) will love this place. You *could* spend hours here and not spend a penny, but parents beware: Everything is available for purchase.

8031 N. Military Trail, Palm Beach Gardens. ⓒ **800/351-8697** or 561/691-9880. Fax 561/691-9517. www.playmobil.com. Admission free. Daily 10am–6pm. From I-95, go north to Palm Beach Lakes Blvd.; then west to Military Trail. Turn left, and the park is about a mile down on the right .

NATURE PRESERVES & ATTRACTIONS

Lion Country Safari 🐾 *(kids)*   More than 1,300 animals on this 500-acre preserve are divided into their indigenous regions, from the East African preserve of the Serengeti to the American West. Elephants, wildebeest, ostriches, American bison, buffalo, watusi, pink flamingos, and many other more unusual species roam the preserve. When I visited, most of the lions were asleep; when they are awake, they travel freely throughout the cageless grassy landscape. In fact, you're the one who's confined in your own car without an escort (no convertibles allowed). You're given a detailed informational pamphlet with photos and descriptions and are instructed to obey the 15-mile-per-hour speed limit— unless you see the rhinos charge (a rare occasion), in which case you're encouraged to floor it. To drive the loop takes just over an hour, though you could make a day of just watching the chimpanzees play on their secluded islands. Included in the admission price is Safari World, an amusement park with paddleboats, a carousel, miniature golf, and a nursery for baby animals born in the preserve. Picnics are encouraged, and camping is available (call for reservations). The best time to go is late afternoon right before the park closes when they herd up all the animals; plus, it's much cooler then, so the lions are more active.

Southern Blvd. W. at S.R. 80, West Palm Beach. ℂ 561/793-1084, or 561/793-9797 for camping reservations. Admission $15.50 adults, $10.50 seniors, $10.50 children 3–9, free for children under 3. Van rental is $6 per hr. Daily 9:30am–5:30pm (last vehicle admitted at 4:30pm). From I-95, exit on Southern Blvd. Go west for about 18 miles.

Palm Beach Zoo at Dreher Park 🐾   If you want animals, go to Lion Country Safari. Unlike big-city zoos, this intimate 23-acre park is more like a stroll in the park than an all-day excursion. It features about 500 animals representing more than 100 different species. A special monkey exhibit and petting zoo are favorites with kids. Stroller and wagon rental available.

1301 Summit Blvd. (east of I-95 between Southern and Forest Hill blvds.). ℂ 561/547-WILD. Fax 561/585-6085. www.palmbeachzoo.org. Admission $6, $5 senior citizens, $4 children 3–12, children under 3 free. Daily 9am–5pm.

Rapids Water Park 🐾 *(kids)*   It may not be on the same grand scale as the theme parks in Orlando, but Rapids is a great way to cool off on a hot day. There are 12 acres of water rides, including a children's area and miniature golf course.

6566 N. Military Trail, West Palm Beach (1 mile west of I-95 on Military between 45th St. (exit 54) and Blue Heron Blvd. (exit 55) in West Palm Beach. ℂ 561/842-8756. www.rapidswaterpark.com. Admission $17–$24 per person; free ages 2 and under. Open mid-March through Sept. Hours vary.

SHOPPING & BROWSING

No matter what your budget is, be sure to take a stroll down Worth Avenue, "the Rodeo Drive of the South," and a window-shopper's dream. Within the 4 blocks (between South Ocean Boulevard and Cocoanut Row on Worth) there are more than 200 boutiques, posh shops, art galleries, and upscale restaurants. Dress as if you were going to an elegant luncheon, and not to the mall down the street, if you want to fit in.

Despite the presence of the usual suspects (Gucci, Chanel, Armani, Hermes, Louis Vuitton, among others), Worth Avenue is not impervious to the mainstream. Victoria's Secret, Limited Express, and several other chains have sneaked in here too, but so have a good number of unique boutiques. **History Buff,** 32 via Mizner (ℂ **561/366-8255**), is a virtual museum, selling every genre of original historical autograph, some dating back to the 1600s, as well as vintage signed photos, first-edition books, and memorabilia. A similar store is **Paper Treasures,** at 217 Worth Ave. (© **561/835-1891**), an autograph gallery with a priceless collection of John Hancocks, including those of Joe DiMaggio, Mickey Mantle, Andrew Jackson, Abraham Lincoln, Howard Hughes, and hundreds more, all displayed in beautiful frames. For privileged feet, **Stubbs & Wooton,** 323 Worth Ave. (© **561/655-4105**), sells velvet slippers that are a favorite of the loofah-ed locals. **The Purple Turtle,** 150 Worth Ave. (© **561/655-1625**) in the Esplanade shopping promenade, sells designer clothes for infants, including Baby Dior and Baby Armani. For rare and estate jewelry, **Richter's of Palm Beach,** 224 Worth Ave. (© **561/655-0774**), has been specializing in priceless gems since 1893. Just off Worth Avenue, at 374 S. County Rd., is the **Church Mouse** (© **561/659-2154**), a great consignment/thrift shop with antique furnishings and tableware. Lots of good castaway clothing and shoes are reasonably priced. This shop usually closes for 2 months during the summer. Call to be sure.

City Place, 222 Lakeview Ave., West Palm Beach (© **561/835-0862**), is a $550 million, Mediterranean-style shopping, dining, and entertainment complex that's responsible for revitalizing what was once a lifeless downtown West Palm Beach. Among the 78 mostly-chain stores are Macy's; FAO Schwarz; Benneton, which has an in-line skating track inside; Armani Exchange; Pottery Barn; and SEE eyewear. Restaurants include a Ghiradelli ice cream shop, Legal Seafood, City Cellar Wine Bar and Grill, and Cheesecake Factory. Best of all is the Muvico Parisian, a 20-screen movie theater where you can wine and dine while watching a feature.

Elsewhere, Downtown West Palm Beach has a scant amount of interesting boutiques along Clematis Street. In addition to a large and well-organized bookstore, **Clematis Street Books,** at 206 Clematis (© **561/832-2302**), there are a few used-record stores, clothing shops, and several art galleries.

The **Palm Beach Outlet Center,** at 5700 Okeechobee Blvd. (3 miles west of I-95), West Palm Beach, is the most elegant outlet mall I have ever seen. Upscale clothing, luggage, and shoes are offered at bargain prices in lushly decorated surroundings. The fully enclosed mall also sports a food court.

WHERE TO STAY

The island of Palm Beach is the epitome of *Lifestyles of the Rich and Famous,* oozing with glitz, glamour, and the occasional scandal. Royalty and celebrities come to winter here, and there are plenty of lavishly priced options to accommodate them. Happily, there exist a few special little inns that offer reasonably priced rooms in elegant settings. Surrounding the island are many more modest places to lay your straw hat.

A few of the larger hotel chains operating in Palm Beach include the **Howard Johnson Palm Beach,** at 2870 S. Ocean Blvd. (© **800/654-2000** or 561/582-2581), which is across the street from the beach. Also beachside is the pricey **Palm Beach Hilton,** at 2842 S. Ocean Blvd. (© **800/433-1718** or 561/586-6542).

An excellent and affordable alternative right in the middle of Palm Beach's commercial section is a condominium that operates as a hotel, too: the **Palm Beach Hotel,** at 235 Sunrise Ave. (between County Road and Bradley Place, across the street from the Publix supermarket; © **561/659-7794**). With winter prices starting at about $105, this clean and comfortable accommodation is a great option for those looking for the rare bargain in Palm Beach.

In West Palm Beach, the chain hotels are mostly located on the main arteries close to the highways and a short drive to the activities in downtown. They include a **Best Western,** 1800 Palm Beach Lakes Blvd. (© **800/331-9569** or 561/683-8810), and, just down the road, a **Comfort Inn,** 1901 Palm Lakes Blvd. (© **800/221-2222** or 561/689-6100). Further south is the **Parkview Motor Lodge,** 4710 S. Dixie Hwy., just south of Southern Boulevard (© **561/833-4644**). This 28-room, single-story motel is the best of the many motels along Dixie Highway (U.S. 1). With rates starting at $50 for a room with television, air-conditioning, and telephone, you can't ask for more.

For other options, try Palm Beach Accommodations (© **800/543-SWIM**).

VERY EXPENSIVE

Brazilian Court ⭐⭐⭐   This bright yellow, Mediterranean-style hotel dates back to the 1920s and exudes a glamour that has been lost through the decades. The rooms, renovated in 1997, are spacious, albeit a bit blasé, but the marble bathrooms are beautiful and modern. Service is doting, but a bit aloof—you won't always be received by smiling faces, but you will get whatever you want. There's even room service exclusively for pets (you know the type: held hostage in Mummy's Gucci bag). A large hotel by Palm Beach standards (The Breakers notwithstanding), Brazilian Court is sprawled over half a block and features fountains and private courtyards.

301 Australian Ave., Palm Beach, FL 33480 © **800/552-0335** or 561/655-7740. Fax 561/655-0801. www.braziliancourt.com. 103 units. Winter $335–$875; off-season $165–$525. Special packages available. AE, DC, DISC, MC, V. **Amenities:** Restaurant, private dining room (up to 12), bar (see below, "Palm Beach After Dark"), heated outdoor pool, exercise room, spa treatments, library, concierge, salon, 24-hr. room service. *In room:* A/C, TV, coffeemaker, hair dryer, iron.

The Breakers ⭐⭐⭐   This 140-acre beachfront hotel is what Palm Beach is all about. Elaborate, stately, and resplendent in all its Italian-Renaissance–style glory, it's where old money mixes with new money, and the old world gives way, albeit reluctantly, to a bit of modernity. In what was a complete juxtaposition of old and new, I spotted rocker Stevie Nicks and her fellow Fleetwood Mac members kicking back in the Breakers lobby. The place is also frequented by Internet moguls who, no doubt, are pleased by the hotel's recent elimination of the jackets-required rule.

Seemingly older and more elegant than the modernized Boca Raton Resort & Club, the Breakers consists of a seven-story building with a frescoed lobby and long, majestic hallways reminiscent of a palace more than a palatial estate. A $100 million renovation took parts of the hotel out of the 1930s and into the 21st century. The indulgent Oceanfront Spa and Beach Club features a spectacular ocean-view fitness center (makes workouts a lot less grueling), four oceanfront pools, cabanas, and saunas. Rooms were also modernized a bit, with Internet access and modem connections, but remain elegant, not sterile, with plush furnishings, huge bathrooms with telephones, and views of the ocean or the hotel's magnificently manicured grounds. A revamp of Florida's oldest existing golf course, led by Brian Silva, transformed The Breakers Ocean Course into a 6,200-yard, championship-level par 70.

1 S. County Rd., Palm Beach, FL 33480. © **800/833-3141,** 888/BREAKERS, or 561/655-6611. Fax 561/659-8403. www.thebreakers.com. 569 units. Winter $405–$1200; off-season $260–$690. Special packages available. AE, DC, DISC, MC, V. Valet parking $17. From I-95, exit Okeechobee Blvd. E., head east to S. County Rd., and turn left. **Amenities:** 5 restaurants, 3 bars, 4 outdoor pools, golf course, 14 tennis courts, health club & spa, watersports equipment (including scuba and sailing), croquet, shuffleboard, and beach

volleyball courts, bike rental, children's programs, game rooms, concierge, business center, shopping arcade, salon, 24-hr. room service, in-room massage, babysitting; dry-cleaning and laundry services. *In room:* A/C, TV, dataport, CD player, minibar, hair dryer.

Four Seasons Resort Palm Beach 𝕽𝕽 Built in 1989 at the edge of Palm Beach's downtown district, this elegant resort has quickly gained accolades from around the world. An incredibly hospitable staff works hard to be sure this beachfront gem lives up to its reputation. The elegant marble lobby is replete with hand-carved European furnishings, grand oil paintings, tapestries, and dramatic flower arrangements—though I did feel like I was in a museum, unable to touch anything. The rooms are spacious with private balconies and lavish bathrooms with color TVs. The main dining room for dinner serves one of the best meals in Palm Beach. An impeccable menu of Southeastern regional cuisine includes daily fish, meat, and pasta specials served in white-glove elegance. Two other less formal restaurants, including a pool bar and grill, round out the dining options.

2800 S. Ocean Blvd., Palm Beach, FL 33480. © **800/432-2335** or 561/582-2800. Fax 561/547-1557. www.fourseasons.com. 210 units. Winter $395–$695 double; from $1,500 suite. Off-season $275–$595 double; from $850 suite. AE, DC, DISC, MC, V. Valet parking $17. Pets under 20 pounds accepted. From I-95, take 6th Ave. exit east and turn left onto Dixie Hwy. Turn east onto Lake Ave. and north onto S. Ocean Blvd., and the hotel is just ahead on your right. **Amenities:** 3 restaurants, lounge, outdoor heated pool, 3 tennis courts, spa, watersports rentals, bike rental, cooking classes weekly, children's programs, concierge, business center, salon, 24-hr. room service, in-room massage, babysitting, dry-cleaning and laundry services. *In room:* A/C, TV/VCR, dataport, minibar, fridge, hair dryer.

Ritz-Carlton Palm Beach 𝕽𝕽𝕽 If the Breakers is too mammoth for your tastes, consider the Ritz-Carlton. A lot warmer than the Four Seasons, the Ritz, though hyperluxurious, manages to lack pretension. Located on a beautiful beach in a tiny town about 8 miles from Palm Beach's shopping and dining area, the Ritz-Carlton is a plus for those who seek privacy but may be a drawback for those interested in the activity of "town." The hotel's elegant and dramatic lobby is dominated by a huge, double-sided pink-marble fireplace, and French 18th- and 19th-century antique furnishings give no hint that the property is not yet 10 years old. Each room has a private balcony and at least a glimpse of the ocean below. All are spacious and decorated in lush contemporary design. Large marble bathrooms are extremely inviting and have telephones. The elegant dining room serves continental-style dinners in ornate surroundings. Other restaurants on the property include a grill, for dinner only; a casual restaurant, open all day; and a poolside cafe and bar. Cocktails are also served in the lobby lounge, where you can often find live entertainment. Afternoon tea is served daily but is best Wednesday to Saturday when a jazz trio entertains. The hotel is so discreet, in fact, that Palm Beach's luminaries often escape here for a rare weekend or night of anonymity.

100 S. Ocean Blvd., Manalpan, FL 33462. © **800/241-3333** or 561/533-6000. Fax 561/540-4999. www. ritzcarlton.com. 270 units. Winter $395–$820; $3,150 suite. Off-season $285–$725; $2,700 suite. AE, DISC, MC, V. Valet parking $15. From I-95, take Exit 45, heading east. After 1 mile, turn left onto Federal Hwy. (U.S. 1). Continue north for about a mile, and turn right onto Ocean Ave. Cross the Intracoastal Waterway; turn right onto Fla. A1A. **Amenities:** 4 restaurants, bar, outdoor pool, health club, Jacuzzi, sauna, watersports equipment/rental, bike rental, children's center/programs, concierge, business center, salon, 24-hr. room service, in-room massage, dry-cleaning and laundry services. *In room:* A/C ,TV, dataport, minibar, hair dryer.

EXPENSIVE
Chesterfield Hotel 𝕽𝕽𝕽 Reminiscent of an English country manor, the Chesterfield Hotel in all its flowery, Laura Ashley–inspired glory is a magnificent, charming hotel with exceptional service to rival that of the Ritz. Warm and

inviting, the Chesterfield is one of the only places in South Florida in which the idea of a fireplace (there's one in the hotel's library) doesn't seem ridiculous. Traditional English tea is served every afternoon, with fresh baked scones, petit fours, and sandwiches. Rooms are decorated with bright fabrics and wallpaper and antiques. The roomy marble bathrooms are stocked with an array of luxurious toiletries. A small heated pool and courtyard are nice, and the beach is only 3 blocks away, but the real action's inside. At night, the hotel's retro-elegant Leopard Lounge (see "The Palm Beaches After Dark," below) serves decent continental cuisine but is better as a later-night hangout for live music, schmoozing, and staring at the local cognoscenti.

363 Cocoanut Row, Palm Beach, FL 33480. ℂ 800/243-7871 or 561/659-5800. Fax 561/659-6707. www.redcarnationhotels.com. 65 units. Winter $309–$350 single or double; off-season $99–$539. Rollaway bed $15 extra. Packages available. AE, DC, DISC, MC, V. Free valet parking. From I-95, exit onto Okeechobee Blvd. E., cross the Intracoastal Waterway, and turn right onto Cocoanut Row. **Amenities:** Restaurant, lounge, small heated swimming pool, access to nearby health club, Jacuzzi, bike rental, concierge, business center, 24-hr. room service, in-room massage, babysitting, dry-cleaning service. *In room:* A/C, TV, dataport, VCR on request, hair dryer.

Plaza Inn 👁👁 This three-story, family-run bed-and-breakfast–style inn located 1 block from the beach is as understated and luxurious as the guests it hosts. From the simple and elegant flower arrangements in the marble lobby to the well-worn period antiques haphazardly placed throughout, the Plaza Inn, whose exterior was renovated in 2001, has the look of studied nonchalance. The courtyard, with its waterfalls and pool, and the intimate piano bar are just two examples of the inn's infinite charms. A small staff is remarkably hospitable and knowledgeable about the island's inner workings. Each uniquely decorated room—Italian, French, or traditional style—is dressed with quality furnishings, several with carved four-poster beds, hand-crocheted spreads, and lace curtains. The bathrooms, renovated in 2000, are lovely if quite small, and the wall-mounted air conditioners can be noisy when they are needed in the warm months. Choose a corner room or one overlooking the small pool deck for the best light. The Stray Fox Pub, a comfortable little bar with mahogany tables, serves cocktails throughout the evening and sometimes has live piano music on the weekends. It's a tough call to decide which is better—the Plaza Inn or the Chesterfield, but the Plaza, unlike the Chesterfield, does include a full breakfast in the price of the room.

215 Brazilian Ave., Palm Beach, FL 33480. ℂ 800/233-2632 or 561/832-8666. Fax 561/835-8776. www.plazainnpalmbeach.com. 48 units. Winter $225–$375; off-season $105–$195. Rates include breakfast. AE, MC, V. From I-95, exit onto Okeechobee Blvd. E. and cross the Intracoastal Waterway. Turn right onto Cocoanut Row; then left onto Brazilian Ave. Small pets permitted. **Amenities:** Restaurant, lounge, heated outdoor pool, exercise room, Jacuzzi, access to nearby health club ($15 per day), bike rental, concierge, secretarial services, limited room service, in-room massage, babysitting, dry-cleaning and laundry services. *In room:* A/C, TV, dataport, fridge, coffeemaker and hair dryer on request.

MODERATE

The Colony 👁👁 The sign outside of this Palm Beach mainstay should read: Roxanne Pulitzer slept here. She did, actually, for quite a while after her 7-week marriage went bust. For years, the colony has been a favorite hangout—hide-out, perhaps—for assorted old timers, socialites, and mysterious luminaries. Beyond that, the Colony is a Georgian-style hotel known for its attentive staff, floral-decorated rooms and, unfortunately, really small bathrooms. The 39 suites and apartments, not to mention the seven two-bedroom villas with Jacuzzis, are much more lavish—and lavishly priced.

155 Hammon Ave., Palm Beach, FL 33480. © **800/521-5525** or 561/655-5430. Fax 561/659-8104. www. thecolonypalmbeach.com. 63 units, 39 suites, 7 villas. Winter $285–$695; off-season $125–$495. AE, DC, MC, V. From I-95, exit onto Okeechobee Blvd. E. and cross the Intracoastal Waterway. Turn right on S. County Rd.; then left onto Hammon Ave. **Amenities:** Restaurant, bar, heated Florida-shaped pool, spa, concierge, limited, seasonal room service. *In room:* A/C, TV, dataport, hair dryer.

Heart of Palm Beach Hotel 🦅

It's this hotel's location—in the heart of Palm Beach, within walking distance of Worth Avenue shopping, and just half a block from the beach—that is its greatest asset. Ongoing renovations since the 1990s have improved the patio space, as well as the rooms in the hotel's two buildings, but there's nothing particularly inspiring about this hotel's rather bland atmosphere and decor. A new exterior paint job and refurbished landscaping have improved the hotel's appearance slightly, however. Most rooms are decorated with modest but new furnishings and fittings in a colorful contemporary style; all come with a balcony or a patio. The tiled bathrooms are small, clean, and functional. Additionally, the staff is particularly outgoing and will help guests plan outings and itineraries. A clubby restaurant serves a mediocre selection of salads, sandwiches, pastas, and cocktails.

160 Royal Palm Way, Palm Beach, FL 33480. © **800/523-5377** or 561/655-5600. Fax 561/832-1201. 88 units. Winter $169–$325; off-season $79–$225 suite. AE, DC, MC, V. Free parking. From I-95, exit onto Okeechobee Blvd. E. and continue over the Royal Palm Bridge onto Royal Palm Way. Pets are accepted. **Amenities:** Restaurant, heated pool, access to nearby health club, bike rental, concierge, room service, dry-cleaning and laundry services, babysitting. *In room:* A/C, TV, dataport, fridge, hair dryer.

Palm Beach Historic Inn 🦅🦅

Built in 1923, the Palm Beach Historic Inn is an area landmark located within walking distance of Worth Avenue, the beach, and several good restaurants. The small lobby is filled with antiques, books, magazines, and an old-fashioned umbrella stand, all of which add to the homey feel of this intimate bed-and-breakfast. In your room, wine, fruit, snacks, tea, and cookies ensure that you won't go hungry—never mind the excellent continental breakfast that is brought to you daily. All the rooms are on the second floor, and each is uniquely decorated and full of frills. Floral prints, sheer curtains, and the plethora of lace can sometimes be overwhelming, masking rather than complementing beautiful antique writing desks and dressers. Happily, there are also fluffy bathrobes, an abundance of towels, and plenty of good-smelling toiletries. Be sure to save some dimes, as 10¢ will buy you an 8-ounce bottle of Coke dispensed by an original 1944 Coca Cola machine.

365 S. County Rd., Palm Beach, FL 33480. © **561/832-4009.** Fax 561/832-6255. www.palmbeachhistoricinn. com. 13 units. Winter $150–$325; off-season $95–$175. Rates include continental breakfast. Children stay free in parents' room. Small pets accepted. No smoking. AE, MC, V. *In-room:* A/C, TV/VCR, fridge, hair dryer.

MODERATE/INEXPENSIVE

Beachcomber Apartment Motel 🦅🦅

It's not just the bright pink building that makes this two-story beachfront motel stand out. For more than 35 years, the Beachcomber has been bringing sanity to pricey Palm Beach by offering a good standard of accommodation at reasonable prices. Squeezed between beachfront high-rises, the motel is located on a 300-foot private beach, adjacent to Lake Worth Beach and a short drive from Worth Avenue shops and local attractions. Every room has two double beds, large closets, and distinctive green-and-white tropical-style furnishings; some have kitchenettes. The most expensive have balconies overlooking the ocean. The bathrooms are basic, and amenities are limited to towels and soap.

Palm Beach & West Palm Beach Accommodations & Dining

ACCOMMODATIONS ■
Beachcomber
  Apartment Motel **20**
Brazilian Court **13**
The Breakers **7**
Chesterfield Hotel **12**
The Colony **18**
Four Seasons Resort
  Palm Beach **21**
Heart of Palm Beach Hotel **9**
Hibiscus House **1**
Palm Beach Historic Inn **14**
Plaza Inn **11**
Ritz-Carlton Palm Beach **23**

DINING ◆
Amici **8**
Bice Restaurant **16**
Big City Tavern **3**
Cafe l'Europe **10**
Chuck & Harold's Cafe **5**
E. R. Bradley's **2**
Galaxy **15**
Green's Pharmacy **4**
John G's **22**
My Martini Grille **3**
Rhythm Café **19**
Ta-Boo **17**
TooJay's **6**

3024 S. Ocean Blvd., Palm Beach, FL 33480. ℂ 800/833-7122 or 561/585-4646. Fax 561/547-9438. 45 units. Winter $95–$250; off-season $55–$130. AE, DISC, MC, V. From I-95, exit 10th Ave. N. Head east to Federal Hwy. and turn right. Continue to Lake Ave. and turn left. Go over bridge and turn right at first traffic light. **Amenities:** Large pool, coin-operated laundry. *In room:* A/C, TV.

Hibiscus House 🌺🌺 *Finds*   Inexpensive bed-and-breakfasts are rare in Southeast Florida, making the Hibiscus House, one of the area's firsts, a true find. Located a few miles from the coast in a quiet residential neighborhood, this 1920s-era B&B is filled with handsome antiques and tapestries in luxurious fabrics. Every room has its own private terrace or balcony. The Red Room has a fabulous new bathroom with Jacuzzi. The backyard, a peaceful retreat, has been transformed into a tropical garden, complete with heated swimming pool and lounge chairs. Also, there are plenty of pretty areas for guests to enjoy inside; one little sitting room is wrapped in glass and is stocked with playing cards and board games. *Beware:* Breakfast portions are enormous. The gourmet creations are as filling as they are beautiful. Ask for any special requests in advance; owners Raleigh Hill and Colin Rayer will be happy to oblige.

501 30th St., West Palm Beach, FL 33407. ℂ 800/203-4927 or 561/863-5633. Fax 561/863-5633. www.hibiscushouse.com. 8 units. Winter $95–$250 double; off-season $65–$170 double. Rates include breakfast. AE, MC, V. From I-95, exit onto Palm Beach Lakes Blvd. E. and continue 4 miles. Turn left onto Flagler Dr. and continue for about 20 blocks. Then turn left onto 30th St. Pets accepted. **Amenities:** Heated pool, concierge. *In room:* A/C, TV, hair dryer.

WHERE TO DINE

Palm Beach has some of the area's swankiest restaurants. Thanks to the development of downtown West Palm Beach, there is also a great selection of trendier, less expensive spots. Dress here is slightly more formal than in most other areas of Florida: Men wear blazers, and women generally put on modest dresses or chic suits when they dine out, even in the oppressively hot days of summer.

EXPENSIVE

Amici 🌺 *Overrated* ITALIAN   This is one of those restaurants in which the scene is tastier than the cuisine. An upper-crusty Palm Beach set tends to convene here and consistently rave about what can only be considered above-average, overpriced Italian food. The best item on the entire menu is gnocchi with white truffle oil, fontina cheese, and spinach. Everything else is fairly standard: grilled sandwiches, pastas with rustic sauces, pizzas, grilled shrimp, and fish. Despite its less than stellar food, it's always crowded and very noisy.

288 S. County Rd. (at Royal Palm Way), Palm Beach. ℂ 561/832-0201. Reservations strongly recommended on weekends. Main courses $18–$27; pastas and pizzas $8–$19. AE, DC, MC, V. Mon–Thurs 11:30am–3pm and 5:30–10:30pm, Fri–Sat 11:30am–3pm and 5:30–11pm; Sun 5:30–10:30pm.

Bice Restaurant 🌺🌺 ITALIAN   Bice's Northern Italian cuisine far surpasses that of Amici's, but as far as atmosphere is concerned, the air in here is a bit haughty, bordering on rude. Servers and diners alike seem to have noticeable attitudes, but you'll forget all that with one bite of the juicy veal cutlet with tomato salad or the pasta e fagioli.

313 1/2 Worth Ave., Palm Beach. ℂ 561/835-1600. Reservations essential. Main courses $20–$32. AE, DC, MC, V. Daily 11am–10pm.

Cafe l'Europe 🌺🌺🌺 FRENCH/CONTINENTAL   One of Palm Beach's finest, this award-winning formal restaurant gives you good reason to get dressed up. The interior is made romantic and luxurious by the tapestried cafe chairs and linen-topped tables set with crystal and china. The enticing appetizers served by a superb staff might include Chinese spring rolls, baked goat-cheese salad with raspberry-walnut dressing, poached salmon, or chilled gazpacho with avocado. Main courses run the gamut from sautéed potato-crusted Florida snapper to lamb chops to roast Cornish game hen. Seafood dishes and steaks in sumptuous but light sauces are always exceptional. Considering that most of the restaurant's devoted diners are either from Europe or travel there often, it's no surprise that Cafe l'Europe in all its European splendor is one of Palm Beach's most popular restaurants.

331 S. County Rd. (at the corner of Brazilian Ave.), Palm Beach. (561/655-4020. Reservations recommended. Main courses $18–$34. AE, DC, DISC, MC, V. Tues–Thurs noon–2:30pm and 5:45–10:30pm, Fri–Sat noon–2:30pm and 5:45pm–1am, Sun 6–10:30pm.

Chuck & Harold's Cafe AMERICAN   This old standby delivers predictable American fare at somewhat inflated prices. But remember, you are paying for one of the area's best people-watching perches. Main dishes include fresh grilled or broiled fish, boiled lobster, and a small variety of straightforward homemade pasta and chicken dishes. If you happen to visit during the season for stone crabs, order them. The crab claws are steamed or chilled and served with a traditional honey-mustard sauce. Considering Chuck and Harold's status as a Waspy enclave, its surprise treat is excellent matzo ball soup!

207 Royal Poinciana Way (corner of S. County Rd.), Palm Beach. (561/659-1440. Fax 561/659-2197. Reservations recommended. Main courses $13–$28. AE, DC, DISC, MC, V. Mon–Thurs 7:30am–midnight; Fri–Sat 7:30am–1am, Sun 8am–11pm.

Galaxy Grille ✦ NEW AMERICAN   Stargazing is certainly at a premium at this deco-inspired Palm Beach hot spot known for a stellar clientele and a menu to match it. Two favorites include a superb horseradish-encrusted yellowtail snapper and an even better grilled swordfish with fresh tomato, black olives, grilled polenta, garlic, and escarole.

350 S. County Rd., Palm Beach. (561/833-9909. Reservations recommended. Main courses $27–$38. AE, DC, MC, V. Daily 5–11pm.

MODERATE

E. R. Bradley's AMERICAN   What used to be a swank saloon on the island of Palm Beach is now a very casual, friendly indoor/outdoor bar in downtown West Palm, attracting a mixed crowd. People don't really come here for the food, though it's quite busy with families during the early evening hours. It's the later-night bar scene that's the real draw. If you are hungry, try the "crab bomb," Maryland lump crabmeat baked in a light cream sauce with steamed vegetables. Sunday brunch is also pretty good.

104 Clematis St. (Datura St.), West Palm Beach. (561/ 833-3520. Main courses $6–$16. AE, MC, V. Sun–Wed 8am–3am, Thurs–Sat 8am–4 am.

Big City Tavern ✦✦ AMERICAN   If the Palm Beach proper dining scene is too stuffy for you, head over the bridge to Clematis Street, downtown West Palm's hub of urban chic, where you will find this yuppie enclave of brick and pressed tin in which people-watching is at a premium. Despite its all-American appearance, Big City Tavern offers a varied menu, including coconut shrimp tempura with a salmon inside-out sushi roll and a delicious bowl of littleneck clams in wine broth with roasted garlic and escarole. On weekends, the Tavern is mobbed, so be prepared for a long wait that's best spent at the action-packed bar.

224 Clematis St., West Palm Beach. (561/659-1853. Reservations suggested. Main courses $7.95–$28. AE, MC, V. Mon–Fri 11am–11pm, Sat. 6pm–1am, Sun 6–10pm.

My Martini Grille ✿✿ ECLECTIC AMERICAN　Reminiscent of a 1930s supper club, this dark wood–lined restaurant is hardly popular with those who lived through those times, but, rather, with retro-loving trendies who really come for the martinis (over 32 flavors). An affordable three-tiered appetizer platter includes just about everything needed to absorb the trail of martinis; special entrees include a rack of lamb with rosemary mint demi-glace and Gorgonzola potatoes.

225 Clematis St., West Palm Beach. ✆ 561/832-8333. Reservations suggested. Main courses $15–$25. AE, MC, V. Tues–Sat 6pm–midnight.

Rhythm Café ✿ ECLECTIC AMERICAN　This funky hole-in-the-wall is where those in the know come to eat some of West Palm Beach's most laid-back gourmet food. On the handwritten, photocopied menu (which changes daily), you'll always find a fish specialty accompanied by a hefty dose of greens and garnishes. Also reliably outstanding is the sautéed medallion of beef tenderloin, served on a bed of arugula with a tangy rosemary vinaigrette. Salads and soups are a great bargain, since portions are relatively large and the display usually spectacular. The kitschy decor of this tiny cafe comes complete with vinyl tablecloths and a changing display of paintings by local amateurs. Young, handsome waiters are attentive but not solicitous. The old drugstore where the restaurant recently relocated features an original 1950s lunch counter and stools.

3800 S. Dixie Hwy., West Palm Beach. ✆ 561/833-3406. Reservations recommended on weekends. Main courses $10–$26. AE, DISC, MC, V. Tues–Sat 6–10pm. From I-95, exit east on Southern Blvd. Go 1 block north of Southern Blvd.; restaurant on the right. Closed in early September.

Ta-boo ✿ AMERICAN BISTRO　Ta-boo is reminiscent of an upscale TGI Fridays—one that caters to a well-heeled crowd—with lots of greenery, a fireplace, and a somewhat cheesy Southwestern decor. For lunch, the kitchen creates California-style individual pizzas with such toppings as barbecued chicken, goat and mozzarella cheeses, and sweet roasted red peppers. The best dinner starter is fresh tuna marinated in ginger and lime. Dinner choices change nightly and may include grilled swordfish topped with olive-caper sauce or grilled veal served on the bone.

221 Worth Ave., Palm Beach. ✆ 561/835-3500. Reservations recommended. Main courses $10–$25. AE, DC, MC, V. Sun–Thurs 11:30am–11pm, Fri–Sat 11:30am–1am.

INEXPENSIVE

Green's Pharmacy ✿ AMERICAN　This neighborhood corner pharmacy offers one of the best meal deals in Palm Beach. Both breakfast and lunch are served coffee-shop style either at a Formica bar or at plain tables placed on a black-and-white checkerboard floor. Breakfast specials include eggs and omelettes served with home fries and bacon, sausage, or corned-beef hash. At lunch, the grill serves burgers and sandwiches, as well as ice-cream sodas and milkshakes, to a loyal crowd of pastel-clad Palm Beachers.

151 N. County Rd., Palm Beach. ✆ 561/832-0304. Fax 561/832-6502. Breakfast $2–$5; burgers and sandwiches $3–$6; soups and salads $2–$7. AE, DISC, MC, V. Mon–Sat 7am–5pm, Sun 7am–3pm.

John G's ✿ AMERICAN　This coffee shop is the most popular in the county. For decades, John G's has been attracting huge breakfast crowds; lines run out the door (on weekends, all the way down the block). Stop in for some good, greasy-spoon–style food served in heaping portions right on the beachfront. This place is known for fresh and tasty fish and chips and its selection of creative omelets and grill specials.

10 S. Ocean Blvd., Lake Worth. ℂ 561/585-9860. www.johngs.com. Reservations not accepted. Breakfast $3–$8.50; lunch $5–$14. No credit cards. Daily 7am–3pm. From the Florida Tpk., take the Lake Worth exit and head toward the ocean.

TooJay's DELI   This simple and predictable restaurant and take-out spot is a favorite with locals and out-of-towners who want good old-fashioned deli. So popular, in fact, that TooJay's now has more than a dozen outlets. This is no Carnegie Deli, but by South Florida deli standards the food is excellent. All the classic sandwiches are available: hot pastrami, roast beef, turkey, chicken, chopped liver, egg salad, and more. Comfort food in the form of huge portions of stuffed cabbage, chicken pot pie, beef brisket, and sautéed onions and chicken livers is sure to satisfy.

313 Royal Poinciana Plaza (3 miles east of I-95 off Exit 52A), Palm Beach. ℂ 561/659-7232. Reservations not accepted. Main courses $8–$13. DC, MC, V. Daily 8am–9pm.

THE PALM BEACHES AFTER DARK
THE BAR, CAFE & MUSIC SCENE: DOWNTOWN WEST PALM BEACH

A decade-old project to revitalize downtown West Palm Beach has finally become a reality, with **Clematis Street** at its heart. Artist lofts, sidewalk cafes, bars, restaurants, consignment shops, and galleries dot the street from Flagler Drive to Rosemary Avenue, creating a hot spot for a night out, especially on weekends when yuppies mingle with stylish Euros and disheveled artists. Every Thursday night is a mob scene of twenty- and thirty-somethings who come out for "Clematis by Night." Each week features a different rock, blues, or reggae band plus an art show. Vendors sell food and drinks, and the street's bars and restaurants are packed. It is a bit raucous at times, but fun. Minors unaccompanied by their guardians are not permitted in the downtown area around Clematis Street after 10pm on weeknights and after 11pm on weekend nights.

Over the bridge, it's a completely different world. Palm Beach is much quieter and better known for its rather private society balls and estate parties. With the exception of some restaurants that are more of a scene—Ta-boo, Amici, and Galaxy Grille—Palm Beach nightlife is more likely to entail sipping port at one of the finer hotels like the Breakers, the Colony, the Ritz-Carlton, Four Seasons, or the Chesterfield.

West Palm Beach

Bliss   With its house music and VIP rooms, this West Palm club seems like it belongs in the velvet-roped world of South Beach clubs. 313 Clematis St. ℂ 561/833-1444. Thurs–Sat. $7 cover.

Liquid Room   Former South Beach hot spot Liquid may have evaporated from the scene, but this Clematis Street location, which shares the building with Bliss located upstairs, is flowing with club kids who revel in the fact that they finally have a chic, celebrity-saturated dance club to call their own. 313 Clematis St. ℂ 561/655-2332. Thurs–Sat. $10 cover.

Lost Weekend   I'm not sure whether it's the local artist displays, the pool tables, or the more than 200 beers from around the world sold here, but for some reason, many of Palm Beach's hipsters love getting lost in this place, which is actually quite nice. 115 S. Olive Ave. ℂ 561/832-3452. Tues–Fri from 4:30pm. No cover.

Monkey Club   This tacky yet trendy Caribbean-inspired dance club is 7,500-square-feet of wall-to-wall, well-dressed revelers. Theme nights are popular here, from ladies nights to the classier version of the wet T-shirt contest—the Miss Hawaiian Tropic Model Search. 219 Clematis St. ⓒ 561/833-6500. Cover up to $10.

Respectable Street Café　This is one of the premier live music venues in South Florida. In addition to the requisite DJs, this grungy bar features an impressive lineup of alternative music acts. The cafe's plain storefront exterior belies its funky high-ceilinged interior decorated with large black booths, psychedelic wall murals, and a large checkerboard-tile dance floor. 518 Clematis St. ⓒ 561/832-9999. Wed–Sat 9pm–4am. Cover varies.

Palm Beach

Brazilian Court Bistro and Rio Bar　Despite its location in the ritzy Brazilian Court Hotel, the bar here is surprisingly laid-back and unpretentious, featuring a mostly older crowd of couples and, at times, swinging singles. 301 Australian Ave. ⓒ 561/655-7740.

The Leopard Lounge (Finds　The Flintstones meets Dynasty at the spotty lounge in the Chesterfield Hotel in which the carpeting, tablecloths, and waitstaff's waistcoats are all in leopard print. There's live music every night from Cole Porter to swing. The crowd's a bit older here, but younger couples and a celebrity or two often find their way here, which makes for an amusing scene. 363 Cocoanut Row. ⓒ 561/659-5800.

THE PERFORMING ARTS

With a number of dedicated patrons and enthusiastic supporters of the arts, this area happily boasts many good venues for those craving culture. Check the *Palm Beach Post* or the *Palm Beach Daily News,* known as "the shiny sheet," for up-to-date listings and reviews.

The **Raymond F. Kravis Center for the Performing Arts,** 701 Okeechobee Blvd., West Palm Beach (ⓒ **561/832-7469**), is the area's largest and most active performance space. With a huge curved-glass facade and more than 2,500 seats in two lushly decorated indoor spaces, plus a new outdoor amphitheater, The Kravis, as it is known, stages more than 300 performances each year. Phone for a current schedule of Palm Beach's best music, dance, and theater.

4 Jupiter ⟨★⟩ & Northern Palm Beach County ⟨★⟩

20 miles N. of Palm Beach, 81 miles N. of Miami

While Burt Reynolds is Jupiter's hometown hero (and Celine Dion just built a sprawling manse there, too), the true stars of quaint Jupiter are the beautiful beaches. In the springtime, you can also catch a glimpse of the St. Louis Cardinals and the Montreal Expos during their spring training seasons. North Palm Beach County's other towns—Tequesta, Juno Beach, North Palm Beach, Palm Beach Gardens, and Singer Island—are inviting for tourists who want to enjoy the many outdoor activities that make this area so popular with retirees, seasonal residents, and families.

ESSENTIALS

GETTING THERE　The quickest route from West Palm Beach to Jupiter is on the Florida Turnpike or the sometimes congested I-95. You can also take a slower but more scenic coastal route, U.S. 1 or Fla. A1A. Since Jupiter is so close to Palm Beach, it's easy to fly into the **Palm Beach International Airport** (ⓒ **561/471-7420**) and rent a car there. The drive should take less than half an hour.

VISITOR INFORMATION A **Visitor Information Center** is located between I-95 and the Florida Turnpike at 8020 Indiantown Rd. in Jupiter (© **561/575-4636;** www.jupiterfloridausa.com) and is open from 9am to 6pm daily.

BEACHES & OUTDOOR PURSUITS

BASEBALL The **Roger Dean Stadium,** 4751 Main St. (© **561/775-1818**), hosts spring training for both the St. Louis Cardinals and the Montreal Expos, along with minor-league action from Florida's state league, the Hammerheads. Tickets range in price from $6 to $18. Call for schedules and specific ticket information.

BEACHES The farther north you head from populated Palm Beach, the more peaceful and pristine the coast becomes. Just a few miles north of the bustle, castles and condominiums give way to wide open space and public parkland. There are dozens of recommendable spots. Following are a few of the best.

John D. MacArthur Beach is a spectacular beach that preserves the natural heritage of subtropical coastal habitat that once covered Southeast Florida. This state park has a remarkable 4,000-square-foot Nature Center with exhibits, displays, and a video interpreting the barrier island's plant and animal communities. Dominating a large portion of Singer Island, the barrier island just north of Palm Beach, this beach has lengthy frontage on both the Atlantic Ocean and Lake Worth Cove. The beach is great for hiking, swimming, and sunning. To reach the park from the mainland, cross the Intracoastal Waterway on Blue Heron Boulevard and turn north on Ocean Boulevard.

Jupiter Inlet meets the ocean at **Dubois Park,** a 29-acre beach that is popular with families. The shallow waters and sandy shore are perfect for kids, while adults can play in the rougher swells of the lifeguarded inlet. A footbridge leads to **Ocean Beach,** an area popular with windsurfers and surfers. There's a short fishing pier and plenty of trees shading barbecue grills and picnic tables. Visitors can also explore the Dubois Pioneer Home, a small house situated atop a shell mound built by the Jaega Indians. The park entrance is on Dubois Road, about a mile south of the junction of U.S. 1 and Fla. A1A.

BIKING Rent a bike from **Raleigh Bicycles of Jupiter,** at 103 U.S. 1, Unit F1 (© **561/746-0585**) for $15.50 per day. Bike enthusiasts will enjoy exploring this flat and uncluttered area. North Palm Beach has hundreds of miles of smooth, paved roads. Loggerhead Park in Juno Beach or Fla. A1A along the ocean has great trails for starters. You'll find many more scenic routes over the bridges and west of the highway.

BOATING & CANOEING You can rent a boat at several outlets throughout northern Palm Beach County, including **Canoe Outfitters,** 8900 W. Indiantown Rd. (west of I-95), North Jupiter (© **561/746-7053**), which provides access to one of the area's most beautiful natural waterways. Canoers start at Riverbend Park along an 8-mile stretch of Intracoastal Waterway, where the lush foliage supports dozens of exotic birds and reptiles. Keep your eyes open for the gators who love to sunbathe on the shallow shores of the river. You'll end up exhausted at Jonathan Dickinson Park about 5 or 6 hours later. A pamphlet describing local flora and fauna is available for $1. Trips run Wednesday to Sunday and cost $25 for a single-person kayak, $35 for a double kayak or canoe.

CRUISES Several sightseeing cruises offer tours of the magnificent waterways that make up northern Palm Beach County. Water taxis conduct daily narrated tours through the scenic waters. One interesting excursion departs from

Panama Hatties at PGA Boulevard and the Intracoastal Waterway. Prices are $17 for adults and $9 for children under 12 for the 1½-hour ride. Call ℭ **561/ 775-2628.** The Manatee Queen, 1065 N. Ocean Blvd. (at the Crab House), Jupiter (ℭ **561/744-2191**), is a 40-foot catamaran with bench seating for up to 49 people. Two-hour tours of Jupiter Island depart daily at 2:30pm, passing Burt Reynolds' and Perry Como's mansions, among other historical and natural spots of interest. Reservations are highly recommended, especially in season; call for the current schedule of offerings. The cruise is wheelchair-accessible. Prices start at $15 for adults and $10 for children. Bring your own lunch or purchase chips and sodas at the minisnack bar.

FISHING   Before you leave, send for an information-packed fishing kit with details on fish camps, charters, tournament, and tide schedules, distributed by the **West Palm Beach Fishing Club,** c/o Fish Finder, P.O. Box 468, West Palm Beach, FL 33402. The cost is $10 and well worth it. Allow at least 4 weeks for delivery.

Once in town, several outfitters along U.S. 1 and Fla. A1A have vessels and equipment for rent if your hotel doesn't. One of the most complete facilities is the **Sailfish Marina & Resort,** 98 Lake Dr. (off Blue Heron Boulevard), Palm Beach Shores (ℭ **561/844-1724**). Call for equipment, bait, guided trips, or boat rentals.

GOLF   Even if you're not lucky enough to be staying at the **PGA National Resort,** you may still be able to play on their award-winning courses. If you or someone in your group is a member of another golf or country club, have the head pro write a note on club letterhead to Jackie Rogers at PGA (see "Where to Stay," below) to request a play date. Be sure the pro includes his PGA number and contact information. Allow at least 2 weeks for a response. Also, ask about the Golf-A-Round program, where selected private clubs open to non-members for free or discounted rates. Contact the **Palm Beach County Convention and Visitors Bureau** (ℭ **561/471-3995**) for details.

Plenty of other great courses dot the area, including the **Golf Club of Jupiter,** 1800 Central Blvd., Jupiter (ℭ **561/747-6262**). A well-respected 18-hole, par-70 course is situated on more than 6,200 yards featuring narrow fairways and fast greens. Fees are $55 until noon, $45 after noon, and $25 after 3pm, and include a mandatory cart. The course borders I-95.

HIKING   In an area that's not particularly known for extraordinary natural diversity, **Blowing Rocks Preserve** has a terrific hiking trail along a dramatic limestone outcropping. You won't find hills or scenic vistas, but you will see Florida's unique and varied tropical ecosystem. The well-marked mile-long trail passes oceanfront dunes, coastal strands, mangrove wetlands, and a coastal hammock. The preserve, owned and managed by the Nature Conservancy, also protects an important habitat for West Indian manatees and loggerhead turtles. The preserve is located along South Beach Drive (Fla. A1A), north of the Jupiter inlet, about a 10-minute drive northeast of Jupiter. Free guided tours are available Fridays and Sundays at 11 am, and no reservations are necessary. From U.S. 1, head east on S.R. 707 and cross the Intracoastal Waterway to the park. Admission is free, but a $3 per person donation is requested. For more information, contact the Preserve Manager, Blowing Rocks Preserve, P.O. Box 3795, Tequesta, FL 33469 (ℭ **561/744-6668**).

SCUBA DIVING & SNORKELING   Year-round warm, clear waters make northern Palm Beach County great for both diving and snorkeling. The closest

Discovering a Remarkable Natural World

North Palm Beach is well known for the giant sea turtles that lay their eggs on the county's beaches from May to August. These endangered marine animals return here annually, from as far away as South America, to lay their clutch of about 115 eggs each. Nurtured by the warm sand, but preyed upon by birds and other predators, only about one or two babies from each nest survive to maturity.

Many environmentalists recommend that visitors take part in an organized turtle-watching program (rather than going on their own) to minimize disturbance to the turtles. The Jupiter Beach Resort (see "Where to Stay," below) and the Marinelife Center of Juno Beach (see below) both sponsor free guided expeditions to the egg-laying sites from May to August. Phone for times and reservations.

Just south of Jupiter, in Juno Beach, is the **Marinelife Center of Juno Beach,** in Loggerhead Park, 14200 U.S. 1, Juno Beach (© 561/ 627-8280). Combining a science museum and nature trail, the small Marinelife Center is dedicated to the coastal ecology of northern Palm Beach County. Hands-on exhibits teach visitors about wetlands and beach areas, as well as offshore coral reefs and the local sea life. Visitors are encouraged to walk the center's sand-dune nature trails, all of which are marked with interpretive signs. This is one place in which you're guaranteed to see live sea turtles year-round, and during high breeding season (June and July) the center conducts narrative walks along a nearby beach. Reservations are a must. The booking list opens on May 1 and is usually full by midmonth. Admission to the center is free, though donations are accepted. Open Tuesday to Saturday from 10am to 4pm and Sunday from noon to 3pm.

coral reef is located a quarter-mile from shore and can easily be reached by boat. Three popular wrecks are clustered near each other, less than a mile offshore of the Lake Worth Inlet at about 90 feet. If your hotel doesn't offer dive trips, call the **South Florida Dive Headquarters,** 23141 Lyons Rd., Boca Raton (© 800/ 771-DIVE or 561/627-9558); or **Seafari Dive and Surf,** 75 E. Indiantown Rd., Suite 603, Jupiter (© 561/747-6115).

TENNIS   In addition to the many hotel tennis courts (see "Where to Stay," below), you can swing a racquet at a number of local clubs. The **Jupiter Bay Tennis Club,** 353 U.S. 1, Jupiter (© 561/744-9424), has seven clay courts (three lighted) and charges $12 per person per day. Reservations are highly recommended.

More-economical options are available at relatively well-maintained municipal courts. Call for locations and hours (© 561/966-6600). Many are available free on a first-come, first-served basis.

A HISTORIC LIGHTHOUSE
Jupiter Inlet Lighthouse ☆   Completed in 1860, this redbrick structure is the oldest extant building in Palm Beach County. Still owned and maintained by the U.S. Coast Guard, the lighthouse is now home to a small historical museum, located at its base. The Florida History Museum sponsors tours of the

Fun Fact **Burt Reynolds Slept Here**

Although there's no sign saying, "Welcome to Jupiter, Home of Burt Reynolds," there may as well be. You see, Reynolds was the ruler of this South Floridian planet, with a park, a museum, a theater, and a ranch that, in better times, all bore his name. Born in Waycross, Georgia, Reynolds grew up in West Palm Beach, where his half-Cherokee father was police chief. While attending Florida State University in Tallahassee, Reynolds injured his knee and lost all hopes of pursuing a pro-football career. That's when he turned to acting. But beyond *Gunsmoke, Deliverance, Smokey and the Bandit,* and that legendary centerfold in *Cosmopolitan,* Reynolds' star faded and the former sex symbol quietly retreated to Jupiter in the early 1980s, where he opened his dinner theater and, later, the Burt Reynolds Ranch, which featured a wedding chapel, the Burt Reynolds Petting Farm, and a Hall of Fame among other things. The restaurant went into foreclosure, and the ranch was sold after Reynolds declared bankruptcy in 1996. Today, the only thing bearing Reynolds' name is the Burt Reynolds Park, 805 U.S. 1. But the legend still lives on. No matter which chapter of his life he's currently on—11 or otherwise—Reynolds will always be responsible for bringing a bit of Hollywood to the little town of Jupiter.

lighthouse, enabling visitors to explore the cramped interior, which is filled with artifacts and photographs illustrating the rich history of the area. First, a 15-minute video explains the various shipwrecks, Indian wars, and other events that helped shape this region. Helpful volunteers are eager to tell colorful stories to highlight the 1-hour tour.

500 State Road 707, Jupiter. © **561/747-8380.** Admission $5. Sun–Wed 10am–4pm (last tour departs at 3:15pm). Children must be 4 feet or taller to climb.

SHOPPING

Northern Palm Beach County may not have the glitzy boutiques of Worth Avenue, but it does have an impressive indoor mall, the **Gardens of the Palm Beaches,** at 3101 PGA Blvd., where you can find large department stores including Bloomingdale's, Burdines, Macy's, and Saks Fifth Avenue, as well as more than 100 specialty shops. A large and diverse food court and fine sit-down restaurants in this 1.3 million-square-foot facility make this shopping excursion an all-day affair. Call © **561/775-7750** for store information.

WHERE TO STAY

The northern part of Palm Beach County is much more laid-back and less touristy than the rest of the Gold Coast. Here, there are relatively few fancy hotels or attractions. In addition to several Holiday Inns, there is a reasonably priced and recently renovated **Wellesley Inn,** at 34 Fisherman's Wharf (I-95, exit east on Indiantown Road; turn left before the bridge), in Jupiter (© **800/444-8888**). Suites include sofa beds, refrigerators, and microwave ovens. Although not within walking distance of the beach, the inn is located near shops and restaurants and Fla. A1A.

VERY EXPENSIVE

Jupiter Beach Resort 🐟🐟   The only resort located directly on Jupiter's beach, this unpretentious retreat is popular with families and seems a world away from the more luxurious resorts just a few miles to the south. The lobby and public areas have a Caribbean motif, accented with green marble, arched doorways, and chandeliers. The simple and elegant guest rooms are furnished in a comfortable island style, and every room has a private balcony with ocean or sunset views looking out over the uncluttered beachfront. A thorough refurbishing in the mid-1990s is responsible for the resort's increasing popularity. In fact, it is so popular that it is being gradually converted into a time-share property. Excursions are available to top-rated golf courses in the area.

5 N. A1A, Jupiter, FL 33477. ℂ 800/228-8810 or 561/746-2511. Fax 561/747-3304. www. jupiterbeachresort.com. 153 units. Winter $170–$450; off-season $97–$205. AE, DC, DISC, MC, V. Valet parking $5. From I-95, take Exit 59A, going east to the end of Indiantown Rd. at A1A. Jupiter Beach Resort is at this intersection on the ocean. **Amenities:** Restaurant, 2 bars, pool, tennis court, exercise room, extensive water-sport equipment/rental, bike rental, children's programs, concierge, business center, room service, in-room massage, dry cleaning. *In room:* A/C, TV, minibar, coffeemaker, kitchenette and VCRs in suites.

PGA National Resort & Spa 🐟🐟🐟   This rambling resort, the national headquarters of the PGA, is a premier golf vacation spot—but its top-rated Mediterranean spa could be a destination in iself. With five 18-hole courses on more than 2,300 acres, golfers and other sports-minded travelers will find plenty to keep them occupied—croquet, tennis, sailing, a health and fitness center, and the sublime spa. Constant updating has kept the grounds and buildings in like-new condition. In 2000 the lobby and all rooms were completely renovated. The par-72 Champion Course, redesigned in 1990 by Jack Nicklaus, is the resort's most valuable asset. More than 100 sand bunkers and plenty of water on 6,400-square-foot greens keep golfers of all levels alert. Watch out for hole 16. Rooms are spacious and comfortable with immense bathrooms. This is not a beach resort, however. Six outdoor therapy pools known as "Waters of the World" are surrounded by mineral pools, which are so sublime, they make the ocean look like a kiddie pool. Don Shula's award-winning steakhouse and restaurant is the hotel's best and most popular restaurant.

400 Avenue of the Champions, Palm Beach Gardens, FL 33418. ℂ 800/633-9150 or 561/627-2000. Fax 561/622-0261. www.pga-resorts.com. 339 units. Winter $319–$389 double; from $489 suite. Off-season $129–$169 double; from $249 suite. Children 16 and under stay free in parents' room. Special packages available. AE, DC, DISC, MC, V. From I-95, take Exit 57B (PGA Blvd.) going west and continue for approximately 2 miles to the resort entrance on the left. **Amenities:** 6 restaurants and lounges, 9 swimming pools, 5 18-hole tournament courses, plus the PGA National's Academy of Golf 19 clay tennis courts, 5 tournament croquet lawns, 5 indoor racquetball courts, Mediterranean spa, aerobics studio, watersports equipment/rentals, concierge, car-rental desk, salon, room service, laundry, babysitting. *In room:* A/C, TV, data-port, minibar, hair dryer, kitchenette in suites.

MODERATE/INEXPENSIVE

Baron's Landing Motel & Apartments 🐟   This charming family-run inn is a perfect little beach getaway. It's not elegant, but it's cozy. The single-story motel fronting the Intracoastal Waterway is often full in winter with snowbirds, who dock their boats at the hotel's marina for weeks or months at a time. Nearly all rooms, which are situated around a small pool, have small kitchenettes. Each unit has a hodgepodge of used furniture, and some have pullout sofas. Bathrooms have been remodeled. Considering that you're a few blocks from some of the most expensive real estate in the country, this is a good deal. Dock rentals are available.

18125 Ocean Blvd. (Fla. A1A at the corner of Clemens St.), Jupiter, FL 33477. ℂ **561/746-8757**. 8 units. Winter $75–$125 double; $1,350–$1,700 monthly. Off-season $45–$75 double; $700–$900 monthly. No credit cards. **Amenities:** Small pool. *In room:* A/C, TV, kitchen, refrigerator, coffeemaker, hair dryer.

Cologne Motel A modest roadside motel, the Cologne is a well-maintained one-story building with a pool but very little in the way of amenities. The small rooms were updated in 1999 with modest but bright bedspreads and curtains, and the retiled bathrooms are small but clean. The area is safe if not scenic and only about a 5-minute drive to the beach. A more direct route by foot gets you there in about 15 minutes. Accesssible rooms are available for travelers with disabilities.

220 U.S. 1, Tequesta/Jupiter, FL 33469. ℂ **561/746-0616**. 9 units. Winter $70 double; off-season $36 double. Weekly rates available. AE, MC, V. **Amenities:** Pool. *In room:* A/C, TV, fridge. No telephone.

WHERE TO DINE

In addition to all the national fast-food joints that line Indiantown Road and U.S. 1, you'll find a number of touristy fish restaurants serving battered and fried everything. There are only a few really exceptional eateries in North Palm Beach and Jupiter. Try those listed below for guaranteed good food at reasonable prices.

Athenian Cafe ✪ GREEK Peter Papadelis and his family have been running this pleasant storefront cafe for more than a decade. Tucked in the corner of a strip mall, this place is a favorite with businesspeople, who stop in for a heaping portion of rich and meaty moussaka or a flaky spinach pie made fresh by Peter himself. You could make a meal of the thick and lemony Greek soup and the large fresh antipasto. In a town replete with tourist-priced fish joints, this is a welcome alternative. Early bird specials, served until 7pm, include many Greek favorites and broiled local fish with soup or salad, rice, vegetables, pita, dessert, and coffee or tea.

In the Chasewood Shopping Center, 6350 Indiantown Rd., Suite 7, Jupiter. ℂ **561/744-8327**. Main courses $5–$16. AE, MC, V. Mon–Sat 11am–9pm; Sun 4–9pm during season.

Capt. Charlie's Reef Grill ✪✪ SEAFOOD/CARIBBEAN The trick here is to arrive early, ahead of the crowd of local foodies who come for the more than a dozen daily local-catch specials prepared in dozens of styles. Imaginative appetizers include Caribbean chili, a rich chunky stew filled with fresh seafood; and a tuna spring roll big enough for two. The enormous Cuban crab cake is moist and perfectly browned without tasting fried and is served with homemade mango chutney and black beans and rice. Sit at the bar to watch the hectic kitchen turn out perfect dishes on the 14-burner stove. Somehow, the pleasant waitresses keep their cool even when the place is packed. In addition to the terrific seafood, this little dive offers an extensive, affordable wine and beer selection—more than 30 of each from around the world.

12846 U.S. 1 (behind O'Brian's and French Connection), Juno Beach. ℂ **561/624-9924**. Reservations not accepted. Main courses $9.95–$18.95. MC, V. Sun–Thurs 11:30am–9:30pm; Fri–Sat 11:30am–10pm.

Nick's Tomato Pie ✪ ITALIAN A fun, family restaurant, Nick's is a popular attraction that's known to bring folks even from Miami for a piece of this Pie. With a huge menu of pastas, pizzas, fish, chicken, and beef, this cheery (and noisy) spot has something for everyone. On Saturday night, you'll see lots of couples on dates and some families leaving with take-out bags left over from the impossibly generous portions. The homemade sausage is a delicious treat, served with sautéed onions and peppers. The *pollo marsala,* too, is good and authentic.

1697 W. Indiantown Rd. (1 mile east of I-95, Exit 59A), Jupiter. © 561/744-8935. Reservations accepted only for parties of 6 or more. Main courses $12–$20; pastas $10–$15. AE, DC, DISC, MC, V. Mon–Thurs and Sun 5–10pm; Fri–Sat 5–11pm.

No Anchovies! ⭐ ITALIAN   This large and colorful restaurant is popular with families that appreciate the large portions and reasonably priced children's specials. An equally colorful menu offers a large variety of pastas, pizzas, salads, and meat and fish specials. Mix and match your pasta with half a dozen sauces. You may also want to try some of the delicious chicken or meats prepared on the oak-burning grill.

2650 PGA Blvd., Palm Beach Gardens. © 561/622-7855. Pizza and pasta $7–$13; main courses $9–$22; appetizers $6–$10. AE, DC, MC, V. Mon–Thurs 11:30am–10:30pm; Fri–Sat 11:30am–11pm; Sun 4:30–10pm.

Sinclair's Ocean Grill & Rotisserie ⭐⭐ CARIBBEAN   As close to upscale as Jupiter gets, Sinclair's is the Jupiter Beach Resort's excellent restaurant overlooking the pool and featuring fresh, locally caught fish as well as an excellent filet mignon. Especially popular are the Sunday brunches.

Jupiter Beach Resort, 5 N. Rte. A1A © 561/745-7120. Reservations recommended. Main courses $9.95–$18. AE, MC, V. Daily 6:30–11am, 11:30am–2:30pm, and 6–10pm.

JUPITER & NORTHERN PALM BEACH COUNTY AFTER DARK

With one notable exception, there just isn't much going on here after dark. **Club Safari,** 4000 PGA Blvd. (just east of I-95), in Palm Beach Garden's Marriott Hotel (© **561/622-8888**), does a hilarious Vegas-style safari theme. The huge, sunken dance floor is surrounded by vines and lanky, potted trees. Nearby, a large Buddha statue blows steam and smoke while waving its burly arms in front of a young gyrating crowd. There is deejay music, a large video screen, and a modest cover charge on the weekends. Open nights, Wednesday through Sunday.

13

The Treasure Coast: Stuart to Sebastian

While the area from Fort Lauderdale to Palm Beach is known as the Gold Coast because of the discovery of priceless treasures in the water, the area north of Palm Beach is known as the Treasure Coast for the same reason—it's been documented that the area was the site of a number of shipwrecks that date back to over 300 years ago. In fact, some historians believe that treasures from these sunken vessels still lie buried deep beneath the ocean floor. The difference, however, is that while the Gold Coast is a bit, well, tarnished as far as development is concerned, the Treasure Coast remains, for the most part, an unspoiled, quiet natural jewel. From the northern tip of Palm Beach County, the Treasure Coast extends through Martin, St. Lucie, and Indian River counties. Miles of uninterrupted beaches and aquamarine waters attract swimmers, boaters, divers, anglers, and sun worshippers who love to dip, dive, and surf. If you love the great outdoors and prefer a more understated environment, the Treasure Coast is a real find.

For hundreds of years, Florida's east coast was a popular stopover for European explorers, many of whom arrived from Spain to fill coffers with gold and silver. Rough weather and poor navigation often took a toll on their ships, but in 1715 a violent hurricane stunned the northeast coast and sank an entire fleet of Spanish ships laden with gold. Although Spanish salvagers worked for years to collect the lost treasure, much of it remained buried beneath the shifting sand. Workers hired to excavate the area in the 1950s and 1960s discovered centuries-old coins under their tractors. The McLarty Treasure Museum at Sebastian Inlet State Recreation Area in Melbourne Beach highlights the history of the 1715 Treasure Fleet. There are also incredible barrier reefs and shipwrecks in St. Lucie County that can be reached from the beaches of Fort Pierce and Hutchinson Island.

Today, on these same beaches you'll find an occasional treasure hunter trolling the sand with a metal detector, alongside swimmers and sunbathers who come to enjoy the stretches of beach that extend into the horizon. The sea, especially around Sebastian Inlet, is a mecca for surfers, who find some of the largest swells in the state.

Along with the pleasures of the talcum powder sands, the Treasure Coast also offers great shopping, entertainment, clubbing, sporting, and numerous other opportunities to take a reprieve from the hubbub of the rat race. The array of wildlife you'll find here is extensive. The endangered West Indian manatee can be spotted along the Treasure Coast's inland waterways. You can learn more about this mammal at The Manatee Observation and Education Center in Fort Pierce. St. Lucie Inlet State Preserve has a wonderful nesting area for loggerhead and leatherback turtles. Take a boat tour through the Loxahatchee Everglades, home to tropical fish, alligators, deer, and exotic birds. Go trolling in Lake Okeechobee for the best freshwater fish around.

If you're a sports enthusiast, you'll enjoy the boundless sporting opportunities here—from golf and tennis to polo and motorcar racing. If you tire from your own activities, take time out to watch the pros play hard. Catch the New York Mets practicing at the St. Lucie City Stadium in Port St. Lucie during spring training.

The downtown areas of the Treasure Coast have been experiencing a rebirth in the past few years, along with the influx of unprecedented numbers of new residents. The area's growth has occurred at a reasonable pace so that the neighborhoods have been able to retain their small-town feel. The result is a batch of

freshly spruced-up accommodations, shops, and restaurants from Stuart to Sebastian.

Southern Martin County's well-to-do Hobe Sound, in particular, is a Treasure Coast hot spot with its pristine beaches, Banyan tree–canopied streetscapes, one-of-a-kind antique shops and art galleries. Hobe Sound rests at the front door of the Gold Coast and the back door of the Treasure Coast, and it has immediate access to the Atlantic Ocean and the Intracoastal Waterway. Real estate here is at a premium, with million-dollar waterfront mansions lining the shores.

For the purposes of this chapter, the Treasure Coast runs roughly from Hobe Sound in the south to Sebastian Inlet in the north, encompassing some of Martin, St. Lucie, and Indian River counties and all of Hutchinson Island.

TREASURE COAST ESSENTIALS
GETTING THERE

Since virtually every town described in this chapter runs along a straight route, along the Atlantic Ocean, I've given all directions below.

BY PLANE   The **Palm Beach International Airport** (© 561/471-7420), located about 35 miles south of Stuart, is the closest gateway to this region if you're flying. See the "Getting Around" section on Palm Beach in chapter 12 for complete information. If you are traveling to the northern part of the Treasure Coast, **Melbourne International Airport,** off U.S. 1 in Melbourne (© 407/723-6227), is less than 25 miles north of Sebastian and about 35 miles north of Vero Beach.

BY CAR   If you're driving up or down the Florida coast, you'll probably reach the Treasure Coast via I-95. If you are heading to Stuart or Jensen Beach, take Exit 61 (Route 76/Tanner Highway) or 62 (Route 714); to Port St. Lucie or Fort Pierce, take Exit 63 or 64 (Okeechobee Road); to Vero Beach, take Exit 68 (State Route 60); to Sebastian, take Exit 69 (County Road).

You can also take the Florida Turnpike; this toll road is the fastest (but not the most scenic) route, especially if you're coming from Orlando. If you are heading to Stuart or Jensen Beach, take Exit 133; to Fort Pierce, take Exit 152 (Okeechobee Road); to Port St. Lucie, take Exit 142 or 152; to Vero Beach, take Exit 193 (State Route 60); to Sebastian, take Exit 193 to State Route 60 east and connect to I-95 north.

If you are staying in Hutchinson Island, which runs almost the entire length of the Treasure Coast, you should check with your hotel or see the listings below to find the best route to take.

Finally, if you're coming directly from the west coast, you'll probably take State Route 70, which runs north of Lake Okeechobee to Fort Pierce, located just up the road from Stuart.

BY RAIL   Amtrak (© 800/USA-RAIL; www.amtrak.com) stops in West Palm Beach at 201 S. Tamarind Ave., and in Okeechobee at 801 N. Parrot Ave., off U.S. 441 north.

BY BUS   Greyhound buses (© 800/231-2222; www.greyhound.com) service the area with terminals in Stuart, at 1308 S. Federal Hwy.; in Fort Pierce, at 7005 Okeechobee Rd. (© 561/461-3299); and in Vero Beach, at U.S. 1 and State Route 60 (© 561/562-6588).

GETTING AROUND

A car is a necessity in this large and rural region. Although heavy traffic is not usually a problem here, on the smaller coastal roads, like Fla. A1A, expect to travel at a slow pace, usually between 25 and 40 miles an hour.

1 Hobe Sound ⟨★⟩⟨★⟩⟨★⟩, Stuart & Jensen Beach

130 miles SE of Orlando, 98 miles N. of Miami.

Once just a stretch of pineapple plantations, the towns of Martin County, which include Stuart, Jensen Beach, Port Salerno, and Hobe Sound, still retain much of their rural character. Dotted between citrus groves and mangroves are modest homes and an occasional high-rise condominium. Although the area is definitely still seasonal (with a distinct rise in street and pedestrian traffic beginning after the Christmas holidays), the atmosphere is pure small town. Even in historic downtown Stuart, the result of a successful, ongoing restoration, expect the storefronts to be dark and the streets abandoned after 10pm.

ESSENTIALS

The **Stuart/Martin County Chamber of Commerce,** 1650 S. Kanner Hwy., Stuart, FL 34994 (© 800/524-9704 in Florida, or 561/287-1088; fax 561/220-3437), is the region's main source for information. The **Jensen Beach Chamber of Commerce,** 1901 NE Jensen Beach Blvd., Jensen Beach, FL 34957 (© 561/334-3444; fax 561/334-0817), also offers visitors information about its simple beachfront town.

BACK TO NATURE: THE BEACHES & BEYOND

BEACHES   Beaches are easily accessible throughout Hutchinson Island, the long, thin barrier island that stretches north and south from Stuart. Look for "coastal access" signs pointing the way to the public beach areas.

The best of them is **Bathtub Beach,** on North Hutchinson Island. Here, the calm waters are protected by coral reefs, and visitors can explore the region on dune and river trails. Pick a secluded spot on the wide stretch of beach, or enjoy marked nature trails across the street. Facilities include showers and toilets open during the day. To reach the park, head east on Ocean Boulevard (Stuart Causeway) and turn right onto MacArthur Boulevard. The beach is about a mile ahead on your left, just north of the Indian River Plantation. Parking is plentiful.

CANOEING   **Jonathan Dickinson State Park** (see "Wildlife Exploration," below) is the area's most popular for canoeing. The route winds through a variety of botanical habitats. You'll see lots of birds and, of course, the occasional manatee. Canoes cost $6 per hour. The concession is open Monday to Friday from 9am to 5pm and Saturday and Sunday from 8am to 5pm.

The Treasure Coast

Coastal Science Center **12**
Dodgertown **5**
Elliott Museum **10**
Environmental Learning Center **4**
Gilbert's House of Refuge Museum **11**
Harbor Branch Oceanographic Institution **7**

Indian River Citrus Museum **6**
McKee Botanical Garden **1**
McLarty Treasure Museum **2**
Mel Fisher's Treasure Museum **3**
Savannahs Recreation Center **9**
UDT-SEAL Museum **8**

FISHING Several independent charter captains operate on Hutchinson Island and Jensen Beach. One of the largest operators is the **Sailfish Marina,** 3565 SE St. Lucie Blvd., in Stuart (© **561/221-9456**), which maintains half a dozen charter boats for fishing excursions year-round. Also on-site are a bait-and-tackle shop and a knowledgeable, helpful staff. Other reputable charter operators include **Hungry Bear Adventures, Inc.,** docked at Indian River Plantation Marriott Resort, 4730-1 SE Teri Place in Stuart (© **561/283-8034;** fishing@tci.net); and **Bone Shaker Sportfishing,** 3585 SE St. Lucie Blvd., in Stuart (© **561/286-5504;** veejay4842@aol.com).

GOLF The pricey **Indian River Plantation Beach Resort** is a terrific destination for golfers, but you must be a guest at the resort or a guest of a member in order to play. Instead, try the **Champions Club at Summerfield,** on U.S. 1, south of Cove Road in Stuart (© **561/283-1500**), a somewhat challenging championship course designed by Tom Fazio. This rural course, the best in the area, offers great glimpses of wildlife amid the wetlands. Winter greens fees are around $60, and carts are mandatory. Reservations are a must and are taken 4 days in advance.

SCUBA DIVING & SNORKELING Three popular artificial reefs off Hutchinson Island provide excellent scenery for both novice and experienced divers. The **USS *Rankin,*** sunk in 120 feet of water in 1988, lies 7 miles east-northeast of the St. Lucie Inlet. The 58-foot-deep **Donaldson Reef** consists of a cluster of plumbing fixtures sunk in 58 feet of water. It's located due east of the Gilbert's House of Refuge Museum. The **Ernst Reef,** made from old tires, is a 60-foot dive located 4½ miles east-southeast of the St. Lucie inlet. Local dive shops have "tips" on the best spots and rules and regulations for safe diving. The Donald F. Welton Scuba Repair Shop (© **561/225-9717;** dfwelton@aol.com) in Jensen Beach is a great place to check out.

SEEING THE SIGHTS

Coastal Science Center 🏖🏖 This is a nature lover's Disney World. Opened by the South Florida Oceanographic Society in late 1994, this 44-acre site surrounded by coastal hammock and mangroves is its own little ecosystem and serves as an outdoor classroom, teaching visitors about the region's flora and fauna. The modest building houses saltwater tanks and wet and dry "discovery tables" with small indigenous animals. The incredibly eager staff of volunteers encourages visitors to wander the lush, well-marked nature trails.

890 NE Ocean Blvd. (across the street from the Elliott Museum), Hutchinson Island, Stuart. © 561/ 225-0505. www.fosusa.org. Admission $6 adults, $3 children 3–12, free for children under 3. Mon–Sat 10am–5pm. Sunday noon–4.

Balloons Over Florida 🏖🏖🏖 *Finds* For a lofty view of Martin County's wildlife, take a hot air balloon ride above the animals' natural habitat. Two fully licensed and insured balloons and pilots will take a maximum of four people up, up, and away for about an hour, depending on wind and weather conditions. After you've landed, drink in the sights over a glass of complimentary champagne and a continental breakfast. A certificate of flight is given to each passenger as a souvenir.

Tours begin at approximately 6:30am from a destination point to be determined. © 561/334-9393. $150 per person, including continental breakfast and champagne.

Elliott Museum 🏖🏖 A treasure trove of early Americana, the Elliott Museum is a rich tribute to inventors, sports heroes, and collectors. A series of life-size dioramas depicts an apothecary, a barbershop, a blacksmith forge,

The Producers

During the land boom in the 1920s, big plans were made for Hobe Sound by the Olympia Improvement Corporation. The company would create a columned, trellised town in the style of a Greek village, one in which movies could be produced. Hobe Sound was renamed Picture City, and street names came straight from Greek mythology: Zeus Crescent, Saturn, Mercury, Mars, Olympus, and Athena. When the boom collapsed in 1928 after a devastating hurricane, the celluloid dreams for Picture City were shattered. The town's old name of Hobe Sound was restored, but the street names remain, as do the cement streetlights on Dixie Highway.

Wildlife Exploration: From Gators to Manatees to Turtles

One of the most scenic areas on this stretch of the coast is **Jonathan Dickinson State Park** ⟨⟩, at 16450 S. Federal Hwy. (U.S. 1), Hobe Sound (© **561/ 546-2771**). The park receives less maintenance intentionally so that it will resemble the habitat of hundreds of years ago, before Europeans started chopping, dredging, and "improving" the area. Dozens of species of Florida's unique wildlife, including alligators and manatees, live on more than 11,300 acres. Bird watchers wiil also be delighted. You can rent canoes from the concession stand to explore the Loxahatchee River on your own. Admission is $3.25 per car of up to eight adults. Day hikers, bikers, and walkers pay $1 each. The park is open from 8am until sundown. See "Where to Stay," below, for details on camping.

Nearby is **Hobe Sound Wildlife Refuge,** on North Beach Road off State Route 708, at the north end of Jupiter Island (© **561/546-6141**). This is one of the best places to see sea turtles that nest on the shore in the summer months, especially in June and July. Because it's home to a large variety of other plant and animal species, the park is worth visiting at other times of year as well. Admission is $4 per car, and the preserve is open daily from sunrise to sunset. Exact times are posted at each entrance and change seasonally.

For turtle walks in Hutchinson Island, call © **877/375-4386.** These walks take place from May 22 through July 22 at 9pm, Friday and Saturdays. Reservations are necessary and should be made well in advance, as walks are limited to 50 people. Reservations are accepted as of May 1.

a clock and watch shop, and other old-fashioned commercial enterprises. Sports fans will appreciate the baseball memorabilia—a half-million dollars' worth—including an autographed item from every player in the Baseball Hall of Fame.

A gallery of patents and models of machines, invented by the museum's founder, Harmon Parker Elliott, and his son, provides an intriguing glimpse into the business of tinkering. Their collection of restored antique cars is also impressive. Expect to spend at least an hour seeing the highlights.

825 NE Ocean Blvd. (north of Indian River Plantation Resort), Hutchinson Island, Stuart. © **561/225-1961.** Admission $6 adults, $2 children 6–13, free for children 5 and under. Daily 10am–4pm.

Gilbert's House of Refuge Museum ⟨⟩   Gilbert's, the oldest structure in Martin County, dates from 1875, when it functioned as one of 10 such rescue centers for shipwrecked sailors. After undergoing a thorough rehabilitation to its original condition along the rocky shores, the house now displays marine artifacts and turn-of-the-century lifesaving equipment and photographs and is worth a quick visit to get a feel for the area's early days.

301 SE MacArthur Blvd. (south of Indian River Plantation resort), Hutchinson Island, Stuart. © **561/ 225-1875.** Admission $4 adults, $2 children 6–13, free for children 5 and under. Daily 10am–4pm.

A BOAT TOUR

The *Loxahatchee Queen* ★★★, a 35-foot pontoon boat (© 561/746-1466) in Jonathan Dickinson State Park in Hobe Sound, makes daily tours of the area's otherwise inaccessible backwater, where curious alligators, manatees, eagles, and tortoises often peek out to see who's in their yard. Try to catch the 2-hour tour, given Wednesday to Sunday as the tide permits, when it includes a stop at Trapper Nelson's home. Known as the "Wildman of Loxahatchee," Nelson lived in primitive conditions on a remote stretch of the water in a log cabin he built himself, which is preserved for visitors to see. Tours leave four times daily at 9am, 11am, 1pm, and 3pm and cost $12 for adults, $7 for children 6 to 12, and free for children 5 and under. See the "Wildlife Exploration" box for more information on the park.

SHOPPING

Downtown Stuart's historic district, along Flagler Avenue between Confusion Corner and St. Lucie Avenue, offers shoppers diversity and quality in a small old-town setting. Shops offer a range of goods: antique bric-a-brac, old lamps and fixtures, books, gourmet foods, furnishings, and souvenirs. For bargains, check out the **B & A Flea Market** (© 561/288-4915), the Treasure Coast's oldest and largest flea market.

WHERE TO STAY

Although the area boasts some beautiful beaches, the bulk of the hotel scene is downtown, where the nicer (and more reasonably priced) accommodations can be found among the shops and restaurants. There are, however, a few excellent beachfront hotels and inns. One of the bigger hotel chains in the area is the **Holiday Inn.** Its recently renovated, stunning beachfront property is at 3793 NE Ocean Blvd., on Hutchinson Island in Jensen Beach (© 800/992-4747 or 561/225-3000). Rates in season range from $130 to $180. Holiday Inn also has a downtown location at 1209 S. Federal Hwy. (© 561/287-6200). This simple two-story building on a busy main road is kept in very good shape and is convenient to Stuart's downtown historic district. Rates range from $99 to $140.

VERY EXPENSIVE

Hutchinson Island Marriott Beach Resort and Marina ★★★   This sprawling 200-acre compound offers so many diversions for active (or not-so-active) vacationers, and families in particular, that you won't want to leave. After a $6 million renovation in 1998, this is definitely Hutchinson Island's best resort, occupying the lush grounds of a former pineapple plantation. Activities include tennis, golfing, and boating. Sportfishing (especially for sailfish) is a big draw here, as are scuba diving and other watersports.

Generously sized rooms, all with fully equipped kitchens, are decorated with colorful spreads and draperies. A complete room renovation occurred in 2000, and in 2001 the hotel's beach building was completely redone. Some rooms overlook the Intracoastal and the resort's marina, while others face the ocean or the gardens.

In the summer months, be sure to sign up for a "turtle watch," during which you can watch the large turtles crawl onto the sand to lay their eggs. Another great activity, offered at an extra cost, is a sightseeing cruise along the St. Lucie and Indian rivers.

555 NE Ocean Blvd., Hutchinson Island, Stuart, FL 34996. © 800/775-5936 or 561/225-3700. Fax 561/225-0003. www.marriott.com/marriott/pbiir. 298 units. Winter $209–$399; off-season $99–$349. AE, MC, V. From downtown Stuart, take E. Ocean Blvd. over 2 bridges to NE Ocean Blvd.; turn right. Pets accepted

with a $50 deposit. **Amenities:** Restaurant, coffee shop, lounge, 4 large pools, 18-hole golf course, 13 tennis courts, fitness center & spa, extensive watersports, bike rental, children's programs, game room, concierge, on-property transportation, limited room service, babysitting, laundry and dry-cleaning services. *In room:* A/C, TV, dataport, kitchenette, minibar, coffeemaker, hair dryer.

MODERATE

Harborfront Inn Bed & Breakfast ★★ *Finds*   A bona fide return to Old Florida, the Harborfront Inn has the advantage of being right on the river, where you can sail, kayak, and water-ski. It consists of a series of little blue-trimmed shingled cottages within walking distance of the restaurants of downtown Stuart. Each room in this highly recommended B&B, which dates back to 1908, has its own private entrance, making it more like a rambling inn. Also, every accommodation has a sitting area and private bathroom. The two best rooms are the bright Garden Suite, which has a queen-size bed, rattan furnishings, and a deck with river and garden views; and the Guest House, which has an extra-large bathroom with two sinks and can be rented with an adjoining full kitchen.

A must-do is the in-room candlelight dinner. The inn's cozy public areas are surrounded by an enclosed porch where breakfast is served. The morning meal usually includes fresh fruit from the trees that grow on the property. No children are allowed here, and smoking is not permitted.

310 Atlanta Ave., Stuart, FL 34994. ℂ **800/294-1703** or 561/288-7289. Fax 561/221-0474. www. harborfrontinn.com. 6 units. Winter $90–$183 double. Off-season discounts available. Rates include breakfast. DISC, MC, V. Free dockage. From I-95 take Exit 61 heading east to U.S. 1 N. Turn left on W. Ocean Blvd. and make the first right (Atlanta Ave.). **Amenities:** Jacuzzi, watersports equipment/rentals. *In room:* A/C, TV/VCR, hair dryer.

Hutchinson Inn ★★   It doesn't look like much from the road—only the tennis court is visible—but you'll soon happen upon striking white gazebos dotting thick green lawns. Located directly on the beach, the Hutchinson Inn is a quiet and charming two-story hideaway. Unfortunately, so many people know about it that it's usually booked a year in advance in high season. The refurbished rooms have rattan furnishings; sofas convert into pull-out beds, and several rooms can be joined to accommodate large families. Some contain kitchens.

9750 S. Ocean Dr. (Fla. A1A), Jensen Beach, FL 34957. ℂ **561/229-2000.** www.hutchinsoninn.com. 21 units. Winter from $125 double; $165–$235 efficiency or suite. Off-season from $95 double; $125–$195 efficiency or suite. Rates include continental breakfast. MC, V. From I-95 take Exit 61, heading east to Monterey; turn right and cross U.S. 1. Go to second light; turn right on E. Ocean Blvd. onto the island. Inn is about 8 miles ahead. **Amenities:** Large outdoor heated pool, lighted tennis court, watersports equipment/rental, bike rental, coin-op washers and dryers. Freshly baked cookies before bedtime. *In room:* A/C, TV, kitchen in some rooms, fridge, hair dryer.

CAMPING

There are comfortable campsites in **Jonathan Dickinson State Park** in Hobe Sound (see the "Wildlife Exploration" box). You can stay overnight in rustic cabins or in your tent or camper in two different sections of the park. The River Camp area offers the benefit of the nearby Loxahatchee River, while the Pine Grove site has beautiful shade trees. There are concession areas for daytime snacks and 135 campsites with showers, clean restrooms, water, optional electricity, and an open-fire pit for cooking. Overnight rates in the winter are $18 without electricity, $20 with electricity. In the summer, rates are about $14 for four people.

For a more cushy camping experience, reserve a wood-sided cabin with a furnished kitchen, a bathroom with shower, heat and air-conditioning, and an outdoor grill. Bring your own linens. Cabins rent for $65 and up a night and sleep four people comfortably, six if your group is really into togetherness. Call ℂ **561/546-2771** Monday to Friday from 9am to 5pm, well in advance to reserve a spot. A $50 key deposit is required.

WHERE TO DINE
EXPENSIVE
Eleven Maple Street ★★★ AMERICAN   The most highly rated restaurant in Jensen Beach, Eleven Maple Street occupies a lovely little house with a white picket fence, French doors, lace curtains, and pink-clothed tables. Dining is both indoors and out, in any one of a series of cozy dining rooms or on a covered patio surrounded by gardens. Straightforward meat and fish dishes run the gamut from local seafood to game and poultry such as venison and duck. Maine lobster, filet mignon, and pastas are also available, and most everything is spiced with fresh-picked herbs from the restaurant's own organic garden.

11 Maple St., Jensen Beach. ℂ **561/334-7714.** Reservations recommended. Main courses $16–$29. MC, V. Wed–Sun 6–10pm. Head east on Jensen Beach Blvd. and turn right after the railroad tracks.

Flagler Grill ★★ AMERICAN/FLORIDA REGIONAL   In the heart of historic downtown, this seemingly out-of-place Manhattan-style bistro serves up classics with a twist. The dishes are not so unusual as to alienate the conservative pink-shirted golfers who frequent the place, yet they're fresh and light enough to quench the appetites of the more adventurous—for example, the saffron and mushroom pasta with Cajun shrimp and roasted tomatoes. The menu changes every few weeks, so see what your server recommends. It's hard to go wrong with any of the many salads, pastas, fishes, or delectable beef choices. The desserts, too, are worth the calories. No smoking is allowed in the restaurant or bar.

47 SW Flagler Ave. (just before the Roosevelt Bridge), downtown Stuart. ℂ **561/221-9517.** Reservations strongly suggested in season. Main courses $17–$25. AE, MC, V. Winter daily 5–10pm. Off-season Thurs–Sat 5:30–9:30pm. Lounge and bar open to 11:30pm. Special sunset menu offered from 5–6pm.

MODERATE
Black Marlin ★ FLORIDA REGIONAL   Although it sports the look and feel of a dank English pub, the Black Marlin offers full Floridian flavor. The salmon BLT is typical of the dishes here—grilled salmon on a toasted bun topped with bacon, lettuce, tomato, and coleslaw. Designer pizzas are topped with shrimp, roasted red peppers, and the like; and main dishes, all of which are served with vegetables and potatoes, include a lobster tail with honey-mustard sauce, and a charcoal-grilled chicken breast served on radicchio with caramelized onions.

53 W. Osceola St., downtown Stuart. ℂ **561/286-3126.** Reservations not accepted. Salads and sandwiches $4–$8, full meals $9–$24. AE, MC, V. Mon–Thurs 5–10pm, Fri–Sat 5–11pm (the bar is open later).

Conchy Joe's Seafood ★★ *Finds* SEAFOOD   Known for fresh seafood and Old Florida hospitality, Conchy Joe's enjoys an excellent reputation that's far bigger than the restaurant itself. Dining is either indoors, at red-and-white cloth-covered tables, or on a covered patio overlooking the St. Lucie River. The restaurant features a wide variety of freshly shucked shellfish and daily-catch selections that are baked, broiled, or fried. Beer is the drink of choice here, though other beverages and a full bar are available. Conchy Joe's has been the most active place in Jensen Beach since it opened in 1983. The large bar is especially popular at night and during weekday happy hours.

3945 NE Indian River Dr. (½ mile from the Jensen Beach Causeway), Jensen Beach. ℂ **561/334-1130.** Reservations not accepted. Main courses $12–$20. AE, DISC, MC, V. Daily 11:30am–2:30pm and 5–10pm (happy hour daily 3–6pm).

INEXPENSIVE

Bubba's Fish Camp *(Finds)* SEAFOOD/SOUTHERN   As you would imagine from its name, Bubba's is an ultracasual spot designed to resemble an old-Florida fish camp. Don't miss the great crawfish gumbo, corn bread, catfish, creamy spinach, hush puppies, and fried green tomatoes, too. After 4pm, you'll find bargain deals on hearty Southern classics like meatloaf, baked Virginia ham with red-eye gravy, fried chicken, and pork chops. Each includes a choice of delicious side dishes. Fresh and crispy onion rings are actually served on tiny bathroom plunger handles. Locals and highway travelers line up outside the screened porch to get into this rustic eatery.

421 S. Federal Hwy. (at south side of Roosevelt Bridge), Stuart. *©* **561/220-3747.** Full meals $8–$10. AE, MC, V. Daily 4pm–10pm and later on weekends. Call about weekend breakfasts.

Nature's Way Cafe *(✦)* HEALTH FOOD   This lovely, clean and green dining room has dozens of little tables, a few barstools, and some sidewalk seating, too. A sort of health-food deli, Nature's Way excels in serving quick and nutritious meals such as huge salads, vegetarian sandwiches, and frozen yogurts. Try some of the homemade baked goods. Sit outside on quaint Osceola Street or ask them to pack your lunch for you to take to the beach.

25 SW Osceola St., in the Post Office Arcade, Stuart. *©* **561/220-7306.** Sandwiches and salads $4–$7, juices and shakes $1–$3. No credit cards. Mon–Fri 10am–4pm, Sat 11am–3pm.

STUART & JENSEN BEACH AFTER DARK

Local restaurants serve as the nightlife centers of Stuart and Jensen Beach. And "night" ends pretty early here, even on the weekends. The bar at the Black Marlin (see "Where to Dine," above) is popular with locals and out of towners alike.

No list of Jensen nightlife would be complete without mention of Conchy Joe's Seafood (see "Where to Dine," above), one of the region's most active spots. Inside, locals chug beer and watch a large-screen TV, while outside on the waterfront patio, live bands perform a few nights a week for a raucous crowd of dancers. Happy hours, weekdays from 3 to 6pm, draw large crowds with low-priced drinks and snacks. No cover.

In a strip mall just outside of downtown, you'll find pickup trucks as far as the eye can see parked outside the **Rock 'n' Horse,** 1580 S. Federal Hwy. (U.S. 1), Stuart (*©* **561/286-1281**). It's a real locals' country-and-western spot and the only real late-night spots in town. Cover varies.

The centerpiece of Stuart's slowly expanding cultural offerings is the newly restored **Lyric Theater,** at 59 SW Flagler Ave. (*©* **561/286-7827**). This beautiful 1920s-era, 600-seat theater hosts a variety of shows, readings, concerts, and films throughout the year.

2 Port St. Lucie, Fort Pierce & North Hutchinson Island *(✦✦)*

7 miles N. of Stuart

Port St. Lucie and Fort Pierce, two Old Florida towns, thrive on sportfishing. A seemingly endless row of piers juts out along the Intracoastal Waterway and the Fort Pierce Inlet for both river and ocean runs. Here visitors can also dive, snorkel, beachcomb, and sunbathe in an area that has been left untouched by the overdevelopment that has altered its neighbors to the south and north.

Most sightseeing takes place along the main beach road. Driving along Fla. A1A on Hutchinson Island, you'll discover several secluded beach clubs interspersed with 1950s-style homes, a few small inns, grungy raw bars, and a few high-rise condominiums. Much of this island is government owned and kept undeveloped for the public's enjoyment.

ESSENTIALS

The **St. Lucie County Chamber of Commerce,** 2200 Virginia Ave., Fort Pierce, FL 34982 (© **561/595-9999**), is the region's main source of information. There's another branch at 1626 SE Port St. Lucie Blvd., in Port St. Lucie. Both spots are open Monday through Friday from 9am to 5pm.

BEACHES & NATURE PRESERVES

North Hutchinson Island's beaches are the most pristine in this area. You won't find restaurants, hotels, or shopping; instead, spend your time swimming, surfing, fishing, and diving. Most of the beaches are private along this stretch of the Atlantic Ocean. Thankfully, the state has set aside some of the best areas for the public.

Fort Pierce Inlet State Recreation Area (© **561/468-3985**) is a stunning 340-acre park with almost 4,000 feet of sandy shores that were once the training ground for the original Navy frogmen. A short nature trail leads through a canopy of live oaks, cabbage palms, sea grapes, and strangler figs. The western side of the area has swamps of red mangroves that are home to fiddler crabs, osprey, and a multitude of wading birds. Jack Island State Preserve, in the State Recreation Area, is popular with bird watchers and offers hiking and nature trails. Jutting out into the Indian River, the mangrove-covered peninsula contains several marked trails, varying in distance from a half-mile to over 4 miles. The trails go through mangrove forests and lead to a short observation tower.

The best beach here, called Jetty Park, lies in the northern part of the State Recreation Area. Families enjoy the large picnic areas and barbecue grills. There are restrooms and outdoor showers, and lifeguards look after swimmers.

The park is located at 905 Shorewinds Dr., north of Fort Pierce Inlet. To get there from I-95, take Exit 66 east (Route 68) and turn left onto U.S. 1 north; in about 2 miles, you will see signs to Fla. A1A and the North Bridge Causeway. Turn right on A1A and cross over to North Hutchinson Island. Admission is $3.25 per vehicle, and the park is open daily from 8am to sunset.

SPECTATOR SPORTS & OUTDOOR PURSUITS

BASEBALL   The **New York Mets** hold spring training in Port St. Lucie from late February through March at the **Thomas J. White Stadium,** 525 NW Peacock Blvd. (© **561/871-2115**). Tickets cost $10 to $15. From April through August, their farm team, the Port St. Lucie Mets, plays home games in the stadium.

FISHING   The **Fort Pierce City Marina,** 1 Ave. A, Fort Pierce (© **561/464-1245**), has more than a dozen charter captains who keep their motors running for anglers anxious to catch a few. Brochures available at the marina list all the privately owned charter operators. The price usually starts at $150 per person for half-day tours, depending on the season. Charters are organized on an as-desired basis. In general, plan to arrive very early in the morning (by 6am) before all the other early birds.

GOLF   The most notable courses in Port St. Lucie are at the **PGA Golf Club at the Reserve** (© **561/467-1300**), at 1916 Perfect Dr. The club's first of three 18-hole public golf courses opened in January 1996 and was designed by Tom

Fazio; another course was designed by Pete Dye. The PGA Learning Center offers lessons for amateurs. The South Course, a classic Old Florida–style course, is set on wetlands and offers views of native wildlife. It is the most popular. The club is open 7am to 6pm daily. Greens fees are usually under $45; after 2pm, $25. Reserve at least 9 days in advance.

SEEING THE SIGHTS

Harbor Branch Oceanographic Institution ⋆⋆   Harbor Branch is a working nonprofit scientific institute that studies oceanic resources and welcomes visitors on regularly scheduled tours. The first stop is the J. Seward Johnson Marine Education Center, which houses institute-built submersibles that are used to conduct marine research at depths of up to 3,000 feet. A video details current research projects, and several large aquariums simulate the environments of the Indian River Lagoon and a saltwater reef. Tourists are then shuttled by minibus to the Aqua-Culture Farming Center, a research facility containing shallow tanks growing seaweed and other oceanic plants. The 90-minute Lagoon Wildlife Tour on a pontoon boat, which examines the Indian River Lagoon, is fascinating and runs from Monday through Saturday at 10am, 1pm, and 3pm. The tour costs $15 for adults and $12 for children 3 to 13.

5600 U.S. 1 N., Fort Pierce. (℄ 800/333-4264 or 561/465-2400. www.hboi.com. Admission $10 adults, $6 children 6–12, free for children 5 and under. Mon–Fri 8am–5pm; Visitor Center Gift Shop Mon–Sat 9am–5pm. Arrive at least 20 min. before tour.

UDT-SEAL Museum   Florida is full of unique museums, but none is more curious than the UDT-SEAL Museum, a most peculiar tribute to the secret forces of the U.S. Navy frogmen and their successors, the SEAL teams. Chronological displays trace the history of these clandestine divers and detail their most important achievements. The best exhibits are those of the intricately detailed equipment used by the navy's most elite members.

3300 North State Road A1A, Fort Pierce. (℄ 561/595-5845. Admission $4 adults, $1.50 children, free for children 6 and under. Mon–Sat 10am–4pm, Sun noon–4pm. Closed Mon in off-season.

Savannahs Recreation Area ⋆⋆⋆ *Finds*   A 550-acre former reservoir, Savannahs is a veritable wilderness, with botanical gardens, nature trails, campsites, a petting zoo, and scenery reminiscent of the Florida Everglades, but in a much more contained environment.

1400 E. Midway Rd., Fort Pierce. (℄ 561/464-7855. Admission $1 per car. Daily 8am–6pm.

WHERE TO STAY

The Port St. Lucie mainland is pretty run-down, but there are a number of inexpensive hotel options on scenic Hutchinson Island that are both charming and well priced. Probably the best option is the **Hampton Inn** (℄ **800/426-7866** or 561/460-9855), 2831 Reynolds Dr., which is relatively new and beautifully maintained. However, if you want to be closer to the water, try the **Days Inn Hutchinson Island,** 1920 Seaway Dr. (℄ **800/325-2525** or 561/461-8737), a small motel that sits along the Intracoastal inlet and is simple but very well kept.

Budget travelers will be glad to know about the **Edgewater Motel and Apartments,** 1160 Seaway Dr. (next door to and under the same ownership as the Harborlight Inn), Fort Pierce (℄ **800/286-1745** or 561/468-3555). Motel rooms start at less than $60 in high season, and efficiencies are also available from $80. Guests can enjoy a private pool, shuffleboard courts, and a nearby fishing pier.

EXPENSIVE

Club Med–Sandpiper 𝒜𝒜 *Kids*   A former Hilton Hotel, the 400-acre Sand-piper resort was purchased by Club Med in 1985 and marketed to Europeans looking for a Florida getaway. They come in droves (Americans, too) with all the kids and nannies for a sunny, active vacation with meals, for a reasonable pre-paid price. The drawback is that guests are 20 minutes from the nearest beach. The buildings could use a major overhaul, but there are plenty of diversions on the grounds, such as golf and tennis, and water-skiing, sailing, and boating on the Indian River. There's even a circus school. The rooms are sparse and small, but not uncomfortable. Because most of the activities here are outdoors, you probably won't spend much time inside anyway.

3500 SE Morningside Blvd., Port St. Lucie, FL 34952. ℂ **800/CLUB-MED** or 561/335-4400. Fax 561/398-5101. www.clubmed.com. 338 units. Winter $170–$280 per person, based on double occupancy. Off-season $150–$275 per person, based on double occupancy. Rates include 3 meals per day. AE, MC, V. From U.S. 1 S., turn left onto Westmoreland Blvd. Make another left onto Pine Valley Rd.; the resort entrance is straight ahead. **Amenities:** 2 restaurants, bar, 4 pools, 3 golf courses, 19 tennis courts (9 are lighted), fitness center, watersports equipment, game rooms, coin-op washers and dryers. *In room:* A/C, TV, hair dryer.

MODERATE

Dockside–Harbor Light Resort 𝒜   Fronting the Intracoastal Waterway, the Harbor Light is a great choice for boating and fishing enthusiasts, offering 15 boat slips and two private fishing piers. The hotel itself carries on the nautical theme with pierlike wooden stairs and rope railings. While not exactly captain's quarters, the rooms, which are simply decorated with pastel colors and small wall prints, are attractive, especially since a thorough renovation was completed in 1999. Higher-priced rooms have either waterfront balconies or small kitchenettes.

1160 Seaway Dr., South Hutchinson Island, FL 34949. ℂ **800/286-1745** or 561/468-3555. Fax 561/489-9848. 64 units. www.docksideinn.com. Winter $55 standard rooms, $69–$115 efficiencies. Off-season $42–$89 standard rooms and efficiencies. AE, DC, DISC, MC, V. From I-95, exit at 66A east to U.S. 1 north to Seaway Dr. **Amenities:** Outdoor heated pool, self-service laundry. *In room:* A/C, TV, minibar,higher-priced rooms have kitchenettes with coffeemaker.

Mellon Patch Inn 𝒜𝒜 *Finds*   The Mellon Patch offers just four bright rooms in what looks like a single-family house. Each room has a large bathroom and sturdy soundproof walls, making it very quiet. The public living room is nicer than any of the small guest rooms. It's designed with a two-story vaulted ceiling, a fireplace, and lots of windows that overlook the Indian River. A gourmet breakfast that might include chocolate-chip pancakes or spinach soufflé is served here each morning. The best part is that there are free tennis courts and a pub-lic beach across the street. The inn is nonsmoking, and children aren't allowed.

3601 N. Fla. A1A, North Hutchinson Island, FL 34949. ℂ **561/461-5231.** Fax 561/464-6463. www.sunet.net/mlnptch. 4 units. $85–$150 double year-round. Rates include breakfast. AE, DISC, MC, V. *In room:* A/C, TV.

Villa Nina Island Inn 𝒜𝒜 *Finds*   A more private option just down the road from the Mellon Patch is Villa Nina, in another simple but new home on the river's edge. Although it's more private, the silence is not nearly as heavy here as it is at the Mellon Patch. In fact, the atmosphere is rather cheery. Innkeepers Nina and Glenn live in the main house and have built rooms along the back, each with a private entrance and either a fully equipped kitchen or a kitchenette. Riverfront rooms are very homey, with comfortable beds and private baths. Enjoy breakfast poolside or delivered to your room (you may also opt out of breakfast for a $10 nightly savings). Smoking is not permitted.

On this stunning 8-acre property, you can find canoes and rowboats for river rides. A nearby shipwreck site makes for an excellent diving excursion.

The nearby **Sterling Casino Lines Cruise ship** welcomes Inn guests with free shuttle service from Vero Beach (✆ **800/ROLL-7-11**).

3851 North State Road A1A, North Hutchinson Island 34949. ✆ and fax 561/467-8673. www.villanina.com. 4 units. Winter $125–$195; off-season $105–$165. DISC, MC, V. **Amenities:** Outdoor heated pool, canoe and snorkel rental, bike rental, free laundry facilities. *In room:* A/C, TV, kitchen or kitchenette, minibar (in most rooms), fridge, coffeemaker.

WHERE TO DINE
There are a number of good seafood restaurants in the Fort Pierce and St. Lucie area, but it's also easy to drive to Stuart for more diverse dining options. See section 1 of this chapter for recommendations in Stuart.

MODERATE
Mangrove Mattie's ★★ SEAFOOD   A rustic restaurant on the Fort Pierce Inlet, Mangrove Mattie's is the best place for outdoor dining, with its priceless location—right on the inlet, affording panoramic views of the Atlantic—and excellent fresh seafood. Weekday happy hours (4 to 7pm) are especially popular, thanks to the view and the free buffet.

1640 Seaway Dr., Fort Pierce. ✆ 561/466-1044. Reservations accepted. Main courses $11–$18. AE, DISC, MC, V. Daily 11:30am–10pm.

P.V. Martin's ★★ SEAFOOD/AMERICAN   This relatively elegant eatery with an eclectic American menu is as funky as it gets in Fort Pierce. The wood floors, beamed ceilings, tiled tabletops, and rattan chairs would be nice anywhere, but here diners enjoy them as they look out through floor-to-ceiling windows onto sweeping ocean vistas. At night the room is warmed by a huge central stone fireplace, and on weekends there's live entertainment in the adjacent bar. Surf 'n' turf dinners run the gamut from crab-stuffed shrimp and grouper baked with bananas and almonds to Brie- and asparagus-stuffed chicken breast and barbecued baby back ribs. An excellent selection of appetizers includes escargots in mushroom caps and a succulent fried soft-shell crab (available in season). Be sure to try the lively Sunday champagne brunch.

5150 North State Road A1A, North Hutchinson Island. ✆ 561/569-0700. Reservations recommended. Main courses $9–$20. AE, MC, V. Mon–Sat 5–9pm, Sun 10:30am–2:30pm and 5–8:30pm.

Theo Thudpucker's Raw Bar and Seafood Restaurant ★ SEAFOOD
Located in a little building by the beach and wallpapered with maps and newspapers, Thudpucker's is a straightforward chowder bar. There's not much more to the dining room than one long bar and a few simple tables. Chowder and stews, often made with sherry and half-and-half, make excellent starters or light meals. The most recommendable (and filling) dinner dishes are sautéed scallops, deviled crabs, and deep-fried Okeechobee catfish.

2025 Seaway Dr., Fort Pierce. ✆ 561/465-1078. Reservations not accepted. Main courses $8–$24. MC, V. Mon–Thurs 11:30am–9:30pm, Fri–Sat 11:30am–11pm, Sun 1–9:30pm.

PORT ST. LUCIE/FORT PIERCE AFTER DARK
ArtWalk, a monthly event to showcase the downtown galleries, restaurants, and shops of Fort Pierce, takes place the second Wednesday of every month from 5 to 8pm and costs $5 per person, beginning in front of downtown's Sunrise Theater (✆ 561/466-3880). The **Friday Fest Street Festival** occurs on the first Friday of every month at the Historic Downtown Riverfront in Fort Pierce and is

free of charge, featuring live music and refreshments for sale. The **St. Lucie Blues Club,** 338 Port St. Lucie Blvd. (© **561/873-1111**), features live jazz, blues, and rock music Tuesday through Sunday nights. Reservations are recommended.

3 Vero Beach ⊀ & Sebastian ⊀⊀

85 miles SE of Orlando, 130 miles N. of Miami

Old Florida is thriving in these remote and tranquil villages. Vero Beach, known for its exclusive and affluent winter population, and Sebastian, known as one of the last remaining fishing villages, are located at the northern tip of the Treasure Coast region in Indian River County. These two beach towns are populated with folks who knew Miami and Fort Lauderdale in the days before massive high-rises and overcrowding. They appreciate the area's small-town feel, and that's exactly the area's appeal for visitors: a laid-back, relaxed atmosphere, friendly people, and friendlier prices.

A crowd of well-tanned surfers from all over the state descends on the region, especially the Sebastian Inlet, to catch some of the state's biggest waves. Other watersports enthusiasts enjoy the area's fine diving and windsurfing. Anglers are in heaven here. In spring, baseball buffs can catch some action from the L.A. Dodgers as they train in exhibition games.

ESSENTIALS

The **Indian River County Tourist Council,** 1216 21st St., Vero Beach, FL 32961 (© **561/567-3491;** fax 561/778-3181; www.vero-beach.fl.us/chamber), will send visitors an incredibly detailed information packet on the entire county, which includes Vero Beach and Sebastian and Fellsmere. You'll find a detailed full-color map of the area, a comprehensive listing of upcoming events, a hotel guide, and more.

BEACHES & OUTDOOR ACTIVITIES

BEACHES   You'll find plenty of free and open beachfront along the coast. Most beaches are uncrowded and are open from 7am until 10pm.

South Beach Park, on South Ocean Drive, at the end of Marigold Lane, is a busy, developed, lifeguarded beach with picnic tables, restrooms, and showers. It's known as one of the best swimming beaches and also attracts a young crowd that plays volleyball and Frisbee. A nicely laid-out nature walk takes you into beautiful secluded trails.

At the very north tip of the island, **Sebastian Inlet** ⊀ has flat sandy beaches with lots of facilities, including kayak, paddleboat, and canoe rentals; a well-stocked surf shop; picnic tables; and a snack shop. The winds seem to stir up the surf with no jetty to stop their swells, to the delight of surfers and boarders, who get here early to catch the big waves. Campers enjoy fully equipped sites in a woody area. Admission to the Sebastian Inlet State Recreation Area, 9700 S. Fla. A1A, Melbourne, is $3.25 per car and $1 for those who walk or bike in.

FISHING   Captain Jack Jackson works 7 days a week out of **Vero's Tackle and Sport-Shop,** 57–59 Royal Palm Point (© **561/567-6550**), taking anglers out on his 25-foot boat for private river excursions. Captain Jackson provides all the equipment. Half-day jaunts on the Indian River cost $250 for two people (the minimum required for a charter), tackle, rigs, and everything included; $50 extra for a third person. You can either bring your own food and drinks or purchase food from the shop.

Many other charters, guides, party boats, and tackle shops operate in this area. Consult your hotel for suggestions, or call the chamber of commerce (© **561/ 567-3491**) for a list of local operators.

GOLF   Hard-core golfers insist that of the dozens of courses in the area, only a handful are worth their plot of grass.

Set on rolling hills with uncluttered views of sand dunes and sky, the **San-dridge Golf Club** (© **561/770-5000**), at 5300 73rd St., Vero Beach, offers two par-72 18-holers. The Dunes is a long course with rolling fairways, and the newer Lakes course has lots of water. Both charge $38, including a cart. Week-ends cost $32 after 12 noon. There is a small snack bar selling beer and sand-wiches. Reservations are recommended and are taken 2 days in advance.

Although less challenging, the **Sebastian Municipal Golf Course** (© **561/589-6800**), at 1010 E. Airport Dr., is a good 18-hole par-72. It's sce-nic, well maintained, and a relative bargain. Greens fees are $35.31 per player with a cart and about half that if you want to play 9 holes after 1:30pm.

Also, see "Dodgertown," below.

SURFING   See Sebastian Inlet details under "Beaches," above. Also, consider the beach north of the Barber Bridge (State Route 70), where waves are slightly gentler and the scene less competitive; and Wabasso Beach, Fla. A1A and County Road 510, a secluded area near Disney's resort where lots of teenage locals congregate, especially when the weather gets rough.

TENNIS   There are dozens of tennis courts around Vero Beach and Sebastian, many of which are at hotels and resorts. Check the local phone book, or try **Riverside Racket Complex,** 350 Dahlia Lane, at Royal Palm Boulevard at the east end of Barber Bridge in Vero Beach (© **561/231-4787**). This popular park has 10 hard courts (6 lighted) that can be rented for $3.21 per person per hour, and two racquetball courts also with reasonable rates. Reservations are accepted up to 24 hours in advance. Nature trails are also on the premises.

SEEING THE SIGHTS

Environmental Learning Center ★★ *Kids*   The Indian River is not really a river at all, but a large brackish lagoon that's home to a greater variety of species than any other estuary in North America. The privately funded Environmental Learning Center was created to protect the local habitat and educate visitors about their environment. Situated on 51 island acres, the center features a 600-foot boardwalk through the mangroves and dozens of hands-on exhibits that are geared to both children and adults. There are live touch-tanks, exhibits, and microscopes for viewing the smallest sea life up close. The best thing to do here is join one of the center's interpretive canoe trips, offered by reservation only ($10 for adults, $5 for children).

255 Live Oak Dr. (just off the 510 Causeway), Wabasso Island. © **561/589-5050**. www.elcweb.org. Free admission. Tues–Fri 10am–4pm, Sat 9am–noon, Sun 1–4pm.

Indian River Citrus Museum   You may as well be in a supermarket, really. The tiny Indian River Citrus Museum exhibits artifacts relating to the history of the citrus industry, from its initial boom in the late 1800s to the present; a small grove displays several varieties. The gift shop sells clever citrus-themed gift items, along with, of course, ready-to-ship fruit.

2140 14th Ave., Vero Beach. © **561/770-2263**. Admission $1 donation. Tues–Fri 10am–4pm.

McKee Botanical Garden ✦✦   This impressive attraction was originally opened in 1932 and featured a virtual jungle of orchids, exotic and native trees, monkeys, and birds. After years of neglect, it was placed on the National Register of Historic Places in 1998. It underwent a top-to-bottom overhaul that was completed in February 2000, and you can now again experience the full charms of this little Eden.

350 U.S. 1, Vero Beach. ℃ **561/794-0601.** Fax 561/794-0602. www.mckeegarden.org. Admission $6 adults, $5 seniors, $3.50 children 5–12. Tues–Sat 10am–5pm, Sun noon–5pm.

McLarty Treasure Museum ✦   If you're unconvinced about why this area's called the Treasure Coast, then this is a must see, along with Mel Fisher's Treasure Museum (see below). Erected on the actual site of a salvaging camp from a wreck in 1715, this quaint little museum is full of interesting history. It may not have the vast treasures of the nearby Fisher museum, but it does offer a very engaging 45-minute video describing the many aspects of treasure hunting. You'll also see household items salvaged from the Spanish fleet and dioramas of life in the 18th century. For the price, you can't beat it.

13180 N. Fla. A1A, Sebastian Inlet State Recreation Area, Vero Beach. ℃ **561/589-2147.** Admission $1; children under 6 free. Daily 10am–4:30pm.

Mel Fisher's Treasure Museum ✦✦✦ *Finds*   This museum is truly priceless. Here's where you can see millions of dollars of treasures from the doomed Spanish fleet that went down in 1715. Although not as extensive as the museum in Key West, this exhibit includes gold coins, bars, and Spanish artifacts that are worth a look. Also, the preservation lab shows how the goods are extricated, cleaned, and preserved.

1322 U.S. 1, Sebastian. ℃ **561/589-9874.** www.melfisher.com. Admission $5 adults, $4 seniors over 55, $1.50 children 6–12, free for children 5 and under. Mon–Sat 10am–5pm, Sun noon–5pm.

DODGERTOWN

Vero is the winter home of the **Los Angeles Dodgers** (at least for the time being; there's been talk of a move), and the town hosts the team in grand style. The 450-acre compound at 3901 26th St. (℃ **561/569-4900**) encompasses two golf courses, a conference center, a country club, a movie theater, and a recreation room. You can watch afternoon exhibition games during the winter (usually between mid-February and the end of March) in the comfortable 6,500-seat outdoor stadium. Even if the game sells out, you can sprawl on the lawn for just $5. The stadium has never turned away an eager fan.

Even when spring training is over, you can still catch a game; the Dodgers' farm team, the Vero Beach Dodgers, has a full season of minor-league baseball in summer.

Admission to the complex is free; tickets to games are $12 for a reserved seat. The complex is open daily from 9am to 5pm; game time is usually 1pm. From I-95, take exit for State Route 60 east to 43rd Avenue and turn left; continue to 26th Street and turn right.

SHOPPING

Ocean Boulevard and Cardinal Drive are Vero's two main shopping streets. Both are near the beach and lined with specialty boutiques, including antique and home-decorating shops.

If you want to send fruit back home, the local source is **Hale Indian River Groves,** 615 Beachland Blvd. (℃ **561/231-1752**), a shipper of local citrus and jams since 1947. Note that it is closed 2 to 3 months a year, usually from summer through early fall, depending on the year's crop; the season generally runs from November through Easter. There are four locations in Vero Beach.

The **Horizon Outlet Center,** at State Route 60 and I-95, Vero Beach (© 877/GO-OUTLET or 561/770-6171), contains more than 80 discount stores selling name-brand shoes, kitchenware, books, clothing, and more. The mall is open Monday to Saturday from 9am to 8pm and Sunday from 11am to 6pm.

The **Indian River Mall** (© 561/770-6255), 6200 20th St. (State Route 60 about 5 miles east of I-95), is a big deal in Vero Beach. This monster mall has all the big national chains, such as the Gap, Structure, and Victoria's Secret, as well as several large department stores, and is open Monday through Saturday from 10am to 9pm and Sunday from noon to 6pm.

WHERE TO STAY

You can choose from accommodations on the mainland or on the beach. Although the beaches in many areas have eroded, leaving only narrow strips of sand, most areas offer pristine beachfronts where turtles lay eggs and sand crabs scurry around. As you might expect, the beachfront accommodations are a bit more expensive—but, I think, worth it. There are deals to be had in the chain hotels and some lovely privately owned properties, especially on weekdays and during off-season. Both **The Palm Court Inn** (© 800/245-3297 or 561/231-2800), at 3244 Ocean Dr., and the **Holiday Inn Oceanside** (© 800/465-4329 or 561/231-2300), at 3384 Ocean Dr., offer oceanfront rooms and suites at comparable prices (from around $80 for a standard room off-season to $185 for an oceanfront suite). The Holiday Inn may be a better choice since it offers discounts to AAA members and its restaurant and lounge directly face the ocean. The Palm Court (formerly a Days Inn) was thoroughly renovated in 1998. Also, a great spot to know, especially if you are planning to fish, is **Captain Hiram's** (see "Fishing," above, and also "Vero Beach & Sebastian After Dark," below), where there are four clean and cozy rooms available adjacent to the restaurant and overlooking the water. Rates are between $80 and $110.

Comfortable and inexpensive chain options near the Vero Beach Outlet Center off State Route 60 include a **Holiday Inn Express** (© 800/465-4329 or 561/567-2500), which opened in June 1998, and a slightly older **Hampton Inn** (© 800/426-7866 or 561/770-4299). Rates for both run between $70 and $80 and include breakfast and free local phone calls.

EXPENSIVE

Disney's Vero Beach Resort 🌟🌟🌟 *Kids*   Situated on the tip of 71 acres of pristine beaches, this Disney time-share resort is reminiscent of a turn-of-the-last-century Florida beach community. The resort takes advantage of its setting by offering exciting children's programs, such as canoe adventures, poolside miniature golf, campfire tales, a trip to a working cattle ranch, and stargazing from a powerful telescope. The best part is a large pool designed like a lagoon with a two-story winding slide that elicits squeals of delight from kids and adults alike. Rooms are bright and spacious, many with balconies. The resort offers reservation-only Disney character breakfasts on select days and is less than 2 hours away from Walt Disney World.

9250 Island Grove Terrace, Vero Beach, FL 32963. © 800/359-8000 or 561/234-2000. Fax 561/234-2030. 112 units, 60 cottages. Winter from $290 ocean-view double, from $355 and way up for villas, from $920 cottages (sleep up to 12); off-season from $170 ocean-view double, from $239 villas. AE, MC, V. From I-95 take

Exit 69 (512 going east); turn right onto County Rd. 510 heading east. Turn right again onto S. Fla. A1A. **Amenities:** 2 restaurants, bar, large pool, miniature golf, 2 lighted tennis courts, health club, Jacuzzi, sauna, watersports equipment/rental, extensive children's programs, game room and sports areas, tour desk, concierge, room service, dry-cleaning and laundry services, babysitting, business center. *In room:* A/C, TV.

Doubletree Guest Suites 🌟 This chain is conveniently located directly on the beach and is close to local restaurants and shops. First-class suites are located in a modern four-story building. The guest rooms are unremarkable, but clean and attractive. Bathrooms are spacious, and most suites overlook the pool or the ocean.

3500 Ocean Dr., Vero Beach, FL 32963. **℃ 800/841-5666** or 561/231-5666. Fax 561/234-4866. 55 units. Winter $235–$265 1-bedroom suite; off-season $125–$185 1-bedroom suite. AE, DC, DISC, MC, V. **Amenities:** Restaurant, bar, outdoor heated pool, kids' pool, access to nearby health club, Jacuzzi, room service, dry-cleaning and laundry services or coin-op washers and dryers. *In room:* A/C, TV, fridge, coffeemaker, hair dryer.

MODERATE

Driftwood Resort 🌟🌟 *Finds* Originally planned in the 1930s as a private estate by eccentric entrepreneur Waldo Sexton, the Driftwood was opened to the public after several travelers stopped by to inquire about renting a room here. Today the hotel's rooms and public areas are filled with the nautical knickknacks collected by Sexton on his travels all over the world. All of the guest rooms were renovated in 2000, and each is unique. Some feature terra-cotta–tiled floors and lighter furniture, while others have a more rustic feel with hardwoods and antiques. Some of the rooms contain Jacuzzis, and all are equipped with full kitchens. The resort is listed on the National Register of Historic Places and, to say the least, has lots of quirky charm.

3150 Ocean Dr., Vero Beach, FL 32963. **℃ 561/231-0550.** Fax 561/234-1981. www.thedriftwood.com. 100 units. Winter $110–$180 double; off-season $75–$130 double. AE, MC, V. **Amenities:** 2 outdoor heated pools, dry-cleaning service. *In room:* A/C, TV, coffeemaker, kitchen (in most 1-bedroom and all 2-bedroom units), Jacuzzi in some rooms.

Islander Inn 🌟 Resident owner Tom Collins runs one of the most comfortable and welcoming inns in the area. Well located in downtown Vero Beach, this small Key West–style motel is just a short walk to the beach, restaurants, and shops. Every guest room has a small refrigerator and either a king-size bed or two double beds. The accommodations are designed in a Caribbean motif with bright fabrics and white rattan furniture.

3101 Ocean Dr., Vero Beach, FL 32963. **℃ 800/952-5886** or 561/231-4431. 16 units. Winter $105–$120 double; off-season $72–$99 double. Efficiencies cost $10 extra. AE, MC, V. **Amenities:** Cafe, pool. *In room:* A/C, TV.

INEXPENSIVE

Davis House Inn 🌟🌟 Each of the dozen rooms in this contemporary three-story, blue-and-white B&B has a private entrance. The rooms are large and clean, although somewhat plain, and each has a king-size bed, a pull-out sofa, and a small kitchenette, making the rooms popular with long-term guests. The bathrooms are equally ample and have plenty of counter space. Guests will find a large wooden deck for sunbathing and a sunny second-floor breakfast room. The inn is a bit out of the way but is within walking distance to some nearby restaurants; the beach is a 10-minute drive.

607 Davis St., Sebastian, FL 32958. **℃ 561/589-4114.** Fax 561/589-1722. 12 units. Winter $69–$79 double; off-season $59–$79 double. Rates include continental breakfast. Nightly rooms are unavailable in February. Weekly and monthly rates available. AE, DISC, MC, V. From I-95, take Exit 69, heading east to Indian River Dr. and turn left. Go 1¼ miles to Davis St.; turn left. **Amenities:** Coin-op washers and dryers. *In room:* A/C, TV.

Sea Turtle Inn & Azalea Lane Apartments ⓡ This two-part property offers the very best value on the beach (just 2 blocks from the ocean). The 1950s motel and an adjacent apartment building have been fully renovated and outfitted with understated but efficient furnishings. You won't find any fancy amenities (or even a phone for that matter, unless you request one), but its price and beachfront location make up for what it lacks in frills. The properties share a small pool and sundeck. Book early, especially in season, since it fills up quickly with long-term visitors.

835 Azalea Lane, Vero Beach, FL 32963. ⓒ 561/234-0788. Fax 561/234-0717. www.vero-beach.fl.us/seaturtle. 21 units. Winter $69–$99 double; off-season $54–$79 double. Weekly and monthly rates available. MC, V. From I-95, go east on S.R. 60 (about 10 miles) to Cardinal Dr.; turn right. **Amenities:** Small pool. *In room:* A/C, TV, small fridge, coffeemaker.

CAMPING
This area is popular with campers, who can choose from nearly a dozen sites throughout Vero and Sebastian. If you aren't camping at the scenic and very popular Sebastian Inlet (see "Beaches," above), then try the **Vero Beach KOA RV Park,** 8850 U.S. 1, Wabasso (ⓒ **561/589-5665**). This 120-site campground is 2 miles from the ocean and the Intracoastal Waterway and a quarter-mile from the Indian River, a big draw for the crowd of regular fishing fanatics. There's access to running water and electricity, as well as showers, a shop, and hookups for RVs. Rates range from $20 to $24 per site, and $19 for tents. To get there, take I-95 to Exit 69 east; at U.S. 1 turn left.

WHERE TO DINE
EXPENSIVE
Chez Yannick ⓡⓡⓡ FRENCH/CONTINENTAL Excellent cooking, a comprehensive wine list, and white-glove service complement the crystal and gilded decor at this French standout. Excellent starters include a succulent sliced duckling breast, cream of lobster soup, and hearts-of-palm salad with a slightly spicy vinaigrette. Some items, like lobster and shrimp in a cognac-dill sauce, are available as either an appetizer or an entree. Other main courses include beef tenderloin stuffed with Gorgonzola cheese and sautéed soft-shell crabs. Desserts might include profiteroles with ice cream and chocolate or raspberry sauce, crème caramel, chocolate-mousse pie, or raspberry sorbet.

1605 S. Ocean Dr., Vero Beach. ⓒ 561/234-4115. Reservations recommended. Main courses $15–$30; fixed-price dinner $19–$21 is available in the off-season. AE, MC, V. Mon–Sat open at 6pm; closing time varies based on last reservation.

MODERATE
Black Pearl Brasserie and Grill ⓡⓡ CONTINENTAL This sophisticated brasserie seems out of place in this beachy town, but it happens to be one of Vero Beach's trendiest spots. The restaurant's small list of appetizers includes salads, chilled sweet-potato vichyssoise, crispy fried chicken fingers with mango dipping sauce, and grilled oysters with tangy barbecue sauce. Equally creative main courses are uniformly good. Don't miss their signature dish, an onion-crusted mahimahi with caramel citrus glaze. Both this original, unassuming restaurant and its newer counterpart, The **Black Pearl Riverfront,** at 4445 N. Fla. A1A (ⓒ **561/234-4426**), serve fantastically fresh *and* inventive food. The riverfront location is more formal and serves only dinner from 5pm.

2855 Ocean Dr., Vero Beach. ⓒ 561/234-4426. Fax 561/234-9074. Reservations recommended. Main courses $12–$21. AE, DC, DISC, MC, V. Mon–Sun 11:30am–10pm, Sun brunch 10:30am–2pm.

Ocean Grill (★★ (Finds) AMERICAN   The Ocean Grill is an institution that attracts locals and faithful devotees with its simple but rich cooking and its stunning locale, right on the ocean's edge. For a dramatic experience, ask for a table along the wall of windows that open onto the sea. This huge and handsome old-timer specializes in steaks and seafood. Try stone crab claws when they are in season, or the house shrimp scampi baked in butter and herbs and served with a tangy mustard sauce, or any of the big servings of pasta or meats. Dinners are uniformly good. The only tacky element of this place is the gift shop.

1050 Sexton Plaza (by the ocean at the end of S.R. 60), Vero Beach. (✆ 561/231-5409. Reservations accepted only for large parties. Main courses $17–$30. AE, DC, DISC, MC, V. Mon–Fri 11:30am–2:30pm and 5:30–10pm, Sat–Sun 5:30–10pm.

INEXPENSIVE

Beachside Restaurant at the Palm Court Resort ★ AMERICAN/DINER
For a great big, cheap American breakfast with an ocean view, this is the place to go. You can get omelets, home fries, cream chipped beef, corn beef hash, pancakes, Belgian waffles, and even grits. Friendly waitresses also serve lunch and dinner in the comfy wooden booths. The best dishes, like chili, fried chicken, and steaks, are hearty and delicious. No smoking.

3244 Ocean Dr., Vero Beach. (✆ 561/234-4477. Breakfast $2–$5; full dinners $8.95 and up. AE, DC, DISC, MC, V. Mon–Sat 6am–2:30pm, happy hour 4–6pm, dinner 5–9 pm, Sun 6am–1:30pm.

Nino's Cafe ★ ITALIAN   This little beachside cafe looks like a stereotypical pizza joint, complete with fake brick walls, murals of the Italian countryside, and red-and-white checked tablecloths. The atmosphere is pure cheese and so is much of the food. Pizza and parmigiana dishes are smothered in the stuff. Still, the thin crust and fresh toppings make the pizza here a cut above the rest. Entrees and pastas are also tasty.

1006 Easter Lily Lane (off Ocean Dr., next to Humiston Park), Vero Beach. (✆ 561/231-9311. Main courses $8.50–$11.95. No credit cards. Mon–Thurs 11am–9pm, Fri–Sat 11am–10pm, Sun 4–9pm.

VERO BEACH & SEBASTIAN AFTER DARK
More than half the residents in this area are retirees, so it shouldn't be a surprise that even on weekends, this town retires relatively early. Hotel lounges often have live music and a good bar scene, especially in high season. For beachside drinks, go to the Driftwood Resort. See "Where to Stay," above.

A mostly 30-something and younger crowd goes to **Bombay Louie's** in Vero Beach, at 398 21st St. (✆ 561/978-0209), where a DJ spins dance music after 9pm from Wednesday to Saturday. Vero Beach is also known as an artsy enclave, hosting galleries such as **The Art Works,** 2855 Ocean Dr., Vero Beach (✆ 561/231-4688) and the **Bottalico Gallery,** 3121 Ocean Dr., Vero Beach (✆ 561/231-0414). **The Civic Arts Center** at Riverside Park is a hub of culture, including the Riverside Theatre (✆ 561/231-6990), the Agnes Wahlstrom Youth Playhouse (✆ 561/234-8052), and the Center for the Arts (✆ 561/231-0707), known for films and an excellent lecture series.

In Sebastian, you'll find live music every weekend (and daily in season) at **Captain Hiram's,** 1606 N. Indian River Dr. (✆ 561/589-4345), a salty outdoor restaurant and bar on the Intracoastal Waterway. The feel is tacky Key West, complete with a sand floor and thatched-roof bar that locals and tourists love at all hours of the day and night.

North of the inlet, head for the tried-and-true **Sebastian Beach Inn** (or SBI to locals), 7035 S. Fla. A1A (✆ 321/728-4311), for live music on the weekends.

Jazz, blues, or sometimes rock 'n' roll starts at 9pm on Friday and Saturday. On Sunday, it's old-style reggae after 2pm. The inn is open daily for drinks from 11am until anywhere from midnight to 2am.

4 A Side Trip Inland: Fishing at Lake Okeechobee ★★★

60 miles SW of West Palm Beach

Many visitors to the Treasure Coast come to fish, and they certainly get their fill of it off the miles of Atlantic shore and on the inland rivers. But if you want to fish freshwater and nothing else, head for "The Lake"—**Lake Okeechobee,** that is. The state's largest, it's chock-full of good eating fish. Only about a 1½-hour drive from the coast, it makes a great day or weekend excursion.

Two things happen in the area surrounding Lake Okeechobee: sugar production and fishing. The area, which actually encompasses five counties, is known as the bass-fishing and winter-vegetable capital of the state.

Okeechobee comes from the Seminole Indian word for "big water"—and big it is. The lake covers more than 467,000 acres; that's more than 730 square miles. At one time, the lake supported an enormous commercial fishing industry. Due to a commercial fishing-net ban, much of that industry has died off, leaving to the sportfishers all the rich bounty of the lake.

As you approach the lake area, you'll notice a large levy surrounding its circumference. This was built after two major hurricanes, including one in 1947 that killed hundreds of area residents and cattle. In an effort to control future flooding, the Army Corps of Engineers, which had already built a cross-state waterway, constructed a series of locks and dams. The region is now safe from the threat of floods, but the ecological results of the flood control have not been as positive. The bird and wildlife population suffered dramatically, as did the southern portion of the Everglades, which relied on the down flow of water from the lake to replenish and clean the entire ecosystem. In early 2001, 30,000 acres of the lake's bottom caught fire due to a severe drought or, some say, arson. Drought had reduced the lake's depth to below 11 feet, provoking officials to impose water restrictions. Surprisingly, however, experts say the fire was beneficial for the lake. High water levels had previously prevented fire, which is a part of the natural cycle of the lake, and surrounding torpedo grass threatened to take over the marshes where native fish tend to swim. The fire brought with it the hope that now that the grass has been burned, the fish and the native plants will return to the lake.

Another threat to the region is posed by the area's largest employer, U.S. Sugar, which owns most of the land around Belle Glade and Clewiston, "America's Sweetest Town."

Still, the area retains its rural charm and boasts the best bass fishing in the state.

ESSENTIALS

GETTING THERE   The best route is to take I-95 south to Southern Boulevard (U.S. 98 west) in West Palm Beach, which merges with State Route 80 and State Route 441. Follow signs for State Route 80 west through Belle Glade to South Bay. In South Bay, turn right onto U.S. 27 north, which leads directly to Clewiston.

VISITOR INFORMATION   Contact the **Clewiston Chamber of Commerce,** 544 W. Sugarland Hwy., Clewiston, FL 33440 (© **863/983-7979;**

www.clewiston.org), for maps, business directories, and the names of numerous fishing guides throughout the area. In addition, you might contact the **Pahokee Chamber of Commerce,** 115 E. Main St., Pahokee, FL 33476 (© **561/ 924-5579;** fax 561/924-8116; www.pelinet.net/pahokee); they'll send a complete package of magazines, guides, and accommodations listings.

For an excellent map and a brief history of the area, contact the **U.S. Army Corps of Engineers,** Natural Resources Office, 525 Ridgelawn Rd., Clewiston, FL 33440 (© **863/983-8101;** fax 863/983-8579). It is open weekdays from 8am to 4:30pm.

OUTDOOR PURSUITS

FISHING   See "Going After the Big One," on p. 375.

SKY DIVING   Besides fishing, the biggest sport in Clewiston is jumping out of planes. Because of the limited air traffic and vast areas of flat undeveloped land, this area attracts novice and expert sky divers alike. **Air Adventures** (© **800/533-6151** or 863/983-6151) operates a year-round program from the Airglades Airport. If you've never jumped before, you can go on a tandem dive, which means, as the name implies, you'll be attached to a "jumpmaster." For the first 60 seconds, the two of you free-fall, from about 12,500 feet. Then, a quick pull of the chute turns your rapid descent into a gentle, balletic cruise to the ground, with time to see the whole majestic lake from a privileged perspective. Dive packages start at $165; group rates start at $150.

WHERE TO STAY

If you aren't camping, book a room at the **Clewiston Inn** ⭐⭐, 108 Royal Palm Ave., Clewiston (© **800/749-4466** or 863/983-8151). Built in 1938 by U.S. Sugar to house executives and visitors, this Southern plantation–inspired hotel is the oldest in the Lake Okeechobee region. It still hosts sugar executives and visiting sportfishers in its 52 simply decorated, nondescript, Holiday Inn–style rooms. The lounge area sports a 1945 mural depicting the animals of the region. Double rooms start at $99 a night; suites begin at $129. All have air-conditioning and TVs.

Another choice, especially if you're here to fish, is **Roland Martin,** 920 E. Del Monte (© **800/473-6766** or 863/983-3151), the "Disney of fishing." This RV park offers modest motel rooms, efficiencies, condominiums, apartments, or campsites, with two heated pools, gift and marina shops, and a restaurant. The modern complex, dotted with prefab buildings painted in white and gray, is clean and well manicured. Rooms rent for $68 and efficiencies cost $88. Condominiums are about $150 a night with a 3-night minimum. RV sites are about $25 with TV and cable hookup.

CAMPING

During the winter, campers own the Clewiston area. Campsites are jammed with regulars, who come year after year for the simple pleasures of the lake and, of course, the warm weather. Every manner of RV, from simple pop-top Volkswagens to Winnebagos to fully decked-out mobile homes, finds its way to the many campsites along the lake. Also, see Roland Martin, above.

Okeechobee Landings, U.S. 27 east (© **863/983-4144**), is one of the best; it has every conceivable amenity included in the price of a site. More than 250 sites are situated around a small lake, clubhouse, snack bar, pool, Jacuzzi, horseshoe pit, shuffleboard court, and tennis court. Full hookup includes a sewage connection, which is not the case throughout the county. RV spots are sold to

Going After the Big One

Fishing on Lake Okeechobee is a year-round affair, though the fish tend to bite a little better in the winter, perhaps for the benefit of the many snowbirds that flock here (especially in February and March). RV camps are mobbed with fish-frenzied anglers who come down for weeks at a time for a decent catch.

You'll need a fishing license to go out with a rod and reel. It's a simple matter to apply. The chamber of commerce and most fishing shops can sign you up on the spot. The cost for non-Florida residents for 7 days is $16.50 and $31.50 for the year.

You can rent, charter, or bring your own boat to Clewiston; just be sure to schedule your trip in advance. You don't want to show up during one of the frequent fishing tournaments only to find you can't get a room, campsite, or fishing boat because hundreds of the country's most intense bass fishers are vying for the $100,000 prizes in the Redman Competition, which happens four times a year in the spring and winter.

There are, of course, more than a few marinas where you can rent or charter boats. If it's your first time on the lake, I suggest chartering a boat with a guide who can show you the lake's most fertile spots and handle your tackle while you drink a beer and get some sun. **Roland Martin,** 920 E. Del Monte (✆ **863/ 983-3151**), is the one-stop spot where you can find a guide, boat, tackle, rods, bait, coolers, picnic supplies, and a choice of boats. Rates, including the boat, start at $175 for a half day. A full day costs $250 and includes all necessary equipment except bait. You'll need a license for this, too, which Roland Martin also sells. They also have boat rentals: A 16-foot johnboat is $40 for half a day and $60 for a full day with a $40 deposit. A 26-foot pontoon is $125 for a full day and $85 for half a day with a $50 deposit.

Another reputable boat-rental spot is **Angler's Marina,** 910 Okeechobee Blvd. (✆ **800/741-3141** or 863/983-BASS). Rentals for a 14-footer start at $40 for a half day, for a maximum of four people. A full day is $60. If you want a guide, rates start at $150 (for two people) for a half day, though in the summer (June to October), when it's slow, you can usually get a cheaper deal.

regulars. But there are usually some spots available for rental to one-time visitors. Rates start at $24.50 a day or $150 weekly plus tax, including hookup. Year-round rates for trailer rentals, which sleep two people, start at $32 from Sunday to Thursday and from $37 on Friday and Saturday.

WHERE TO DINE

If you aren't frying up your own catch for dinner, you can find a number of good eating spots in town. At the **Clewiston Inn** (see "Where to Stay," above), you can get catfish, beef stroganoff, ham hocks, fried chicken, and liver and onions in a setting as Southern as the food. The dining room is open daily from 6am to 2pm and 5 to 9pm, and entrees cost $9 to $18.

Index

See also Accommodations and Restaurant indexes, below

RESTAURANTS

FROMMER'S® COMPLETE TRAVEL GUIDES

Alaska
Amsterdam
Argentina & Chile
Arizona
Atlanta
Australia
Austria
Bahamas
Barcelona, Madrid & Seville
Beijing
Belgium, Holland & Luxembourg
Bermuda
Boston
British Columbia & the Canadian Rockies
Budapest & the Best of Hungary
California
Canada
Cancún, Cozumel & the Yucatán
Cape Cod, Nantucket & Martha's Vineyard
Caribbean
Caribbean Cruises & Ports of Call
Caribbean Ports of Call
Carolinas & Georgia
Chicago
China
Colorado
Costa Rica
Denmark
Denver, Boulder & Colorado Springs
England
Europe

European Cruises & Ports of Call
Florida
France
Germany
Greece
Greek Islands
Hawaii
Hong Kong
Honolulu, Waikiki & Oahu
Ireland
Israel
Italy
Jamaica
Japan
Las Vegas
London
Los Angeles
Maryland & Delaware
Maui
Mexico
Montana & Wyoming
Montréal & Québec City
Munich & the Bavarian Alps
Nashville & Memphis
Nepal
New England
New Mexico
New Orleans
New York City
New Zealand
Nova Scotia, New Brunswick & Prince Edward Island
Oregon
Paris
Philadelphia & the Amish Country
Portugal

Prague & the Best of the Czech Republic
Provence & the Riviera
Puerto Rico
Rome
San Antonio & Austin
San Diego
San Francisco
Santa Fe, Taos & Albuquerque
Scandinavia
Scotland
Seattle & Portland
Shanghai
Singapore & Malaysia
South Africa
Southeast Asia
South Florida
South Pacific
Spain
Sweden
Switzerland
Texas
Thailand
Tokyo
Toronto
Tuscany & Umbria
USA
Utah
Vancouver & Victoria
Vermont, New Hampshire & Maine
Vienna & the Danube Valley
Virgin Islands
Virginia
Walt Disney World & Orlando
Washington, D.C.
Washington State

FROMMER'S® DOLLAR-A-DAY GUIDES

Australia from $50 a Day
California from $70 a Day
Caribbean from $70 a Day
England from $70 a Day
Europe from $70 a Day

Florida from $70 a Day
Hawaii from $70 a Day
Ireland from $60 a Day
Italy from $70 a Day
London from $85 a Day

New York from $80 a Day
Paris from $80 a Day
San Francisco from $60 a Day
Washington, D.C., from $70 a Day

FROMMER'S® PORTABLE GUIDES

Acapulco, Ixtapa & Zihuatanejo
Alaska Cruises & Ports of Call
Amsterdam
Australia's Great Barrier Reef
Bahamas
Baja & Los Cabos
Berlin
Boston
California Wine Country
Charleston & Savannah
Chicago

Dublin
Hawaii: The Big Island
Hong Kong
Houston
Las Vegas
London
Los Angeles
Maine Coast
Maui
Miami
New Orleans
New York City
Paris

Phoenix & Scottsdale
Portland
Puerto Rico
Puerto Vallarta, Manzanillo & Guadalajara
San Diego
San Francisco
Seattle
Sydney
Tampa & St. Petersburg
Vancouver
Venice
Washington, D.C.

FROMMER'S® NATIONAL PARK GUIDES

Family Vacations in the National Parks
Grand Canyon

National Parks of the American West
Rocky Mountain
Yellowstone & Grand Teton

Yosemite & Sequoia/ Kings Canyon
Zion & Bryce Canyon

Frommer's® Memorable Walks

Chicago
London

New York
Paris

San Francisco
Washington, D.C.

Frommer's® Great Outdoor Guides

Arizona & New Mexico
New England

Northern California
Southern California & Baja

Southern New England
Vermont & New Hampshire

Frommer's® Born to Shop Guides

Born to Shop: France
Born to Shop: Hong Kong,
    Shanghai & Beijing

Born to Shop: Italy
Born to Shop: London

Born to Shop: New York
Born to Shop: Paris

Frommer's® Irreverent Guides

Amsterdam
Boston
Chicago
Las Vegas
London

Los Angeles
Manhattan
New Orleans
Paris
San Francisco

Seattle & Portland
Vancouver
Walt Disney World
Washington, D.C.

Frommer's® Best-Loved Driving Tours

America
Britain
California
Florida

France
Germany
Ireland
Italy

New England
Scotland
Spain
Western Europe

The Unofficial Guides®

Bed & Breakfasts in California
Bed & Breakfasts in
    New England
Bed & Breakfasts in the
    Northwest
Bed & Breakfasts in Southeast
Beyond Disney
Branson, Missouri
California with Kids
Chicago
Cruises
Disneyland
Florida with Kids

Golf Vacations in the
    Eastern U.S.
The Great Smoky &
    Blue Ridge Mountains
Inside Disney
Hawaii
Las Vegas
London
Mid-Atlantic with Kids
Mini Las Vegas
Mini-Mickey
New England with Kids

New Orleans
New York City
Paris
San Francisco
Skiing in the West
Southeast with Kids
Walt Disney World
Walt Disney World for
    Grown-ups
Walt Disney World for Kids
Washington, D.C.
World's Best Diving Vacations

Special-Interest Titles

Frommer's Britain's Best Bed & Breakfasts and
    Country Inns
Frommer's France's Best Bed & Breakfasts and
    Country Inns
Frommer's Italy's Best Bed & Breakfasts and
    Country Inns
Frommer's Caribbean Hideaways
Frommer's Adventure Guide to Australia &
    New Zealand
Frommer's Adventure Guide to Central America
Frommer's Adventure Guide to India & Pakistan
Frommer's Adventure Guide to South America
Frommer's Adventure Guide to Southeast Asia
Frommer's Adventure Guide to Southern Africa
Frommer's Gay & Lesbian Europe
Frommer's Exploring America by RV
Hanging Out in England

Hanging Out in Europe
Hanging Out in France
Hanging Out in Ireland
Hanging Out in Italy
Hanging Out in Spain
Israel Past & Present
Frommer's The Moon
Frommer's New York City with Kids
The New York Times' Guide to Unforgettable
    Weekends
Places Rated Almanac
Retirement Places Rated
Frommer's Road Atlas Britain
Frommer's Road Atlas Europe
Frommer's Washington, D.C., with Kids
Frommer's What the Airlines Never Tell You

Let Us Hear From You!

Dear Frommer's Reader,

You are our greatest resource in keeping our guides relevant, timely, and lively. We'd love to hear from you about your travel experiences—good or bad. Want to recommend a great restaurant or a hotel off the beaten path—or register a complaint? Any thoughts on how to improve the guide itself?

Please use this page to share your thoughts with me and mail it to the address below. Or if you like, send a FAX or e-mail me at frommersfeedback@hungryminds.com. And so that we can thank you—and keep you up on the latest developments in travel—we invite you to sign up for a free daily Frommer's e-mail travel update. Just write your e-mail address on the back of this page. Also, if you'd like to take a moment to answer a few questions about yourself to help us improve our guides, please complete the following quick survey. (We'll keep that information confidential.)

Thanks for your insights.

Yours sincerely,

Michael Spring

Michael Spring, *Publisher*

Name (Optional) _____

Address_____

_____

City_____ State_____ ZIP_____

Name of Frommer's Travel Guide _____

Comments_____

_____

_____

_____

_____

_____

_____

_____

_____

_____

Please tell us a little about yourself so that we can serve you and the Frommer's community better. We will keep this information confidential.

Age: ( )18-24; ( )25-39; ( )40-49; ( )50-55; ( )Over 55

Income: ( )Under $25,000; ( )$25,000-$50,000; ( )$50,000-$100,000; ( )Over $100,000

I am: ( )Single, never married; ( )Married, with children; ( )Married, without children; ( )Divorced; ( )Widowed

Number of people in my household: ( )1; ( )2; ( )3; ( )4; ( )5 or more

Number of people in my household under 18: ( )1; ( )2; ( )3; ( )4; ( )5 or more

I am ( )a student; ( )employed full-time; ( )employed part-time; ( )not employed at this time; ( )retired; ( )other

I took ( )0; ( )1; ( )2; ( )3; ( )4 or more leisure trips in the past 12 months

My last vacation was ( )a weekend; ( )1 week; ( )2 weeks; ( )3 or more weeks

My last vacation was to ( )the U.S.; ( )Canada; ( )Mexico; ( )Europe; ( )Asia; ( )South America; ( )Central America; ( )The Caribbean; ( )Africa; ( )Middle East; ( )Australia/New Zealand

( )I would; ( )would not buy a Frommer's Travel Guide for business travel

I access the Internet ( )at home; ( )at work; ( )both; ( )I do not use the Internet

I used the Internet to do research for my last trip. ( )Yes; ( )No

I used the Internet to book accommodations or air travel on my last trip. ( )Yes; ( )No

My favorite travel site is ( )frommers.com; ( )travelocity.com; ( )expedia.com; other_____.

I use Frommer's Travel Guides ( )always; ( )sometimes; ( )seldom

I usually buy ( )1; ( )2; ( )more than 2 guides when I travel

Other guides I use include _____

What's the most important thing we could do to improve Frommer's Travel Guides?

_____

_____

_____

Yes, please send me a daily e-mail travel update. My e-mail address is

_____

Mail to: Michael Spring, Publisher and Vice President, Frommer's Travel Guides
909 Third Ave., New York, NY 10022   FAX: 212.884.5432